Others:
The Evolution of Human Sociality

Others:
The Evolution of Human Sociality

Edited by
Kaori KAWAI

Translated by
Minako SATO

Kyoto University Press

First published in Japanese in 2016 by Kyoto University Press. This English edition first published in 2019 jointly by:

Kyoto University Press
69 Yoshida Konoe-cho
Sakyo-ku, Kyoto 606-8315
Japan
Telephone: +81-75-761-6182
Fax: +81-75-761-6190
Email: sales@kyoto-up.or.jp
Web: http://www.kyoto-up.or.jp

Trans Pacific Press
PO Box 164, Balwyn North, Melbourne
Victoria 3104, Australia
Telephone: +61-3-9859-1112
Fax: +61-3-8611-7989
Email: tpp.mail@gmail.com
Web: http://www.transpacificpress.com

Copyright © Kyoto University Press and Trans Pacific Press 2019.
Set by Sarah Tuke, Melbourne.
Printed by Asia Printing Office Corporation, Nagano, Japan.

Distributors

Australia and New Zealand
James Bennett Pty Ltd
Locked Bag 537
Frenchs Forest NSW 2086
Australia
Telephone: +61-(0)2-8988-5000
Fax: +61-(0)2-8988-5031
Email: info@bennett.com.au
Web: www.bennett.com.au

USA and Canada
Independent Publishers Group (IPG)
814 N. Franklin Street
Chicago, IL 60610
USA
Telephone inquiries: +1-312-337-0747
Order placement: 800-888-4741
  (domestic only)
Fax: +1-312-337-5985
Email: frontdesk@ipgbook.com
Web: http://www.ipgbook.com

Asia and the Pacific (except Japan)
Kinokuniya Company Ltd.

Head office:
38-1 Sakuragaoka 5-chome
Setagaya-ku, Tokyo 156-8691
Japan
Telephone: +81-3-3439-0161
Fax: +81-3-3439-0839
Email: bkimp@kinokuniya.co.jp
Web: www.kinokuniya.co.jp

Asia-Pacific office:
Kinokuniya Book Stores of Singapore Pte., Ltd.
391B Orchard Road #13-06/07/08
Ngee Ann City Tower B
Singapore 238874
Telephone: +65-6276-5558
Fax: +65-6276-5570
Email: SSO@kinokuniya.co.jp

The translation and publication of this book was supported by a Grant-in-Aid for Publication of Scientific Research Results (Grant Number 17HP6011), provided by the Japan Society for the Promotion of Science, to which we express our sincere appreciation.

All rights reserved. No reproduction of any part of this book may take place without the written permission of Kyoto University Press or Trans Pacific Press.

ISBN 978-1-925608-83-0

Contents

Figures	vii
Photographs	viii
Tables	ix
Acknowledgements	x
Contributors	xii

Introduction—Finding "Others" from an Evolutionary Perspective: The Search for the Evolutionary Historical Foundations of Human Sociality *Kaori Kawai* — 1

Part I: Aspects of Others: Emergence, Formation and Transformation

1 Approving Others and Incomprehensible Others in Primate Society *Suehisa Kuroda* — 25
2 Are Animals "Others" or Are There "Others" to Animals? *Michio Nakamura* — 47
3 When Others Appear *Toru Soga* — 69
4 "The Other Who Can Refuse": A Precondition for Transition to Human Society *Kōji Kitamura* — 91
5 Empathy and Social Evolution: The Human History of Understanding Others *Hitoshige Hayaki* — 109

Part II: Others and Other Groups: How to Interact with the Counterpart

6 Who Is the Alpha Male? The Appearance of the "Other" in Chimpanzee Society *Hitonaru Nishie* — 127
7 Encountering the "Other": How Chimpanzees Face Indeterminacy *Noriko Itoh* — 149
8 When Pricking Up One's Ears for the Voices of Strangers: Others in Chimpanzee Society *Shunkichi Hanamura* — 177
9 The Origins of "Consideration for One's Enemy": What Kind of Others Are Neighboring Groups to the Dodoth? *Kaori Kawai* — 217

Part III: The Representation and Ontology of Others in Humankind

10 The Ontology of the Other: The Evolutionary Basis of Human Sociality and Ethics in the Formation and Continuation of Inuit Society *Keiichi Omura* 237
11 Ancestral Spirits, Witchcraft and Phases of the Other in Everyday Life: The Case of the Bemba People of Zambia *Yuko Sugiyama* 257
12 The "Face" and the Other: Muslim Women Behind the Veil *Ryōko Nishii* 283
13 Morality and Instrumentality: A Practical Approach to Theorizing the Other *Masakazu Tanaka* 303

Part IV: The Expanding Horizons of the Theory of Others

14 The Spirit as the Other: From the Iban Ethnography *Motomitsu Uchibori* 325
15 A History of the Distance Between Humans and Wildlife *Gen Yamakoshi* 347
16 Toward the Environmental Others: An Ethological Essay on Equilibrium and Coexistence *Kaoru Adachi* 365
17 Society as a "Story": Work Sharing, Cooperative Breeding and the Evolution of Otherness *Yūji Takenoshita* 387
18 The Turing Test in the Wild: When Non-Human "Things" Become Others *Ikuya Tokoro* 407

Epilogue—Future Agenda, Others as an Affliction: Tripartite Relationships and the Tetrahedral Model *Takeo Funabiki* 425

Notes 443
Bibliography 465
Index 498

Figures

3.1 Attitude toward a third term (X) and the perception of otherness — 79
3.2 Strong "involvement" and the perception of otherness — 84
3.3 Reference standard and the perception of otherness — 85
3.4 Direction of the actor's attention — 88
5.1 Timeline of major human fossils — 119
8.1 The usual ranging area (or home range) of chimpanzees of Mahale M group in Tanzania — 185
11.1 Divisive narrative — 275
11.2 Mode of division and othering by narrative — 276
15.1 Changes in the population of Bossou chimpanzees — 361
16.1 A mixed-species association of Diana monkeys and red colobuses and the distribution of conspecific groups in the Taï National Park — 375
18.1 The "other" is a being that is open to the possibility of communication — 411
E.1 Tripartite relationships and the tetrahedral model — 431
E.2 Three ritual exchange roles in *nimangki* rituals — 434

Photographs

1.1	A bonobo infant and its mother	35
1.2	Bonobo peering behavior	44
2.1	A female chimpanzee named Nkombo	49
2.2	Grooming is a routine interaction for chimpanzees	57
2.3	Emory spying on a warthog	60
2.4	Carmen carrying around a genet carcass	63
2.5	A giraffe and oxpeckers	64
3.1	Gabra Miigo children learning the Qur'an	83
6.1	Fanana (right) receiving grooming from Kalunde (left) an old male	134
6.2	Alofu	134
7.1	Exploratory action: "Looking"	155
7.2	Playing	167
7.3	Stopping	169
9.1	Morning at a Dodoth animal (grazing) camp	220
9.2	A ritual to repel Turkana raids performed at a Dodoth animal camp	227
11.1	Villagers folded their hunting net and conversed between hunts	267
11.2	Net cleansing ritual	269
15.1	Sacred chimpanzees of Bossou, Guinea, intrude into the village and eat cultivated papaya	352
15.2	Wildlife tour in Nairobi National Park	357
16.1	A mixed-species association in the Taï National Park	379

Tables

11.1 Events involved in the division and revival of B village 273
15.1 Comparison of two types of wildlife tourism in Africa 359

Acknowledgements

This book is the culmination of a joint research project entitled "Human Society in Evolutionary Perspective (3)", conducted at the Research Institute for Languages and Cultures of Asia and Africa (ILCAA) of the Tokyo University of Foreign Studies over a period of three years from 2012 to 2015 and published with the support of a Grant-in-Aid for Publication of Scientific Research Results (Grant Number 17HP6011), provided by the Japan Society for the Promotion of Science (JSPS). This collaborative research project comprises a series of ongoing joint studies with long-range outlooks, and has so far been undertaken in three phases over ten years from 2005. Researchers primarily studying extant wild primates and those working on extant humans convened for the purpose of exploring the evolution of human society and sociality, and continuously engaged in collaborative research by developing a new theme every three or four years. This book is the third volume in the series, after *Groups* and *Institutions*, with the subtitle *The Evolution of Human Sociality*, and presents the outcomes of the Otherness Research Project (ORP) on the theme of *Others*. Although the three books are not specifically labeled as a series, they have all been published as the fruits of the above joint research project and their contents share a strong level of connection and continuity. From April 2015, the project entered its fourth phase of research activity under the banner "Human Society in Evolutionary Perspective (4): Existence, Environment, Extremity", with the added participation of experts in the fields of primate social ecology and historical geography in addition to the contributors to this book.

* * *

As with *Groups* and *Institutions*, the publication of this book has been realized with the tremendous assistance of many people and organizations. I would like to take this opportunity to express my gratitude to them.

In the academic specialties of our contributing authors, namely, primate sociology, ecological anthropology and sociocultural anthropology, field research forms the foundation, as researchers draw on their own field data as primary evidence. So, first of all, I would like to thank the local people who allowed our researchers to stay and undertake fieldwork in their areas, those who acted as research assistants and the primates who tolerated "(persistent) following" by researchers, and apologize for not being able to mention their names individually here. This book would not have been possible without the various forms of "cooperation" they provided.

The following organizations and the people who work for them helped us greatly in facilitating the conduct of our field studies: JSPS Nairobi Research Station, the Institute of Ethiopian Studies (Addis Ababa University), the Department of Social Sciences (Makerere University), Nairobi National Park (Kenya), Tanzania Commission for Science and Technology, Tanzania Wildlife Research Institute, Tanzania National Parks, Mahale Mountains National Park (Tanzania), The Embassy of Japan in Guinea, Directorate General for Scientific Research and Technological Development (Guinea), Bossou Environmental Research Institute (Guinea), Higashiyama Zoo and Botanical Gardens (Nagoya City Zoo) and Chubu Gakuin University Child and Family Support Center "La Lura".

Finally, Mr. Tetsuya Suzuki, the chief editor at Kyoto University Press, and Professor Yoshio Sugimoto of Trans Pacific Press, helped us throughout the publication process of this English edition from the planning stage to the final proofs, as they did with *Groups* and *Institutions*. They patiently waited for the authors, who tended to lag behind schedule in writing and proofing, and always supported this perpetually inexperienced editor.

I extend my sincere gratitude to them all.

Spring 2019
Kaori Kawai

Contributors

Kaori Kawai (Introduction, Chapter 9)
Professor, Research Institute for Languages and Cultures of Asia and Africa, Tokyo University of Foreign Studies

Suehisa Kuroda (Chapter 1)
Emeritus Professor, the University of Shiga Prefecture

Michio Nakamura (Chapter 2)
Associate Professor, Graduate School of Science, Kyoto University

Toru Soga (Chapter 3)
Professor, Faculty of Humanities and Social Sciences, Hirosaki University

Kōji Kitamura (Chapter 4)
Emeritus Professor, Okayama University

Hitoshige Hayaki (Chapter 5)
Professor, Faculty of Humanities and Sciences, Kobe Gakuin University

Hitonaru Nishie (Chapter 6)
Postdoctoral Research Fellow, Japan Society for the Promotion of Science

Noriko Itoh (Chapter 7)
Researcher, Wildlife Research Center, Kyoto University

Shunkichi Hanamura (Chapter 8)
Researcher, the Center for African Area Studies, Kyoto University

Keiichi Omura (Chapter 10)
Professor, Faculty of Liberal Arts, the Open University of Japan

Yuko Sugiyama (Chapter 11)
Professor, Faculty of Humanities and Social Sciences, Hirosaki University

Ryōko Nishii (Chapter 12)
Professor, Research Institute for Languages and Cultures of Asia and Africa, Tokyo University of Foreign Studies

Masakazu Tanaka (Chapter 13)
Professor, Institute for Research in the Humanities, Kyoto University

Motomitsu Uchibori (Chapter 14)
Professor Emeritus, Hitotsubashi University and the Open University of Japan

Gen Yamakoshi (Chapter 15)
Associate Professor, the Center for African Area Studies, Kyoto University

Kaoru Adachi (Chapter 16)
Associate Professor, Faculty of Sociology, Kyoto Sangyo University

Yūji Takenoshita (Chapter 17)
Professor, Faculty of Nursing and Rehabilitation, Chubu Gakuin University

Ikuya Tokoro (Chapter 18)
Professor, Research Institute for Languages and Cultures of Asia and Africa, Tokyo University of Foreign Studies

Takeo Funabiki (Epilogue)
Emeritus Professor, Graduate School of Arts and Sciences, the University of Tokyo

Introduction
Finding "Others" from an Evolutionary Perspective: The Search for the Evolutionary Historical Foundations of Human Sociality

Kaori Kawai

Living with others

Humans know how to live with others in groups of various sizes such as the family, community, state and nation. As an animal species, humans (*Homo sapiens*) are part of the order Primates, of which each species has evolved its own specific mode of living upon the common foundation of gregariousness. Humans as well as non-human primates (hereafter called "primates") gather and assemble in various forms according to the species, or often the group within a species, and live with others peacefully or agonistically or while maintaining minimal involvement[1].

There is no doubt that in humans the most prominent feature of living with others is that it takes place in groups that are multi-layered, multi-faceted, flexible, complexly intertwined, sometimes entangled and often enormous. While these qualities have become more prominent since the modern age, it is likely that the use of linguistic representation that is only found in humans plays a crucially important role in the formation of these diverse groups and in the possibility for individuals to belong to different groups and live as a constituent member of each group simultaneously. Although language itself can be regarded as an institution, human societies have produced various other rules, norms and institutions to facilitate the coexistence and co-presence of multiple individuals, i.e., to enable people to live together. In the case of contemporary society, the most fundamental and important device must be that of the social contract, which was progressively inherited from Hobbs to Locke and Rousseau and precipitated the development of the modern nation-state system.

Nevertheless, humans were evolving and advancing the means to live with others in various forms well before the establishment of language (as an institution) and the invention of the social contract. This would have occurred in the process of expanding a person's associative capacity from other co-present members of their group to others belonging to neighboring groups, others not currently present whom they might encounter at some point and others living far away whom they might hardly ever or never encounter – a possibility that probably only arose when humans acquired language. On the other hand, it is the basic position of this book that primates without human-like articulated speech language also generate institutions in the broadest possible sense, including arrangements and standards that can be called rules, norms, customs and conventions – the archetypal or proto-institutions discussed by the authors of this book in the preceding volume, *Institutions: The Evolution of Human Sociality* (Kawai (ed.) 2017), including the *natural institutions* discussed by Kuroda (1999) – and live together while interacting with others in species-specific manners in groups with species-specific structures[2].

To elaborate on this position, I shall first explain the way the word "others" is used in this book. We do not limit the usage to "others" as an abstract concept that emerged as the other (other mind) in contraposition to the self (own mind) along with the discovery of the "individual" in the academic fields that pioneered the discourse on others such as philosophy and ethics, as I discuss below. We consider others to be other individuals when one individual becomes the subject on the basis of the obviousness or universality of the visible and tangible individual organism. Thus we address not only conspecific others as "other individuals", but also any being that approaches an individual and compels this individual to choose an action to take, i.e., in this book we deal with a broad range of cases, including heterospecifics, the environment and things (non-organic or inanimate objects). We expect that the mechanism for the generation of others, where some individuals within the category of conspecifics emerge or do not emerge as others, in other words, the othering process and mechanism or the ontological state of others, depends on the relationship, situation and context. We hope to deepen our study of living with others in a concrete way based on the manner of social interaction (reciprocal action)[3] with these wide-ranging and variable others.

This position is aligned with the approach we took in considering gregariousness in humans and primates in the first volume we collaborated on, *Groups: The Evolution of Human Sociality* (Kawai (ed.) 2013b). Here we began with "groups" as the constituent and underlying entities of society instead of directly approaching "society" at an abstract level. We observed, analyzed and discussed gatherings of individuals (assemblies) as relatively visible, substantial and actual objects, or in other words, gambled on the tangibility of the group phenomenon.

The means to live with others, which we humans have acquired in the process of evolution, is almost synonymous with "sociality" that implies "reciprocal exchanges" and "smooth relations" between individuals. The English word "sociality" is thought to be an appropriate translation of the Japanese word *tasha* used in our studies, as it denotes "social nature, group-forming nature and gregariousness (in humans and animals)" as well as "social intercourse and sociability". In this book, we take "sociality" to mean "the social ability to live with others sympatrically". While this type of sociality is also found in non-human species, it can be regarded as one of the prominent characteristics involved in the establishment of the human species itself in the sense that we have evolved in an extremely diverse and complex fashion[4]. The aim of this volume is to reach a new vantage point in the quest to locate the evolutionary historical foundations of the sociality that humans have acquired in their process of evolution. We do this by elucidating the specifics of that which is other, the emergence of others and the state of the relationship called "otherness" on the basis of social interactions between individuals.

It is not easy to discuss others in the context of evolution. Just like the evolutionary foundations of social, cognitive and psychological mechanisms such as society, social structure and the mind, others and sociality hardly leave any vestiges of their physical traits or materials (objects) in the form of fossils. Consequently, a comparative study or joint discussion involving researchers of extant human societies and those of extant wild primate societies is likely to be an effective means to theoretically and empirically examine them. On the assumption of this methodological inevitability, this volume comprises studies of extant human societies, studies of extant wild primate societies and studies of both. To rephrase the specificity (peculiarity) of our approach to others in this book, it is an empirical science that pays attention to interactive actions and behaviors between individuals in humans and primates and establishes the origins of the emergence of others in them. This constitutes an attempt to focus on the othering process, i.e., the mechanism that generates others in terms of "when and how others appear to an individual and how they meet face-to-face and relate with an individual", and to understand how the relationship is maintained and the condition of the relationship from the viewpoint of its situation- or context-dependent and interactive aspect, i.e., the "scene of interaction". While the collection of narrative data through interviews and oral surveys is one of the main methods of qualitative research in anthropology (sociocultural anthropology in particular), we considered that another key anthropological method, observation (detailed direct observation and participant observation of people's actions and behaviors), is important and aimed to adopt it as much as possible here to enable us to see humans from the same viewpoint as that used to look at primates.

As I shall explain in detail below, we employ two distinct stances toward others in this book, namely, "heterogeneous others" or "others belonging to different groups" and "homogeneous others" or "others belonging to the same group". The latter viewpoint has rarely been adopted intentionally in studies on others in sociocultural anthropology, which has placed greater emphasis on others as other cultures/societies. However, in the joint research project this book is based upon we attempted to bring the perspective and methodology of primatology (hereafter referring to "Japanese primatology" unless otherwise stated; to be explained in the next section) to the forefront and also to clearly highlight the focus on interactive actions and behaviors between individuals in anthropological research. If not for a joint project with primatologists (hereafter referring to "primatologists in the tradition of Japanese primatology" or "primatologists descended from the Japanese primatology school", unless otherwise stated), sociocultural anthropologists would never have ventured to emphasize this perspective and ecological anthropologists might never have been able to maintain this approach. Both the first and second phases of the joint research project on the evolutionary historical foundations of human sociality, on the theme of groups and institutions respectively, were collaborations between primatologists (primate sociologists and primate ecologists) and anthropologists (ecological anthropologists and sociocultural anthropologists). It is likely that they laid the groundwork for sociocultural anthropologists, whose central themes have been representation and imagination, to discuss the origin of these very human matters and phenomena on the basis of interactions in primatological situations.

The chapters in this book examine the overlapping but distinct domains (and attributes) of meaning of others as well as the dynamic process of othering, in which others are generated through specific interactions between individuals. The others addressed here include those far exceeding the denotation of others in common usage or as used in discussions in the humanities in terms of heterospecifics, the environment and things (non-organic or inanimate objects), as mentioned earlier. We do not offer a strict definition of "others" or aim to do so here. This may be a logical inevitability in view of the fact that this book is an attempt to analyze and consider others in primates, including humans, i.e., it includes others from the perspective of pre-language, pre-human individuals in its scope. Having recognized the broadness and diversity of the subject, we shall position the zoological meaning of "conspecifics" as the central usage of the word "others" in this book in principle (however, I shall discuss this from another angle later). The word "others" is used in this sense below for the purpose of discussing the possibility of broadening the starting point and destination of our search, rather than to define others itself.

Recent discourse on evolution involving others and sociality

In recent years, evolution has become a highly popular topic in the academic world. Discourses on evolution have featured not only in the academic fields founded on biology, such as evolutionary biology and evolutionary psychology, but also in a broader range of fields from evolutionary linguistics, cultural evolution and evolutionary arguments on the legal system to a philosophy of evolution in the philosophy of science. The evolution of what we call human "sociality" is the area that contains the most extensive and complex themes and offers the greatest scope for arguments among these threads.

Especially in ethology, comparative cognitive science and related areas, evolutionary discussions have been actively developing on the theme of what kinds of relationships individual animals form with other individuals for their survival. These discussions can be summarized in plain language as an endeavor to elucidate the origin and evolution of the mind for the purpose of coexistence between individual animals on biological and evolutionary grounds. Numerous books and academic papers containing the word "mind" in their title or subtitle are being published daily. As they contain some important arguments directly and indirectly related to our themes of "others" and "sociality", we must engage with them before we can move forward. So, before I introduce the specifics of this book, I provide a brief overview of the essence of the current trend in the discourse on evolution – a comprehensive explanation would require more than one thick volume.

While the current trend involves many distinct themes in several fields of study, the central theme, to put it plainly, is the fundamental question of "Why do humans help one another?". Let's recall our everyday life. Mutual help between strangers, not to mention acquaintances, occurs in our lives every day and everywhere. In human society, cooperation is very common and widespread and extends beyond kinship relations. A more abstract or technical view of this phenomenon centers on the theory of "reciprocally altruistic behavior" used by Robert Trivers to explain altruism between non-related people, who proposed important basic theories in sociobiology in the early 1970s. Trivers deepened his inquiry into the emotional system as the evolution of the mind, which has evolved out of reciprocal altruism. The question "Why do humans help one another?" – or in other words, "How did humans' remarkable reciprocal altruistic behavior evolve?" – has moved beyond the realms of evolutionary biology, evolutionary psychology and the fields of primatology and anthropology that underpin this book and greatly expanded by straddling adjoining academic fields such as developmental psychology, cognitive science and behavioral science (e.g., the proposition of theory of mind as a mechanism to read the minds of others), brain science and neuroscience (the discovery of mirror neurons, the social brain hypothesis etc.) and physiology and genetics (the relationships with the endocrine system and hormones, selection pressure on groups etc.), and continues to produce new results. This focus on altruism has emerged as one of the hottest research themes and drawn arguments from numerous other academic disciplines ranging from humanities fields such as history and archaeology to social sciences such as sociology, political science and economics.

Research on reciprocal altruism from an evolutionary viewpoint is highly diversified. In this area, remarkable progress has been made, for example, in studies on the origin and evolution of the active food sharing behavior and orientation toward the spirit of sharing and fairness found widely across human societies, the reason for or origin of morality and ethics that are thought to be universal in humans, the process and mechanism of the development of cooperative behaviors and the origin and evolution of psychological mechanisms such as synchronizing behavior, cooperativity and empathy that are thought to be highly developed in humans.

This book shares the same curiosity with this current trend as it approaches the origin and evolution of others and sociality, especially their formation and foundations, from the angle of empirical sciences such as primatology and anthropology, as mentioned earlier, and discusses similar social events and phenomena by addressing actions and behaviors such as food distribution and sharing, inquiring into the generation of morality and ethics and considering the evolution of synchronizing behaviors, cooperativity and empathy. In this sense, I have no qualms about locating this book as part of this trend and in fact I am confident that this book can make a positive contribution to this discourse. Nevertheless, I would like to make it clear that this book was not conceived directly out of this trend in academic discourse, or by tapping into it. Before I explain chronologically how this book came about, I present its premises concisely, focusing on two major points here.

Firstly, a clear point of difference is that all studies presented here are from empirical science based on field research of wild primate societies or extant human societies, whereas the main areas of the aforementioned academic trend including psychology and behavioral science center on experimental science conducted in laboratories with primates in captivity or human infants/children as test subjects. Still, this does not mean that our arguments here are entirely irreconcilable with lab-based studies. Achievements in the experimental sciences are extremely valuable and informative. It is our view that collaboration between them should result in more productive and fruitful discussions. In fact, many of the theses (chapters) here cite various findings of experimental science.

Secondly, I, the editor of this book, specialize in ecological anthropology, but my long and deep involvement in the tradition of Japanese primatology, both theoretically and methodologically, means that it forms the foundation of my thinking, which, along with the primate sociology-related chapters in the book, is not premised on the aforementioned experimental academic trend. In Japan, primatology based on the study of wild Japanese macaque troops was born independently from the Western discipline in the late 1940s, soon after the Second World War, and was led by Kinji Imanishi and his student (successor), Jun'ichirō Itani. Within ten years of its inception, this young academic discipline positioned the unraveling of the mystery of human social evolution and the reconstruction of early human societies as its clear goals, shifted its research field to the African Continent as the cradle of human evolution and accumulated field research based on long-term ongoing studies in two streams, namely, primate sociological studies on great apes and ecological anthropological studies on hunter-gatherer peoples, nomadic pastoralists and shifting cultivators whose livelihoods continue to rely heavily on nature. In addition to the historical background, the tradition of Japanese primatology also entails an attention to society (community, group) as the basic unit of study. This means that even observational studies of individual behaviors have been analyzed and examined on the assumption that there is society (community, group) in the background. This characteristic forms a contrast to the emphasis on the individual as the subject of study of Western primatology that has inherited the tradition of ethology. Correspondingly, it appears that there has been a contrast in the unit of evolution between society (synusia) in the former and the individual (and genes in recent years) in the latter. Japanese primatology is also noted for methodological characteristics such as a thorough understanding of social relationships between all individual members of each group (BSU: Basic Social Unit), as well as a meticulous attention to the details of interactive behaviors between individuals based on the active use of individual identification from an early stage.

On the basis of the above, I provide more specific explanations of the contents and topics addressed in this book below.

The background: From "groups" to "institutions" to "others"

Firstly, I briefly explain the origin of this book. As mentioned above, this book has been compiled from the outcomes of a joint research project carried out by researchers working in primatology and anthropology – primate sociology, ecological anthropology and sociocultural anthropology to be more exact. This project was named "Human Society in Evolutionary Perspective (3)" and was based at the Research Institute for Languages and Cultures of Asia and Africa (ILCAA) of the Tokyo University of Foreign Studies. The participants met fifteen times on the theme of "others" (hereafter called the Otherness Research Project: ORP) and convened two associated symposiums over the three years from 2012 to 2015. This project was numbered (3) as it followed the first and second phases on groups and institutions, respectively (hereafter called the Groups Research Project: GRP, and the Institutions Research Project: IRP). The two preceding volumes mentioned above, *Groups: The Evolution of Human Sociality* (Kawai (ed.) 2013b)[5] and *Institutions: The Evolution of Human Sociality* (Kawai (ed.) 2017)[6] were published as the fruits of these phases of the project and the outcome of each symposium was reported on the project's website. As the details can be accessed through these publications, I shall only attempt a quick overview of the preceding phases here to provide the minimum information required for an understanding of the position of this book.

Human Society in Evolutionary Perspective (1): GRP 2005–2008
In order to hone in on the sociality that humans have acquired in the evolutionary process, the GRP put forward the clear position of starting from the very simple and concrete fact that humans and primates gather (or assemble). It aimed to elucidate the tangible condition of the coexistence and co-presence of individuals without letting it be reduced to or absorbed by a more abstract concept such as "society". I highlight the following two points as the main results.

The first point is the importance of the concept of "non-structure" (or anti-structure). Examples of non-structured assemblies include mixed-species associations of cercopithecines in West Africa, which are loose and flexible communities of heterospecific monkeys who feed and range together as well as performative groups gathered for specific activities such as assemblies of seafaring people congregating across the boundaries of their villages, islands or ethnic groups to engage in piracy. They share the common characteristics of being loose and free assemblages of autonomous individuals as well as being dynamic groups because of their transience. This theme emerged as an attempt to actively recognize that the reality of groups always contains not only a structure but also some form of non-structure, because these gatherings were found to occupy a considerable proportion of daily life and should be given due recognition.

The second point relates to the representational ability we humans have acquired. We have the ability to perceive even an absent and invisible entity as a companion or an enemy. It is possible to say that this expansion has been achieved by the acquisition of the linguistic representational ability that enables perception beyond our field of vision, i.e., "here, now". The perception of companions is made possible by the representational action of "we", which is supported by identity as a sense of belonging to, for instance, a patrilineal group or other cultural category, ethnicity or nation-state. In this type of association, it is very common that members do not actually know each other despite sharing the same "we consciousness". This is homologous to the situation in which a linguistic representation such as "so-and-so patrilineal descent group", "so-and-so ethnic group" or "so-and-so nation" reinforces the image of one's enemy in referring to them. This is a mode of existence of groups that is peculiar to humans. Needless to say, because language is one of the most characteristic institutions acquired by humans, this representational ability-based grouping demonstrates that human groups are bundles governed by institutions. Thus, questions on the principle and dynamics of coexistence and co-presence of individuals were passed on to the IRP.

Human Society in Evolutionary Perspective (2): IRP 2009–2011

Groups have some kind of principle or dynamics that generates and sustains them. Conversely, the fact that multiple individuals form and live in a group in reality indicates the existence of some principle or dynamics for the coexistence and co-presence of multiple individuals. We attempted to find the origin or beginning of institutions there.

Institutions permeate the human life-world sometimes as explicit legal regulations and at other times as semi-explicit moral codes or more implicit conventions (customs and mores). It is certain that these institutions are mediated and constructed by language, and the ordinary social scientific theories of institutions are based on this assumption. However, our scope extends to the evolutionary historical foundations far beyond this usual assumption. As language itself is one of the institutions humans have developed, we cannot possibly approach the evolutionary historical foundations of institutions via a theory that requires language as a precondition. At the same time, we can raise the following question when we do not presuppose language: will we find a principle that is not or cannot be linguistically represented even in the foundations of language-mediated institutions? A behavioral principle that regulates relationships between individuals can be called an "archetypal institution or proto-institution" that can be understood only when we broaden our field of vision to non-human primate societies. Unless we turn our gaze to this place, we cannot expect to gain an understanding of institutions that includes a view to human social evolution.

The fruits of the IRP can be summarized into the following three points.
1. When we consider the most primordial form of institution, it is not necessary to assume the existence of a transcendental being (god, law or anything else), i.e., an external third term.
2. It is not necessary to assume the existence or otherwise of a legal system, especially penalties that are essential in modern law, as a condition for the formation of institutions.
3. Conventions that manifest at the behavioral level are thought to be of crucial importance in the evolutionary process of institutions.

In light of these three points, it seems that institutions have already emerged at the great ape stage in the embryotic form of archetypal institutions or proto-institutions and that there is no need to consider human-like articulated speech to be the determinant factor in the formation of institutions. Even today, we humans continue to live by the bundles of conventional actions and practices inherited from archetypal institutions or proto-institutions as the core of institutions in the continuum of the incessant repetition of ordinary interactions.

Institutions are realized firstly by the actions and behaviors of individuals within a group. There are individual actions and behaviors that connect to those of other individuals and lead to the generation of various social phenomena. Be it a group or an institution, living with others is the precondition. "Others" was chosen as our next theme in order to approach the evolutionary historical foundations of human sociality from the process behind the emergence of others (or the diversity and commonality of their emergence in different species or locales) and to re-examine the group and institution phenomena from that angle. Looking back, however, I do wonder if the progression of our themes from "groups" to "institutions" to "others" may appear circuitous in a sense. Could we move directly from "groups" to "others"? It may have been a possible route, but I am certain that making a detour to "institutions" helped to deepen our understanding of the evolutionary historical foundations of human sociality.

Others as the counterpart: Positioning "others" in this book

I would like to reiterate that the aim of this book is to approach a higher-order sociality that humans have acquired in the process of evolution using what is described by the word "others" as a clue. This viewpoint is based on the results of our joint research project in primatology and anthropology, as mentioned above. Accordingly, the "others" addressed here stand in a different place from the subject of contemplation and speculation in academic fields such as philosophy and ethics. These others emerge as individuals or assemblies of individuals in a real and specific context or situation as the counterpart in social interactions based on empirical evidence from primatology and anthropology. In this case, the self is also considered to be an individual or an assembly of individuals that emerges with others in a real and specific context or situation. Others are not static beings that are there from the start (as pre-existing beings); they are beings that emerge (are generated) dynamically through the process of othering in specific interactions between individuals. The process of the emergence or generation of others, i.e., the othering process, is that of the formation of a social relationship between an individual and another individual giving rise to the emergence of sociality by which society is formed. In reality, or in the flow of physical time, society is there before individuals are born and pre-existing society continues to exist, but in this book we consider that theoretically others and societies are formed through this process. This view of others can be found throughout the book, whether the subject is humans or non-human primates.

The Japanese word for "others" (*tasha*) is ambiguously defined and used in a wide range of contexts. It is certainly a concept word as a technical term (and a relatively new concept) in philosophy and ethics, but it is also used to mean "persons other than oneself (from a given individual's viewpoint)" in everyday contexts. It is similar to "strangers" (*tanin*) in that sense, but there is a clear difference in the referent range between the two words as, for instance, one's family and relatives are others (people other than oneself) but not strangers. By way of experiment, I looked it up in a Japanese dictionary called *Shin meikai kokugo jiten* (Sanseidō), renowned for its unique semantic interpretations. To my surprise, the word *tasha* could not be found in the fourth edition (1997)[7]. Does this mean that the word was not a common Japanese word in 1997? That seems unlikely. This prompted me to check another dictionary, *Kōjien* (sixth edition, 2008; Iwanami Shoten), which resulted in another slightly unexpected finding. There was an entry for *tasha*, but it gave the short and blunt definition of "person(s) other than oneself" together with an arrow symbol instructing the reader to refer to the entry for *tashasei* (otherness). When I looked that word up, I found the following philosophical explanation: "(philos.) Refers to the characteristics of others that cannot be reduced to the consciousness or abilities of self (I), e.g., asymmetry, transcendence and externality; a term to re-acknowledge the individuality and heterogeneity of others that have been lost by modern philosophy that started from the absolute certainty of ego".

It appears that *tasha* is not regarded by the world of Japanese linguistics and dictionaries as an everyday word used in common parlance. Although I could have continued to look it up in other dictionaries at hand, I decided to refrain as I might have been caught up in the depths of the history of humanities, and any further linguistic pursuit would have been superfluous for the purpose of this book. In any case, *tasha* is apparently a rather tricky word in the context of the everyday Japanese language. It seems to be positioned at quite a distance from common words that generally refer to anything that is different from oneself, such as other(s) in English and *autres* (*autrui*) in French.

On the other hand, outside of such everyday linguistic contexts, *tasha* has become a major topic that is important enough to occupy its own area of study not only in philosophy and ethics, but also in phenomenology, psychology, sociology, history, political science, economics, psychiatry, neuroscience, biology and many other fields. As for other disciplines that have a stronger association with this book, I have already mentioned the discourses in evolutionary biology, evolutionary psychology and ethology that are areas adjoining primate sociology, ecological anthropology and sociocultural anthropology on which this book is based, as well as the ongoing publication of numerous books and papers in these fields. If I may say so, "others" is trendy in the academic world of 2019. This book may be seen as another that jumped on the bandwagon, and we cannot do much about this. Still, as I detailed in the previous section, this book is a collection of the results of the ORP in the third phase of a joint primatology-anthropology research project entitled "Human Society in Evolutionary Perspective" that began more than a decade ago. In other words, "others" is a theme that was formulated independently in the process of investigating human sociality from "groups" and "institutions" and being on trend has never been our aim. It is my view that we can take a radical approach to various issues faced by humankind today (e.g., conflict resolution and coexistence[8]) because of this.

Two aspects of the discourse on others

During our ongoing discussions on others in the joint primatological-anthropological research project, different perspectives on or aspects to others came to the surface. These differences are thought to highlight problems associated with addressing others in an evolutionary context. In this section, we shall examine the usage of the word "others" and the axis and spread of the way others are discussed from the perspective of the aspectual difference. This is a discussion on the possible viewpoints toward others rather than on the topic of others itself.

Others in the two broad categories in this book, namely, "others in one's own group" and "others thought to belong to other groups" or "others as individuals in other groups" can be rephrased as "others of the same kind as oneself" and "others of a different kind from oneself". In the case of humans, the former refers to others who are fellow members of the same group as oneself (I), including parents and siblings as others to oneself (I) within one's family as a group, or others in various peer groups such as schools, classes and workplaces. Here, both self and others belong to the same population at various levels – for instance the "Japanese nation" or "human beings"– to constitute "we". There is no limit to the membership or size of "we". On the other hand, the latter others belong to groups that are seen as different from the self (I) in some respects. For example, they are people outside of one's own family or belonging to ethnic groups other than one's own. As you can see, the difference between the two categories is that between the frame of reference with respect to others as the subject and not the difference in the subject itself. In other words, the same others from an objective or third-party perspective can be others from the former or latter perspective.

We must be aware of these two aspects when discussing others. In this book, due to the methodological requirement of being a collaborative project involving anthropologists and primatologists, i.e., a comparative examination of human and primate societies, ecological anthropologists and sociocultural anthropologists also address "others in one's own group" (the first aspect) in most cases, and attempt as much as possible to pay close attention to any observable interactions, i.e., concrete and specific exchanges between people in daily practices seen in the field, and to describe them in detail.

Sociocultural anthropology has historically studied others belonging to other groups such as ethnic groups, societies and cultures that are foreign to Western modernity and other strangers/others who are different from I/we. Others in this sense have always been "person(s) different from oneself" as strangers, albeit to various degrees. Even when the anthropologist's own culture or modern Western society was the subject, they still found "different" cultures such as minorities and subcultures and studied them as "person(s) different from oneself" who are strangers.

Thus, sociocultural anthropology traditionally emphasized the heterogeneous part of self and others. Here the most straightforward form of comparative studies involving "one's own culture (society)" versus "another culture (society)" took center stage, while the question of "individuals" or inter-individual relations within the same society (group) receded into the background; or rather, the heterogeneity of other cultures in relation to one's own culture surfaced prominently before any discussion of "individuals" within the subject society could take place. The question of "sociality" in the context of investigations focusing on heterogeneous societies was established in the form of the case study method led by the Manchester School of social anthropology in England that emphasized interactive relationships between individuals from a critique of structural functionalism as early as in the 1960s, and transactionalism which became active during the 1970s. In Japan after these periods, however, the school of symbolic and interpretive anthropology in American cultural anthropology became mainstream and the interactive others at the individual level did not receive attention until the end of the twentieth century[9].

The situation was very different in primatology. Primates as the study subject for primatologists are of biologically different species and therefore they can be regarded as even more distant than strangers are for anthropologists. In principle, primatologists as observers cannot (do not) assume commonality with the primates they are studying. At the same time, primatologists have endeavored to avoid reduction to that which is internal to the individual, such as "an intention" and "a will". As I mentioned earlier, others as well as the self are beings that emerge concretely through interactions and there is no need to evoke their internal world. At the start of Chapter One, Kuroda considers the significance of introducing "others" and "otherness" as concepts for analyzing primate societies. Primatology has seldom used philosophical terms such as "others" and "strangers", while analysis of the subject comprising multiple individuals has normally focused on the relationship between single individuals, for instance, two monkeys or chimpanzees. The adoption of the term "inter-individual relationship" is a natural consequence of in-principle abstention from taking the viewpoint of the primate (self) that is the subject of observation and seeing the counterpart in an interaction as the other; here primatologists are attempting to avoid the trap of anthropomorphism[10]. Ultimately, this relates to the essential question of whether primates have the concept of self (self-recognition), but there is no reliable means to test this objectively. This also means that primatologists have been maintaining their observer's standpoint and deliberately refrained from seeing other individuals from a primate's perspective, while paying attention to the details of the actions and behaviors of primates as their subject as closely as possible.

Consequently, what we have here is not a simple problem of language (terminology). Primatologists have been looking at inter-individual relationships from the objective standpoint of a third party and distancing themselves from the self/other distinction between two (or more) interacting individuals (or an assembly). Thus, it is appropriate to say that primatologists have been looking at inter-individual relationships neutrally from a third-party perspective. Despite this, primatology has been inclined to pursue research that questions the sociality of the target species itself. Accordingly, others addressed by primatologists are in principle "others in one's own group" (the first aspect).

As I have reiterated, I am arguing about the purely "in-principle" facet. It is true that assuming commonality with humans has been criticized as anthropomorphism, but it is also true that not assuming a certain degree of commonality will make it difficult to understand the behaviors of the monkey or chimpanzee subjects in social (sociological) context. The empirical fact is that when a primatologist follows their subject in the field, they have the tendency to "back" this individual, and normally record observations from the subject's viewpoint. In other words, the primatologist is absorbed in or integrates with the subject and describes the behavior of the monkey or chimpanzee as a subjective actor/experiencer, so to speak. Under these circumstances, some Western primatologists such as F. de Waal (2006 and many others) have emerged with a positive attitude toward the methodological utility of anthropomorphization or anthropomorphic thinking, which is also called "strategic anthropomorphism". Although since the earliest stage of Japanese primatology that began in the 1940s anthropomorphization or the anthropomorphic technique premised on individual identification has been an important methodology, especially in primate sociology, it was not recognized as a "scientific" (biological) method by Western researchers who were rooted in the tradition of ethology.

On the other hand, as I mentioned earlier, recent advancements in cognitive science have encouraged research, mainly by experiments in captive conditions, involving reduction to the individual's inner world such as will and intention from the perspective that the individual's actions and behaviors are based on its will and intention. Active discussions about the commonality and difference in the interior, or cognitive abilities, of humans and primates are taking place through comparative experiments on human infants/children and great apes. However, we must say that these studies are after all reductionist to the individual level, because they explain actions and behaviors according to the will and intention of individual parties. This probably indicates that although this viewpoint deals with others and sociality in one respect, it is not focused on understanding these phenomena in themselves. By contrast, this book pays meticulous attention to the details of observable empirical facts that emerge as the individual's actions and behaviors, and examines others and sociality mainly on the basis of interactions between individuals. Although this standpoint represents a small minority in contemporary primatology that is dominated by studies aligned with evolutionary ecological theory integrating neo-Darwinism, sociobiology, ecology and ethology, I would like to position it as one particular current in primate sociology.

    I have now explained that there are two aspects to discussing others and that this book mainly focuses on the first, which is to look at "others in one's own group". Furthermore, I would like to reiterate that the anthropologists and primatologists involved have endeavored to pay close attention to the details of empirical facts in the field and to avoid speculation as much as possible.

Discussing "others" in the context of evolution

What is the significance of discussing social phenomena surrounding others in the context of evolution? Since the subject of our research includes extant primates and humans, specific time factors are not relevant, unlike paleoanthropology and archaeology that deal with early human remains and fossils. This is why our aim is an exploration of the evolutionary historical foundations rather than the evolution of human society itself. Although references to human ancestors and branch lines of early (fossilized) humans such as Australopithecus and Neanderthal are normally expected in discourse on evolution, they are not mentioned in most of the chapters here. One of the reasons is that, unlike human bones and stoneware, hardly any physical remnants (objects or materials) are left by the mode of existence of others and sociality. After all, our inquiry along the evolutionary axis does not entail that we follow the chronological (historical) development of the evolutionary transition or gradual path of evolution of otherness. As we cannot help but remove the "time" axis, we have no choice but to discuss the theoretical process of evolution and to develop an abstract argument. However, this is in fact where the strength of our argument lies. There is no doubt that the theoretical foundation for a comparison linking primates to humans has to be evolution, and we are attempting to explore sociality in primates and humans using this foundation. The process of constructing the social in a concrete manner from that foundation is the theory of social formation, and we have treated this theoretical process as the evolutionary historical foundations in both the GRP and the IRP. The ORP was established with the intention of digging deeper into the layers underneath groups and institutions for the very purpose of elucidating the more biological (physical) foundations of sociality. I would like to stress here that the methodological prudence of this book is in the thoroughly stoic attitude adopted by both anthropologists and primatologists in their consideration of the evolutionary historical foundation of sociality on the basis of diverse and minute facts actually observed and experienced in the field rather than narrating it historically and chronologically as if it were a story of human evolution.

The concept of "others" is defined variously and broadly in individual chapters because there is no common strict definition shared across chapters, as mentioned earlier. The above explanations have largely covered this. One thing I would like to add is the concern that provisionally defining "others" as "other conspecifics" from the outset may give the false impression that others in primates are basically of the same species (other conspecifics) and that heterospecific others (heterospecifics) have rarely been assumed. However, this is not the case as there are examples such as mixed associations of cercopithecines in which animals of multiple species coexist sympatrically and synchronize their activities; and for wild primates, predators and prey of other species can be treated as important others. Moreover, I have stated above that the environment and things (inorganic or inanimate objects) can become others in the same way. The individual chapters in this book actively and meticulously address various expanses around others without dismissing them as exceptions or deviations.

Conversely, others in anthropology have their individual attributes (sociocultural attributes) at the forefront and cannot be "bare others" with no such attributes (see Chapter Six by Nishie). Accordingly, the self/other distinction is reclaimed by or reduced to more specific entities such as natal family groups, ethnic groups or nation-states. This may be a natural attitude or standpoint considering that sociocultural anthropology in particular has been dealing with the question of others mainly by looking into otherness (alterity) itself that emerges in or through other ethnic groups, cultures and societies. However, this book does not intend to follow this polarizing tendency between anthropology and primatology. As I mentioned above, anthropologists are also endeavoring to address others within groups at certain levels on the basis of the arguments made by collaborative research in order to avoid this issue.

Contents

After this Introduction, this book presents eighteen chapters in four parts and concludes with a final chapter entitled "Future Agenda" that discusses our argument on others on a more abstract level. I provide a brief overview of each part and chapter below.

Part I: Aspects of Others: Emergence, Formation and Transformation

Part I comprises studies in primatology and anthropology – from the fields of primate sociology and ecological anthropology to be more precise – that present introductory arguments for the analysis and examination of individual cases in relation to the evolutionary historical foundations surrounding others to be addressed from Part II onward. They raise questions about a mechanism or process in which social phenomena such as that which is other, otherness and others as a relationship emerge, form and transform in primate and human social groups.

More specifically, Chapter One by Kuroda discusses the mechanism that allows the subject (individual) to form a community called "*we*" with another individual as the other through approval, while a deviation by the other individual disaggregates *we* and the deviating party emerges as the incomprehensible other in the two species of the genus *Pan*. In Chapter Two, after removing the assumption that others are human (one's conspecifics), Nakamura provides a comprehensive examination of that which is other to various animal species ranging from chimpanzees to social insects. Chapter Three by Soga posits that others always emerge where communication takes place and discusses the sensing of otherness and the understanding of others by seeking the mechanism for its emergence in a reference standard as well as interaction or "involvement". Chapter Four by Kitamura discusses the platform of "communication in interaction systems" common to primate and human societies and attempts to elucidate the kind of other that was introduced to it to prompt the emergence of human society and the stage at which it was introduced. In Chapter Five, Hayaki argues that humans' exceptional ability to synchronize with others is the biological (evolutionary) foundation of empathy and that the co-evolution of cognitive capacities and empathy gave rise to the emergence of *we-ness* in the history of humankind and enabled the formation of multi-layered human society, including familial units.

Part II: Others and Other Groups: How to Interact with the Counterpart

Based on the discussion in Part I, how do others, and other groups as an extension, appear in actual scenes of real life or survival? Studies in Part II consider the appearance of specific others and how the being who interacts with these others confronts and deals with individual situations. Three are studies on groups of wild chimpanzees based on detailed primary data and grounded in immediacy and the fourth study describes and discusses the appearance of other groups in relationships between ethnic groups of pastoralists.

Chapter Six by Nishie recounts how chimpanzees mutually perceive the "yet-to-be encountered somebody" in an extraordinary situation involving the disappearance of the alpha male in a unit-group and arrives at "bare others" as the characteristic condition of others in chimpanzees. In Chapter Seven Itoh proposes that the evolutionary historical foundations of others are contiguous with the way animals face various phenomena they encounter, and locates the way chimpanzees face otherness (indeterminacy) rather than others themselves at the center of concern. Chapter Eight by Hanamura considers wild chimpanzees' experience of others (other groups) based on their out-of-the-ordinary behaviors and interactions when they hear the voices of individuals belonging to other groups (unit-groups) thought to have been inherently their enemies (in hostile relationships). Following Chapter Eight, Chapter Nine by Kawai continues to look at others at the group level (other groups), albeit shifting attention to pastoral peoples, and discusses how neighboring groups exist side by side based on agonistic and non-agonistic interactions between adjacent ethnic groups from the viewpoint of empathy and mutual approval.

Part III: The Representation and Ontology of Others in Humankind

While the first two parts offer a mixture of studies on both primate and human societies, studies in Part III are exclusively about human society. They describe, analyze and examine the specifics of the mode of existence of others and the conditions of relationships with others mediated by linguistic representation that is unique to humans and highlight the ontological characteristics of others in human society.

Chapter Ten by Omura reports that there is an established relationship in Canadian Inuit society between hunted wildlife and humans in which animals give themselves to humans as food and command people to share food among themselves, and describes the way this relationship forms the ethical foundation that guarantees the existence of others. Chapter Eleven by Sugiyama discusses the excessiveness and multilayeredness produced when a reality is constructed through the sharing of narratives in the group structuralization phase as well as the emergence of various concomitant aspects of others in association with the fission and fusion of groups in Bemba society in Zambia. In Chapter Twelve Nishii looks at the face that is the part of the body with the power to evoke images as the intersection of the biological body and social relations, and puts forward an ontology of others based on the act of covering the face with a veil among Muslim women in South Thailand. Chapter Thirteen by Tanaka examines the variability of the self-other relationship and the representation of others, i.e., the way close others (insiders) and not-so-close others (outsiders) are easily switched, using a practical approach focusing on morality and instrumentality, which are two attitudes governing people's actions. Chapter Fourteen by Uchibori explores the ontological question of how psychic or spiritual others, which are almost definitely unique to humans, emerge in contrast with the emergence of others as other individual actors of almost equal capacity on the same plane as the self.

Part IV: The Expanding Horizons of the Theory of Others

While the previous chapters and parts have dealt with others where the counterparts in interactions were generally conspecific individuals or groups, Part IV attempts to gaze out into the expanses of the discourse on others through studies that try to discuss relationships between humans and other animals (mainly wild animals) on the same horizon, as well as studies that expand the scope of others to include not only heterospecific individuals and groups, but also the environment and things (natural and artificial objects).

Chapter Fifteen by Yamakoshi seeks to understand the relationship between humans and wild animals focusing on the behaviors such as physical distance that manifest on the boundary between "we" humans and wild animals as others, both of which are biological beings, while referring to some examples of excessive human habituation, crop damage, observation and tourism. Chapter Sixteen by Adachi explores the possibility that there is a phase that is open to others in the discipline of biology that normally does not deal with others overtly by examining interactions with the environment performed by life forms where dealing with the environment "modestly" well is a universal characteristic. Chapter Seventeen by Takenoshita compares collaborative child-rearing in gorillas and cooperative breeding in humans and argues that humans intertwine their own and others' stories to share and act out a "saga", while each great ape creates their own story out of the real world and both the self and others play their respective characters. Chapter Eighteen by Tokoro examines the phenomenon of the expansion of the denotation of others by hypothesizing non-human beings (non-human animals, natural and artificial objects) as others and argues that they can emerge as others in specific social or cultural situations or contexts.

The final chapter, entitled "Future Agenda", is a study by Funabiki that attempts to develop a model for the argument on others presented in this book without neglecting the viewpoint of modern Western philosophy and ethics as the location of the birth or discovery of "others". Funabiki's model is abstract enough to be called mathematical, because a bold abstraction was thought to be necessary to allow us to present our argument founded on observed biological phenomena and everyday practices in a way that would mesh with those from other academic fields, especially philosophy and ethics.

In other words, it is the fundamental standpoint of this book that it is essential to move back and forth between a careful and prudent observational and empirical approach and bold theorization in order to explore the roots or essence of the problem of "others", which can be regarded as the greatest challenge for humanity in this century, without being driven by trends in academia. Consequently, cases and key concepts presented in each chapter are wide-ranging. Yet, it is possible to think that they converge on one place both methodologically and epistemologically, as explained here in this introductory chapter.

Our next goal, i.e., the theme for Human Society in Evolutionary Perspective (4) that follows the ORP, is "Existence, Environment, Extremity" – "extremity" is mentioned in "Future Agenda" as well – on which collaborative research began in Spring 2015. This is an attempt to bring the "environment", which has been present as basso continuo for "groups", "institutions" and "others", and "existence" to the forefront of our awareness and to ascertain their "extreme" phases. "Existence" can be understood biologically/ecologically to begin with, but because it contains social elements as long as primates, including humans, live with others, the method for existence (survival strategy) has to be non-deterministic, variable and communicational. We aim to create a fresh vantage point from which to view the evolutionary historical foundations of human sociality by focusing on this postulate.

Part I
Aspects of Others: Emergence, Formation and Transformation

1 Approving Others and Incomprehensible Others in Primate Society

Suehisa Kuroda

Key ideas

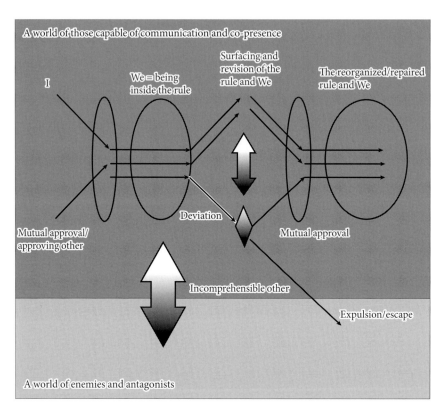

A subject forms "We" (a community/performative group) through mutual approval with the other individual(s) or acceptance by the approving other(s). When "We" is broken down by a deviation, the outer boundary of the rule and "We" surfaces in consciousness and the deviant appears as an incomprehensible other. The subject is faced with the other with salient otherness and chooses either to expel them or to repair/reorganize the rule and "We". This process is applicable to play in primates as well as the formation of alliances and the transfer of individual members to other groups in chimpanzees, but the reorganization resulting in the change of the rule and "We" is seldom found in the genus *Pan*. On the other hand, the reorganization of the rule and "We" happens frequently in human society. In other words, the incomprehensible other serves as a person who demands a renewal of the world of "We".

Bringing "others" into primate sociology

Is it meaningful to bring the concepts of "others" and "otherness" (see Kawai's Introduction) into an analysis of non-human primate societies?

No human can be as a human being by themselves alone. Nevertheless, modern philosophy since Descartes has been founded on solipsism with self as the starting point, and therefore cannot logically deal with the existence of others. The concept of "others" (hereafter used without emphasis) has been introduced to philosophy in order to compensate for this deficiency (Nakayama 2007). In psychology and sociology, it has been thought that the identity and norms of an individual are acquired through interactions with people around them who embody the culture of the community they were born into (Erikson 1973; Mead 1991). Others in this context are an existence that guides the socialization of the individual as a member of their community. Accordingly, the concept of "others" used in these fields incorporates such things as self, identity and norms, and therefore it seems reckless to apply it to primates who have no language and for whom a methodology to clearly demonstrate the existence of self has not been established.

On the other hand, Japanese primate sociology was launched and developed by the hypothetical application of human sociological and anthropological concepts (Itani 1987). Even the concept of "institutions", which is unique to human society, can be used in comparisons with primate societies (especially of chimpanzees and bonobos of the genus *Pan*, the two species most closely related to humans) to study the evolutionary historical foundations of the appearance of human social institutions, provided that conditions for rules and norms are slightly relaxed (Kuroda 1999, 2017; Nishie 2017). This is possible because the origin of society is far older than sociologists and philosophers think, and the basic social structure of great apes shares common characteristics with that of humans. In his attempt to connect Jean-Jacques Rousseau's *The Discourse on the Origin of Inequality* and his theory of coexistence in primate societies, Itani (1987) argues that society preceded what Rousseau calls a solitary and free "natural human"; that is, the solitary and free "natural human" has never existed and therefore the discourse on the beginning of human society must start from the point of transition from anthropoid society. This argument is further supported by the fact that in societies of the genus *Pan*, a close relative of humans, the equality principle preponderates and individuals have the ability to behave in a manner that embodies this principle according to their social status, i.e., social consciousness (Kuroda 1999). Finding the prototypes and variations of human social traits in anthropoid societies entails seeking a deeper understanding by unearthing and relativizing the evolutionary historical foundations of human society, and cannot be construed as an archetype-hunting game.

The problem of others originates in the relationships with other people and societies that humans inevitably become involved in as they grow and live. If so, the joy and suffering associated with our co-presence with others did not necessarily begin in human society. For example, Nishida (1981) made the following observations on chimpanzees. A male chimpanzee often tries to leave his group with an estrous female in order to maintain their sexual relationship, but the female does not always comply, so the male makes continual efforts to secure her company. In another more specific observation, an alpha male, who was losing ground in a contest for dominance, kept walking alone in a dark forest even after his challenger had gone to bed, drank water from a stream twice (a rare behavior), sighed and let out a low groan before he finally made a bed and went to sleep. Can we disregard these behaviors as cases of superficial similarity to human behaviors?

Of course, when we discuss non-human primates in whom we cannot prove the existence of self, we are discussing "something otherness-like" to be exact, as we have no choice but to deviate from the original philosophical, psychological or social meaning of otherness. Yet, I believe that this attempt can deepen our understanding of the evolutionary historical and social foundations that produce others and the manner in which we deal with the existence of others, including their origins (see Parts I and II of this volume).

In the first of the two preceding volumes in this series (*Groups*), I argued that groups based on the equality principle, which is the coexistence principle for *Pan*, are unstable and that the collective excitement (anti-structure phase) that occurs when an aggregation of many individuals goes into a state of excitement is the mechanism that maintains coexistence by resolving this instability problem (Kuroda 2017). In the second volume (*Institutions*), I pointed out that the equality principle is a mechanism prone to produce deviations and that deviations offer important opportunities to bring to the fore the rules and conventions we follow subconsciously, and proposed that when we explore *Pan* societies for the emergence of institutions as coexistence mechanisms, collective excitement can be one of its foundations (Kuroda 2017). While our search for the appearance of others in this chapter centers on *Pan* societies, what we can find there is a deep link between the equality principle underpinned by a patrilineal social structure and the appearance of others with "otherness". Itani (1987) regards this social structure and this coexistence principle as the basic foundations of human society (although not all researchers agree). If so, it can be stated that the appearance of others with otherness (as in Lévinas, to be discussed later) is something that characterizes the lineage of this structure and the coexistence system. This provides one answer to the question about bringing the concept of others into primate sociology.

This attempt has another meaning for primate sociology itself, because the study of others requires the detailed observation and analysis of interactions between the subject individual and others from the former's perspective. This is not limited to primates, but after many years of intensive research, researchers become so attuned to the behavioral patterns of the subject animal both visually and aurally that they become able to sense when the observed individual is sensing the presence of another individual behind it, to identify the subtleties of its deportment such as the length of response intervals and minute changes in its gaze or posture and to guess what this means. There are two types of data involved, namely a detailed description of the subject's actions and a description of the subtle manifestation of its interest in another individual. In the case of focal animal sampling (tracking an individual animal), there are more descriptions of such subtleties. However, the latter type of data may be reported in books intended for a general readership, but it is seldom used in academic theses about social relationships because this type of data is visible or invisible depending on the observer's interest. More clearly describable and quantifiable data tend to be favored for the purpose of academic publications. Above all, because research topics that require this subtle and detailed data (Kuroda 2015) did not attract much attention in primate sociology in the past, much of it had to be put aside even though it was the very source of the palpability of the existence of the subject primates in the minds of many observers.

The attempt to bring others into primate sociology will set the stage for these hidden gems (see Chapters Six, Seven and Eight). Moreover, the nature of data that relies on the individuality of each observer means that it needs to be described in a manner that is unconstrained by the regular style. In other words, in order to let these gems shine, the observer must modify the setting to find a better way to illuminate them. Thus, the attempt to introduce others into the study of primate societies has the potential to create new ways to describe them.

Approving others and incomprehensible others

We shall simplify the concept of others to the extent that it does not contradict the regular usage in its application to primate societies, and examine how the argument can be expanded from that point in primate sociology. As the concept of others has widely varying contents depending on the field or the individual philosopher or researcher, we shall consider just two concepts of others that seem to be in opposition.

One is drawn from the argument of E. H. Erikson (1959, 1973) and G. H. Mead (1991) that the self and identity of a subject are formed in interaction with others. Erikson (1959) recognized five stages of psychosocial development in childhood up to adulthood, where the successful completion of each stage results in the acquisition of basic virtues. He emphasized the importance of parents' acceptance (= approval) of children's increasing independence and encouraging rather than criticizing the child for failures by which they become more confident and secure in their own ability to survive in the world. Erikson (1973) also argued that it is essential for both self-development and recovery from mental trauma that others approve the existing self. According to Mead, a person is socialized through the internalization of others, which is directed by others' approval or disapproval. I shall call others that are defined by this developmental self-other relationship "approving others".

The concept of "approving others" comes into being only if there is a need to be approved of or a need for recognition within the subject. If we keep to the developmental framework, the relationship between the need to be approved of and approval/disapproval parallels the child-adult (especially guardian) relationship, and this kind of approval has a strong connotation of an "acceptance of one's existence itself" or an "approval of one's identity". However, we shall adopt a broader application rather than this limited one. The spectrum of approving others adopted here includes such cases in which an approval function becomes a privilege and hence a power in society, parties working together on equal standing become symmetrically and reciprocally approving others and a passive approval is given in the form of acquiescence. If approval is given in accordance with the rules of a social group, this approval/disapproval is analogous to the dichotomy between "permission/rejection", which was emphasized by Itani (1987) as an act involved in the formation of primate social structure.

The other concept of "others" draws on Lévinas's understanding that highlights otherness (see Chapter Ten by Omura). This other is the other self or the other mind and "an existence that always flows over and out of my understanding" (Nakayama 2007) whom I can never understand in the way I understand myself. However, Nakayama sums up Lévinas's otherness as follows: "The 'resistance' (= otherness) of the other does not do violence to me, does not act negatively". In other words, the other is someone who is co-present with me while carrying in them something incomprehensible to me, but that is not all. I cannot put aside this incomprehensibleness because I seek co-presence and understanding, which is also a demand of otherness, or I realize that the other is an existence that flows over and out of my understanding because I feel that I understand the other. Thus, the other with otherness appears because of the subject who seeks co-presence with the other, just as the approving other appears vis-à-vis the subject who seeks approval. Seeking co-presence with the other precisely means that human beings are social beings. We shall call others with otherness or others who impose a strong sense of otherness on us "incomprehensible others" here.

In the mind of the subject, other people who are different from the self present with some level of otherness, but such realization tends to be reflective. We do not normally see incomprehensibleness in others with whom we socialize regularly, and we even push aside incomprehensibleness and give priority to "understanding" if we are trying to communicate with people from foreign cultures. Consequently, the other's otherness disappears in the mind of the subject when some affiliative act is being performed or when co-presence is occurring (this performative group and the co-presence group in it are represented as "We" from the subject's standpoint: Kuroda 2017). Therefore, an appearance of an incomprehensible other is unexpected, at least initially. For the subject, who thought the self and the other were in agreement that they were in the same world, or in other words, who thought that they constituted "We", this is the moment of realization that the other was protruding from or strayed out of the "We" framework.

In this way of interpretation, incomprehensible others appear in places of deviation where they protrude from the framework of the community values that the subject follows or the mutual understanding within a performative group. If the subject desires co-presence in spite of this, the subject must request the other to return to or review the mode of co-presence (rules and conventions) and "We". In the latter case, the subject is faced with the decision of whether the subject must change themselves accordingly or reject and exclude the other, that is, whether to change the rules and reorganize "We" or retain the rules and dissolve or split "We" (Kuroda 2017).

Although the two types of others look different, they share the common characteristic of appearing from an existence involved with oneself. Accordingly, they may appear in one person in an intertwined manner. A rejection of approving others leads the self to the social isolation of a closed self, while a rejection of incomprehensible others leads to diminished activity in self-preservation. This is why the subject must accept and face up to others first, even though they present with otherness. As in the case of a mother to her weaning infant, for example, when the other, who used to accept everything, suddenly declines to breastfeed or cuddle, the mother turns into an incomprehensible other in the mind of the infant. If, however, separation from the other is not an option, the subject must search for a new way to realize co-presence. In this case, the incomprehensible other is an existence that forces a renewal of the subject's world.

By combining the above, we can also compare the two types of others in the following way. Approving others are those who form, maintain or deepen "We" because they affirm the values and actions of the person who seeks approval, whereas incomprehensible others are those who bring "We" to the front of consciousness and to the verge of change.

We shall attempt to apply the concept of "others" to primate societies below, based on the above descriptions of the two types of others. Nevertheless, we shall adopt a loose definition of otherness as stated above, and broaden incomprehensible others to "people in whom the appearance of otherness is inferable" for reasons such as hesitation in communication with an unfamiliar other, the moment of breakdown of the ongoing joint action or co-presence, a special action against an other who engages in unusual behavior, a gap before the initiation of communication and so on. If the subject wishes to maintain the existing relationship with the incomprehensible other, then the subject needs to change or adjust their behavior afresh. In other words, the incomprehensible other is a person who brings otherness to the forefront and compels the subject to change themself.

Absence of approving others in early developmental stages

Approval covers a wide range of acts because, while it is an act of affirming a certain existence or action, it sometimes becomes clear through the opposite act of rejection in the form of acquiescence. Accordingly, we shall categorize typical human cases using two examples – one revolving around the approving others thought to be important in the developmental process and who appear in relation to coexistence, and one revolving around the asymmetry and symmetry of an act of approval – and attempt to apply them to non-human primates.

The first form of approval that appears between an infant and a guardian in the human developmental process is a total mutual acceptance, which is outside of the scope of our discussion here. What we need to note with regard to early stages of human development is that an infant constantly expresses its need for approval and this is the origin of the appearance of the developmental approving others.

A human infant begins to exchange smiles ("social smile": Takeshita 1999) and vocalizations with its mother around four months after birth. This exchange soon develops into a form of call-response in which the infant calls the mother a short distance away and responds to the mother's call. This type of vocalization by the infant can be regarded as a request for approval, and the mother's response can be regarded as approval. Conversely, mothers generally report that they experience the great joy of motherhood when the infant smiles back or responds vocally, so the infant can be regarded as the other who accepts and approves of the mother, even though this is not the infant's intention.

As the infant develops an ability to play with building blocks after the first year, it begins to delight in being praised for stacking blocks well, that is, its act is approved. After reaching the age of two, the infant goes on to demand approval for any accomplishment verbally by shouting, "Look! Look!". A joy of achievement and a need to gain approval from an intimate other are expressed together at this moment and, if approval is given, further enhance the infant's sense of achievement and desire for a new challenge.

While this type of request for approval combines a representation that the infant is "an existence that meets the expectations of surrounding adults" and a request for the recognition of this fact, the adults need to accommodate the infant's ability and perspective in making judgment. Consequently, this constitutes a request to "Look at my achievement from my standpoint", which is in fact an excessive and unreasonable request to "Make my world your world", but the surrounding people accept it with little awareness of this fact. Let us call this interaction a "deep engagement". A desire for "deep engagement" with one's surroundings may not be expressed overtly by adults who have acquired inhibition and self-control (exceptions might occur between lovers), but it has been inherited as a human trait. Otherwise, "the agony of co-presence" (see Chapter Ten by Omura) would not exist and hence "incomprehensible others" would not appear.

The infant's request for approval of its act already incorporates the adults' expectations, that is, the values of their community, and therefore it is an act of orienting oneself as a member of the community. In response, the approving adults apply their values and cultural attitudes to the infant through approval/disapproval and make corrections. Where the adults indicate which matters need approval emphasizing the act of approval/disapproval, it amounts to "training" or "teaching" which produces role models or teachers. On the other hand, it is well known that the child's behavior grows similar to that of its parent over time without intentional training. This is thought to happen because the child identifies with the parent while facing the same objects and the infant's body becomes attuned to the parent's in their sympathetic relationship (see Chapter Five by Hayaki).

The need for approval that causes the appearance of approving others forms the basis for not only the socialization and education of infants, but also the formation of desires towards society such as for expression, fame, recognition and so on. In other words, approving others have the same origin as these basic social desires that underpin human society.

Does the need for approval and approving others during the developmental process also appear in primate societies, especially in chimpanzee and bonobo societies? In these settings, the infant-mother relationship is no different from the full acceptance relationship between the human infant and mother. In subsequent stages of development, however, the need for approval and approving others do not appear clearly nor are simple acts of discipline or training found in chimpanzees and bonobos. When chimpanzee and bonobo infants go near hazardous objects, their mothers either stop them or pick them up and run from or attack the threat. This is sufficient because the infants eventually stop going near potential aggressors or dangers, but the mothers almost seem indifferent in our eyes as they do not scold mischievous children nor do they express pleasure with their achievements. Paired with this lack is a lack of need for approval in children. As a result, there is no appearance of an approval-like act in which mother and child share in "the result of an action". This is a major psychological divide between humans and their most closely related species.

One example that confirms the lack of the need for approval and the act of approving is video footage broadcast in a program called *Ikimono chikyū kikō* on NHK, Japan's national broadcaster (1998). The chimpanzees living in the forest of Bossou Village, the Republic of Guinea, use a stone anvil and hammer to crack hard oil palm seeds to eat highly nutritious endosperms. Young chimpanzees begin to use the stone tools by trial and error as they imitate their mothers from around the age of 3.5 years, but they only occasionally succeed by chance. They become skilled enough to choose an appropriate anvil/hammer pair and to control the hammer for optimal cracking by around the age of seven. The video footage shows a four-year-old chimpanzee watching its mother use the stone tools and slapping a seed with its hands, a seed rolling down a crooked stone anvil and then the young chimpanzee accidentally succeeding in cracking the seed. What surprised me was that the infant slowly ate the endosperm expressionlessly while its mother and other chimpanzees nearby, who would have seen the infant's success, showed no change in their demeanors at all and continued to do whatever they were doing.

Photo 1.1 A bonobo infant and its mother
A bonobo infant is highly dependant on its mother and cries loudly if it lags behind her even slightly when travelling. Like a human child, it demands "deep engagement" from its mother.

This case was not exceptional. I have asked multiple researchers involved in testing various problem-solving capabilities of chimpanzees in captivity, and none of them have reported that they exhibit any special expressions or gestures when they succeed in solving problems. As mentioned earlier, a human child would say such things as "I did it!" and "Did I get it right?" to seek agreement or look to a nearby adult with a proud expression[1]. Here the child is seeking approval. However, chimpanzees do not show a joy of achievement nor request approval. Consequently, approving others do not exist in this context[2].

Bonobos are slightly different from chimpanzees. Bonobo infants start crying out for guardians if they are left unattended[3]. If they lag behind their mothers a little while marching in a procession on a tree, they start bleating loudly. Researchers who have cared for bonobos say that bonobo infants are a handful, but they do try to understand the other's intention. This propensity can lead to a request for "deep engagement", albeit not to the degree of human babies (Kuroda 1999). In comparison, chimpanzee infants are more independent. The following is an observed case, although it is exceptional.

Four-year-old male bonobo infant TW sits face-to-face with, almost touching, alpha male KM, who is eating sugarcane, peers into KM's face and begs for food by reaching his hand toward KM's mouth. After a while, KM drops small pieces of sugarcane from his mouth into TW's hand twice. TW runs to his mother, touches her, and returns to KM to continue begging. TW runs to CHT, about a year older than him, touches him and returns to KM. TW fetches a piece of sugarcane by himself, returns to KM and eats it in front of him, then runs to CHT again, immediately returns to KM and receives a piece of sugarcane. CHT approaches YS, the second-ranked male also eating sugarcane, and peers into his face, but YS does not respond. CHT approaches MN, a young male eating sugarcane, then returns to YS and sits in front of him, but YS still does not respond. CHT glances at YS, and then returns to his mother. TW again receives sugarcane pieces from KM twice in a row.

Judging from CHT's reaction, we can surmise that TW communicated to his mother and CHT that he received or tried to receive sugarcane from KM. Why did he do so? In my mind, TW was showing his joy upon receiving sugarcane from KM to his mother and his playmate. It is the equivalent of "Look! Look!" in human infants. Even though approving others did not appear in the end because his mother did not seem to respond, we cannot rule out the possibility that bonobos have something similar to a need for approval.

A subject seeking approval for co-presence and approving others

An important approval behavior that can be observed in *Pan* is approval in relation to co-presence or cooperation when participating in some group or occasion. An asymmetrical form of approval for co-presence or cooperation is that by the leader of the group or occasion, which is what Itani (1987) calls "permission". Here, we shall call the act of mutually approving co-presence "mutual approval". The asymmetrical and symmetrical forms of approval are not always clearly distinguishable in the real world, but we shall not go into details here. See Chapter Five by Hayaki and Kuroda (2017) for a discussion of mutual approval in play among primates.

I must explain the social structure of *Pan* briefly as a premise for our discussion below. Chimpanzees and bonobos live in social groups consisting of several dozen to over one hundred individuals. These are patrilineal groups where females transfer between groups and males remain in their native group. There is one major difference between the two species – chimpanzee males form a male group with an alpha male at the top and stand against neighboring groups, whereas bonobo males do not form a male group and they build peaceful relationships with neighboring groups even though they sometimes antagonize them. If an individual chimpanzee encounters a hostile neighboring group, it may be attacked or even killed, but such cases have never been observed in bonobos. As bonobo females get together to confront males, females ultimately have the advantage in their power relationship (Furuichi 1991; Kanō 1986; see Chapters Two, Six, Seven and Eight regarding chimpanzee society).

In chimpanzees, the subject seeking approval and the approving others appear in greeting behavior when a late-adolescent male approaches and tries to join a group of adult males, and when a transferred young female forms a relationship with a senior female. Greeting is considered to be an act to resolve tension and confirm a relationship when a chimpanzee encounters another in their fission-fusion society. Adult males hug or kiss on an equal footing, whereas a female or adolescent male who encounters a dominant male extends a hand while showing a submissive expression and uttering grunts, and settles down when the counterpart responds by gently touching their hand. Some interpret this as a display and confirmation of a relationship rather than a greeting, because some females do not act in this way when they encounter a dominant male.

To male chimpanzees, adolescence is a period of struggle when they stop following their mothers around and try to join the adult males. This is not the case in bonobos, as they continue to follow their mothers into adulthood and males do not form groups[4]. In adolescence, male chimpanzees first challenge adult females to gain dominance over them. When they more or less succeed in doing so, the late-adolescent males begin attempts to participate in adult male gatherings. Adolescent males approach adult males while vocalizing pant-grunts, usually uttered by submissive individuals, extending their hands or bowing. If they are permitted to touch, they follow them around for grooming. Adult males initially chase them away by threatening or attacking, but adolescent males continue to approach and eventually gain approval to join them (Goodall 1986; Hayaki 1991). As mentioned in an example in the next section, young males gradually join the rank order of adult males by challenging lower-ranked adult males to gain dominance over them.

The initial rejection by adult males is an act that complies with the existing rank order and apparently keeps out those who try to enter. However, if a young male is unable to join the adult male group, he not only remains in a status below the lowest rank, but also becomes exposed to the danger of being killed by another hostile group if he acts alone outside of his community. This means that the only course of action for adolescent males that is adaptive to their social structure is to keep trying to become part of a male group. Thus, the subject who continuously seeks approval despite rejection appears, and eventually approving others will also appear.

For young female chimpanzees and bonobos, it is essential to gain approval for co-presence in the group they transfer into. Even if they do not like their new group, they must eventually join a group somewhere. They have no other choice. In chimpanzees, a transferred female often stays on the fringe of a gathering and behaves cautiously. Males and infants are receptive to the new female and invite her to play or mate, but the existing females often threaten or attack her. The new female approaches a receptive high-ranking male to avoid being attacked by other females or follows a receptive dominant female, and gradually blends in with the rest of the group. What we find in this process are the subject's efforts to become a member of the group and the others who give their approval almost in the form of acquiescence.

In the case of bonobos, a new female is welcomed by males and infants and actively and tirelessly interacts with them by mating and playing (Kuroda 1982), but the existing females are not necessarily welcoming. An infant may be playing with a new female, but the mother may threaten and exclude her. Unlike in chimpanzees, however, the situation can take a different turn in bonobos as females engage in the practice of genito-genital rubbing to defuse tension and reconcile. Dominant females are generally receptive to new females and often permit their co-presence as they respond to an invitation for genito-genital rubbing from young females. Eventually, the new female follows a particular dominant female (Idani 1991).

Let me introduce one observed case. After transferring to E1 group in Wamba, a young female named Aey mated with males and played with infants, but she was ill treated by other females. Then, she repeatedly engaged in genital rubbing with a dominant female named Hal and began to follow her. When Hal was stung in the face by a bee and let out a small cry, other bonobos nearby did not react at all, but Aey, who was five to six meters away, ran to her and gently touched her face. This incident demonstrates the degree of attention Aey was paying to Hal at the time. A few days later, Aey got into a struggle with a young male over sugarcane. Hal ran to her aid and together they chased the male away (Kuroda 1982). Hal not only approved Aey for co-presence, but also acted as her guardian or ally. Nonetheless, young females frequently switch the others they follow and stop following particular individuals once they have their own babies.

These examples indicate that young *Pan* males and females become subjects seeking approval for co-presence because it is deeply related to their social structure and there is no other option for them. The appearance of approving others is a consequence of that. The mode of co-presence achieved as a result is the very foundation of their social structure and not mediated by any particular values or the like separated from it.

Incomprehensible others in chimpanzees

I stated earlier in the chapter that incomprehensible others appear in places of deviation where they protrude from the framework of the community values that the subject follows or the mutual understanding within a performative group. I also stated that incomprehensible others force the subject to rethink the mode of presence (rules and conventions) as well as "We" as a community.

According to these definitions, individual relationships surrounding a transferred individual from another group (young female) of chimpanzees or bonobos are not where the incomprehensible other appears. This is because, although the transferred individual is an unknown other to the existing members of the group and all of the existing members of the group are unknown others to the transferred individual, the relationships therein precede mutual understanding and shared values. Therefore, either party may be attacked or welcomed, but it cannot be an unexpected response or a deviation from an agreement.

However, it may be possible to say that an incomprehensible other appears in the lead up to the transfer of a female out of her native group. In bonobos, a daughter slowly reduces the frequency of social interactions from the age of seven or eight and spends significant time on her own when resting and ranging. It seems rather odd to find a daughter hiding in a bush like a recluse away from her mother at the center of her ranging party. Her younger brothers and infants invite her to play or groom, but she withdraws and disappears from the group by the age of around nine. The daughter may become an incomprehensible other to the other members of her native group, but none of them attempt to restore co-presence with her and instead simply let this member of "We" fade away. Observers have trouble understanding this strange incongruence between the way the daughter leaves her group and the aforementioned active effort she makes in her new group.

In relation to transfers, there is a possible appearance of an incomprehensible other in chimpanzees when a new female gives birth to a male baby within six to twenty-four months of her arrival. The frequency of this has been declining in the

Mahale Mountains in recent years, but in the past male chimpanzees used to engage in cannibalism by killing the first baby of a new female (Nishida 2011, Nakamura 2015). If the males with whom the new female have built friendly relationships in the new group snatch, kill and eat her baby, it is reasonable for us to imagine that these males must appear as incomprehensible others in her eyes. Yet, the loss of the baby leads the disheartened mother to become estrous again, mate with the males who killed her baby and become pregnant. After that, the female tends to act more closely with the males. The reason for the selective killing of the first male baby is unclear, but the new female's second baby is spared. Hence it is ultimately reasonable for the female to recognize the existence of violent incomprehensible others and deal with them by seeking closer co-presence.

In chimpanzees and bonobos, there are frequent instances where a young male suddenly begins to challenge a senior male after a period of submission and persistently attempts to move up in the rank order. These contests are quite fierce, particularly among chimpanzees, and we can surmise the appearance of an incomprehensible other in the process. This was particularly true with the case of Goblin reported by Jane Goodall (1986, 1994).

In the Kasekela community in Gombe Stream, Figan rose to the top through a firm alliance with his older brother Faben and maintained his alpha male status for ten years after his brother's death by securing another ally. A male infant called Goblin began to follow Figan, who took him under his wing by grooming, and grew up by repeatedly imitating Figan's display and other behaviors. When he reached fourteen years old, Goblin began to challenge adult males despite his young age. He would ambush his opponent or make a surprise attack from above or behind. It was obvious that he had learned these tactics from Figan, who had been using them to compensate for his small stature. The targets of his challenges seldom put up a fight in fear of reprisal from Figan. Even if they fought back and repelled Goblin, he never gave up and continued to challenge tenaciously. Goblin climbed to a high rank that was disproportionate to his young age and finally challenged Figan and caused him to fall out of a tree. Adult males banded together to beat Goblin and inflicted severe injuries on him. Once his injuries healed, however, Goblin resumed his persistent attacks on Figan and others. Figan looked increasingly unsettled, and for an unknown reason disappeared from the group. Goblin gained an older ally named Jomeo and became the alpha male at the unusually young age of seventeen. Goblin was aggressive by nature and often attacked even females and infants mercilessly. Perhaps because of that, the entire group turned against him and twice inflicted major injuries on him. In the end, Goblin died of his injuries.

According to Goodall, Goblin's case was highly unusual in that he kept challenging on his own without an ally until he reached the top. When Goblin attacked Figan, whom he had been following and receiving protection from since he was an infant, Goblin must have appeared as an incomprehensible other in Figan's eyes. It is also possible that all other members were apprehensive when, despite many setbacks, Goblin persisted. Otherwise Goblin could not have been victorious considering his physical disadvantage and lack of allies. At first, male chimpanzees attempted to beat and exclude this incomprehensible other, and when the attempts failed, they oddly resorted to ignoring him. On one occasion when Goblin approached them with furious displays, the other males repeatedly ignored him by intently engaging in grooming for more than ten minutes (Goodall 1994). In the end, Goblin jumped in and scattered them.

Although Goblin reached the top on his own, he approached an older male named Jomeo to form an alliance with him through grooming and meat sharing. The alliance eased Goblin's tension, cut the frequency of his aggressive displays by half and settled him down. He began to behave more like an alpha male and the two always shared meat from hunting between them. This indicates that alliance for male chimpanzees is mutual approval and shows how important allies are. In a way, mutual approval turned the incomprehensible other (Goblin) back into a co-present other. Even then, Goblin's tyrant-like behavior did not stop and he continued to suddenly go into displays and attack other individuals. Finally, the entire group set upon and killed Goblin in the end, because he became the other the group could no longer live with, that is, an enemy.

While Goblin was the alpha male, he exhibited another aspect of the incomprehensible other when he tried to coerce his estrous mother into copulation (Goodall 1994). Goblin was nineteen years old at the time and had not shown sexual desire toward his mother before. In this incident, the mother became enraged and counterattacked as Goblin tried to force her into copulation, but Goblin did not give up easily and attempted to mount her many times. She somehow avoided mating with him, but she became fearful of Goblin and avoided his company from then on. She had no choice but to abandon her co-presence with a son who had become an incomprehensible other. Several incest attempts between siblings were observed at Goodall's study field, and normally it was the female sibling who would scream and run away. These instances were very rare compared with other mating combinations, and perhaps it is reasonable to say that an incomprehensible other appeared in these cases. The possibility of incest involving siblings arose in Goodall's study field, as almost half of the females remained with their mothers even after adolescence instead of transferring to another group.

The equality principle and incomprehensible others

Itani (1987) found two principles underpinning the mechanism of coexistence by which primates form groups, namely, the inequality principle and the equality principle. The inequality principle is a means for coexistence by fixing a dominant-subordinate relationship into a rule. The equality principle is a means for coexistence by either interacting on an equal footing or acting as if members are equal, despite the dominance relationship between them. He also argued that the matrilineal social groups of the superfamily Cercopithecoidea are generally dominated by the inequality principle, whereas chimpanzees and bonobos, the closest species to humans, have patrilineal social groups in which the equality principle is gaining power after the inequality principle-based order began to break down.

To put it simply, a chimpanzees' social group has a nuclear group of adult males that is joined by females who transfer from other groups. While the male members maintain strong unity in standing against neighboring groups, they are also rivals who compete for ranks and mates, as the frequency of mating with a fertile female increases according to rank. In order to maintain a high rank amid this competitive environment, it is indispensable to find a male ally for mutual assistance (Goodall 1994; de Waal 1987; Nishida 1981).

Besides the above, the following two points are more important in understanding interactions between male chimpanzees. Firstly, male chimpanzees have more or less equal strengths and capacities, and many of the individuals are resilient enough to try to regain dominance when an opportunity arises even when they are defeated in a fight to increase their rank. Secondly, while they have the ability to secure a special ally in order to gain and maintain a higher rank, they are also capable of betraying their current ally depending on the situation. Consequently, the rank order and the associated peaceful state built by the males are more like provisional contracts temporarily entered into on the basis of the balance of power. If the alpha male wishes to keep his status, he must serve his allies and supporters who are in fact subordinate to him (de Waal 1987, 1993; Kuroda 2017).

Thus, although a clear rank order exists among males, it is quite different from a stable rank order based on the inequality principle and requires all members, including the alpha male, to exercise self-restraint if they want to maintain it. Nevertheless, those who act on the equality principle to become equal or superior are cultivating future betrayals. One day, they may appear as incomprehensible others who tear up the provisional contract.

On the other hand, it is likely that there is another mechanism that maintains this unstable group order – the way a release of the males' self-restraint turns into a communitas-like collective excitement and reinforces the group's solidarity (Kuroda 2013, 2017). Especially in chimpanzees, collective excitement manifests strongly when the group encounters or fights a hostile group. In a whirlpool of fear and aggression, male chimpanzees hug each other to fire themselves up and in doing so conflicts among individuals dissolve into solidarity in mutual dependence. It is possible to say that otherness between group members vanishes completely in this communitas-like situation.

Japanese macaques, whose society is based on the inequality principle, act collectively in hostilities with other groups, but they never enter into this communitas-like situation. As the balance of power between Japanese macaque groups is determined by the relative strengths of their alpha males, occasions of intergroup hostility have no effect on the relationships between the individual members of the same group. It is possible to say that the disappearance of otherness in chimpanzee social groups is structurally connected to the equality principle, just as is the appearance of incomprehensible others.

While we have discussed the equality principle in relation to male chimpanzees, it of course applies to female chimpanzees as well, going beyond their practice of food sharing or the fact that the dominance/subordination principle is not the rule governing interactions between individuals (Kuroda 1999). In both chimpanzees and bonobos, the female's ability to transfer between groups under the patrilineal system means that females are released from blood ties and acquire the freedom to move to another group if they do not like their new group, even though it comes at a price. In matrilineal primate species on the other hand, blood relation is the main determinant of rank among females and they have no way of escaping males who come into a female consanguineous group, therefore they have far less freedom to act on their own. In short, we surmise that females in a patrilineal society enjoy a higher degree of freedom than females in a matrilineal society and their rank order, if it exists, is determined by the relative strengths of individuals and hence entails a higher degree of freedom (fluidity) than the consanguinity-based rank order. From a female point of view, the equality principle is strongly linked to patrilineal society.

44   Chapter 1

Photo 1.2 Bonobo peering behavior
A young bonobo male peers into a female's face at close range. This behavior is inferred as an act of deferring a decision about engagement to the other.

An act to recognize otherness

Peering behavior, the intent gazing of one individual at another in close proximity, is observed in gorillas, bonobos and chimpanzees. Bonobos in particular engage in prolonged peering (several tens of seconds) with one's forehead almost touching the other's face (Photo 1.2). Bonobos in captivity engage in peering behavior with human researchers as well. This behavior is yet to be fully understood, although researchers interpret it as an interrogative behavior judging from the situations in which it manifests (private communication from P. M. Greenfield). In the case of peering among bonobos in Wamba, it is sometimes followed by genital rubbing or grooming, but on most occasions nothing happens and the peerer quietly leaves the scene. On all of the occasions when something happened, the peeree made a small body movement and the peerer responded to it. Based on these observations and the fact that an invitation to engage in genital rubbing or grooming is accompanied by a clear signal, an act of peering without any signal can be understood as an open invitation for interaction leaving the choice of what to do to the counterpart (Kuroda 1999).

According to this interpretation, peering behavior indicates that one wants to do something but does not know what the counterpart wants, therefore one waits to see how the counterpart reacts, or, one relinquishes one's agency and lets the counterpart choose what to do. In other words, one suppresses one's wishes and accepts the counterpart without knowing their wishes. This suggests that one not only has full confidence in the counterpart, but also recognizes that the counterpart has something one does not have. This suggestion is worth considering, because bonobos in captivity exhibit an attitude of trying to listen to and comply with what their researcher-carers want (Savage-Rumbaugh 1993) and because it can solve the theory of mind problem (NHK 2000). The following behavior has been commonly observed both in the wild and in captivity: in grooming, one party pulls the other by the hair on their head and moves for more than ten meters. The individual who is being pulled with its head down cannot see where it is going, but it follows the counterpart's lead without resistance.

We can derive the following hypothesis if the above supposition is correct. In the earlier discussion about incomprehensible others in chimpanzees and bonobos, an incomprehensible other suddenly appeared in the form of a deviant. The only ultimate response by a subject to it (except where it was a mother in the weaning period) was exclusion (by stopping the interaction, severing a relationship etc.). In other words, incomprehensible others who appeared to chimpanzees and bonobos did not become others demanding the transformation of "We". However, if peering behavior means, without knowing what the other wants, that one waits to see how the other reacts or that one defers one's subjectivity to the other's wishes, then this behavior contains a different attitude toward otherness – recognizing otherness in the other and accepting it. While this otherness is different from the incomprehensibleness that appears in deviations, peering can be regarded as approval for otherness and a behavior that allows the other to have its own subjectivity. Still, this remains a hypothesis at this stage, as in most cases the other does not respond and nothing follows.

A behavior such as peering by putting one's face very close to the other's face cannot happen in inequality principle-based species such as the Japanese macaque, because the subordinate individual would run away. Peering, which seems to allow this otherness to appear, is possible precisely because the species operate according to the equality principle.

The narrative begins with a deviation

We have so far examined the appearance of others in *Pan* societies in terms of developmental approving others and incomprehensible others with salient otherness. I stated in my thesis in *Institutions* that rules and "We" who assume these rules are brought to the forefront of consciousness and renewed by deviations in natural institutions, but our discussion here has now arrived at the same conclusion. A deviation that triggers the appearance of an incomprehensible other leads to rethinking the subject and the rule and opens a door to a renewed world. While this rarely occurs in *Pan* societies in reality, the door often opens very wide in human society. It also entails the destruction of an existing world. All myths and folktales begin their narratives with a deviation and end with the emergence of a new order. This counterposing of a rule and a deviation can be regarded as one of the unique characteristics of human society.

2 Are Animals "Others" or Are There "Others" to Animals?

Michio Nakamura

Key ideas

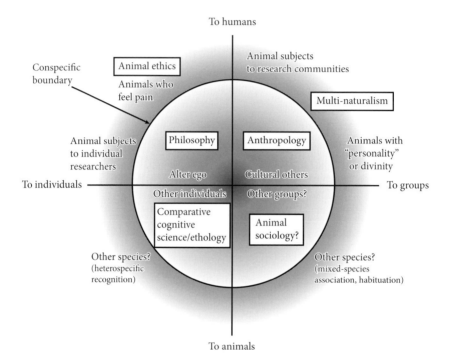

Within each quadrant, others may be differentiated on the basis of whether they are conspecifics or heterospecifics (inner circle). Discussions on others are usually confined to human-to-human interactions shown in the top half of the circle. Unless we consider that others exist only to humans, we need to explore the bottom half of the circle as well as the outside of the inner circle. Boxed labels signify corresponding academic disciplines.

Photo 2.1 A female chimpanzee named Nkombo
While she is a chimpanzee individual, she is a specific other called "Nkombo" with characteristics that are distinct from those of other chimpanzees in the minds of researchers in Mahale.

Others and animals

Discourses on "others" in disciplines such as philosophy and anthropology are often based on the implicit assumption that both parties (self and others) are human (*Homo sapiens*). If we are to discuss others from the position of "Human Society in Evolutionary Perspective", however, we need to consider whether non-human animals can be others and whether others exist for non-human animals in the first place. In this chapter, I examine whether the concept of "others" is applicable to animals, instead of assuming that others = human. In doing so, it should be noted that the concept of "others" varies among different academic disciplines.

Let us first establish the following points.

In my studies of wild chimpanzees (*Pan troglodytes*) in Mahale, Tanzania, the chimpanzees are others to me. It seems to me that way at least (Nakamura 2009). It also seems to me that exchanges between them are interactions between others. The chimpanzees I am referring to here are not chimpanzees in general, but rather they are specific and individual beings whose faces and characteristics I can recall (Photo 2.1).

The second point is that humans are ambiguous beings who are *animals and non-animals at the same time*. While human (*Homo sapiens*) is an animal species (an organism that belongs to the kingdom Animalia), it is often believed that humans differ from *mere* animals (beasts) because they are equipped with so-called "humanity". Although this is a very anthropocentric categorization, we shall use the term "animals" to refer to "non-human animals" in this chapter.

What are others?

There are two aspects to others: that which we understand because of similarity and that which we do not understand because of dissimilarity. In daily life, (we think that) we are able to understand people around us and to interact with them. We do not imagine that our friendly conversation partner might attack us in the next breath. We tacitly understand that the person would never act in such a manner. On the other hand, others are different from "I" in a strict sense. Some people think that "only I can feel my pain", and that it can never be established in principle whether the color red I am seeing is qualitatively the same as the color red others are seeing.

An attempt to discuss others in relation to animals gives rise to the question, *to whom* are they others? While others signifies "other humans" to humans in many of the discourses on others, it would be useful to clarify that there are two distinct questions involving animals: whether animals can be others *to humans* and whether conspecifics and other animal species (including humans) can be others *to animals*.

There is another dimension to this discussion. In the case of others to humans, a distinction between others as individuals and as groups appears possible. In the case of the philosophical problem involving self (ego) and others (alter ego), the other can be a single individual. On the other hand, others in cultural anthropology, for example, often tend to be groups (be they cultural or ethnic) other to one's own group (see Key Ideas Diagram).

Who are others to humans?

Conditions giving rise to others

We begin our examination by looking at the conditions that generate others to humans[1]. For the purpose of this chapter, the conditions need to include animals as potential others. The code *h* in the section below denotes a human.

Condition 0(*h*): "Others are those of the same species as *h* (i.e., are humans)".

As mentioned earlier, this is the most common – but seldom expressed – assumption[2]. This assumption is not applicable to our current examination as it completely excludes animals.

Condition 1(*h*): "Others are those who have X similar to that of *h*".

These are beings not entirely the same as "I" (ego), but they (seem to) have X similar to "my" X (thus, alter ego). The X can be substituted with subjectivity, mind, soul, reason, cognitive capacity and so on. The X is usually seen as some internal/mental function that characterizes "I" (and humans by extension). The key feature of the X is that in many cases it is not easily verified by empirical science.

In this sense too, animals are usually not others (or it is more appropriate to say that they are not considered as a subject for such discussion). The assumption is that animals have no X (Cartesian "reason": Descartes 1953) or impoverished X (Heidegger's "world-poor", cited in de Fontenay 2008). Such assumptions appear to be prevalent even today. For instance, "becoming animal" in Azuma (2001: 127) means "the erasure of this kind of intersubjective structure and the arrival of a situation in which each person closes various lack–satisfaction circuits". In this sense, others do not exist to animals.

Conversely, the recognition that animals "have X" will lead to the logical conclusion that animals are others. The same line of reasoning is followed (albeit in reverse) by, for example, Singer (2011), who uses "a capacity to feel pain" as X in recognizing animal rights. This line of reasoning argues that it is outrageous to eat animals (others) that can feel pain.

This type of argument is closely intertwined with the so-called "problem of ego and alter ego". It seems that this is fundamentally a problem between individuals premised on the modern Western idea of the autonomous "individual"[3]. *Cogito, ergo sum* (I think, therefore I am). And the "I" asks, "How about you?"

Condition 2(*h*): "Others are those who do not belong to Y, to which *h* belongs".

These others are complements of a set Y: those who do not share an understanding with us; those who speak a different language or who are outside of the bounds of our communication; those who are culturally different from us. Y can be "the

Japanese nation" or a "village population". Foreigners and outsiders are considered to be others.

Being outside of the bounds of our communication does not mean a total inability to communicate in reality. For example, communication is possible between Japanese people and foreigners, or villagers and outsiders. To be more accurate, it probably signifies different manners, styles or frequency of communication. This view is similar to the "society" in sociobiology as described by Wilson (2000: 8), where "its boundaries can be defined in terms of the curtailment of communication".

Unlike Condition 1(h), Condition 2(h) is used in the context of others to "us" rather than "I" as an individual. It may be premised on the existence of groups.

Animals can be others in this sense. The recent discourse on animals in anthropology (e.g., Okuno et al. 2012) appears to be aligned with this view. In short, it attempts to explore the existence of non-human beings outside of the bounds of normal human (linguistic) communication.

Those who were outside of the bounds of communication might not have even been "others" initially (e.g., the Barbaros[4] to the Hellenes (Greeks) in ancient Greece). Considering that those barbarians and foreigners who were not others in the past have since been promoted to the status of others, however, animals are perhaps going through this stage (a transitional stage from non-others to others). Humans may always need to be able to point to others "who are not us" whenever they question their own identities.

In practice, however, we do not think about the "modern individual" and something internal pertaining to Condition 1(h) or the entire group pertaining to Condition 2(h) every time we face others. Are there more real-life conditions?

Condition 3(h): "Others are those able to interact socially with h"[5].

This condition can include the following two conditions.

Condition 3(h)-1: "Others are those who actually interact (have interacted) socially with h".

Condition 3(h)-2: "Others are those who can potentially interact socially with h".

The Condition 3(h)-1 is easy to understand, as it is actually observable. Yet, Condition 3(h)-2 is also necessary because there are cases in which others are recognized in the absence of actual interactions. For instance, we might not actually speak to persons who sit beside us on a train[6], but we would be unlikely to kick them without warning as if they were pebbles on the ground. This is because we recognize our neighbors as others with whom we could potentially interact.

Let us use this Condition 3(*h*) to determine whether non-human beings are others to humans in some examples.

Those who are others to humans?
When one is playing with one's pet animal, unless one is a real contrarian, one is likely to agree that there is a social interaction occurring. In this sense, pets are others to their owners.

Similarly, Derrida (2014) felt "ashamed" when his cat saw his naked body, thus he considered the cat to be his other. It is unlikely that a sense of "shame" would arise in the absence of the other's gaze.

Zhuangzi, an ancient Chinese thinker, saw some fish leap in a river and knew the joy of the fish (Kanaya 1975). It is possible to consider that the fish appeared as the other to Zhuangzi at that time. We do not normally consider that there is a social interaction between leaping fish and the human watching them. When Zhuangzi was able to feel the joy of the fish, however, they became the other with whom he could potentially interact.

Those who are not others to humans
When we buy a package of pork at a supermarket and eat it, we almost never think of the pig it came from as the other. The person eating the pork never thinks about socially interacting with the pig. This is not simply because the pork is a lifeless object. For example, the ashes of a deceased son (lifeless objects) are probably an other to his parents, who have not yet been able to lay them in a tomb.

To Nagel (1989), who contemplated what it would be like to be a bat, the bat was not an other[7]. To him, the bat was merely the object of hypothetical reasoning and not actually there with him.

In a similar example, Huizi, a debater strolling with the aforementioned Zhuangzi, responded, "You are not a fish. How do you know the joy of the fish?" (Kanaya 1975). Both Huizi and Zhuangzi saw the leaping fish. If Huizi denied the possibility of interacting with the fish by declaring that "the joy of the fish is unknowable", then the fish could not be an other to Huizi, even though he witnessed the same phenomenon as Zhuangzi.

Ambiguous cases

Some examples are not so clear-cut. One is the case of a certain alien (the Magu-magu) in a science fiction story entitled *Saiaku no sesshoku* (Worst contact) by Tsutsui (1979). An earthling and the alien can converse on a superficial level, but they never understand each other. While the human thinks he has built an amicable relationship with the alien, the Magu-magu abruptly attacks or attempts suicide without warning. Can we consider such beings to be others when humans cannot interact with them properly?

In the case of robotic pets such as AIBO, we initially get the feeling that we can interact with them as living pets. AIBO can be considered to be the other as long as this relationship continues, but once the owner gets bored and puts it away in a closet, the switched off object is no longer the other to the owner. A live pet cannot be switched off and put in a closet. It demands to be fed and excretes bodily waste, which needs to be disposed of. Nevertheless, when the owner rejects the possibility of interacting with a live pet and abandons it, it may at that point cease to be the other to the owner.

While robotic pets are programmed to "respond" to human actions in some ways, ordinary dolls do not respond at all. In this sense, they are theoretically incapable of interacting with us. Yet, can we say with confidence that a doll is not the other to a child playing with it?

In some cases, children's playmates are not "real" in the usual sense. A certain proportion of children create imaginary companions invisible to adults (Mitchell (ed.) 2002). The imaginary companions can be "realistic" beings to the imagining children whom they can see, hear and/or touch. To observers, the children may look as if they are interacting with "empty space" (treating empty space as the other).

How about people on television? Are the celebrities talking on a TV screen interacting with you[8]? The same questions can be asked about animals. We encounter various animals on a TV screen as we watch nature documentaries. However, this experience seems very different from the actual experience of coming face-to-face with animals (Nakamura 2015a), in that it lacks the possibility of direct response.

Thus, others fluctuate considerably when we ask who others are to humans. Animals are excluded only when a condition such as Condition 0(h) is adopted. The answer depends on X and Y in Conditions 1(h) and 2(h) (i.e., depending on the definition). Under Condition 3(h), the boundaries of the perceived others fluctuate depending on the situation.

Who are others to animals?

Now, let us consider who can be others to animals. We shall simply swap h indicating a human with a signifying an animal, while maintaining the same pattern.

    Condition 0(a): "Others are those of the same species as a".

Concepts such as "cognition of the other" in comparative cognitive science and "the other individual" in animal behavioral science generally assume this condition. In this sense, it is assumed that others exist to those animals with cognitive capacities that are relatively close to those of humans.

    Condition 1(a): "Others are those who have X similar to that of a".

This is not very useful here, as X tends to be something unique to humans and often difficult to verify by empirical science. It becomes meaningful only if X is an ability that is recognized in humans and just a small number of animal species, but the question remains in terms of how far it can be extended. "The ability of mirror self-recognition" in the place of X seems to make sense, while "the ability of visual perception with eyes" seems to hardly serve the purpose. This condition appears to be susceptible to anthropocentric demarcation after all.

    Condition 2(a): "Others are those who do not belong to Y, to which a belongs".

There can be others to animals under this condition. To those animals who form groups with clear membership, for example, there must be others who are not "members of their own group" (i.e., members of other groups). At the least, their behavior toward members of other groups is clearly different from their behavior toward members of their own group. Not confusing the members of one's own group with those of other groups is almost synonymous to forming distinct groups.

    In many species, it is also rare for animals to confuse their own conspecifics with members of other species[9]. For instance, to chimpanzees it is conceivable that those who are not chimpanzees (e.g., gorillas, humans etc.) appear as others. It is unlikely that chimpanzees confuse chimpanzees with gorillas or humans, as the former behave differently from the latter.

    Can any of these self/other distinctions be applied as a condition that gives rise to others? There are some questionable cases. For example, certain insects may clearly distinguish their conspecifics through "automatic" reaction to wing color patterns. Similarly, ants may distinguish the members of their own colony (group) from those of other colonies through odorant response. Is it appropriate for us to equate these cases with the human propensity to exclude the members of other groups?

> Condition 3(*a*): "Others are those able to interact socially with *a*".

This condition can include the following two conditions.

> Condition 3(*a*)-1: "Others are those who actually interact (have interacted) socially with *a*".

> Condition 3(*a*)-2: "Others are those who potentially can interact socially with *a*".

The aforementioned cases of "automatic" reaction to colors and smells (and if we thus do not considered them "social") under Condition 2(*a*) can be excluded under this condition. Where interactions resulting from automatic reaction are considered "social", then those who engage in such interactions can be included in others. Let us look at specific examples of animals under Condition 3(*a*).

Others to chimpanzees

We shall consider others to the chimpanzee, my study subject, here. They can be broadly divided into other conspecific individuals and animals of other species.

Conspecific individuals

As chimpanzees live in a steady form of group called a unit-group (or community), the fellow individuals in the same group (i.e., familiar individuals) can be considered others. They engage in a wide range of interactions with these others on a daily basis including grooming, meeting, parting, greeting and fighting (Photo 2.2).

These interactions between chimpanzees within a group appear "social". In terms of Condition 3(*a*), this means that chimpanzees live with a large number of others on a daily basis, just as humans do.

Then, how about the chimpanzees of other groups? Intergroup relationships between unit-groups are said to be antagonistic, and chimpanzees do not routinely

Photo 2.2 Grooming is a routine interaction for chimpanzees

interact with individuals belonging to other groups. In other words, the individuals of other groups are strangers who should be avoided.

Below are some examples of intergroup encounters in my research field of Mahale, Tanzania.

Case 1: The cause of a commotion

The chimpanzees of M group, my study subject, are on a hill ridge in the southern part of their home range. At least all adult males and most adult females of M group are located in the vicinity. Many of the individuals suddenly turn their heads to the south and raise ear-splitting screeches. Males hug one another or put their arms around other males' backs. A few chimpanzees venture into bushes to the south of the ridge. There is a mountain named Mkulume about one kilometer by straight-line distance to the south of the ridge. Then, the voices of other chimpanzees reach my ears from the northern side of Mkulume. As all the males of M group are here and some of the voices from Mkulume sound like male voices, the source of the voices is probably N group, which is the southern neighbor of M group. Calls are produced by M group, followed by vocalization by N group, followed by vocalization by M group, and this exchanging of voices continues. It is unlikely that the groups have direct visual or physical contact, as there is a considerable distance between them. After continuing the vocal exchange for a while, the individuals of M group begin travelling northward and the voices supposedly from N group are no longer audible.

This example can be considered as an interaction with unknown parties via voices. There may be different views on the question of whether this can be called "social" or not. It is possible to interpret this as simply a reaction to an unfamiliar sound. However, their reaction in this case is not the same as their reaction to the voices of chimpanzees of their own group or other animals, or the sound of an airplane. Therefore, if we assume that the chimpanzees are screaming and huddling together while thinking about the chimpanzees of another group, we can say that others with whom they potentially can interact have appeared to them.

In this way, other groups constitute potentially antagonistic parties to adult males, but the situation is slightly different as far as females are concerned. In particular, for the sexually mature females who were born into M group, other groups are potential destinations for transfer. While males nervously engage in vocal exchanges, young females may be evaluating the other group as to whether it is a good place to transfer to in the future.

What happens immediately after the transfer of a female? According to a case study of a female newly immigrated to M group from another group (Nakamura and Itoh 2005), the resident group members show a level of interest that is clearly stronger than usual by gathering around the immigrant female (i.e., treating her differently from the known members). Nevertheless, they engage in usual interactions with her such as mild intimidation and grooming. In other words, they seem to accept the unfamiliar individual as the other with whom they can interact.

A case that differs from that of a normal other individual involves playing with an imaginary playmate (e.g., Hayaki 1990). Although there is no other party to the social interaction in such a case (at least it is invisible to the observer's eyes), this involves an act of trying to interact socially. This is no different from the aforementioned human imaginary companion in this sense. It is possible that chimpanzees share this ability to create in their minds "others" who do not exist in reality[10].

Animals of other species
Chimpanzees live in a variety of relationships with other sympatric animals. Among them, those who most frequently encounter and have diverse relationships with chimpanzees at Mahale are red colobus monkeys. The red colobus

(*Procolobus rufomitratus*, hereafter just "colobus") is a primate species belonging to Cercopithecidae, Colobinae. Although this monkey species is well known for being frequently hunted and eaten by chimpanzees, the relationship with chimpanzees is not confined to predator-prey. I discuss some examples below.

Case 2: Hitting a colobus monkey
One day, an adult male catches a colobus monkey. The male is holding the tail of the colobus, which is still alive and squeaking. Nkombo, an adult female watching by his side, lightly raps the colobus in the head with her fist several times. The colobus squeaks every time it is hit.

As chimpanzees are inept at finishing off their prey, it is common for a captured colobus to be still alive. This gives rise to the seemingly grisly situation where a colobus can be eaten alive. Chimpanzees normally just eat the animal they have caught and rarely engage in any other act. I wonder whether they would feel uncomfortable eating prey once it had become the other through interaction?

Case 3: Provoking a colobus
A young female named Serena taps a tree trunk as she climbs. Colobus monkeys upon the tree emit alarm calls. She climbs higher and a male colobus makes a short run in her direction. Serena descends a little. She repeats the game of approaching and being chased off by the colobus.

It is difficult to regard Serena's act as a serious attempt to hunt the colobus, as it is not easy for a lone chimpanzee, especially a young female, to catch prey. In fact, she appears to enjoy the colobus' reaction. If this is the case, the colobus must appear to Serena as "the other" rather than "the prey".

Case 4: Being intimidated and chased off by a colobus
Linda, an adult female, is feeding on fruit a short distance away from other chimpanzees. A troop of colobus monkeys arrives from the south over the tree branches. As a male colobus runs toward Linda, she descends the tree halfway. The colobus continues to act in a threatening manner, and Linda reaches the ground and hurriedly travels in the direction of her group.

In this case, we could interpret that a social interaction was certainly occurring if the intimidating colobus were replaced with another chimpanzee. This case is

Photo 2.3 Emory spying on a warthog

the same as Case 3 in the sense that an interaction is happening, except that here "an object of playful teasing" is replaced with "an object of fear".

While it is difficult to see edible meat as the other, it is possible to interact with a living colobus in various ways. It is therefore not appropriate to say that chimpanzees' relationship with colobus is always that of predator-prey.

In the case of humans also, social interaction can take place even with beings that are primarily for consumption. For example, humans sometimes eat their livestock as meat, even though they have looked after them with care.

Chimpanzees have an ambiguous relationship with leopards (*Panthera pardus*) as well. It is probably that the leopard is primarily an object of fear for chimpanzees. Cases of leopard attacks on chimpanzees have been observed in a West African study site (Boesch 1991), and chimpanzee bones have been found in a leopard scat in Mahale (Nakazawa et al. 2013). Accordingly, leopards are chimpanzees' potential predators and chimpanzees basically maintain vigilance against and avoid them.

Yet, chimpanzees sometimes act in a threatening manner toward leopards, and there is one reported case in which chimpanzees killed leopard cubs (Hiraiwa-Hasegawa et al. 1986). Also, chimpanzees have been observed to show interest in the dead body of a leopard (Nishida 2012).

In Mahale, encounters between chimpanzees and warthogs (*Phocochoerus africanus*) are not uncommon. While there are only two cases of predation of a warthog in 1966–1995 data (Hosaka et al. 2001), interactions such as warning, provocation, running away in fright and chasing are more frequent. Here is one example.

Case 5: An encounter with a warthog
An adolescent male named Emory is spying on a warthog (Photo 2.3). Whether being bothered by the attention or not, the warthog trots toward Emory. Emory backs off when the warthog approaches. Once he is farther away, Emory resumes his observation of the warthog and takes various actions such as shaking a tree and getting a little closer.

In this case, for some reason Emory became curious about the warthog, even though he did not seem intent on "eating" it. It was not easy to interpret his behavior, but it appeared to be a response suggesting a mixture of "curiosity" and "vigilance".

We should not forget that humans are also animals of another species to chimpanzees. In some regions, humans eat chimpanzees or hunt them for their skins or as sources of traditional medicine, and a majority of chimpanzees in zoos today were captured as infants (when their mothers were killed) or are their descendants. In general, therefore, humans are dangerous animals to chimpanzees.

As an exception, a particular type of human called "researchers" approach chimpanzees with the intention of habituating them (see Yamakoshi in Chapter Fifteen). Chimpanzees exercise vigilance at first, but they drop their guard and begin to act normally when researchers slowly increase the frequency of encounters and continue to demonstrate their harmlessness.

Nonetheless, they do not necessarily treat all humans equally, even when they have become habituated. Their attitudes toward tourists are sometimes clearly different from the way they behave toward familiar researchers (Nakamura 2009).

We have so far looked at cases involving live mammals. Let us now consider examples of other animals (e.g., insects) and dead animals.

Case 6: Playing with a moth
A juvenile female named Imani catches a moth alive. Instead of killing it, she grips its wing in her lips and plays with the flapping wings. She throws the moth away when its flapping motion slows and catches and holds it in her lips again when it resumes flapping (Nakamura 2013).

This case may not exactly be what we could call a social interaction. Yet, the moth's motion (i.e., being animate) appears to have generated the pleasure of engaging in this act as play. In this sense, we can perhaps treat this as a marginal case of the appearance of an other.

The next case involves a mammal that is already dead.

Case 7: Being afraid of the dead body of a bushpig
Chimpanzees come across the partially decomposing body of a bushpig (*Potamochoerus larvatus*). Some of them move closer and sniff, while several climb trees to watch and emit frightened wraa calls.

Chimpanzees are known to respond with a mixture of curiosity and fear to the corpses of other chimpanzees (Hosaka et al. 2000) and aardvarks (*Orycteropus afer*) (Hosaka et al. 2014). These cases are equally difficult to interpret. It is possible that this is associative learning linking an animal carcass to the presence of a leopard (that may have killed it) – the possibility that chimpanzees are spooked by the potential presence of a predator nearby rather than the dead body itself[11]. On the other hand, we cannot rule out the possibility that they are reacting to the dead body itself differently from the way they react to a mere object. If the state of "being dead" evokes a sense of fear, this would indicate that chimpanzees understand "death" to a certain extent. More prudently, however, we may say that they are avoiding an "unfamiliar object"[12] or "something in an unusual state".

In the meantime, chimpanzees' attitudes are somehow different in relation to the dead bodies of small animals.

Case 8: Transporting a dead genet
The genet (*Genetta* sp.) is a small mammal about the size of a kitten. An adolescent female named Carmen found the decomposing body of a genet and carried it around on her back for a while (Photo 2.4).

Photo 2.4 Carmen carrying around a genet carcass

The dead genet of course did not move, therefore this is different from Case 6 in which a chimpanzee appeared to enjoy the animacy of her plaything. As young females often transport items such as tree bark, branches and man-made objects, it is perhaps unnecessary for us to speculate that she was carrying it because it was a dead animal. On the other hand, because the sense of fear shown in Case 7 is absent in this case, we suspect that a mere "*dead* animal" is not a trigger for fear.

Animals other than chimpanzees

The chimpanzee obviously does not represent all "animals". As Derrida (2014) points out, "animals" are not at all homogeneous enough to be bundled together in opposition to "humans". We must remember that there is difference between one species and another to the same extent as (or more than) the difference between humans and chimpanzees.

If we do not stand on the premise that the appearance of others is a rather recent event in evolutionary history (i.e., it happened in the evolutionary lines

Photo 2.5 A giraffe and oxpeckers

of anthropoid or primate, for example), it will be meaningful for us to study whether others can exist in animals that are phylogenetically remote from *Homo sapiens*. As we cannot possibly consider all animals here, we shall venture to look at the cases that do not permit interpretation by our chimpanzee-based reasoning so easily.

Intraspecific

Social insects are animals with a very different kind of sociality from that of mammals. Taking a line of ants as an example, individual ants contact one another by touching each other's bodies with their antenna or crossing their antennae. Through this form of communication, a colony of ants as a whole can accomplish feats such as marching in a perfect line, catching much larger prey or dissecting and transporting it to their nest.

Let us look at the classic case of territorial defense among the three-spined stickleback (a small freshwater fish) (Tinbergen 1957). In the breeding season, males become territorial as their bellies turn red. They respond to the red bellies of conspecific males by attacking them.

In both the above cases, the phenomenon of social interaction emerges between conspecifics. However, an individual ant is no longer regarded as an individual from the same colony if its smell (pheromone) is artificially changed. Three-spined stickleback males tenaciously attack an elliptically shaped plate with its bottom half painted red, even though it is an inanimate object. Given that they respond to "incorrect" information provided by humans, their interactions seem to be more of an automatic/physical response.

I am not trying to assert that the interactions among ants and three-spined sticklebacks are non-social. However, we need to recognize that they are qualitatively different to our usual social interactions in some sense. There may be others to ants, but their others may not be understood in the normal way we understand our others.

Interspecific

Interactions between animals of two different species can be often observed in predator-prey relationships, symbiotic or parasitic relationships and mixed-species associations.

Predator-prey interactions are easy to imagine. They include a lion eating a zebra and a spider eating a trapped moth. Parasitic interactions are also simple. Lice and ticks parasitize humans as well. Symbiotic interactions can be found between giraffes and oxpecker birds, for example. These birds are often seen perched on the neck or shoulder of large herbivorous animals such as giraffes (Photo 2.5), and benefit from eating parasites on them, while giraffes benefit from having parasites removed by the birds. A mixed-species association is a phenomenon involving the formation of a group by animals of multiple species (Adachi 2003) and is common among primates and birds.

These interspecific relationships between various animals have often been discussed from an ecological cost-benefit viewpoint, but it seems that the question of whether social interactions are taking place between different species has rarely been examined. Is the other party in such an interspecific relationship merely an "environmental" factor that benefits (or harms) one, or is there already an embryotic sign of otherness here? There seems to be scope for future exploration.

In closing: For an evolutionary historical understanding of others

To the question posed in the title of this chapter, "Are animals 'others', or are there 'others' to animals?", my tentative answer is a rather indecisive "Yes and no, depending on the conditions and the situation". This is because to begin with the word "others" is ambiguous and has different meanings in different academic disciplines even when it is used in relation to humans.

In this chapter, we have taken the standpoint of trying to understand "others" in the broadest possible sense without assuming a human-like mind. I believe that we should better expand the concept of "others" as much as possible before we approach the evolutionary historical basis of others (and it is more important to expand the concept of others *to animals* rather than *to humans*). If we approach this with the understanding that others are social counterparts[13], we can recognize the common presence of others among various animal species (or it is at least possible for observers to interpret in this way), and there is no need to limit the possibility to conspecific individuals. I am certain that there will be many people who will not accept some of the possible cases of others I have mentioned in this chapter. However, I believe that the task of recognizing others (or if this term is not acceptable, "the primordial form of otherness") in various animal species and identifying and comparing similarities and differences between them is an important task in considering the process by which human "others" emerged.

On the other hand, we need to be careful about many things when we expand the concept of others to animals. For example, it is easy for observers to read "others" into the behaviors of animals who are human-like in their appearance and behavior such as chimpanzees[14], but such inference is more difficult in the case of animals with sociality that is dissimilar to human sociality such as ants. And it is possible that, *because of* the abilities for representation and imagining which humans have specialized, human observers read "others" into animal interactions *as they wish*. However, these problems theoretically arise when we study humans as well. Unless we assume a priori that there are others to humans, we cannot rule out the possibility that observers are just reading "others" into interactions between other humans (who, after all, resemble the observers more closely than other animals do).

My intention in this chapter has been to outline the issues relating to others in animals in the simplest format possible, rather than to arrive at a conclusive answer. I am prepared to accept criticism for oversimplification. Nevertheless, it is almost impossible for us to come to a common understanding if individual researchers and academic disciplines simply continue to define others from their own standpoint (and in a complex manner that defies mutual translation) and to limit their discussion to "my idea of others" and "others in this academic field". I believe that the first task we need to carry out in an attempt to understand "others" in the evolutionary historical context is to identify the relationship between the concepts of others in various disciplines and clarify which aspect is being discussed. It is my expectation that this task will lead to the creation of an environment that fosters multifaceted discussions of others inclusive of the societies of other animal species.

3 When Others Appear

Toru Soga

Key ideas

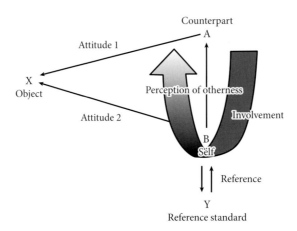

Otherness is perceived in the context of a triadic relationship. (1) Where there is a large gap between Attitude 1 disclosed by the counterpart and Attitude 2 of oneself toward the same Object (person/thing/event), one perceives otherness in the counterpart. (2) Where the counterpart asserts the righteousness of their own value judgment or attitude and demands one's involvement, one perceives otherness in the counterpart. (3) Where the counterpart's action toward the Object deviates from one's own reference standard, one perceives otherness in the counterpart.

Perceiving incomprehensible "otherness"

There is a social networking service called Facebook. After the terrorist attacks carried out by Islamic extremists in Paris, France, in November 2015, Facebook offered the option of adding an image of the French national flag to the user's profile picture to show sympathy for the victims and solidarity with France. A great number of users immediately took this option.

However, this innocent expression of sentiment was met by an unexpected backlash. People complained that it was not right to single out France when greater numbers of people were being killed in frequent terrorist attacks in places such as Syria and Iraq. Aside from the question of morality, it was very interesting to me that a considerable number of people expressed their discomfort when Facebook users began to display the French flag. I suspect that their apparent distress came from a visual form of peer pressure as their lists of friends quickly filled with French flags. In this chapter, I would like to discuss the perception of otherness that occurs when one feels as if one's close friends are suddenly becoming distant.

Others are significant in considering the evolution of human sociality. Humans have built diverse types of society by modifying their relationships with others. In Bushmen hunter-gatherer society for example, it is customary for people to try to resolve interpersonal tension by leaving the location where the tension was expressed and maintaining spatial distance between the parties involved. As they choose not to get involved with incompatible others, they have built a society with a high level of fission and fusion and a low level of political integration. In Gabra pastoralist society on the other hand, people are willing to give unconditional support to their clan members, even if they have committed heinous acts such as murders. They use the clan system to "assimilate" or "dissimilate" others. The Gabra have built a society in which relationships with others are automatically handled in relation to clan membership (Soga 2017). Meanwhile, in our civil society, we have been trying to achieve coexistence by assuming the existence of others who differ from us and providing appropriate institutions. At the same time, we have made it possible to fight others with the use of such institutions.

These three types of society can be summarized as follows: "society that avoids confrontation with others" (the Bushmen); "society that institutionally expels others from a clan and avoids having others within the clan" (the Gabra); and "society that institutionally seeks to coexist with others" (civil society). This classification is of course conceptual. In reality, the Bushmen sometimes live with unresolved friction with incompatible others, and the Gabra sometimes fight or quarrel with members of the same clan. Our society features bullying and insidious violence where civil rules cannot penetrate.

In previous publications, I have considered the formation of human "groups" and "institutions" (Soga 2013, 2017). While these subjects have dealt with how relationships with others are formed, I shall reverse the direction of my thinking here and consider a mechanism that results in the appearance of others. Others appear constantly in all societies. They appear among those who are close to us and create a rift. We sometimes perceive people of other ethnicities outside of our society as others and they become targets to kill, or sometimes we extend our hospitality to heterogeneous others. Let us now examine the ways we perceive or do not perceive others.

To "understand" others

I begin by looking at how others have been treated in philosophy. From the outset, others have been dealt with as obscure beings. The question has been how to understand others rather than how others appear. Philosophy has put forward two major positions in understanding others. One treats them as capable of being understood, while the other treats them as the "absolute other".

Comprehensible others

The notions of "intersubjectivity" developed by Husserl and "intercorporeality" proposed by Merleau-Ponty support the position that others can be understood. Various academic disciplines with a passion for understanding others such as anthropology, sociology, sociopsychology and ethnomethodology have looked to Husserl's and Merleau-Ponty's theories of others for methodological bases in the understanding of others.

The principle here, as explained by Tsuru (1998), can be summarized as follows: In Husserl's phenomenology, "the other" is seen as a "modification of the self" rather than simply as a "duplicate of the self". When many people share similar experiences, "the other" to "me" will come to see "me" as "the other". Based on this shared subjectivity formed in this way, or "intersubjectivity", the belief that all of us must be seeing the same world is created. For this reason, "my" subjectivity and "the other's" subjectivity basically share the same structure, even though they appear in different ways, and hence "I" can understand "the other".

Anthropologists conduct fieldwork and attempt to understand others experientially. The key to this endeavor lies in the intersubjectivity and intercorporeality shared by "I" and "others". Yet, this does not mean that anyone can understand others instantly just because we are all equipped with intersubjectivity and intercorporeality. Long-term fieldwork is indispensable perhaps because researchers need a great deal of experience before they can acquire the same subjectivity as that of their participants.

Even then, there are others who defy understanding. For instance, there is no guarantee that a researcher will be able to understand others who engage in headhunting or cannibalism, even after many years of fieldwork. However, sometimes shocking experiences can help to overcome this hurdle. The following passage describes a striking scene where his wife's death helped anthropologist Renato Rosaldo (1993: 3–9) understand an impulse for headhunting, which he had previously had difficulty comprehending.

> When Ilongots told me, as they often did, how the rage in bereavement could impel men to headhunt [...] no personal experience allowed me to imagine the powerful rage Ilongots claimed to find in bereavement. [...] In 1981 Michelle Rosaldo and I began field research among the Ifugaos of northern Luzon, Philippines. On October 11 of that year, she was walking along a trail with two Ifugao companions when she lost her footing and fell to her death some 65 feet down a sheer precipice into a swollen river below. Immediately on finding her body I became enraged. How could she abandon me? How could she have been so stupid as to fall? I tried to cry. I sobbed, but rage blocked the tears.

Through his experience of profound loss, Rosaldo understood the rage Ilongots felt in bereavement. He admits that his anger was not necessarily identical to that felt by Ilongots. For instance, the Ilongot people channeled their rage into headhunting, whereas Rosaldo did not. Nonetheless, this example shows us the possibility that things that initially seem almost incomprehensible may be understood through cumulative experience.

Incomprehensible others

When we become convinced after years of fieldwork or radically different experiences that we "understand others", what do we become able to do? Let us consider the case of East African pastoralist societies.

Any anthropologist who has conducted field research in an East African pastoralist society will have been beset by the pastoralist custom of begging. Begging among the Turkana people is particularly intense, and anthropologists have been trying to understand it while being tormented by its persistence. For example, Ohta (1986) finds two main characteristics of begging – emphasis on the general reciprocity of altruistic giving and unilateral dominance of the begging party over the other – and points out that a sense of indebtedness that supports reciprocity is placed in an inactive state. Kitamura (1991, 1996b) notes that the Turkana confront what is presented "here, now" in a fully positive manner and understands that their society demands "deep engagement".

Nevertheless, no matter how one perceives begging, one cannot escape from communication with the Turkana facing one. In his struggle to understand begging, Kitamura (1991: 141) states "The difficult path of attempting to understand a foreign culture is open only in the direction of escaping from the state of maladaptation". What does he mean by this?

Even if we are convinced that we "understand others", it does not mean that we understand them in every detail. For argument's sake, if we understood the other in front of us completely, we would probably not enter into conversation with them, as there would be nothing to talk about. However, the opposite is true in reality. We tend to converse or get involved with others more by understanding them. What Kitamura is trying to say is that an understanding of others is available only in the process of escaping from the state of maladaptation occurring between us and them. When we understand begging, we become caught up in "deep engagement". We can escape from awkward exchanges by understanding others, but the more successful we are in escaping, the closer we are drawn into engagement with others.

We shall examine this direction in Lévinas, a leading figure behind the argument that others are incomprehensible.

In commenting on Lévinas's understanding of otherness, Tsuru (1998) sharply critiques Husserl's intersubjectivity and Merleau-Ponty's intercorporeality as they negate "the otherness of the other". As the "otherness" of the other is "that which is absolute other", turning it into something that is comprehensible on the basis of "intersubjectivity" means taking away not only the "otherness" of the other but also the "individuality" of "I". So, what did "the other" mean to Lévinas, who regarded "the other" as "that which is absolute other"?

> Lévinas argued that involvement with the other should be considered on a practical level instead of under the framework of the other as an object of perception, and constructed his unique theory of otherness *guided by the question of what the heterogeneity of the other brings to me* and not by similarity between I and the other. According to Lévinas, the other appears in a unique manner called "visage". When I am "face-to-face" with

the other, *the other is that which imposes a responsibility to "respond" on me and not an object to be perceived.* (Tsuru 2012: 28; emphasis added)

Lévinas's theory of the other asks what does heterogeneity bring to me rather than aiming to understand the other as an object of perception. Here, the other is a party who forces a face-to-face interaction on me. Because the other constantly destroys and deviates from my ideas, communication between myself and the other continually produces unexpected reactions and diverse responses. The heterogeneous other can be regarded as a partner in weaving a world for my self. The other brings meaning to the self through verbal interaction, reading each other's body language and facial expressions and connecting to communicate with each other.

If this is the case, it is not strange that we do not feel that we have understood others in everyday interactions even when we feel that we have understood others phenomenologically. Tsuru (1998) makes the point that "I" never asks "the other" anything, or vice versa, in the relationship between "I" and "the other" assumed by the phenomenological theory of the other. It is a silent understanding of the other, so to speak. We must instead position the other in a face-to-face interaction and avoid heading in the direction of the silent understanding of the other.

A dynamic understanding of others

In this chapter, we shall consider others who inevitably appear in human interactions based on Lévinas's theory of the other, rather than trying to understand them as an object of perception. While Lévinas regards the other as a necessary condition for interaction, it is also a sufficient condition. Where there is an interaction, the other necessarily appears. We must remember the following two points when we consider the problem of the other.

First, we must adopt a broad scope for the other both temporally and spatially. Some academic disciplines consider that the other is an agent who affects the self that belongs to a particular period of time. In psychology, for example, it has been argued that the existence of others is essential for the formation of a self-image. The speech, actions and attitudes of the other are considered to play an important role in self-development (Mizokami 2008). In this chapter, I would like to treat others as counterparts in interactions at every stage in life, and avoid limiting the focus to adolescence. These others may not be involved in the development of the self, but they may bring about a transformation of it. While elders may be others to young people involved in the development of their self-image, young people can be others to elders as well. Let us assume that others appear in interactions between various generations of people rather than limiting the significance of self and others to certain life stages or generations.

The same applies to spatial broadness. In anthropology, the other ethnic group in an interaction has been treated as the other. There are various manners of interaction. For instance, the agro-pastoralist Hor people in southwestern Ethiopia are said to categorize neighboring peoples into three types: "enemy people", "unclean people" and "friendly people". The Hor communicate with these peoples differently – negative exchanges such as war with enemies, coexistence with friendly peoples and no communication with unclean peoples (Miyawaki 2006). We shall treat these other ethnic peoples as others who appear in different kinds of communication. Moreover, the development of the media and the Internet has enabled us to communicate with those who live on the other side of the world. These days, opinions are exchanged worldwide on global-scale issues such as global warming. There are cases where diasporas who have fled political persecution lend support to conflicts on the other side of the world. In these contemporary situations, people living on the other side of the globe can become others. Although we shall not focus on this kind of other here, we need to keep in mind that others always appear where communication takes place.

The second point is that we must treat the other as a changeable being. In the aforementioned field of psychology, the other is conceptualized as a being that influences the formation of the self. Conversely, it points to the perception that "others become less important after adolescence". The significance of others to the self during the development of a self-image tends to change after that period. Others are not static beings; change in the state of the self changes the nature of others. Let us assess this fluctuation below.

Changes in how others are positioned may be similar to the swing of a pendulum. While studying the agro-pastoralist Daasanach people in southwestern Ethiopia, Sagawa (2011) noticed that their relationships with neighboring peoples cycled repeatedly between amity and war. Based on this discovery, he pointed out that peoples could not be characterized as having a fixed nature, for example a "peaceful people" or a "militant people". In this context, interethnic relationships vacillate between war and peace, and this dynamism is what we need to examine. Further, Sagawa states that potential impetuses toward opposite forms of the relationship exist behind each interaction, be they hostile or amicable.

In terms of Lévinas's theory, these potential impetuses are related to the other being "that which is absolute other". Referring to Lévinas (2006, cited in Sagawa

2011), Sagawa states, "What follows is the paradox that a group of people capable of waging war is capable of achieving peace as a manifestation of diversity, while a group of people capable of achieving peace is prone to go into a state of war as a consequence of diversity" (Sagawa 2011: 423–424). This chapter also pays attention to this type of fluctuating relationship in discussing the other.

The other is not a fixed being. When we feel that we understand the other completely, a sense of the heterogeneity of the other disappears even if "that which is absolute other" is still lurking deep inside them. We sometimes feel a complete agreement of thoughts, or being "on the same page", in complementarity with a counterpart. Conversely, a feeling of the other's heterogeneity increases when ways of thinking move apart. We may feel that we have nothing in common, sense a rising anger or lose trust.

The heterogeneity of the other (incomprehensibility) represents only a small aspect of their being. While keeping "that which is absolute other" deep inside, the other can be understood in some aspects and appears as an incomprehensible being in other aspects in everyday interactions. Everyday interactions are formed by connecting one's own action to the counterpart's action; a heterogeneous other appears when a rift emerges in such interactions. In which situations do we sense otherness in those close to us in everyday living? We now look at such situations.

The triadic relationship and others

The self-other-object model

In psychology, the formation of the self is thought to be carried out through the internalization of the speech and actions, views, thoughts, norms and values of others. In which relationships does this internalization take place? According to Tomasello (1999), babies in their early infancy live in a dyadic relationship in which they imitate the other's actions in face-to-face situations or touch a thing. Their communication between self and a familiar other (the mother in most cases) is closed. When a baby turns its attention to the other, it does not pay attention to nearby things, and when it turns its attention to a thing, it does not pay attention to the other. After nine months, however, infants begin to live in a triadic relationship consisting of self, other and object (i.e., thing, event or person). They can not only pay attention to a thing (object), but also have the awareness that the other is also paying attention to the thing (object) at the same time (Hamada 1988; Tomasello 1999).

The formation of the self in infancy occurs in this triadic relationship. The self sees an object (thing, event or person) and at the same time learns how the other behaves, thinks and understands in relation to the object (thing, event or person) in the triadic relationship consisting of self, other and object. The self is formed through the internalization of such views and thoughts. If we consider this internalization in terms of the aforementioned "fluctuation of the other", we can interpret this as one phase in an approximation of self and other.

Besides the formation of a self-image, where the self internalizes the other, there are situations in which both parties mutually internalize, or the other internalizes the self. It is clear that what the self internalizes is a certain aspect (a behavior, view, thought etc.) of a certain other expressed toward a certain object. When we say that the self internalizes the other, we mean a very small part of the other. "That which is absolute other" in the other relates to our only partial ability to internalize.

If the formation of the self in the triadic relationship between self, other and object is one of the phases of an approximation of self and other, we must be able to detect the appearance of the other if we make use of this triadic relationship. While the formation of the self was an effect of the internalization of the other, what we need to detect here is the distancing of self and other or a dissimilation action. Clues to sensing dissimilation include behaviors, views, thoughts and values expressed by a "potential other (A)" and "I (B)" toward a third term (X) (thing/event/person). When a "potential other (A)" expresses some opinion or value judgment about a third term (X) and "I (B)" feel that they are dissimilar to mine, "I (B)" get a sense of heterogeneity toward my "counterpart (A)".

This heterogeneity manifests to a greater degree when the "potential other (A)" involves "I (B)" in their opinions or values. Although this "involvement" is not a necessary condition for the sensing of the other, one is generally inviting people around one to agree when one expresses an opinion or value judgment. This force for agreement is involvement, and this chapter pays attention to this aspect as well.

Otherness perceived from an attitude toward a third term

Let us look at the case of perceiving otherness based on the other's response to a third term (thing/event/person). When (A) exhibits a certain attitude toward (X), (B) sometimes sympathizes with (A) and at other times feels uncomfortable with (A).

It appears that the pastoralist people of Gabra Miigo in Ethiopia with whom I have been conducting research perceive this kind of otherness. An unexpected statement led me to this realization. In 2002, I was looking for people with knowledge of history in my attempt to reconstruct the history of the Gabra Miigo. There is a position of political and ceremonial leadership in the Gabra Miigo called "Father of Gada". I was trying to identify the names of past Fathers of Gada. The people immediately

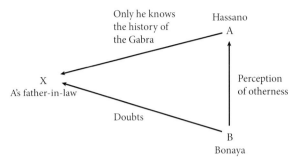

Figure 3.1 Attitude toward a third term (X) and the perception of otherness

understood what I was researching and became quite enthusiastic. When I presented my research results to them daily, they identified the history experts as if competing with each other, and put forward their assertions as to who knew more or better. The Gabra Miigo love heated discussions.

One day, a man named Hassano boasted that his wife's father was "Far more knowledgeable than anyone else. He knows what no other Gabra Miigo knows". People continued to argue about his statement, but eventually Bonaya, Hassano's friend, said under his breath, "If there is part of Gabra Miigo history that is known only to him, it means what he knows is not part of Gabra Miigo history".

When I heard Bonaya's muttering, I was struck by several aspects. Firstly, his delivery was calm and showed no sign of excitement, unlike the typical mode of expression in all other Gabra Miigo men. The content of his statement had no competitiveness, but it refuted Hassano's comment transcendentally on the basis of his argument. At that moment, I suspected that Bonaya was feeling some degree of heterogeneity toward Hassano. This is schematized in Figure 3.1. Hassano (A) made the exaggerated claim that his wife's father (X) was more knowledgeable than anyone else. At that moment, Hassano (A) appeared to Bonaya (B) as the other.

Here is another example. This case involves the Gabra Malbe people, who live in Kenya. Unlike the boisterous Gabra Miigo, the Gabra Malbe are a quiet people. The late Reizō Harako, who studied the Gabra Malbe, called them a "philosophical people". When I visited the field in 1997, however, they were engaged in a fierce contest surrounding several traditional leadership positions, casting off their mask of serenity.

Kenya was in the middle of a general election at the time. The Gabra Malbe experienced division in their society as they were caught up in electioneering. The political campaigners exploited the authority of the traditional office bearers in order to undermine the supporters of their rival candidates. Although it was not customary for the traditional office bearers to behave in an authoritarian manner, they exercised their influence during the election and attracted people's attention. In addition, the fact that election candidates offered large amounts of campaign funds to these traditional officials in order to secure their support motivated more people to seek these positions (Soga 2002).

One day, an elderly Gabra Malbe man named Shafi watched this tumult amongst his people and muttered, "No one wanted to become an office holder in the old days. When you are in that position, you become so busy with mediation and ceremonies that you have no freedom to put your animals to grazing when you want to". In the past, he had served in a traditional position called *jallaba*. He probably could not understand the young people's desire to hold such a post, as he knew how busy this would make them.

This situation can be represented using a triadic relationship. The younger generation (A) wished to gain the position of traditional office holder (X) and fought over it. However, Shafi (B) could not understand the fuss. Shafi (B) perceived otherness in the younger generation (A) as he watched how they reacted to (X).

Otherness perceived by the observer

When I (B) perceive otherness in the counterpart (A) in the process of communication, the perception is a phenomenon occurring inside my mind and is supposedly invisible to the eye of an external observer. Yet, the remarks made by Bonaya and Shafi told the observer that they were perceiving otherness. Which aspect of their remarks conveyed their perception of otherness?

Firstly, both Bonaya and Shafi made their remarks at a certain distance from the center of people's concentration. Bonaya kept himself out of the debate over the question of "Who knows better?", while Shafi kept his distance from those who coveted the position of traditional office bearer. The fact that their remarks were made in the form of "muttering" is also relevant.

If Bonaya and Shafi had thrown themselves into the debate and loudly tried to convince others of their argument, this would show that they did not sense otherness in others. When two parties have differing opinions at a particular moment, the party that is attempting to convince or refute the other party does not perceive otherness in the other party. This is because of the expectation that the party they are confronting will "soon" have the same opinion, even if they hold a different opinion "now".

On the other hand, the "muttering" of Bonaya and Shafi (B) was not intended to convince the counterpart (A). When those observing from the outside hear a remark devoid of an intention to persuade (A), they sense that (B) perceives otherness in (A).

Now, why did Bonaya and Shafi perceived otherness in Hassano and young people, respectively? Otherness was perceived simply because they are "different". As Lévinas says, others carry "absolute otherness" in them, and it is natural that they exhibit different opinions and attitudes in everyday interactions. Nonetheless, some differences are great while others are only minor. Minor differences can actually make conversation livelier. Major differences, however, lead to the perception of otherness.

A third term (X) acts as a trigger for the manifestation of major differences. The very existence of (X) brings both major and minor differences to the surface. The way a person (A) relates to an object (X) produces various differences. It can be said that the difference is the root of otherness. A person forms various opinions and attitudes toward various third terms (X, X', X'' and so on). Otherness may or may not be perceived depending on which third term is in focus. This means that the perception of otherness is context-dependent.

Otherness perceived by strong "involvement"

Next we examine the case in which otherness manifests when the counterpart (A) presents its opinion or value judgment about a third term (X) and "involves" I (B). I stated earlier "The very existence of (X) brings both major and minor differences to the surface". The next case describes the way two ethnic groups that were approaching one another with regard to multiple third terms (X, X') began to perceive otherness through involvement surrounding a certain third term (X''). We shall confirm that the perception of otherness is context-dependent while we examine a mechanism by which involvement causes I (B) to perceive otherness as it forces (B) to play along.

Although the Gabra Malbe and the Gabra Miigo consider themselves to be of the same ethnicity based on the common Gabra designation, until recently they did not often interact. This is because the agro-pastoralist Borana people occupying the area between the two groups are hostile to them. However, the two groups began to increase cooperation rapidly from around 2000 in order to deal with certain situations, including an election in North Kenya and ethnic conflicts in South Ethiopia.

In electorates in and around the city of Marsabit, North Kenya, ethnic minorities such as the Gabra Malbe, the Burji, the Rendille and the Samburu have been actively cooperating in their election campaigns in order to take seats from the majority Borana. Meanwhile, seats in the electorate of Moyale near the North Kenyan border had been held by the majority Borana. The Gabra Miigo residents near the city of Moyale were trying to capture the seats from the Borana with the cooperation of the Gabra Malbe. In this situation, the Gabra Malbe (B) and the Gabra Miigo (A) cooperated in order to take seats from the rival Borana candidates, and (B) did not perceive heterogeneity in (A) in doing so.

Similarly, the Gabra Miigo and the Borana had been engaged in frequent ethnic conflicts in South Ethiopia, but the Gabra Miigo began to attack the Borana on both sides jointly with the Gabra Malbe. Again, the Gabra Malbe (B) and the Gabra Miigo (A) shared the same attitude toward their common enemy in the Borana (X'), and (B) did not perceive heterogeneity in (A).

As the Gabra Malbe and the Gabra Miigo increased their interaction, however, another third term (X'') came to draw attention from both sides. This was conversion to Islam (X''). A majority of Gabra Malbe worshipped their traditional one and only god named *waqa*, while small numbers were Catholic Christians or Muslim. The relationship between Christianity and the traditional religion has been positive and without conflict. However, almost all of the Gabra Miigo people were Muslim. The Gabra Miigo near Moyale in particular were ardent members of a Wahhabist mosque with strong fundamentalist leanings. It appears that they actively tried to convert non-Muslim Gabra Malbe to Islam. A Gabra Malbe man (Christian), who was my research assistant, told me that the Gabra Malbe were starting to grow tired of the Gabra Miigo people because of their persistent attempts to convert them.

Let us ascertain the context-dependency of otherness first. Otherness is perceived as a difference in attitude toward a third term (X). When the third term (X) is switched to another third term (X'), Otherness in relation to (X) recedes into the background and otherness in relation to X' is newly perceived. In this example, the relationship between the Gabra Miigo and the Gabra Malbe grew amicable in relation to "seats (X)" and "the Borana (X')", and the two groups approached one another. In relation to "Islam (X'')" however, their friendly relationship receded into the background and the Gabra Malbe perceived otherness in the Gabra Miigo.

Photo 3.1 Gabra Miigo children learning the Qur'an
Almost all of the Gabra Miigo people are Muslim. In a village with a resident Islamic teacher (*malim*), children are taught Qur'an in the early morning.

Nonetheless, it is important to note that what made the Gabra Malbe perceive otherness in the Gabra Miigo was not Islam (X") itself. Some of the Gabra Malbe were Muslim and the Gabra Miigo's faith in Islam in itself was not the reason behind the perception of otherness. They perceived otherness because they were subjected to "involvement" in the form of persistent proselytizing. Conversion is a typical involvement. A strong involvement leads to the perception of otherness perhaps because every person has "that which is absolute other" in them. Be it a conversion or something else, a strong involvement allows the absolute difference lurking between self and other to come to the surface.

Whatever the issue may be, when someone (A) tries to persuade me (B), (A) thinks that "I can persuade (B) if we talk it over". Persuasion is an act attempted by (A) who feels "closeness" to (B) rather than by a person who senses heterogeneity in (B). This is the very reason (A) trying to persuade (B) sometimes has a love-hate feeling toward (B) (and this is also a perception of otherness) when (A) has failed to persuade (B) despite much effort.

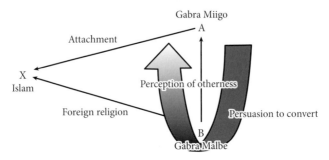

Figure 3.2 Strong "involvement" and the perception of otherness

Conversely, I (B) feel otherness in an advocate (A) when (A)'s argument in relation to a third term (X) is unacceptable to (B), and (A) is attempting to involve (B) by way of persuasion, for example (Figure 3.2). As we have seen in the above example, there are occasions when otherness is perceived by the act of involvement itself rather than by the content of a third term (X). This is because involvement can be considered as control over (B) by (A). The concept of otherness becomes apparent and is perceived as resistance against the exercise of control by (A) over (B).

Reference standards and others

Perception of otherness based on a reference standard

We have so far examined the perception of the other in everyday life. Our discussion has centered on the other perceived in everyday interactions among people who are familiar with one another. Now we shall consider otherness perceived in less familiar persons. Otherness in this discussion is perceived in situations where people with different cultural, social or religious backgrounds have contact. In other words, it is otherness that manifests in so-called cross-cultural situations.

The mechanism by which one perceives otherness in people from a remote world is somewhat different from the aforementioned triadic relationship. When one sees or hears the attitude or behavior of foreign people toward an object, one uses one's own attitude or behavior as a reference standard. Let us see how it differs from the triadic relationship.

For instance, one topic that comes up frequently in conversation among the Gabra Miigo (B) is the manner of eating (X) of the white people (A). The white people eat food served on their own plates, whereas the Gabra Miigo sit around a dish and share the food. One of the virtues of the Gabra Miigo is "sharing joys and

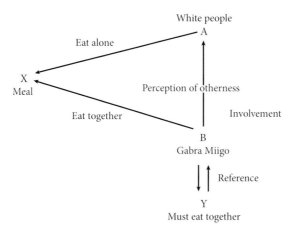

Figure 3.3 Reference standard and the perception of otherness

sorrows with others", and the sharing of a plate of food is an embodiment of this virtue. This is why the Gabra Miigo (B) have a strong sense of otherness toward white people (A) when they see (A) eating from their separate plates (Figure 3.3).

Sagawa (2011) has also noted the perception of otherness in relation to eating. The Daasanach people (B), the subject of Sagawa's research, are both hostile and hospitable toward their neighboring pastoralists. However, Ethiopian highlanders (A) in the town do not antagonize nor share meals with the Daasanach, and would not think of extending hospitality toward them (X). In this context, the hostile neighboring pastoralists are not others to the Daasanach. Rather, the Daasanach perceive otherness to a greater degree in the Ethiopian highlanders.

In this situation, very little interaction takes place between self and other. The perceived otherness here is perceived in observing another group of people from afar, rather than in everyday interaction. The mechanism of perceiving others without interaction is different from the triadic relationship between self, other and object in our earlier discussion. Otherness is perceived in others in relation to their behavior in relation to an object (eating) by referring to their own standard.

Here is another example of this way of perceiving otherness. The Gabra Malbe talk a lot about their neighboring Turkana. For instance, "Turkanans get pregnant every year", "Mothers get large bellies with babies while they are still breastfeeding" and so on. These comments are based on the Gabra Malbe's belief that it is best to conceive at three-year intervals according to their reference standard. When people see or hear of behaviors that deviate from their own reference standard in this way, they perceive otherness along racial or ethnic boundaries. A reference standard (Y) that has been developed within each group functions to reinforce the boundaries with other groups and exclude them as others, and in doing so, the reference standard itself is reproduced continuously.

However, there are situations in which multiple ethnic groups share the same reference standard, as in the case of the Daasanach and neighboring groups who exchange hospitality. Many of the North Kenyan pastoralist societies are known to have myths, rituals and age systems that are common to multiple ethnic groups (Schlee 1989; Kurimoto and Simonse 1997). While reference standards certainly exist within each ethnic group, they are sometimes shared by more than one ethnic group. I must stress that otherness is not always perceived along ethnic or racial boundaries.

Understanding others based on a reference standard

While a reference standard enables one to perceive otherness without interacting with others, it can also serve as a tool to understand others without interacting with them. Let us look at the human propensity to easily understand others by using a reference standard.

In the aforementioned case of Renato Rosaldo (1998), he tried to understand the rage that drove Ilongots to headhunt by using a rather handy device, before he himself confronted the death of his wife.

> My own inability to conceive the force of anger in grief led me to seek out another level of analysis that could provide a deeper explanation for older men's desire to headhunt. [...] I explained the anthropologist's exchange model to an older Ilongot man named Insan. [...] He looked puzzled, so I went on to say that the victim of a beheading was exchanged for the death of one's own kin, thereby balancing the books, so to speak. Insan reflected a moment and replied that he imagined somebody could think such a thing (a safe bet, since I just had), but that he and other Ilongots did not think any such thing. (Rosaldo 1993: 3–4)

Initially, Rosaldo tried to understand Ilongots' emotions by relying on a suitable anthropological theory instead of trying to gain a direct understanding of their feelings. This attitude should not be considered to be mistaken. We go out into the field in search of new ways of understanding on one hand, and on the other hand we teach our university students various theories and encourage them to use them to understand various phenomena.

Rosaldo tried to rely on a theory formulated by "experts", but all sorts of lay theories (Furnham 1988) are bandied about in daily living. For example, when the Gabra Miigo were faced with the threat of disintegration around 2005, they interpreted various circulating rumors using the lay theory of matrimonial relationships as follows.

In 1994, Ethiopia enforced an ethnicity-based federation. Both the Oromo and the Somali asked the Gabra Miigo to choose which group they wanted to align with. The Gabra Miigo continued to debate which group they would join until around 2005. However, the debates revealed the breadth of a gap that could not easily be filled. At that stage, the Gabra Miigo were split between the Oromo faction comprising those who lived in the Oromo area and the Somali faction comprising those who lived in the Somali area. I was living in an area of predominantly Oromo supporters, and one day I heard them talking about a man who had made some comments favoring Somalis at a meeting. They said that the man sided with the Somalis because his second wife was Garre Somali.

This man might have made comments favoring the Somali because he thought it would be better for the future of his people, but others would not listen to his argument. People had made up their mind that "He has a Somali wife, therefore, he sided with the Somali". They interpreted the man's action by relying on their lay theory that the matrimonial relationship would determine his attitude. Whether it is an academic theory or a lay theory, it is possible that someone perceives otherness or understands others by using a reference standard without interacting with the other party.

Relationship between reference standard and interaction

Why is an interaction ignored when a reference standard is used? Isobe (1998) discusses a triadic relationship between "actor", "object" and "regulator" using René Girard's "triangle of desire" as a clue. According to Isobe, when an actor is aware of the presence of a regulator, in some cases the actor may not form a full relationship with the object. For instance, a daughter (actor) who is told to be kind to her younger brother (object) by her mother (regulator) may carry her "kindness" to excess regardless of his feelings. In this case, her kindness toward him is extended in order to be recognized by her mother (arrow (2) in Figure 3.4), and hence her kindness becomes excessive. She does not pay attention to her brother (arrow (1)) in this instance. Although she is supposed to extend her

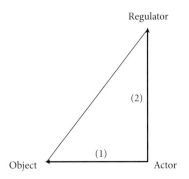

Figure 3.4 Direction of the actor's attention

kindness to him because she cares about him, her interest in the object vanishes when the regulator appears.

This composition is similar to that of the situation in which Rosaldo (self (b)) attempted to understand the Ilongot (object (X)) using anthropological theory (reference standard (Y)). When Rosaldo tried to understand a phenomenon using a theory, he looked as if he had an interest in the other as the subject, but actually he did not. In the Gabra Miigo example, the comments of the Somali-leaning man (object (X)) were interpreted on the basis of the lay theory that his wife was Somali (reference standard (Y)). The man's true intention was ignored.

Be it an academic theory or a lay theory, understanding the object by referencing a theory results in a loss of interest in it. However, what is important here is the fact that the norm (regulator) appeared because there was an interest in the object in the first place. Anthropologists have produced theories (regulator) in their struggles with others (object) and the Gabra Miigo people have produced various lay theories in their everyday living. These theories (regulator) serve as a device to reduce the complexity of society. A reference standard causes people to perceive otherness in others without interaction and at the same time functions as a device to facilitate an understanding of others.

Three mechanisms for perceiving others

We have so far examined mechanisms for perceiving others. A person may: (1) perceive otherness based on the other's attitude or behavior toward an object (X), (2) perceive otherness based on the other's attempt to involve the person or (3) perceive otherness by reference to a reference standard.

However, these mechanisms not only enable the perception of otherness, but also contain impetuses in the direction of incorporating the other into oneself. For instance, the triadic relationship concept was originally borrowed from the infant development model for the internalization of the other's behaviors, attitudes and values toward an object. In this model, the other's attitude toward an object (X) (mechanism (1)) became the source of the transformation of the self. Although self-development after adolescence is rarely studied in psychology, it does not mean that the impetus to internalize the other's behaviors, attitudes and values ceases in adulthood. One may attempt to transform oneself by choosing a role model from among the people around one and mimicking and practicing their behavior. The triadic relationship is simultaneously a mechanism for perceiving otherness and a mechanism for transforming oneself to emulate the other.

While the other's attempt to involve one can trigger the perception of otherness (mechanism (2)), one may willingly get involved with the other in some cases. Persuasion immediately comes to mind. Especially in the world of business, various communication techniques have been developed for the purpose of persuading people. This is based on the empirical rule that involvement in the form of persuasion may sometimes arouse antipathy, but even someone who is resistant at first can be persuaded and turned into a collaborator in the end. And as mentioned above, one may understand the other easily by referring to a standard (mechanism (3)). These mechanisms explain the impetuses to not only perceive otherness, but also incorporate the other into oneself.

From an evolutionary perspective, it is noteworthy that humankind is equipped with a mental faculty to understand others or perceive otherness based on reference standards and not just in face-to-face interactions. After millennia of living by hunting and gathering, humankind went on to engage in farming and animal husbandry, built cities and created "imaginary communities" called nations. Unlike large apes, humans are able to live in larger societies with many more members. It is likely that this was made possible by the understanding of others and the perception of otherness based on reference standards such as culture, language, religion, laws and institutions, rather than through interactions.

When humans encountered strangers, they might have attacked or even killed them in some cases, but they also had the ability to accept and coexist with them. In other words, humankind has evolved in such a way that they perceive and exclude heterogeneous others by constructing value systems (cultures and morals) on one hand, while they permit coexistence, if not close connection, by understanding others on the basis of theories and norms. This ability to reduce complexity while partially understanding others must have played an important role in the evolution of human sociality.

In the meantime, the understanding of others and the perception of otherness through interaction provide the momentum to shake up reference standards that have a tendency to become rigid. For example, where all kinds of people are regarded as "we" by reference to a particular standard, face-to-face interactions that take place within the "we" sometimes cause us to perceive otherness in "we". Similarly, even when I regard certain others as "they" by reference to a standard, I sometimes feel that "they" and I are alike through personal encounters and face-to-face interactions with some of them.

I once witnessed an exhausted Turkana traveller arrive in a Gabra Malbe village late at night and ask for lodging for the night (Soga 2013). The villagers listened to what the traveller said for a while, then allowed him to stay and gave him tea. It was just after the end of an ethnic conflict between the Turkana and the Gabra Malbe that had left both peoples deeply scarred. A young man from this village had been killed. As all Gabra Malbe people saw the Turkana as their enemy and all Turkana people considered the Gabra Malbe as their enemy by reference to their respective standards, the traveller must have come to the Gabra Malbe village because he had no other option.

To the man's "visage" requesting a night's lodging, the villagers responded with deep sympathy. A face-to-face interaction allows people to have a fresh experience. This act of the villagers exerts an effect in the direction of weakening or pushing back or raising doubts about the reference standard that the Turkana were their enemy. Of course, a single act or experience seldom shakes an entrenched reference standard. Yet, interaction can continually exert its effect on a reference standard and result in weakening or strengthening it.

A person attempts to internalize the other or perceives otherness in the other surrounding various objects. The perception of otherness and the understanding of the other happen by way of a reference standard, interaction or involvement. These mechanisms are mutually related and sometimes the reference standard dominates the interaction and at other times the interaction dominates the reference standard. This brings me to the understanding that otherness is sometimes perceived, and the perceived otherness sometimes vanishes amid a power relationship between a reference standard and an interaction.

4 "The Other Who Can Refuse": A Precondition for Transition to Human Society

Kōji Kitamura

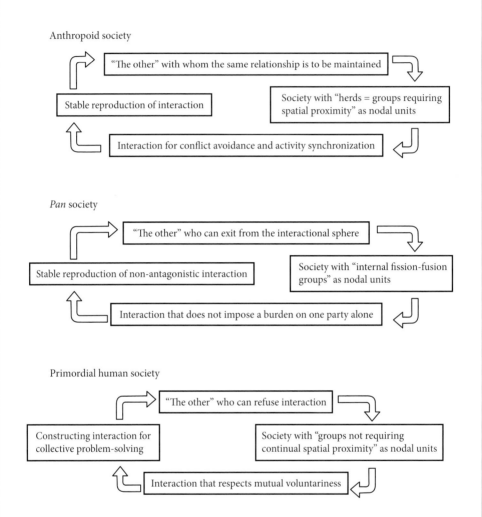

This chapter examines what occurred in the transition from non-human primate society to human society centering on the communication in interaction systems that is commonly found in these societies. The discussion focuses on what kind of "other" people assumed and what type of interaction they intended to carry out with "the other" in their communication. The differences in these factors between these societies are thought to correspond to the differences in their social structure and form of social order incorporated in the respective recursive processes shown above and reproduced in each system continuously.

Communication in interaction systems

The purpose of this chapter is to examine "communication in interaction systems[1]" as a mode of communication that is common to human and non-human primate societies. An interaction system refers to a set of communications carried out by two parties in an attempt to realize a certain outcome by connecting reciprocal acts based on the precondition of co-presence (being in the same place together). This set or communication system is destined to be continually abandoned and begun anew. A system of this nature and the individual communications comprising it are thought to be common to human and non-human primate societies. Therefore, from the perspective of this chapter in considering the characteristics of human society in the context of the evolution from non-human primate society to human society, the question becomes, "What were the changes to this common ground that led to the emergence of human society?".

In terms of the conditions of society and the form of social order in individual species, on the other hand, we must conceptualize a societal foundation that transcends individual interactions if an interaction system is to become reproducible through the process of continual ending and starting at the beginning (Luhmann 1995). In other words, we must assume that society chooses to establish an order that covers a broader range, encompassing the before, after and outside of individual interactions. And we must assume that it is realized by communication in an interaction system itself, rather than via some special means in the animal and primordial human societies we are considering here. In this chapter, we shall examine interactional communication in the societies of individual species to identify the nature of "the other" assumed by a party as the communication counterpart and the type of interaction the party intends to engage in with the other. We anticipate that this exercise may clarify differences in terms of the choices made by individual societies.

In this discussion, we consider that in connecting communication in an interaction system each individual is attempting not only to realize a certain outcome as a consequence of an interaction, but also to establish social order beyond the scope of an individual interaction. We then examine what kind of other is assumed and what kind of order is intended in their choice to establish the social order necessary for the reproduction of such an interaction system at different stages in the history of evolution.

Interaction systems in pre-human societies

Mammalian societies in the gregarious form of living

The precondition for communication in an interaction system is the co-presence of parties. The societies of nearly all primate species adopt a form of gregarious living in the sense that multiple individuals coexist in the same place and engage in the same activities together. In fact, many mammalian species live in societies based on the gregarious form of living in which coexistence is thought to be realized under two principles, namely "social facilitation" by sharing the outline of activity now and then with peers, and "social inhibition" to avoid conflicts with peers that tend to manifest in such settings (Kummer 1971).

A behavioral tendency thought to be established by social facilitation is sharing a particular motive with conspecific individuals (others) nearby in their relationship with an environmental resource and synchronizing activities at that particular time. Based on this very common tendency, others are seen as counterparts in the synchronization of the general outline of a particular activity. This will likely lead to the realization of the situation of engaging in the same activity together at a particular time and place, but also the establishment of the social order that makes this situation recursively reproducible at different times and places.

What we must remember here is the question of what each individual gains by mutually synchronizing their activities, because the genetically-based behavioral tendency to try to synchronize one's behavior with those of others in the vicinity is likely to be established only if it results in a higher likelihood of survival for those behaving in that manner. In this case, it is thought that this behavior can result in the discovery of precious resources out of reach for a lone individual, or the effect of confusing or distracting predators by being in a group. In short, the mechanism allows each individual to secure an advantage in their relationship with an object in the environment while trying to adjust their relationship with others at the same time.

On the other hand, the general behavioral tendency under the social inhibition principle is to try not to get too close to others at all times in order to avoid conflict as much as possible, while attempting to synchronize one's activity with those of others nearby. In these instances, others are seen as counterparts in mutual conflict avoidance. It is thought that the state of conflict avoidance becomes reproducible repeatedly in one's relationship with others. On that basis, the ongoing use of this general behavior of synchronizing one's activity with those of others without getting too close to them is likely to help them to realize mutual behavioral adjustments effortlessly when the potential for conflict actually manifests.

It is thought that "social facilitation" and "social inhibition" define the general framework of the mode of activity in the societies of species adopting a gregarious form of living and are essential in establishing the social order that extends beyond interactions in individual situations. Nevertheless, we must not overlook the fact that by selecting a specific behavior in a specific situation, each individual produces order at a behavioral chain level that is expected for that situation as well as an outcome that leads to gains for each individual's survival at the same time. Therefore, it should be understood that it is not a mere accumulation of these general behavioral tendencies adopted by individuals that creates social order; it is an accumulation of the process consisting of the choices of specific behaviors in specific situations by individuals and the adjustments made in mutually connecting them that puts coexistence with others into an orderly state.

From the viewpoint of the organization of society as a whole in each species, on the other hand, we must pay attention to the possibility that the overlapping of these two principles adds uncertainty to the reproduction of such social order. The principle of social facilitation is thought to enable recursive reproduction of an orderly situation in which conspecific individuals engage in the same activity together in the relationship of fellow conspecific individuals relying on the behavioral tendency to mutually synchronize activities at the time on the basis that they are present in the same place at the same time. The principle of social inhibition, on the other hand, makes them refrain from getting too close to conspecific individuals according to the behavioral tendency to avoid conflict with them as much as possible and may well promote the tendency to move away from each other. It is conceivable that this will bring about a situation where there are no conspecific individuals nearby for one to mutually synchronize activities with.

Despite this, many species maintain social order in the form of gregarious living possibly because even if conspecific individuals go on to live separately in the course of the aforementioned process, it seems that they are disposed to return to the process of continually reproducing a situation in which they engage in the same activity together with others at the same place in response to change in the condition external to their social relationship world, such as a concentrated distribution of important food resources. Consequently, we cannot go so far as to say that the form of order in each society is directly produced by the manner of interactional behavior itself in gregarious societies at this evolutionary stage.

Herd societies in anthropoids

In comparison, the herd societies of anthropoids (e.g., the Japanese macaque) that are thought to be at a higher evolutionary stage than gregarious mammalian societies appear to be closer to a condition in which the manner of interactional behavior itself produces a form of social order. A herd society is one formed by herds as groups with fixed membership. In such a society, a herd is the unit-group determined by the nodal concentration of the members of a conspecific society in a spatial distribution where the relationship between fellow members of the same herd becomes important. The principles of social facilitation and social inhibition, which are means to maintain order in the state of coexistence of fellow conspecific individuals in gregarious mammalian societies, are replaced with those of fellow herd members. In other words, it is likely that the formation of multiple nodal concentrations within a conspecific society sets off a recursive process in which actions are connected to reproduce the nodality in the relationship between the fellow members of each unit on the basis of spatial aggregation, and thereby herds are maintained in a stable condition.

For the recursive decision-making process to continue working to reproduce order in herd societies, an obstacle that causes uncertainty in the reproduction of social order in gregarious mammalian societies must somehow be removed. The obstacle stems from the fact that a general behavioral tendency required under the principle of social facilitation and that required under the principle of social inhibition are not naturally compatible; and the change that has contributed most to their transition to herd societies in which this obstacle has been resolved took place in an area involving the principle of social inhibition.

Anthropoid herd societies adopted completely different forms of response in realizing a state of conflict avoidance in the area of social inhibition, while simply replacing the behavioral tendency for social facilitation between members of the same species with that between members of the same herd. Whereas a general behavioral tendency complying with this principle was required regardless of the target of that behavior in the earlier-stage societies, it became important in herd societies to assume what kind of other the counterpart in that behavior was, and to figure out what kind of order should be created in the relationship with the other.

In this case, the assumed other as the target of an inhibitive behavior to realize a conflict avoidance situation is the other who is regarded as an individual with dominance over oneself. The response one adopts is to create a situation free from any possibility of conflict by acting like a subordinate individual that is subservient to the counterpart in connecting one's behavior to that of the other. This approach eliminates the element of incompatibility between a behavior for social inhibition and one for social facilitation. For example, acting as a subordinate to a dominant other among members of the same herd enables one to avoid conflict by submitting to the other's will and at the same time to strengthen mutual activity synchronization by following them.

Acting as a subordinate in behavioral connection with a dominant other is a highly effective means for conflict avoidance through individual inhibitive behavior. In fact, order for coexistence might be impossible without this response in anthropoid herd societies, as all members of a herd constantly engage in the same activity together in such a closely unified group that the potential for conflict could surface at any time. However, this apparently ironclad approach has a weakness. This relationship between one dominant individual and one subordinate individual must be shared by the involved parties as a reliable arrangement if this approach is to be effective for the formation of social order. To ensure that the potential conflict does not become a reality, members of the herd must continually confirm the invariability of this relationship by recursively connecting behaviors between various combinations of members. We can surmise that the said recursive process initiates in this case as well, where an established relationship serves as a reference pattern and connecting the behaviors that confirm and reproduce the relationship increases the invariability of the relationship. Just as in the case of the formation of groups with fixed membership in these societies, the phenomenon generated by the recursive process seems very reliable, but the state of social order in these societies can be fundamentally overturned if some of the underlying conditions are altered.

Next, we examine the society of the genus *Pan*, which is thought to generate a form of social order similar to that in human society. In *Pan* society, members of a group are not always inclined to stay in the same place together, and therefore the importance of the dominant-subordinate relationship between individuals for conflict avoidance is clearly diminished. How does this change influence the assumption about the other and the form of order to be produced in the relationship with the other? We shall consider this question in the context of the evolution toward human society.

Evolution toward human society

The fission-fusion society of the genus *Pan*
The fundamental difference between *Pan* society and anthropoid society is that the former are formed by groups that frequently undergo fission-fusion, as described in

Chapter Six by Nishie. In chimpanzee and bonobo societies, which are the species comprising the genus *Pan*, groups merge and split frequently and repeatedly while members periodically form larger ranging groups, and it is thought that they have a form of organization called a "unit-group" that makes this behavior possible (Nishida 1968; Kuroda 1982). It is envisaged that this state of group organization was brought about by a change in the area of social facilitation that involved a transition from the approach of synchronizing the outline of activity with any members of the same group to that of providing an option to live apart from some members. We must remember, however, that the possibility of reuniting is also provided in this case. If we focus on this point, we can say that individual members have become able to choose the option of temporarily living separately from some members as the need arises. It is likely that the primary function of living separately in this case is to preclude the possibility of conflict.

Although it is unclear whether chimpanzees and bonobos are doing so for this purpose, at least it is obvious that the importance of the approach of relying on the dominance-subordination relationship between individuals for conflict resolution has decreased in *Pan* society compared with anthropoid society. In the anthropoid approach, a subordinate individual forestalls a possible conflict when it surfaces by disengaging from an interaction in progress, while trying to stay within the range of the interaction in order to continue to share the outline of the activity. This response is thought to ensure the stability of their coexistence while effectively precluding the possibility of conflict. In *Pan* society on the other hand, the availability of the option of living apart as needed increases the probability that the disengagement of one of the parties from an interaction in an effort to remove the possibility of conflict will lead to a group member's exit out of the sphere of the interaction. And the "social choice" they have adopted to deal with this problem is to provide certain restraints rather than allowing it to happen.

The first restraint is to avoid laying the whole burden of removing a potential for conflict on the shoulders of one party alone. The second restraint is to require both parties to cooperate in order to generate a non-antagonistic interaction between them. These restraints ensure that neither party has to disengage from the interaction at the time when the possibility of conflict surfaces, and that the possibility of stable coexistence afterward is maintained. It is likely that these measures properly remove the potential for conflict and reduce the risk of an exodus of group members from the sphere of interaction leading to the disintegration of the group.

Such measures typically involve an attempt to constitute, as required operationally, a non-antagonistic interaction that is easily identifiable by its characteristic pattern in order to actively preclude the potential for conflict and to maintain order for coexistence. For instance, when two adult male chimpanzees are on the brink of a hostile clash, they engage in reciprocal grooming thus avoiding conflict and enabling them to coexist peacefully afterward (de Waal 1994). In addition, they commonly engage in a stylized non-antagonistic interaction called "greeting behavior" or "appeasement behavior" to resolve tension or to remove the potential for conflict in the situation and to ensure peaceful coexistence afterward.

Food sharing, which is a central topic in the study of *Pan* society, is another typical example of interaction engaged in for the purpose of stopping the other from disengaging from an interaction and maintaining the possibility of stable coexistence afterward. Aside from the type of food sharing that can be interpreted as "parental investment", such as the feeding of a child by a parent, food sharing between adults is considered unique to humans and the genus *Pan* (Nishida and Hosaka 2001). In the food sharing interaction of the genus *Pan*, it appears that the party asking for a share of food is prepared to wait until the other party voluntarily responds, and the party with food tries to maintain calm in the situation without reacting negatively to the request. In this way each party takes care not to force the other out of the interaction while altering their behavior to avoid conflict.

Food sharing in *Pan* society is different from that in human society in the following respects: food sharing is not carried out unless there is a request; a food sharing request is sometimes not responded to for a long time; and the share of food given to the requester is smaller or less palatable than that retained by the requestee (Nishida 1973; Kuroda 1999). It is possible to say that in making a request the requester is simply attempting to extract a response from the other party that may result in the consumption of food by the requester, while the requestee is simply trying to avoid a conflict and to realize an outcome that is compatible with what the other party is attempting in that situation. In that case, it cannot be regarded as an event realized by mutual agreement between parties about the act of "sharing".

This form of interactional behavior can be considered as a behavior conducted when assuming that the other in an interaction is an individual who can disengage from the interaction and step outside of its sphere any time, and when attempting to maintain order for coexistence at the time by preventing that from happening while generating a non-antagonistic interaction in the situation. However, one remaining problem is that group members have no reliable means to verify an individual's membership of the same unit-group that is necessary when an individual tries to return to the group after temporarily separating from some members. In fact, the re-merging of a ranging group after a period of separation usually causes tumult due to a strong sense of resistance among its subgroups.

It appears that members of *Pan* society now have the option of living away from group members as needed, but this limiting condition prevents them from freely using this option as an expedient means to avoid conflict. They are therefore normally considerate of one another so as not to compel the other party to disengage from an interaction. In the human society that followed, this limiting condition was resolved brilliantly by an evolutionary historical watershed called language acquisition, which is thought to have given rise to different ways of responding.

The form of order in human society

In pre-human primate society, each individual in an interaction chooses their actions to secure their own advantage and tries to generate a behavioral chain-like order in the situation by connecting their action to that of the other party. At the same time, they assume the other in an interaction is a member of the same category and respond to them in the same way, regardless of which individual it is, and consequently establish social order with a broader influence beyond individual interactions. In this instance, a recursive relationship in which one is both the cause and the effect of the other is established between the reproduction of communication in an interaction system and the establishment of a spatial aggregation with stable membership, and the parties must make constant efforts to maintain this state of coexistence (Kitamura 2013).

On the other hand, communication in an interaction system in human society is not premised on the recursive reproduction of the condition requiring members of the same group to stay together in the same place. Communication can be performed with the other at any time thanks to the ability to identify group members based on linguistic information available to any third party. In other words, an individual can start a new communication more easily even after stopping an interaction with a fellow group member for some reason and separating, thus one is released from the previously unavoidable burden of constantly engaging in the maintenance of spatial proximity to one's peers. Consequently, human society has gained a greater degree of freedom in securing the possibility of reproducing interaction systems, and each individual has more scope to engage in an activity to more actively secure their own advantage.

The activity in question is trying to cooperate with one's peers in dealing with problems that are difficult for an individual to resolve alone. Humans even try to cooperate with their peers in solving problems entailing a high risk of resulting in conflict due to the parties' competing interests. In this case, they are compelled to produce a solution that is satisfactory to both parties through a collective response by working out an approach that seems effective in solving the issue at hand rather than by simply removing the potential for conflict. In interactional communication in pre-human society, each individual was in principle merely trying to obtain an advantage for themselves indirectly by creating an order for coexistence to secure the possibility for interaction through the synchronization of activities with peers and precluding the possibility of conflict. In comparison, it seems that in human society the individual more actively tries to obtain an advantage for themself. It follows that this ensures not only the reproducibility of interaction systems in general, but also the establishment of the social order that makes interaction for collective problem-solving recursively reproducible.

Even in human society, it is essential to establish a platform of "social choice" that transcends individual interactions where communication in interaction systems, which is only possible when parties are present at the same place, is necessarily reproducible through constant stops and restarts. Next, I hypothesize a primordial human society that followed pre-human societies in which this kind of social choice is realized by communication in interaction systems, just as it was in preceding societies. We shall consider what kind of "other" is assumed and what kind of order for coexistence is the aim in such communication. This primordial society is a simple form of society in which a hierarchy based on political and economic dominance is not yet formed, and absolute standards exogenous to interactions such as institutions as well as the social authority underpinning them have not yet come to the fore.

Let us examine what kind of response is required at the level of "the manner of interactional behavior" by the new condition of "facilitating the easy resumption of an interaction with a peer after a discontinuation" brought about by language acquisition. It is conceivable that this condition has the ironic consequence of actually increasing the possibility that the other will disengage from the interaction and exit the interactional sphere. Therefore, each party is compelled to not only devise a way to induce the other party's active participation in a problem-solving interaction, but also to try to ensure the possibility that the interaction can be resumed on another occasion, even if the other party refuses to continue the interaction and exits the sphere. In this instance, the other becomes an object consciously identified as a being able to exercise the freedom of refusal while engaging in an interaction.

One of the important means to maintain the substance of an interaction with another in collectively resolving a problem at hand is to behave in a manner that expresses respect for the voluntary choices made by the other. When the other party responds as if respecting one's choice, one will not abandon such an interaction voluntarily because each party is trying to secure their own advantage. When dealing with a problem involving parties' competing interests, however, each party will naturally try to extract a concession from the other in order to secure their own advantage while behaving toward the other in the aforementioned manner. Consequently, their interaction becomes a negotiation that is difficult to conclude. When a stalemate is reached, the parties can shift emphasis from the realization of a settlement advantageous to one party to the establishment of an order to make the performance of the interaction easier and more desirable. The following two typical responses are possible.

The first type is where both parties respect each other's voluntary choices and refrain from abandoning their interaction, even if the choices fail to meet expectations; they try to reach a settlement that is satisfactory to both parties by further advancing their common understanding through connecting communications. The ingenuity of this approach lies in their willingness to let the negotiation take its course and accept the outcome of the cumulative common understanding as "our choice", the making of which they both participated in[2].

On the other hand, the second type of response also involves mutual respect for each other's voluntary choices, but in this case the parties try to create a situation where the other's voluntary participation becomes a matter of course, as they completely avoid any approach that directly prescribes the other's response in an interaction. By doing so, they make the outcome of the interaction agreeable to both parties. Meanwhile, each party tries to extract a concession from the other in the sense of securing their own advantage and can possibly refuse to continue the interaction if the other party is not willing to cede more ground. Even in this case, however, it can be deemed that the cessation takes place as a consequence of a series of voluntary choices made by both parties, and that both parties agree to the outcome.

The ingenuity of this approach is that the parties accumulate mutual agreement to each of the outcomes produced in the course of their interaction, while letting the negotiation take its course regardless of whether a settlement is reached or not. In this way they treat their interaction as something that guarantees the reproduction of peaceful coexistence, no matter how the interaction progresses. With this kind of interaction, the parties can easily decide whether to conclude the interaction, leave it open or resume it at a later date, no matter when a discontinuation takes place.

In the first approach, the parties try to overcome the hurdle of having completely incompatible goals and to reach a settlement that is satisfactory to both in collectively dealing with a problem with competing interests. Their motivation to confirm that they are compatriots who share the same choice is obvious in this approach. In the second approach on the other hand, the parties try to pursue negotiation with emphasis on their respective voluntary choices while letting the negotiation take its course regardless of whether or not they will reach some form of settlement. It is likely that each party is trying to create a minimum level of order in their relationship with the other that can constitute a conflict-free interaction that is reproducible.

While the first approach suggests something akin to a shared value among the members of society, the second seems to indicate that adjustments in the manner of interactional behavior as an accumulation of individuals' voluntary choices directly lead to the generation of the minimum level of social order. This second approach can be considered the simplest response required for a transition to a new stage of social evolution entailing the appearance of "others who can refuse", in the sense that they can exercise the freedom to refuse while voluntarily engaging in an interaction. In the next section, we shall explore the manner of communication in Bushmen hunter-gatherer society in my research field of Botswana to identify some concrete examples of this approach. I would like to re-examine the conventional argument that hunter-gatherer societies are "egalitarian", and propose a new alternative interpretation by reference to understanding developed through the evolution-based hypothesis above.

Communication in the Bushmen's interaction system

In my investigation of communication in Bushmen society, I have looked at the manner of giving and receiving in exchanging objects for collective consumption (food sharing is one well-known example that is) and highlighted that adjustments to the manner of behavior in such interactions create "social order" that can be recursively reproduced. Using the example of sharing a tobacco pipe that I have frequently discussed in my studies (Kitamura 1996a, 2013), I shall re-describe what takes place in this situation using the terminology outlined in our analysis above.

In Bushmen society, when a person finishes smoking and tries to pass the pipe to the next person in the practice of tobacco sharing, it is quite common, albeit not always the case, that the next person fails to notice their action. The first person then retracts their extended hand and waits a few moments before offering the pipe once again instead of trying to catch the second person's attention, and this time the second person notices and receives it. What the first person is doing in this situation is behaving in a manner that expresses respect for the other's voluntary choice by waiting until the other notices and voluntarily receives the pipe. The first person extracts the other's voluntary response to receive it by offering the pipe a second time. On the other hand, the second person creates the situation of non-receiving by not immediately receiving the pipe when it is offered the first time, thereby prompting the first person to try to pass it on again. While the connection of the parties' behaviors produces the event of pipe passing, it also ensures that the parties mutually agree that the outcome was brought about through the accumulation of their voluntary choices.

The same can be said about food sharing, which is practiced routinely in many hunter-gatherer societies. One notable characteristic of the manner of behavior in this type of interaction is that both the giver and the receiver are required to behave in a discreet and restrained manner (e.g., Lee 1979). From the perspective of this chapter, the requirement for this manner of behavior not only means that this form of sharing is different from food sharing in the genus *Pan*, which is initiated by the requester, but also provides a reasonable explanation for the argument that this sharing is not practiced obligatorily according to some rule.

These societies choose a way of life where the collective consumption of hunted large game by those who live in the same camp is taken for granted, but the manner of behavior in interactions to realize this collective consumption is determined neither by one party following the other's direction nor by both parties submitting to a rule. It is in fact determined where the parties to an interactional communication mutually make adjustments as the situation progresses by each respecting the other's voluntary choices while trying to secure their own advantage. They make the outcome of the interaction acceptable to both giver and receiver by conducting the communication between them in this manner, and at the same time turn the interaction into a special opportunity to confirm the reproducibility of their order for coexistence.

Naturally, this manner of behavior is not exclusive to interactions involving collective consumption; it has become a characteristic approach of Bushmen societies in all sorts of situations. For instance, it can be observed in an idiosyncrasy employed in their conversation, which is the most common form of interactional communication in daily life. When I began living with the Bushmen people, the most striking behavior that differed from my own was the phenomenon of "speech overlap". Of course, it is not part of every conversation, but their speech overlaps very frequently and for a considerable length of time. Between Bushmen, it is common for one party to ignore the other's speech and start talking over the top of them. As the two parties ignore each another's speech and continue talking at the same time, the phenomenon of speech overlap routinely occurs.

I observed the following episode. A man was persistently nagging another man. When the second man eventually began to refute his complaint, the first man suddenly turned away and began to talk loudly to a passerby at a distance. The second man whose reply had been ignored continued to talk as if nothing had happened, thus making their speech overlap last for some time. First, in terms of our discussion thus far, ignoring the counterpart's reply and starting a new monologue is a manner of behavior that emphasizes the voluntary nature of the participation of the individual. On the other hand, the ignored man continued his own monologue because the other man's decision to begin talking at the same time was his voluntary choice and was unrelated to the ignored man's speech and should be respected as such, and therefore the ignored man should continue his own speech irrespective of the other man's actions.

In the above example of "conversation", the man effectively refused to listen to the other man's speech by talking at the same time, and even though the two men continued their monologues, the "interaction through conversation" was discontinued and subsequently abandoned. While this type of event might sour a relationship in our society, it does not hinder the reproduction of peaceful coexistence between concerned parties in Bushmen society because it is accepted as the outcome of an accumulation of voluntary choices made by both parties. On the other hand, in the aforementioned case of interaction for collective consumption, the expected outcome of connecting one another's actions is clear to both parties, and although each party may be dissatisfied with the way their interaction was progressing and expressed this, in the end the parties are inclined to adjust their respective actions in the direction of the expected outcome.

In his study of !Kung Bushmen, Lee (1979) observed that "men who went to dismember a kill with the hunter expressed their disappointment one after another and insulted the hunter". This behavior becomes understandable using the above logic. The hunter sharing the kill and the men receiving their shares may become dissatisfied with the way the distribution is carried out and express this feeling, but that does not stop the process of sharing. Where each party tries to secure their own advantage while respecting the other's claim, the parties mutually adjust their actions so that in the end sharing is realized as expected.

The episode described by Lee became famous because he recognized the effect of the norm underpinning the foundations of egalitarian society that "the arrogant behavior which a successful hunter is prone to exhibit should be dampened". However, he was able to develop this argument simply because he and many other anthropologists believed that hunter-gatherer society was "egalitarian" and therefore the behaviors of hunter-gatherers would be governed by egalitarian principles. As explained in our discussion here, there is no need for us to assume any special norm or value that can be called "egalitarianism" in order to understand the manner of behavior among the Bushmen (Kitamura 1996a). I shall discuss this point in the closing section below.

The form of order in primordial human society

As I summarize the above discussion, I offer the possibility of a new understanding of how we should interpret the form of order chosen by primordial human societies.

According to our discussion, a major change that emerged in the transition to human society is likely to have derived from the ability to easily resume communication in an interaction with peers after a discontinuation, which was precipitated by language acquisition. In other words, the identification of group members using linguistic clues enabled people to more easily start and restart communication with their peers after a period of separation on the basis of their relationship as "fellow members of the same group". The resultant change is important for the following two reasons. First, as people acquired a greater degree of freedom in establishing the reproducibility of interactions with their peers, they were given latitude to make active attempts to secure their own advantage by cooperating with their peers in tackling problems that could not be solved individually. Second, as they needed to assume that their counterpart in communication after this change would be "an other who can refuse" with the ability to exercise the freedom of refusal while actively participating in communication, they were compelled in communicating with this type of "other" to behave in a manner that facilitated their counterpart's active participation and ensured that their counterpart's refusal would not hinder the reproduction of peaceful coexistence between them.

"The Other Who Can Refuse": A Precondition for Transition to Human Society 107

With the change in relation to the first point, communication in an interaction system with peers became not only an activity aimed at the creation of social order to make its reproduction easy and desirable, but also an attempt to pursue an outcome that would enhance the possibility of the survival of individual parties. For this reason, the parties must make certain choices as to how to handle the desirable but barely feasible goal of reaching a settlement that satisfies both parties in dealing with a problem, especially where they have conflicting interests. We surmised that hunter-gatherer society adopted the approach of giving priority to the establishment of social order to make such communication recursively reproducible while letting communication take its course regardless of whether it would reach a settlement in their collective response to a problem.

With regard to the second point, people adopted the approach of firstly creating a situation in which voluntary participation by the counterpart in communication was a matter of course by explicitly indicating one's utmost respect for the other's voluntary choices presented in their communication with "an other who can refuse". As at the same time they also try to extract a concession from their counterpart in order to secure their own advantage, the counterpart may refuse to further connect communication. Even if this occurs, the discontinuation is accepted by both parties as the outcome of an accumulation of their voluntary choices and therefore does not pose any impediment to the subsequent reproduction of interactions between the parties.

Communication executed in this manner becomes a negotiation in which the parties put their respective voluntary choices to the fore and certainly constitutes an "egalitarian" interaction engaged in by two parties in basically an equal relationship with no differentiation in their status or function. However, if we are to explain their behavior on the basis that there is what we call an established "egalitarian norm or rule" as an antecedent to their interaction and that they are complying with this thing that has been introduced from the outside, we must question what it actually is and how it has been introduced to their society. On the other hand, our evolution-based argument here suggests that a situation that is seemingly complying with a rule external to an interaction is in fact brought about through an accumulation of the voluntary choices of the parties within the interaction. The cornerstone of this interpretation is the understanding that this "egalitarian" manner of behavior manifested as the direct consequence of individuals' attempts to ensure the reproducibility of the interaction aiming to deal with a problem in cooperation with their peers as the aforementioned change took place in the process of transition to human society. At the same time, as people accepted and practiced this manner of behavior as absolutely imperative in realizing a desirable outcome, this "egalitarian" social order came to be reproduced recursively. In other words, this hypothesis proposes that the form of order chosen by primordial human society was brought about not by relying on a rule introduced from the outside of an interaction, but rather by the onset of the recursive self-productive process within the interaction as described above.

Although a phenomenon produced by this type of recursive process appears to be very stable, we know for a fact that in some cases the mode of social order can be altered fundamentally when the underlying condition changes. It is also important to note that this kind of major change triggered by a shift in the underlying condition cannot be explained by a simple causality theory. The evolutionary study of human society proposed here is still at a trial stage, and further development is anticipated.

5 Empathy and Social Evolution: The Human History of Understanding Others

Hitoshige Hayaki

Key ideas

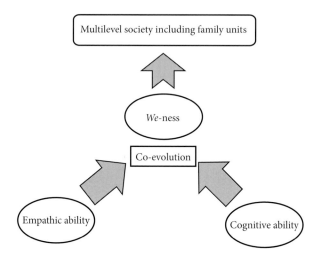

This chapter presents the following hypothesis (*we*-ness hypothesis) focusing on the evolution of the understanding of others in humans. In early humans, a better understanding of others' intentions and the meaning of their actions – thanks to the development of their cognitive ability that took place probably at the time of *Homo erectus* – greatly expanded cooperative relationships between the constituent members of a group and enabled them to perform joint actions efficiently for shared purposes. This change triggered the co-evolution of their empathic ability to give rise to "*we*-ness". The emergence of "*we*-ness" allowed the formation of multilevel societies containing family units.

Synchronizing with others

A migrating school of sardines in underwater footage appears as if it were a giant gleaming silvery animal itself. When tuna and other predators attack the school, it eludes them by instantly changing its configuration before returning to the original large formation. Individual sardines synchronize and coordinate with each other as if parts of a giant animal in order to maintain the aggregation. The individuals of many animal species that form "anonymous groups", such as flocks of migrating birds and herds of wildebeests seasonally migrating over a long distance, have the ability to achieve remarkable synchronization with others in the group in order to maintain the aggregation.

I shall call this ability to tune in to the others around one and integrate one's action with theirs *synchronization ability*. This ability is thought to have evolved for the purpose of defense against predators and to have ancient origins.

It is thought that animals that form a group with stable membership such as the Japanese macaque can range while maintaining their group because they synchronize their activity rhythm, including travelling, resting and feeding, with the others in the group. When foreign enemies or predators appear, they flee in the same direction in a synchronized manner and sometimes collectively make threats against the enemy. Scenes of individual group members synchronizing and engaging in the same behavior can be found in all sorts of situations.

On the other hand, perhaps no animal (mammal) can synchronize its actions with others' as perfectly as humans can. The total synchronization of movements found in military marches and when sports fans cheer involves intentional synchronization through sharing the schema of action. Musical performance, choir and mass dance also demand perfect synchronization. When people cooperate to lift a heavy object, they use an interjection (such as "heave-ho") to synchronize their actions, allowing them to lift a heavy load that could not be moved by a single person.

Behavioral synchronicity also influences the feeling, mood and atmosphere of the individuals co-present at a scene. A "coo" call is uttered when a troop of Japanese macaques settles down in a forest. One macaque's coo call tends to trigger many such calls from all over the area. Japanese macaques cry "hoyaa" in a slightly excited voice when waiting for food at a feeding station. When one starts the call, others begin calling from all over the place. The calls somewhat resemble the sound of shrieks emitted by fans at a pop idol's concert.

In the case of humans, even laughter, sadness, anxiety and anger can spread to those nearby. I once experienced the transmission of yawning while following a wild chimpanzee. I was following a young female named Pulin, who had quickly become accustomed to humans after migrating from another troop only a few years earlier. As Pulin stopped travelling and lay down on her back in a bush, I sat down by her side. She yawned and I subsequently yawned contagiously. Looking at me, she yawned again. Again I yawned contagiously. To my surprise, Pulin yawned again. After that, I yawned intentionally and ended up yawning alternately with Pulin almost ten times (Hayaki 1990).

Synchronization can be separated into weak synchronization and strong synchronization. In humans, weak synchronization is a phenomenon that relates to activity rhythm, emotional state and the atmosphere or mood at the scene, and is produced when people become involved in a familiar activity with familiar people in a familiar way. They lead their usual, ordinary lives while sharing the same landscape of life and synchronizing with each other. They find a sense of security in that life is proceeding as usual. On the other hand, strong synchronization tends to be brought on by events such as the appearance of an enemy and makes people instantly share some strong emotion once they understand the situation. If we describe weak synchronization as the sharing of the "*back*ground", strong synchronization can be called the sharing of the "figure", using terms from Gestalt psychology. Human beings have created a wide variety of means to artificially generate strong synchronization. Music and dance can be regarded as typical examples.

The sharing of emotions and feelings with others based on synchronization ability can be called "empathy". According to F. de Waal (2010), empathy activates an area of the brain that has been present for over 100 million years. This ability developed in the ancient past together with movement imitation and emotional contagion and added many new layers over the subsequent course of evolution until our ancestors finally became able to not only feel what others felt but also to understand what others wanted and needed (see also Chapter Nine by Kawai).

It is likely that domestic dogs and cats read their owner's feelings to some degree. Animals, especially mammals, are equipped with an ability to sense the feelings and emotions of others in the vicinity. Without this ability, behaviors such as appeasement, reassurance and reconciliation to calm the other's excitement, remove the other's fear, comfort the other and so on, which are often found in chimpanzees and other animals, would be impossible. This way of understanding others can be regarded as understanding others through empathy. An empathic understanding of the other's emotions happens instantaneously, but this alone may be insufficient to enable one to lie to the other or to detect the other's lie. The development of cognition is essential for the understanding of others.

Generation of self and other

If we focus on individuals in society, birth is the first situation where the other emerges. For the newborn baby, the birth means that it is separated from its mother's womb and abruptly ejected into the world. The formation of a perception/cognition of self and other must be a challenge for the baby. In this sense, the other is generated alongside the self in the growth process. On the other hand, to the mother the baby is like a part of her body that has been separated from it, but the baby emerges as the other whom the mother cannot control. Studies on rhesus monkeys reared in isolation have reported cases of mothers who reject their babies immediately after giving birth and attack them or treat them as foreign objects. A study of Japanese macaques in Takagoyama, Chiba Prefecture, has reported that younger mothers handle their babies poorly and the baby mortality rate is considerably higher in primiparous mothers than in parous mothers (Hasegawa 1983). In the case of wild chimpanzees, females often move away from their peers to give birth alone, but they are often observed to return to their groups with their newborn babies in their arms and present them to their peers. To the peers who come to look at the babies, the latter must be others who are new group members. In chimpanzees, the inexplicable phenomena of infanticide and cannibalism occasionally occur in relation to babies[1]. It is suspected that the problem of "others" is relevant to these phenomena.

Supposing *self* and *other* are formed in the growth process, what does this process entail? According to E. S. Reed (2000), by the third month of its life a human baby begins to understand their agency (the ability to act independently) and the other's agency, to anticipate external phenomena (especially animal phenomena) and to learn to control their own agency. The baby selectively explores the affordances[2] of things, anticipates inherent characteristics of certain things and verifies the anticipation through its own actions. A dyadic interaction emerges as the baby uses the rhythmic structure of the adult's gestures and vocalizations as clues (in anticipating the other's behavior). From the perspective of a rule, it can be said that forming anticipation about things is the learning of regularity, while having anticipation in relation to others is the learning of contingency (incidental relationships accompanying uncertainties). The baby establishes a habitual way of dealing with the caregiver and forms familiar interactions through their recurring dyadic interactions. With unfamiliar people other than the caregiver, it gradually develops familiarity as it continually adjusts its anticipation.

From the age of nine months or so, human infants acquire the ability to focus attention on one object or phenomenon jointly with the caregiver and develop a triadic interaction (Reed 2000) or a joint attentional frame (Tomasello 2008) to share environmental affordances with the other, thereby starting to understand the other as an intentional being. This ability is thought to play an important role in language acquisition.

There have been no reports of the development of this triadic interaction in infancy in non-human primates, but a broader view of primate social behaviors often finds cases in which multiple individuals focus their attention jointly on a single phenomenon. For instance, Japanese macaques often look to an influential individual when they begin travelling and many individuals turn their attention to the object of alarm when alarm calls are uttered. A joint attack on a particular individual is also triadic. Group hunting[3] and the gang attack of a particular individual observed in chimpanzees (Nishida et al. 1995) can also be considered triadic. Although a triadic framework is certainly established in these examples, it is uncertain whether they are always performing a dyadic interaction while maintaining attention on the object (the third term) using it as a mediating term, as in a human triadic interaction. In many cases, it can be interpreted as a simultaneous performance of distinct actions toward the same object.

The "peering" behavior of chimpanzees can be considered similar to a triadic interaction in human infants. Young chimpanzees often draw very close to the hands of an adult who is doing something (e.g., preparing food to eat) and watch intently for a long time. The watched adult shows no reaction to the watcher, but it is possible to argue that an interaction is taking place between the two parties in a passive sense in that the adult does not reject the youth.

If a common intersubjective field is created through the recurrent performance of triadic interactions, it must also act as a field to create trust in and empathy with others. Once human infants reach the age of four or five, it is said that they come to understand that the other has not only intentions and attentions that manifest in its behaviors, but also thoughts and beliefs that may not be expressed in its behaviors; in short, they understand that the other is "a being with a mind" (Tomasello 2006). This can be called a cognitive understanding of the other.

As in the emergence of joint attention, the cognitive understanding of the other is thought to originate in synchronization and identification with the other (normally a caregiver). When one understands that the other also has its own intentions, i.e., the self-ness of the other, one becomes able to see things from the other's viewpoint. However, we must remember that this understanding of the other corresponds to the level of maturity of one's understanding of the self. Two- or three-year-olds absorbed in pretend play gain much experience of becoming someone or something other than themselves in the process. Playing a role in pretend play means operating from the other's perspective. Nevertheless, children do not develop a sufficient understanding of "theory of mind" until they turn four or five. Perhaps at this stage their *empathic understanding of the other* and *cognitive understanding of the other* are still undifferentiated and need to develop through reciprocal influence.

The developmental process of understanding the other in human infants can be identified in the history of human evolution after some modification (see the discussion on the evolution of human groups below). Perhaps at around the time of the emergence of the genus *Homo*, humans developed the cognitive capacity to understand the other as a being with a mind, which in turn further developed the empathic understanding of the other. When humans' understanding of the other deepens, the extent of their empathic capacity must broaden in response. It is thought that the cognitive understanding of the other and the empathic understanding of the other evolved side by side through reciprocal influence.

Growing familiar with the others in a group

While primate social structures are diverse, there is no doubt that consanguinity through the mother-daughter connection exerts a major influence on relationships between individuals within a group in a matrilineal society such as that of Japanese macaques. When we pick an individual in a group and observe its relationships with those around it, we find a clear difference in the manner of association between its blood relatives (consanguineous group), including its mother, sons and daughters, and the other individuals in the group. Let us call the former "relatives" and the latter "acquaintances" here. Besides these group members, strangers occasionally appear from outside of the group.

Favoring one's relatives over others is called nepotism, which has a biological foundation called kin selection[4] (Hamilton 1971; Trivers 1991). However, it is improbable that animals recognize their own relatives and non-relatives as categories. In mammals in which the mother raises her offspring with her own milk, it is thought that nepotism arises as a result of using the degree of familiarity, such as proximity and contact since infancy, as a behavioral indicator (Hasegawa and Hasegawa 2000). If this is the case, for individual Japanese macaques, the difference between relatives and acquaintances must be a quantitative difference in the degree of familiarity rather than a categorical qualitative difference. This means that it is the researchers observing them who create the categories of relatives and acquaintances, not the Japanese macaques.

However, the difference between acquaintances and strangers seems to be more than a matter of varying degrees, even for Japanese macaques. There is a discontinuous distinction between knowing and not knowing or being somewhat familiar and not familiar. This distinction is demonstrated by strong vigilance and hostility exhibited in encounters with strangers. Yet, strangers are not simply excluded. For instance, well-built solitary males that turn up during the mating season often seem to be very attractive to troop females. These solitary males manage to mate with a few females on the sly, despite being attacked by many troop males. For the solitary males, becoming acquainted and familiar with some troop members through mating relationships with females can lead to a successful transfer into the troop.

Relatives and acquaintances within the troop are companions or peers who have formed varying degrees of familiarity through all sorts of interactions. A certain level of predictability regarding each other's behavior must engender a certain level of trust and security about co-presence with them. They do not have this sense of security in relation to unfamiliar strangers from outside the group. Intergroup encounters are generally hostile and outsiders are non-companions (i.e., enemies?) from the viewpoint of a troop individual. However, troop individuals are not necessarily adversaries from the perspective of a solitary male, for example, outside of the troop. It seems that the relationship between strangers is not always symmetrical.

In patrilineal societies such as chimpanzee groups, consanguineous groups are not formed as the mother-daughter connection is severed by the daughter's migration, unlike in Japanese macaque society. Nepotism is limited to relationships between mothers and their mature sons and between uterine brothers, except while individuals are immature. A strong connection between mother and son is found in bonobos, who have a similar social structure to chimpanzees, whereas it is not marked in chimpanzees. There have been observed cases of cooperation between brothers (Goodall 1990), but the presence of adult brothers within a group is not very common[5]. Consequently, a chimpanzee unit-group[6] is mostly comprised of a limited number of relatives and a large number of acquaintances. Females grow up in this group and migrate to other groups when they reach sexual maturity. In other words, female strangers come into a unit-group. Newly immigrated females are sometimes attacked or bullied by resident females (Itoh 2013), but males seldom attack them. Newly immigrated females may find former female acquaintances from their natal group who can help them fit into the new group. As the new females interact with various individuals within the group, the other members gradually become familiar with them.

Primate societies are fundamentally groups comprising acquaintances. Although group members generally exclude strangers, they accept them on occasion. The immigrants gradually become part of the group through a repetition of various interactions with group members. In other words, strangers are no longer strangers when they stay with and coexist in the group.

Group-forming primates loosely synchronize their activity cycle with others in daily living. From the perspective of individual development, the baby's first object for synchronization is its mother. Cognitive understanding also develops through dyadic interactions with the mother. As the infant's physical abilities increase, the object for synchronization expands to children of the same or similar ages. Because synchronization is closely linked to physical function, it is more easily achievable between individuals with similar physical abilities. Play offers a field where the infant can directly experience physical synchronization with others. As the infant grows, it expands its scope of synchronization and begins to loosely synchronize with the others in the group. At the reproduction stage, synchronization with a reproductive partner of the opposite sex looms as a major challenge. A unique courting behavior system can be regarded as a device for synchronization.

The above course of individual development is a process of familiarization with the others within a group. "Familiarity" is a type of learning, including acclimatization and habituation, and is hence applicable in relation to animals, plants and the environment. One can become familiar with a pet or farm animal and even relate well with a dangerous object while maintaining a certain relationship. When one has become familiar with one's environment, one can live in it safely.

The evolution of human groups

We have no material evidence that directly tells us what kind of society our ancestors lived in when they emerged six to seven million years ago[7]. Fossil evidence shows that the brain volume of early hominins[8] is similar to that of extant great apes, but their erect bipedalism and smaller canine teeth are notable features.

Societies and behaviors in the extant species that are closest to them, including chimpanzees, bonobos, gorillas and humans (*Homo sapiens*), highlight some commonalities. Firstly, the brain volume suggests that their level of intelligence was about the same as that of chimpanzees and gorillas. They would have lived in a community, although we do not know what type. They would have had a long childhood where infants were breastfed until the age of three to five and accompanied their mothers at all times. The young would not have travelled alone without their mother until they reached sexual maturity at the age of seven to nine. Sexually mature females would have left their natal group to migrate to another group or to a male and produced and reared their offspring there[9]. They would have given birth every five years or so and raised five or six children at most in their lifetime. We shall refrain from speculating on the male life history here, because it greatly differs between chimpanzees and gorillas. The longest lifespan would have been around fifty years, and hence their community would have included a maximum of four generations down to grandchildren or even great-grandchildren. In view of the migration of sexually mature females, they would not have formed a consanguineous group based on the mother-daughter blood relation.

We do not know whether the earliest hominins formed one-male groups as gorillas do or multi-male groups as chimpanzees and bonobos do, or neither type of group, but they would certainly have formed some kind of group. Based on forest animal fossils found with *Sahelanthropus* and *Ardipithecus* (Figure 5.1), early hominins are thought to have lived in or on the fringes of forests and slept in beds made on branches at night. As they certainly would have adapted to a gradually drying environment from that point, it is highly likely that they formed multi-male groups to protect themselves against predators. If they were travelling between forest and grassland, it is possible that they had a system of fission and fusion whereby they dispersed into smaller parties in the forest and re-merged into a large party when they entered the grassland. The reduction in the size of canine teeth also suggests decreased competition and increased tolerance between males, and therefore it is more plausible to think that males coexisted within a group.

The genus *Homo* first appeared from among early hominins, probably the slender species of *Australopithecus*, about 2.5 million years ago. The use of Oldowan stone tools began around that time[10] and brain volume began to increase rapidly[11]. They had slightly larger bodies, perfected erect bipedal walking no different from the way modern humans walk and changed their feeding habits from a plant-centered diet high in nuts and fruits to a more meat-centered diet. Their range expanded greatly and some groups moved out of the African Continent for the first time and spread

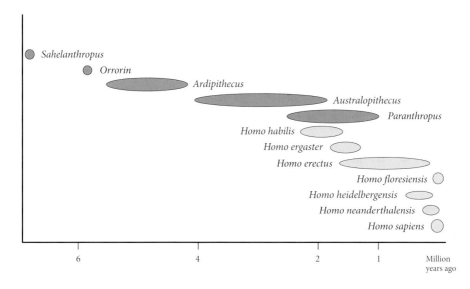

Figure 5.1 Timeline of major human fossils

into Eurasia. As these changes clearly indicate a marked rise in their cognitive capacity, the emergence of the genus *Homo* is perhaps the most appropriate point in the history of human evolution to mark the development of a cognitive understanding of others based on theory of mind. As the early genus *Homo* evolved into *Homo ergaster* and *Homo erectus*, it is highly likely that they began to recognize the other they lived with as "a being with a mind". It is thought that early childhood, a stage that had been previously nonexistent, manifested between infancy and childhood at the time of *Homo erectus* (Thompson and Nelson 2011). If so, their child-rearing system and the pattern of development of an understanding of the other might have changed at that time. According to Mithen (2006), early humans with theory of mind would have been able to understand the other's feelings, beliefs, wants and intentions well and to predict the other's behavior in a way that is not possible for modern monkeys and apes. It is considered that the development of theory of mind as well as communication between mother and child was essential for the development and transmission of skills to make tools from stone flakes from one generation to another.

If sustained bonds were established between particular females and males at the time of *Homo erectus*[12], they might have formed multilevel societies similar to that of hamadryas baboons where a number of such units assemble to form a large group (Yamagiwa 2015a). This is equivalent to the structure in the pre-band theory of family precipitation posited in a study of the origins of the family by J. Itani (1983). T. Nishida (1999b) conjectured that early hominin society already had this type of multilevel structure. The following is purely a hypothesis.

If a unit formed by a particular female and a male had a basically monogamous structure including some polygamy, its superordinate group would comprise a number of such family units in addition to a male-only unit of young males. Children would grow up in each family unit until they reached maturity when males would leave their families to join the male unit. As early humans who forayed into savannas would have dramatically expanded their range, they might have lost their territoriality at that stage, as with the case of gorillas (Yamagiwa (ed.) 2007). Such a group is expected to have travelled all over their range in loose formation or merging and parting frequently and would have encountered other groups in the process. Whereas intergroup encounters end in intense hostility in chimpanzee society, early humans with smaller canine teeth and lower levels of rivalry between males might have achieved a temporary fusion between groups, as with the case of bonobos (Kanō 2001). I imagine that young females migrated in the midst of riotous confusion and excitement (Kuroda 2013) and formed new units with new males in the new group.

The multilevel society of early humans hypothesized here is structurally similar to those of hamadryas baboons and gelada baboons, but it belongs to a different class substantively. In hamadryas baboons, females in a one-male unit go off by themselves away from the male. On each occasion the male has to bring them back forcefully by biting their necks (Kummer 1972). He must always keep a watchful eye on the movement of females in his unit. In a one-male unit of gelada baboons, its cohesion is maintained by consanguineous bonds between females and in a sense the male is simply slotted into an aggregation of females. If the early human unit had a patrilineal structure based on female transfers, it would be similar to hamadryas baboons' one-male unit, but the human male would not have been able to supervise his females all the time in contrast with the case of hamadryas baboons.

It is supposed that early humans, especially at the *Homo erectus* stage, manufactured sophisticated stone tools such as hand axes and engaged in frequent hunting. If their cognitive understanding of others made great advances around this period, they would have developed an ability to understand the intention and meaning of the other's actions better and to engage in various cooperative behaviors to achieve shared goals. By sharing one another's goals, they could intentionally divide roles and efficiently carry out collaborative activities to accomplish things that had been done by one person previously. If so, it is unlikely that all unit members participated in carrying out various activities. Perhaps multiple units would gather and males would engage in all sorts of collaborative work while females cooperated in child-rearing and other activities. This would indicate that early humans maintained the cohesiveness of each unit while unit members sometimes temporarily went separate ways (i.e., fission and fusion)[13]. This situation might happen occasionally in chimpanzees if a unit was comprised of females and their offspring, but it would not be so easy to maintain if a non-sanguineous male was included.

In fact, in chimpanzee society there are occasions when a particular male and a particular female form a couple and maintain an exclusive sexual relationship, albeit temporarily. One type of this mating behavior is called "consortship" involving the alpha male and the other type is called "safari behavior" involving a middle- to high-ranked male. In the former, the alpha male constantly accompanies his favorite estrous female and intercepts any other male trying to approach. While this behavior is possible because of his dominant status in the group, it has been observed that some females sneak off to copulate with another male when the alpha lets them out of his sight, later returning and pretending nothing has happened. In the latter type, a middle- to high-ranked male takes a non-estrous female to range in an area away from the rest of the group for a period from a few days to a few months, during which they mate repeatedly.

These two types of pairing are temporary and do not lead to a stable female-male relationship afterwards, but they represent two possible ways to maintain a monogamous mating pair in primate society. One way is to use force, as seen in hamadryas baboons. The other method is to stay away from competitors, as seen in groups of gibbon pairs or one-male groups in gorillas. Both involve an attempt to maintain pairing by restraining one party in the couple from having contact with other group members.

In the above-hypothesized multilevel society of early humans, the couple must remain together while maintaining each party's freedom to have contact with other group members, including those of the opposite sex. An essential factor in the establishment of a multilevel society is that early human females do not express estrous cycles as obviously as chimpanzees and bonobos do. Two opposite vectors would need to be reconciled within the group, namely the expansion of cooperative relationships between individuals and the stabilization of female-male relationships.

In modern human society, family members are partially segregated from others through the sharing of a closed space called home, while they are guaranteed free contact with non-family members. What makes this possible is perhaps the existence of various social norms and institutions. Early humans would not have had social institutions like ours, as they would not have acquired language yet, but the embryonic form of social norms and natural institutions (Kuroda 1999) would have emerged at the time.

The generation of *we*

The advancement of the cognitive understanding of others that took place in early humans, probably at the time of *Homo erectus*, dramatically expanded cooperative relationships between the constituent members of a group through a better understanding of others' intentions and the meaning of their behaviors. They were able to engage in joint actions to accomplish shared goals to improve efficiency in various activities, including hunting, dissecting prey, gathering food and rearing children. The repeated participation in these joint actions would have exponentially improved their ability to communicate through gestures and voices and engendered trust relationships beyond a sense of security based on familiarity, as discussed above. The clear realization that a goal is achieved by connecting one's actions with others' in a joint action for a shared goal must have generated a sense of *we*-ness (Tomasello 2013) among the participants.

Becoming familiar with other group members may form a background for loose *we*-ness as an accumulation of dyadic relationships. However, the familiarity relationship is formed by repetitions of dyadic interactions between two parties and does not result in the clearly outlined aggregation of *we*. The emergence of *we*-ness requires strong rather than weak synchronization. When strong synchronization is incorporated in joint actions based on the cognitive understanding of others, the empathic understanding of others is enhanced and *we*-ness emerges.

I would like to think that the generation of *we*-ness and the engendering of trust within the group facilitated the emergence of the social norms required for the maintenance of multilevel society in early humans. The couple in a family unit was formed on the basis of the approval and guarantee of the other constituent members of the group (i.e., third parties) rather than within the dyadic relationship alone[14]. The other group members approved the couple's relationship within that family unit and the couple accepted it. Because of this, the couple could temporarily disperse at any time and a social norm emerged when it became the way of *we*.

Incidentally, non-human primates, even great apes such as chimpanzees, are generally uninterested in relationships between others that do not directly concern themselves, although they show a strong interest in the actions of others that directly concern them. For example, incest avoidance between a mother and son or siblings that is commonly found in primate societies is purely a rule between two parties, and therefore a third party shows no reaction to those who deviate from this rule (Kuroda 2017). It seems that great apes are highly capable of finding a conventional rule in a dyadic interaction and coordinate their behaviors as parties to the interaction, but they are unable to separate it from "here, now" or to apply it to a third party objectively. Although great apes exhibit a wide range of behaviors involving social norms (de Waal 1998; Kawai (ed.) 2017), Tomasello (2013) argues that social norms are not found in great apes if they are defined as "socially agreed-upon and mutually known expectations bearing social force, monitored and enforced by the third parties".

Kuroda (2017) uses the term "We-type institution" to describe a phenomenon in which chimpanzees gang up to intrude on and commit bloodshed in the neighboring group's range in intergroup aggression. It certainly feels that *we*-ness is manifesting in the way multiple males go on a rampage amid strong excitement and synchronicity for the common goal of killing members of a neighboring group. However, it is very rare to see three or more chimpanzees involved in a joint action with a shared purpose in their everyday activities. In humans, when one declares that a doll is a baby, all other children, even infants, in pretend play will instantly share that goal and continue to play with the doll as a baby. Humans use language to easily share a purpose and create *we* who act jointly. In view of the rarity of triadic play and the complete absence of team competition play in chimpanzees (Nishida 2008), the difference between them and humans is clear. It appears that chimpanzees are yet to be equipped with a sufficient ability to create *we*. This was probably the case with early hominins as well.

"*We*" is a representation and an imaginary construct without substance. It sometimes represents you and I who are "here, now", or some friends and I, or my family and I, or my school or company or humankind as a whole. It is an ambiguous and flexible existence. On the other hand, *we* accompanies the realistic sense that we have something in common. It seems that the generation of *we* has steered the subsequent history of human society.

The strong empathic ability enhanced by the development of the cognitive understanding of others sometimes promotes the blending of the self and the other, extinguishes the self/other distinction and creates the *we* that accompanies intense emotions. At that moment, new others emerge outside of *we*. Are the newly emergent others potential *we*, or irreconcilable and incomprehensible others? It is reasonable to state that the contraposition between *we* and others has always been exploited politically in the history of *Homo sapiens*.

Part II
Others and Other Groups: How to Interact with the Counterpart

6 Who Is the Alpha Male? The Appearance of the "Other" in Chimpanzee Society

Hitonaru Nishie

Key ideas

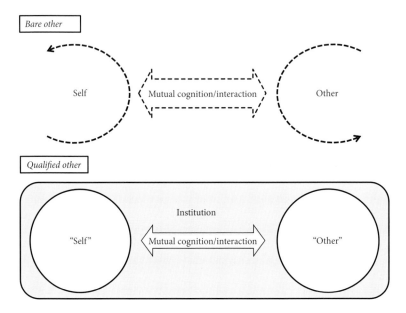

The *self* and the *other* have an ambivalent relationship in which they mutually trigger cognition/interaction, but they cannot comprehend one another completely. Confronted by the "contingency" inherent in the *other*, the range of mutual cognition/interaction broadens and the mutual relationship inevitably becomes unstable, so the parties must develop an *ad hoc* relationship by resorting to "exploratory" cognition/interaction on each encounter (the *bare other*). On the other hand, the *qualified other* is a device to produce a construct that makes one feel "as if one can have a full view" of the *other* whose totality is incomprehensible. In human society this has made it possible to mitigate cognitive load by subsuming the contingency of the *other* into an "institution" and narrowing the range of mutual cognition/interaction.

Because the "institution" merely "conceals" the contingency of the other, however, abrupt appearances of the *bare other* make our cognitive/interactional selection difficult. We then attempt to stabilize the mutual formation of a relationship by reclaiming the other as quickly as possible. The human way, marked by this strong predilection for a stable relationship with the *qualified other,* can be regarded as a "vulnerable" attitude in the sense that we are not tolerant enough to accept *bare others* as they are.

> A chance encounter that is not framed by a shared interest destabilizes the other's outline, and I begin to search for the further meaning of the other's action. In fact, this is the very place where I meet the mind of the other who I cannot fully comprehend or perceive.
>
> (Noya 2012: 227)

In Chapter Six of *Institutions: The Evolution of Human Sociality* that preceded this volume, I presented a detailed account of the disappearance of an alpha male (the highest-ranked male) in wild chimpanzee society, outlined "an exploratory approach to deal with an unstable social encounter using conventional manners of action" observed in the process and theorized the emergence of an "institution" as a "spontaneous order" created by repeated employment of these conventional manners (Nishie 2017, hereinafter called "Part I"). I described the difficulty of selecting mutually appropriate actions in the unstable social encounters that occurred due to the uncertainty of relationships between group members (i.e., "We do not know who the alpha male is") in the wake of the extraordinary state of the prolonged absence of the alpha male, and examined the way the initial instability and confusion at scenes of social encounters gradually converged as they resorted to conventional manners (such as emitting pant-grunts and grooming as discussed later) to produce a certain degree of order and relied on that temporary social order in selecting their next actions. In other words, my argument about institutions in chimpanzee society in Part I was that the chimpanzees generated an improvised and local order through the exploratory application of conventional actions, and used that order in subsequent action selection to create a "spontaneous institution" on each occasion instead of relying on the predetermined institutions that can be referred to by anyone at any time.

The idea of "spontaneous order" as a primordial form of institution is derived from the discourse of social philosopher F. A. Hayek (1967a, 1967b, 1973), but I believe that the originality of Part I rests in its concrete description of order formation in chimpanzees' languageless society. On the other hand, as it was bound by the theme of "institutions", Part I downplayed the confusion and instability in actual encounters between chimpanzees, and focused its discussion on the subsequent convergence of chaos and the formation of order. Consequently, I was unable to fully describe and discuss such questions as "Why did the (former) alpha male go missing again after the apparent convergence?" and "How should we interpret the situation of 'continuous disappearance' and 'not encountering other individuals' for more than a year?", or in other words, the aspect of "divergence" associated with encounters with *others* as the opposite of convergence, so to speak.

For this reason, my aim here is to describe the aspect of "divergence caused by *others*" based on specific interactions between chimpanzees. This entails addressing "a prolonged state of not encountering each other" as the opposite of "a scene of encounter" (discussed in Part I from a phenomenological perspective) as well as "a viewpoint/actor that causes a divergence of meaning in the world = *other*" as the reverse of "an order spontaneously formed out of chaos = institution" (discussed in Part I from a theoretical perspective). It is anticipated that a discourse combining both aspects ("institution" and "other" from phenomenological and theoretical perspectives) will describe the *bare other* who is not subsumed under institutions in chimpanzee society and the *qualified other* compressed by institutions in human society.

The *other*: That which enables/summons institutions

Before I begin discussing the *other* in chimpanzee society, I shall clarify its relationship with institutions, which I addressed in Part I.

Firstly, my discussion on institutions in Part I already assumed the existence of the *other*. In short, an institution without an *other* is impossible, and an institution can come into being only with the existence of an *other*. I maintain my position in Part I here, in that an institution for me alone (private institution) is impossible and nonsensical. In this sense, the *other* was the precondition that made institutions possible.

On the other hand, the *other* is not only the precondition for institutions, but also that which summons institutions. The *other* is a subject who defines the world from a different perspective from that of *I*, and brings another aspect to the meaning of the world (Noya 2012). In the co-presence of "the *other* as the ultimate uncertainty" (Nishie 2017) who interprets the world differently from the way *I* do, a spontaneous institution is formed, used, maintained and reproduced in which a local pattern is produced and used in selecting the next action. This was the substance of my argument on "institutions" in Part I. Here, an institution, which would be impossible and unnecessary in a world without *others* (if such a thing were possible), was required and summoned as a technique to enable co-presence with "the *other* who brings a divergence of meaning to the world" (Noya 2012) and to manage social life without difficulty.

Based on this model of the (minimum) relationship between the *other* and institution, how do we describe this *other*?

Firstly, an *other* is a being *I* recognize and interact with (who *I* demand recognition/interaction from) as a cognitive agent/actor with certain cohesiveness. In simpler terms, the *other* is "somebody" rather than "something". In this sense, it differs from an inorganic "thing" that exists in the general environment (something), but in some cases a thing can have certain agency and *I* can recognized it, or *I* can act on/be acted on by a thing as an object with agency (somebody) (see "*things* that exercise agency" in Chapter Eighteen by Tokoro). Further, the *other* is not necessarily a single biological individual; in some cases an aggregation of individuals (e.g., a group with a certain cohesiveness) or one part of an individual (e.g., a certain behavior) can be perceived as *other*. In either case, that which *I* recognize/interact with (or *I* demand recognition/interaction from/ with) as a cognitive agent/actor with certain cohesiveness exists as somebody with certain agency and not something as a mere object. In this instance, a "readiness (possibility) for mutual cognition/interaction" arises between *I* and the *other* rather than *I* unilaterally recognizing/acting on the *other* as somebody.

The *other* who appears as a cognitive agent/actor with certain cohesiveness is also a being whose totality cannot be perceived. The *other* brings a different framework of meaning to the world because the *other* interprets the world from a different perspective and therefore *I* cannot completely grasp the *other's* viewpoint (in theory) (Noya 2012). As long as the *other* is *other*, *I* cannot see all of its being or viewpoint. Perceiving the "*other* whose entirety cannot be grasped" gives rise to not only the "readiness (possibility) for mutual cognition/interaction", but also the "falteringness (difficulty) of mutual cognition/interaction" at the same time. In daily life, when a conversation is flowing smoothly we simply "chatter" (without using a subject in the case of the Japanese language) without consciously distinguishing self and other all the time in terms of "*I* am talking" and "*they* are listening". We perceive *otherness* in our daily interactions in the moment when "an interaction falters" (e.g., when we do not understand what the other is saying) and the *other* and *I* appear as subjects who interpret the world from different viewpoints amidst the "faltering interaction".

In this way, the *other* simultaneously appears in the "readiness (possibility) for interaction" and the "falteringness (difficulty) of interaction". While the *other* as a cognitive agent/actor that is different from *I* activates the readiness for mutual cognition/interaction, the *other* as a being whose "whole" cannot be seen from the viewpoint of *I* causes mutual cognition/interaction to falter. In short, the *other* provides the impetus for an interaction and at the same time poses difficulties for it. *I* am required to connect with the *other* in the initiation phase of each interaction (readiness for interaction) and as *I* cannot see the whole of the *other*, I am unable to predetermine the appropriate manner of relating and therefore forced to keep feeling my way forward as I continue interacting (faltering interaction). This is because the "incomprehensible whole" that forms the *other* in turn forms part of the entirety of the possible relationships between the *other* and *I*, and hence *I* must create a new path in the world, not as a stable and consistent perspective, but as an unstable existence that appears in the ad hoc relationship with the *other*.

The *other* that appears in this "readiness for/faltering interaction" is thought to appear in the various forms of concreteness depending on the situation in various social lives. I shall describe below the concrete forms of appearances of the *other* in chimpanzee society and discuss how they differ from those in human society.

Disappearance of the alpha male and subsequent instability

Background and circumstances of the incident

Wild chimpanzees live in unit-groups consisting of multiple males and females. Each unit-group maintains a basically stable membership aside from fluctuations due to births and deaths as well as intergroup transfers of young females at sexual maturity. Male chimpanzees basically stay with their natal group for life (male philopatric social system). M group in my study field of the Mahale Mountains National Park in Tanzania has maintained a membership of approximately sixty individuals since I began studying them in 2002.

Although the unit-group membership is relatively stable, it is very rare that all members assemble in one place. Members usually break into subgroups (parties) to range together. Party membership is flexible, and it is rare to see the same combination of individuals together all the time; they repeatedly encounter and separate routinely as they range along. This flexible party composition in chimpanzees is specifically called "fission-fusion" (see Chapter Seven by Itoh). In relation to the cases in our discussion below, I shall add that while "not encountering someone for a period of several days to several weeks" is a very common phenomenon as chimpanzees in Mahale routinely encounter and separate from other individuals in their lives, the "non-appearance of a particular individual for over several months" or "no encounters between particular individuals for over several months" is relatively rare. Particularly, the phenomenon of the prolonged disappearance of a socially prominent individual such as the alpha male is an extraordinary event that has so far happened only once in a decade or so in Mahale.

It is believed that there is a linear dominance rank between males within a chimpanzee unit-group which permits researchers to understand their rank order based on the direction of aggression, intimidation and pant-grunts, which is considered to be submissive vocalization[1]. The top-ranking male is called the alpha, at whom other individuals utter pant-grunts unilaterally; he does not utter pant-grunts at others.

Although dominance rank in male chimpanzees is thought to be understood on the basis of indicators such as aggression, intimidation and pant-grunts, the linear order is not always verifiable as there are pairs of individuals seldom observed to engage in such interactions and occasions where the direction of interaction is unclear. However, the direction of pant-grunts from other individuals to the alpha male or intimidation and attacks by the alpha male towards other individuals can be observed with relative stability, and therefore researchers regard the existence of the alpha male in chimpanzee society as almost self-evident.

Thus, matters such as the "(stable membership of the) chimpanzee unit-group" and "(the alpha male in) dominance rank among males" are assumed by human observers in the abstract as a "bird's-eye view ideal type", so to speak, despite (or because of) the virtual lack of opportunity to see the "whole" of them.

Nevertheless, this self-evident assumption was overturned out of the blue. The occurrence of the disappearance of the alpha male incident, which I address here to follow up my discussion in Part I, was the beginning of the upending of the assumption as far as I was concerned. Members of the stable group appeared to have been interacting with one another according to their dominance ranks until the day before the alpha male suddenly went missing. I noticed no signs of the impending disappearance at all, and the cause of the event remains a mystery to this day. Fanana, the alpha male at the time (Photo 6.1), went missing literally out of the blue.

The second-ranked male, Alofu (Photo 6.2), had the unusual habit of holding his own nipple with one hand when nervous, and used to vocalize pant-grunts while holding his nipple on most encounters with Fanana. Alofu had no one to pant-grunt to after Fanana's disappearance, and became the receiver of unilateral pant-grunts from others. In other words, Alofu became the alpha male by default in the sense that all other individuals uttered pant-grunts at him. It was, however, difficult for me to determine who the alpha male was during this extended period of time, as Alofu could potentially utter pant-grunts at Fanana upon his return. As the period of disappearance continued, I was also unsure whether Fanana could continue to be regarded as "a stable member of the group" because he rarely encountered other

Photo 6.1 Fanana (right) receiving grooming from Kalunde (left), an old male

Photo 6.2 Alofu

group members. It seemed that these senses of "uncertainty about the identity of the alpha male" and "uncertainty about who can be considered stable members of the group" were shared by all of the chimpanzees, including Fanana and Alofu, as some "sense of instability" or "sense of discomfort", rather than being just my impression.

Fanana, who went missing after 26 November 2003, was not observed at all during December. He was observed alone or together with a small number of individuals sporadically in January 2004, but encounters with Alofu were rarely observed. During my stay until September 2004, a direct encounter between them was observed only twice (16 April and 25 August). These scenes of encounter were discussed in Part I. In this chapter, I focus on a side of the story I could not discuss previously, that is, how "missing" Fanana and the "stable members of the group", including Alofu, managed to elude one another. In the state of not encountering one another, the situation develops while the parties cannot be certain "where, with whom and who the other is". The aim of this chapter is to depict the appearance of the *other* in chimpanzee society by describing how chimpanzees deal with this "yet-to-be encountered *other*".

The first "near miss": Fanana sightings and escapes

Let us look at how Fanana managed to avoid encounters with other individuals during his disappearance.

As mentioned earlier, Fanana was sighted sporadically in January 2004 and looked healthy and no different than prior to his disappearance (except that he was alone) as far as I was able to observe. Because some wild chimpanzees quietly disappear and die when they become sick or seriously injured, I was worried about Fanana's safety when he had been missing for over a month. When I actually followed and observed him when occasionally sighted in January, I was relieved to find him healthy and unchanged, as he fed normally, sometimes vocalized long-range pant-hoots and vigorously charged with his hair bristled to kick buttress roots.

As I observed Fanana behaving like his usual self, however, I could not understand at all why this seemingly "normal Fanana" remained "in hiding". In fact, in late January Fanana joined a party of about twenty individuals, including an old male (Kalunde: on the left in Photo 6.1), two young males and multiple females, and ranged with them for two days, and I continued my observation with the expectation that things might return to the state prior to his departure. However, Fanana subsequently left the party seemingly on a whim and again disappeared.

On the morning of 1 February, I set off to conduct observation with my assistant as usual, sighted Fanana alone at 8:50 and began to follow and observe him. The chimpanzees' habitat is a large forest (M group routinely ranges an area of approximately twenty-five square kilometers) with dense undergrowth, which obstructs our vision on the ground level and makes finding a silent solitary individual extremely difficult. On that day, as we began our observation I was delighted with the good fortune of encountering Fanana unexpectedly. Still, it is easy to lose sight of a solitary individual on the move, and it is very difficult to find them again once visual contact is lost. On this occasion, I was more nervous than usual as we followed Fanana, especially because he was avoiding others and it was unpredictable whether he might encounter any of them.

For a while after we began to follow Fanana, he slowly travelled to the east along the valley. At 8:59, Fanana suddenly vocalized pant-hoots loudly, kicked buttress roots and ran away eastward, so my assistant and I lost sight of him soon after we began following. We did not hear any response (voice) to Fanana's pant-hoots from other individuals, possibly because we were in the valley.

We were rather disheartened by the early loss of our target, but we continued to search for him in the area on the eastern side. At 9:26, we luckily found Fanana again, feeding on fruit alone upon a tree about 100 meters to the east of where we had lost him.

About three minutes later, Fanana stopped feeding, descended the tree and began travelling southward. Four minutes later (9:33), he paused at a research trail intersection[2] and sniffed the ground on the eastern side. He then sniffed the ground on the southern side and began to travel southward along the research trail. He walked quietly and slowly in a much more cautious manner than usual, as he frequently sniffed at the ground and occasionally paused to look to the south (in the direction of travel) and the west.

At 9:58, Fanana paused on the research trail and looked to the south and west alternately. About thirty seconds later, barks from more than one chimpanzee rang out intermittently from a relatively close position on the southwestern side. Fanana immediately left the research trail, entered a bush on the southeastern side and quickly travelled away from the source of the voices. In contrast to his previous measured walk, he rapidly accelerated and ran eastward through the undergrowth as fast as he could. My assistant and I desperately tried to keep up, but our longer limbs were hindrances to running in the bush. Although my assistant ran much faster than I did and tracked Fanana to another research trail about 300 meters to the east, he could not see Fanana after that point.

As we were able to hear intermittent barks from multiple individuals from the southwest even after Fanana's escape, we went to check the source of the voices and discovered a party of twenty-five or so individuals, including Alofu and four other adult males, about 100 meters southwest of the spot where Fanana fled. The chimpanzees in this party did not seem to notice that Fanana had been close by, and slowly travelled to the northwest for the rest of the day.

In this case, we observed how the solitary and "missing" Fanana quickly fled upon hearing the voices of multiple individuals. We are unsure whether Fanana was able to identify "who" the vocalizing individuals were, but we expect that he at least understood that there were multiple individuals. He might have understood that there were multiple males, as male and female voices are different in quality, and he might even have understood that Alofu was there. For now, we shall adopt the interpretation that Fanana recognized a group of multiple individuals and avoided (fled from) the group.

Nevertheless, are we correct in saying that Fanana recognized a group of other individuals only upon hearing their voices? Of course, he would have recognized the vocalizing group when he heard their voices, but a close review of Fanana's behavior leading up to the vocalization suggests that he was already searching for "(perhaps unspecified) others".

For example, a pant-hoot is a vocalization commonly used for long-distance communication, and the vocalizer is often observed to "wait for a reply" from another individual (Hanamura 2010a). In other words, a pant-hoot is an exploratory behavior in search of an unspecified "somebody" rather than a call to a specific individual. As it is unspecified, it does not always draw a reply, and it is up to the counterpart whether they reply or not. For this reason, "searching for somebody" may be too strong an expression. However, considering that Fanana would be difficult to find if he remained quiet, and that he was spending most of his time alone during his disappearance, making loud noises in the form of pant-hoots or kicking buttress roots would increase the possibility of being found or replied to by "somebody". Behaviors to increase "the possibility of ending a solitary life", or in other words, "the possibility of encountering somebody", would at least trigger an interaction with "somebody". In the sense that Fanana's pant-hoot would trigger a "reply" from "somebody", it could be regarded as an exploratory call to (an unspecified) somebody.

Fanana travelled southward along the research trail cautiously, pausing to smell the ground repeatedly. We suspect that this behavior was in anticipation of an encounter with "somebody" and enabled Fanana to ready himself for the possible encounter (including the option of avoiding it).

If he detected the smell of another individual on the ground, the most he would be able to deduce from it would be that "the individual (the source of the smell) had been there", and not where the individual was or what the individual was doing now. He might be able to deduce from a fresh smell that the individual was "still nearby" or "went that way", but available information would be very limited. If we suppose that a smell can be used to identify the source individual, but that it is difficult to gain detailed information from the smell about who else was present and what they were doing, then at most the information that Fanana gained by sniffing at the ground is likely to be that "(specified/unspecified) somebody has been (might have been) here". Again, this behavior is an exploration for a yet-to-be encountered "somebody".

Following this cautious behavior, Fanana came close to a party of many individuals, heard their voices and fled hurriedly in sharp contrast to his previous measured walk. In other words, Fanana repeated his "exploration" as he anticipated an encounter with "somebody" and managed to avoid it just before the encounter became a reality. Consequently, Fanana's relationship with "somebody" was postponed without being reclaimed by relationships based on ordinary interactions, and he was able to continue the life of the missing.

The panic-like confusion that occurred at the time of encounters between "missing" Fanana and other individuals and its convergence were addressed in Part I (Nishie 2017), but a resolution of the state of "disappearance" requires an "encounter" (in the sense that the state of "disappearance" is a "continuous avoidance of encounters"), whatever the outcome. As the encounter was not realized because Fanana fled, the state of disappearance remained after this episode.

Thus, the relationship between Fanana and other individuals was postponed in a state of "suspension", so to speak. How can we describe this "suspended" relationship between Fanana and other individuals?

Needless to say, Fanana was a member of a stable group before his disappearance. "Member of a stable group" here means a "counterpart in various manners of interaction in daily life" through routinely encountering and separating, ranging together and separately for a period, exchanging pant-grunts, grooming and fighting with one another, napping together when they meet, uttering or hearing pant-hoots and knowing or not knowing where the others are when apart. Fanana's "disappearance" meant that he avoided routine interaction by not encountering group members on an ongoing basis, and shook "the stability of group membership" as a result. In other words, what is projected as a silhouette in the background by the "encounters" discussed in Part I and the "near misses" here between Fanana and the other members includes not only the individual relationships between them, but also "all possible but invisible relationships" in the form of a unit-group normally comprised of a stable membership.

Fanana was the alpha male prior to his disappearance. When he encountered other individuals, he received pant-grunts from them and rarely met with intimidation or attacks from them. Even if this could be called a kind of "institution" based on some "bottomless reason" (Nishie 2017), the recursive formation of a mutually stable relationship and the utilization of this relationship made the next action selection easier. However, a stable relationship between the alpha male and a subordinate individual could be sustained and reproduced through mutual encounters; the prolonged lack of encounters makes the recursive interactions (e.g., pant-grunts, intimidation and aggression) that form this stable relationship impossible, and hence the mutual relationship becomes unstable. In fact, panic-like chaos broke out at the scenes of encounters after Fanana's disappearance, as discussed in Part I, and this chaos was most likely brought about by the "destabilization of the relationship". The "absence of the alpha male" caused by Fanana's disappearance highlights not only the individual relationships between Fanana and the other members, but also "all possible but invisible relationships" between "the alpha male and subordinate individuals" that enable the usual stable relationships.

The second "near miss": Alofu and others encounter Fanana

After that episode, Fanana appeared to spend most of his time alone, although he encountered other group members on several occasions. When he encountered a large party including Alofu in August, he uttered a pant-grunt at Alofu. This made me think that Alofu had become the new alpha male, and that Fanana's disappearance and the unstable relationships that had continued for more than a year would finally end (Nishie 2017). Yet, Fanana continued to avoid contact with the other individuals and remained "missing". I was due to finish my study and leave for Japan at the end of September and hoped to witness a "resolution" before leaving, but Fanana was slow to appear.

On 25 September 2004, the voices of some chimpanzees had been coming from somewhere high up in the eastern hills since morning. As many individuals, including Alofu and Kalunde, had come down to the lowland by around 11:00, we decided to follow Alofu for the day. Until about 13:30, Alofu and his party slowly traversed the lowland southward and passed their time idly by feeding on fruit on the treetops and grooming each other. Loud vocalizations such as pant-hoots and pant-grunts rang out frequently as they ranged as usual with a large ranging party.

At 13:32, a bark rang out suddenly from a nearby location to the east of where Alofu was. Alofu, with his hand on his nipple, immediately began to walk along the research trail southward together with Kalunde, Nkombo, an older female, and others. Seven minutes later, Alofu paused at an intersection and sniffed at the ground. Orion (young male) arrived and stopped just south of the intersection. For a few minutes, Alofu smelled the ground as well as fresh chimpanzee feces nearby.

At 13:44, Orion and Alofu began to walk along the research trail southward together. Orion initially walked ahead of Alofu, then later Alofu overtook him and continued to travel southward while sniffing at the ground repeatedly. We noticed that their penises were erect perhaps due to tension.

Four minutes later, Alofu and Orion turned westward at an intersection while uttering pant-hoots. Again, four minutes later, they turned to the south at another intersection. Alofu walked ahead of Orion at a relatively fast pace and rarely paused.

At 13:56, Alofu and Orion produced pant-hoots and soon after stopped together, where Orion began to groom Alofu. About four minutes later, pant-hoots from a single individual rang out from a distant location to the southwest. Alofu and Orion immediately began to walk southward along the research trail.

The two headed south at a very brisk pace and turned west at a fork in the trail at 14:06. At 14:09, Alofu and Orion produced pant-hoots at the next intersection, then Alofu with his hair standing on end headed to the northwest along the research trail.

At 14:13, Alofu and Orion merged with Bonobo and Masudi (both adult males) in a bush on the eastern side just off the research trail, but none of them uttered a pant-grunt or any other vocalization. The four sat there for a while. At 14:19, Alofu picked up fallen leaves to smell them and busily looked to the northwest and the north. The four made no move for a time and began to lie down to rest on the spot.

At 14:44, the four suddenly got up and began to walk to the southeast while producing loud barks and pant-hoots. Alofu soon reached the research trail and began to double back in the direction of where he had left off. Masudi and Orion gradually lagged behind, but Alofu retraced his path quickly with Bonobo. We could hear many voices from the northern and northwestern sides of where Alofu was, which presumably came from the large number of individuals who had been with Alofu earlier. At 14:58, Alofu and Bonobo uttered pant-hoots and Alofu made loud noises by kicking some buttress roots. Soon after, some adult females, Kalunde and others arrived from the north side one after another.

Alofu spent some time feeding on fruit in the treetops with Kalunde and others, then at around 15:30, set off on the same southward research trail he had hurried along with Orion a short while ago and headed south, this time at a leisurely pace together with Bonobo, Kalunde, some young males and adult females. As every female who encountered Alofu uttered pant-grunts at him, it began to get very noisy around him.

At 15:59, Alofu reached an intersection, where he had previously turned to the northwest at 14:09, and this time turned to the southwest and walked down a slope. Alofu paused occasionally, looked back, and resumed walking upon catching sight of his male followers such as Masudi and Pimu.

At 16:12, Alofu smelled the surface of the research trail and at 16:16 began to pick up and eat fallen fruit. Up in a nearby tree, Kalunde and Nkombo were already feeding on the same fruit. At 16:20, Kalunde finished eating and descended the tree. In turn, Alofu climbed the tree and fed on fruit for about six minutes, then came down to the ground and lay down by Kalunde. At around 16:30, Nkombo finished feeding and descended from the tree, and the three lazed around nearby.

At 16:58, Alofu and Kalunde uttered pant-hoots and heard many voices in reply from a wide area on the north side. At 17:02, as we stopped following and reached the research trail to head to our camp, we saw Fanana on his own coming from the north and approaching the location of Alofu and Kalunde. Fanana entered a bush on the south side and slowly approached Alofu's location.

At 17:03, Fanana uttered a pant-grunt in the direction of Alofu, Kalunde and Nkombo from a spot approximately five meters north of where they were lying. At that moment, Kalunde jumped out of the bush at a furious speed and attacked Fanana, who momentarily bared his teeth and immediately began running northward at great speed pursued by Kalunde. Alofu and Nkombo began to run after them. Although we normally rarely had to run while following chimpanzees, on this occasion my assistant and I ran after them. Still, we could not keep up with their speed and soon lost sight of them. As we kept running, other chimpanzees, who had been staying on the north side, came out of the bushes on both sides one after another, overtook me and ran northward in the likely direction of Fanana's escape. The area was in utter tumult and the voices of the chimpanzees were moving northward fast.

At 17:13, we finally caught up with a gathering of Alofu, Kalunde, Nkombo, Masudi, Orion and others on the research trail about one kilometer to the north.

Fanana must have gotten away as he was nowhere to be seen. Alofu was nervously sniffing at fallen leaves in the area repeatedly.

In the case of this "near miss", I was able to observe Fanana's approach from Alofu's viewpoint, as opposed to the previous case. As the above account is a substantially compressed version of an event that took place over a long period of six hours or so, some points may not be clear and I would like to review the situation with emphasis on my points of discussion.

Firstly, let us look at the "search" conducted by Alofu and Orion from around 13:30 for about one hour.

Alofu and others had been feeding and lounging around until that point, but a barking voice from a nearby source prompted him to walk southward in a nervous manner (holding his nipple). Alofu sniffed at the ground and chimpanzee feces nearby and pant-hooted several times as he walked southward at a relatively fast pace accompanying Orion. Alofu and Orion stopped, but set off again as soon as they heard a pant-hoot from a single individual at some distant southwestern location and headed south along the research trail at a fast pace in the direction of the voice. When they merged with adult males including Bonobo and Masudi at 14:13, Alofu kept checking the smell of fallen leaves.

As I walked behind Alofu, the way he hurried southward while nervously sniffing at the ground seemed to indicate that he was "searching for the individual who had produced that faraway voice". I could not identify the source of that voice, but considering that many individuals were in the vicinity of Alofu and the faraway pant-hoot from a single individual prompted him to head in that direction hurriedly (and nervously), I suspect that the voice (faraway pant-hoot) represented some "unexpected vocalizer, location and timing" for Alofu and others. It is possible that the vocalizer was Fanana (whom they would almost encounter afterward) and that Alofu and others recognized his voice, but this point is uncertain. At least, though, it is possible to say that their "approach in the direction of that voice" with their nervous demeanors (Alofu holding his nipple, the erect penises, bristled hair and moving at a fast pace) was an act of heading to "explore" for a "yet-to-be encountered somebody" in readiness for some sort of "encounter with an unexpected counterpart". Alofu's act of repeatedly "smelling the ground (fallen leaves, feces)", similar to Fanana's act described in the previous section, can also be regarded as an exploratory behavior in an effort to detect the arrival of a "yet-to-be identified somebody".

Nevertheless, this exploration turned out to be fruitless (not encountering "somebody") and Alofu reunited with other males and backtracked. During my time following chimpanzees, this was one of the few occasions when I saw them travel fast so nervously for such a long period or distance, and end up backtracking without much happening. Seeing Alofu and others "backtrack without much happening" was another reason that gave me the impression that their previous "hurried southward walk" had some special meaning.

After that, Alofu merged with the original party, fed occasionally while travelling slowly southwest with Kalunde (old male) and Nkombo (old female) and relaxed until the late afternoon. Then, the second "near miss" with Fanana occurred (17:03).

Immediately before the near miss, Alofu and Kalunde uttered pant-hoots and received many voices in return from a wide area to the north (16:58). Considering that Fanana appeared from the north, he approached the location of Alofu and others upon hearing their pant-hoots and replies. While it is uncertain whether Fanana recognized the voices as those of Alofu and others, at least his behavior of approaching the location of multiple pant-hoots was clearly different from his behavior in the first near miss incident in which he ran away upon hearing many voices.

Fanana approached within five meters of the location where Alofu, Kalunde and Nkombo were lying around and uttered a pant-grunt. While a pant-grunt is a very typical interaction at the time of an encounter, the ferocity of Kalunde's reaction (charging at Fanana at a furious speed) in this instance was almost unprecedented. And the strength of agitation and the speed of chase exhibited by Kalunde, Alofu, Nkombo and the other individuals coming to join them in their pursuit of Fanana were something I had never witnessed before. If Fanana had stayed instead of fleeing, he might have been subjected to severe attacks. Although occasional attacks by the receiver of a pant-grunt on the utterer have been observed under ordinary circumstances, it seemed to me that the ferocity of the charge and the level of agitation demonstrated by the individuals on this occasion were clearly different from "the ordinary manners of interaction at an encounter".

The pant-grunt is a pattern of interaction commonly used in ordinary encounters between chimpanzees, and I described the way it is used as "a conventional technique to manage the unstable context of an encounter" in Part I (Nishie 2017). However, Fanana's pant-grunt in the present case clearly fails to perform the (conventional) function as "a cue to trigger the convergence of contextual instability". In fact, we can say that confusion brought on by "the unexpected encounter itself" overwhelms and threatens the stability of the convention. In other words, a "bare encounter" with "that which is other" that arrives from the outside of the convention causes such a strong reaction, chaos and a surge of excitement that it overwhelms the stability of the convention. It is conceivable that what I call "that which is other" here is not limited to "the other individual" such as "Alofu to Fanana" and "Fanana to Alofu", as it brought confusion and excitement to both Fanana and other members as "all possible relationships between Fanana and other members" (such as "group member" and "alpha male") which they could not fit into any of their conventions nor understand which single aspect to choose.

Just as in the first near miss, the second near miss led to the highlighting of "all possible but invisible relationships" such as unit-group member and alpha male at once upon Fanana's approach to other individuals. The "unstable encounter" did not fit in any category of "convention = usual manner" and their mutual relationship was "suspended" and postponed by Kalunde's charge and chase and Fanana's subsequent escape. If this kind of interaction were to continue, Fanana would be unable to resume interacting not only with other males based on their dominance rank, but also with other individuals as group members; he might lead the life of a solitary male without belonging to any group, which is normally inconceivable in male philopatric chimpanzee society. While I was only able to observe the circumstances of Fanana's "disappearance" for about one year up to the second near miss, I have been told that Fanana seldom encountered other group members even though he stayed in their ranging area for the next several years, leaving their relationships in suspension (Nakamura 2015b: 205).

Based on these two cases of near miss involving Alofu and other stable group members and the "missing" Fanana, we shall next consider how to interpret the appearance of "that which is other" in chimpanzee society.

The *bare other* and "cognitive toughness"

What insights can we gain about *others* as the reverse side of institutions mentioned earlier from the above interactions among chimpanzees, especially the state of "disappearance" that was prolonged by the near misses and subsequent escapes?

Firstly, chimpanzees engaged in various exploratory actions with regard to the "yet-to-be encountered (specified/unspecified) somebody" and tried to identify who that "somebody" was. In the first near miss, Fanana created an opportunity for "somebody" to respond by uttering a pant-hoot, and approached "somebody" as he repeatedly sniffed at the ground. In the second near miss, Alofu and Orion hurriedly headed in the direction of a faraway pant-hoot and explored for traces of "somebody" on the ground and fallen leaves.

However, these exploratory actions failed to culminate in the formation of a clear relationship, which was postponed in a state of suspension due to Fanana's escapes. In other words, the relationship between these individuals failed to fit into a particular stable framework and caused great confusion on the point of encounter, thus the period of non-encounter continued. The suspension and postponement of a relationship in one sense appears to be rather incomprehensible and "seemingly irrational" in the eyes of us observers. For example, Fanana repeatedly approached a group of individuals or produced a long-distance pant-hoot, even though he was supposed to be in a state of "disappearance" – an ongoing state of not encountering many individuals. If Fanana wished to remain in such state, he should have stayed quiet and refrained from approaching the voices of other individuals. In fact, he behaved accordingly most of the time, but for some reason he occasionally engaged in behavior such as long-range vocalization and approaching other individuals which sometimes resulted in utter tumult (as we saw in Part I and the second near miss in this chapter). On the other hand, even though Alofu and others nervously went to explore a faraway voice, they failed to "reconcile" with Fanana, who was pant-grunting, and chased after him escalating the utter tumult (as we saw in Part I). How can we interpret these chimpanzee behaviors, which I often struggled to understand as I observed them in the field, in the context of the appearance of the *other*?

The seemingly irrational chimpanzee behavior constitutes an *ad hoc* way, so to speak, to "get through" a situation by leaving the *otherness* of the approaching that which is other alone, i.e., responding in an *ad hoc* manner and postponing it, instead of reducing cognitive load by placing a relationship within some "system of symbols that can be referred to by anybody at any time" such as a rule or an institution. In other words, when confronted by "all possible relationships" brought by the *other*, they resort to a very limited *ad hoc* interaction by exploring a mode of relationship and dealing with each response locally; they do not aim to immediately transition to a stable relationship through mutual adjustments to their interaction by reference to "some order referable by anybody at any time (rule or institution)". And the incomprehensibleness and irrationality we observe in their *ad hoc* interaction in turn illuminate our usual practice of squeezing the *otherness* brought by the *other* into some convention or institution and dressing it up as something comprehensible.

As I stated earlier, *others* can be *others* because they bring other viewpoints to the world that do not fit into that of *I*, and as long as *others* exist as beings who cannot be contained in the world operable by *I*, the arrival of *others* is destined to destabilize the relationship between *I* and the world (and the existence of *I* itself). When we confront *others* in this unstable state, the most familiar course of action is perhaps to try to transition to a stable relationship by referring to "the manner of relating to one another". Take for example self-introduction as typical human behavior when we encounter a stranger. The "introduced self" here largely consists of "information that can be used in building a relationship with the counterpart" such as name, place of birth, occupation, hobbies and personal history. In short, self-introduction is primarily an interaction to present various aspects of the self to the counterpart for the purpose of creating a cue to build a relationship with them. The intention here is to explore what kind of relationship can be formed depending on how the counterpart responds to the presentation of multiple aspects of the self. If the counterpart shows an interest in my hobby, I build a relationship on that basis. If occupation or personal history becomes a significant topic, then we can initially form a relationship within those parameters.

If we consider a more everyday situation in which we sense something unusual about a person we know well, we try to bring the situation back into a framework that is comprehensible as quickly as possible by posing various questions such as "What's happened?" and "How are you feeling?" to the counterpart to explain the behavior. What is being done here is the presentation of a mutually referable relationship framework, and its aim is to converge our relationships with *others* under this frame. It is possible to say that in this way we are trying to stabilize the relationship between self and other by reclaiming *otherness* into a mutually referable framework.

The chimpanzee behavior seems irrational and incomprehensible to us probably because their interactions do not easily converge under this mutually referable relationship framework. In the first near miss, Fanana avoided an encounter with "somebody" on one hand, and ran away after searching for that "somebody" on the other hand. In the second near miss, he arrived at a place where he knew many individuals were gathering and was ferociously charged and chased by Kalunde and others who drove him away. Kalunde, who led the charge and chase, had spent two days ranging with "missing" Fanana only a few days before the first near miss and seemingly interacted with him as usual at the time. Considering that Alofu received a pant-grunt from Fanana about one month before the second near miss (Nishie 2017), he was already in a stable position as the alpha male. Despite that, Alofu nervously went to search for a faraway vocalizer and restlessly sniffed at fallen leaves even after Fanana fled at the time of the second near miss. In the end, they were unsure about the status of their relationships and continued to interact in a way that increased their confusion and left Fanana in a state of "disappearance" with no fixed place in their social relationship. This uncertainty about the status of their relationship was the reason for the incomprehensibleness we observed.

This relationship destabilization brought about by *others* originates in their inherent contingency, that is, the possibility of being other. I argued at the beginning of the chapter that the *other* appears in two aspects, in that the *other* presses *I* to recognize/interact (readiness for mutual cognition/interaction) while it always evades recognition/interaction by *I* (faltering mutual cognition/interaction). In other words, the relationship between *I* and the *other* (and their respective existences) inevitably becomes *ad hoc* and unstable in the face of all possible relationships brought about by the "contingency = all possibilities beyond reach" inherent in the *other*. When chimpanzees are faced with this unstable relationship, they get through this suspended situation by continually exploring various *ad hoc* relationships instead of recognizing/interacting by placing the *other* in a mutually referable framework. Therein lies the characteristic of their way of mutual cognition of/interaction with the *other* in their society.

In another publication I introduced the concept of "cognitive toughness[3]" (Nishie 2010) to describe this characteristic way of mutual cognition of/interaction with the *other* in chimpanzees. Similarly, in describing the chimpanzee's sociality created by the process of fission-fusion, Itoh (2013) counts "autonomy, flexibility and tolerance" as its characteristics. By extension, we can surmise that the incomprehensibleness of the chimpanzee behavior discussed in this chapter is supported and made possible by cognitive toughness or tolerance for uncertainty to withstand the contingency inherent in *otherness* in its "bare state", rather than subsuming it into a mutually referable framework.

Evolutionary foundations of *others*: *Bare* and *qualified others*

We have seen in this chapter that the *other* in chimpanzee society was dealt with by way of postponing and tolerating it in its *bare* state, rather than promptly fitting it into a framework referable by anybody at any time such as rules and institutions. On the other hand, humans have shifted to "the construct that a stable relationship can be achieved" by compressing, so to speak, the contingency inherent in the *other* using rules and institutions. This is our final point of argument in this chapter. I shall discuss what I consider to be a typical example below, as this contrast seems to be highlighted clearly in the relationship between researcher and research subject.

As a researcher of wild chimpanzees, I search for, follow and observe wild chimpanzees living in the forest. As my research subjects, the chimpanzees are already well habituated to human observers and do not seem to be bothered by my presence. This does not mean that they pay no attention to me; in fact they closely monitor humans, including myself. For example, they try to keep their distance if humans get too close, or run away or intimidate in some cases. They do not seem to consider me as a chimpanzee (member of the same group) either, because they have never invited me to engage in grooming or mating. They would not know that I am studying them (I have never tried to explain this to them as they would not understand my explanation) and they do not seem to perceive me as an obvious "enemy" either (they would run away if they did). So, who do the chimpanzees think I am? To be frank, I have no idea. They continue to disregard me (i.e., not get involved with me actively) most of the time, despite being persistently followed and observed by me, who is probably an incomprehensible being in their minds.

By contrast, I imagine that the situation would be different if the research subject was human (although I have no experience in that field). The first thing attempted by an anthropologist in a cross-cultural social study is to occupy a stable position in the subject society. Typically, the researcher can establish a certain position in the subject society by finding a cooperative person and being accepted as a member of that person's family. If the researcher was not able to become a member of this society, they would arouse suspicions such as "Who are they?" and "Are they doing anything undesirable?" which would make the researcher's study rather difficult. Some may think that this is because the researcher and the subject are both human conspecifics, but if a chimpanzee (or an alien) followed us humans continually, would we be able to tolerate the persistent following without asking the follower "Why are you doing it?". This suggests that when we humans are faced with the arrival of an *other*, we have a strong inclination to stabilize our relationship with them by taking in the entire view of our framework of relationship and locating the self and other within that framework.

If one of the things humans have acquired in the process of evolution is institutions such as language, perhaps one of its primary functions is to establish a framework for relationships with others that is referable by anybody at any time. It is possible that this function has allowed humans to reduce the cognitive load by "compressing" the chaos caused by the contingency inherent in *otherness*, and as a result enabled us to increase the size and complexity of social relationships. Conversely, this has led to the obscuring of the contingency as if it did not exist. It seems that in humans the *bare other* is reclaimed, compressed and concealed by rules and institutions as something whose existence is undesirable. In the evolution of human society, humans have come to exhibit a strong preference for a stable relationship with the *qualified other* after compressing and concealing the *bare other*. We have become vulnerable creatures who can no longer tolerate the acceptance of the *other* in a "bare state".

7 Encountering the "Other": How Chimpanzees Face *Indeterminacy*

Noriko Itoh

Key ideas

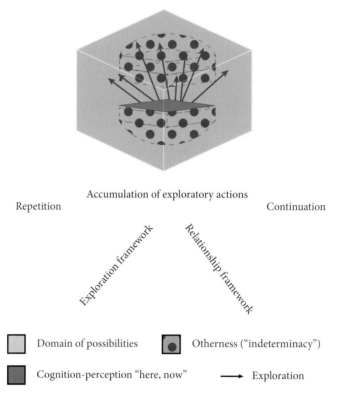

We notice all sorts of occurrences as we follow chimpanzees in the forest. They face these phenomena in an exploratory manner whether they are conspecific or heterospecific, alive or dead, living or non-living or perceived or not perceived. Exploration is an act of "feeling" for the possibility that the given phenomenon is different from one's cognition-perception "here, now", that is, "indeterminacy", rather than trying to grasp a complete picture of the phenomenon. In this chapter, the attitude of facing indeterminacy openly as it is contiguous to various other possibilities is called "staying with indeterminacy". Unlike highly structured gregarious (cohesive group) primate and human societies, chimpanzees form unstable social relationships that necessitate exploratory actions. The mode of group formation involving repeated encounters and separations (fission-fusion), and the inevitability of the exploratory approach to each encounter because of it, form the foundation of their exploratory way of life where they remain "indeterminate" even with their fellow group members.

Facing *indeterminacy:* "Others" beyond human perception

The aim of this chapter is to explore the world of the "other" for chimpanzees. To achieve this, we need to somehow sort out a dual problem deriving from the assumption that the commonly supposed "other" is another human being relative to the "self" (human being), as well as the fact that I, who observe chimpanzees, am myself a human being.

The concept of the "other" implicitly assumes, to a certain extent, that the self who perceives the other is human. This constitutes the first obstacle in considering what the other is for non-humans (see Chapter Two by Nakamura). The assumption of humanity means that the discernment of the other relies on a self that is a human being equipped with "advanced" cognitive ability. In this case, that which is other to non-humans is precluded and at the same time the other to humans may be reduced to the cognitive ability of the self. This appears more of a "self" cognition problem than an "other" problem. A prime example of this may be the act of discussing the "other". The act of discussing the other here encompasses narrating, analyzing, explaining and classifying the other. This "other" is a recalled other. Considering that human cognition has changed and continues to do so, the other that is reduced to the human cognitive ability is outside of our interest in this chapter.

On the other hand, the other is also that which we encounter. The major concern on such encounters is the "otherness" (*indeterminacy*; see below and Chapter One by Kuroda) of the encountered other in relation to the self, which cannot be reduced to the ability of the self. By referring to the otherness – whether as something that is comprehensible or not – however, humans can reclaim it back into the cognitive framework of the self as a characteristic of the other recollected by the self. This is equivalent to the "qualified other" who appears as a result of the subsumption of the contingency of the other under a rule or institution framework, as discussed by Nishie in Chapter Six (p. 147). This cognitive predilection is so strong and natural for us humans that it becomes the second obstacle for human observers in their consideration of the other in non-humans.

Still, humans are not the only species that is subjected to this cognitive/perceptive constraint. The human cognitive/perceptive constraint comes with each person's "place of living" (following Adachi 2013, 2017) (hereafter, "field") rather than their individual ability. All living things, including humans, relate to the environment through living (Adachi 2013: 36), constitute species and in some cases form groups. At the same time, this "field" provides behavioral guidelines to the living things (Adachi 2017). The field is a domain of interaction for living individuals realized by (and only to the extent of) interactions specific to each living thing that has adopted the physical structure-environment (ecological and social). In other words, living things are also subjected to a constraint as they face *indeterminacy*, albeit in a different mode from humans.

For these reasons, we need to meet the following challenges in this chapter: firstly, refraining or maintaining a certain distance from subsuming the discussion into a human cognitive framework; and secondly, examining how non-humans face *indeterminacy*, including the possibility that they are subsuming it into some kind of framework. In this chapter we address various phenomena that chimpanzees encounter and look at how they discern and face *indeterminacy* in scenes of encounter, although this will be a considerable deviation from the commonly assumed other (i.e., human, the other individual). We continue contrasting the human "qualified other" and the chimpanzee "bare other" initiated in Nishie's discussion in the previous chapter and consider the condition of the chimpanzee "other" from the viewpoint of its interactions with their living environment and their mode of group formation and continuance. The difference between the ways *indeterminacy* is faced in chimpanzee society and in human society has continuity with the distinctions between the ways *indeterminacy* among group members is faced in other primate groups. At the same time, it is likely to have continuity with the exploratory action employed by chimpanzees and other living things when they confront their environment (other than group members).

Exploring *indeterminacy*

In my investigation of otherness = *indeterminacy* in the field of encounter, I limit the field of encounter to one where a cognitive-perceptive process is taking place based on the exploratory approach of "discerning as a phenomenon that involves oneself", as described below. There is a tendency to distinguish between cognition and simple perception (passive response to stimuli). However, here we adopt the view that, regardless of who or what the observer is, perception is a cognitive process of the "characterization of external reality" rather than the "comprehension of external reality" (Maturana and Varela 1991)[1].

The environment is full of various things and occurrences, but they are not necessarily what or how the living things perceive them to be. Living things interact directly or are forced to interact in an exploratory manner with such encountered phenomena (including potential phenomena). This appears in the act of discerning the environment as a phenomenon that involves oneself. Simply put, it is more than a mere encounter – it is a situation in which one is required to meet (or there is a possibility to meet) and to explore who or what is being met.

What necessitates an exploration is found not only in the explored phenomenon, but also in the explorer. In other words, interacting in an exploratory manner means becoming aware of the possibility of the phenomenon being different from one's cognition-perception "here, now" (otherness), or to put it more simply, *indeterminacy*. For the explorer, this is also an act of trying to come up with a prognosis as to how to behave next. It can be described as a discovery of obscurity that involves an exploration of *indeterminacy* in the liminal space between the comprehensible and the totally incomprehensible. Accordingly, it does not matter whether an encountered phenomenon can be clearly identified (in a human sense) or not.

Is it possible to observe the exploratory action performed by living things? As long as the observer is human, it is impossible to observe (cognize) all of the exploratory actions practiced by non-humans. However, it is possible to a certain extent. When a human observer is observing living things with the intention of recording their behaviors, it is of course impossible to record something when nothing is happening, but it is too late to observe *after* something has actually happened. The act of observation requires continual preparedness for things to happen next from the position where nothing is happening now. At this point, the observer may feel an *interstice* (*sukima*) prior to the next situation, as they presage that something will happen, but still nothing is happening. In more positive terms, observation and recording in the field are realized through the discovery of this *interstice* prior to the occurrence of a possible phenomenon.

From the standpoint of the observed living thing, this *interstice* is the place where it confronts *indeterminacy*. In the sections below, I look at what living things do and how they do it in this *interstice* in order to examine how they face *indeterminacy* (otherness).

Into the wild: The other as a sign

The most straightforward example of an *interstice* would be an exploratory interaction between animals and the environment called "vigilance", which is commonly observed in a wide range of species. Living things go into vigilance mode before they face danger and not when they are in danger. They search for signs of danger. These "signs" can be defined rather broadly. For instance, many people have seen footage of the way prairie dogs stand on their hind legs to keep a lookout. They look for signs of danger continually. These signs alert the seeker to possible yet unconfirmed phenomena, and in this sense the sought signs are the *indeterminacy*.

To the observer, the observed living thing's exploratory action (vigilance) toward its environment feels *interstitial* because of the absence of a concrete action by the external world "here, now" toward the explorer (as long as the vigilance is successful).

On the other hand, the explorer creates an *interstice* between its existence and various phenomena that have the potential to threaten it by exploring for the signs of danger rather than the danger itself. To other individuals who coexist with this individual, this *interstice* also serves as a cue for exploration for and discovery of signs. The *interstice* that becomes this cue is a sign for those who use it as a cue.

Vigilance is a behavior that has evolutionarily accumulated and engendered a series of measures, consisting of a relatively stable exploratory framework for avoidance and exploratory actions corresponding to various signs, in the co-presence of living things and the phenomena that threaten their lives and the repeated encounters between them. At the same time, the range of exploratory actions that individuals can take "here, now" is limited, and this limitation leaves moment-to-moment prognostication open to various other possibilities.

My research has focused on studying a group of wild chimpanzees (M group) in Tanzania's Mahale Mountains National Park. Interactions between chimpanzees and their environment are continuous with explorations in vigilance, but in addition to avoidance there are numerous exploratory acts that can be put down to curiosity or interest.

The forest where M group chimpanzees live is labyrinthine; thick vines and shrubs hinder visibility and make walking difficult. They utilize an area of approximately thirty square kilometers (Nakamura 2015c), most of which is a complex forest including patches of diverse flora at various stages of growth or transition on land cultivated prior to the national park designation. Its topography is complex, comprising countless small ridges, valleys and streams (Itoh and Nakamura 2015a).

Diverse varieties of living things inhabit this forest. Chimpanzees are sensitive to all sorts of phenomena, including sounds from the undergrowth and wafting smells. Sounds, shapes, odors and movements discerned "here, now" are not only taken as they are, but are also acted upon as they are explored further beyond the realm of cognition-perception "here, now". Chimpanzees instantly turn around

Encountering the "Other": How Chimpanzees Face *Indeterminacy*

Photo 7.1 Exploratory action: "Looking"

Chimpanzees employ various modes of "looking", including "glancing", "watching" and "peering" as shown in Photos 7.1a and 7.1b (a chimpanzee leaning over and peering up into the treetop in 7.1a and another peeking into an ablution area over a fence at the research camp in 7.1b – there was no one inside and nothing happened this time, but I have also been peeked at during bathing). The "looking" action of another individual seems to concern them as well (7.1c). The old female in the foreground was looking at the treetop and the old male arriving after her also stopped and looked up at the same treetop. Like in this case, it is often unclear what they are looking at. Humans are also often "looked at" (7.1d).

to look upon hearing the loud thud of a falling tree branch behind them, wait and see for a period when they are startled by thunder and act in various ways towards not only unfamiliar beings (e.g. the corpse of an aardvark), but also other animals, including potential predators (e.g., leopards) (see Nakamura in Chapter Two) and pythons (Zamma 2011).

Because these encounters do not involve an across-the-board regularity of action, such as always avoiding or acting in certain ways in certain cases, the (human) observer is unable to extrapolate any relationship framework and hence finds it all very difficult to comprehend. However, on each occasion chimpanzees create an *interstice* by acting in an exploratory way and construct a relationship framework. Here is one observed case that can serve as an example.

Case 1: Audible but invisible (22 October 2005)
I had been following an adult male named Darwin since morning. While Darwin was on an observation trail, I noticed that another adult male, Alofu, was in a bush away from the trail looking somewhat scared (at 13:43). There were other chimpanzees nearby, including infants, adult males and females, who were feeding or simply resting. Darwin seemed to be concerned about Alofu and sniffed at trees around him. Alofu was whimpering[2] and touching his nipple[3], as he habitually did when he was nervous.

At 13:49, Alofu moved a little southward in the undergrowth. Darwin repeatedly took a step and scratched his body while paying attention to Alofu. Cadmus (young male) came out of the forest onto the trail. Darwin climbed up a vine as if he was looking out for something. Cadmus looked to Alofu in the brush and immediately followed Darwin. From the vine with an unobstructed view, they both looked out to Alofu and over a far distance in an "exploratory" manner in the southerly direction towards which Alofu's body was facing.

At 13:50, Cadmus climbed higher and Darwin descended a little. They alternately looked to the south and to Alofu, who was still whimpering in the brush.

At 13:52, Alofu continued to whimper as he climbed a vine. Darwin and Cadmus looked to the south and to Alofu alternately. Alofu moved from the vine to a tree and climbed higher. A young female followed him. Alofu continued to whimper.

At 13:53, Alofu reached the treetop and sat down. Cadmus began to feed on leaves nearby. At 14:06, Darwin finally descended from the vine and began slowly departing southward along the trail, just after Cadmus began to travel in the same direction at 14:05.

Darwin and Cadmus initially scanned the far distance rather agitatedly and nervously and turned to Alofu when they found nothing, but all they could perceive was Alofu's whimpers. I, too, looked through my binoculars and strained my ears wondering if there was anything in the direction Darwin and Cadmus were scanning, but all I found was an *interstice*.

Darwin and Cadmus treated Alofu's behavior as something that concerned them as well; they literally tried to see this yet-to-be-perceptible something arriving from the outside, and even attempted to get a clearer view by climbing up the vine.

To Darwin and Cadmus, the identity of "it" they are searching for (the thing that was making Alofu anxious in this case) was unclear. Consequently, they had no way of figuring out how to act or what to look for.

Nevertheless, "it" gradually responds in an unstable but somewhat coherent way to their exploratory action performed on the basis of the phenomenon that "Alofu was afraid" and an accumulation of such exploratory actions. In this case, a series of exploratory acts of "looking" gradually confirmed that they actually could not see anything (nothing was happening).

They tried to figure out what to do next based on the outcome of their exploratory actions, but the situation of not seeing anything "here, now" is contiguous to the possibility that it is not the case, because they had no prognostication for their exploration in the first place. In other words, they cannot prognosticate whether their cognition-perception "here, now" is sufficient or whether they need to engage in further exploration (i.e., they cannot decide when to stop the search). Consequently, the prognostication about what to do next is deferred.

Of course, they would not (or cannot) keep searching forever. As they gradually ascertained that "there is nothing", to that extent "it" was set aside as something harmless enough for them to return to their ordinary living, which they had been engaged in before they noticed Alofu's whimpering (see Note 2). When Alofu left the field and moved up on a tree, "it" "disappeared".

Darwin and Cadmus did not see anything after all. However, they went on the watch for someone's unheard voice and something unseen that concerned them while they monitored Alofu's behavior. What they were doing was accumulating exploratory acts towards something that was or might be coming from the outside while being open to other possibilities, in other words, staying with the *indeterminacy*. This is different from my attitude in the following where I try to identify exactly what "it" is (to categorize "it" as something).

It seems that Alofu was unnerved by the presence of a thin white string between the observation trail he wanted to get to and the undergrowth he was in, rather than something in the far distance that Darwin and Cadmus were looking out over. The string, which appeared suddenly in the forest, had been left there by a visiting conservation group after they had measured distances by putting the string along some of the trails at a height of one meter above the ground[4]. After this episode, I observed how Alofu behaved when he came across the string every time I had an opportunity to do so, as did other researchers. Based on our observations that Alofu was the only individual who was unnerved by the string and it prevented him from getting to the trail in other places, I inferred that "it" was the string.

I attempted to identify exactly what Alofu was afraid of because I am an onlooker who is studying chimpanzees. As far as the chimpanzees, who are trying to survive in a complex environment, are concerned, however, it is probably more important to prognosticate whether "it" is significant enough to interrupt their daily routine rather than to make an accurate identification[5]. "It" remained an unknown phenomenon to Darwin and Cadmus, while in Alofu's eyes it was some frightening unknown phenomenon rather than just a piece of string. The attitude of staying with *indeterminacy* entails continuing to face it in an exploratory manner while being open to the possibility that what is nothing now may become something in the next moment, instead of trying to resolve or reduce the *indeterminacy* by reference to a framework outside of the encounter.

There is another noteworthy characteristic to this example. Darwin and Cadmus found an *interstice* between the phenomenon of Alofu's whimpering and an unknown phenomenon that was "supposed" to be involved in it on the basis that Alofu was whimpering. This is analogous to my behavior of observing chimpanzees and recording my observations. They created a new *interstice* through exploratory interaction with an unknown phenomenon (*indeterminacy*) with an *interstice* created by Alofu as a clue.

Chimpanzee interactions

We now examine the *interstices* found in interactions between chimpanzees. They consistently employ the attitude of staying with *indeterminacy* here, as Darwin and Cadmus did in Case 1 above. Chimpanzee interactions are more reliant on chance in the sense that they act in a more trial-and-error way rather than follow a stylized pattern[6].

A continuous exploration for signs
The following case is about a young female named Serena, who had just lost her mother and infant sister (presumed to have died). I saw Serena and Bonobo (adult

male) begin to approach Fanana (adult male) at the same time and braced myself, thinking "This may end in trouble", when I realized that Serena was slow to notice Bonobo's movement.

Case 2: Serena, Bonobo and an accident (2 October 1997)
Masudi was grooming Kalunde, Kalunde was grooming Fanana and Fanana was grooming Serena (hereinafter called the "grooming party"). Serena was lying on her belly. The place was on a hillside of the three-way intersection of a north-south observation trail and another trail extending to the eastern hill. Two other parties (a party of females and their infants and a party of adult males and young males) were resting nearby farther up the hill trail and farther south along the north-south trail respectively. Outside of these parties, one young male was resting alone about three meters to the south of the grooming party and Bonobo was also resting alone in the brush on the western side just before the north-south trail.

This episode took place in a very short period of time (12:58:59–13:02:09) and "nothing" happened after all, but the chimpanzees engaged in a surprising array of acts as summarized below. I attached a transcript of a time-series video at the end of this chapter because details are very important here (see Appendix on p. 174).

As mentioned earlier, Serena was being groomed by Fanana as part of a grooming party where the other two members were both adult males. Bonobo, who had been sitting a little away from this party, began to approach them. When he was about to sit in front of Fanana, Fanana shifted his position slightly away from both Serena and Bonobo.

The accident occurred immediately after that when Serena and Bonobo began to approach Fanana at the same time. Serena seemed to notice the situation two seconds later as she looked to Bonobo, but she did not (or could not) stop moving. At that point, Bonobo also noticed that Serena was approaching Fanana and changed his course slightly as if to give way to Serena. Serena sat by Fanana while Bonobo continued to move until he sat by Kalunde. It took seven seconds from their simultaneous approach to this point. Thereafter they repeatedly looked at one another, and Serena groomed Fanana for a fleeting moment before leaving the scene at 13:02:09.

Bonobo and Serena glanced at one another many times (see Appendix, underlined). Although the matter appeared to have been settled when Bonobo belatedly noticed Serena's movement and gave way, Serena hesitated to begin grooming even though she had directly approached Fanana. The fact that Serena frequently looked at

Bonobo while rarely looking at Fanana suggests that her attention had shifted from grooming with Fanana to Bonobo's movement.

Serena must have been "bothered" by Bonobo's intermittent glances. Serena solicited Fanana for grooming at 12:59:13, but she turned to look at Bonobo one second later as if she was preoccupied. Immediately after that (12:59:19–20), she even attempted to move from the "prized" position near Fanana. She could not focus on grooming and engaged in self-scratching four times in a short period of twenty-eight seconds from 13:00:26 (see Appendix, double-underlined). Self-scratching is literally the act of scratching oneself when there is an itch, but this kind of self-touching behavior is also engaged in when one is nervous. Thus, Serena's restless grooming of Fanana soon came to an end.

Serena's persistent glancing at Bonobo was probably driven by her sense of "anxiety" about not knowing what would happen next. Her action happened to be in competition with Bonobo's action, and Bonobo subsequently changed his course of action but continued to look towards Serena with Fanana. Bonobo's intermittent glances kept in the foreground the possibility that their relationship surrounding Fanana had become an awkward/uncomfortable one. This suggests that what Serena was exploring was the *indeterminacy* of Bonobo's next action as a possibility based on the "accident" of simultaneous approach and Bonobo's subsequent intermittent glancing in her direction; this is where an *interstice* is formed.

Serena's next action was dependent on Bonobo's action, but Bonobo was not doing anything other than "looking". To Serena, in this situation Bonobo continues to be the "other" as a sign of the possibility of directing some action towards her, and hence the *interstice* is produced continually. That nothing is happening in one moment does not mean that nothing will happen in the future. That nothing is happening "here, now" remains contiguous with various other possibilities. The only way to confirm that "nothing happened" is to accumulate moments in which nothing is happening, that is, to keep exploring. What she got at any moment was probably not strong enough to be called a confirmation. While the males in the party were enjoying grooming, Serena left the scene alone. At this point, the outcome of "nothing will happen" was finally realized (in a way retrospectively as "nothing has happened").

In general terms, it may be more difficult to maintain a state of not making any interaction happen than actually making some interaction happen in a situation where some interaction is expected. While both Bonobo and Serena continued to explore one another, Serena's restless demeanor suggested that she was at least constantly confirming that Bonobo was taking no action. Yet, she could never confirm that and therefore an *interstice* had to remain as such after they happened to approach Fanana simultaneously. It was also supported by Bonobo's exploratory attitude of not doing anything other than "looking". This situation made it even more difficult for Serena to ignore the *interstice*. It may have been better for Serena if this *interstice* had disappeared, but if it did (or if she ignored it), it would become impossible for her to confirm that nothing was happening.

This way of facing *indeterminacy* in which chimpanzees endlessly stay with the *indeterminacy* about what will happen next would be, in human terms, a very troublesome situation. We would wish to resolve it by referring to the accident (simultaneous approach) itself and enquiring about or apologizing for what had gone wrong. Conversely, chimpanzees even leave the *indeterminacy* as it is rather actively in some cases, as we shall see in the next example.

Deferring *indeterminacy*

In the next case, things continue to happen and an *interstice* is created repeatedly, but for us humans, what the chimpanzees are doing as a whole is puzzling.

Case 3: A maneuvering between Alofu and Caliope (12 October 2005)

I was following Alofu (male aged twenty-three), who was fixated on an estrous female named Caliope (estimated age forty-five). Alofu was completely under her thumb, as Caliope frequently sat down and frustrated his intention to travel. While Alofu had resorted to direct action many times already by trying to move her by grabbing her hand, arm, foot, nape and pubic mound, Caliope had held on to a nearby shrub as she sat down as if to resist him.

At 13:16:32, Alofu began to try to remove Caliope's fingers from the branch she was holding.

At 13:16:49, Alofu tried to insert his fingers in the mouth of immobile Caliope and pull her head, but Caliope straightened her posture every time and did not move. Alofu tried to pull her by the arm but she shook his hand off.

At 13:17:34, Alofu tried to grab her other hand. Caliope shook it off. Alofu was about to put his hand in Caliope's mouth, but immediately when Caliope adjusted her grip, Alofu tried and finally managed to remove her hand from the branch. Caliope immediately grabbed the branch again. Alofu pulled her hand but Caliope shook it loose and hid her arms between her legs and chest.

> At 13:18:41, Caliope uttered a pant-grunt[7] at Alofu and they exchanged open-mouth kisses[8]. They kissed on their chins as well. Alofu <u>tried to pull her by the arm</u> again, but Caliope began to <u>move her mouth toward and away from Alofu's chin repeatedly using the recoiling action of the branch she was holding</u>. Caliope at least appeared to be playing. Caliope finally began to travel at 13:20 and Alofu followed her.

This interaction between the two adult chimpanzees continued without abating for a long time. Moreover, Caliope's behavior appeared to show that she knew what Alofu wanted her to do, but she calmly and firmly resisted it (double-underlined). On the other hand, Alofu responded with all sorts of maneuvers, including pulling and loosening her grip (underlined). I have previously described a similar interaction between a male and an estrous female (Itoh 2003). The females eventually moved, and they were not busy with other matters like feeding or interacting with others while they were refusing to move. Nevertheless, females protracted the interaction by using various tricks against the males' attempts to travel together, and the males responded with various tactics.

It is difficult to describe with certainty what Alofu and Caliope were doing in this protracted interaction as a whole. Yet, it was certainly not the case that nothing was happening. As soon as an *interstice* was formed, Alofu proposed "travelling together", and Caliope's refusal caused a new *interstice* to form, and this cycle of action was repeated. The observer did not know how it would end and perhaps neither did they.

When we look in more detail, we notice that they gradually changed their tactics. However, a clear direction (e.g., stronger refusal, escalating demand etc.) cannot be identified, as they resorted to all kinds of tricks. These tactical changes failed to advance the situation. Nevertheless, I suspect that these minor changes were employed in order to create a new *interstice*, and the next tactic was selected to produce other possibilities instead of concluding their interaction at the end of the previous cycle of proposition-refusal.

In hindsight, we can suppose that this interaction as a whole was carried out so as to prevent the individual proposition-refusal cycle from becoming something definitive for both of them (e.g., a fight). In the meantime, the opposing "intentions" of Alofu, who wanted to travel together, and Caliope, who refused to do so, were secured continuously. In the normal (human) sense, such conflicting intentions cannot coexist. In this interaction, however, we can find a situation in which a new *interstice* is created and a new proposition is put forward as if the preceding proposition-refusal cycle a moment ago did not happen, while this contradiction is preserved – an *interstice* is rolled forward, so to speak. In other words, we can surmise that refusing a proposition is not categorized as a refusal; it is left (rather actively) to stand as *indeterminacy* contiguous to other possibilities and rolled forward to the next proposition.

The way the chimpanzees continue to stay with *indeterminacy* that is common to the three cases above is continuous with the highly redundant interactions engaged in by chimpanzees at the scene of ant fishing involving fishing tools, ants and ant nests as described by Nishie (2010). Various situations occur repeatedly, including one in which a chimpanzee takes a tool from another but does not use it, and "equivocal responses" continue endlessly in which they seem to be somewhat bothered but do not clearly refuse to give the stick. This attitude for interaction commonly found in the ant-dipping example and the aforementioned cases can be called one of "surrendering oneself to the 'contingency' of the other's action […], to 'tolerate' a state of continually surrendering oneself to this kind of uncertainty"[9] (Nishie 2010).

The situation between Caliope and Alofu might have been coming close to reaching the limit of their "tolerance". Although the contrast between Caliope's somewhat teasing manner and Alofu's desperate maneuvers was quite amusing, I became a little worried that the repetition of such blatant rejections might eventually drive Alofu to violence (as sometimes occurs). This tension was demonstrated by Caliope's greeting behavior of kissing and pant-grunting at the end of this episode. Greeting behavior is commonly seen at the time of an encounter accompanying some kind of tension or excitement. In this sense it was unusual that greeting was being performed between two who had been together for a long time, but the greetings employed in this case may well express their state of tension. It is possible to suppose that these acts triggered the transformation of their simple proposition-refusal interaction to become a more playful interaction, thereby resolving the heightened state of tension between them.

Creating an *interstice*

Prior to the episode in Case 3, Alofu was putting forward his propositions in a less direct form, engaging in acts such as "shaking a branch/grass", "tapping the ground with his foot" and "looking back" toward Caliope a short distance from her without touching her directly. Ethologically, these acts fall into the category of a behavioral pattern called "solicitation" (see Nishida et al. 2010 among others;

"pulling" in Case 3 is also classified as solicitation) and are commonly observed in many living things, including chimpanzees. From the perspective of an *interstice*, solicitation can be regarded as a behavior specialized for *interstice* creation.

The most typical solicitation behavior among living things is the courtship display performed in relation to breeding (see also Chapter Five by Hayaki and Chapter Sixteen by Adachi). In addition, chimpanzees are known to engage in the aforementioned proposition to travel together as well as some solicitation prior to so-called social interactions such as grooming and play (Nishida et al. 2010).

A solicitation is made to the other party before an actual activity begins. If what is taking place here is compared to the prey's behavior of "searching for signs of a predator based on the eat-be-eaten relationship framework", for example, it can be described as "an activity specifying/clarifying the relationship framework 'here, now' through a disclosure of signs made by the predator (the soliciting party in this case) to the prey (the solicited party in this case)". The disclosure of signs is an exploratory activity on the part of the soliciting party. For the solicited party, on the other hand, the supposed/expected relationship that forms an exploratory framework is specified; in other words, the provision of an *interstice* to delimit an opening to other possibilities serves to reduce the scope of an exploration of *indeterminacy* "here, now"[10].

Chimpanzees engage in various solicitation behaviors, which (including courtship behavior) vary from one group to another and lack the stylized patterns of beautiful ritualistic displays found in other species (Nishida et al. 2010 among others). In fact, they exhibit rather equivocal and ambiguous behaviors in the context of soliciting (which also seem to be found in other primates besides chimpanzees). This actually makes sense considering that these individuals move (transfer) between groups and that intergroup mutation is "normal". At the same time, the provision of an *interstice* means that further exploration is needed on the part of the solicited party.

Cohesiveness and anti-cohesiveness

The impetus to reduce the scope of exploration to one's next action "here, now" as in the above example of solicitation can be found in the way a group is formed and maintained. Adachi (2017) discussed the function of a group as a social "field". The field functions as a behavioral guideline and is constructed as a result of behaviors.

When the individuals who were born in the group perform participatory functions for the formation of the group during their developmental process, the group comes to possess multi-generational inheritability.

Itani (1987) pointed out the difference between chimpanzees and other primates in the way groups are formed and maintained. Itani used the term "cohesiveness" (*shūchūsei*) to describe the primate groups that are well organized, close-knit or coherent while illustrating chimpanzee groups using the term "anti-cohesiveness" (*hishūchūsei*). This cohesive/anti-cohesive trait is considered to provide an impetus to reduce exploration in interactions between group members in the former, whereas recursive (repeated) action and exploration are essential in the latter.

Anti-cohesiveness is likely to be a background condition that forms the basis of chimpanzees' exploratory way of life in which they continually live with *indeterminacy*. In order to consider this point, we must first make a detour to understand cohesive society.

Social relationships and *interstices*

In cohesive-gregarious primate society with inheritability, a bundle of relationships that can be called a "social structure" can be found (typically, the dominance rank relationship and the matrilineal kin relationship), and these structured relationships are relatively stable (e.g. the dominance rank seldom changes).

This social structure is portrayed based on the measurement of who engages in what type of explicitly social behavior to whom at what frequency (see also Chapter Sixteen by Adachi). This relationship improves the observer's prediction about how two parties will behave upon encountering, and this social structure is regarded as an important element for the formation and maintenance of social groups.

On the other hand, the structural trait of the "field" serves as a behavioral guideline for the individuals living there and allows group members to engage in action selection based on stable "relationships" (see Chapter Five by Kitamura and Chapter Sixteen by Adachi). Here, exploration for a "relationship" brings about an *interstice* and at the same time offers a relationship framework, thus extinguishing the need to perform mutually and constantly exploratory actions that are open to various possibilities.

Although the relationship reduces the need for exploration, it does not mean that these individuals are not exploratory. Sustaining the relationship as well as the social structure is founded on their continual functioning to recursively produce their mutual relative physical positionings prior to direct actions (Mori 1977; Rowell and Olson 1983).

Rowell and Olson (1983) appear to consider, although they do not state it explicitly, that this relative positioning between individuals creates a structure (coherence of the group as well), and that explicit social behaviors are displays that manifest when this guideline is eroded or actively breached (e.g., intimidation in the former and grooming in the latter). In this case, "production of a certain distance" involves not only producing a physical distance but also a social distance called "a relationship", as well as continuously producing a social structure.

In addition to these activities, individuals carry out an exploratory activity in the form of aggregation (behaving gregariously) (Itoh 2010) and exist as a group to that extent. In this way, they continually create appropriate distances that are neither too close nor too far, and by giving them regularity they simultaneously realize their being as a group and the structuring of the group in a stable manner[11]. This spatial relative positioning is also important in humans, and the distance between individuals varies depending on the social relationship and the social group (culture) (Hall 1970).

In the structured group, a relationship framework formed by a certain type of regularity in the production of appropriate distances precedes a framework for specific interactions, and at the same time restricts its opening to other possibilities. The stability of encounters in this situation may be threatened by an encounter with a roving solitary monkey that has transferred out of a group and has no position in the social structure (see Adachi 2013), or a discontinuation of the exploratory activity of aggregation such as group fission.

Meanwhile, consanguinity is very limited in chimpanzee society as it is patrilineal (females transfer out of their native group at sexual maturity while males spend all their lives in their native group) (see Chapter Five by Hayaki). They have dominance ranks (see also Chapter Six by Nishie), but these are highly unstable. In *Chimpanzee Politics*, de Waal (1994) describes the way chimpanzees employ various measures to reverse or maintain their ranks. "Politics" among male chimpanzees has also been drawing the attention of researchers in Mahale.

Conversely, the dominance rank order in chimpanzee society cannot function without exploratory actions, and this is why it can become destabilized (rank reversal). Accordingly, it is essential for chimpanzees to remain exploratory in the formation of a relationship framework even when there appears to be a stable

Photo 7.2 Playing
Chimpanzees of all sexes and ages play together. These two adult males engaged in play for over five minutes, first tickling one another, then chasing one another around a tree as shown in the photo, with slapping, light biting and tumbling in between for variety's sake, and ending by chasing one another around the tree in larger circles. Their mouths were open as they were "laughing hard" (play-panting) during play.

relationship. In other words, the state of the relationship here continues to retain an element of otherness and continues to be *indeterminate*. The practices of food sharing and play in adult relationships demonstrate the importance of composing an exploratory action toward the other individual instead of giving precedence to a structured relationship such as dominance rank; the attitude of remaining *indeterminate* continues to function here.

It seems that the situation in which a relationship does not always precede an action and the exploratory attitude of remaining *indeterminate* as we saw in the cases above are inextricably linked to the fact that chimpanzees continue to form groups despite their lack of cohesiveness, as we shall discuss next.

Fission-fusion

Chimpanzees remain *indeterminate* in facing fellow group members as well as other living things (or possible phenomena). The aforementioned situation in which a "relationship" (social structure) does not necessarily precede action selection (how to act in a situation) is also part of their exploratory attitude of staying *indeterminate*. To elaborate the latter, greeting, for example, is used as an indicator of a dominance relationship by researchers, but it is not that simple, because it is common for a subordinate to be punched or chased by the dominant when the former greets the latter. Although this is a very unreasonable situation if we give precedence to the framework of dominance rank, chimpanzees face other individuals in a place where a relationship (social structure) is not sufficient to define how one should act (i.e., there is no right action) in their everyday life.

Next, we shall recap the chimpanzee social group that lacks cohesiveness from the perspective of *interstices* and examine their exploratory attitude of staying *indeterminate*, as well as look at the relevance of the way anti-cohesive society is formed and maintained.

The most confusing thing for me in observing chimpanzees is the frequent occurrence of encounters where they meet, do nothing and move apart. In the second volume of this series, *Institutions: The Evolution of Human Sociality*, I explained that more often than not, nothing happens when individual chimpanzees encounter, despite their rowdy image (Itoh 2017). I pointed out that while the contingency and repetitiveness of their encounters are relevant to the difficulty of starting a specific interaction, this is why the synchronization of activities that involve no need for interaction – such as feeding and resting – is in itself an important form of interaction for them. Let us look at chimpanzee encounters in which nothing happens from another perspective.

Chimpanzees in Mahale form a group (unit-group) of sixty or so members, but the individual members repeatedly meet and part (fission-fusion) rather than gathering together in one place. Up to their juvenility (around age five to eight, Matsumoto and Hayaki 2015) they are either held by their mothers or follow them around unless they are lost, and their mothers wait for them. Newly transferred females often follow other adults around as well. On the other hand, most adults and adolescent individuals, including mothers, participate in the fission-fusion phenomenon on their own. It is impossible to predict when, where, whom and how they will encounter and their behaviors appear to be random in general.

There is no shortage of opportunities to observe chimpanzee encounters, as they frequently get together and separate. Perhaps because I am hoping to collect data, my expectation for something to happen may be too high, and chimpanzees let me

Photo 7.3 Stopping
Chimpanzees repeatedly encounter and separate at the individual level. They encounter each other many times in the process. As shown in the photo, a travelling individual stops in front of the counterpart in an encounter and "looks" at the counterpart (the two chimpanzees on the right in 7.3a and the one chimpanzee on the right in 7.3b were the individuals who arrived). They may further approach their counterpart and engage in some form of interaction, but often leave the scene without interacting. In the cases photographed here, they left without interacting. The "stopping" position can be quite far away as in 7.3a, or within a few paces as in 7.3b.

down without fail. A majority of my notes read as follows: "X:X:X, P arrives", "X:X:Y, Q walks past", "X:Y:Y, P travels in the direction of A" and then P disappears.

Although in my eyes they appear to behave indifferently, they are not uninterested in one another. When they see another individual, they often look at that individual and pause for a few moments. The seen individual is also aware of the other's presence. If the counterpart is in brush with poor visibility, the individual may crouch down to get a better look.

As the chimpanzees become aware of one another and one stops momentarily, my expectation as to what will happen next increases, but this expectation is betrayed more often than not as mentioned above. From another perspective, the occurrence of the action of "pausing" may mean not only that I am sensing an *interstice* in this encounter, but also that the chimpanzees are creating the *interstice*.

This is because something does happen in some cases, and also because the way it happens seems to be continuous with the approach of "pausing momentarily" rather than continuing what they were doing before the counterpart's appearance. In some cases, one pauses, slowly approaches the counterpart and starts grooming; in others, the counterpart approaches and starts playing. One may either initiate the interaction or leave it to the counterpart, but each party seems to weigh up the timing of interaction.

Even when we cannot identify that something has happened, chimpanzees look at the counterpart and pause momentarily probably because they are compelled to explore what the counterpart is doing and going to do next, regardless of what they themselves want to do. Even when they do nothing, they do so on the basis of their mutual action to do nothing or to move away rather than doing as they please. As we saw in Case 2, confirming that "nothing will happen" can only be attained through exploratory means.

If this is the case, their way of life filled with fission and fusion is full of contingent *interstices*. The recurring fission-fusion at the individual level can create and maintain a kind of totality in the form of a group (Itoh 2003) perhaps because it is supported by their activity to create *interstices* in the field repeatedly in that they are faced with action selection each time and each time create an interaction (including doing nothing) "here, now" in an exploratory manner.

Chimpanzees form a group through recurrent encounters. At the same time, their rank order and associated male alliances (Hosaka and Nakamura 2015) or female friendships (Itoh and Nakamura 2015b) are unstable because they are built into these recurrent encounters. As *indeterminacy* is guaranteed in this way, it becomes possible for exploratory actions to take precedence over relationships.

With regard to the unstable nature of the rank order in chimpanzee society, Itani (1987) argues that chimpanzees are in need of more multi-dimensional social rules or means for coexistence as structures such as dominance rank no longer provide reliable bases (see also Chapter One by Kuroda). I agree that structures do not provide reliable grounds, but I am not sure whether or not they have some sort of consistent rules (whether multi-dimensional or not). In my view, the way chimpanzees face *indeterminacy* suggests that the flexibility to face "others" in their unit-group or other "others" in an exploratory manner as well as the flexibility to construct or destroy interactions through the recurrent performance of them are indispensable for their way of life. I suspect that such exploratory attitude is boundlessly similar to a kind of leeway toward the surrounding world (for instance, following a python in defiance of fear, or refusing a proposition even though it may upset the counterpart) or the realm of play (as they actually play in some cases) rather than rules.

Anti-cohesiveness, which is the formative condition of groups that carry out fission and fusion at the individual level, is the source of their exploratory nature as well as the consequence of it. At the same time, having fission as a requirement for group formation makes it possible to keep exploration recursive rather than continuous. This seems to be more in line with the way living things face the *indeterminacy* of an unknown phenomenon that they encounter and explore in a complex and diverse environment as we have seen above, rather than the way other gregarious living things that highly structure their groups reduce the need for exploration through structuralization when they continue to stay within a proximal space.

Staying with *indeterminacy*: Spoken and encountered "others"

Living things interact with the environment in an exploratory way. Chimpanzees in Mahale might chase a python (Zamma 2011), bark at an aardvark corpse or play with a moth (Chapter Two by Nakamura). They exhibit a mixture of emotions such as interest, curiosity, fear and pleasure. Chimpanzees in Gombe play with a baboon (Goodall 1986), Koko the gorilla looks after a kitten (Patterson and Linden 1984) and various other living things interact with humans. They are capable of performing such interactions precisely because they find *indeterminacy* in the counterpart's next action in their encounters and continue to stay with the *indeterminacy* by maintaining their exploratory attitude.

What do humans do? They also interact with other living things and also know them very well. However, while humans may face *indeterminacy* at the moment of an encounter, they bring in an apparently different type of interaction as outside observers. This is a descriptive interaction performed in the framework of the human cognitive domain from the outside of the encounter (Maturana and Varela 1991). It is probably this shift that has created our extremely human new (and beyond human control) way to interact with the environment, i.e., to attempt to control nature. This can be regarded as anti-environmental from the perspective of the living field we used to form by linking human activities with the environment.

In their field of living, chimpanzees create a group together with other chimpanzees. They engage in exploratory actions amongst themselves in continuity with their interactions with the environment. In societies of humans and other gregarious primates (cohesive society) on the other hand, the burden of exploration is mitigated by structuralization. Even here, humans attain the position of being outside observers of the society they live in. For instance, after going through the age of reason (etiology), we have entered the age of probability where "self" and "other" become data points in an arbitrary yardstick in arbitrary data sets such as various social groups, states and the whole world, and the self is continuous with the other on the same plane (Hacking 1999). In this case, *indeterminacy* is positioned as the determinate within a gradation measured by the arbitrary yardstick (the normal and various degrees of deviation from it) rather than becoming contiguous to various other possibilities.

Becoming an observer of the society one lives in means that one is leaving the activity of generating society through interactions with others, and it is antisocial in this sense (Maturana and Varela 1991). Yet, if one continues one's social involvement with the society one lives in, albeit as an observer, rather than just being antisocial and letting the society collapse, to that extent one can provide an impetus for the reorganization of individual human societies. Hacking (1999) argues that the probability classification carried out by humans not only creates new classifications, but also influences human behaviors in turn as well as what is considered to be normal. In other words, *indeterminacy* to humans produces new *indeterminacy* when it is turned into the determinate, thus *indeterminacies* continue to intertwine and fluctuate at various levels from the individual to the state.

There appears to be a major disconnect in the attitude toward *indeterminacy* = otherness between humans and other living things. In either case, however, it seems to be founded on the exploration of *indeterminacy*. No matter how hard humans try to put a strong lid on *indeterminacy* using every available means, it is probably impossible to remain an outside observer at the field of encounters. On the other hand, it seems that staying with *indeterminacy* in actual encounters in the lives we live (even if we cannot do so continuously) sometimes plays an important role.

Appendix 7

Detailed record of Serena, Bonobo and the accident (02 October 1997)

12:58:59 BB begins to approach FN and his grooming party.

12:59:03 BB is about to sit down with his back toward FN.

12:59:04 FN starts to move westward, BB half-rises to his feet and pant-grunts.

12:59:09 FN sits down. SE and BB begin to approach FN simultaneously.

12:59:11 SE <u>sees</u> BB and continues to approach FN. BB <u>catches SE's eye</u> and pauses with his left foot in the air. SE <u>gazes at</u> BB. BB moves slightly to the left.

12:59:12 Immediately following BB's move, SE looks down at the ground and proceeds to take a step forward with her right foot.

12:59:13 BB <u>looks back</u> toward SE and FN (hereafter, SE-FN stands for SE and FN resting area). SE turns her back to FN. FN follows BB with his eyes.

12:59:14 SE <u>looks</u> toward BB, BB averts his gaze and proceeds eastward toward DE. SE <u>tilts her head</u> toward BB as she sits down.

12:59:15 BB <u>glances</u> toward SE-FN again. SE continues to watch BB. FN looks toward BB and others.

12:59:16 BB <u>glances</u> toward SE-FN again. SE continues to watch BB. BB looks at the ground and moves near the head of DE, who is lying down. SE and FN are diagonally across (west) from them (SE is behind FN). FN moves his left hand to the left from the front of his body.

12:59:17 FN moves his right hand to the left. BB sits down at this moment.

12:59:18 FN stands up and turns his back to SE. SE continues to watch BB. As soon as BB sits down, DE begins to groom BB.

12:59:19–20 FN brushes off leaves from the sole of his left foot as he sits down. At the same time, SE moves as if to move westward.

12:59:21 FN lies on his belly. SE looks back to FN and quickly turns her body to him. BB <u>watches</u> SE-FN.

12:59:23 SE begins to groom FN.

12:59:38 BB shifts his gaze from SE-FN to the ground (also seems to be glancing upwards).

12:59:43 BB looks at his left hand, and almost simultaneously SE <u>looks</u> up toward BB. Grooming for FN stops temporarily.

12:59:45 BB <u>looks</u> toward SE-FN.

12:59:48 SE looks down and resumes grooming.

12:59:49 SE abruptly looks westward. BB is still looking toward SE-FN.

12:59:50 BB looks in the direction of SE's gaze.

12:59:51 SE resumes grooming. BB returns his <u>gaze</u> toward SE-FN.

12:59:57 approx. BB gazes away from SE-FN.

13:00:11 BB looks up, scratches his right shoulder with his left hand, and looks at that hand (with his face toward the north).

13:00:26 SE <u>scratches</u> (1) her left hand with her right hand as she turns her face to the south.

13:00:29 SE momentarily <u>turns her face</u> toward BB-DE (the area where BB and DE were resting as it was difficult to identify where SE was looking) while <u>self-scratching</u> (2).

13:00:30 BB <u>looks</u> toward SE and wipes his face with his hand.

13:00:31 SE looks at the part she is scratching (north and down). BB raises his right hand a little while <u>keeping his face</u> to SE-DE.

13:00:32 BB begins self-grooming with his right hand.

13:00:33 SE opens her mouth and <u>looks</u> toward BB-DE.

13:00:36 SE <u>scratches</u> (3) her right hand again and turns her head down.

13:00:49 BB <u>looks</u> toward SE-DE. FN is wriggling on the spot.

13:00:54 SE straightens her back a little and <u>scratches</u> (4) her left shoulder with her right hand from the front.

13:00:58 FN wriggles again. BB is still looking.

13:01:02 An interruption (another individual nearby leaves the scene to the south).

13:01:13 DE sits up with his left hand lightly placed on BB and begins to groom BB. BB watches SE-DE. SE tilts her body to the left (westward), to the left of FN (as if to peek at BB).

13:01:19–21 SE tilts her body deeply to the right (eastward) and comes back up.

13:01:21–24 SE tilts her body again and comes upright to the north this time.

13:01:25 SE reaches her right hand toward FN.

13:01:29 SE grooms FN.

13:02:09 SE leaves.

Note: BB = Bonobo, DE = Kalunde, FN = Fanana, SE = Serena. I found SE several minutes later sitting alone on a trail just one to two meters south as I followed FN travelling southwards where barks from chimpanzees rang out at 13:04. FN, SE and BB did not get together. FN went with DE for a while as they travelled and engaged in displays.

8 When Pricking Up One's Ears for the Voices of Strangers: Others in Chimpanzee Society

Shunkichi Hanamura

Key ideas

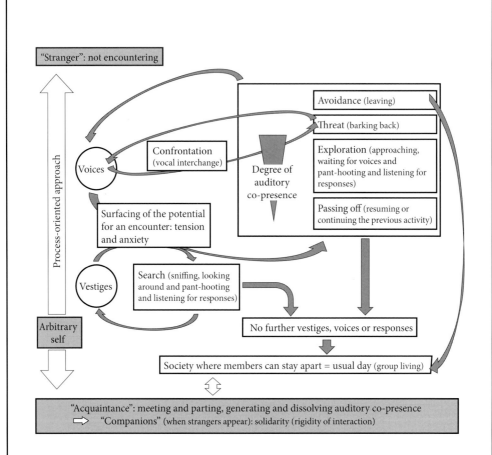

Others emerge to chimpanzees in a way that is different from how they emerge to humans, who tend to use institutions to reduce their otherness (the unpredictability and contingency of their presence/absence and behavior) and predefine the content of their interaction with individual others. For instance, when a potential for encountering "strangers (whom they do not routinely encounter)" surfaces through voices emanating from or vestiges discovered around the periphery of their group's home range, chimpanzees adjust their action choices on a case-by-case basis with the process-oriented attitude of "depending on the other party's action" using the strangers' otherness as a resource without predefining how to interact with them (or what existence the strangers are to them) while exhibiting tension and anxiety. Consequently, chimpanzees exhibit various behaviors in response to strangers' action and the level of auditory co-presence with strangers: they may "pass off" the arising potential to interact with strangers for now, start an "exploration" for the presence/absence and behavior of strangers in preparation for a possible sudden encounter and end it when nothing happens, "threaten" and sometimes come to a "vocal confrontation" or "avoid" further contact. On the other hand, they also interact with their "acquaintances (whom they have been repeatedly meeting with and parting from)" though voices with the same process-oriented attitude. In such interactions, they can either attempt to construct and continue auditory co-presence through vocal exchange, suspend the interaction to resume their own activities or let each other's voices pass and go their separate ways without exhibiting tension or anxiety when the potential for an encounter surfaces. Thus, chimpanzees form a "society where they can stay apart from one another". When strangers emerge, however, chimpanzees show solidarity with their "companions" to deal with them together and cannot continue their flexible fission-fusion grouping and interactions through voices in the usual manner. In this sense, strangers are the others who threaten the stability of their everyday living. Nevertheless, it seems strangers emerge to newly immigrated females in a way that is different from how they emerge to resident individuals and that resident females with experience of transferring between groups are not fazed by the emergence of strangers to the same extent that males are.

Emergence of the stranger, how to deal with its otherness

Living things encounter various kinds of others. The other is a being with its own agency that is different from the self who emerges when living things perceive its otherness (i.e., the unpredictability and contingency of its presence/absence and behavior) and fundamentally defies full comprehension. Living things explore its presence or absence and behavior through observation and/or interaction while making a prediction by referring to the outcomes of such previous interactions or the way other individuals behave toward the other. Knowing what form of existence the other is, that is, how the other concerns oneself, is almost synonymous with living with the other, and the self, regardless of self-recognition or lack thereof, also emerges and is altered through interactions with such others. The social lives of animals, including humans, have evolved along with the evolution of ways to deal with otherness in conspecific individuals, who concern them more than any other kind of other.

Unlike anonymous groups (i.e., groups with no fixed membership where a majority of constituent individuals do not identify one another) of conspecifics formed by animals such as migratory fish and birds and seasonally migrating gnu, many primates form "groups" with stable membership that are spatially separated from other groups. When they form this type of group, the individuals belonging to other neighboring groups they occasionally encounter emerge as "strangers" with strong otherness according to the difference from the "acquaintances" (i.e., group members) they associate with on a daily basis. While for an individual an acquaintance is an other whose otherness the individual deals with in daily interactions, and vice versa, and based on the way each deals with the other's otherness, they shape a unique group living, a "stranger" is an other who threatens the stability of such everyday living. It is supposed that one deals with the otherness of such strangers in cooperation with one's "companions" on the scene at the time, and based on the way they deal with it, they shape various intergroup relationships with those strangers.

Chimpanzee groups (or unit-groups) in the wild have a multi-male, multi-female structure between which a majority of females transfer at the age of puberty. After transfer, females basically remain in the group where they give birth. Unlike the type of groups formed by many other primate species whose members range in one troop, all the members of a chimpanzee group, except for dependent infants and juveniles, are able to range individually. They repeatedly meet and part and in the process of fission-fusion grouping they form temporary parties (i.e., gatherings of individuals who remain in or are ready to have visual contact with each other) with different members each time (see Hanamura 2015 for an overview). The same individuals may meet again several minutes or hours after parting or may not meet again for several weeks or even months. Chimpanzees leading this way of group living use a long-distance vocalization called a pant-hoot (see Hosaka et al. 2015 and Hanamura 2017 for details), which can be heard in a radius of one to two kilometers. Pant-hoots are often uttered in chorus among individuals within a party, and such choruses or solo pant-hoots are exchanged between parties. Yet, they do not always range together through vocalization. Instead, they can be far apart beyond the audible range; or may not utter any voice for days and thus may pass close by each other without noticing.

In Chapter Eight of *Institutions: The Evolution of Human Sociality* (Kawai (ed.) 2017) preceding this volume, I analyzed interactions via pant-hoots among the chimpanzees of M group in Mahale, Tanzania, and pointed out that their process-oriented way of connecting actions (or way to deal with each other's otherness) serves as a device (i.e., convention or institution) to support their "society where they can stay apart from each other". Through the exchange of pant-hoots within a timeframe of ten seconds that takes on the meaning of "call-response", they accomplish non-face-to-face encounters and create temporary fields (i.e., a state of auditory co-presence) in which they can continue further interaction with the mutual expectation that "the other party is aware of my/our presence". However, they do not know when, where and whose voices will emanate and their call is not often responded to, while it sometimes attracts an unexpected response. Instead of setting a predetermined common goal for their interactions (e.g. maintaining or achieving a specific condition or a certain order such as continuing the vocal exchange and meeting visually) that can reduce each other's otherness and limit their choices of action, they coordinate their action choices with the process-oriented attitude of "depending on the other party's behavior" by using each other's otherness as a resource while being influenced by activity rhythm and interaction among visible individuals in each party. By mutually coordinating their action choices with this attitude without prescribing how to develop their interaction, while they are able to attempt to construct a field and continue the auditory co-presence through exchanging pant-hoots any time they range within the reach of each other's voices, at the same time they are able to suspend the interaction to resume their own activities or let each other's voices pass and go their separate ways even beyond the audible range. When another party's voice sounds, they sometimes listen to whether any other party will respond; their social space extends beyond a dyadic relationship here.

However, the voices of other individuals who are outside the field of vision that reach their ears do not always come from members of their own group; they – often pant-hoots – may be the voices of individuals of another group. In this chapter, we shall consider such situations and analyze how chimpanzees deal with the otherness of individuals belonging to other groups and their intergroup relations, including comparison with those of humans. We shall also explore various aspects of their experience of others and the characteristics of their group living, focusing on the similarities and differences in interactions with individuals of another group through voices and with individuals of one's own group, and by looking at differences in behavior between newly immigrated females and resident individuals.

Intergroup relations in chimpanzees

Primate individuals belonging to different groups basically have an antagonistic avoidance relationship, aside from those who transfer between groups, but intergroup hostility or xenophobia has been emphasized in chimpanzees based on reports such as the following (reviews: Wrangham 1999; Mitani et al. 2010). Chimpanzees, mostly males, sometimes "patrol" (i.e., fast-paced and silent travelling while peering around to check for the presence/absence or vestiges of unknown individuals for reconnaissance) the ranging area that overlaps with their neighboring groups and "intrude" into another group's home range, and an encounter with individuals belonging to another group can develop into an intensely antagonistic interaction that sometimes leads to someone's death due to injuries sustained in the confrontation. If such "confrontations" occur repeatedly and the population of one group declines, female emigrations, including secondary ones after childbirth, can be also promoted and on rare occasions the dissolution of the group ensues, resulting in an increase of the female population and an expansion of the ranging area of another group.

The first reported case can be called the invasion of Kahama group by Kasekela group in Gombe, Tanzania (Goodall 1990), where many cases of "patrol" and "intrusion" involving antagonistic interactions and the death of attacked individuals have been confirmed. This is the only case in which it is almost certain that a hostile intergroup relationship resulted in the extinction of one of the groups. Wrangham, who was at the scene and shocked by the brutality of the attack, characterized the "intrusion" as "lethal raiding into neighboring communities [or groups] in search of vulnerable enemies [e.g. those raging alone] to attack and kill" (Wrangham and Peterson 1996: 24) that is not found in the intergroup interactions of other primates which center on "threatening" and "avoidance" in the overlapping range, and discussed the evolution of intergroup violence from the perspective of male reproductive strategy, including comparison with that in humans.

As the two groups in Gombe were created when the original group split, their relationship cannot be generalized across all intergroup relationships in chimpanzees. However, several more cases of "patrol" and "intrusion" by the remaining Kasekela group and other groups as well as antagonistic interactions between these groups and the death of attacked individuals have been either confirmed or suspected in Gombe since that time. Similar cases have also been reported in some other study sites. In Mahale, the individuals belonging to K group, which had been the main research subject since research began in the late-1960s, were confirmed to range in a way that "avoided" encounters with neighboring M group when they heard their voices, and several incidents as follows were also observed: one case of an "intrusion" by M-group chimpanzees into the home range of K group and the subsequent heated display contest between them, two cases of attacks by K-group chimpanzees on M-group chimpanzees upon encounters in the overlapping range and some cases of vocal interchange between them (Nishida 1979). The number of K-group individuals gradually decreased, including through female transfers and atypical secondary transfers after childbirth, until only one male remained in the first half of the 1980s, but it is difficult to attribute this to the antagonistic intergroup interactions because no such interactions with M-group chimpanzees were observed prior to the disappearance of K-group chimpanzees and other factors such as the off-center population structure of K group at the time can naturally explain the decline (Nakamura and Itoh 2015b).

Through these reports, the chimpanzee has been portrayed, especially in the mass media, as a purposive, bellicose and male-centered species that "engages in daily patrol in fear of invasion by other groups and attempts to expand its range or acquire more females by invading other groups when the opportunity arises". However, to a great extent this is merely an image formed by equating the ultimate male reproductive strategy that is supposed on the basis of behavioral ecology and the proximate factors that are somewhat anthropomorphically assumed to explain the behaviors (e.g. motivation or intention, here) as well as projecting human views of war (especially those such as the image of *imaginary* "savage war in primitive societies" abstracted by Clastres (2003)). In the first place, a majority of contact between individuals belonging to different groups is auditory and the incidences of visual contact vary greatly depending on the subject group and the research period (Boesch et al. 2008; Wilson et al. 2012). In M group of Mahale, no visual contact with individuals from other groups has been observed, aside from newly immigrated females, for the last fifteen years (as at 2015). In order to explore the reality of their intergroup relations, we need to focus on non-face-to-face interaction via voices between individuals from different groups and analyze the process that culminates in "patrol", "intrusion", "confrontation" or "avoidance" and their behaviors in these situations. Another question we must ask is how they distinguish the voices of the individuals belonging to their own group from those of non-members and how they share that distinction among group members.

Interactions with strangers through voices and/or vestiges

The voices of strangers from the outer edges of the home range

M group (with around sixty members) has been ranging within approximately thirty square kilometers of the forest zone between Lake Tanganyika spreading to the west and the Mahale Mountains rising up in the east (see Figure 8.1). Areas used by other groups for ranging extend to the north and the south of this area. The aforementioned K group, which finally disappeared in the 1980s, ranged in an area covering the northern part of M group's current home range and extending further north. It is known that Y group began to use this area by the second half of the 1990s and at least in recent years, both M and Y groups use an area between the Nkala River in the northernmost part of M group's home range and the upper Kashiha River in the northeastern part. Mount Mkulume in the southernmost part and the upper Sansa River in the southeastern part of M group's home range are used by a southern neighbor called N group. In recent years, however, there have only been two reported cases in which individuals belonging to other groups were found to be in the home range of M group (see Sakamaki and Nakamura 2015 for a review of intergroup relations among Mahale chimpanzees). When many M-group chimpanzees were staying in the northernmost part of the home range for a few days in 1998, some chimpanzees not of M group were spotted in the southeastern part at a distance from them. No contact between them and M-group chimpanzees was observed at that time. In 2000, an attack on an adult female and presumably her infant of an unknown group by some M-group chimpanzees took place in the northern part of the home range.

In the following analysis, we shall focus on the "voices emanating from the outer edges of the home range" (north of the Nkala River and the upper Kashiha River and south of Mount Mkulume and the upper Sansa River) presumed to be those

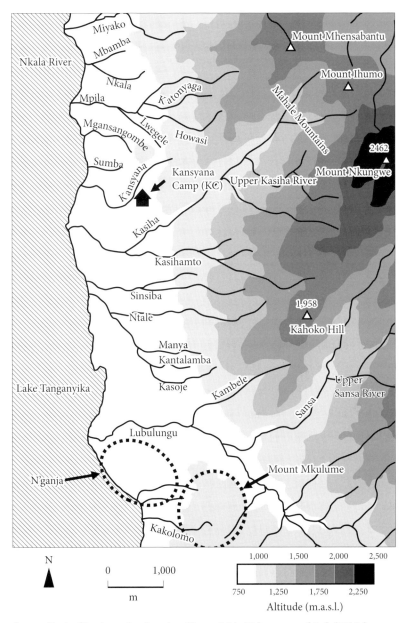

Source: Revised by the author based on Figure 2.7 in Nakamura and Itoh (2015a).

Figure 8.1 The usual ranging area (or home range) of chimpanzees of Mahale M group in Tanzania (covering from the Nkala River in the north to Mount Mkulume in the south and from the lake shoreline in the west to at least half-way up the mountains in the east) and its surrounds.

of chimpanzees of other groups (hereinafter referred to as <voices> accordingly: eighteen cases in seven episodes) out of all the voices coming from outside the field of vision while I was observing chimpanzees during my research over twelve months from 2005 to 2006 and a total of four months between 2012 and 2014. They exclude voices judged to be those of M-group chimpanzees based on the ranging and grouping situations recorded by multiple researchers on the day of observation and a few days before and after that day. In these cases, it is likely that the chimpanzees under observation were also able to identify the voices.

The chimpanzees of M group use the northern and southern "peripheral parts of their home range" (the approximately one kilometer zone inside the outer boundary) where <voices> can be audible throughout the year, although the frequency varies depending on the phenology (fruiting seasonality) and distribution of their staple fruits. Of 186 days on which chimpanzees were observed during my 2005–2006 study, <voices> were heard sixteen times in five episodes (north: eight times in three episodes; south: eight times in two episodes; mostly pant-hoots or mixed vocalizations of pant-hoots and barks and/or screams). There was a lower likelihood of hearing <voices> while ranging in the peripheral parts (north: three days out of seventeen; south: two days out of twenty-four). As other voices presumably uttered by M-group chimpanzees outside of the field of view rang out much more frequently during observation, with pant-hoots and mixed voices including pant-hoots alone emanating once or twice per hour on average (though sometimes none per day and at other times close to 100 times per day), the sounding of <voices> can be considered a rare occurrence.

When the <voices> rang out (within thirty seconds on all eighteen occasions), at times the chimpanzees exhibited behaviors they rarely exhibit when they hear other voices (for their usual reactions, see discussion on page 200 below). These (observed within thirty seconds after hearing the <voices> on all eighteen occasions) included diarrheic defecation, nipple touching or fumbling (a habit of some individuals), clumping among individuals in visual range on the scene, physical contact such as hand reaching and embracing, all of which can be regarded as expressions of tension and anxiety, and "wraa calls" that are usually uttered when chimpanzees encounter extraordinary phenomena such as the corpse of a conspecific or heterospecific animal, earthquakes and falling trees or dangerous beings such as a snake or a leopard (Hosaka et al. 2015). Considering that the type of <voices> are no different from those they ordinarily utter and hear, it is likely that they perceived the <voices> as the "voices of strangers" that differed from the familiar "voices of acquaintances". There must have been many occasions when they were unsure whether or not the vocalizers were strangers, but we can consider that they would sense "stranger-ness" in the voices based on not only their ranging and grouping situations ("Acquaintances would not be there now"), but also on the location ("Voices do not usually emanate from that area") and in some cases the quality of the voices. This is because they exhibited the aforementioned behaviors upon hearing <voices> even when they had not met any individuals or heard any voices outside the field of vision for several days, and hence appeared not to know where their acquaintances would be. When they discovered the vestiges of feeding, defecating, bedding and so on in the peripheral areas or near the source of <voices>, they sometimes exhibited behaviors such as smelling the vestiges and the ground around them as well as diarrheic defecation, clumping together and engaging in physical contact. We suppose that they can sense the presence of "likely strangers" (who may still be in the vicinity) from the vestiges based on their location and/or smell.

In some cases, they barked back in chorus at <voices> and not necessarily within thirty seconds after they rang out they produced pant-hoots and listened for the presence or absence of a response in the same way that they emit "calls" to another party in their ordinary interaction, but these were clearly directed at strangers. Their ranging patterns and activities following the sounding of <voices> were also diverse: in some cases, they hurried toward the <voices>, but in other cases, moved away from them; they also sometimes stayed on the spot and resumed their previous activity.

Accordingly, we can surmise that chimpanzees do not perceive strangers that emerge through voices and vestiges as certain beings with a fixed visage (or attributes), and thus their behavior toward the voices and vestiges varies greatly depending on the situation. As many of the <voices> in the eighteen occasions rang out sequentially from around the same area over a short period and chimpanzees often encountered vestiges before or after the sounding of the <voices>, we shall analyze their behaviors toward these together with their ranging and grouping situations before and after each episode.

Exploration and confrontation

Let us first look at an episode in which a "patrol"-like behavior was observed. Here we analyze how chimpanzees deal with the otherness of strangers with particular attention to whether the behavior has the goal-oriented aspect that the term "patrol" implies, such that it is "carried out to keep a lookout for an already-known enemy or danger". While "patrol" behavior used to be observed at least once per week among chimpanzees in Gombe in the past (Goodall 1990), it was not observed among M-group chimpanzees in Mahale during a one-year study period from 1999 to 2000, except for one suggestive case (Sakamaki and Nakamura 2015), and the following two are the only cases I have observed myself in a total study period of sixteen months.

In Episode 1, which was observed over four days from 20 to 23 December 2005, a majority of M-group chimpanzees arrived in the north in the afternoon of 20 December after ranging in the south until the day before (19 December), and encountered the voices presumably of Y group to the north (1 case) and vestiges (2 cases) over this period.

Episode 1: 20–23 December 2005
At sunset on 20 December, four males parted from a large number of individuals, after discovering and smelling vestiges of feeding that had been left around noon on the same day, in the northeastern part of M group's home range, began diarrheic defecation and hurried northward silently for one hour or so while sniffing the ground and looking around them. The four reached the northernmost part of the home range and produced pant-hoots, but they seemed to have doubled back as there was no response. The whereabouts of the four on the next day, 21 December, was unknown, but they had re-merged with many individuals by the morning of 22 December. These multiple individuals all spent their time as usual, sometimes spreading out and exchanging pant-hoots with one another in the northern part of the home range until the early afternoon. Pant-hoots emanated from the outer edge (about one kilometer to the north) in the early afternoon. Seven males, some of whom began diarrheic defecation, and five females clumped and moved toward the voices while pausing many times to prick up their ears, or sitting down and remaining silent for a while to keep their ears open for any voices. I do not know where they went after that due to their fast-paced and silent movement, but I aurally confirmed that there were no voices from them or northern <voices> around the area at least until the early evening. In the morning of the next day, 23 December, mostly the same individuals were found to be resting in a place one kilometer southwest of the location. Seven males and eight females headed north in the midmorning and then found numerous vestiges, such as beds and feces, that had been left presumably on the day before, in the northernmost part of their home range. After embracing or clumping together, they began to search the vicinity in the same manner the four males had employed on 20 December. Their whereabouts after that are unknown,

but it was confirmed that many of them travelled southward on 24 December and almost all of them were ranging in the south by 26 December.

In this episode, the chimpanzees exhibited tension and anxiety (diarrheic defecation, clumping together and physical contact) on all occasions of "encounters with voices or vestiges". After hearing <voices>, they began to explore the movement of the strangers supposedly around the source of the voices without disclosing their own location by silently approaching or waiting for the next vocalization. Because the voices rang out sometime after they had exchanged pant-hoots among themselves, this would have made them realize the possibility that the strangers were aware of their presence. Following the discovery of vestiges, they explored the whereabouts of the strangers who supposedly had been there in the recent past by searching the vicinity in silence and producing pant-hoots afterward. In other words, they felt ill at ease in the situation where the "potential for an encounter with strangers" surfaced through their voices and/or vestiges ("Strangers over there are likely to be aware of our presence"; or "Strangers are likely to be nearby"), and therefore they were "exploring" their behavior and presence/absence in preparation for a possible sudden encounter, including the avoidance of it. Nevertheless, in any "exploring" cases in this episode, it appears that there were no further "encounters with voices or vestiges" as a result of their "explorations", and they subsequently ended their "explorations".

December falls in the congregating season when a majority of M-group chimpanzees form a loose gathering through voices and range over a long distance from north to south and from south to north while repeatedly meeting and parting from one another[1]. During the few days when this episode took place amid such large-scale ranging, strangers emerged through their intermittent encounters with voices or vestiges, and hence they carried out "explorations", although "nothing happened" and hence the presence of the strangers also faded away.

In Episode 2 observed on 6 May 2006 (see Appendix 8.1 at the end of this chapter), an "exploration" triggered by an "encounter with voices" brought further "encounters with voices and/or vestiges", and the development of this cyclic process resulted in an "intrusion" into Y group's home range which culminated in a "confrontation" through voices with presumably Y-group chimpanzees. May is in the dispersing season when M-group chimpanzees separate into small parties and range in different areas with little vocalization. However, on that day I happened to observe a relatively large party travelling northward in the northern part of the home range. I shall summarize and analyze the episode below.

Summary from Scene 1 to the middle of Scene 5 in Episode 2 (6 May 2006)
<Scene 1> When pant-hoots emanated from the outer edge of the home range to the north (about one kilometer away) for the first time, many individuals produced wraa calls, but during the vocalization they resumed their previous activity including a display contest among males over proximity to a semi-estrous female. They had a relaxing time while grooming one another thereafter. <Scene 2> They moved a little northward and began hunting red-colobuses with loud vocalization. As soon as the tumult settled, pant-hoots rang out in the north for the second time. Males barked back while engaging in displays followed by a chorus of pant-hoots by some males. After raising the chorus, the vocalizers and many other individuals, including females, around them stayed motionless to listen for a response, but they received nothing from the north. Around that time, nine individuals, including three females, hurried northward while pausing many times to prick up their ears, while the remaining three females and one young male travelled southward or remained on the spot. I lost sight of the nine there, but about ninety minutes later, I rediscovered them. They had regained calm and were feeding a short distance to the north (across the Nkala River in the northernmost part of the home range). <Scene 3> After feeding, the nine discovered some fresh vestiges of feeding nearby. They clumped together while sniffing them, then moved northward silently while smelling the ground and looking around. Some males kicked tree buttresses while emitting low, pant-hoot-like voices. As the nine continued travelling northward while pricking up their ears, pant-hoots accompanied by screams rang out in the north shortly after. They clumped together again, and one male fumbled his nipples. After that, one female left the party, but the remaining eight individuals continued to travel northward. <Scene 4> Once the eight reached a mountain ridge, they sat down and pricked up their ears for a while as if waiting for the next round of voices, but none came. They then began feeding again, but stopped after a short time, circled the vicinity at a fast pace and waited for voices on another ridge on the way. <Scene 5> When they returned to the ridge where they had stayed a short time ago, pant-hoots mixed with barks and screams emanated from a place nearby to the north (a few hundred meters away). They all made a dash to the north while barking back, pant-hooting and displaying and what ensued was a stormy interchange of voices.

In this episode, they exhibited a sense of surprise or alarm (by emitting wraa calls) at the first unexpected <voices>, but immediately resumed their previous activity without carrying out any "exploration", that is, "passed off" the potential for interaction with the strangers that was afforded by the voices. This was perhaps because the strangers were not likely to be aware of their presence, as they had not been emitting any types of loud vocalizations leading up to it, unlike the scene when the <voices> sounded in Episode 1. However, when the <voices> sounded for the second time immediately after they raised a clamor in the hunt, the strangers that had previously manifested only vaguely seemed to emerge clearly as an existence who had remained in the same place, certainly behaved toward them with awareness of their presence and hence demanded some reaction (including the option to not react). After "threatening" by barking back at the voices, they began to take an exploratory approach by producing pant-hoots and moving toward the source of the voices while pricking up their ears in order to explore the behavior and whereabouts of the strangers, such as whether they would take further action or not and whether they would continue to stay there or would be heading somewhere else. Because they began feeding after travelling northward, I began to feel that "nothing happened" after all, but they resumed their "exploration" as they discovered some fresh vestiges presumably of the strangers nearby by smelling the ground to check their whereabouts and kicking buttress roots and listening for a reaction to find out if they were around. The <voices> sounded for the third time amid this exploration making them realize that the strangers "were still in the vicinity", and accordingly they came to carry out further "exploration"; after moving toward the voices, they waited for the next round of voices and searched the vicinity.

In the deep forest, however, it was impossible to see the strangers or to know how many individuals were involved. In addition, the next voices took a long time to emanate despite their intensive waiting and only a few clues were found despite their intensive searching. Their tension and anxiety heightened inevitably in this situation where they might encounter strangers suddenly somewhere in the vicinity, i.e., they could not predict where the strangers were now, when and what action they would take next, even though they were certainly in the vicinity and aware of their presence. It is conceivable that as the strangers were also placed in a similar situation, they waited for voices from the chimpanzees I was observing and produced pant-hoots to explore their reaction while retreating. Under these circumstances, the <voices> sounded for the fourth time from a nearby location and they barked back uproariously. The strangers barked back in a similar manner, and the stormy interchange of voices continued for ten minutes.

By then, they had reached ("intruded on") an area that M-group chimpanzees rarely range in and was probably more frequently used by Y-group chimpanzees. However, firstly, there is no evidence that they perceived the area as "Y group's range". They probably understood that they were moving from a familiar area into an unfamiliar area, but there is no such thing as a clear-cut border line delineating the range's boundary like those humans draw on maps, and in any case we are unsure if they are capable of a categorization such as "Y group" in their languageless world. Secondly, the interchange of voices began mostly with barking but half way through became uproarious with wraa calls and screams (see the middle of Scene 5 in Appendix 8.1), indicating that they went into a state of panic. For this reason, it is difficult to suppose that they continued to "explore" to achieve a specific purpose (i.e., goal) such as "to antagonize through voices", let alone "to find and attack" the strangers. It seemed to me that they "did not know what to do" when they ended up in a shouting match, even though it was the outcome of their own "exploration". After the strangers stopped responding in the middle of the vocal interchange, they sat down, waited for the possible next voices for a short while and then turned back to the south. They no longer waited for voices or exhibited tension or anxiety after that (see the latter half of Scene 5 and Scene 6 in Appendix 8.1), even though the strangers remained invisible as before. As they ended their "exploration" and regained their composure at this point, they probably judged that "the strangers had left and no further action was expected", i.e., "there was no potential for further encounters with them" for the moment, based on the movement of the strangers' voices and the absence of their reaction and further vocalizations.

The series of behaviors the chimpanzees exhibited, including those in Episode 1, suggests that they were coordinating their choice of action each time using the otherness of strangers (i.e., the unpredictability or contingency of their presence/absence and behavior) as a resource, without pre-defining the course of potential interaction that could develop (or what existence the strangers could be to them), while showing tension and anxiety about the "potential for an encounter with strangers" that rose to the surface through voices and/or vestiges. In other words, the process-oriented approach to the otherness of their fellow group members involving "seeing what the other party will do", which characterizes their interaction through pant-hoots (see the beginning of this chapter), is thought to also apply to their interaction with strangers. They therefore exhibited various behaviors depending on the strangers' behavior and the degree to which they were aware of their presence (i.e., the level of auditory co-presence with the strangers): "passing off" the potential for an encounter for the time being, starting an "exploration" to prepare for a possible sudden encounter and ending it when nothing happened, or escalating from "threatening" to a "shouting match" and continuing their "exploration" until the potential for an encounter dissipates. Incidentally, many of them travelled southward on the day after Episode 2 (7

May), and stayed in the southern part of M group's home range on the following day as well; they did not "go on patrol in the north against another intrusion by strangers". This also offers a glimpse into their process-oriented attitude toward the otherness of strangers.

Of course, this does not mean that they did not anticipate at all how their interaction with the strangers would develop. They arrived at "confrontation" through voices in Episode 2, and there have been observed cases of antagonistic interactions involving physical contact in the past, as mentioned earlier. If they have had such experience in the past, no matter how rare, it is not surprising that they might begin to anticipate the possibility of an antagonistic interaction as the "potential for an encounter with strangers" or the "possibility that strangers would behave toward us" increased. In fact, the heightened tension among the chimpanzees made me think that an encounter with strangers would cause a huge tumult. My assistant and I hastily tried to check if anyone was injured after the shouting match in Episode 2 (and confirmed that no one was injured). Just after mostly male chimpanzees began their "exploration", following the sounding of the <voices> for the second time, two females left the party. Another female left the party soon after the <voices> sounded for the third time following the males' buttress kicking. Given that these females were carrying their infants, it is likely that they did so to avoid getting caught in a potentially dangerous situation as they acutely sensed the other individuals' demeanor of becoming absorbed in the "exploration" and the possible course of their interaction with strangers. Accordingly, it is conceivable that they anticipated at the time of the "exploration" that "We do not know what will happen if contact with strangers continues, including the possibility of resulting in an antagonistic interaction". If we accept that they had this anticipation, we must emphasize their "tolerance" or "toughness" toward the otherness of strangers in that despite this they continued to coordinate their action choices in response to the strangers' behavior on each occasion.

Avoidance

In Episode 3 below, which was observed on 8 August 2006 (see Appendix 8.2), some chimpanzees of M group were approached by chimpanzees presumably of N group in the south and behaved in a way to "avoid" further contact with them.

August is in the beginning of the congregating season when many M-group chimpanzees begin to range together forming a loose gathering, while repeatedly meeting and parting from one another. In this episode, the chimpanzees were ranging near Mount Mkulume in the southernmost part of the home range in mostly three parties (A, B and C), while switching members through occasionally meeting and parting, exchanging voices and letting others' voices pass. Then, pant-hoots and barks from many individuals, presumably of N group from the south, rang out from a relatively near location (a few hundred meters away) as if to overlay their voices. Accordingly, it is conceivable that it was obvious to the M-group chimpanzees without needing to "explore" that the strangers took that action in awareness of their presence, unlike when <voices> sounded in Episode 1, and that they might be "threatening" as their voices included barks. For this reason, we can surmise that from the start the strangers emerged as an existence demanding some reaction (including not reacting), and that therefore the M-group chimpanzees had no option to "pass off" as they did when <voices> sounded for the first time in Episode 2. Moreover, soon after that the voices of many individuals presumably of N group rang out for a second time from another location a short distance away from the source of the first voices. This suggests that there were at least two parties of strangers in this episode. Under these circumstances, although I had been feeling that I was inside the expanse of the social space of M-group chimpanzees through voices as usual until then, I felt a vague sense of unease about the sudden emergence of many likely strangers and the possibility that I might have been inside the expanse of their social space.

On this occasion, Party A clumped and stood on their hind legs to stare in the direction of the <voices> from the south when they rang out the first time. They barked back in an undertone and engaged in displays toward the <voices> in the second round, but in the end they headed in the opposite direction (northward). Party B, who had until then been intermittently exchanging pant-hoots with Party A and were feeding on treetops on this occasion, fell silent and remained on the spot when the <voices> sounded twice in succession. When the southern <voices> again rang out twice about twenty minutes later, one or two individuals on a treetop began diarrheic defecation. After that, when pant-hoots from Party A sounded from the east, all Party B members clumped and headed in the direction of the voices (eastward) while responding.

It seemed that strangers had emerged as an existence that demanded some reaction when the chimpanzees in Episode 2 barked back at the second <voices> that sounded immediately after their vocalization. This scene in Episode 3 was different from that occasion in that the chimpanzees were barked back at suddenly at closer range, <voices> continued to ring out in succession and (it felt as if) they were outnumbered. These circumstances are considered to be the major reasons for them choosing actions such as "avoiding while issuing half-hearted threats" (Party A) and "attempting to merge with companions" (for the meaning of "companion" see next section) (Party B). Nevertheless, they did not "escape immediately as a precaution against a possible attack by the strangers" either. While both parties exhibited a sense of tension and anxiety, they first silently remained on the spot and waited for the next possible voices for a while to explore the strangers' movement and action (in response to their silence). They did not seem to be so vigilant as to avoid being located or barked back at by the strangers, as they subsequently resumed pant-hoot exchanges with their own group members. It is possible to say that although in the end they "avoided" further contact with the strangers by leaving the place, both parties did so while "exploring" the strangers' behavior (and that of their own companions) with a process-oriented attitude. Incidentally, many of the observed individuals in Episode 3 were found in the central part of the home range by the day after next (10 August). On 29 August, most of them returned to the southernmost area where this episode had taken place, but their demeanors were no different to usual.

Solidarity with companions and the rigidity of interaction

Let us look at interactions among M-group chimpanzees upon hearing <voices> and what impact these intragroup interactions had on, and received from, their interactions with external "strangers".

In all of the episodes so far, we have seen that the individuals on the scene engaged "together" in actions such as silently approaching the source of the <voice> and quietly waiting for the possible next <voice>, emitting wraa calls, barking back or leaving the scene after remaining silent for a while. It is likely that the synchronization of their actions led them to perceive themselves, who were dealing with strangers' otherness together while sharing in tension and anxiety, as "companions" (in the sense of being more than mere "acquaintances" with whom they routinely associated), and this solidarity in turn promoted their immersion in their interactions with the strangers[2]. Here, I show that the circle of such companions can spread beyond individuals within sight and elicit the characteristics of interactions among companions.

As I mentioned in the previous section, Party B in Episode 3 remained silent when the southern <voices> rang out in succession, but when a chorus of pant-hoots was raised by Party A in the east, with whom they had exchanged pant-hoots intermittently, they headed in that direction (east) while responding to the chorus. We shall focus on what happened after that. When another pant-hoot chorus was again emitted by Party A, which had moved slightly to the north, four chimpanzees in Party B adjusted their direction of movement from east to northeast (i.e., the direction from which the second chorus of Party A was heard). About ten minutes later, they "called" by pant-hooting and listened for a response. Party A did not respond, but they heard a response from Party C (west) as well as another round of southern <voices> (barks and pant-hoots). At that time, some in Party B huddled together while grimacing (a so-called cry face with the ends of the mouth pulled back and the upper and lower teeth exposed) or screaming. After coming to a standstill in this manner, when pant-hoots from Party C rang out again, they hurried westward while responding to the voices; they then merged with Party C and headed north together.

It is common for M-group chimpanzees to not merge with the other party after exchanging pant-hoots. In addition, they are generally unperturbed when the other party in an ongoing pant-hoot exchange does not respond to their pant-hoots produced as "calls" (which accompanies the behavior of "listening for a response") or when another party responds to them unexpectedly (Hanamura 2017; see also its summary at the beginning of this chapter). Accordingly, the movement of Party B and the loss of composure exhibited by some individuals at this scene suggest that they were, as an exception, strongly aiming to achieve a specific goal, such as merging (i.e., achieving visual co-presence) and/or exchanging pant-hoots (i.e., constructing or maintaining auditory co-presence) with the other party, from whom they had been staying apart and with whom they had not always exchanged pant-hoots. In other words, the circle of companions to deal with the strangers' otherness together spread to other parties with whom they had been ranging while forming a loose gathering with intermittent pant-hoot exchanges on that day.

Thus, in all episodes we can confirm solidarity among companions mediated by the encounters with strangers. From another perspective, however, this kind of solidarity means that they were unable to continue fission-fusion grouping (or repeatedly meeting and parting) and interactions via pant-hoots "in the usual manner". Meetings and partings seldom occur while chimpanzees are banding together to "explore" or "avoid", except for some individuals who depart or merge before or after the act. The membership of a "party", which is supposed to be essentially fluid, remains almost constant as if they were a "troop" or "team". The aforementioned movement of Party B and the perturbation exhibited by some of its members in Episode 3 indicate that they were no longer able to "coordinate their action choices with their usual process-oriented attitude" in interactions via pant-hoots with the other individuals in their own group. In short, when strangers emerge, chimpanzees lose their usual "autonomy, flexibility and tolerance for ambiguous interactions" (Itoh 2013: 119) in fission-fusion grouping and interactions via pant-hoots among acquaintances/companions, and those interactions become rigid (see also Itoh 2017 and Chapter Seven by Itoh for their usual manner of fission-fusion grouping, i.e., the way they meet and move apart).

Process- and goal-orientation in dealing with strangers' otherness

The M-group chimpanzees sometimes heard the voices that came on rare occasions from the outer edges of their home range as the "voices of strangers" and exhibited tension, anxiety and surprise or alarm toward the "potential for an encounter with strangers" that surfaced through such voices or the vestiges discovered in the vicinity of the source or the peripheral part of the home range. Yet, when they ranged in the peripheral part, they did not appear to take any special measures against strangers unless they encountered voices or vestiges presumably of strangers. Even when strange voices rang out, at least in the case where they had not produced loud vocalizations for a while until that point and hence the strangers were unlikely to be aware of their presence, they "passed off" the arising potential to interact with them for the moment and continued ranging and engaging in activity with vocalizations in the same way as before (Scene 1 in Episode 2). Because of their continued ranging and activity, strangers might come to notice and take action (Scene 2).

In some cases (Episode 1), strangers are potentially aware of their presence due to the fact that they had been vocalizing shortly before the strange voices rang out, but auditory co-presence with the strangers was unclear unlike in the cases where they barked back at or were barked back at by strangers. On these occasions, they began to explore the strangers' movement – while the state of co-presence remained uncertain – by silently "approaching and waiting for voices". When they discovered strange vestiges, they also kept silent and began to "search" the vicinity to explore the strangers' whereabouts. Because such "explorations" rely on the other party's next voices and/or vestiges exclusively, they attempted to maintain (unilateral) auditory and/or olfactory contact with the strangers. They sometimes took an "exploratory approach" by emitting pant-hoots or kicking buttress roots in order to explore the strangers' reaction or presence/absence. If there was no further encounter with voices or vestiges and "nothing happened", they ended their "exploration".

In other cases, it became clear that strangers were staying there and making an approach to them because the strange voices sounded repeatedly and overlapped with their own vocalizations. In these cases auditory co-presence with the strangers was unlikely to be avoidable or was forced upon them. On these occasions, they might bark back to "threaten", and if the strangers barked back in response, the situation could lead to a stormy interchange of voices ("confrontation"). However, whether the strangers had "left" or would "take no further action" could only be judged by the repetition of "the absence of the ensuing vocalization or reaction" when they approached and waited for voices, took an exploratory approach by pant-hooting or threatened by barking, as well as "their absence or the absence of vestiges and other clues" when they searched (Scenes 2–6 in Episode 2). When they were barked back at suddenly and outnumbered by strangers, they might turn back to "avoid" further contact with them while staying put in silence for a while to explore the movement and next action of the strangers or attempting to merge with other companions (Episode 3).

Thus, when strangers emerged through voices and/or vestiges, while exploring their unpredictable (as to when and where the next voices or vestiges would be encountered or how they would take action) and contingent (i.e., no voices when waited for, no presence or clues when searched for or no reaction when an approach was made) presence and behavior, chimpanzees coordinated their action choices according to what the strangers did or did not do next (e.g., the type and timing of vocalization and the number of the vocalizers, etc.) and the degree of auditory co-presence. We can say that through this exploratory manner they felt for a possible relationship or way of association with strangers in each case such as "what kind of interaction could we develop (or not)" and "which party leaves". However, they were not committed to determining the type of relationship; they sometimes left it unclear by ending an "exploration" when they did not encounter further voices or vestiges or simply "passing off" the arising potential to interact without even exploring.

In the evolutionary history of human society, strangers must also have constantly emerged. Our ancestors presumably lived in groups, expanded their area of inhabitation and travelling distance through the usage of fire and technical innovation and broadened their symbolic world through the acquisition of language. Consequently, we humans would have encountered aliens who appear very rarely, the dead or ghosts as well as the living, and spirits, specters or deities that cause extraordinary phenomena. While feeling awed by such various strangers, we have weaved "stories of relationships" with them through rituals and have built up pluralistic (or multi-dimensional) societies by sublimating their otherness into those stories. For outsiders, who belong to other groups with relatively higher frequencies of contact, we have tended to categorize them according to the groups they belong to, assigning "visages (attributes)" to each "them" of those groups, such as "friends" with whom we should trade, "guests" whom we should welcome, "enemies" whom we should exclude and so on, and have built up polyptychial (or multi-layered) society by reclaiming their otherness into these "frames of relationship"[3].

Thus, when humans encounter strangers, they reduce the strangers' otherness and limit their own action choices by referring to the institutions (i.e., stories or frames of relationship) that have been precipitated external to their actual interactions in each case and hence take on apriority. This manner of dealing with the otherness of strangers can be called "goal-oriented" in the sense that the content of the interaction to be performed (or what existence the strangers are to them) is determined in advance of actual interactions and the relationship (i.e., the *goal*, which is a specific condition or a certain order directed by the story or the frame) is reproduced stably. Of course, the relationship has to be felt for or modified for newly encountered strangers or those who no longer fit into the existing story or frame. Even in these cases, however, what humans have been doing is deciding which story or frame to adopt by using the existing ones as clues, or creating new stories or frames that can stabilize relationships.

On the other hand, when chimpanzees encounter strangers, they coordinate their action choices using the otherness of strangers as a resource where they find few clues for what kind of relationship they can form. This manner of dealing with the otherness of strangers can be called "process-oriented" in the sense that they either feel for a possible relationship with the strangers or leave it undetermined, depending on how the potential interaction unfolds (i.e., the *process*) in each case (without predetermining what existence the strangers are to them). Unlike humans, they would not aim for a stable relationship with strangers, and the strangers would also not seek a stable relationship with them. Accordingly, they "passed off" the voices of strangers that were unlikely to concern them. Even with those voices likely to concern them, they "explored" the whereabouts and behavior of the strangers only when continuing to encounter their voices and/or vestiges, and did not seem to act with the purpose of achieving a clear state of hostile or non-hostile co-presence. Where co-presence (or encounter) was unlikely to be avoidable, they attempted to dissolve the co-presence by "threatening" or "avoiding", just as in the case of intergroup interactions in other primate species (see the second section of this chapter).

Now, why can encounters between chimpanzees belonging to different groups lead to intensely antagonistic interactions that have not been reported in other primates? While chimpanzees have no voices entirely dedicated to coordinating intergroup spatial distance, their very loud vocalizations such as pant-hoots used mainly in intragroup interactions can reach individuals of neighboring groups. While they also have no explicit marking behaviors that can function to restrain "intrusions" by individuals of neighboring groups, they are sensitive to smells and vestiges as they acquire some information from them left by other individuals of their own group on a daily basis. These auditory and olfactory intragroup interactions produce chances for individuals belonging to different groups to notice each other's presence, but the voices and vestiges do not provide unambiguous meanings such as "Stay away" or "This is our area". Although they can bark back or scream at strangers upon hearing their voices, it is difficult for them to clearly "threaten" or "avoid" them in non-face-to-face interactions through nonlinguistic vocalizations. It is thought that these characteristics of their intergroup interaction partly contribute to their process-oriented attitude with which they "explore" one another's whereabouts and behavior through voices and vestiges. However, their "explorations" seldom result in visual contact, and the size of the other party remains unclear as both parties range over a large area while merging and separating repeatedly, heightening tension and anxiety before visual encounters. This situation promotes solidarity among individuals acting together in each group and elevates the interaction between individuals belonging to different groups to an interaction between monolithic "teams", thus producing strong tension and anxiety such that could send them into a panic in the stormy interchange of voices in Episode 2. In this way, before encountering visually, the situation where an intensely antagonistic interaction can easily occur upon encountering is already ripe, even though and precisely because visual encounters seldom take place[4].

The way chimpanzees deal with the otherness of strangers and the characteristics of their auditory and olfactory interaction as discussed so far are also considered to be the background reasons for the frequent "patrols" and "intrusions" reported in some research sites. Let's say the incidence of encounters with voices and vestiges increases temporarily, triggered by an abundant production of delicious fruits in an overlapping area of the home ranges of two neighboring groups or any other phenomenon, and results in a frequent occurrence of events similar to Episode 2. In some cases when they range in this area, their tension and anxiety may be aroused in anticipation of the presence of strangers even without encountering voices or vestiges. Such anticipation would be able to lead them to repeat "explorations" (or "patrols"), resulting "intrusions" and vocal interchanges (or "confrontation"). Once an intensely antagonistic interaction accompanying physical contact arises, it can aggravate their tension and anxiety further, which, together with growing anticipation of physical danger, may convert their process-oriented attitude into a goal-oriented one. Consequently, the strangers may temporarily materialize as "enemies" amongst some individuals who have had repeated encounters with them, even though language would be needed for this "visage" to become fixed and decontextualized and to develop apriority[5].

As far as the invasion of Kahama group by Kasekela group in Gombe is concerned, Goodall (1990) and Wrangham (Wrangham and Peterson 1996) were shocked by the "killings" committed by former acquaintances that had belonged to one group prior to a split. Yet, it is also conceivable that because "former acquaintances had become strangers they did not know well", they repeatedly felt for a way of associating with them but in the process their mutual otherness at the time was highlighted by the gap with that in the past when they had been acquaintances, leading to frequent antagonistic interactions. In human society, separation and hostility can result from the continuation of the "activation of difference" by which people who have been living without any hostility are divided into two sub-groups on the basis of a particular difference identified in relation to some sort of problem, other pending problems are also reclassified on the basis of that particular difference and various traits emphasizing the difference, from symbols such as clothing, rituals and flags to legal systems, are rediscovered or newly invented on both sides (Fukushima 1998; see also "symmetrical schismogenesis" in Bateson 1972). It is suspected that in chimpanzees in Gombe, their separation and hostility were brought on because a particular difference surrounding some sort of problem (e.g. a slight bias in affiliation and/or the range of their main use) they shared was continually activated, and that the problem persisted even after separation until one of the groups disappeared. According to the description by Goodall (1990), in this process that lasted many years, elder males who had lived together previously appeared to have continued their affiliative interactions beyond group difference, but eventually they, too, were caught in the activation of difference and one of those males ended up as a victim of violence.

The Gombe case is a valuable example that suggests that chimpanzees can create and maintain the boundary between "companions and strangers" monolithically among individuals within a group, and come to produce their spatial separation according to the boundary after the fact without language (that is the basis of category, symbol and institution)[6]. It is conceivable that on this occasion they assigned the "visage" of "enemy" to the strangers and limited their action choices according to the "frame" of that specific (i.e., hostile, here) relationship, although it happened by force of circumstances based on the actual unfolding of their interaction. If this is the case, we can state that the process-oriented way is pregnant with the potential for precipitation of the goal-oriented way and its "frame". In this sense, the process-oriented way forms the evolutionary foundation of the way to deal with the otherness of strangers that is common to humans and chimpanzees, but as demonstrated by Itoh (Chapter Seven) and Nishie (Chapter Six), chimpanzees have been evolving in the opposite direction from humans, strengthening the process-oriented attitude, that is, tolerance to the otherness of various others. This tolerance or "toughness" would have enabled chimpanzees to continue interactions with a "flexible and ambiguity-tolerant" attitude without fixing ideas about what form of existence various "others" or the "self" were, unlike interactions among humans living in a language world, and in turn would have been underpinned by such interactions.

It is a fact that in some cases hostility between chimpanzees belonging to different groups intensifies unusually. In both academic and public media, there has been a tendency to emphasize chimpanzees' hostility against individuals of neighboring groups via their behaviors on these occasions, and the behaviors are easy to regard as those adopted with a goal-oriented attitude (see the second section of this chapter). As discussed above, however, such hostile events are thought to occur precisely because they adopt a process-oriented attitude and hence refrain from determining their relationship in advance. No former-Gombe-like situations have taken place, at least between the individuals of M group and their neighboring groups, in Mahale in recent years. I suspect that where there are multiple neighboring groups in other research sites, which have always been separate groups[7], the chimpanzees lead their lives primarily within their respective groups without much intergroup contact; of course they would from time to time encounter one another's voices and vestiges, but their behaviors in such circumstances would be rarely "confrontation", instead usually "exploring" or "passing off" the arising potential to interact, or "threatening" or "avoiding" in an attempt to dissolve the resultant state of co-presence against the background that they "know little" about the strangers. In any case, historical and context-sensitive analysis appears to be indispensable in the study of intergroup relations in chimpanzees.

Others in chimpanzee society: Strangers and acquaintances

Society where members can stay apart

There is no doubt that the way we humans associate with others was dramatically altered through the acquisition of language. Humans have been shaping their group living by dealing with the otherness of not only individuals of other groups, but also of their own group using the "goal-oriented way" supported by language and institutions. For instance, we not only perceive "those" with whom we conduct trade to be "our" "friends", but we also mutually perceive "each" of us to be "somebody" with a particular "role" to play in the division of labor and cooperation (see Chapter Seventeen by Takenoshita). Similarly, the "process-oriented way" of M-group chimpanzees toward the otherness of individuals of other groups was found to be essentially the same as the way they dealt with the otherness of their fellow group members in non-face-to-face interactions through pant-hoots (see the beginning of this chapter). However, there were major differences in terms of the options for action they could choose and interactions that could unfold, though there was a degree of overlap, depending on whether the other party in the interaction was "strangers" or "acquaintances". Let us look at the differences in order to examine what existence "strangers" and "acquaintances" are to them, and explore the characteristics of their group living.

When strangers who emerged through voices were "likely to be aware of our presence" or when chimpanzees discovered fresh vestiges suggesting that strangers were "likely to be still in the vicinity", they attempted to maintain auditory and/or olfactory contact with the strangers in order to "explore" their whereabouts and behavior, while exhibiting tension and anxiety and refraining from ordinary activity with vocalizations. For this reason, we can say that "strangers" to chimpanzees are others who unnerve them under the condition that they "do not know where they are now, where they have gone – when and where we might encounter them visually or aurally" as long as the potential for an encounter is arising. We can rephrase this as others whom they "cannot stay apart from" in preparation for a possible sudden encounter, in which they do not know what will happen because they "do not routinely encounter" them and have no previous experience of non-hostile co-presence. When an auditory co-presence (or auditory encounter) with strangers occurs, they "avoid", "threaten" or sometimes come to a "vocal confrontation" with them while "exploring" their whereabouts and behavior; as a result, they repeatedly end up "not encountering" them visually, and accordingly these others become distinguished from "acquaintances".

On the other hand, chimpanzees do not show a distinct sense of tension or anxiety toward voices of their acquaintances unless they are screams, barks or wraa calls. If the voices are pant-hoots, even when the vocalizers are unlikely to be aware of their presence, the hearers sometimes attempt to create auditory co-presence by making an approach such as responding or calling anew after listening for the presence/absence of other parties' responses to the voice they have heard. What I would like to stress here is that even when the vocalizers are almost certainly aware of their presence or making an approach to them, the hearers are able to "defer" or "pass off", not particularly avoid or explore, the arising potential for an encounter or further interactions (Hanamura 2017). When they discover fresh vestiges, they often smell them and sometimes the surrounding ground, but most of the time they "pass off" the arising potential for an encounter without pertinaciously searching the vicinity. In contrast to "strangers", "acquaintances" to them are others who do not unnerved them under the condition that they "do not know when and where they will encounter them" when the potential to encounter them is arising. They are rephrased as the others whom they "can stay apart from" without particularly preparing for a possible sudden encounter with them as the result of the repetition of visual meeting and parting (i.e., fission-fusion grouping) and the generation and vanishment of auditory co-presence (i.e., interactions through pant-hoots).

When strangers emerged through voices and/or vestiges, chimpanzees were no longer able to continue their usual "flexible and ambiguity-tolerant" fission-fusion grouping or interaction through pant-hoots as they sought solidarity. For this reason, we can surmise that their "society where they can stay apart from one another" is realized on the premise that "there are no strangers", although it is normally self-evident and they would not be conscious of it. However, there is no guarantee that they can maintain non-hostile co-presence in the future with others with whom they sometimes go without encountering for months, even in the case of acquaintances. In fact, there has been an observed case of a "solitary male" who spent a long period of time ranging on his own and avoided encounters with others in his group, especially other males, for months or years (during which he refrained from recurrent non-hostile co-presence) in Mahale. The solitary male and some other males in the group exhibited tension and anxiety toward each other's voices and vestiges similar to those exhibited toward "strangers", and sometimes engaged in persistent "explorations" (Chapter Six by Nishie). In addition, newly-immigrated females (who have still little experience with recurrent non-hostile co-presence) seem to tend to follow another individual when ranging and stay within the audible range of other individuals' voices especially when they venture alone (Hanamura, unpublished data), suggesting that they "cannot stay apart from" other group members compared to resident individuals who were born in the group or have spent many years in the group after immigration.

In view of the above, for individuals who have not met or heard each other's voices for some time, it is apparent that it is not easy to associate in the same way as before when they reunite, to construct a state of co-presence through pant-hoots, to continue their respective activities under such visual or auditory co-presence and to again go their separate ways even beyond the audible range. As Kitamura (Chapter Four) and Itoh (Chapter Seven) state, their group living is a very fragile phenomenon operating based only on the repetitions of non-hostile visual and auditory co-presence in the sense that it provides no other clues to confirm "membership of the same group", unlike in the case of humans who can utilize language and institutions as the clue nor in the case of many other primates who can utilize their own spatial proximity (i.e., troop or cohesive aggregation). In this style of group living, the frequent emergence of strangers would hinder its stable reproduction or alter its mode from a "flexible" to a "rigid" one. It is uncertain whether they are aware of this, but strangers are certainly others who threaten the stability of their everyday living. Nevertheless, as if to maintain this vulnerability of group living to strangers rather than resolve it, the chimpanzees in the episodes discussed above dealt with the otherness of strangers with a process-oriented attitude, probably because this way of interaction is essential for reproducing their unique style of group living.

Acquaintance/stranger boundary, and strangers in the eyes of females

It must be important for the stable reproduction of chimpanzees' group living that the voices of "acquaintances" and "strangers" are distinguished, and that the distinction is shared among all group members. As mentioned in the section entitled "The voices of strangers from the outer edges of the home range", it is thought that they perceive "stranger-ness" in voices emanating from the outer edges of the home range where they ("we") rarely range. However, because of their fission-fusion grouping, they have no direct means of confirming that their individual ranges are roughly the same area. Therefore, it is unlikely that "the boundary between acquaintances and strangers" (i.e., voices emanating from which area are perceived as "strangers' voices") rooted in each individual's ranging area is monolithic or previously shared among all members. Now we shall review the analyzed episodes above by focusing on the behaviors of newly immigrated females.

In Episode 2, when individuals in the party raised wraa calls successively upon hearing the northern <voices> for the first time, Tarnie, the only new female in the party, gazed in the direction of the voices (north) intently and watched other individuals producing wraa calls without uttering the call herself. In the middle of Episode 3, when resident individuals in Party B (Kalunde and Nkombo) were upset that southern strangers reacted to their voices and their interaction with Party A did not go as expected, two new females (Vera and Tarnie), who had been following the two residents, watched them without exhibiting similar perturbation. When the two residents turned around to merge with Party C, Vera followed them whereas Tarnie remained on the spot and even began to nap. When the southern <voices> sounded from a slightly more eastern location, she began to travel eastward in parallel to the voices. On the way, she met Qanat, another new female who was travelling in the direction of the voices (south) after parting from Party A, which had headed north upon hearing the southern <voices>. The two females were completely separated from the other M-group chimpanzees, who all ended up choosing "avoidance" and went north, and continued to travel eastward in parallel to the southern <voices> that were also heading east.

In this way, newly immigrated females do not seem to hear <voices> in the same way as resident individuals, because they sometimes behave in a distinctly different manner toward the <voices>. If new females are not yet familiar with the home range of their new group, they cannot be sure where the outer edges are. Even when they are familiar with the range, "over there" can be an appealing or very familiar place for them, considering that they sometimes transfer between multiple groups or temporarily return to their native group until they give birth. The two females in Episode 3, Tarnie and Qanat, were found to be ranging with other M-group chimpanzees in the central part of M group's home range two days later, but newly immigrated females (as well as pre-emigrated young females) may end up transferring to other groups on these occasions, sometimes without knowing it.

On the other hand, in all of the episodes, like the males, resident females heard the <voices> as "strangers' voices" that aroused tension and anxiety, indicating that females eventually take on the attitude toward strangers as residents after immigration. In fact, in February 2014, some eight years after Episode 3, I observed Qanat, who had, after all, remained with M group and had two children, upon hearing <voices>, standing up on her hind legs ahead of other individuals in the party and engaging in nipple fumbling while holding on to another female. In addition, around thirty years before Episode 2, in which a resident female of M group, Gwekulo, took part in a vocal confrontation with individuals presumably of

Y group while stomping on the ground, she who had still not immigrated into M group and had been a member of K group at that time had been observed to take part in a similar confrontation with M-group individuals (Nishida 1979). While the newly immigrated females in Episode 2 and 3 behaved differently from the rest, they observed the way resident individuals in the party behaved unusually in response to <voices> and sometimes came to range in the same way as the resident individuals through their involvement in interactions between the residents and strangers. As newly immigrated females experience these events repeatedly, albeit infrequently, they would come to learn through the behaviors of various resident individuals on each occasion to hear the voices emanating from certain places – which eventually become the outer edges of the group's home range – as "strangers' voices" in the same way that resident individuals did, and come to share with resident individuals the experience of interactions with strangers while learning their conventional ranging area.

Nevertheless, the attitude of resident females toward strangers was slightly different from that of males. It appeared that resident females exhibited less tension and anxiety than males and tended to "pass off" strangers' voices, even when the strangers were likely to be aware of their presence, with an attitude that was somewhat closer to the attitude they would exhibit upon hearing acquaintances' voices. For instance, only males had diarrheic defecation in Episode 1 and Effie, a resident female, was feeding nonchalantly while males were kicking buttress roots and pricking up their ears for a reaction half way through Episode 2. In Episode 3, after Nkombo, a resident female, headed to the west in an upset manner, she returned when she heard Vera's scream. The behavior of the resident females with infants in Episode 2, leaving or not following the party when most members of the party were absorbed in "explorations", can be interpreted as an expression of their attitude of not being overly concerned about the presence of strangers in addition to avoiding a situation that was potentially dangerous for their infants. I suspect that females' experience of transferring between groups is a factor behind this attitude. Perhaps strangers are simply "an unfamiliar existence" to male chimpanzees, who have no opportunity to live outside of their own group, whereas it is easier for strangers to emerge as "beings similar to us who could be acquaintances although they are not acquaintances now" to female chimpanzees who have come from the "outside".

There is no doubt that intergroup transfer and traffic have fostered the community consciousness that unites multiple groups in the evolutionary history of human society as well. As Kawai (Chapter Nine) discusses, our empathy with individuals of other groups and consequently diverse intergroup relationships are thought to have evolved alongside this consciousness; such empathy would have also helped to alter intergroup relationships from hostile to hospitable ones as it has the power to shake the existing relationship frames.

Appendix 8.1

Arrow legend

⟶ Ranging route in each scene

⋯▶ Estimated ranging route

⟶ Ranging route in previous scene

Case 2 (6 May 2006)

Scene 1

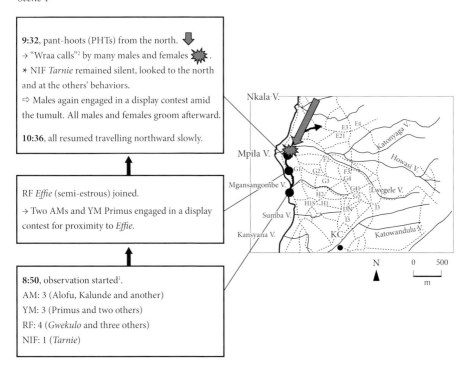

9:32, pant-hoots (PHTs) from the north. ⬇
→ "Wraa calls"[2] by many males and females ✸.
★ NIF *Tarnie* remained silent, looked to the north and at the others' behaviors.
⇨ Males again engaged in a display contest amid the tumult. All males and females groom afterward.

10:36, all resumed travelling northward slowly.

⬆

RF *Effie* (semi-estrous) joined.
→ Two AMs and YM Primus engaged in a display contest for proximity to *Effie*.

⬆

8:50, observation started[1].
AM: 3 (Alofu, Kalunde and another)
YM: 3 (Primus and two others)
RF: 4 (*Gwekulo* and three others)
NIF: 1 (*Tarnie*)

Notes: Abbreviation, age class and immigration status: Adult Male (AM: ≥ 16 years old); Young Male (YM: 9–15); Resident Female (RF: ≥ 5th year since transfer); Newly-Immigrated Female (NIF: ≤ 4th year, nulliparous); Young Female (YF: born in M group, 9–12). [1] Only individuals aged 9 or older are shown (females in italics). [2] See text in the section entitled "The voices of strangers from the outer edges of the home range".

Scene 2

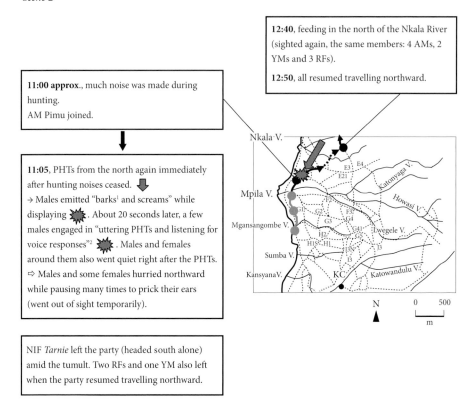

11:00 approx., much noise was made during hunting.
AM Pimu joined.

11:05, PHTs from the north again immediately after hunting noises ceased.
→ Males emitted "barks[1] and screams" while displaying. About 20 seconds later, a few males engaged in "uttering PHTs and listening for voice responses"[2]. Males and females around them also went quiet right after the PHTs.
⇨ Males and some females hurried northward while pausing many times to prick their ears (went out of sight temporarily).

12:40, feeding in the north of the Nkala River (sighted again, the same members: 4 AMs, 2 YMs and 3 RFs).
12:50, all resumed travelling northward.

NIF *Tarnie* left the party (headed south alone) amid the tumult. Two RFs and one YM also left when the party resumed travelling northward.

Notes: [1] Uttered mostly at conspecifics (rarely heterospecifics such as humans and snakes) in the context of intimidation, accusation and protestation, and sometimes accompany screams from individuals who are barked at or nearby. [2] Staying still and listening for about 10 seconds after the end of the utterance according to the customary pattern of vocal exchange within 10 seconds: a behavior to listen for a "response" to a PHT ("call") one has just emitted; note, however, that a PHT is uttered in various other contexts and often without accompanying the behavior of "listening for" (Hanamura 2017).

Scene 3

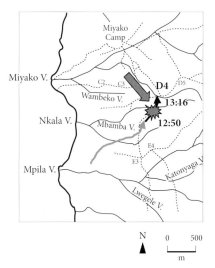

12:50, fresh feeding vestiges on an observation trail.
→ Many individuals sniffed the vestiges and the ground around them.
⇨ All clumped together and travelled northward in silence while pausing and looking around many times.
12:54, some males kicked buttress roots a few times while emitting PHT-like "fow" sounds in low voices 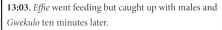, then hurried northward while pricking their ears.

12:57, PHTs and screams from the north ⬇.
→ All clumped again, AM Alofu engaged in "nipple fumbling"[1] with his mouth open.
12:59, all resumed travelling northward.

RF *Fuji* departed, leaving 4 AMs, 2 YMs and 2 RFs (*Gwekulo* and *Effie*) in the party.

13:03, *Effie* went feeding but caught up with males and *Gwekulo* ten minutes later.
13:16, the party reached D4 ridge.

Note. [1] A habit of some individuals, often accompanying a grimace (cry face) or hand reaching to another individual and occasionally wraa calls.

Scene 4

13:16~, all (4 AMs, 2 YMs and 2 RFs) clumped and sat down at D4 ridge for some time while gazing in the northerly direction, and then began feeding nearby.

13:32, all around D4 suddenly rushed into bushes to the north.

All reached C4 ridge, sat down for a while, and hurried back to the south via D3 (only intermittent observations due to the rush through the bush).

14:45, all returned to D4.

During this scene, all remained silent and no voice emanated from the north either.

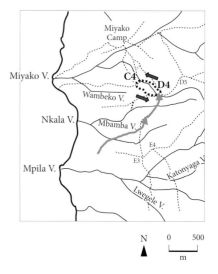

During this scene, the membership remained unchanged.

Scene 5

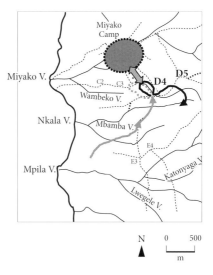

14:47, two minutes after returning to D4, PHTs from 🌀. ⬇
→ Males raised PHTs and barks ⬆ while displaying and entered the northern bush again.
→ RF *Gwekulo* also uttered PHTs ⬆ while slapping the ground and *Effie* uttered barks. ⬆

14:49, PHTs, barks and screams rang out from 🌀 again. ⬇
→ The observed party issued PHTs, barks, screams and wraa calls, although observation was impeded by thick bushes. ⬆

14:53, raucous voices rang out from 🌀 again and lasted for 1 minute or so. ⬇
→ The observed party raised raucous voices, including wraa calls.

14:56, the observed party raised barks and screams. ⬆
→ No voice from 🌀.

15:02, the observed party raised PHTs and barks. ⬆
→ No voice from 🌀.
⇨ All sat down for a few moments and then changed their course to the east and return to the south.

15:30, all returned to D4, continued on to the east, and turned southward just before D5.

The membership remained unchanged from Scene 4.

Scene 6

I got ahead of them and waited at E3.

16:20, PHTs from the observed party a short distance to the north ✳.

16:56, all (4 AMs, 2 YMs and 2 RFs, unchanged) reached E3.

All travelled slowly southward while feeding intermittently.

On the way, RF *Fuji*, who had departed before D4 in Scene 3, rejoined.

18:00, end of observation.

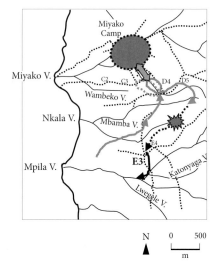

Appendix 8.2

Episode (8 August 2006)
In the morning, four AMs (Alofu, Kalunde, Bonobo and another), three YMs, four RFs (*Nkombo* and three others), two NIFs (*Qanat*, in the fourth year after immigration and *Tarnie*, in the third year) and one YF ranged in loose formation while exchanging pant-hoots occasionally in a low-lying area in the southernmost part of M group's home range (N'ganja: see Figure 8.1). I observed *Tarnie* and my research assistant observed Alofu. It was either confirmed or presumed that many of the other M-group members were not in this area on that day.

At around **11:30**, Alofu, one YM and five females (Party A) climbed Mount Mkulume on the eastern side (see Figure 8.1) and engaged in feeding and hunting there until 14:25. Meanwhile, Kalunde, Bonobo, *Nkombo* and *Tarnie* incrementally moved eastward while exchanging pant-hoots with Party A to the east and other parties intermittently. On the way, an NIF named *Vera* (in the second week) joined and Bonobo departed to the west, and the party (Party B) began feeding before Mount Mkulume at **13:28**. Bonobo merged with three males just to the west (Party C[1]).

14:25 Party B responded to pant-hoots from Party A in the east. Overlapping the response pant-hoots, pant-hoots and barks from many individuals rang out in the south. Although Party B feeding on the treetop was out of sight, no movement was detected and feeding sound stopped.

14:27 Pant-hoots from many individuals again rang out from the same area in the south, although slightly away from the previous location. Party B remained silent.

Meanwhile in Party A, Alofu and some females clumped in response to the first round of southern voices and stood on hind legs to gaze in the direction of the voices. They barked back at the second round of southern voices in an undertone while engaging in displays and then headed north.

14:50 Pant-hoots and barks from many individuals sounded twice in succession from the south. About thirty seconds later, diarrheic feces dropped from the tree on which Kalunde and *Nkombo* were staying.

14:58 Pant-hoots from Party A rang out in the east twice, slightly to the north of the previous location. Party B descended the tree in a hurry while responding to the second chorus of pant-hoots and ran eastward; Kalunde, *Nkombo*, *Tarnie* and *Vera* clumped and began to ascend Mount Mkulume in that order.

15:08 Pant-hoots from Party A rang out again in a location further north of the previous position. Kalunde changed his course to the northeast upon hearing the voices and the other three followed.

15:19 Kalunde, *Nkombo* and *Tarnie* uttered pant-hoots and listened for a response. At that moment, barks and pant-hoots rang out again in the south. At the same time, pant-hoots presumably from Party C[1] rang out from the west. No response from

Party A. Kalunde looked toward each source of voices while grimacing (cry face), and *Nkombo* made physical contact with Kalunde while screaming in an undertone. *Tarnie* and *Vera* sat down nearby and watched Kalunde and *Nkombo* without grimacing or screaming.

15:21 Pant-hoots from presumably Party C rang out in the west again. Kalunde and *Nkombo* doubled back to the west while responding to the voices and descended the mountain[2]. *Tarnie* also responded, but she did not follow the two. *Vera* did not respond and began uttering "hoo, hoo, hoo"[3] while gazing in the direction where the two went.

15:22 *Vera* continued to utter the same voice, and when *Tarnie* tapped *Vera's* arm, she screamed. *Nkombo* came back and charged at *Tarnie*, then turned back to the west in a hurry. *Vera* followed her to the west[2] while looking back at *Tarnie* a few times. *Tarnie* leaned on a nearby shrub.

15:40 *Tarnie* bagan to nap.

15:59 Individuals in the south appeared to have moved slightly to the east as pant-hoots rang out from a location slightly to the east of the previous position. *Tarnie* got up, looked in the direction of the voices, got off the shrub and began to climb the mountain to the east.

16:09 *Qanat* appeared (who was seen with Party A at least until 15:15, so presumably she subsequently left Party A and travelled southward). *Tarnie* uttered "ha" at *Qanat* and the two climbed further to the east together.

16:13 Pant-hoots rang out from the southeast again. The two paused and looked toward the voices, then resumed travelling to the east.

16:25 I lost sight of the two due to rugged terrain.

Notes: Abbreviations as per Appendix 8.1. [1]Another research assistant, different from the assistant observing Alofu (Party A), confirmed that Party C was in the low-lying area in the west (N'ganja: see Figure 8.1) until around 15:30. [2]Because a research assistant lost sight of Alofu and other members of Party A, who were travelling northward, at 15:15, he descended the mountain to listen for voices in the low-lying area. The assistant, there at 15:50, saw all of Party C as well as Kalunde, *Nkombo* and *Vera* (all of Party B except for *Tarnie*), who were travelling from the west to the north. [3]This voice is commonly made by infants calling their mothers nearby. It is sometimes uttered by mothers who lose sight of their infants, and on rare occasions, uttered by an adult who has lost sight of his/her friends.

9 The Origins of "Consideration for One's Enemy": What Kind of Others Are Neighboring Groups to the Dodoth?

Kaori Kawai

Key ideas

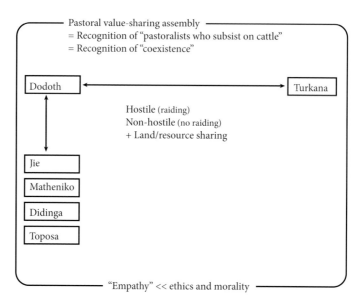

The pastoral people of Dodoth in Uganda live adjacent to the Turkana (Kenya) as well as the Jie (Uganda), Matheniko (Uganda), Didinga (South Sudan) and Toposa (South Sudan). Relations between these neighboring groups oscillate over time between a "hostile" relationship involving mutual livestock raiding and a "non-hostile" relationship involving the joint use of the same grazing areas and watering places without raiding. It is thought that these groups consciously/subconsciously form a higher-order assembly of "pastoralists who subsist on cattle" called the "pastoral value-sharing assembly". It is considered that ethics or morality is shared within the assembly and is engendered by "empathy" as a biological and evolutionary mental foundation.

Coexistence in mutual raiding

The Dodoth peoples are cattle pastoralists living on the northeastern edge of the Karamoja region in the northeastern part of the Republic of Uganda, East Africa. Several pastoral ethnic groups live around the Dodoth's area of residence/activity where Uganda shares borders with Kenya and South Sudan. Five of them adjoin the Dodoth: the Jie and Matheniko of Uganda to the south, the Toposa and Didinga of South Sudan to the north and the Turkana of Kenya to the east. These groups engage in mutual raiding that involves forming armed parties of various sizes to rustle each other's cattle herds. Although ethnographic records and colonial government archival records have been prone to emphasize the hostility in their intergroup relations, their conflicts are not necessarily constant or permanent. Through reconciliation negotiations, they have been transitioning to non-hostile ("friendly") relationships and accumulating practices such as sharing grazing areas and watering places, building personal friendships beyond ethnic boundaries, visiting each other's homes and gifting or exchanging livestock[1].

In this chapter, I discuss the case of pastoral peoples who engage in opposing types of interaction oscillating between the hostile interaction of mutual raiding and the non-hostile interaction of not raiding. This process has occurred on a backdrop of not invading each other's territory, not annihilating each other and not amalgamating with each other; they resolutely continue coexisting as separate groups who live side by side. I analyze this case from the perspective of "what coexistence with others (people of other groups) means" and "what kind of mentality toward others (people of other groups) supports this". In doing so, I consider recent discourses on the biological (evolutionary) foundations for morality and ethics as well as empathy that is deeply intertwined with the former.

The Dodoth's area of residence/activity extends over approximately 7,800 square kilometers along the borders with Kenya and South Sudan, and the settlements and animal camps[2] I stayed at were in Kalapata district, ten to twenty kilometers from the Kenyan border. Kalapata is on the frontier between the Dodoth and the Turkana. The Dodoth in this district have stronger relationships, both good and bad, with the Turkana than other neighboring groups due to this geographic factor. For this reason, our discussion in this chapter mainly focuses on Dodoth-Turkana relations.

Photo 9.1 Morning at a Dodoth animal (grazing) camp
More than 100 families with respective herds of cattle, goats and sheep gather and jointly set up a large-scale camp. Herders engaged in grazing at the camp mainly include boys over the age of ten and unmarried adolescent men, who are joined by some married young men and occasionally middle-aged men.

Evolutionary foundations for "empathy"

In recent years, the biological (evolutionary) foundations for ethical views and morality have been actively studied in many academic fields such as evolutionary anthropology, cognitive archaeology, neuroscience and primatology. What is being questioned here is the fundamental basis for ethics and morals, which is "how to relate to others (appropriately)" or "What is the (appropriate) way to relate to others?". It is possible to state that this is an approach based on the premise that we humans (should) have acquired the art of "living side by side with others" biologically (evolutionarily) as primates, who have evolved and developed their foundational gregariousness into various modes.

It is said that being able to empathize with others is an essential basis for the standards used to facilitate judgment about what is good and bad, such as ethics and morals. The foundations and process of the evolution of empathy are described and analyzed in detail in a series of books by F. de Waal, including *Good Natured: The Origins of Right and Wrong in Humans and Other Animals* (1998), *The Age of Empathy: Nature's Lessons for a Kinder Society* (2010) and *The Bonobo and the Atheist: In Search of Humanism Among the Primates* (2014). De Waal (1993 and others) is a primatologist who has come to consider the evolution of empathy and ultimately morality in humans from the starting point of the study of cooperation and conflict resolution in primates. According to de Waal, human empathy is backed by a long history of evolution. We are at the tail end of a very long line of primates with a high level of mutual dependency who live in communities (de Waal 2010). The important feature of human empathy is the ability to put oneself in another person's position and to be attentive to others *without losing one's own identity*. To be able to do this, certain cognitive capabilities, especially sufficiently developed senses and the ability to see things from another's perspective, are required (de Waal 1998; emphasis added).

One of the behaviors that are thought to manifest from empathy is called "reciprocal altruism". This type of behavior has been theorized by social biologist R. Trivers and refers to an animal behavior entailing risking one's own welfare for the benefit of another non-consanguineous individual (Hasegawa and Hasegawa 2000). De Waal states "a behavior to offer a helping hand to others has evolved for self-serving reasons" (2010). If the object of one's altruistic behavior is a close associate such as a family member or friend who is willing to return the favor, it is certainly self-serving. In the long-term or on average, natural selection produces behaviors that reward the individual who behaves altruistically. This does not mean that humans and animals give reciprocal help only for self-serving reasons. Individuals are sometimes altruistic as a result of learned behavior (inclination), even when they gain nothing from it. For instance, some people would jump in front of an oncoming train in order to save a stranger's life. It is difficult to imagine that these people are motivated by the prospect of a future reward. We are pre-programmed, so to speak, to "offer a helping hand". Empathy is an automated response only amenable to limited self-control. Most of us cannot help but be emotionally affected by others' circumstances. If all that was required of us was to use others, evolution would never have furnished us with the ability to empathize (de Waal 2010). Clearly, we often make an instant moral judgment instinctively. Our emotions make the judgment, followed up by our reasoning ability acting as a spin-doctor who formulates a plausible explanation (de Waal 2010).

It is said that peers surprisingly easily influence human emotions. The origin of empathy is found here, and not in the domain of more sophisticated imagination or in the ability to think consciously about how one would feel in the other's position. It is argued that empathy began in a very simple form together with physical synchronization (de Waal 2010). Physical synchronization is discussed in detail in Chapter Five by Hayaki, who concludes that no other animals (mammals) can synchronize action with others as perfectly as humans. According to him, the sharing of emotions and feelings with others based on various synchronization capabilities can be called *empathy*. This ability "developed in the ancient past [...] and added many new layers over the subsequent course of evolution until our ancestors finally became able to not only feel what others felt but also to understand what others wanted and needed". Hayaki calls this way of understanding others an "empathic understanding" and points to the immediacy of understanding others' emotions in this way. He names another way of understanding others a "cognitive understanding" that is based on the human ability that develops by the age of four or five to understand that people other than oneself are also "intentional beings" (Tomasello 2006). Hayaki argues that at around the time of the emergence of the genus *Homo*, humankind probably developed the cognitive ability to understand the other as "a being with a mind", which in turn enhanced their empathic ability to understand the other, and posits that the deepening of an understanding of others would go hand in hand with the broadening of the scope of empathy for others. He suspects that these two ways of understanding others have co-evolved through mutual influences.

Returning to de Waal, he refers to the following view of Theodor Lipps (1851–1914), a German psychologist credited as being the father of the modern concept of empathy. We feel nervous when we watch a circus performer walking on a tightrope, because we feel we are inside their body and thus share their experience. We are walking on the rope with the performer. De Waal states as follows while reminding us that Lipps was the first to recognize the existence of a *special transmission channel* we have with others. "By unconsciously merging self and other, the other's experiences echo within us as if they are our own. Such *identification*, argued Lipps, cannot be reduced to other capacities, such as learning, association or reasoning. Empathy offers *access* to 'the foreign self'" (de Waal 2010; emphasis added).

Now, in light of the above discussion on morality, ethics and empathy, we shall examine the state of the relationship between the Dodoth and the Turkana, who "live side by side" in a specific area while oscillating between hostility and non-hostility.

"Consideration" for the Turkana, a supposed enemy?

Since I began my study on the Dodoth peoples in 1996, aside from some short periods of non-hostility, the Turkana and Dodoth have mostly been in a hostile relationship involving a series of raids on one another. The Turkana were the "enemy" of the Dodoth and embarked on raids to rustle their livestock, while the Dodoth also frequently attempted to rustle the Turkana's livestock[3]. People in Kalapata county earnestly prepared against Turkana raids on a daily basis by patrolling watering places and grazing areas, relocating their animal camps frequently, performing rituals to fight off the Turkana and placing fetish objects to ward off their approaches (Kawai 2002a, 2004). However, I was bothered by an unusual statement made repeatedly about the Turkana, supposedly the dangerous enemy who steal the Dodoth's livestock and the object of anger and hatred. The statement could be interpreted as an expression of "consideration" for the Turkana involved in raids on the Dodoth and is outlined below. This particular example was uttered by an old man whose entire herd of cattle had been rustled by an armed Turkana gang while out grazing.

On the day in question, after the raid the cattle herders returned to their settlement and repeatedly expressed condemnation of and anger toward the Turkana. They said, "Terribly bad (*erono*), bad, bad, really bad". An old man whose livestock had been stolen at first listened quietly and eventually began to speak as follows.

> The Turkana's land is a low land down the cliff [of the Great Rift Valley] unlike the Dodoth's land [at 1,300–1,700 m a.s.l]. It is an extremely hot place. Sorghum is planted in the rainy season[4], but the rain soon stops and crops largely die before harvesting. Bird damage is also severe. The Turkana do not have settlements [*ere*]. They only have *awi* [animal camps][5]. So, men, women, children and old people, they all lead a nomadic life. It is a hard life. But all Turkana people must love their livestock very much [an explanation for why someone would lead a nomadic life with their animals all the time].

When I heard this statement, I could hardly believe my ears. They could not be the words of a man who had just lost his entire herd of cattle to the Turkana. Aren't the Turkana his enemy who rustled his cattle? Wouldn't it be a more natural expression of his feelings to reproach, condemn and hate their barbarous act rather than to consider their circumstances? The man was of course disheartened and distressed by the loss of his herd. Nevertheless, in reality it is extremely difficult to retrieve a stolen herd. There are no legal means to reclaim a herd of livestock once it has been taken to the Turkana's land. It is not uncommon for the Dodoth to resort to raiding in order to recover a lost herd, but the target of such a raid is not necessarily the Turkana individuals who actually rustled the herd. In the case of this Dodoth man, his sons carried out frequent raids after the incident, but they targeted the Jie, their southern neighbor, instead of the Turkana. In any case, the words of this man, who seemed to accept the harm done by raiding in acquiescence and even to show consideration toward the Turkana perpetrators, are difficult to understand from our outsider's perspective.

Regarding this situation, I once called a superordinate assembly of "multiple pastoral ethnic groups whose inter-relations oscillate between hostility and non-hostility", or a meta-ethnic assembly, a "supracommunal pastoral value-sharing sphere", or "pastoral value-sharing sphere" for short (Kawai 2017; hereinafter called the "pastoral value-sharing assembly"). Those belonging to individual ethnic groups were loosely associated as a whole while maintaining their own identities as members of separate ethnic groups and while oscillating between hostile and non-hostile inter-ethnic relations over time. This associative framework somewhat resembles the mixed-species association of cercopithecines as a loose assembly discussed by Adachi in Chapter Sixteen. As the act of "showing consideration" toward members of other, hostile groups means seeing them on the same plane as members of one's own group, it is reasonable to assume the existence of a loose assembly or a group of loose coexistence that has fostered the unfettered, higher-order identity of "We the pastoralists who subsist on cattle" (see below).

In addition to actions mainly and directly involved in their subsistence activities, such as raiding during hostile periods and livestock exchange and the shared use of grazing areas and watering places during non-hostile periods, the pastoral value-sharing assembly shares socially and culturally similar institutions, behavioral norms and conventions such as age systems or generation systems, ritual types and procedures, the manner of bridewealth negotiation, a musical genre called "ox songs", the practice of divinatory intestine-reading at the time of animal slaughter and the existence of diviners and witch doctors (traditional healers) called *emuron*[6]. The greatest commonality is the importance of livestock (cattle in particular) that is central to their lives and lifestyle. This situation may correspond to a "saga" shared with others as discussed by Takenoshita in Chapter Seventeen. Raiding is one of the means to acquire livestock to which this pastoral value-sharing assembly assigns the highest value not only economically, but also culturally and socially. It seems to me that raiding is positioned as a social phenomenon that is expected at any time, and is neither a war nor a consequence of extraordinary enmity within this assembly. Raiding cannot be regarded unequivocally as an unreasonable, unjust and antisocial act; it appears to be one that is beyond morality, or which they do not or cannot judge in moral terms.

Even when I interpreted raiding in this way, however, I still had some questions. Why and how can the violent act of raiding be accepted as "legitimate"? Raiding is an unreasonable event for its victims whose livestock are taken by force, but it is a reciprocal act of which they too can become perpetrators. Perhaps they cannot reject or condemn the act as wrong when they find themselves on the receiving end because they, too, commit the same act. Do they resign themselves to accept the damage when they fall victim to a raid for this reason? How can the old man's statement, as if showing consideration for the Turkana, help me find answers to these questions? Did he take pity on the Turkana's life in a harsh natural environment and feel compassion for them? Even if he did, to my mind he should have been hurt by the loss of his cattle as the backbone of his and his family's lives and subsistence. Let us next examine these points.

Characteristics of Dodoth raiding and interactions with neighbors

I have repeatedly discussed Dodoth raiding from various angles (Kawai 2002a, 2004, 2006, 2013, 2017 etc.), but I would like to offer a brief overview of its characteristics once again here.

Raiding is the act of rustling by force of arms a whole herd of livestock, which is the only and most highly valued property of the pastoralists in this region. A raiding party consists of a few dozen to hundreds of men armed with AK47 automatic rifles and other small firearms, and it is not uncommon for people to get killed or injured in the ensuing gun battle. Because it is an interaction involving the use of force, raiding among the eastern and northeastern African pastoral peoples has often been described as one of the primordial forms of war or warfare in both the Japanese and English languages. There are certainly some regions where this description is apt, such as those occupied by the pastoral peoples of southwestern Ethiopia and South Sudan (Fukui 1993; Fukui et al. 2004; Kurimoto 1996; Miyawaki 2006; Sagawa 2011; Hutchinson 1996; Simonse 1998 etc.). However, raiding carried out by cattle pastoralists in the border zone between Uganda, Kenya and South Sudan, including the Dodoth, lacks some characteristic elements of war. Firstly, the use of arms is purely for the rustling of livestock and not aimed at invasion, persecution, domination or genocide. Although it is true that the number of casualties has been climbing due to an influx of small firearms, it seems that the Dodoth do not necessarily aim to kill people (Kawai 2017). They carry guns to intimidate their target rather than to shoot them; the most expedient outcome for them is that the firing of warning shots induces the target to flee, leaving their animals behind. Although they form a gang to carry out raids, I have never seen them practice shooting in preparation for gun battles. Based on these observations, I can say that raiding in this region is similar to war in appearance, but quite different in nature. For this reason, I have consistently been using the term "raiding" to describe the phenomenon called *ajore* in Dodoth in the sense of "mounting a raid to steal livestock" rather than engaging in "war" or "battling".

Another characteristic of Dodoth raiding is the absence of acts that can be called "vengeance", such as payback or retaliation. They sometimes make statements to the effect that "We are justified in going on a raid because the Turkana are stealing our livestock so often", but they are not convincing, as they may mount an attack on another ethnic group instead of the Turkana. Some who lose livestock in a raid choose to reacquire a herd via raiding. It appears that the Dodoth lack an inclination toward vengeance that would motivate them to attack the Turkana in retaliation for livestock raiding or because some Dodoth people were killed by the Turkana. Although it can be interpreted as an effort to break and avoid the endless cycle of violence through paybacks and retaliation between two given ethnic groups, it seems to me that each raid is a stand-alone event of livestock rustling, where the raiders' purpose is purely the acquisition of livestock while the outcome of the raid for its victims is a loss of livestock; nothing more, nothing less.

The Turkana call for peace talks during the dry season when cattle grazing becomes difficult in the harsh living environment, as cattle are vulnerable to dryness. The Dodoth agree and their relationship becomes non-hostile. Many Turkana bring their animals to the Dodoth's land to share their grazing areas and watering places and to set up joint animal camps. More surprisingly, I have seen passing Dodoth herders help a Turkana stranger lift water for his cattle.

The Dodoth never say things like "The Turkana of Kenya should not come to Uganda" by brandishing the logic of a "modern nation-state" as an exclusion zone, or turn down requests from the Turkana on the grounds that "The Turkana stole our livestock in the past". What is the origin of their tolerance and generosity? The Dodoth allow the Turkana to use their pastureland and water resources because the Turkana have difficulty grazing their livestock on their own land during the

Photo 9.2 A ritual to repel Turkana raids performed at a Dodoth animal camp
A "black ox" is sacrificed according to instructions in their prophecy book. After a congratulatory prayer is recited, the ox is dissected, grilled and consumed, including meat and innards, by participating men.

dry season. During this period, the Dodoth and the Turkana temporarily set aside their hostile relationship based on mutual livestock raiding and encounter each other as members of the same pastoral value-sharing assembly as "pastoralists who subsist on cattle"[7].

I did not provide a detailed explanation in the previous section, but what I call a "pastoral value-sharing assembly" refers to the following situation. The Dodoth and their neighboring ethnic groups have never chosen amalgamation, no matter how close a relationship they build or how many times they overlap their spheres of activity by setting up animal camps in the same location or sharing the same grazing areas and watering places. There have been cases of intermarriage between ethnic groups, but they are extremely rare. As far as I can see, it is very much a situation in which each group has built hostile/non-hostile relations with its neighbors while continuing to maintain its own ethnic identity. I mentioned earlier that raiding is just one of the means to acquire livestock (cattle in particular), but it is very difficult to find an adult male who has never participated in a raid.

Similarly, very few men would live their lives without falling victim to raiding. Raiding is an extremely common social phenomenon.

The pastoral value-sharing assembly has certain arrangements (or proto-institutions; see Kawai 2013) built into it so that while the hostile interaction called "raiding" is carried out repeatedly, the parties do not aim at invasion, persecution, domination, genocide or other wartime atrocities. In other words, they mutually choose the path of "continuing to live in the region as neighbors" as the premise. Raiding is one of the means for livestock acquisition that is used as the need arises, and no one carries out repeated raids in order to endlessly amass livestock. During an attack, they do not seem fixated on shooting their guns nor do they gun down all of the herders of the other group every time they take their animals. There are set patterns as to where and how the attack will take place[8], and guns are used mainly for intimidation. When the raided group immediately tries to retrieve the rustled herd, there is an "arrangement" as to how far they can pursue the raiders, as follows: "Should the rustled herd of cattle be herded into the animal enclosure of one of the members of the raiding group, then the game is over at that point" (Kawai 2017: 228). In other words, some type of inhibition is built into the ritual of raiding. Based on their interactions with others belonging to other groups, I surmise that the Dodoth and the Turkana, and probably the other ethnic groups in the pastoral value-sharing assembly as well, share some explicit or implicit or conscious or unconscious mental reasons and/or foundations that function to regulate their actions and behaviors towards one another that can be called "ethics" or "morals".

Origins of the cognition of others/other groups in the Dodoth

Another point of note about the pastoral value-sharing assembly is the way it has been sustained over the long-term.

Although raiding is a hostile interaction carried out by armed groups, it is quite different from war, as discussed above. Livestock are shifted between the Dodoth and the Turkana through violent means, but each group continues to dwell in its own sphere of living/activity. The Dodoth and the Turkana both recognize that they "exist side by side" and make no attempt to change that situation on the basis that they are both "pastoralists who subsist on cattle".

This reminds me of the concept of "recognition" in terms of our relations with others as theorized in *The Phenomenology of Spirit* by Hegel (1807), an influential theorist in the school of thought known as German idealism. Kumano explains

Hegel's argument on the possibility of strongly perceiving the emergence of others as follows.

> **Otherness** precisely means being *different* from the I while belonging to the *same* dimension of existence as the I in some way. Sameness and otherness are unified within the other. Sameness and distinctness emerge in the same dimension in the form of existence as the other to the I. (cited in Kumano 2002: 176–178; emphasis added)

If this is applied to Dodoth-Turkana relations, we can say that the Dodoth and the Turkana belong to the *same* dimension as "pastoralists who subsist on cattle"[9], but they are *different* from one another as ethnic groups. To the Dodoth, the Turkana "emerge in the same dimension in the form of existence as the other[s] to the I [we]".

Kumano explains Hegel's theory of "mutual recognition" further as follows. "The other appears to the I and the I knows that the being is the other. [...] In other words, in an existence distinct from myself, it is at one with myself. [...] The other and the I are simultaneously equal and different". As if to correspond to Hegel's words, the Dodoth and the Turkana perhaps mutually recognize the mutual recognition between them. They mutually recognize that each group recognizes the other as "pastoralists who subsist on cattle", although they are different at the level of ethnicity. The Dodoth and the Turkana mutually recognize that they mutually recognize each other's existence. In this kind of relationship, Hegel states, "Where the other emerges as the other, all acts are simultaneously one's acts and the other's acts and 'one-sided acts come to nothing'. What matters here is not the 'object' but 'the independent other'" (cited in Kumano 2002: 189). If we apply this logic, we can infer that the Dodoth and the Turkana mutually recognize that they repeatedly engage in raiding one another as independent beings, while they engage in gifting or exchanging livestock and grazing in the same locations as friends.

Hegel's argument pertains to the individual relationship between self and other rather than the intergroup relationship. Nevertheless, the argument is applicable to the Dodoth-Turkana relationship as above because the narrative about their relationship does not necessarily intend to locate each ethnic group as a monolithic entity. In both groups, individuals lead highly autonomous lives and are very independent-minded[10]. Although raiding is carried out by an organized gang, demonstrating strong solidarity as an action group, the solidarity arises from bonds between individuals such as friends, relatives and in-laws and is not based on the logic of ethnicity. In some cases, raiding parties are formed across ethnic boundaries (as a coalition force). Further, the bonds have no power to compel, and hence any person who is asked to participate in a raid can decline the request (choose not to participate) for any reason. We must remember that the Dodoth and the Turkana place more importance on interpersonal relations than ethnic identity, and their ethnicity is not an overarching imperative in their understanding of relationships and groups. Both the Dodoth and the Turkana try to consider "others" as specific individuals. While tragedies brought by an understanding of others (other groups) as a monolithic existence are told by the history of numerous wars and persecution, the Dodoth-Turkana relationship has avoided such horrors. As I have mentioned repeatedly, their relationship has been devoid of invasion, persecution, domination and genocide. Perhaps one of the reasons for this is based on the following.

A Dodoth man is simultaneously a being with the attribute of belonging to the ethnic group of Dodoth and a pastoralist in possession of cattle that are indispensable for his own survival and subsistence; and a Turkana man is a being with the attribute of belonging to the ethnic group of Turkana and also a pastoralist in possession of cattle that are indispensable for his own survival and subsistence. In the mind of the Dodoth man, the Turkana are probably not understood as a monolithic group of "faceless" people. A Turkana raiding gang has gathered around a man who requires cattle that are indispensable for the survival and subsistence of himself and his family. The gang is formed by his associates at his request. Raiding is a desperate, do-or-die act, as it entails the risk of being killed in a counterattack or pursuit. In one sense, the raided Dodoth man acts with an extremely generous attitude toward the Turkana man who chose this act. That is, he does not retaliate or take revenge on the men who rustled all of his cattle. He even speaks as if he has consideration for the raiders.

In the mind of the Dodoth, the Turkana ethnic group is different from their own, but the Turkana people are not always their enemy. While I have been translating the Dodoth word *emoit* as "enemy", it also means "other ethnic groups". To the Dodoth, all neighboring ethnic groups can become hostile or non-hostile. "Hostility" here refers to a situation involving the occurrence of a hostile interaction called "raiding" between two groups, and does not extend to any other situation as far as the Dodoth and their neighboring ethnic groups are concerned. The harshness of the Turkana's living environment is beyond anyone's control. The Turkana live in a baking hot land, but they do not attempt to invade the cooler highland domain of their Dodoth neighbors. They continue to live in their hot, arid land without complaint, and only temporarily go to use the Dodoth's grazing areas and watering places when they run out of grass and water to feed their livestock in the driest part of the dry season. The Dodoth show their generosity by allowing them to do so.

The Dodoth's views on the Turkana's poor living environment are expressed on a daily basis, and they repeatedly speak as if they have consideration for the lives of the Turkana people not only during periods of non-hostility, but also while hostilities are ongoing and even immediately after falling victim to the Turkana's raids, as in the case of the aforementioned old man. Their remarks can be summarized as "Although I am a victim whose cattle have been rustled, I recognize that the Turkana perpetrator had a reason that compelled him to resort to this act". Do the Dodoth not find this logic contradictory? Does this statement mean that the Dodoth have consideration for the Turkana? Are the Dodoth such an understanding, easygoing people? I hardly think so. In that case, what is the cognitive process involved in the Dodoth's acceptance of raiding by the Turkana? I would like to examine this question in closing my discussion.

Living side by side with the Turkana

Raiding is organized when a person who requires livestock for whatever reason recruits his associates to form a gang and mounts a raid to rustle a herd of livestock owned by a member of another ethnic group. It is an unreasonable and unacceptable act of violence for the victim, but the raided Dodoth does not choose to deal with it by way of retaliation or revenge. Neither does he make circuitous explanations for it, such as "I cannot complain when Turkana people rustle our livestock as Dodoth have rustled their livestock in the past", or "I may end up going to raid a Turkana in the future, so I must accept the damage I have suffered in this raid". In other words, raiding exists as an ordinary event that is potentially carried out or suffered by anyone, and it cannot be legitimized or justified on a logical basis. While falling victim to a raid is no doubt an unhappy and unfortunate situation, the act of raiding itself does not seem to be understood as an unjust event.

The action selection of "not repaying evil with evil" appears to be rooted in their empathic understanding of why one would resort to the act of raiding. It supports the legitimacy of resorting to the hostile act of raiding as an available option when one is under overwhelming pressure to acquire livestock. It is unlikely that the old Dodoth man's words of "consideration" for the Turkana were an expression of his sympathy or pity. Quoting de Waal once again, "Sympathy differs from empathy in that it is proactive. […] Sympathy, in contrast, reflects concern about the other and a desire to improve the other's situation" (de Waal 2010). The action selection "not repaying evil with evil" differs from relinquishing one's livestock voluntarily. And of course the Dodoth do not voluntarily give their livestock to the Turkana without request. The aforementioned old Dodoth man may have simply uttered what came into his head at that moment in regards to a particular man belonging to the neighboring Turkana group. He may have simply stated what he thought about another man, who is "a pastoralist who subsists on cattle" just like himself, rather than falling into the contradictory position of showing consideration for one's enemy. He was not taking pity on the Turkana man's circumstances by imagining that he was in need of livestock for whatever reason and happened to choose raiding as a means for livestock acquisition. He does not have to imagine the Turkana man's circumstances; the fact that "He needed livestock" is sufficient. I remember his detached tone of voice. It gave me the impression that he was deliberately bypassing his circuit for sympathy.

Based on past experiences, it is a well-known fact that hostility between neighboring groups can become non-hostile over time. For this reason, the Dodoth do not attempt to change the situation in which the Turkana people are others who continue to coexist as members of a neighboring group. They have chosen the path of jointly using and owning the resources available in their region, while oscillating between hostile and non-hostile relations. Pastoral values held by the pastoral value-sharing assembly are means to coexist in the form of ethics and/or morals, which have a biological (evolutionary) foundation in empathy, as noted earlier. According to de Waal (1998), there are only two realistic alternatives in an imperfect world with limited resources: (1) unmitigated competition; or (2) a social order partly shaped and upheld by aggression. Monkeys, apes, humans and many other animals choose the second option.

The Dodoth and the Turkana share the higher-order (meta-)identity of "pastoralists who subsist on cattle" belonging to the pastoral value-sharing assembly. Consequently, their aggression does not result in complete destruction with the potential to bring ruination upon others. Moreover, although I coined the term "pastoral value-sharing assembly" to describe the assemblage as a concept, I suspect that both the Dodoth and the Turkana already "know" this condition – or this existential situation. If so, they must recognize that the hostile act of raiding is a phenomenon inherent to this assembly.

To each Dodoth, each Turkana is the other with whom he has maintained (and will continue to maintain) coexistence through empathy underpinned by its biological (evolutionary) foundation. A Dodoth man who becomes the victim of raiding instantly "understands" the Turkana perpetrator's feelings rather than their circumstances. He probably has travelled to the Turkana's land to visit a Turkana friend. He knows from experience that their land is a wilderness much drier and hotter than that of the Dodoth. He knows that Turkana families have no settlements and therefore men and women of all ages live nomadically, moving from camp to camp. The aforementioned old Dodoth man spoke as if he had "consideration" for the Turkana because he inferred the Turkana's circumstances, consciously constructed a situation where the Turkana man felt compelled to resort to the hostile act of raiding and rationally simulated it. In other words, it was not the result of sympathy or theory of mind (cognitive understanding of others). Rather, he instantly knew the other's feelings and emotions through empathy (empathic understanding of others) and accepted the damage he had suffered. This can be regarded as an expression of an ethical and moral attitude engendered by the empathy that is a biological and evolutionary mental foundation of the mode of coexistence with others who continue to live as neighbors in the same region.

Furthermore, the following point can be made about social significance provided by this ethical and moral attitude. The behavioral tendencies of the Dodoth, including considerate remarks and a lack of an inclination toward revenge, a certain type of inhibition during raiding and tolerance for sharing resources during the dry season, can only be realized on the assumption of their equality with the Turkana as groups as well as individuals. For this reason, these behaviors are believed to function as a set of mechanisms to sustain the pastoral society in the region as a whole that constitutes the pastoral value-sharing assembly and as a compass indispensable in maintaining its social order.

Part III
The Representation and Ontology of Others in Humankind

10 The Ontology of the Other: The Evolutionary Basis of Human Sociality and Ethics in the Formation and Continuation of Inuit Society

Keiichi Omura

Key ideas

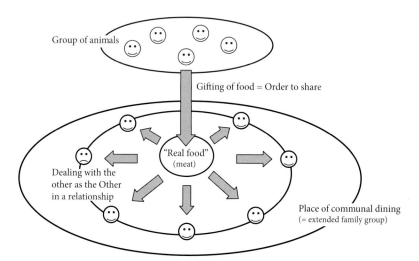

For the development of a society in which everyone deals with the other as the Other separate from and unassimilable to themselves, a device is needed to prevent the act of treating the other as the Other from being exploited by the other, and to protect those who act in this way from being dominated, controlled, used as a tool or killed. In Inuit society, their subsistence system has established a relationship between wild animals and the extended family group in a cyclical pattern, which provides the option of treating the gift of food from animals as a gift to the extended family group instead of as the property of the hunter. This ensures that the hunter and other members of the group can share food at the place of communal dining and interact with one another as the Other without fear of domination and control by anyone, as long as they demonstrate through their actions that they have chosen that option. If ethics is about enabling the other to exist as the Other, then an exploration of human ethics from the perspective of the evolutionary basis is about exploring the genesis and evolution of social systems that guarantee the other's existence as the Other from an ontological perspective.

A starting point: Lévinas's two questions for anthropology

"Subjectivity" is "a relationship, but one where there is no disjunction between the terms held in relationship" (Lévinas 1978: 108). A relationship with the Other is unavoidable for me and I am already saddled with a relationship with the Other inside my body. The Other is wedged into "I", and I gestate the Other within my body. And the Other is wedged into me with its insurmountable distance, vast difference, intact. […] Between the different terms, in fact the terms separated by the difference, a relationship forms regardless, and I become both the relationship and a term of the relationship. The relationship cannot be undone and the relationship with the Other never ends. That is why I "cannot be indifferent" to the Other. Therefore, the Other always compels. I am possessed by the Other. (Kumano 2012: 225)

To approach the Other is to put into question my freedom, my spontaneity as a living being, my emprise over the things, this freedom of a "moving force", this impetuosity of the current to which everything is permitted, even murder. The "You shall not commit murder" which delineates the face in which the Other is produced submits my freedom to judgment. […] It [the moral justification of freedom] consists in addressing an infinite exigency to one's freedom, in having a radical non-indulgence for one's freedom. Freedom is not justified in the consciousness of certitude, but in an infinite exigency with regard to oneself, in the overcoming of all good consciences. But this infinite exigency with regard to oneself, precisely because it puts freedom in question, places me and maintains me in a situation in which I am not alone, in which I am judged. This is the primary sociality. (Lévinas 1969: 304)

As in Lévinas's insight above, if the Other that is incommensurate with the Self already possesses the conscious subjectivity of a "human" before the beginning of "human" consciousness, before all cognition and practice, as one who is impervious to not only being known but also being subsumed or controlled by the Self, who inexorably forces an infinite responsibility for the Other upon the Self, then the formation and continuation of social groups, in no matter what form, must be a necessity for human consciousness. If so, we may be able to say that sociality, as an infinite responsibility[1] for the Other, is a fundamental condition of human conscious subjectivity, and that being human is about forming and maintaining social groups, in no matter what form. This is the very reason why "morality is not a branch of philosophy, but first philosophy" (Lévinas 1969: 304)[2] because, as the underlying thought behind all philosophies, including ontology and epistemology, it explores our relationship with the Other that is a fundamental condition of the human conscious subject, i.e., human sociality.

Lévinas's reflection immediately poses two questions to anthropology, which is a field that explores human universality through human diversity. One of the questions asks whether sociality, being an inevitable relationship with the Other, which Lévinas finds to be a fundamental condition of the human conscious subject, is a universal condition of human consciousness. Despite the brilliance of Lévinas's insight, arrived at after his deep exploration of the tradition of European philosophy, it still remains an insight on "the human being" from the history of European knowledge as it is based on the localized context of twentieth century Europe. The other question relates to the type and function of social groups that are formed and maintained by sociality, and the processes involved in their formation and continuation. Lévinas found the inevitable sociality in human consciousness by delving deeply into phenomenology, and did not touch on the reverse process, that is, the process through which a social group is formed and maintained by sociality, other than offering the loose guideline that a just society or state should be grounded upon this type of primordial sociality.

The purpose of this chapter is to address these two questions by analyzing the process through which an extended family group is formed and maintained in the Inuit, the indigenous people of the Canadian Arctic[3]. Firstly, I examine what the Inuit consider to be the ideal personality. In doing so, I shall discover that, as Lévinas found in human subjectivity, Inuit subjectivity is already and always possessed by others, who impose a responsibility for others on the self. The Inuit are thus faced with a dilemma concerning their responsibility for others, and theoretically become unable to interact with them. I then look at their subsistence system, which is a device for the formation and maintenance of the Inuit extended family group, and reveal that the extended family group is formed and maintained in the dynamic process of deferring the dilemma concerning responsibility for others through this device. Lastly, based on this analysis of the subsistence system, I shall consider the two questions that Lévinas has raised for anthropology.

The "real Inuit" dilemma

Previous studies on the Inuit personality in Arctic anthropology (e.g., Briggs 1968, 1970; Brody 1975) have demonstrated that there is an ideal personality called "real Inuit" (*Inunmariktuq*) in Inuit society. According to Briggs (1968,

1970), "real Inuit" refers to a mature adult with a balanced ratio of two qualities, namely, "reason" (*ihuma-*) and "affection" (*naglik-*).

"Affection" refers to qualities and emotions that are expressed in words by the stem *naglik-*, and serves as a criterion of human goodness. In concrete terms, it is about the spirit of kindness that motivates one to help people physically and mentally by, for example, sharing food or a warm place ungrudgingly instead of keeping it all to oneself, and willingly offering a helping hand to people in need. The Inuit word for "thank you", *qujanaqutit!*, means "You are generous and giving", which also suggests that affection is an important quality for them. Emotions that are opposite to affection include hostility toward others and withdrawn or depressed feelings such as hatred and jealousy. In this sense, affection includes the quality of sociability – being open to others without being hostile toward them, withdrawn or depressed.

On the other hand, "reason" covers qualities that are expressed in words using the stem *ihuma-*, and articulates the condition of being an autonomous "adult" (*inirniit*). A reasonable adult refers to an autonomous person who behaves in a socially acceptable manner, maintains equanimity in the face of difficulties and maintains self-control without being prone to anger. The mature adult respects not only their own autonomy, but also that of others. The reasonable adult can deal with each situation pragmatically and flexibly without having preconceived ideas about other people or things, and maximize their potential in an adaptable manner.

While affection is believed to be an innate and universal quality a human (*Inuit*) is born with, it is thought that infants (*inuuhaat*) and children (*nutaraat*) are yet to be equipped with reason, which is a quality that is acquired gradually as one matures into an adult. Infants and children are therefore incapable of socially appropriate behaviors through well-balanced self-control; they are overcome by their emotions and desires, quick to become frustrated and angry, become upset and unable to deal with a situation calmly, infringe upon the other's autonomy and try to monopolize. Because they lack reason, infants and children are seen to be vulnerable and in need of constant care.

Thus, infants and children are definitely weak physically, mentally and socially, and should be protected affectionately. They are looked after in everything, and their displays of lack of reason arouse in adults an intense desire to protect them. Adults' affection for children is so strong that they wish to be with them day and night, and they even say that they should not love their children too much because they miss them too much when they part from them for a day of hunting or trading (Briggs 1968, 1970).

It is important to note here that expressing affection openly toward adults with reason and even adolescents (*inuuhuktut*) with growing reason is considered to be disrespectful of their autonomy. Accordingly, people refrain from openly expressing affection toward adults with reason so as not to disrespect their autonomy. They avoid ordering and forcing adults and even adolescents as well as instructing and teaching them to do things, as they need to show respect for their autonomy. Violating their autonomy in this way would indicate not only that one does not appreciate others' autonomy, but also that one's reason is questionable.

Respecting others' autonomy, of course, does not mean avoiding all approaches to them. One would be regarded as malicious if they failed to immediately help someone in trouble, to share food and everything else and collaborate or to express their affection. However, one's affection must not be intrusive, as this would be a violation of the other's autonomy, and a blatant demonstration of affection could be regarded as patronizing. Thus, affection and reason need to be balanced and controlled. Growing and maturing into a "real Inuit" means achieving this exquisite balance by developing the difficult art of caring for others without becoming too explicit, and expressing affection while respecting the others' autonomy[4].

This is, of course, an ideal and not very easy to achieve in reality. If all Inuit adults were "real Inuit", this would mean that it was a very natural, ordinary state, and would not have to be held as an ideal. The fact that people are expected to strive to be "real Inuit" indicates that the Inuit recognize that a "human" (Inuit) in a natural state often has hostility toward others, gets in a bad mood and becomes depressed or withdrawn, becomes upset in the face of an unexpected situation or failure, wants to monopolize everything and wants to dominate or control others without regard for their autonomy. For the Inuit, maturing into adulthood means overcoming this natural state and striving for the ideal, even if they do not actually reach the state of being "real Inuit".

However, the commitment to be a "real Inuit" is the inner state of each individual and is not directly accessible to others. This means that one must continuously demonstrate their commitment through their actions in order to gain social recognition as an adult. Others observe one's actions and judge whether one is committed to the ideal. One may think or claim this commitment to the ideal to be the case with oneself, but the others do not recognize it unless it is demonstrated by one's actions. Because the natural state of "humans" (Inuit) is considered to be the opposite of "real Inuit", failing to demonstrate one's pursuit of the ideal in every action will lead the others to judge that one has reverted to the natural "human" state and that one is immature and lacks reason or is malicious.

It is clear that the subjectivity of the Inuit adult, who must continuously show others that they are committed to achieving the "real Inuit" ideal, is what Lévinas calls subjectivity that is "a relationship and a term of the relationship" with the Other. Prior to taking any action, the Inuit adult has already been called by others that are lodged within to interact with them in a manner that shows their commitment to the ideal, and has already been compelled to respond to the call. Because the Inuit adult has already responded and has been saddled with the responsibility of showing their commitment to the ideal through their actions, the Inuit adult has no choice but to proactively interact with the others through such action. No matter how many times one responds to the call, one can never stop responding. Although the subjectivity of the Inuit adult is impregnated with others, others will never be assimilated into the self; others as what Lévinas calls "the Other" will continue to call the adult while keeping their unassimilable alterity. The adult can continue to be an adult only by continuously responding to the call of such others by enacting their commitment to the "real Inuit" ideal.

Another element that indicates that the subjectivity of the Inuit adult is located in the relationship between the mutually unassimilable and separated self and other is that the "real Inuit" ideal, to which the Inuit adult is forced to show commitment through their action in their interactions, is a figure who embodies both reason and affection. The quality of reason that demands respect for the autonomy of both oneself and the others precisely means mutually recognizing that the self and other are mutually unassimilable and separated by a great distance while mutually respecting the alterity of each other. Interacting with each other despite the separation must be carried out via acts such as helping and caring for the others and giving food to them, that is, acts to express one's affection for the others, rather than trying to assimilate the others into the self and eliminate alterity from them by imposing one's self-centered interpretation upon them or exploiting, dominating or controlling them, not to mention hurting or killing them. In this sense, the "real Inuit" ideal is synonymous with the subjectivity that interacts with the others as what Lévinas calls "the Other" while being separated from them and respecting their unassimilable alterity.

What is important here, however, is that the Inuit adult is unable to know whether the others are similarly committed to the "real Inuit" ideal, and consequently runs into the following logical dilemma in trying to interact with the others through actions that express their commitment to the ideal.

The other who is not aiming to become a "real Inuit" may remain in the natural human (Inuit) state and disrespect one's autonomy or take advantage of one's affectionate acts such as giving food or assistance in order to assimilate, dominate or control one. Conversely, the other who is not committed to the ideal may give food or help with the intention of dominating and controlling the recipient. As long as the natural Inuit state is considered to be the polar opposite of "real Inuit", this possibility will continue to exist. Moreover, the person who is exploited feels compelled to accept the other's domination and control because they must respect the other's autonomy in order to demonstrate their maturity. However, this contradicts the "real Inuit" ideal to respect one's own autonomy.

In addition, because one has no direct access to others' feelings or intentions, one is unable to judge the personality of the other in advance of one's enactment of the ideal in one's interaction with the other; one can only judge in hindsight, based on the other's responses. Of course, one can ask the other if they are aiming to be "real Inuit", but one must not accept their response at face value. This is why one must demonstrate one's maturity via actions rather than words. The very act of asking the question not only suggests one has doubts about the other's voluntary commitment to the ideal, but also exposes one's lack of trust in the other and hence one's immaturity.

In this situation, it would be safer if one were to wait until the other has acted, judge the other on the basis of the action and take action in response. However, because the same situation would apply to the other as well, both Inuit adults are possessed by the responsibility for others and trying to fulfill that responsibility, but at the same time they are prevented from doing anything because of their doubts about the other[5]. This is also applicable when one is the recipient of food or help. Thus, although Inuit adults try to act as adults who are committed to the "real Inuit" ideal, they run into a dilemma before they perform an action and get stuck in the mire as they wait for the other to make a move. This dilemma is inexorably built into the "real Inuit" ideal and, logically, the harder Inuit adults try, the more entangled they become in the dilemma, motionless in great distress as they are weighed down by the responsibility imposed by others[6].

Of course, the Inuit people do not simply stand around burdened by their responsibility for others; they actively engage in real-life interactions. Otherwise they would remain isolated from one another without developing social relationships or forming social groups such as extended family groups. In this case, how is the dilemma surrounding "real Inuit" resolved, and how are social groups created and maintained? We shall look at how the Inuit resolve the dilemma by analyzing the subsistence system that creates and maintains the extended family groups that form the basis of their everyday social life.

Subsistence system: Forming the life-world and the extended family

Arctic anthropologists have pointed out that the existence of a social-cultural-economic system called "subsistence" is commonly observed among the Inuit and Yu'pik peoples who are distributed widely from the Arctic zone of easternmost Siberia through North America to Greenland (e.g., Bodenhorn 1989; Fienup-Riordan 1983; Kishigami 2007; Nuttall 1992; Stewart 1995, 1996; Wenzel 1991)[7]. The subsistence system generates and maintains the relationships between the Inuit and wild animals as well as those among the Inuit and is governed by their worldview conceptualized as an ideal world order to be realized (Omura 2012, 2013a). Under this system, the extended family group[8], which is the basic unit of Inuit sociality, is generated and maintained through the distribution and consumption of resources acquired through the relationships between the Inuit and wild animals. The mechanism by which this Inuit subsistence system produces extended family groups sustainably can be represented in the following cyclic system model (Omura 2012, 2013a).

Firstly, the Inuit people enter into a food giver-receiver relationship with individual wild animals using their subsistence skills such as hunting, fishing, trapping and gathering. The sharing of food and other life resources acquired as the products of such a relationship leads to the formation of each extended family group, which forms the basis of everyday social relations among the Inuit. What is important here is that food sharing has become the rule in Inuit society because, in their ideal world represented in their worldview, the following reciprocal relationship is aimed for as the ideal relationship between the Inuit and wildlife that must be achieved in subsistence activities.

In the Inuit worldview, wild animals are believed to have "spirit" (*tagniq*), which remains after their bodies perish. However, this spirit can only be reincarnated in another body if – and only if – the Inuit collectively consume all the flesh; therefore, the spirits of wild animals voluntarily offer their bodies to the Inuit for sharing and consumption so that they can be reborn in new bodies. From the point of view of the Inuit, wild animals help them because they are given the resources for their survival. Thus, what is aimed for in the Inuit worldview is a reciprocal relationship by which wildlife help the Inuit to survive by offering their bodies as food and the Inuit in turn assist them to be reborn in new bodies by sharing and eating the food.

Because of this guiding principle set out in their worldview, the Inuit as "food receivers" are subordinate to wild animals and must always share food with each other. This sharing thus becomes a norm: if food is not shared, the wildlife cannot reincarnate, and people become afraid that the wildlife will stop offering their bodies as food. Importantly, what is ingenious here is that the food-sharing rule is articulated as if it were set by wildlife, not the Inuit. This is why cooperative relationships are realized in which every Inuit shares food according to the common rule, without anyone ordering them to do so.

Among the Inuit, the equal sharing of food engenders trust relationships in which they mutually expect the other not to monopolize food and mutually rely on the other's willingness to cooperate in the act of food consumption. Consequently, the Inuit have managed to do away with dominant-subordinate relationships and to realize relationships of trust, equality and cooperation among themselves by positioning themselves as food receivers who are always subordinate to wildlife and allowing wild animals to impose the food-sharing rule on them.

However, animal domestication is prohibited in Inuit society as the price of this arrangement. If the Inuit domesticated wild animals, the food-sharing rule would be imposed by the Inuit who domesticated the animals, not the animals. This would mean that the Inuit were dictating the other Inuit and the once expelled dominant-subordinate relationships would return to Inuit society. For equal trust relationships to arise among the Inuit, wildlife must be held in a dominant position over each and every Inuit. As a result, the Inuit are compelled to engage in subsistence activities such as hunting, fishing, trapping and gathering in which they, as the dependent in a weak position, use techniques to entice animals, as they are unable to adopt any methods that involve the control and management of wild animals such as pastoralism.

Moreover, the sharing rule not only promotes food sharing among the Inuit, but also the sharing of skills and knowledge for subsistence activities and collaboration. Because the rule dictates that the Inuit must always share the food acquired in subsistence activities, it enables them to willingly collaborate in them without worrying about usurpation or betrayal. In fact, because they must always share the food acquired in subsistence activities without monopolizing, acts such as engaging in hunting or fishing alone or keeping skills and knowledge to themselves take on a negative meaning, while sharing skills and knowledge and collaborating with one another acquire a positive one.

Once sharing and collaboration become the norm, the knowledge and skills required for subsistence activities are developed and enriched, increasing the probability that the Inuit and new wild animals will re-enter the relationship between "the receiver of food and those who accept the sharing order" and "the giver of food and those who issue the sharing order". When this relationship is actually realized, all will return to the starting point of subsistence and the same cyclical process will be repeated. Thus, the rebirth of an animal spirit into a new body is achieved in the form of the reproduction of the Inuit-wildlife relationship in the cyclical process of subsistence as depicted in the Inuit worldview. The animal spirit that is reproduced without perishing refers to the relationship between the Inuit and wildlife.

When the "enticement–order" relationship between the Inuit and wildlife continues to operate cyclically while being intertwined with the "trust and collaboration" relationship among the Inuit, two categories surface: namely, the Inuit, whom one must trust and cooperate with and wildlife, who are the object of enticement and the imposers of order. Of course, their relationships with wildlife that are formed and renewed in the cyclical process involve various animal species, not just one. Accordingly, each Inuit extended family group is formed at the nodal point of various relations cyclically created with multiple animal species through subsistence practices, and looms as one of the nodal points that are blended into the interlinked network of countless nodal points of various animal groups. This network is the life-world of the Inuit called *nuna*.

Communal dining: Deferring the dilemma through food

The important feature of the Inuit subsistence system, which continuously creates the life-world *nuna* involving their relationships with wildlife and forms and maintains the extended family groups that are embedded in it, is the ingenious way in which the dilemma embedded in the "real Inuit" ideal is deferred through the practice of food sharing imposed by wildlife, even though it does not resolve the issue.

If a hunter, to whom a wild animal has directly given its body for consumption, is aware of his responsibility for others as an adult committed to becoming a "real Inuit" and wishes to fulfill a reciprocal relationship with the animal, he is compelled to share the gifted food with the others rather than keeping it for himself in order to continue to receive food from wildlife and demonstrate his commitment to be a "real Inuit", regardless of whether the others are committed to the ideal or not. If the hunter fails to share the gift of food with the others, he becomes afraid that he will not be given the bodies of wild animals in the future and would be regarded as malicious or anti-social by the others.

However, if the hunter keeps his own share and gives the rest to a particular other, and then if the other to whom the hunter has given food is not committed to the "real Inuit" ideal, the other may grab it all and keep it for himself instead of sharing it with the others. If this happens, food is not distributed among the Inuit, and the condition for receiving the gift of food from wild animals is not fulfilled. There is also the risk that the other who has received food from the hunter may consider the hunter's act of offering food to indicate the hunter's subordination to him and exploit the hunter's act to dominate and control him. On the other hand, because the hunter's commitment to "real Inuit" is not obvious to people other than the hunter himself, the people become afraid that their act of receiving food will be considered to indicate their subordination to the hunter and will be exploited in order for the hunter to dominate and control them once they have received food from him.

There is one simple way for the hunter to solve all of these problems – laying all of the food given by wildlife out in front of all of the members of his extended family group and participating in communal dining where food is freely available to all diners, instead of keeping his own share and giving the rest to the other members of his extended family group. In other words, the hunter confines his role to delivering the received food, and shares the food in a communal dining style where he can freely consume his share on an equal basis with the others.

Of course, if every Inuit were committed to the "real Inuit" ideal, the hunter would be able to share food with the other Inuit, and they would share it with other Inuit and the food would be passed on from one Inuit to the next until all of them had partaken of it. However, the chain of sharing may be interrupted if even one of them is not committed to the ideal and keeps food to themselves[9]. This risk is removed if the hunter assumes the role of a carrier of the given food, lays everything out before all of the members of his extended family group and joins in communal dining, sharing the food with all the others at once.

It is true that the hunter's act of handing everything over to all members of his extended family group, including himself, indicates his subordination to the extended family group as a whole. However, the hunter is subordinate to the extended family group *as a whole* and not to its individual members. Therefore, even from the perspective of someone who is not committed to the ideal, the hunter's act indicates that he is subordinate not to him or her, but to the extended family group on an equal basis with the other members. From the perspective of someone who is committed to the ideal, on the other hand, the hunter's act follows the order issued by the wild animals to achieve a reciprocal relationship with wildlife, and indicates that the hunter is subordinate to wildlife as well as to his extended family group. Anyone who is committed to the ideal will not exploit the hunter's act to their advantage, because they respect others' autonomy. Thus, the hunter can remove the risk that his act of offering food will be considered to indicate his subordination to someone in his extended family group and be exploited by them.

In this situation, the Inuit who are given food from wildlife via the hunter can safely consume it without fearing the possibility of being dominated or controlled by the hunter, because the hunter's act has indicated that he is subordinate to the extended family group and is sharing food on an equal basis with them. Thus, the hunter and the others are able to simultaneously satisfy the animal's order and their responsibility for others by helping the animals to be reborn and demonstrating their commitment to the ideal of the "real Inuit" through the act of eating their share of gifted animal body without fearing that their autonomy will be violated. They can follow the wildlife's order, respect each other's autonomy and express affection toward each other by simply taking and eating their share of food – as long as they refrain from taking more than they can eat – and redistributing some of it to the others[10]. Moreover, the subordination of everyone to an extended family group, which in turn is subordinate to wildlife, is demonstrated the moment this communal dining is realized through the act of taking and eating a share of food. Through this process, the extended family group, which is subordinate to wildlife and to which all members are subordinate, comes into existence.

In reality, although Inuit hunters sometimes eat part of their catch on the spot in order to relieve their hunger, they basically bring all of it back to the storage room at the household of an elder or seasoned hunter, who is the mainstay of the extended family group, instead of sharing it with another. Generally speaking, a large freezer capable of storing a large amount of catch is found only at the household of the leading elder or seasoned hunter of the extended family group comprising several nuclear family households. The dissecting and processing of the catch is carried out in front of the elder's or seasoned hunter's home, and the food is stored in the large freezer in his house. As details of the hunt are reported to the extended family group by radio or verbally every day, all group members are thoroughly familiar with the food stock in storage. When they are hungry or at meal times, they bring food out of the freezer and prepare and consume it.

In the basic eating style of communal dining in Inuit society, several people sit in a circle around some slabs of meat or a few fish, which they call "real food" (*niqinmarik*). Although these days they live in houses with modern kitchens and tables, on each occasion they spread a sheet of cardboard on the floor and lay "real food" on it to share among several people. As the average extended family group has around ten adults and twenty children, they cannot all sit in a circle at once. Those who have finished eating leave the circle and others come in to fill the vacant spots to continue communal dining involving four to five people. Participation in this style of communal eating itself is a clear demonstration of their willingness to share food, and at the same time the participants are judged to be adults who are committed to the "real Inuit" ideal.

In this style of communal dining there are certain eating customs that are followed implicitly. For instance, a few whole fish might be served half-thawed on the cardboard sheet and have to be cut in round slices with a cooking knife called *ulu*. The starter would cut a whole fish into four to five pieces of the correct size, place them in the middle, and each person would take a piece to eat as they wished. Alternatively, one person might cut a piece out of a whole fish for themselves, returning the rest to the middle, and the next person would do the same until everyone had their own share. Their tacit manners require them to show subtle courtesy to one another in various ways. For example, one may avoid taking the other's favorite part of fish, prompt the other to take their share first or take turns cutting the fish (cutting a semi-frozen fish requires considerable strength and skill).

These courteous gestures are made discreetly, because overt solicitude is regarded as interference with the others' autonomy. Communal diners refrain from talking so as not to interrupt the others' enjoyment of food and vacate their seats as soon as possible for those who are waiting. Meals are enjoyed basically in silence, except when diners occasionally burst into laughter at some child's temper tantrum when they are teased about their poor manners. Diners engage in conversation for about one hour after finishing a meal while drinking tea. Communal dining in a circle serves as a perfect place for participants to demonstrate their mutual attentiveness toward not interfering with one another's enjoyment of "real food", and to mutually express and confirm their commitment to be "real Inuit" upon whom wildlife's order and the responsibility for others are imposed.

Of course, this mutual display of adult attitudes during communal dining does not necessarily resolve the "real Inuit" dilemma. The other who acts like an Inuit adult may be putting on an act while secretly plotting to gain dominance over others. Will this person act like an Inuit adult next time? Once suspicions arise in this regard, they never go away. Distrustfulness is a natural human (Inuit) condition, and therefore the others are likely to harbor the same suspicions about oneself. Even though each other's adulthood might be mutually confirmed this time, one can never know the others' true intent and how they will act next time. Their interaction may have gone well this time, but their suspicions are never quelled. The dilemma is merely postponed.

Conversely, Inuit adults passively and voluntarily choose to dine communally at every meal in order to be recognized as an adult precisely because their dilemma is never resolved, and each other's intent can only be confirmed through interactions. One may wish to eat to relieve hunger, but if one eats alone, their action will be judged to be anti-social. However, if one is paralyzed by the "real Inuit" dilemma and does nothing, they will suffer not only being seen as an immature person lacking reason or a malicious person, but also will eventually starve to death. One can overcome the dilemma and eat food only by participating in communal dining and mutually confirming one another's adulthood through the exchange of careful civilities mediated by "real food". Nevertheless, no matter how many times they confirm each other's adulthood through exchanges of subtle actions during communal dining, their mutual suspicions will never go away because they can never know the others' true intent and how they will act in the future, and hence the dilemma is simply deferred. Thus, they are prompted to continue the practice of communal dining, and through this dynamic process, an extended family group as a group of Inuit people who gather to share food is formed and maintained.

What is important here is that communal dining is not possible unless the relationship between wild animals and the extended family group is established cyclically as one between "the receiver of food and those who accept the sharing order" and "the giver of food and those who issue the sharing order" by the subsistence system. Embedded in this process is the option for people to think that food is given to the extended family group rather than being owned by the hunter who catches it, even though it is the hunter who is given food directly by animals. From the hunter's perspective, if the food becomes his property, handing over the food to the others becomes difficult because he becomes afraid that his act of offering may be considered to indicate his subordination to the others and be exploited by those who are not committed to the "real Inuit" ideal. From the perspective of Inuit other than the hunter, they would feel reluctant to receive food from the hunter if it was his property, as they are afraid that their act of receiving it might be considered to indicate their subordination to the hunter and allow them to be exploited by him.

If the option is available to interpret that it is the Inuit extended family group that is given food from wildlife and the food then becomes the group's property, the hunter can hand over his catch to the group by demonstrating that he has chosen this option and that he is subordinated to the group without worrying about being subordinated to someone in the group. Likewise, the other who is offered the food can demonstrate their subordination to the group by taking and eating it without worrying about being subordinated to the hunter, as long as the hunter's action has indicated that the food is owned by the group. Thus, both the hunter and the others can share the food in a communal setting without being subordinated to an individual in the group in exchange for their subordination to the group. For the Inuit, the subsistence system provides the basis for communal dining and allows them to defer the "real Inuit" dilemma by giving them the option to treat food as a gift from animals to the extended family group through its cyclical process.

The ontology of the Other: Human sociality and ethics

The mechanism of the Inuit subsistence system teaches us a few lessons with regard to the two questions that Lévinas posed to anthropology.

One is the possibility that sociality, which Lévinas located at the root of "human" subjectivity, is universally found in humankind. The subjectivity of the Inuit adult is already and always burdened with a responsibility for others in the form of a compulsion to show one's commitment to the "real Inuit" ideal through their actions. Sociality in interactions while mutually respecting each other's autonomy is the fundamental condition governing the subjectivity of the Inuit adult. In this sense, it is possible to say that Inuit society is one in which what Lévinas calls subjectivities, each of which is "a relationship" with what he calls "the Other" and "a term of the relationship", interact while recognizing the difference between a separate self and other and respecting the unassimilated alterity of each other. Consequently, the underpinning of the conscious subject by human sociality, which is already and always responding to the call of others as "the Other" and passively burdened with the responsibility for others as "the Other", might be a universal characteristic of all humankind in the sense that it applies to not only "humans" in Europe but also to Inuit adults.

We must remember, however, that the "real Inuit" who interacts with the others while mutually respecting their own and the others' autonomy is the ideal that one aspires to, not the natural state of the Inuit (human) – in fact, the existence of the ideal means that their natural state is just the opposite. If every Inuit were born with a sociality to respect their own and the others' autonomy during interactions, they would not have to aspire to this ideal. Instead, the natural state of the Inuit (human) is pregnant with impulses to ignore their responsibility for others, to disregard the others' autonomy, to dominate and control them as if the others were objects, to reject interaction with others out of hostility and to ignore the others as if they were irrelevant objects. The Inuit adult oscillates between the ideal sociality that entails treating the others as separate from and unassimilable to themselves, that is, what Lévinas calls "the Other", during interactions and the impulse to objectify, dominate and control the others by eliminating alterity from them and assimilating them into themselves.

This is clear from the view in Inuit society that infants and children are not equipped with the sociality to deal with the others as separate from and unassimilable to themselves in their interactions with them. Infants and children are yet to develop "reason" and unable to recognize their own and the others' autonomy, to say nothing of respecting it. In fact, infants and children have no autonomy in the first place, as they are utterly dependent on others. Infants and children might keep food to themselves, reject interactions with others out of hostility or treat the other as a tool in disregard for their autonomy. They would be unaware of their responsibility for others enacted by demonstrating their commitment to be "real Inuit" by action, even if it is in fact imposed upon them. Infants and children must learn to respect their own and the others' autonomy as they are raised, and in the process develop an awareness of the responsibility for others imposed upon them and become liable for it[11].

Thus, the existence of at least one society, in which the process of cultivating respect for their own and the others' autonomy is needed as a condition for the acquisition of a sociality to interact with the others while treating them as "the Other", and where this sociality is held up as an ideal, speaks eloquently to the fact that this form of sociality is not a universal biological trait of humankind, even if human sociality is underpinned by the condition where one is already and always responding to the call of others as "the Other" and passively burdened with a responsibility for them. If this form of sociality were biologically essential for the human species, neither its idealization nor the cultivation process to acquire it would be needed. People would naturally grow to respect their own and the others' autonomy and be burdened with their responsibility for others. The "real Inuit" ideal teaches us that human beings have a universal urge to dominate and control the others by eliminating alterity from and objectifying them, and they have been attempting to fight this urge and treat the others as "the Other" unassimilable to oneself in interactions. This is the second lesson that the Inuit subsistence system teaches us.

Considering that the impulse to eliminate alterity from the others and objectify them to dominate and control them is universally found in humans, if a real society is to arise from sociality, there is a need for some device to prevent those who have the urge to dominate and control others from exploiting the actions of those who treat others as "the Other", even if the sociality that treats others as "the Other" in interactions is built into the subject. One may respect the others' autonomy and treat them as separate from and unassimilable to oneself in interactions, but if the other is a person who disregards others' autonomy and tries to eliminate alterity from them and objectify them, one's action may be exploited for domination and control or in an extreme situation, one may be killed. In order to build a society in which all members treat one another as "the Other", there needs to be a device to prevent anyone who attempts to dominate or control others from exploiting the actions that treat the others as "the Other", as well as to prevent the objectification and killing of those who act in this manner.

In Inuit society, their subsistence system is such a device. Because the subsistence system establishes the relationship between wild animals and the extended family group in a cyclic pattern, and provides an option to treat food as a gift to the extended family group rather than the hunter who received it directly from wildlife, by choosing this option and being subordinated to the extended family group the hunter and all other members of the group can share the food and interact with one another as "the Other" without fear of domination or control by someone in the group. The Inuit subsistence system is designed to allow every Inuit to treat one another as "the Other" in interactions without fear of being dominated or controlled by any individual by choosing the option it provides to prevent anyone who is motivated by an impulse to objectify, dominate and control the others from attempting to exploit the actions of the hunter or other people.

Of course, as long as everyone has the impulse to eliminate alterity from the others and objectify, dominate and control them there is no guarantee that people will share food and treat one another as "the Other" in every interaction. Although the Inuit subsistence system provides an option to prevent the exploitation of the action of treating others as "the Other" for domination and control, it cannot stop the hunter from taking ownership of food and dominating or controlling others through food distributing, or another Inuit from keeping it all and trying to dominate and control the others by distributing it to them. The appearance of a person who attempts to dominate or control the others is one of the central themes of the Inuit myths and folklore that are told repeatedly with a sense of trepidation (Boas 2011; Saitō et al. 2009).

Because humans have both the built-in sociality to treat others as "the Other" as a condition of conscious subjectivity and the universal impulse to eliminate alterity from others and objectify, dominate and control them, everyone must demonstrate through their actions that they are treating the others as "the Other" every time one acts. A society is formed and maintained in this dynamic process of endlessly repeated interactions to confirm one another's intention of treating the others as "the Other". In this sense, tension between the impulse to eliminate alterity from the others and what Lévinas calls a responsibility for "the Other" serves as the driving force for the generation and maintenance of concrete social groups. Thus, the state of being charged with a responsibility for others as "the Other" while keeping an urge to eliminate alterity from the others and assimilate them into the self as the objects of domination and control can be regarded as the evolutionary foundation of human sociality. This is the third lesson that the Inuit subsistence system teaches us.

Nonetheless, tension between the impulse and the responsibility concerning others may be the evolutionary basis for human society, but a society in which everyone treats each other as "the Other" cannot be realized without a device to prevent the exploitation of the act of treating others as "the Other" for the purpose of domination and control, because otherwise no one would feel safe to act in that manner. In this situation, people would refrain from interacting with one another out of fear of exploitation, and therefore there would be no possibility of forming a social group. Even if some kind of social group were formed, the act of treating the others as "the Other" would be exploited and those who acted in that manner would be dominated and controlled by those seeking to objectify, dominate and control the others.

It is conceivable that social systems are developed so that conditions for the adequate functioning of the evolutionary basis of human sociality are ensured, including the prevention of exploitation, the protection of those who treat the others as "the Other" against domination and control and the imposition of a responsibility for others as "the Other" to counter an impulse to eliminate alterity from the others and assimilate them into the self. This is the last lesson the Inuit subsistence system teaches us. A social system is required so that those who respond to the call of others as "the Other" and treat the others as "the Other" can be protected; others can exist as "the Other" without being assimilated, dominated and controlled only under the protection of such system. In this sense, it is possible to say that an ontological consideration of others is related to considering the way social systems exist to protect others' existence as "the Other". If ethics is about enabling others to exist as "the Other", then an exploration of human ethics from the perspective of the evolutionary basis is about exploring social systems that guarantee others' existence as "the Other" and ensure the functioning of the evolutionary foundations of human society based on the tension between the impulse and the responsibility concerning others. The ontology of others as "the Other" is the ontology of society, and the evolutionary basis of ethics in human society lies in the ontology of others and society.

11 Ancestral Spirits, Witchcraft and Phases of the Other in Everyday Life: The Case of the Bemba People of Zambia

Yuko Sugiyama

Key ideas

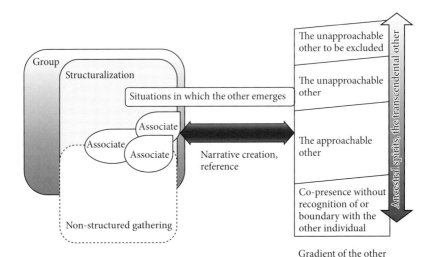

Gradient of the other

The residential group of the Bemba village is made up of the layers of non-structured gatherings of focused affinity, co-presence and scenes of concretization and structuralization of genealogy, generation and gender. The everyday life in the village contains situations in which various phases of the other emerge in interactions among people. The emergence of the other is variable and situation-responsive along a gradient of otherness. As people recount events according to the situation and weave a common narrative through polyphonic dialogues, they generate mutual association among them and structuralize a group.

The other individual and the other

Forming a "social field of encounter" by sensing each other's "intention" is commonly found in chimpanzees and other great apes when two individuals have an encounter (Nakamura 2003; Yamagiwa 2007, 2015c). This phenomenon is also shared in humans. The ability to sense each other's intention to form a social field is considered to constitute the nucleus of sociality that humans and great apes have developed in their evolutionary history.

However, the coalescence of multiple dyadic encounters does not generate a society, that is, a structured group. The relativization of one's own position is necessary to recognize a structure led by the categorization of collective "us" and "them", which is less likely to occur in a dyadic relationship. When a structured group is formed, it affords encounters between three or more parties in which "the other" necessarily emerges. In order to allow appropriate action selection in the sequences of communication, an encounter between three or more parties requires each to have two different perceptions to figure out the intention of each of the other individuals around them, and the ability to sense their own position in the "whole" group they are included in. Selecting which party one should approach first or move away from is based on the judgment as to which party is one's closer *nakama* (associate) (or perhaps a more political judgment), and at that moment one categorizes all individuals present, oneself included.

Categorizing the individuals in an encounter based on levels of association creates a set of similar individuals called "we", as well as a set of "them" = "other" who are different from us. In other terms, where the categories of "I" and "them" are created, one becomes aware that the "I" is the "other" to the "them". It is important to note that in each case the other emerges in a situation-responsive and multilayered manner. It is supposed that the other and the associate emerge as if nested in various social situations and act as structural elements of a group to create its entirety[1].

At the individual level, the boundary between self and other fluctuates easily. With a passing nod to Turner's communitas concept, we have all experienced situations in which the boundary between the other and ourselves almost disappears, or a tool or some inorganic object felt as if it were an extension of our own body. Conversely, we sometimes feel as if a thing has a mind of its own.

The perception of "the other" does not always come to the surface. As I discuss elsewhere (Sugiyama 2013) on gatherings, based on the argument by Adachi (2013), the central theme at non-structured gatherings tends to be the joint creation of a social field rather than distinguishing the self from the other, and hence, interactions to construct a field of affiliative co-presence repeatedly occur. Upon structuralization of a group, affinity adds reality to its existence and deepens the bonds between its members.

Our cognitive ability to discriminate between the self and other individuals comes with boundary variability and situational responsiveness. When "the other" is categorized, it is also expected to emerge with variability and situational responsiveness in a multilayered manner. The flexibility and multilayeredness of the emergence of the collectivized other is an integral part of the conditions of a group as a whole, i.e., its size, pattern of environmental use and way of life such as migration and settlement. It is perhaps reasonable to say that for humans and other great apes who have been leading highly migratory lives with recurrent fission-fusion, the condition of the other that has enabled them to simultaneously maintain group cohesion and flexible fission-fusion has been a significant development in the history of evolution. This is a mechanism that structures groups through the creation of "associates" in a nested pattern by the creation of "the other", while at the same time preventing their boundary from being completely fixed.

Another point to consider is the "gap" that occurs when an individual senses the other individual's intent. Although we have the ability to sense the other's intent, we also know that there is always the possibility that it is not their real intent, or that we have misread it in the sense that it is only speculative knowledge after all. This makes tactical deception possible, as mentioned by Takenoshita in Chapter Seventeen. While this gap can be a hindrance to smooth action connection, it created room for social negotiations and politics to arise and offered humans and great apes an opportunity to hone their social skills. It appears that the allowance of a gap in understanding at the individual level functions effectively in the collective formation of the other.

Humans have come to use "the other" more operationally due to their acquisition and development of language. By using the gap operationally through the use of language, they can find a common channel with the other individual(s) and create an association. They are able to leave "here, now", create "others" in a situationally responsive manner, convert them into the collective other beyond the individual's experience and utilize it as a resource in group formation.

This chapter treats the other as a phenomenon that appears as relationality in the practice of interaction, and focuses on the process in which it is collectively created. Our discussion aims to consider the other in humans in relation to group formation by describing various phases of the emergence of diverse others amongst the Bemba people.

Self/other as relationality, narrative and collective others

According to Stern's research on infant development (1983), self and other are differentiated from birth onward. Stern stresses the importance of mother-child interaction, which he called "state sharing". After the age of eighteen months, the establishment of self-awareness and the emergence of empathy are observed in combination with mirror self-recognition. Empathy is also said to be an ability that develops hand in hand with self/other distinction. The development of empathy is closely intertwined with the developmental stages of social perspective-taking (role-taking) over a long period. After going through egocentric role-taking at around age four, followed by subjective role-taking and self-reflective role-taking, one becomes able to take a third person's perspective by considering one's own and the other's perspectives by the time one reaches the mutual role-taking stage (age thirteen to sixteen). At this stage, one can associate one's own and the other's perspectives simultaneously and reciprocally and realizes that people interact by mutually considering each other's thoughts and emotions (Ito and Hirabayashi 1997; Kubo 1997). Humans thus discover the other at the same time that they discover the self, but "the other's perspective" taken at the time is the other's perspective inferred by "I", and not truly the other's. In this process they acquire the framework of "characters" and "actors", as discussed by Takenoshita in Chapter Seventeen.

Social psychologists Hermans and Kempen (1993) propose the concept of the dialogical self, inspired by James' (1993) theory of cognitive self and combined with the concept of polyphony. A polyphonic dialogue arises as a set of different interpretations about a single event in the form of the vocal exchange of actors in different positions in an imaginary space, and continues to create narratives about the world. In this space, the self is conceptualized through dialogue (including with imaginary others) that oscillates between a number of perspectives. The self is a relational phenomenon that transcends the boundary between the internal and the external, and self and other appear simultaneously within interactions in polyphonic dialogues.

What is noteworthy is that Hermans and Kempen translate the idea of *I*-positions and *Me*-positions for the analysis of narrative to establish the framework of polyphonic dialogue. They cite Mancuso and Sarbin (1983) who introduced the

I-Me distinction into a narrative framework: "*I* stands for the author, the *Me* for the actor or narrative figure". With this framework in mind, narrative construction becomes "a means for organizing episodes, actions, and the significance of the actions" (Hermans 2004: 18). *Me* in this discussion is relatively autonomous and independent from author *I*, and speaks freely regardless of the author's will[2]. The voices of "characters" in this dialogue are those of the others as inferred by "I", but the *I*-position is not constant.

Hermans and Kempen (1993: 167) cite Sarbin's version of the self-narrative:

> [A] single author is assumed to tell a story about himself or herself as an actor, the conception of the self as a polyphonic novel goes one step further. It permits the one and the same individual to live in a multiplicity of the worlds with each world having its own author telling a story relatively independent of the authors of the other worlds. Moreover, at times the several authors may enter into dialogue with each other.

They continue,

> In the polyphonic translation of the self, [...] the spatial character of the polyphonic novel leads to the supposition of a decentralized multiplicity of *I* positions that function like relatively independent authors, telling their stories about their respective *Me's* as actors. The *I* moves, in an imaginal space, from one to the other position, from which different or even contrasting views of the world are possible.

Through this imaginary dialogue involving multiple voices on different experiences and from different perspectives, the experiences are structured into a narrative form and a world is created. This implies that individual narratives continue to exist even when they are contradictory and can be altered by the voices of narrative figure. In this regard, the dialogical-self framework is useful here in considering the emergence of the other and the creation of association amongst the Bemba. This is because the collective "other" comes into being in the Bemba when other people envision the intention of the person regardless the person's true intent or actual action. Also, situational retelling allows contradictory narratives to be supported and the transformation of the other on the spot, so to speak, while other conflicting narratives also run in parallel.

Bruner (1998, 1999) argues that in the narrative mode of thought, stories deal with the intentions and actions of those who characterize the progression of narratives or their backgrounds, and are interpreted to convince people of their verisimilitude. There, concrete and idiographic human experience takes center stage and is positioned in time and space. While Hermans and Kempen's discussion of narratives is useful, I would like to emphasize here, in order to consider the collective other, that narratives are told in the voices of real people and enacted in a social space rather than in an imaginary space. This is because the collective other we are attempting to discuss in this chapter is considered to generate communication between multiple *I*-positions in a narrative format involving different individuals using their real voices and actual interactions, which in turn leads to the formation of the collective other. Each concrete idiographic experience is interpreted so as to convince people of its verisimilitude, as Bruner argues.

In the following examples, narratives are told in real voices, actually enacted and interacted with. When the framework proposed by Takenoshita in Chapter Seventeen is superimposed here, we can incorporate the aforementioned "gap" in the field of interaction and hear far freer voices of the "characters" themselves. A human who has acquired language conveys the truth-likeness of a series of events through narration, and shares the experiences of other individuals in a nesting pattern. Through the process of co-creating a narrative by telling/retelling it, people position each of their experiences in a particular time and space and share realities. By creating a particular narrative in the retelling, people make the temporal course of their experiences reversible and form the collective "we = associates", including the others. Based on this viewpoint, we next analyze the phases of the emergence of the other through ethnographic descriptions of the Bemba[3].

Bemba everyday life and ancestral spirits

An overview

The Bemba are a group of Bantu speaking peoples who reside in *miombo* woodland in the Northern Province of Zambia. After originating from a place near modern-day Angola and the Democratic Republic of Congo, by the end of the seventeenth century they had settled in the Kasama district in northern Zambia and eventually established a matrilineal chiefdom with various nearby ethnic groups under its control (Roberts 1974).

The chiefdom's political organization has a centralized structure comprising the Paramount Chief, *Chitimukulu*, at the top, three senior chiefs, including *Chitimukulu*, at the next level, and fifteen junior chiefs below it. Each chief is a highly autonomous king, who has his own territory and governs a wide range of legal and political matters as well as ritual and ceremonial matters within it. This political system was further consolidated upon colonization by the British at the end of the nineteenth century, and has been preserved to date after the country's independence[4]. The Bemba population has increased from just over 100,000 recorded in the 1930s to more than two million today[5].

While the Bemba people uphold the identity of "We, the Bemba" as members of the Bemba Chiefdom, they live in small villages as the basic residential unit ranging from ten to seventy households, mostly comprised of a headman and his matrilineal siblings. Due to the village's matrilineality and matrilocal residence system, most men other than the headman's matrilineal kin are from another village. The high divorce rate and high ratio of female-headed households are notable features (Kakeya and Sugiyama 1987, Sugiyama 1992). Villager mobility is relatively high, and it is common for people to travel to another locality to visit friends and relatives and stay there for long periods. When they run short of the nearby *miombo* woodland suitable for shifting cultivation, a number of villagers will set up a satellite hut in the woods several kilometers from their village suitable for cultivation. In any case, ten to thirty years after the establishment of the village settlement, the whole village migrates in search of adequately regenerated *miombo* woodland. In times of generational transition, internal conflicts cause many villages to break up, but this phenomenon synchronizes with the village's developmental cycle that is characteristic of matrilineal-matrilocal society (Sugiyama 2013; Oyama 2002, 2011).

The Bemba people have subsisted on their unique *chitemene* system of shifting cultivation as their main livelihood, combined with gathering, hunting, fishing, peddling and seasonal work in cities. They believe that the affluence in the villagers' lives is protected by the blessing of their ancestral spirits who live among *miombo* woods. Ancestral spirits command the weather and wild flora and fauna, and control the fertility of *miombo* woodland and peace in the villages. There are many conventions for the use of *miombo* woodland, including cultivation rituals, which are supported by the worship of the ancestral spirits and deeply involved in the rules of etiquette that govern behavior toward ancestral spirits. The ancestors' anger manifests as calamities and diseases and punishes those who breach the rules. Phases in which the other emerges are also generated through the involvement of the ancestral spirits.

Bemba witchcraft and ancestor worship

Witchcraft in the Bemba is more deeply associated with ancestor worship than animistic worship, as was the case in Audrey Richard's classic monograph (Sugiyama 2004; Richards 1950). For the villagers, the ancestral spirits are both objects of awe and familiar beings they know through rituals and the "name of the navel" practice. They are well versed in the names and personalities of the ancestral spirits and know the genealogical relations between them (Sugiyama 2004, 2017).

The ancestors who are well known to the villagers are mostly limited to a dozen or so chiefs a few generations down from the founding chief of the Bemba Chiefdom. The villagers' lives are deeply connected to the names and genealogies of these past chiefs through the naming practice of "name of the navel", where it is believed that an ancestral spirit enters a woman's womb through her navel when she becomes pregnant and influences the child for its lifetime. The newborn child is thus first given this ancestor's name. This is the "name of the navel".

The Bemba people learn the names of their ancestors through these navel names and position themselves in the genealogies of the Bemba chiefs. Theoretically, any Bemba is able to trace any other Bemba's ancestral genealogy by reference to their navel name and place them according to that genealogy. When they form a relationship with someone other than their kin or in a particular situation such as a ritual to treat an illness, they can mutually adjust their relationships by referring to the genealogies of the Bemba chiefs connected through their navel names (Sugiyama 2013).

Chiefs and village headmen are proficient in rituals to approach ancestral spirits and responsible for celebrating them. This is why chiefs and headmen are believed to have supernatural powers under the patronage of the ancestors and are thus given authority and political power. Headmen can appeal to the ancestral spirits to sanction those who disrupt the order of the village or deviate from the norms. They are also said to keep sorcerers and misfortune out of the village territory. On the other hand, it is believed that sorcery to harm others for personal gain or because of envy or a grudge is possible by manipulating the ancestral spirits in a broad sense. Whether to maintain the norms or for evil purposes, rituals to approach the ancestors produce forces that directly influence the stability of villagers' lives and the maintenance of the residential group. Besides chiefs and headmen, the mediums of the ancestral spirits (*ngulu*) and witch doctors have the skills to understand the intentions of the ancestors and communicate their words to the villagers.

The most fundamental principle governing life in Bemba villages is sharing. The failure to share can arouse envy and anger in other people, which can lead to witchcraft to bring trouble to the village or offend the ancestors and cause diseases or crop failures (Richards 1950; Kakeya 1983, 1987). When a sudden illness or disaster strikes an individual or the village as a whole, witchcraft and the ancestors' anger are used as tools to explain its causal link and offer guidance in the search for a solution. Conversely, these elements can also trigger a split between those who have been living together. The other in the Bemba often forms in a fissure in human relationships through the creation of narratives about calamities or witchcraft.

The formation of the other in a collective sense can provide the impetus to divide a group.

Witchcraft, calamities and the other

Phases of the other and narratives

Various phases of the other manifest in multiple situations involving the ancestral spirits and witchcraft such as net hunting, healing rituals and the ritual to please the ancestral spirits.

Situation 1

Intention of ancestral spirits in net hunting: From atypical to approachable other
In August 1984, I was staying in B village of the Bemba with my supervisor, Professor Kakeya, and became acquainted with the villagers. When Prof. Kakeya asked to accompany a net hunting party one day, the headman and other villagers firmly rejected his request, as the hunt on that day was a special hunt pertaining to a promotion ritual for a female medium. The hunt was intended as divination to find the intention of the ancestral spirits in relation to a decision on whether the medium should start training to become a witch doctor. The headman and other villagers said, "This is our important ritual. The presence of a white man will offend the ancestors. It will hinder the promotion ritual, so we are not allowing a white man to participate". This was tantamount to declaring that Prof. Kakeya, a "white man", was an "atypical other" who should not be involved in the village's important rituals.

In the end, the hunting party failed to catch anything. Divination by a witch doctor who had accompanied the party revealed that there was trouble in the village and that someone who had remained in the village and failed to participate in the hunt was harboring strong anger. The ancestral spirits were angry because that person had "quietly uttered a curse in expressing his anger"[6]. Upon hearing the revelation, the headman and many of the hunters said that they "immediately recognized that it was referring to Mr. Kakeya". After a whole day of hunting without success, the villagers returned home empty-handed.

In addition to the practical purpose of obtaining meat for food, net hunting in Bemba villages also serves as divination to ascertain the ancestors' intentions based on

Ancestral Spirits, Witchcraft and Phases of the Other in Everyday Life 267

Photo 11.1 Villagers folded their hunting net and conversed between hunts

the results of the hunt. A failed hunt indicates that the ancestors are angry. Catching a male animal means that the ancestors are indicating there is a problem, whereas a female animal indicates that the village is at peace and the ancestors are pleased. Witch doctors rarely accompany net hunting expeditions, except on important occasions such as promotion or harvest rituals. Once the result of a hunt is known, they conduct divination in *miombo* woods to determine a problem or to offer a prayer to the ancestral spirits.

On the following day, the headman visited Prof. Kakeya to apologize and asked him to participate in the next net hunt. Although Prof. Kakeya did not actually "utter a curse in anger", upon hearing the witch doctor's revelation, the villagers assumed that "he must have done so (otherwise we would have caught an animal)"[7]. With the participation of Prof. Kakeya, the next hunt quickly caught a female animal and the promotion ritual was completed without mishap.

The villagers loved to discuss this episode. While the main theme was the promotion of the female medium to the position of witch doctor, peppered with what each villager saw and heard, Prof. Kakeya was given an important role in everyone's story. The story went as follows: The "white man", who was initially regarded as the atypical other who had nothing to do with the core elements of our life, turned out to be a source of witchcraft through angry words and a being who had influence over our lives; although he was once angry, he was good enough to respond to the headman's apology and request for participation and to cooperate in the successful conduct of an important ritual; and it was confirmed that the ancestral spirits wished to treat the "white man" as a member of our village. Largely regardless of Prof. Kakeya's own motive or actual behavior, he came to be called "our white man", and his position was shifted from "atypical other" irrelevant to their life to "approachable other" who was a member of the same village.

Situation 2
Agreement between villagers in net hunting: From associate to approachable other
The failure of net hunting is taken as a sign of trouble in the village. The person who is determined as the source of trouble must undergo a ritual to cleanse their hunting net. In 1985, I joined in a hunt unaccompanied by a witch doctor that was unsuccessful. Without a witch doctor, villagers could not communicate with ancestral spirits to determine the reason for the hunt's failure. The male participants started joking with each other lightheartedly in guessing who the culprit was. This kind of situation is often observed during net hunting. On such an occasion, if some of them remember that someone has made trouble or suppressed his anger in the past, they hint at the past deed and jokingly identify him as the problematic person. This provides an opportunity for villagers to vent their relationship concerns in public that they cannot speak about in normal circumstances.

In many instances the named troublemaker does not accept the blame, and thinks that blaming him is not right. However, it is usually the case that he grudgingly kneels before the hunting net and hits the net with a bunch of twigs several times while muttering, "It is not me, but if you say I am to blame, I apologize, I apologize, I apologize". After that, the other villagers clap their hands, the headman declares that "Trouble has been cleansed", and they start the next hunt. If hunting failures continue, they ask a witch doctor to accompany the net hunt for divination.

This is a process in which a failed hunt leads to a situation where a villager initially participates in the hunt as an associate, but other villagers conveniently assign a social meaning to his past action and regard him as an other. To other villagers, this villager is "the approachable other" who has the ability to take the blame for the village's troubles and to conduct a cleansing ritual to solve the problem. "The other" thus formed is that created collectively, albeit temporarily, in a way that does not correspond with the

Photo 11.2 Net cleansing ritual
After a failed hunt, a man named as the cause of the failure performs a net cleansing ritual using a tree branch

named villager's intention. However, he reverts to the position of an associate when the headman declares that the "trouble has been cleansed".

Nevertheless, his temporary assumption of the role of the other in this situation is committed to memory and may manifest on a later occasion of misfortune or conflict as "the unapproachable other", as discussed next. In the case where conflict leads to the disintegration of the village in the next section, the naming of the headman as the cause of the ancestors' anger in this phase resulted in a serious problem.

Situation 3
Naming in healing rituals: Approachable/unapproachable other
When the villagers suffer disasters or major illnesses in quick succession, they seek treatment from a witch doctor. A diagnosis is made as to the cause of the illness or disaster, and the person causing the trouble is identified rather specifically. The most common causes include "a human-derived illness", indicating witchcraft, and the ancestors' anger. If witchcraft is diagnosed, the attributes of the responsible person are

mentioned in detail and those concerned with this matter are gathered for the conduct of a healing ritual. If the ancestors' anger is diagnosed as the problem, the particular event that triggered it is indicated and those who are concerned are gathered[8].

In either case, the person who is accused of witchcraft denies the charge. Yet, if others support the witch doctor's diagnosis, the accused must attend the healing session and cooperate with the ritual even if they profess their innocence. This is because if they refuse to cooperate, the accused runs the risk of being labeled as the "harmful other" and excluded from the group, whereas cooperation in the healing ritual will place the accused in the category of "the approachable other" able to participate in the rectification of the unfortunate situation. In some cases, the expedient explanation that the accused was compelled by envy inside him to unintentionally commit witchcraft or the act that angered the ancestors is used to pave the way to a possible reconciliation (Sugiyama 2017).

There are times when the accused is categorized as "the unapproachable other" who should be excluded. In most of these cases, a close relative of the victim is identified as the source of witchcraft, because in this situation witchcraft is regarded as real sorcery invoked with an intention to harm the target. This is seen as an evil plot to gain more power by killing a close relative rather than a mere manifestation of envy or anger via the ancestral spirits.

According to villagers, "Close relatives are to be feared most". Powerful sorcerers gain more power and authority by killing close relatives using sorcery and rejoice in it. It is impossible to coexist with sorcerers, who are malice and avarice personified. However, it is considered that the only way to deal with already existing sorcerers is to exclude them as "unapproachable others", and sometimes such accusations are taken as far as the chief's court. As mentioned earlier, these accusations tend to coincide with generational transitions and sometimes escalate into village breakups.

Situation 4

Pleasing the ancestral spirits: Ancestral spirits as the transcendental other
There are two types of rituals "to please the ancestral spirits", where the village's mediums gather to commune with them; one is a regularly conducted event and the other is organized as needed. The regular ritual is called "drinks to thank the ancestral spirits" and is held annually around October in conjunction with divination by net hunting. The mediums gather at the headman's home and invite the ancestral spirits to possess their bodies and speak their words. On these occasions, the headman is chastised for errors he has made in rituals and hidden issues among the villagers are

made public. The chastised headman and others apologize to the ancestral spirits according to the ritual and obtain their forgiveness.

When a hidden problem is revealed, the name of an ancestral spirit is mentioned in identifying a concerned party by their navel name. The other concerned party is also named in this way. The named parties among the drinkers sitting outside of the headman's home are called into the house for talks to settle the dispute. As there is more than one villager identified collectively according to their navel name, all of those named thus become involved in the ritual as concerned parties.

The ancestral spirits' allusion is often based on an actual conflict between villagers, and therefore some among those who are called into the house may have knowledge of it. Sometimes they come forward claiming, "It is my dispute" and assert their point of view. If no one comes forward, all of the suspected parties say, "It is not me, but if you say I am to blame, I apologize", and all clap their hands. After that, the headman declares reconciliation by saying, "The trouble has been resolved".

What is curious here is that the named villagers admit fault, even if they do not think they are parties to the supposed trouble, before reconciliation is declared. The villagers identified by the named navel names are collectively turned into the other in the negotiation and assigned the role of settling the dispute in the staged reconciliation.

As in Situation 2, they all revert to being associates after reconciliation has been achieved. The kind of troubles mentioned on these occasions are understood to be akin to witchcraft problems, and therefore may be linked with serious illnesses or disasters in the future and used to explain their cause.

The non-regular ritual to "please the ancestral spirits" is a more entertaining event, where villagers enjoy themselves as they watch the ancestral spirits sing and dance. Sometimes a problem in the village is mentioned between songs and dances. Although the parties to the issue are not named on this occasion, the ancestral spirit who alludes to the existence of trouble is identified through medium possession, and consequently the villagers try to figure out who among the villagers with that navel name could be involved. These episodes are also recalled when future misfortunes occur and used as causal factors.

According to "the name of the navel" practice, all villagers are supposed to have their ancestral spirits inside their bodies. On various occasions the spirits expose hidden troubles by expressing their anger. The named villager is accused of a certain action by the ancestral spirit inside their body as the transcendental other, and at the same time treated by other villagers as "the approachable other" and assigned the role of repairing the situation. However, the villager is thrown into the multilayered emergence of the other as they do not remember committing the act, and the named villager is also the other unknown to themselves.

Through these occasions, the villagers who have the same ancestral name as their navel name come to understand that they are irrevocably connected by the same ancestral spirit. The system of naming according to the spirit's name also provides a loophole for the village to discuss trouble between actual villagers as if it were trouble between their ancestral spirits as transcendental others.

Group fission-fusion and creating the other through narrative

A chain of events and a narrative of division

The other emerges with different phases in multiple situations. Utilizing this situation, people connect various occurrences in everyday life and collectively create a narrative. As shown in Situations 1 and 2 above, narration is often combined with a collective response to a problem at hand and oriented toward reunification, such as the resolution of the problem or the repairing of associations, but it occasionally develops into a relationship breakup. Especially in times of generational transition, narrative creation acts to sever connections with some fellow villagers as "the unapproachable other". On these occasions, conflicting narratives are created regarding the same event, and the villagers are divided into smaller groups depending on which narrative they retell (support). The following is a case involving the division and reformation of B village (Sugiyama 2004).

I have listed various events associated with this narrative chronologically in Table 11.1. This village was established by the previous headman together with his siblings in 1958. The whole village shifted to another location due to pest and disease problems in 1963, and in 1982 the previous headman relinquished his position to his younger brother.

The younger brother who succeeded the headmanship dealt with the sons of his sisters strictly. Based on the matrilineal system in the Bemba, the sons of the headman's sisters are supposed to be future successors to the position, but in this case the relationship between them and the headman had deteriorated[9]. The young and middle-aged sons of his sisters set up a satellite hut in *miombo* woods several kilometers away from the village, as they wished to open up a larger field for shifting cultivation. For a period of six months or so while they cleared the woodland, they stayed away from the village together and strengthened the affinity between them.

What gave rise to the narrative that led to division was a series of tragedies that started in 1984. In that year, a theft occurred as well as an incident in which a

Table 11.1 Events involved in the division and revival of B village

Year	Event in B village	Event in the chief's territory
1958	Founding of B village	
	Frequent pest damage and illnesses	
1963	B village moved to a new site	The previous chief passed away
1982	The previous headman relinquished his role to a younger brother	
1983	Relations between the headman and a group of younger men deteriorated	A new chief was appointed
1984	Several younger men set up satellite huts for *chitemene*	Edible caterpillars suddenly disappeared
	Net hunting failures	
	The previous headman fell seriously ill	
	A theft	
	A baby was bitten by a snake	
1986	A yellow fever outbreak, deaths of children	Arbitration at the chief's court
	A young woman suffered a strange illness and came back to life after dying	
	The previous headman was discovered to have a magical item	
	The previous and incumbent headmen were condemned as sorcerers	
1987	The village split	Enquiry to deregister the village
	The aforementioned young woman was bitten by a poisonous snake	
1996	The village was reinstated	

baby was bitten by a snake, and a succession of net hunting failures aroused some voices of concern about the ancestral spirits' anger or problems in the village. In October that year, edible caterpillars had suddenly disappeared despite an earlier forecast of a bumper catch. From the end of 1985 through 1986, an outbreak of yellow fever in the region killed several children in the village. Then, a young female villager caught a strange disease and died before diagnosis was possible. As one of the yellow fever victims was her daughter, the villagers lamented her misfortunes and many attended her funeral. However, bizarrely, the woman came back to life in the middle of her funeral.

As she failed to regain full consciousness even though she was alive, a witch doctor was asked for a diagnosis. In the process, it was discovered that the previous headman was in possession of a magical item. He claimed that he had placed the magical item to detect thieves, but his excuse was rejected and he was accused of sorcery in 1987. The incumbent headman was also accused of abusing his authority in approaching the ancestral spirits, angering them and causing the snakebite incident.

From then on, various misfortunes that happened in and after 1984 were retrospectively told as causally-related narratives, as follows.

> Poor hunting results, the deaths of children from yellow fever, the young woman's strange illness and the disappearance of edible caterpillars are all connected. Witchcraft by the previous headman and the ancestral spirits' anger toward the incumbent headman are the cause. Anger toward the headman for his mistakes in ritual procedures has made the situation worse. This problem was indicated in net hunting. Although the headman has lost the ancestral spirits' protection, he abused his authority to appeal to them in relation to the theft incident and consequently aroused their anger. What triggered this series of misfortunes was the establishment of a new ancestral shrine by the headman using an "improper" method. The snakebite incident was a manifestation of the ancestors' anger toward the headman, who tried to abuse his power. It was a sign of major misfortunes to come, including yellow fever and the woman's illness, and a warning from the ancestral spirits. The headman forgot his responsibility to protect the villagers and used the ancestral spirits and cursed his relatives for his selfish desires, as did the previous headman out of personal enmity. Their actions aroused strong anger in the ancestral spirits and brought misfortune to the villagers. The headmen are sorcerers.

This narrative was not constructed overnight. As shown in Figure 11.1, it was completed in a process in which those who were involved in the events told their stories respectively, and those who heard them added their own interpretations and retold them from different points of view.

The narrative goes back to the existence of trouble indicated in net hunting a long time ago, and treats the errors supposedly made by the headman in dealing with the ancestral spirits as the beginning of all the misfortune. The incident in which a baby was bitten by a snake was positioned as a sign of a series of misfortunes to come (Figure 11.1). The headman and the previous headman were accused of causing this situation and their authority was questioned. They were condemned as sorcerers and mediation attempts at the chief's court also failed. The villagers who supported this narrative accusing the headmen migrated to C village

Ancestral Spirits, Witchcraft and Phases of the Other in Everyday Life

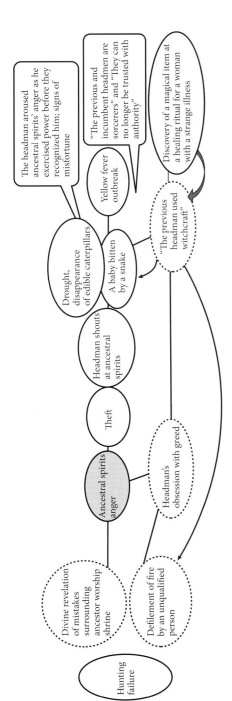

Figure 11.1 Divisive narrative

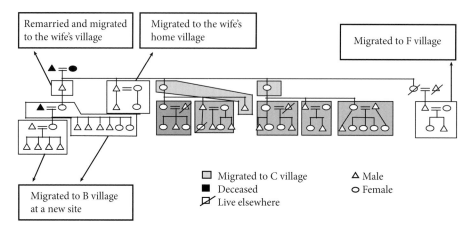

Figure 11.2 Mode of division and othering by narrative

together. The headman and the previous headman who rejected the accusations moved to different villages. Those who were neutral migrated to F village. Thus, the village divided and ceased to exist (Figure 11.2). In this narrative leading to the division, the headman and the previous headman were deprived of the legitimacy of their authority and condemned as sorcerers who cursed their close relatives out of enmity and greed. The past events that had happened in Situations 2, 3 and 4 in relation to the emergence of the other were remembered and used as the important foreshadowing elements of the narrative. When the narrative integrating all these causative elements was shared by the villagers, the headman and the previous headman were collectively turned into the other, categorized as "the unapproachable other" and even the excluded other, and the residential group of B village broke up and scattered.

A narrative for reunification
About a decade after the disintegration of B village, the village was reformed with the sons of the sisters of the previous headman who were eligible to succeed the headmanship and their siblings as its core members. What gradually took place over several years in the lead up to the reunification was the retelling of the narrative behind the division from a different perspective. Those who had previously supported the accusatory narrative against the headmen constructed one of reconciliation and reunification about the same series of events by talking about them on various occasions. The story goes as follows.

The "alarming problem" indicated by poor hunting results and divination pointed to the conflict between the headmen and some young and middle-aged men that brought the village to the brink of a break up. The ancestral spirits were warning about it. We should have talked it over but we did not understand the ancestors' warnings and made them angrier.

As yellow fever and deaths of children spread throughout the chief's territory, errors in ritual procedure were committed by the chief, not the headman, and angered the greater ancestral spirits. Rain stopped and edible caterpillars disappeared because of the chief's mistakes and we experienced terrible hardships. And it was the chief who sold our land to the government.

The woman's strange illness was caused by witchcraft carried out by a woman with whom her husband was having an affair, and had nothing to do with the previous headman's magical item. This was because her misfortune continued even after the previous headman left the village and she ended up losing her toe from a poisonous snakebite. The previous headman actually used his knowledge of herbal medicine to save her from the mistress's witchcraft. It was inappropriate for the previous headman to place a magical item, even in the name of justice, but that's all water under the bridge. The act of remembering his duty and saving the woman was more important and should be respected.

This explanation was formulated dialogically by rearranging the same events to make a different story. Interestingly, it was told by the very people who had previously created the narrative that led to the division of B village. Its characteristic is found in the disassembling of the elements that had been causally connected in the divisive narrative for the purpose of demonstrating that the series of misfortunes had not been triggered by the headman's mistakes. The "alarming problem" indicated in net hunting divination was reinterpreted as a rift among the village men, while the yellow fever outbreak was attributed to the ancestral spirits' anger at the chief's mistakes. Further, the village woman's strange illness was brought back into the narrower, interparty context of sorcery carried out by her husband's mistress.

The new interpretation largely followed the narratives given by the previous and incumbent headmen to justify their actions at the time. In other words, the people who tried to revive B village created a narrative able to be shared once again amongst themselves and the previous headman by rearranging the events of that time from a different perspective from that at the time of the division (the position that located the previous headman as the other). The previous headman, who had been condemned as a sorcerer and excluded as "the unapproachable other", was welcomed back as "the approachable other" and included in the association of the new B village with a view to its reinstatement.

There was a reason behind revising the divisive narrative and repositioning the previous headman from "the unapproachable other" to "the approachable other". A successor to the headmanship must receive special training from a village elder to learn the rituals for the ancestral spirits and become initiated into the art of their worship. The person able to teach the most effective rituals to the relatives was the previous headman, who was their maternal uncle with experience as headman. For this reason, he had to be recast in the position of "the approachable other". The young and middle-aged men of B village, who had once condemned and parted ways with the previous headman, later created the unifying narrative by following the composition of his excusatory narrative and adding subsequent events to it. They eventually achieved reconciliation by sharing the narrative of reunification among the constituent members of the new village, including the previous headman.

It should be noted that the elements incorporated in the reunification narrative were mostly the same as those told in the division narrative. However, while the division narrative attributed the ancestral spirits' anger to individual errors made by the previous and incumbent headmen in the village-level context, the reunification narrative shifted the context in which the ancestral spirits' anger was aroused to the chief's territory level while retaining that anger as the key element, and at the same time found fault with "we" as a whole rather than the headmen as individuals, thus closing the way to collectively turn the headmen into the other.

In these narratives, the ancestral spirits as the transcendental other play a significant role. The villagers face one another as individual beings "here, now". However, the belief that the individuals are directly connected to their respective ancestors through their navel names and given peace and security by *miombo* woodland ruled by the ancestral spirits enables the narratives to address the events experienced by the villagers "here, now", while indicating causal relations on the other layers to socialize the individuals' experiences.

We need to remember that the issues relevant to the peace and security of the entire village such as a lack of rain, crop failures, pest damage and plagues are linked to the intention of the ancestral spirits as the transcendental other, not people, in the narratives. When a major disaster strikes, people begin to talk about interpersonal disputes, which have been understood in individual contexts, in a narrative linked to the intention of the ancestral spirits. This way of making a narrative was used as a representation of a certain political standpoint and a tool to eclipse the power and authority of the village elders. When they revised the narrative to follow the previous headman's perspective from the new position of "we", he regained his authority.

Alignment of narratives and formation of the collective other

In the everyday life of the Bemba, various situations see the emergence of different others, ranging from the submerged other through to the atypical other, the approachable other and the unapproachable other along a gradient, and people move back and forth along this gradient according to the situation that creates the other through narratives. Under normal circumstances, people tell their individual narratives from their respective positions, but when they come to a situation in which the other is created, the narratives that are told individually are given a certain direction by "the ancestral spirits' intention" and turn a particular villager or villagers into the other as a result.

At a gathering of three or more villagers, people make a hidden problem visible by using the ancestral spirits' intention as a pretext, determine the party to the problem, temporarily create the approachable other and assign the role of correcting the problem. On the back of the presented "intention of the ancestral spirits" in this situation, people engage in a dialogue in an attempt to bring their narrative viewpoints closer by aligning each other's narratives. For instance, the process of guessing "the party" through an exchange of innuendoes between participants after the problem has been brought to the surface, as in Situation 3, clearly demonstrates people's attitude to collectively create and share a narrative told from the viewpoint of "the party" (*I*-position) they determine. It seems that people endeavor to align their viewpoints and narratives to achieve cooperation precisely because they presume the existence of a "gap" between them.

The situations in which the other emerges saliently involve crises for the village as a residential group, including a series of misfortunes, disputes, conflicts, crop failures due to bad weather and plagues. In these situations, using a collective approach people turn some villagers they normally associate with into "the other", and assign the role of repairing their social life that has been disrupted by "the ancestral spirits' anger" or "witchcraft" at times through a ritual apology to the ancestral spirits and at others through a condemnation of sorcery[10]. As demonstrated by the schism between the group of young and middle-aged men and that of older men, including the previous and incumbent headmen, at the time of the village split, people use the sharing of events as a series of narratives to socialize each individual's experience, form associations according to the situation and structuralize the group. Although each villager's experience of a given event is specific and different from any other villager's experience, the process of aligning each other's narratives leads to their consolidation around one viewpoint and the formation of the other.

I would like to point out that the person who is made "the unapproachable other" and subjected to condemnation is not necessarily completely ostracized. The "name of the navel" practice dictates that each Bemba carries an ancestral spirit as the transcendental other inside their body from birth. The same ancestral spirit resides in the bodies of other Bemba as well. They separate out "the unapproachable other, the other to be excluded" from among their associates while maintaining the setting in which their pre-existing relationships cannot be severed completely. This is where a device for the division and reunification of the group is found.

The power of the narrative is also important. As a new narrative was retold from a different viewpoint at the time of the reunification of B village, a different context was created. The same series of events creates a narrative that shapes a different worldview while forming a completely different other, and prompts fission-fusion through the reorganization of their association. The events are freely rearranged from a different viewpoint and the experienced facts take on the appearance of manipulable objects. In the case of B village discussed in this chapter, the narrative for reunification was born at the point of resolution of the conflict between the competitor's viewpoint and the successor's viewpoint surrounding power and control over the village. The use of language there allowed the free retelling of the narrative and made the chronology of the events reversible in that sense.

Particularly in the case of the Bemba, by positioning the ancestral spirits as the transcendental other along the gradient of the phases of the other, they have made it possible to position practically uncontrollable events such as bad weather and plagues as something they can deal with. They come up with a means to handle these misfortunes collectively by turning a person who has been named as the cause of "the ancestral spirits' anger" into the other, and assigning the role of an intermediary to placate this anger.

The Bemba collectively deal with village-wide crises such as disputes, conflicts, plagues and crop failures due to bad weather by creating the other for the purpose of repairing the environment and social relations and maintaining the group. They also make use of the individual's experiences such as illness and hardships to create and share narratives. In doing so, they have created the other arbitrarily, converted them into the collective other that transcends each individual's experience and repeatedly carried out fission-fusion and migration in a flexible manner by reorganizing their association through division and reunification. "The other" in the Bemba serves as a resource to generate a group that is sustainable over the long-term as it changes in size and composition.

In light of this example, it is reasonable to say that the possibility of a "gap" in the sensing of one another in interactions between individuals not only provides the impetus to create diverse others, but also generates directionality toward the sharing of a worldview in a social field that is reshaped every time individual narratives are "aligned" through polyphonic dialogues mediated by language. This strategy has something in common with the formation of the "qualified other" discussed by Nishie in Chapter Six. The question of whether this directionality has emerged specifically in humans will have to be discussed further through a comparative analysis of non-human great apes, as attempted by Takenoshita in Chapter Seventeen, including an analysis of the function performed by language through dialogically created narratives.

12 The "Face" and the Other: Muslim Women Behind the Veil

Ryōko Nishii

Key ideas

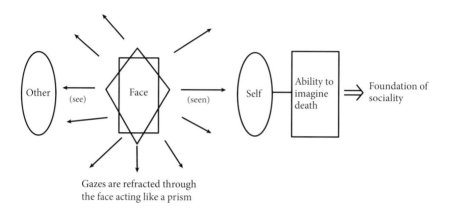

Gazes are refracted through the face acting like a prism

People are compelled to enter into responsive relationships with others by their physical presence. By meeting face-to-face, the other affects and generates the self, and the face is the keystone of this affective relationship. A human being is considered to be a being that receives the other through the face, and performs a leap from the other in front of one to the non-phenomenal other = the transcendental other. A human being who has developed an ability to imagine death acquires a face that inspires the formation of an ethical self beyond the face as the symbol of a biological individual. This perhaps means that humans have come to form the basis of their sociality through their faces in the process of their evolution.

The veil

The "face" on the boundary between self and other

The custom of covering the face of the dead with a piece of cloth is not exclusive to Japan. In the southern Thai village with a mixed population of Muslims and Buddhists where I have been conducting ethnographic research, local people from both religions lay the deceased person on a bed and cover their face with a cloth. In fact, the Muslims cover the whole body of the deceased with a white cloth, and the Buddhists cover the body with a blanket until it is placed in a casket, while the Japanese place a small cloth only over the face of the deceased[1]. On these occasions, the cloth covering the face of the deceased looks as if it were a marker distinguishing the dead from the living. The cloth indicates that the body of the dead is no longer in the same condition as the body of a living person, no matter how peaceful the face appears. Why do we cover the face of the dead? It probably has something to do with the unique, evocative power of the face.

The face possesses individuality that allows us to distinguish between one individual and another. In the process of evolution, the formation of a face begins with the mouth to take in energy, followed by sensory organs such as the eyes, nose and ears (Baba 2009: 12–14). At the primate stage, the shifting of the eyes from the sides to the front of the face allowed stereoscopic vision, which led to the enlargement of the brain. In primates, the importance of facial expressions in communication has been highlighted, based on the fact that facial muscles of expression are equally developed in both gorillas and pithecanthropus[2].

Early on in the field of psychology, it was pointed out that facial expression recognition forms the basis of social relations. In the 1980s, Ekman and others published their highly influential theory that the characteristics of facial expressions for six basic emotions – anger, disgust, fear, happiness, sadness and surprise – are universal in humankind (Ekman and Friesen 1987). In recent years, research on facial recognition has flourished and studies on cultural differences in facial expression recognition have been attracting attention[3].

In this chapter I consider the existential human condition involving the self and the other in relation to the "face" as a significant factor in social relationships. More specifically, I look at the act of covering the face with a veil among female participants in the Da'wa movement[4], one of the Islamic revivalist movements[5] in Thailand, and link it to our broader discussion of the other[6]. This constitutes an attempt to elucidate some part of the formation of human sociality while encompassing a wide range of phenomena, from that concerning specific "faces" to the ethics for living outlined in Lévinas's non-phenomenal "face" in face-to-face situations[7].

The absence of the face

Muslim women wear diverse forms of veils. Besides the niqab and the chador that cover the entire body, including the face, the commonly worn veil such as the hijab in Indonesia, Malaysia and Thailand is a short type that covers the hair but not the face[8].

Among these types of veils, I consider the use of face-covering veils in particular here. In the Thai language, the expression *pit na* (to cover the face) consists of *na* meaning "face" or "front", and *pit* meaning "to close" or "to block", though they have no particular name for face-covering veils. In this chapter, I attempt to demonstrate that "closing the face", i.e., "the absence of the face", conversely highlights the meaning of the face or the phenomena manifested by it.

Washida (1998: 34) states, "The absence of the face makes people feel uneasy perhaps because the face has transitioned to an obscure existence that can no longer be identified as something". In face-to-face situations, "The absence of the face means an inability to enter into a relationship of mutual understanding in which people mutually see themselves in their counterpart as if seeing their reflection in a mirror, and therefore covering one's face with a hood or a mask signifies a unilateral refusal to enter into a smooth communicative relationship between I and the other" (Washida 1998: 36).

I am certainly not the only person who has felt uncomfortable looking squarely at or communicating with a Muslim woman with her face covered by a veil. I suppose that one reason for this is that my inability to see her facial expressions prevents me from checking how my remarks have been received, and makes me hesitant to continue speaking.

Once I have seen a woman's face without a veil, however, I feel much less hesitant in subsequent conversations with her, even when she is wearing a veil. If I have never seen her face, I continue to have this sense of uncertainty, as I do not know whom I am talking to. In other words, the face serves as a crucial element in perceiving the entire personality of one's conversation partner. The other is a counterpart whose face makes one feel that one has understood that person.

The Da'wa movement and women's activities

The characteristics of the Da'wa movement

The Da'wa movement emphasizes edification through physical movement and travel as a means of personal reform. The conversion of an individual to Da'wa cosmology transforms their entire world. The new world is established in the deepest part of the inner self of the believer (Masud 2000). In short, the movement aims to transform an individual's worldview and inner world through individual practices, and by extension their overall attitude to life or way of living in the direction of Islam.

In practice, followers form a group of ten or so members called the Jama'at under a leader called the *shuro*, and visit mosques in various areas for either three days per month, or in blocks of forty days or four months per year. They stay at each mosque for three days to study Islam and visit local villagers to invite them to join the movement. They carry their own cooking equipment and eat and sleep at each mosque. During Da'wa, participants completely "isolate" themselves from the secular world outside of the mosque to devote themselves to worship and learning. They are required to fully abide by the rules of the mosque.

These travels are normally organized for men only. Special travel parties that include women are organized separately (see below).

For Da'wa participants, the Da'wa principles must be reflected in their family and marital relationships. Da'wa teachings start with wives and children. The husband is instructed to pay attention to how his wife dresses. A Da'wa leader in southern Thailand told me in an interview, "Those who participate in Da'wa treat their religion sincerely and never leave the clothes of their wives and children alone". He said that his wife had changed since she began to participate in Da'wa with him after marriage. She used to leave her face uncovered, just as many other women in southern Thailand do, but she now covers her face except her eyes when she goes out.

The Da'wa movement in Mae Sot

It is said that Da'wa was introduced to Thailand in 1966 by Haji Yusuf Kan of Mae Sot in Tak Province at the border between Thailand and Myanmar[9]. Over ninety percent of Muslim men in Mae Sot have participated in Da'wa. There are arguments for and against Da'wa, even among past participants. Regarding the Da'wa movement in the Muslim community of Mae Sot today, there is a clear difference of opinion between the pro-Da'wa camp led by recent Muslim arrivals from Myanmar and the anti-Da'wa camp of mostly Thai Muslims who used to participate in the movement but are now critical of it. This is the current condition of the Da'wa movement, which has been undergoing a transformation triggered by the recent phenomenon of an influx of Muslims from Myanmar escaping from persecution by the Myanmar government and the Buddhist majority[10].

Da'wa activities amongst women

A study meeting called *talim* is exclusively for women and attracts active participation. In Mae Sot where both Burmese and Thai are spoken, *talim* is organized for women in each language once per week. When I conducted a survey in 2013, Burmese-speaking *talim* meetings were held on Fridays and Thai-speaking meetings on Sundays at the homes of the participants on a rotation basis. Most *talim* participants wear face-covering veils outside of their homes. When they are inside the room where *talim* is held at the host's house in the presence of women only, they remove their veils and expose their faces[11].

The Burmese-speaking *talim* I observed on 31 August 2012 was conducted in the following manner. For thirty minutes from two o'clock in the afternoon, participants recited passages from a Tabligh textbook or the Qur'an. A male Islam expert arrived halfway through to give a lecture, but he remained invisible behind a curtain for the duration; the lights were turned on behind the curtain while the women's side of the room was darkened during the fifteen-minute lecture so that the women could not be seen by the man. The study meeting lasted for two hours or so. After the meeting, refreshments were served and the women chatted for a while before they put their veils on and left. At this Burmese-speaking *talim*, I hesitantly asked if I could photograph the participants in the room. They all put their veils on and allowed me to do so. The face-covering veil is part of their standard dress here.

Cases of women who wear the face-covering veil (*pit na*)

Motives for covering the face with a veil

In Mae Sot, it is not compulsory for women to cover their faces. Many of the veil-wearing women there say that they were motivated to wear veils because other women were doing so. Here are some examples.

Suniya[12] (age twenty-three), whom I met at a Thai-speaking *talim*, has a Muslim father from Pakistan while her mother is a former Buddhist who converted to Islam upon marriage. She was born in Nakhon Sawan Province, northeastern Thailand, and moved to Mae Sot when she was four months old. She is strikingly beautiful with fine facial features, but she always wears a veil to cover her face when she is outside. She said that she first wore the veil when she was in the second year of junior high school. Since she attended a three-day Da'wa for the first time at the age of ten with her aunt, she has participated in Da'wa many times with her relatives and went to Bangkok to study Islam for one year when she was a second-year junior high school student. She explained her motivation to cover her face: "I saw my brother's wife and other women around me covering their faces and wanted to do so myself; I got permission to cover my face from my mother". She returned to Mae Sot at the age of nineteen and married an Islamic teacher; she now teaches Islam to children.

When a woman participates in Da'wa, she must be chaperoned by her husband or a male relative who cannot marry her, such as her father or brothers; women cannot go on their own. Men and women, even married couples, stay in separate places while participating in Da'wa. Men stay at the mosque while women stay at a nearby house together – male members of the family who owns the house cannot go home for the duration. The form of Da'wa attended by these male-female pairs is called *masturo*.

Many Da'wa participants feel an extraordinary sense of elation or solidarity during the event. Many women reported that they got the desire to cover their faces while participating in Da'wa and wanted to continue doing so after returning home. Saida (age thirty-eight) explains as follows: "While at Da'wa, all women other than myself were covering their faces. After returning from the forty-day Da'wa, I felt the desire and covered my face, too". In this way, many women are motivated to cover their faces by their relationships with other women at Da'wa.

Reasons for covering the face

Besides their initial motivation, women mention other reasons for covering their faces.

Firstly, it is often said that women are "precious properties". They say that women cover their faces because "women are like diamonds; they should be stowed away in a drawer and not be taken out" or "women are like bananas; they stay fresh covered, but they spoil quickly when they are peeled; that is why women must cover their faces when they go outside". These words were heard at a gathering of women who visited Da'wa (*masturo*) from Myanmar.

Another reason women mention is that they cover their faces to avoid committing a sin, because arousing desire in men is a sin. Zainab is a former schoolteacher who has devoted herself to Da'wa activities since retirement and wears the veil. The youthful and beautiful woman, who does not look her age (over sixty), says as follows: "If a woman goes out not properly covered and arouses desire in men, she is committing a sin. It is worse than killing someone. You can only kill one person. If she is improperly dressed and arouses desire in many men, she is causing many people to commit a sin".

Similarly, at the same Da'wa another beautiful woman with an air of glamour says as follows[13].

> My husband's father has never seen me. I have three children but I try not to let him see me. If he sees me, he may think I'm beautiful or he may think something bad. People's minds change. My religion does not allow showing [my face]. Only my father and brothers [see my face]. I don't show my face to my husband's brothers either. If I live my life in this way, God will reward me in the afterlife. It is like an unpeeled fruit. I don't show my hair because if I do, each hair will turn into 70,000 snakes and bite.

Saida (age thirty-eight) says that covering her face helps her avoid risks. Let us look at her case in more detail below.

In Bangkok, she worked for an IT company and her husband worked in the air force. Her husband started participating in Da'wa through a friend before urging her to participate as well. In 2003, they left their jobs at the age of twenty-eight and returned to Mae Sot.

Saida says as follows: "If I cover my face, I'll be rewarded in the afterlife and I get safety in this life… Men do not dare to flirt with me. It's self-defense. Covering my face makes everything better". The "safety in this life" she points to derives from "becoming invisible" to others.

> I won't be punished after death. If I cover my face, men cannot see. Whether my face is beautiful or not. They can't do anything bad to me. We don't have to look at men either. Men may look at me but they cannot see me. Men cannot harass me. And women covering their faces cannot gaze at men. They stay calm. They don't want to look. Covering the heart [*klum citcai duai*], too.

This suggests that covering the face can sever the see-seen relationship and that it is possible to strategically manipulate relationality itself by doing so. This is apparent in the case of Fatima below.

Fatima (age twenty-eight) is a Burmese Muslim who migrated to Mae Sot with her seven brothers fifteen years ago. She acted as my interpreter with her fluent Thai at the first Burmese-speaking *talim* I participated in. She lives with her ten-year-old son. When she was twenty, her parents tried to marry her off to a Burmese Muslim and she ran away to a relative's house in Bangkok. She was eventually persuaded to marry him by her parents, who told her that he was a good man. When she was seven-months pregnant, her husband, a motorbike-taxi driver, died in an accident in Bangkok. She returned to Mae Sot and remarried a forty-five year-old man, twenty-two years her senior, when her child was eighteen months old. Although he already had a wife, he said that it was pitiful to raise a child without a father and visited her parents three times to propose marriage. She finally agreed to marry him. The second husband was a roti[14] vendor on Samui Island in southern Thailand, who was Muslim but living with a Buddhist wife. He often returned to Mae Sot, where his parents lived, and gave her 100 baht per day[15]. Soon after her remarriage, however, she discovered that her new husband was quick to anger and behaved violently toward her and her son. She was sometimes strangled to the extent that she was unable to eat. He beat her son with an electrical cord. She said that she could endure violence toward her, but not toward her son. Her son hated his stepfather and said, "I will avenge you, mother, I will stab him with a knife".

Fatima participated in Da'wa for the first time four years ago. Her son warned her, "Mother, don't go to the mosque. Father will punch you again". During Da'wa, she was surprised at how helpful and caring people were toward each other. "They take food from the same plate by hand to share with everyone. They do the dishes and sleep together even though they are not brothers or sisters. Allah is great and Muhammad is great. After three days in Da'wa, we all cried when we left, even though we all live in the same community". When she went to Da'wa in Pakistan later on, a Pakistani asked her why she did not cover her face. The Pakistani told her: "Everyone has his own taste. One person likes fair skin, another person likes dark skin. Men desire women [if women do not cover their faces]. It causes problems. The Prophet did not like women showing their faces". Although Fatima claims that she is not beautiful because she does not have fair skin, from my point of view she has an attractive face with chiseled features and large eyes. Upon returning from this Da'wa, she decided to cover her face.

Fatima was initially unsure whether she could cover her face, but she liked it when she tried. Her husband did not like it and tried to prevent her from doing so. About two years ago, she finally got a divorce and ended her seven years of marital misery, during which her husband beat her daily when he was staying in Mae Sot. "Nowadays, I pay no attention when he returns to Mae Sot. I do not greet him. I'm covering my face, so I ignore him". Thus, Fatima was able to sever an abusive interpersonal relationship by covering her face.

Criticism toward face covering

Many Thai Muslims, who do not normally cover their faces, voice their criticisms of this practice. The population of the southern Thai village where I conducted my research is equally divided between Muslims and Buddhists, but only three women wear face-covering veils and only one of them, a former Buddhist who recently migrated from Myanmar, wears it constantly when out of the home. She converted to Islam when she married a Muslim man. Kop, who is involved in Da'wa activities in the village, began to take his wife to Da'wa just one year ago. His wife started wearing the veil at around the same time. However, she wears it only when attending Da'wa with her husband and she shows her face in her day-to-day village life, just as other Muslim women do. Kop explains why his wife does not always wear the veil as follows.

> Covering the face is prescribed by God's law. A woman cannot have the courage to cover her face because she is afraid of people. Afraid of being criticized. Being talked about behind her back. If the king orders a soldier to wear a particular uniform, villagers criticize that he looks like a Likay [village theater] actor, and the soldier takes his uniform off. The villagers cannot be punished, but the king can pass a death sentence [on the soldier who did not follow his order]. This is why one should fear God instead of fearing people [who criticize face covering].

Kop's wife does not wear a veil every day, as she is afraid of being criticized by other villagers.

The parents of Saida in the earlier example initially strongly disapproved of face covering.

> They complained to me every day that they did not like [face covering], and why I quit a good job in Bangkok. They kept telling me day after day until they stopped eventually. When I came home covering my face for the first time after a forty-day Da'wa, my mother didn't let me in the house. They opposed, but my mother eventually stopped complaining. In those days, there weren't many [people who covered their faces]. Many [of those who covered their faces] came from Myanmar. …No matter what they say, I won't remove [a face-covering veil]. I must stand firm. My father says "why do I cover my face?", criticizes that it's too strict, and does not greet me when he passes me outside because he says he can't tell if it is his daughter. When there are many people covering their faces when he is walking outside, he can't see which person is his child. That's why he doesn't greet. They are all black.

These criticisms seem to arise from people's rejection in response to the act of covering the face itself, rather than for religious reasons. Some people argue against it on the grounds that face covering causes practical problems.

Practical inconvenience was mentioned by the principal of an Islamic school, claiming that students in Arabic lessons cannot see the mouth of their teacher if she covers her face. He asks the female teachers who wear veils to show their faces during lessons, as it is important to show their mouth movements and only children and no male adults are present in the classroom. Zainab, a Thai Muslim from Myanmar I met at a *masturo* study meeting, used to be an English teacher, and she was not allowed to cover her face with a veil while working. She began to wear it only after her retirement.

Some Muslims other than those who participate in Da'wa offer different interpretations about covering the face for religious reasons.

Farida (age forty-two) worked as a teacher for six years at an Islamic school in Chachoengsao in central Thailand, and now teaches Islam to children at home. She migrated to Mae Sot upon marriage. Her husband is an imam at a leading mosque in Mae Sot. She says that it is not compulsory for women to cover their faces and hands; they are completely free to choose.

Harima (age seventy-eight) is a cheerful and active woman who volunteers at hospitals and in the community and continues to go to Bangkok by overnight bus every weekend to attend lectures on Islam. She also takes gemstones and other merchandise from Mae Sot to do business during her visits. She has been studying in Bangkok for over twenty years. She proudly claims to be more proficient in Islam than anyone else in Mae Sot. "Islam does not command women to cover their faces and hands. The Qur'an simply says, 'Tell female believers to look downward modestly, guard the genitals and hide other beautiful parts from other people except the visible parts. Cover the chest'".

Changes triggered by face covering
In women who cover their faces

Common comments made by many women about the impact of covering their faces are as follows.

"My mind calms down [*citcai sagop khun*], feels happy [*mi khwam suk*] and feels comfortable [*sabai cai*]". "I gain merit in the afterlife and safety in this life. I believe in God. I can gain virtue in the afterlife". Aisha (age thirty), whom I met in a Burmese-speaking *talim*, says as follows: "Everything got better. My mind is more relaxed. I have changed a lot".

Zainab, a Thai Muslim, says, "I feel relaxed when I cover my face. It's uncomfortable [embarrassing] to be looked at by men. My husband, father and brothers are the only exceptions". About not wearing a veil, Saida says, "If I don't cover my face, I don't know what to do when I go outside. It's uncomfortable [*mai sabaicai*]".

In men whose wives cover their faces
How do the husbands feel about their wives covering their faces?

One benefit is the ability to avoid the gaze of other men. Alam is an Islamic teacher from Myanmar who is also a Da'wa leader.

> Covering the face is wonderful. It's a hallmark of the religion (Islam). It's written in the Qur'an. It can't be helped if she can't cover her face at work. But it is not the best. Men do not need to cover. Women must cover. It's not good when men look at them. Covering reduces the risk. You can't tell if she is beautiful. Women are important. That's why it's best for them to cover up and stay home. The wives should stay home and do nothing.

Similar to the reasons cited by women above, Kop, the aforementioned Da'wa participant in southern Thailand, identifies religious sin and the value of women as property as reasons for women to cover their faces.

> According to the Islamic code, women are men's properties. Not only their faces, but if they go outside, they arouse sexual desire. Wearing revealing clothes is a sin. It is difficult to practice. But it is seen as strange. It is right in Islam. You don't see their faces unless you are a family member. You don't know whose children they are. What their faces look like. They are covered. It's a human resource [*sapayakon butkhon*], a valuable resource. Forestalls desires. Just as we forestall a brain drain [of highly trained workers to foreign countries], or just like natural rubber or jasmine rice, we protect them.

He also feels that his wife has become beautiful since she began to cover her face. In Thailand, fair skin is considered to be one of the most important requirements for female beauty. Kop says rather joyfully, "She has a lighter complexion. I feel bad [*huacai sia*] if [other men] look at her face wondering whose wife she is". This schema follows the logic that men are actors while women are property, and therefore men must protect women in the house and fend off dangers from the outside. In support of this, the wife is not addressed by her personal name when participating in Da'wa. If her husband's name is Kop, she is addressed as "Ariya Kop". "Ariya" means a person under protection, and therefore "Ariya Kop" means "a person under the protection of Kop" (Kop's wife). When it is time for the wife staying at the women's accommodation to leave, she is summoned thus: "The person under the protection of Kop, come outside. Your car is waiting". It is also said, "Just like a detergent [and other products]. They have brand names such as Breeze, Pao" – in other words, the wife and the husband are one, and the husband is a label that indicates his wife.

The other confronted by veil wearers

I have discussed above that wearing a veil dramatically changes the world in which the wearer lives. In this section, I examine three types of "others" that women face when they form their own selves, as told by women, who are properties and resources from the male point of view. These others are God, the husband and the outside of Da'wa. This may give us some glimpses into the world these women inhabit.

Facing God: The world of Da'wa

Once people become devoted to Da'wa activities, their involvement in the world outside of Da'wa becomes secondary. Many of the Da'wa participants do not have a television set at home. They do not watch the news. They seem to be only interested in their peace of mind and their afterlife. When I was conducting a survey in December 2013, there were large-scale anti-government rallies in Thailand and most Muslim families other than the Da'wa devotees left their televisions on day and night and remained glued to the screens. In Mae Sot, large buses were mobilized for those going to participate in rallies in Bangkok. However, those involved in Da'wa told me that the wave of demonstrations did not concern them. The answers were the same for male Da'wa leaders and female *talim* participants alike.

I got the impression that the veiled women in Da'wa had chosen to lead a peaceful and religiously satisfying life under their veils. Saida said that she used to regard doctors and lawyers highly, but she now had different values. She said that she wanted her children to lead a religious life in Da'wa and find husbands in Da'wa, because things wouldn't work well otherwise.

The former English teacher Zainab has been devoting herself to Da'wa activities since her early retirement. When I asked her what changed after she began to participate in Da'wa, she responded as follows.

> Changed, changed a great deal. I left Mae Sot and went to university in Phitsanulok. But I did not discard my religion and did not discard prayer. I did not stop reading the Qur'an. I continued. I feel comfortable working in Da'wa. My mind is calm. I don't think anything. I know contentment. All my children are good human beings. God made

all my children good human beings. I thank God. Because we have this environment now, the children stay in the religion. None of them misbehave. They don't smoke or drink. … My two-year-old granddaughter mimics what she sees on TV. She walks like a fashion model or presses cheeks together. We turn the TV off and don't let her watch because she mimics it. But sometimes we let her watch religious videos, thinking of and singing about God. We let her watch animal shows. Many TV ads show naked bodies. It is not good to broadcast things that are forbidden by Muslims. It was not as bad as this in the old days. Television influences children. If we watch ads of beautiful cars day after day, we will want to have one. It's the same with children. It gets into their brains.

Saida clearly states that covering her face means facing God in daily life, as follows. "When I cover my face, I offer prayer more promptly. Automatically. When I don't cover my face, I sometimes miss my prayer and don't do five times. I do all of them. Reverence. I revere and worship God. When the face is not covered, people may get lazy or go out". Saida continues. "I can concentrate better. I concentrate when I offer prayer. My mind is calm. I want to study the religion more. I have a stronger desire to understand the religion. And I have a stronger desire to help other people".

In this way, by wearing a face-covering veil, women spend more time meeting face-to-face with God in everyday life[16].

Facing the husband: Family life in Da'wa

Saida says that her relationship with her husband changed when she started going to Da'wa. "If we have the religion, we love more. The religion teaches us to love our children and family. When I do something related to the religion, I feel joy. I enjoy talking. When there is the religion, he is content. I think he is pleased that his wife covers her face".

I asked Saida how a married couple devoted to Da'wa lives day-to-day.

When Adhan is called [call to worship from a mosque made at prescribed times] at five o'clock in the morning, I wake my children up to offer prayer. We read the *talim* together with my husband at home. For about ten minutes. Then he speaks like [he did at the study meeting] yesterday. He goes to the mosque. At around half past five. After worship [at the mosque], he goes to his parents' café to help them. He delivers the cakes he has made. I take our eldest daughter to school on my bike at half past seven. She is a first-year student at an Islamic school. My husband takes our sons to a kindergarten at half past eight. He returns to the mosque by nine. He discusses Da'wa [activities] from nine to eleven every day. He makes time for it. He sometimes visits people. Visits their homes, visits the sick at hospitals. He comes home at around noon to eat lunch and rest. Then he goes back to the mosque. I make lunch early and go to the café at ten. Women offer prayer at 12:40 and my husband prays at one o'clock. He sometimes stays at the mosque or sometimes comes home. He goes to pick up our sons at three o'clock. Our daughter walks home. I close the café at four and go home. My husband fetches our sons by four [and drops him at home] and goes to the mosque to worship at half past four. A teacher arrives at five and reads Qur'an with our daughter. Seven or eight children from Da'wa gather and study from five to seven every day. Except Friday. They stay at the mosque until the night prayer [Isha'a][17] finishes at around half past seven. Our family eats dinner together. My husband bakes cakes. I put our children in bed. We make cakes until about ten o'clock. We make them every other day, ten cakes each time.

This is their daily routine when her husband is not participating in Da'wa.

Saida's husband participates in Da'wa for four months each year, during which she cannot contact him at all. He was not present at the birth of their child or his father's death. He came home four months later to see the baby for the first time, but Saida fully accepted it because she was also devoted to Da'wa.

He does not contact me at all for four months while he is participating. He does not ring. I don't know where he is. He rings me at the end of the four months. "The four months have passed. I'm coming home". Every year. When I gave birth to our second child, I did it on my own at the hospital. Where my husband was, in Pakistan or somewhere, I don't know. He returned to Bangkok on the final day and he found out. "Have you had the baby? A boy or a girl?", he asked. He knew nothing.

She continues.

I have no problem with my husband. He doesn't drink or smoke. He doesn't play around. He goes away for his religious work, not for play. Everyone is delighted. Women also gain merit. …I'm convinced that God will look after us. What would I do if my husband died? I can't rely on anyone. I rely on God. We can't stay together forever. If he dies, we will have to support ourselves. I will have to raise three children on my own. It's only four months and we'll see him soon. …God takes care of us. It's not my husband that takes care of us. What if he dies? I must keep going. No one knows who will die first.

She appears to be philosophical about life.

There is a different kind of benefit to participating in Da'wa as a couple; Saida finds that her relationship with her husband feels fresh after doing so.

> After participating in *masturo* together, I feel very happy when I come home as if I'm newly married. Men and women are separated in *masturo*. Men stay at the mosque and women stay in a house. Each couple calls for one another to meet. We feel shy, as if we were new lovers. Happy. We don't argue, we are not bored. Just like the newly married. It is like that every time. After participating in *masturo*. We understand each other. We don't fight. Feel like we've just got married. Feel like we are out on a date.

Although Saida used to earn more income than her husband did, now she feels happy deferring to him.

> Many women work in Thailand. They have self-confidence and feel superior to men. But in Islam, we can't say women are better than men. If the head of the family follows the religious principles [*lak satsana*], we follow him. There is no problem. Happy. He has reasons. It doesn't mean that we never argue. Sometimes he accommodates me. Sometimes I accommodate him. We help one another. I'm not just following. He listens to me, I listen to him. We've been together for thirteen years, but we've been helping each other more since we had children.

Others also say that participation in Da'wa has improved their relationship with their husband. They say that the husband loves the wife more. Rafmat (age forty-two) came to Thailand from Myanmar twenty years ago, and has been covering her face for nine years. She married at the age of twenty and has a sixteen year-old daughter. Her husband (age fifty-three) left Myanmar for Thailand to trade. "I didn't fall in love, my mother married me off to him. I like him now. Because God injected love. …God injected love in him because I cover my face and look different from other women. Other men cannot see my face. I look beautiful forever in his eyes. He always tells me, 'You are beautiful'. God injected in his heart. It's God's command".

As above, where both husband and wife are devoted to Da'wa, they focus their attention on one another. When the wife wears a veil to cover her face, she severs relationships with other men and goes under the protection of her husband, thereby making their relationship more secure. Where only one spouse is devoted to Da'wa, on the other hand, the face-covering veil can block the relationship between husband and wife, as in the case of Fatima presented above.

Relations with people outside of Da'wa

In covering their faces, whom are these women hiding from? It is not from God, not from their husbands and not from their fathers, brothers or relatives. Specifically, their faces are concealed from any men outside of their family, regardless of their religion. They have no problem showing their faces to me, a non-Muslim, as long as there is no man present. At the scene of Da'wa where men and women are completely separated, women expose their faces in women-only spaces.

In public places outside of Da'wa where men and women are not segregated, such as markets and schools, however, their faces are concealed because of the presence of men. In other words, the face is covered and kept private in public spaces containing unspecified men and women. Before identification as an individual, a veiled woman becomes an anonymous existence that is not easily accessible to people other than certain individuals. The absence of the face functions as a device to turn her into a being that should not be seen, even though she is physically present. Accordingly, criticisms against covering the face in public spaces such as a village, as mentioned by Kop, may stem from the problem of keeping one's identity private. Perhaps Saida's parents were expressing their concerns about and disapproval of the anonymization of their daughter in a public space. Conversely, the absence of the face implies that one's physical presence essentially renders one already open to others.

The others that trigger the formation of the self for the face-covering woman here are mainly God, her husband and those involved in Da'wa. She lifts her veil to God, her husband, other male relatives and women, and she uses it to shut out the rest of society.

Discussions on the face and the other

We take on overwhelming passivity by existing as a physical body. Yet, the boundary between self and other exhibits fluctuations beyond the boundary that appears to be physically clear-cut in the form of the body covered with the visible skin. As in the cases of spirit possession, for example, our existence is open enough to allow the possibility of a switch between self and other (Tanabe 2013; Nishii 2013). Even in these cases, a responsive relationship with the other is made possible by our physicality.

The other here exists as a being that affects and generates the self through meeting face-to-face[18]. Washida states as follows, by converging the entire skin of the being on the face. "An operation to convert the entire body surface to the *plain face*, together with the entire membrane of our being converted by it, forms the *face*. And what we ordinarily call the 'face' is no other than this *face* that has converged and condensed on the facial surface" (1998: 135–136). In other words, the face is the condensed form of the entire being acting as the keystone and the prototype image in this self-other affective relationship. It is thought that "Seeing the face and identifying the face have some critical significance in the process of composing an image" (Uno 2012: 146).

Lévinas defined the face as a symbol of the other that cannot be incorporated into the subject (Uno 2012: 157). According to Uno, however, Lévinas treated the face simply as the symbol of otherness and a sign of transcendence without a careful examination of the fact that the composition of an image by the face is involved in the composition of the subject at the same time (2012: 158). While Lévinas considered that the other transcended the subject, this perhaps indicates in some sense that a human being is one that receives the other through the face and performs a leap from the other before one's eyes to the non-phenomenal other = the transcendental other. A human being who has developed an ability to imagine death acquires a face that inspires the formation of an ethical self beyond the face as the symbol of a biological individual. This perhaps means that humans have come to form the basis of their sociality through the face in their process of evolution.

It is possible to say that a Muslim woman who covers her face with a veil is trying to limit the others who can meet her face-to-face while composing a religious and ethical self in that place by "closing" her "face" = "making it absent". The covering of the face is a device to transform physical presence into absence quite radically, and the absence of the face may conversely lead to a transcendental other = God in a warped way.

According to Lévinas, the composition of the self takes place after a face-to-face encounter with the other. This sense of time lag is perceived as an awareness of a "gap" in living in Luhmann as well. According to N. Yoshizawa (2002: 141), Luhmann believes that there is already a gap between living and what is perceived as living. This constantly produced gap enables us to have all sorts of experiences in the world, and at the same time frustrates our recognition of all sorts of experiences at the last moment (Yoshizawa 2002: 141). Because of this gap, Luhmann also considers otherness as an absolute difference that can never be overcome by any measure, and assumes that it is the root of the formation of society as the paradox of the "coexistence of I and the other" promotes the generation of events. The other who is encountered in an event can only be perceived in the state of moving away from me, and I can only coexist with the other in the movement of evading[19].

Yoshizawa also states that, to Luhmann, "the other that is sensed in 'movement' manifests as something always interchangeable with I that is sensed as I for the first time in an interaction with the other. …The experiencing of the other contains a highly dangerous aspect in which the identity of I is composed simultaneously with the other, and hence I may no longer be I" (2002: 187–188). In this sense, the veiling of the face is possibly being used as a strategy to avoid confronting the difficulty the other and the self have in standing face-to-face.

Let us finally return to the question raised at the start of this chapter, that is, why do we cover the faces of the dead? This relates to the existential condition of the other that could have been the self. It is thought that a transformation of the other's being into something mysterious and eerie manifests most clearly in its face. It thrusts at us the gap between the dead body and its recent state of animation in a compelling manner, and once again questions the life of the self that has been formed face-to-face with the other. The gap bounces on the self and destabilizes its existence. This is perhaps why we need to indicate explicitly that the other with whom we used to have a responsive relationship in face-to-face situations is already a dead person. This is a strategy adopted by those facing the dead to preserve their selves. The cloth covering the face of the dead may be a device to fend off the situation in which the level of threat to the root of the life of the living itself has reached its maximum.

It is possible to say that the veil covering the face of Muslim women and the cloth covering the face of the dead protect the seen and the seer by covering the face from opposite directions.

13 Morality and Instrumentality: A Practical Approach to Theorizing the Other

Masakazu Tanaka

Key ideas

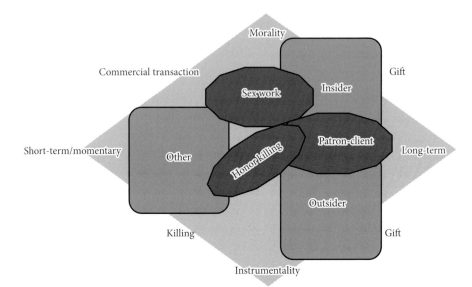

The insider, outsider and other are arranged along two axes – morality/instrumentality and long-term/short-term (or momentary) relationships. The base schema is superimposed with the possibilities of the other becoming the insider (i.e. sex workers) and the insider becoming the other (i.e. honor killing victims), as well as a relationship that is neither insider nor outsider (i.e. patron-client).

Insiders, outsiders, others and strangers

Organ transplantation currently practiced in Japan is divided into two broad types. One is live organ transplantation that is permitted only between close relatives, and the other is transplantation from declared brain-dead donors. The former act is considered the ultimate gift made by sacrificing part of one's body to save the life of a close family member. However, it is also commonly understood that there is nothing exceptional about organ donation between close family members. On the other hand, the latter process involves organ donation by a stranger. The organ recipient cannot find out the identity of the donor, and even if they do, they cannot meet the donor as they have already died. One of the issues surrounding organ transplantation is the commoditization of organs. We need to avoid inhumane situations (involving ultimate othering reminiscent of Auschwitz) such as the selling of one's own organs, killing people to sell their organs or "breeding" future organ donors. Live organ transplant is restricted to close relatives, while the other type of organ transplant is carried out anonymously precisely to distance the process from commercialization. Altruism is assumed between close relatives, whereas commercial exchanges are assumed between complete strangers. This chapter is interested in the formation of the social relationships that underpin these assumptions, based on the categories of "insiders" and "others".

To think about others is to consider (the boundary of) oneself at the same time. Where is the boundary of *I*? My body is normally considered to be my boundary, but there may be occasions when I get the sense that I am outside of my body, or conversely, a familiar tool might feel like an extension of my body. A typical approach to explore the self-other relationship or embodiment is to examine them from the perspective of philosophy, especially phenomenology[1]. While I pay due regard to the findings of this approach, here I discuss (the self and) the other in a more social context with a particular focus on practices involving the other (solicitation, interaction).

The purpose of this chapter is to consider self-other relationships, or representations of the other, from a practical approach using morality and instrumentality as keywords. What I call "morality" here is the regulatory ideal that one must not act out of self-interest, the ultimate form of which is either self-sacrifice or self-denial. On the other hand, instrumentality includes the attitude and view that treats the other in a self-serving manner, and the self-affirming or self-aggrandizing attitude that positions the other as an object to be used to serve one's self-interest. In our practical approach, we focus on everyday interactions and "things" that mediate such interactions, and examine the process (practice) that distinguishes closer others (insiders) and more distant others (outsiders)[2]. In contrast, the method of studying self-other relationships from a fixed standpoint based on existing social groups and categories (family, kin, ethnic groups etc.) is called a structural approach[3].

In this chapter, I examine the others one has practical relations with in some form by dividing them into two broad categories, namely, "insiders" and "outsiders". "Insiders" generally refers to others one is related to by blood, such as immediate relatives and family members, but in this chapter it refers to interpersonal relations and groups governed by moralistic values. In contrast, relationships with outsiders are governed by instrumental values; but this is not to say that this occurs *because* they are outsiders. Whether or not one's counterpart is an outsider is determined by whether or not the relationship is governed by instrumental values. In other words, the insider/outsider distinction here is an operational concept in which the insider-other is in a relationship governed by morality, whereas the outsider-other is in one governed by instrumentality. An outsider can be turned into an insider through moral practices, while an insider can become an outsider through instrumental practices. Practices based on moral versus instrumental values serve as the criteria for the distinction between insiders and outsiders, respectively. The type of practice separates others into insiders and outsiders, or generates and constructs them.

We must also take note that besides insiders and outsiders in long-term relationships, there are also people around us we have short-term (or momentary in most cases) relationships with. They are referred to as the "other(s)" in this chapter. This term specifically assumes others mediated by currency. On the other hand, all beings other than the self are referred to in italics as the "*other(s)*". This is a collective term that includes insiders and outsiders as well. Accordingly, the others mentioned in the previous paragraph are *others* in a strict sense. The contrast between morality and instrumentality does not correspond to that between gift and currency. We establish a long-term relationship with the other through gifting (we gift to seek such a relationship). However, this does not directly produce a moral relationship. Gifting is used to establish an instrumental relationship such as a patron-client relationship (see "Use, distribution and sharing of resources" below) in some cases. In contrast, currency is used for short-term commercial interactions and does not produce long-term relationships with customers, except when debts are incurred. The beings mediated by currency are mostly "others" (see "Social capital" below). Moreover, those who have been regarded as insiders can suddenly become subject to exclusion. The beings excluded in this way can also be called "others" (in the sense that one will try to minimize one's subsequent relationships with them) (see "Relatedness" below).

While I discuss the insider, the outsider and the other in this chapter, I also assume one more type of being, which is the stranger. These four types comprise *the others* that are addressed in this chapter in a limited way. The stranger is a more mysterious being than the other. It remains on the periphery and destabilizes the symbolic order, while helping to maintain it at the same time. In the progression from tradition to modernity and primitive to civilization, the stranger has been the substitute for the other. The stranger is a peripheral existence and its peripherality defines its attributes. In this sense, it has been actively discussed using the structural approach rather than the practical approach[4]. The stranger does not necessarily have a short-term relationship with the self. In fact, long-term relationships with strangers are established through gifting, for example. Nevertheless, the stranger is not strictly an insider or an outsider, but should perhaps be considered in a context different from the domain of practices to distinguish the relational categories discussed here. I shall return to this question at the end of the chapter.

In this chapter, I examine a wide variety of cases using a microscopic approach taking morality and instrumentality as key concepts to identify the fuzziness of the insider/outsider boundary, while focusing on the performative aspect in which certain practices can transform a person into an outsider, an insider or even an other[5].

Firstly, I shall demonstrate that morality and instrumentality are opposing concepts central to the consideration of social relations by critically examining three concepts discussed in anthropology and sociology in recent years, namely, resources, social capital and relatedness. Although there is a general tendency to assume that the concepts of social capital and relatedness (bonds) have a moral characteristic, it is important to note that they also have an instrumental characteristic. Secondly, I attempt to analyze the insider-outsider relationship in order to clarify that the boundary between them is not set in stone, and in turn delve into the ambiguity of our self-other relationship.

Morality and instrumentality

Use, distribution and sharing of resources

A major project entitled "Distribution and sharing of resources in symbolic and ecological systems: Integrative model-building in anthropology"[6], mainly based at the Tokyo University of Foreign Studies, was undertaken from 2002 to 2006. The project leader, Motomitsu Uchibori, describes the project as follows[7].

> **The purpose and significance of the research area**
> As suggested by the abbreviated name "resource anthropology", this research area is being established for the purpose of understanding the symbolic (cultural) and ecological (natural) systems, the two foundations underpinning human society, from the perspective of their interrelation by using the manners of distribution and sharing of "resources" as the research keystone, and constructing a new integrated area of anthropology to study the condition of this interrelation empirically and theoretically. It aims to establish a new perspective from which to see the manners of distribution and sharing of "resources" in a broad sense, including human-made secondary physical resources and intangible intellectual and cultural resources as well as natural resources derived directly from the ecological system, as the fundamental composition of human society.

Behind the concept of "resource" lies the "human-centered instrumental worldview". This viewpoint sees humans as tactical beings. Humans select their actions of their own free will for the purpose of their own survival or the survival of their group. In doing so, they bestow value to resources, including primary resources such as things, life forms and others around them and secondary resources such as knowledge and culture, on the basis of whether they can be utilized for the survival of the self or the group or whether they are scarce (for example, air is necessary, but it is not scarce and therefore is not a resource). As long as we hold the view that resources are defined by their usefulness for humans, we cannot truly overcome the mechanical-technological understanding of them.

As outlined in the passage quoted above, however, the question in the resource anthropology project is "the distribution and sharing of resources" and not "the utilization of resources". The words "distribution and sharing" imply cooperativity or sociality in humans in relation to resources. People distribute and collectively own (ownership adjustment) resources through conventions. What emerges there is morality rather than instrumentality. People need to collaborate rather than compete, and what is required to facilitate this is morality that governs how to behave as human beings, parents, children or siblings. In this sense, resource anthropology ought to be understood as a project about morality more than anything else. Nonetheless, we must remember here that whether a resource is regarded according to morality or instrumentality is determined by human practices – utilization or sharing – and not by the nature of each resource.

Social capital

A book written by political scientist Robert Putnam drew attention to social capital, which is the third type of capital along with physical capital and human capital, and refers to "connections among individuals – social networks and the norms of reciprocity and trustworthiness that arise from them" (2000: 14). Social capital "makes people smarter, healthier, safer and richer, and better able to govern a just and stable democracy" (Putnam 2000: 290). In a healthy democracy, abundant social capital allows people to lead economically affluent lives. It naturally results in more efficient government, fewer crimes and less expenditure for crime prevention. According to a "bold" conclusion made by Haruya Sakamoto (2010: 15), social capital theory asserts, "If everyone gets along and trusts and helps each other, everything will turn out all right in the world". It is possible to say that social capital is close to the concept of "merit" in Buddhism. People practice good deeds in day-to-day interactions and accumulate merit, which enriches society. Through these practices, others transform into insiders and a good society is created.

In contemporary society, however, intimate relationships among people are in decline and ceding ground to paranoia about others. According to Putnam, civic-mindedness is waning and the crime rate is escalating. Putnam described this situation as diminishing social capital. This argument aptly captured people's vague feeling of anxiety about society, and at the same time the rebuilding of networks that was presented as the solution, i.e., the revitalization of various civic groups (voluntary associations), suited the social trend.

Social capital also has some negative aspects that cannot be ignored. In this respect, Putnam divides social capital into "bonding" and "bridging". The former reinforces inward-looking, exclusionary and homogeneous groups. The latter is outward-looking and actively welcomes openness and diversity. Putnam mentions "ethnic fraternal organizations, church-based women's reading groups, and fashionable country clubs" as examples of bonding social capital, while "the civil rights movement, many youth service groups, and ecumenical religious organizations" are examples of bridging social capital (Putnam 2000: 22). Putnam states that the former type has numerous negative effects, stemming from its exclusivity. These are described in such terms as "the dark side of social capital" and "negative social capital". Bonding social capital that strengthens existing ethnic and religious groups can escalate intergroup conflict and threaten the unity of a nation, while making a considerable "social contribution" internally[8].

As is clear from the aforementioned definition of social capital ("connections among individuals – social networks and the norms of reciprocity and trustworthiness that arise from them"), it has a close association with morality. Relationships formed through individuals' everyday practices are reciprocal and generate trust. This supposes the existence of people who are considerate of others, are trustworthy and always think about what is important for society (networks) when they act.

On the other hand, Putnam's emphasis on morality leads one to overlook the aspect of social capital that permits the justification of exploitation and domination. We also cannot ignore the existence of people who exploit social capital (social capitalists) (Tanaka 2015). One example of the social capitalist is a charismatic cult leader who exploits the social capital people produce and appropriates it to gain access to other domains (e.g., political power, financial capital). Besides religion, this has been practiced as a matter of course in the political world.

Putnam once argued that democracy was more highly developed in northern Italy that was better endowed with social capital than the south of the country, after analyzing the various factors considered to be the indicators of social capital in that country (Putnam 1993). However, what is important here is how the various factors are combined, rather than their individual values and sum total. Even if particular factors such as the activity of self-help organizations may be prominent, they are meaningless as indicators of social capital unless they are functioning democratically.

The concept of social capital thus implies morality on one hand and instrumentality on the other. What is important is that capital has these two characteristics. Putnam seems to believe in the possibility that moral relationships generated through intimate interactions (reciprocity, trust) will proliferate. Similarly, in the final chapter of *The Gift*, Mauss (1954) suggests the possibility of the gift economy in society covering a large area. This argument assumes the linking of gift giving, moral values and long-term relationships. However, gifting does not always carry moralistic connotations (see "Insider or outsider? The patron-client relationship" below). It is possible to say that currency has a better chance of creating balanced interpersonal relations (see "Maintaining a relationship as others: The case of sex work" below). According to the classification here, Putnam was aware of the question of how to turn the other into a moral agent (insider), but he lacked a perspective on the outsider.

Relatedness

While I have mentioned that social capital is accumulated through day-to-day interactions, a similar concept has been proposed in the field of anthropology. This concept is "relatedness".

British anthropologist Janet Carsten proposed the concept of "relatedness" to replace "blood relations" in order to relativize the biological nature presupposed by the concept of "kin" in Europe (1995, 2000). It puts a broader range of human relations, including kin, within the scope of anthropological studies, and allows various "kin relationships" generated by modern reproductive technology to be studied from a cross-cultural perspective. The significance of the concept of relatedness for the discussion here goes beyond this methodological issue, because it questions the actual substance of a relationship (interactions between the individuals), which tends to be overlooked in the concept of social capital. In other words, things and bodies are included in the concept of relatedness. It attempts to understand human relationships – including those seemingly determined biologically, such as a mother-child relationship – as those formed through everyday practices or as a kind of developmental process rather than as a given. An apparently fixed group also becomes an aggregate of relatednesses created through the day-to-day activities of its constituent members. To rephrase in terms of our interest here, people become insiders through their intimate interactions.

Relatedness as outlined by Carsten can be regarded as a morality concept similar to social capital. While insiders are created through relationships via things and bodies, they (of which the mother-child relationship is a typical example) are people who are connected by moral bonds. Nevertheless, as we saw with resources and capital (social capital), we can identify the same two aspects – instrumentality and morality – in relatedness.

What Carsten seems to overlook is the negative aspect of relatedness. For instance, violence between a couple (domestic violence), child abuse and family murder-suicide cannot be explained by Carsten's argument. Unity between parents and children or siblings may simultaneously create a sense of ownership of others. Intimacy may lead to the belief that children must follow their parents or that the wife must obey her husband. Even in the theory of relatedness that emphasizes morality, we must not ignore its instrumental side. Relatedness looks at exchanges of things and body contact, and focuses on the process that creates insiders through it. From the same viewpoint, we must understand that it can produce outsiders that are convenient to the self.

Insiders, outsiders and others

I have so far looked at capital, social capital and relatedness as concepts in my analysis of social relationships and pointed out their dual quality based on instrumentality and morality. In the next section, I examine several specific examples in order to consider the process in which insiders and outsiders are created through practice, as well as some cases of othering and exclusion.

Insider or outsider? The patron-client relationship

We shall begin with a situation where a gifting relationship becomes instrumental. In this example, one attempts to use an interpersonal relationship created through the gifting and exchange of things as a tool to serve their own interest-base on the assumption that it is founded on morality. People are persuaded to follow a moral request from an insider, but this practice aims to exploit insiders and results in their othering.

Chihiro Nakayashiki (2014) has studied a kin organization called *nirin* in Tibetan society in India. *Nirin* are kindred recognized by the self and include relationships involving a rather complex entanglement of morality and instrumentality. When an election date approaches, political candidates and their supporters try to fully capitalize on their *nirin* relationships to secure the votes of their *nirin* members. When people are asked to vote for someone, they agree according to their idea of morality on the basis of *nirin* relationships. However, as *nirin* boundaries are unclear, people sometimes find themselves in a quandary when multiple candidates who claim membership of the same *nirin* ask them for their vote. When an election looms, those who seldom associate with one another on a day-to-day basis begin to negotiate, saying, "We belong to the same *nirin*". In this way, *nirin* members are utilized instrumentally. In this situation, a person is used upon becoming an insider, and thus becomes an outsider.

Further, there has been a reported case involving the dramatic transformation of *nirin* itself. Here, *nirin* transforms from the essentially ego-centered flexible network of relationships with obscure boundaries, unlike unilineal descent groups, into a kin group named after a major figure (leader). The group boundary becomes clearer and its membership definitive. The leader's intent determines which candidate the members must vote for. In other words, votes are influenced by a top-down decision. Instrumentality rather than morality wields overwhelming power here. In this way, *nirin* sometimes generate interpersonal relationships involving a subtle balancing of morality and tactics, and at other times create inflexible and instrumental relationships (leader-follower relations). Nevertheless, it is likely that morality is not completely negated even in the latter.

If its constituent members are more open and less tied to blood relations or territoriality, the case of inflexible *nirin* reported by Nakayashiki would be similar to the patron-client relationship (leader-follower) or faction in general terms[9]. The leader (patron) recruits and turns outsiders into insiders, irrespective of their blood or territorial connections. The leader uses various resources in their possession (distributing gifts at times) to attract followers, and looks after them to secure their support. What is sought in exchange is their allegiance that compels them to support the leader as required. When one supports the leader and attaches oneself to the faction, some degree of political and economic calculation is at work. Although the patron-client relationship can be regarded as an institution that turns others into insiders, political and economic motives are found on both sides. The leader imposes debts on the followers through gifting, and uses morality to ensure their support. The quid pro quo that the leader requests of their followers is political and sometimes self-sacrificial support. The followers enter into a close relationship with the leader in search of profits (increased political protection or economic benefit). Thus a long-term relationship is formed and comes to carry a moral characteristic.

Maintaining a relationship as others: The case of sex work

Gifts and commodities or currency have always been discussed contrastively in the field of economic anthropology. The usual subject of study is the social relationship between giver and receiver or buyer and seller. While our discussion in this section focuses on social relations found in monetary exchanges, we shall attempt to examine them from the perspective of the relationships they create, maintain or reject rather than the sorts of relationships they reflect.

In a commercial transaction that involves selling something, the client is usually assumed to be a complete outsider (the other). The price of the object or service is not assumed to be dependent on the interpersonal relationship between them. In the field of economic anthropology, however, the buyer-seller relationship and its impact on the transaction, or conversely, the transformation of the transactional relationship caused by the buyer's "regularity of patronage", have been the main topics of study (Tamura 2009; Watanabe 2015). This problem appears prominently in the area of sex work (prostitution) that provides sexual services to clients. For instance, in order to maintain certain levels of income female sex workers in Japan try to increase their number of regular customers by expressing affinity for their clients. In other words, they attempt to establish long-term relationships with clients through emotional labor (Tanaka 2014a).

Sex workers behave in the manner of "lovers" in order to win their client's favor. Because of this, some men angrily complain about paying for their services based on the fact that the women have affection for them. One woman commented to the author as follows.

> I think it's risky to deal with a man as if he were more than a customer. Dangerous. Once you've acted in that way, the customer tends to get carried away. I've upset many customers, who confronted me, like, "I, what am I? What am I to you!" [angrily].

Somewhere along the line, the client begins to think of the sex worker as an insider (lover), and a monetary transaction (outsider-outsider relationship) is incompatible with that relationship. Once this happens, her tactic of showing affection in order to secure regular clients backfires. While this is applicable to other jobs in addition to sex work, it tells us that the successful operation of sex work requires a delicate balance between conflicting factors, which are affection and financial exchange (Tanaka 2014a, 2014b).

There are hardly any women with regular clients in the red-light district in Mumbai, India, where I have been conducting ethnographic fieldwork since 2014. One of the reasons for this is that men stop paying for services once they become regulars. Each session only takes five to ten minutes, and the minimum rate is the equivalent of US$4.00. In such a short time and at such a low price, women cannot afford to engage in intricate emotional labor.

The dilemma entailed in sex work in Japan is also applicable, to a certain degree, to service jobs involving emotional labor in general. It is not the case that customers at MacDonald's outlets never take a customer service representative's smile as an expression of favor. Sex work differs from other jobs in that the services it sells are sexual acts, which typically represent intimacy. As demonstrated by arguments on relatedness, the exchange of bodily fluids enhances intimacy. There is nothing more suggestive of intimacy between parties than sex. This gives rise to the argument that sex work cannot be recognized as a legitimate job[10].

On the other hand, we can suppose the following counterargument. By charging customers money for their services (maintaining commercial transactions), sex workers are refusing to form intimate relationships. By receiving currency immediately prior to the act, the nature of sex itself changes. This interpretation may appear forceful, but I would like to discuss a study on sexual services for women provided by men (erotic massage) as an example.

According to Kyomi Kojima (2004), male erotic masseurs gain enjoyment from providing sexual services to women, unlike "hosts" or male companions at Japanese "host clubs" who ask female customers for more drinks and gifts, alluring them to love and have sex with them. Their relationships with the female customers are motivated by money only, not sexual desire. Many erotic masseurs make a living from another job and consider erotic massage as a service (volunteering) rather than work. They are not really interested in making money and rarely set a time limit on their interactions with clients. Their motto is to devote themselves to their service until the woman is satisfied. However, their female clients insist on paying them, even if it is a small amount. This is because if the client does not pay the masseur, the relationship will become ambiguous, putting the woman in a passive position in her sexual relationship just like in many other intimate relationships. She buys a service from him to avoid such a situation. The payment practice guarantees her initiative position and indicates that she does not have a private relationship with him ("refusing a romantic relationship" in Kojima's words).

From this perspective, by receiving money female sex workers are demonstrating that their sexual services are not of a private nature, although they are in the opposite position to male erotic masseurs. Currency is a medium to prevent one from becoming an insider here. Sex workers do have regular clients; yet, they are not allowed to pay on credit, unlike in hostess bars and pubs. This is because the formation of a long-term relationship without monetary transactions blurs the boundary between sex work and a more intimate romantic relationship in that scenario, whereas credit payment is used to strengthen trust relationships in the case of bars and pubs.

As the saying goes, "The end of money is the end of love". This refers to the situation in which one is loved and given attention while one has money, but spurned and shunned as soon as the money runs out. In this case, money is a means to create insider-like relationships. A client visits the same sex worker as long as he has the money to pay her, and he may eventually be able to continue his relationship even when he has no money. In most cases, however, the client is refused service when he runs out of money, which is hardly surprising. What can be construed from the example of erotic masseurs is that the act of paying each time severs a tie that could potentially continue the relationship into the future.

In contrast, the same currency can create a tie if it is in the form of debt (credit) (Tanaka 2007).

An intimate relationship mediated by currency is typically a short-term one. The client receives a service in exchange for money. Yet, when this relationship is sustained, that between self and other changes. The change is favorable in some cases and unfavorable in others. In one example of positive change, a client becomes a regular and the woman begins to see him outside of the business premises, eventually becoming his mistress on a monthly allowance. The woman may become a lover instead of a mistress and eventually marry the man. If the client and the worker become lovers, gifts will be exchanged instead of currency. Conversely, in order to avoid entering into an undesirable relationship, currency can play an important role as in the aforementioned example.

In the above section, I have attempted to highlight the difficulty of maintaining a relationship between others and clarify the function of currency.

The other among insiders: Honor killings

I now look at a situation in which the other emerges among insiders. This case cannot be explained in terms of the contrast between insider and outsider discussed thus far. As I mentioned at the start, the other is an object with which a momentary and anonymous relationship is formed, and is neither an insider governed by moral values nor an outsider dictated by instrumental values. The other has rarely attracted as much attention as the insider in traditional societies studied in cultural anthropology because of this brevity of relationship.

The case below involves honor killing, which is a common occurrence in the region from North India to the Middle East[11]. "Honor killing" is defined as an act of violence (lethal incident) committed as a means to remove the disgrace brought on a woman's family and groups (family, kin, village, caste, religious group etc.) by her "immoral" behavior and to restore their honor. Here immoral behavior includes such acts as premarital sex, ignoring her parents' advice and eloping with a man of her own choice, being the subject of rumors about affairs, cheating on her husband and so on. If any of these things happen, a woman's father and brothers are considered to have failed to control her sexuality and the family's honor is tarnished. Besides her own family, members of other groups she belongs to are also dishonored in some cases. The supposedly only way to restore honor is to kill the guilty woman. In 2007, 655 murder incidents in India were recognized as honor killings (Sharma 2008). According to more recent United Nations statistics, around 1,000 people out of a total of 5,000 honor killing victims were killed in India. The actual number is likely to be higher[12].

Female sexuality is strictly controlled in India. Premarital sex is of course forbidden. Outside of marriage, an intimate relationship with a particular man is not permitted, even if it is not sexual. The discovery or rumor of a supposedly immoral sexual relationship can become a legitimate reason to carry out an honor killing. Cases of marriage between different castes (especially between a lower-caste man such as an untouchable, and a higher-caste woman), between different religious faiths, within the same village (consanguineous marriage) and within the same *gotra* (patrilineal clan) are strongly opposed by not only the parents of the parties, but also their entire villages and castes. In the case of a married woman, her adultery or suspected adultery becomes the reason for honor killing. In one shocking case, a husband killed his wife just because he dreamed she was unfaithful. When a woman is raped, it is she who is killed because she is considered to have dishonored her family.

> In July 2004, a girl [age fifteen] belonging to the higher Gurjar caste in Rajasthan had a relationship with a seventeen-year-old Dalit [untouchable] man and eloped. Her family reported to the police that the young man had abducted her. The police searched for the couple and found them living in Mumbai. The girl was subsequently murdered by her father and uncles on 22 September. The family reported that she had died of a snake or insect bite. The police arrested thirteen people, but a state MP belonging to the same Gurjar caste was reportedly lobbying to reduce their sentences. (*Deccan Herald* 2004)

As this example shows, people who carry out or ask someone else to carry out an honor killing think that their family name has been damaged by the daughter's actions, including her father, brothers, uncles, mother and sisters. There have been cases in which the suspected perpetrators were the victim's mother and sisters. If the matter involves the honor of not only one family, but also a whole village or kin group, the violence takes on a more collective nature. The victims can be the woman alone, both the woman and man or the man alone. In the process associated with honor killings, the police and judiciary naturally become involved at various stages, including when an elopement is discovered, upon application for protection and when arrests are made and perpetrators are prosecuted after a crime has been committed. However, the immediate arrest or felony conviction of perpetrators are rare because local courts, the police and the suspects often share the same views or values about honor, while local politicians often intervene to protect the suspects. As in the case of the Gurjar caste mentioned above, politicians interfere with the police and judiciary to defend the suspects because they do not want to lose votes by upsetting the members of a locally influential caste.

In Indian society where caste endogamy[13] is the norm, marriage between a woman and a lower-caste man is unacceptable. When this happens, the boundary separating the inside of the caste from the outside is destroyed by the woman's immoral action. This destruction of order is expressed verbally as a loss of honor. Beyond a single family, the inside can extend to a kin group, village community or entire caste. They can only clear the dishonor brought by the woman by killing her. For this reason, honor killing is an act of violence, but it is justifiable violence (from the viewpoint of the insiders she used to be one of). The insiders are primarily governed by morality. An honor killing is the consequence of the primacy of the morality of the inside and leads to the further strengthening of their morality. By committing a supposedly immoral act, the woman transforms from insider to other. She would be abandoned or disowned (cast out) in most societies – merely becoming the other. In societies where honor is considered important, however, her othering would affect the rest of the family and threaten the family's social life. This is because her othering signifies an exclusion from the inside that is broader than the family (kin group, village or caste) (hence her sisters may not be able to marry, for example). They have no choice but to eliminate her if they want to prevent the rest of the family from becoming other as well. She becomes the threatening other rather than the mere other, and has to be killed as a result.

From the viewpoint of the killers, the daughter or sister who eloped with an outsider has been their alter ego. In Indian society where "dividualism" is a dominant idea, a person is thought to be dividual and share bodily substances with those close to them rather than an individual (not dividual), and therefore parents, children and siblings who have been sharing food can be regarded as having obscure boundaries between them. The woman who commits an immoral act is a foreign body intruding into the world of blended self-others and has to be removed. She is an alter ego as well as a foreign body. The daughter becomes the other because of her own mistake. Moreover, she becomes a traitor who remains as a foreign body in the eyes of her family and kin group. This foreign body can infect the rest of the group, and for this reason they have to eliminate it by killing her.

The boundary separating the insider and the other is fragile, and people thus frequently engage in practices that reinforce it through various cultural practices. On the other hand, they try to denounce and exclude (kill) the insider who has become the other (for example, the woman who is thought to have committed a sexual transgression) in order to maintain order among the insiders.

The ultimate other

So far we have discussed the relationship between the insider and the outsider, and the dynamics of the transformation of the insider into outsider or other, by focusing on gifting, commoditization and currency. As I mentioned above, a long-term relationship is assumed in the insider/outsider case, whereas a relationship with the other is short in principle. The ultimate momentary relationship is one in which an encounter spells the death of either party. The "relationship" vanishes as soon as it is formed. Bar and Ben-Ari (2005) surveyed the Israeli military to find out how snipers shoot to kill distant enemy soldiers, and argued that the ability to see an enemy soldier as a depersonalized existence, i.e., an object rather than a person, was important. At the moment the person is objectified, the rifle trigger is pulled and a bullet is fired. This is the moment when the possibility for human interaction collapses in an instant[14].

The battlefield is not the only place we can find a world consisting of others who can only expect momentary relationships. A more general example is an extermination camp, which is a world controlled by anonymity. The others are addressed by numbers and deprived of their names and various individual elements associated with them. Prisoners are given the same close-cropped haircut and the same prison uniform. There is no individuality there. Although they are biologically alive, the prisoners are not socially alive. They are the living dead, the depersonalized and "things" rather than human beings (Agamben 1999). Large quantities of belongings, wearable articles, hair and other remnants of the Jews sent to Auschwitz in Poland are impersonal. Human hair, which supposedly is of a most personal nature, is merely a material for use in industrial products. It is unilaterally seized and exploited, just as its owner is. Morality associated with a gifting relationship does not exist here[15]. Even if prisoners are not immediately sent to the gas chamber, they are treated as less than other, materials (things), from the moment of their arrival. It would not be surprising if the aforementioned human organs for transplantation were among such materials[16].

The disappearance of the stranger

In this chapter I have been focused on practices that separate others into insiders, outsiders and others. We have seen that these practices are closely related to the self's intention about whether to form a moral relationship or an instrumental relationship. My analysis of various examples has found that there is no fixed dichotomy between the insider world governed by morality and the outsider world controlled by instrumental relations and values. We have discussed what kind of relationship the parties are trying to form (or to refuse to form) by focusing on transformation between insider and outsider as well as gifting and commodity exchange. The concept of relatedness proposed by Carsten predominantly reflects moral relationships because of its origin in insider relationships, and gives little regard to instrumental relationships. Putnam's social capital is a concept proposed to cover a far broader society than Carsten's. Yet, it too places greater importance on moral relationships. It is imbued with the practical motive regarding how to revitalize civil society. The ideal civil society envisaged by Putnam is at the opposite extreme of the world of extermination camp prisoners I called the "ultimate others" in the previous section.

When we turn our attention to intermediaries for practices such as currency exchange, shooting a rifle or the workings of an extermination camp, the emergence of the people we call "the others" in this chapter is modern. Currency and weapons have of course existed since ancient times. However, the roles they played then are far removed from those they play in modern society. Currency had a magical function in the past, and some coins were too large to transport. Weapons always demanded close combat and although they were made to kill, they did not assume momentary encounters in mass slaughter from remote locations (e.g., aerial bombings). So, were insiders and outsiders the only people who existed in pre-modern times? Of course not. However, we should think that what existed outside of long-term human society of the selves comprising insiders and outsiders was "the stranger" mentioned at the beginning rather than the other we have been discussing here. The stranger situated on the periphery of society was a being that was given all sorts of symbolic added value as a "signifier minus the signified", a "floating signifier" or with a "symbolic value of zero". This being has been called a "trickster" and a "third term" (Imamura 1982). This type of being is observed in contemporary society as well; however, the role played in this setting is much smaller than in the past or in traditional societies studied in anthropology. We who live in contemporary society encounter the other before we encounter the stranger. Nevertheless, we must not assume that the stranger always belongs to the peripheral world or we only form a short-term relationship with him or her, even in traditional societies.

The commoner society of the Azande described by Edward Evan Evans-Pritchard (1937) is a world where witches are prevalent, hiding among the insiders. The process of discovering them, inhibiting their powers and sometimes ostracizing them is one of transforming the insider into the stranger (rather than the other). Yet, this does not involve casting out witches completely. Although some have been killed in exceptional cases, many continue to live in society even after they have been identified as such. This is where this example differs from honor killings.

If this chapter can contribute to our evolutionary historical discussion, it is located in this question on the disappearance of the stranger somewhere along the line. We can perhaps say that what emerged to take the stranger's place was primarily the other mediated by currency. There were many mysterious strangers and many opportunities to encounter them in the old days[17]. In contemporary society, the dark corners that could harbor strangers have been eliminated literally by enlightenment, modern technology and currency pervading all corners of the world. What exists in our familiar world are insiders and outsiders, and anonymous others exist outside of it. Once again, the insider, the outsider and the other are not fixed beings; they change gradually (regular clients in sex work) or instantaneously (honor killings) through people's practices. However, these days there are hardly any instances in which they transform into strangers (e.g., ghosts). This may be a process that can be called the "secularization of the stranger". I would like to position this chapter as the first attempt to theorize *the other* with one eye set on the study of secularization.

Part IV
The Expanding Horizons of the Theory of Others

14 The Spirit as the Other: From the Iban Ethnography

Motomitsu Uchibori

Key ideas

Layers of existence and behavior in the Iban's world

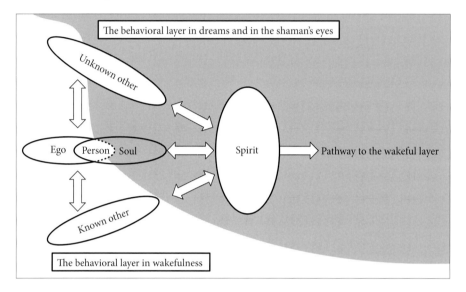

Each oval indicates the being that acts in the two layers. Overlapping, transformation and interaction between them are indicated by ⇔. While the ego and soul in part overlap, which constitutes the person, the key characteristic of the Iban's theory of human existence lies in the idea that the ego and soul act independently in different layers.

Almost entirely (exclusively) others: Degrees of otherness

Individuals belonging to a sympatric communal group or community are mutually others on a certain behavioral plane, and many of the chapters in this volume address them in this sense. When we avoid the distinction between the absolute self and the absolute other and take into account the relativity of otherness and its degree, we can reasonably say that individuals who share an understanding and sense of their world are others with a low degree of otherness. On the other hand, others who live separately and encounter only infrequently have a high degree of otherness, but their otherness has the potential to be lowered infinitely as long as they mutually recognize the attribute of being others on the same behavioral plane as the self. In the case of human society, the variability of the degree (or density) of otherness has been dealt with as a very ordinary research topic in many fields within the timeframe of evolution and history in an expansion of the outer edges of society, as well as the timeframe of the life history of the individual. In either timeframe, the topic has been considered in relation to the interactional (behavioral) plane or the plane of subjective proximity and companion identity. It is possible to say that the degree of otherness did not demand fundamentally different research approaches within those limits.

The other that is the subject of my discussion in this chapter is not on the same behavioral plane as the self in the above sense. If we are to talk about it in the context of continuity with ethology or primatology, what is on the same behavioral plane should be referred to using the concept of *the other individual*, even if it is a human being. The other in my discussion here is not the other individual in that sense. However, this does not mean that it exists on a plane that never intersects with that on which the self exists – a parallel plane, so to speak. The two planes sometimes intersect, and these beings may have the same existential value and mutually interact on overlapping lines. It is possible to think that the duality of the human behavioral plane manifests because of the existence of this type of other. If we are to refer to the other individual that is applicable to primates, including humans, and animals in general as the other, what we are trying to discuss here requires a different approach and perhaps should more appropriately be called "the stranger-other" to distinguish it.

What I discuss below is the stranger-other in this sense as well as what can be spoken of as an illusion depending on one's point of view – in other words, the question of how that which can be seen as something psychic, spiritual or divine in a person's lived experience emerges as the other or the other individual in the capacity of an almost equal agent to the self on the same behavioral plane. We shall explore the conditions behind its emergence by contrasting it with the other as the other individual. Viewing this as a critical momentum in the evolution of human sociality will be the main point of contention of this chapter.

The existence of something illusory that emerges in the form of the other is understood and accepted collectively – this kind of other almost definitely and characteristically appears in human species. The phenomenon of transient hallucination itself is likely not unique to humans. However, it is difficult to imagine that any group in other animal species in general or primates in particular has the collective understanding that an illusion experienced through various senses, including hallucination, actually exists on the same plane as the self in the world. In this sense, a discussion on "others-as-strangers" as illusions is expected to be directly relevant to the question of the understanding and acceptance of reality among the constituent members of a group or community with borders that can be established in some form, and perhaps to the question of what constitutes communal senses as well.

An episode from the Iban life-world

I would like to begin by discussing a brief episode from the past. I experienced the following in the gallery of an Iban longhouse by the upper Skrang tributary of the Lupar River in southern Sarawak, Malaysia, in the western part of Borneo on one evening in October 1976 (on this part of Sarawak, see Uchibori 1996).

A shamanic ritual called *serara' bungai* in the Iban language was conducted that night. This ritual was frequently conducted in the communities of those classified as the Saribas and Skrang Iban who live near the Layar, Skrang and Krian rivers, among the many Iban settlements that spread throughout the state of Sarawak today. The word *bungai* means "flower", which refers to an invisible plant that represents the state of life of the family (or household) as a whole in this context. It is said that each family (household) has one "flower"[1], part of which withers when a family member dies. Although the individual performances of this shamanic ritual vary in detail depending on the particular case or shaman, the central motif remains the same. The shaman emulates the act of severing (*serara'*) the part of the family's "flower" that corresponds to the life of the recently deceased member. For this reason, the ritual is usually conducted some days prior to the end of the mourning period that applies to the entire longhouse community. However, the ritual conducted by the shaman may have a function of more practical importance than the visual representation of the symbolic separation of life and death. This is based on the fact that many community members use this occasion to consult the shaman about their recent experiences and ask him for an explanation and possible solutions in some cases. I shall focus on this function in the current example.

In the evening, in addition to his own ritual items, the shaman arranged those provided by the deceased's family, including a small pot, a blowpipe, a ritual ikat cloth (*pua' kumbu'*) made for the rite and as a prestige possession and narrow and long-segmented variety bamboo shoots. Older women gathered in the gallery and sat around the shaman. One woman began to talk about her dream from the night before, as follows. She was walking in the woods near the longhouse and encountered the deceased man in question. He was coming from the opposite direction with a spear in his left hand and accompanied by two dogs. She was frightened by the sudden appearance of the deceased, and asked him what he was doing. He replied that he was hunting (*ngasu*, meaning hunting with dogs). Upon hearing this, she shouted: "Stop, Uncle, don't attack me, we are relatives". Those around her interpreted her dream as a sign that the dead, who was a shaman in life, was still wandering around and hunting the living. Another woman opened her mouth and said that she, too, encountered the deceased in her dream.

What transpired from the conversation that followed was that the "soul" (*semengat* in Iban) of the deceased shaman was thought to have occasionally turned into "a wicked *antu*, a demon spirit", which had hunted his fellow humans' souls even before his death. They associated the death of an infant in a nearby longhouse several years earlier with the then living shaman's hunting escapades. I will describe the varied faces of what is called *antu* in detail later. Suffice to say that it is what can be described as a demon when it is evil and a spirit when it is not, and that to the Iban, it is a being with opposite attributes to humans in many respects, while it has many commonalities as an individual actor in the world envisioned by the Iban in which it acts. It had been said that the deceased shaman's soul had occasionally been "evil" (*jai'*). However, in the conversation after the discussion of dreams at the ritual, the elderly women did not say that his "personality itself" – tentatively speaking – had evil intentions. Instead, it was claimed that "It was not his fault; it was his soul that was bad".

The ritual in the gallery proceeded amid this conversation. After the completion of the main procedure that involved cutting and disposing of part of the outer sheath of a bamboo shoot with a small knife, one of the elderly women asked the shaman to deal with what was happening. The shaman gently declined, reasoning that an effective measure against the deceased shaman's evil soul would require ongoing ritual service by a shaman, and their longhouse no longer had a resident shaman – this shaman was called out from another longhouse. He added in the end, "It is the soul that is bad, not him [the deceased shaman]".

Narrating one's experience: The soul and the dream

On first glance, the above episode is not unusual for those familiar with the Iban's belief in the existence of souls. According to Freeman (1970), an authority on Iban ethnography, the Iban have an "unshakable belief" in the existence of what Freeman translates as "souls" in English. "Unshakable belief" sounds like an antiquated expression, but we can at least recognize the fact that Freeman did not encounter a single Iban who was skeptical about the existence of souls at the end of the 1940s when he conducted his research. Even in a study I conducted in the mid-1970s, elderly people as well as young men and women in their twenties talked about the existence of souls as a matter of course. They frequently mentioned it as part of their everyday experience, rather than as something confined to special occasions such as rituals. In ethnological discussions, the existence of concepts that correspond to souls is so commonplace that it is rather difficult to focus on it as a theoretical question. If we are going to talk about souls, the most convenient discursive frameworks would be around "concepts of personhood" from anthropology in the recent past and "ontology" from anthropology today. While either of these could be relevant to this chapter in general, here I shall adopt "how we speak about our experiences" as the initial framework.

Among the opportunities for the Iban to talk about their everyday experiences, chitchat in the "common gallery", called *berandau ruai*, attracts the biggest audience. The word *ruai* means "longhouse gallery", and *berandau* is likely a verb derived from the word *randau* that refers to "long trailing vines". This term aptly expresses the manner of purposeless meandering conversation. Although the aforementioned episode took place at the scene of a ritual, the women conversed in the style of *berandau*. The topics of their ordinary *berandau* range from gossip about the residents of other longhouses to information about farm work, hunting and gathering – "ordinary" experiences of activities and hearsay – and also frequently relate to their dreams. It is mostly their own recent dreams that feature, but sometimes another individual's dream is discussed. In the latter case, what motivates people to talk about it is the peculiarity of the content of the dream or the peculiarity of the connection between the dream and some actual event. Many of their experiences of a spiritual nature occur in dreams.

A dream is an experience of an objective sort for the Iban. The Iban language has no comprehensive abstract expression corresponding to "experience", but it is possible to state that, if experience means acting while exploring the details of the world around oneself through sensations (the five senses) and establishing them in one's consciousness through reflection, the Iban raise their dream in their consciousness through talking about it in *berandau* and elevate it to the level of experience. In this sense, as far as the Iban are concerned a dream and an experience outside of a dream share the same pattern. The question we need to ask here is how the two exist in parallel as different kinds or phases of experience, even though they share the same pattern.

According to a "theory" put forward by the Iban, this is based on the idea that each person has two agents – or rather, they perceive two aspects to human agency as such. The soul is the agent that acts in dreams, whereas the body or part of it represents the agent that acts during wakefulness. The question here relates to the extent of the effectiveness of this explanation, that is, to what extent are the Iban convinced by this explanation, in what kinds of situations do they refer to it and are they aware of any contradictions contained in it? By examining these points, I expect to reveal the reality behind their unshakable belief in the existence of souls.

I would like to introduce the idea of "behavioral layers" (or layers of "action") here. This is similar to the vogue word "perspectives", but "layers" emphasizes the synchronicity and multilayered structure of the foundation for diverse behaviors. This is because while "perspectives" implies the *switching* of the focus or viewpoint – even if continuously – depending on the time and situation, I instead want to turn my attention to *concurrency* here. There are broadly two layers. One is the behavioral layer in dreams, which is equivalent to the layer where shamans perform their abilities to be discussed below. The other is obviously the behavioral layer represented by wakefulness and the body, which is a physical layer accompanying the usual human intentions and sensations. I call them "behavioral layers" instead of "experiential layers" here because an experience is clearly formed only when it is raised in one's consciousness, as mentioned earlier, and it should be called a behavior (or an action) prior to this stage. The two behavioral layers are brought to consciousness through, for example, conversation in the form of *berandau* and become the integrated experience of a certain individual. My use of the word "experience" earlier in this section was slightly premature in this sense, but I would like it to be taken as a preemptive usage, so to speak.

The behavioral layers here can be regarded as the internal strata of what Hallowel (1955) called a "behavioral environment". The behavioral environment contains various actors, or rather, every constituent of the behavioral environment is a potential actor who takes on a real form depending on the behavioral layer at the time. One thing we need to pay attention to is that, as we all know, the agent who talks about their dream during wakefulness is different from the agent who acts in their dream. In other words, no matter how realistic a dream is thought to be in a meaningful behavioral layer, its integration into the individual's experience takes place in the layer of reality during wakefulness. The reality in a dream in this sense is situated in an upper layer of the reality that overlays its substratum. However, this does not immediately lead to the conclusion that the agent during wakefulness is ego while that in a dream is non-ego. It is perhaps better to say that if we separate the agent into A during wakefulness and B in a dream, ego is the field where agent A and agent B appear in an *asymmetrical* manner. For, although ego is more often than not talked about in the words of agent A, a certain type of infiltration is recognized between A and B, as what transcends A is also ego. Shamans are those who can – or who say they can – experience this infiltration with certainty[2].

It follows that what is seen in a dream (and seen by shamans) and objects of experience in wakefulness are entities in the aforementioned dual world, but they do not exactly correspond. The world in waking hours and the world in a dream are only parts of the world as a whole, and they cannot be experienced simultaneously. One can get to know another person's dream only through experiencing it as a narrative in waking hours. This is the very ground that gives rise to a contradiction. Let's say there is world A and world B and agent A and agent B. The As and Bs in the two terms correspond with one another in my world, but I can only hear and know the B of the other in layer A indirectly. The soul is generally considered to reside in the skull, indicating that a person is living with consciousness. It is said that the soul leaves the body temporarily when a person is dreaming or sick, and death represents a complete and permanent separation between soul and body. This is all very straightforward up to this point. However, as evident in the above episode, in the Iban's understanding, the soul is not completely identical to the person or his/her personality (Uchibori 2013). This is rather difficult to understand as it is fundamentally different from the Christian view of the soul, and leads to the development of what can be called a peculiar contradictory space comprising incompatible logics.

One of the consequences of the theory of divergence between the agent in a dream – called the soul – and the ego, or the logic that they are separate beings, is that the latter is not (cannot be) responsible for the former's actions. While the actual narration and feeling of an episode like that discussed in the previous section indicates how this is reflected, another curious question arises concerning the existence of the spirit and ghost of the deceased at the center of this episode. The question is somewhat beyond the case of a dream becoming an experience. In association with this question, we shall advance our discussion from experience to existence.

The existence of spirits

The episode discussed above involved an encounter with a "known other" in a dream. This known other was identified as *antu*, a being that could be a spirit or a demon, in the conversation between the women and the shaman. This probably stemmed from the perception they had prior to his death that he could have turned into an *antu*. As I said earlier, according to the Iban's rationale, an experience in a dream is experienced by the soul of the person who is dreaming, and things that are seen in a dream are the souls of the seen things. It is as if they literally follow the intellectualistic core rationale employed in Edward Burnett Tylor's classical conceptualization of animism. This theoretical assumption, as well as the act of passively assigning various interpretations to the actual dreams they have on a day-to-day basis, in a sense, and in some cases actively seeking a particular dream, constitute dreaming folklore in the Iban. A majority of their day-to-day dreams are "culturally patterned dreams", which are interpreted in a highly automatic manner according to patterns and responded to with automatic solutions such as not going to work in the field or changing one's plans. This can be regarded as a mechanism that prevents special meaning from being attributed to individual dreams. On the other hand, when an unidentifiable person appears in a dream and approaches the dreamer in an unusual way, people tend to consult a shaman to deal with it whenever possible. This is because unidentifiable figures, like some animal species (land and water creatures) that appear in dreams, tend to be regarded as *antu*.

From the above it is clear that in Iban ontology, the soul of the dreaming person and *antu* exist on the same behavioral layer. Actually, during an interaction in a dream it is *antu* who actively has an effect, be it positive or negative, and in most cases the dreaming person's soul takes a passive role. It is common practice to actively seek an encounter with *antu* in a dream, and many people claim to have acquired various magical objects or knowledge in such encounters. These encounters are essential in acquiring spiritual abilities required to qualify one to work as a shaman. Even in these cases, however, *antu* are still the active party in the sense that the dreaming person is the beneficiary. From this viewpoint, *antu* can be seen as the origin of some kind of power, whether beneficial or harmful. It is not the case that there is something behind *antu* that manifests via *antu*. *Antu* is the origin or source of power, and not a messenger or an intermediary of any other more fundamental source of power.

There is a lingering sense of "incomprehensibility" about *antu*, and it comes from this sense of their being the origin of power. This gives the word a semantic nuance close to that of *kami* (spirits, forces) in Japanese, but *antu* offers a far broader range of reference than *kami* in everyday language. Its usage, which ranges from overripe fruit and vegetables to photography at a certain point in history (Jensen 1974), perhaps corresponds to that of the Japanese term *obake* (monster, specter or ghost) in Japanese. In relation to human death, *antu* is used to refer to "the dead" in general, including the physical being of the corpse during a funeral service – equivalent to *hotoke* ("the deceased" deriving from the term Buddha), as in the Japanese police drama jargon – and the spiritual being of the deceased – like *hotoke sama* (the departed soul) in everyday Japanese. It is used on its own or in combination with *sebayan*, a more specific collective term for the dead. The word *antu* referred to in the episode under discussion was used partly in this way, but it was in fact referring to an Iban folk entity with a more specific name, Antu Gerasi. This was almost self-evident to the Iban. The meaning of *antu* in this case is closer to a "demon" or "bogeyman". Among many kinds of demonic *antu* in the Iban world, Gerasi is perhaps the most feared and is said to go hunting with dogs, as seen in the woman's dream. It is said that in his eyes humans take on the appearance of wild boars. It follows that a demonic spirit such as Antu Gerasi is a harmful being to humans, but for specific people he sometimes acts as a guardian spirit. In this sense, it is not definite whether *antu* are essentially good or evil. This ambiguity also applies to *petara*, generally regarded as spiritual beings good for humans, which we will discuss further below.

When we look at the overall picture of *antu*, which are discussed in various contexts and relate to humans in various ways, one thing I must emphasize is that the ongoing existence of the deceased in the form of a ghost occupies a special position within the Iban's theory of souls. In this case, for example, the soul and the spirit not only exist in the same behavioral layer, but also confirm the equation "soul (*semengat*) = spirit (*antu*/ghost)". This equation allows all the responsibility for the personal character and behaviors attributed to the agent in life, especially during waking hours, to be placed on the soul of the deceased. In other words, the separation between "the person's self" and "the person's soul" is dissolved upon death. The person is absolved of blame for the behaviors of the mischievous or evil soul as long as they are alive. This is why a man can get away with confessing that he sneaked a visit to another man's wife in his dream by making the excuse that "My soul is behaving badly". The same defense is accepted for the behaviors of the deceased shaman's soul while he was alive. However, the Iban's soul theory is supposedly not designed to provide a defense for attacks on people by the deceased shaman in someone's dream. If the dead has a personality, it has to be the soul's personality. A logical contradiction is found here.

The folk theory of dreams and the ontology of souls and spirits are, after all, the wrong place to look for logical consistency. Because the theory that the soul permanently resides in the skull and wanders out when a person is dreaming during sleep or when sick already contains a number of contradictions (inconsistencies), it is certainly useless to try to argue about an episode of contradictory discourse here[3]. Nonetheless, identifying small contradictions is also important in measuring the place and weight of these theories in people's lives. By doing so, we are able to recreate the scenes of the practical application of folk theories, and determine in which parts of social life these logical contradictions produce the desired effects.

It is uncertain whether the contradictory statement of the shaman who conducted the ritual in the aforementioned episode was made intentionally or inadvertently. If it was intentional, he might have said it to be evasive as he made little of the old women's concerns and tried to avoid further involvement, or if it was inadvertent, he might have been being careless about the theories of spirits and ghosts, at least on that occasion. While the former case would not require further explanation, the latter case warrants further investigation as to the cause of this carelessness. A consideration of the cause would require thinking somewhat more broadly about the issue.

In my view, the factor behind this is, in abstract terms, the epistemological gap between the established cultural representation and the tendency of human memory and recollection to focus on particularities. In more concrete terms, the equation "the deceased = the soul of the deceased" represented theoretically among the Iban falls, at least sometimes, in failure when the person in life is recollected. Talking as if the personality of the deceased remains separate from the soul after death is an *abuse of the logic* of their theory about the personality of the living. This abuse becomes possible because people's recollection of the personality represented by the body of the recently deceased overrides the theory. This is particularly so when this remembering accompanies strong emotions. The elderly women who talked about the horrifying encounter with a "known other" in a dream was party to such recollection, and perhaps the shaman was influenced by it and unintentionally appropriated the common phrase that was supposed to be applied to the living and his soul.

The role that a memory would have played in this appropriation has almost fundamental importance in our discussion of the meaning of dreams for the Iban. Memory and the narration of it are activities that take place in the wakeful behavioral layer. The figures and events recollected in the narration of a dream derive from the wakeful behavioral layer of the past. When they interfere with behaviors in a dream, a pathway is formed between the two behavioral layers. If we turn our eyes from the bilayer behavioral structure to the dual world of beings, we can say that the process of narration builds a bridge between the two worlds. Dreams become meaningful experiences in the wakeful behavioral layer in the form of signs and warnings to the Iban precisely because this pathway or bridge has been formed. We must remember, however, that the pathway or bridge is normally a one-way road. Dreams exert some influence on wakeful life, but not the other way around. The Freudian theory of "day's residues" is not a concern of the Iban. In our search for the background factors to the episode under discussion, we have established that they are blind to the role of memory and recollection. This is why they have discovered the origin of independent meaning and unique emotions (fear and anxiety) in dreams.

In closing this section, I would like to add a few points. The possibility for *antu* and the soul to be actors in the same behavioral layer is demonstrated not only by what we have discussed so far, but also by the fact that some Iban people call *semengat padi* – the soul of rice – *antu padi* (Iwata 1972). As far as I can remember, I have never heard it said that *antu* have a soul or the expression "the soul of *antu*". Again, overall, the equation "soul $\approx$ spirit" holds[4]. However, this is only in one aspect of the relationship. In another sense, an *antu* can be an actor in a different behavioral layer from the soul, that is, an actor in the wakeful behavioral layer of humans. This is the transcendence of *antu* in the Iban world. I use the word "transcendence" to describe its ascent beyond a certain horizon, which is the boundary zone between the behavioral layer of the soul and that of the person in an ordinary condition. *Antu* refers to beings that can freely move between the two behavioral layers, and it can be regarded as a collective noun for such beings.

The wakeful behavioral layer of humans is a physical world comprising physical "things", and the physical existence of a person has primacy there. Accordingly, *antu* also emerge as something that is sensed physically there. In other words, *antu* are perceived via the physical senses (five senses). The *antu* thus perceived becomes a real thing to the Iban. Reality is firstly physical – the Iban introduce the topic of their own actions and experiences by saying, "My body itself…". It is their internal physical organs and not their "mind" or "soul" that sense the outside world and internalize the sensations.

Spirit = other as the mirror image or inversion of the self

Antu that appear in the wakeful human behavioral layer almost always take on human form. Although it may be bald or unusually large or with a hole in its back, it never appears in the form of a non-human thing – as some Japanese demons do – or a non-human animal. Some animal species are said to become *antu*, but they still appear in human form when they interfere in the human world. The predominance of what can be called anthropomorphism in some areas of the Iban's physical behavioral layer needs to be given sufficient attention. This focus on the human form is probably recognized by the Iban themselves. They use the word *utai* ('thing') to refer to an obscure entity that sexually attacks women in their dreams, or an unidentifiable (or unidentified) entity that is believed to bring harm[5]. On the other hand, *antu* are far more concrete and human-like, and in this sense are on a continuum with humans. Perhaps it is rather appropriate that the human corpse is called *antu*. As I mentioned earlier, *antu* can transcendentally move between the two behavioral layers, whereas humans can only do so in different times and spaces by splitting the "self" into the physical body and the soul. This is the crucial difference between them, and a human can become *antu* only in the existential mode of being the soul. This is the sole basis for the whole story told in the episode under discussion here.

What this reveals is that to the Iban, *antu* are beings that are very close to what the human "other" is to the self; they are counterparts one can interact with in a similar way that humans interact, although they are transcendental "strangers-others" that are not human. *Antu* are certainly other on the far end of the otherness spectrum, but here I depict the human-like "strangers-others" condition of *antu* evident in specific interactions.

Let us begin with Antu Gerasi that appeared in the above episode. The name *gerasi* is not uniquely Iban, as a demon spirit called Geregasi is also known to the Malay people in the Malay Peninsula (Skeat 1900). However, there are very close parallels between Gerasi's attributes and the lifestyle of the Iban. His hunting dog is called Pasun, and Gerasi goes hunting with his dog, kills and eats humans. As humans are said to look like wild boars in the eyes of Gerasi and Pasun, their existence reverses the position of the Iban in the "hunter" versus "hunted" relationship. Seen from the other side, Gerasi is an *image bearing the negative meaning* of Iban men in the act of hunting, or an "inversion". To hazard the risk of reading too much into this, the Iban may be projecting their guilty feeling as hunters = "animal killers" onto Gerasi (Uchibori 1980; Burkert 1989). Although the Iban routinely assert their strong sense of identity as rice cultivators, Iban men have an equally strong passion for hunting. Iban women are often critical of this, and even dismiss men's bias for hunting as a "pastime". This conflict between farming and hunting along gender lines literally displays gender imbalance, as in the case of the next *antu*. In fact, there is a marked contrast between men and women in various kinds of *antu* in the Iban, be it in the form of gender or sexuality.

The greatest gender imbalance is found in Antu Koklir. Women who die in childbirth turn into this *antu*. As with the case of a demon spirit called Pontianak found across Southeast Asian islands, the transformation is triggered by events surrounding childbirth. While Pontianak is usually said to attack pregnant women and cause miscarriage and stillbirth, Koklir is believed to attack womanizing men in the habit of sneaking into women's beds by pecking at their testicles (*pelir*). Pontianak is driven by jealousy toward pregnant women and a vendetta on their babies (*anak*), but Koklir in the Iban, by contrast, has hostility toward men in sexual relationships or the sexual relationship itself. Among animals, a civet species called *binturong* (*enturon* in Iban) is said in some cases to turn into this *antu*.

A group of *antu* that is the extreme opposite of Gerasi to the Iban is called Orang Panggau (people of Panggau). In general, these are the central characters that reside in the world of a set of heroic folktale cycles called Ensera Panggau[6]. The main hero's name is Keling, which is a term of Sanskrit origin found throughout Southeast Asia and refers to a person from the Indian subcontinent in the Javanese language, for example, but it does not have this meaning in Iban. These folktales are characterized by various forms of representation of the elements of heroic folktales, as formulated by Vladimir Propp early last century. The main protagonists include Keling, his lover/wife Kumang and their cousins, and the story is populated by numerous other characters, including their adversaries and supporters (Uchibori 1979). Antu Gerasi sometimes appears, not always as an antagonist but also as Keling's supporter.

The narrative is easy to understand up to this point. What requires some explanation is the Iban's idea that a certain pathway connects this world of heroic folktales to the real world of humans. More specifically, Keling and other characters are regarded as *antu* who in ancient times were beings in the real world and members of the same community as the Iban. Just as humans and Gerasi have a continuous pathway in the sense that the soul can become Antu Gerasi, the Iban and the characters in Panggau have a pathway in the sense that they once belonged to the same community. However, there is no "transformable" connection between humans in the real world and Panggau heroes, as one cannot become the other. The heroes appear in the real world in the form of cobras and other venomous snakes. Some Iban people are prompted by the appearance of one of these snakes inside their homes in conjunction with a revelation in a dream to adopt one of the Panggau heroes – corresponding to the kind of snake that appeared; Keling if it was a cobra, for example – as a guardian spirit. Thus, they acquire the status of *antu* that are basically benevolent toward humans in the two behavioral layers of the human empirical world beyond that of folktales. The most noticeable features of the folktale heroes of Panggau are their headhunting exploits, good harvests and winning over women by sneaking into their bedrooms, which are ideals blatantly enacted by Iban men in the real world. On this point, the Panggau heroes are the projection of the Iban onto the spirit world, just Antu Gerasi is, but they are in a sense a straightforward, positive, upright image of themselves without the negative connotation of Gerasi.

Further from the group of Panggau heroes, there is another group of spirits known as *petara*. As mentioned earlier, *petara* in the Iban language has been translated by most scholars, native or foreign, into English as gods or deities. This translation is not incorrect in the sense that the beings basically carry out favors for humans. However, I must point out that the reference that locates *petara* in stark opposition to *antu* found in much of the ethnographic (folklore) literature, including those works written by Iban researchers, lacks precision. All of the old Iban men I spoke to in hill villages in the mid-1970s considered *petara* at least as a type of *antu*, i.e., a subcategory. Where did this difference of opinion come from?

I suspect that *petara* came to be regarded by scholars as a different category from *antu* due to the following circumstances. The word *petara* is derived from the Sanskrit term *bhatara*, the variant words of which are widely used to refer to divine beings in both the island and continental parts of Southeast Asia. In many areas, the *bhatara*-derived words seem to be distinguished from those related to the Iban word *antu*, such as *hantu* (Malay and Javanese) and *hantuen* (Ngaju Dayak) (Stöhr and Zoetmulder 1965). The distinction applied to the Iban case may be an effect of this broader-region ethnography, or interference from some monotheistic bias. In any case, there are reasons to suspect that a desire to recognize a superior divine being, if not the only god, in the Iban's worldview is (was) at work in the process of describing them. These days, some people even talk about *petara* not as a category name, but as a supreme god transcending the individually named beings the term includes.

This detour aside, I wish to emphasize that *antu* is the uppermost category of transcendental beings in the Iban, and that it can be regarded as the equivalent of *kami* in the Japanese language, therefore various beings called *petara* carry the common traits of *antu*. The well-known *petara* names include Singalang Burong the war deity, Pulan Gana the god of land, Sempandai the forger of humans to be born and Manang Menjaya the god in command of shamans, who are the major gods invited to rituals for headhunting, farming, healing, ordination and accompanying festivities respectively. Like other *antu*, they are perceived in human form, but their involvement in people's everyday lives is certainly not as pervasive. Aside from verbal citations in depictions in folk or mythological tales, or appeals made in prayers and songs in rituals and at festivities, the relative strength/density of the relationship of those spiritual beings with humans in terms of interaction can be described as follows.

> Demonic beings such as Gerasi > Heroic beings such as Keling > *petara*

A strong/dense relationship indicates that there is a more ambivalent one in reality. This has greater positive and negative effects on humans, stemming from the content of the mirror-image effect of *antu* on the Iban. I stated earlier that Gerasi is an inverted image with a negative value, while Keling is a positive, upstanding image; however, each also carries some degree of the reverse value. Gerasi as the strongest hunter-*antu* can become a guardian of humans, while from the outset Keling and the other heroes embody contradictions contained in the Iban's ethics of the past. In comparison, the ambivalence surrounding *petara* is at most that they are "cumbersome beings"[7]. To follow this up, I would like to explore the ambivalence found in the ethics of Iban society of the past, i.e., ambivalence toward others, a little deeper in the next section.

The spirit as alter ego

Is it possible to state that *antu* and humans engage in "social communication"? I can only respond to this question by saying that they certainly do within a community of individuals who share the understanding of the existence of *antu*.

This is because the existence of *antu* and their ability to intervene are inherent in the basis for the formation of social relations within such a community. In most cases, communication that occurs between *antu* and a human individual is confined to a dream, and the other individuals in the community of shared understanding do not participate in it in any sense. Although what takes place individually is fundamentally incomprehensible to others to some degree, a narrative about it can be formulated in a spatiotemporally remote place and, needless to say, this remains meaningless unless it is narrated. We must consider the narration of dreams by the Iban in this context, and the same applies to their "encounters" with *antu*.

The existence of *antu* such as Gerasi and Keling as the mirror images of humans means that every Iban individual harbors an internal ethical ambivalence. We can say that a basically evil *antu* such as Gerasi can be the soul of a human because the Iban recognize somewhere in their consciousness that humans indeed have Gerasi-like attributes. Let us say that *antu* is the embodiment of the "ogre of the heart" (conscience) in the context of the early medieval Japanese language, or the super-ego in a psychoanalytical sense, and is something that lies midway between solidity and abstraction. *Antu* are the invisible other within, or the other as one's own reflection, so to speak, and this is why they emerge in the form of the other that simultaneously appears human-like and non-human-like. The incomprehensibility of *antu* ultimately stems from their comprehensive nature as beings that contain all these values. Because of this incomprehensibility, *antu* cannot reside on the same behavioral plane as the human self and they must be represented as "strangers-others" when they are represented tangibly.

In the past, headhunting offered a stage for competition among the Iban men. Some say that education has replaced headhunting these days, but in any case, the emphasis is placed on competition and social prestige that connote *success with women* (Masing 1980). However, headhunting achieves prestige only through the act of killing, and this is where it is crucially different from education. Further, education offers prestige that can be achieved by both men and women. Aside from prestige and competition among peers, however, education is a long way from replacing headhunting in terms of its relevance to the Iban's view on life and gender (and sexuality). The old ethics and values that revolved around headhunting constitute a specific complex that is irreproducible in the new reality. I argue, with some reservation, that the act of murder that leads to the acquisition of a trophy head has something in common with the killing of animals in hunting. Both acts accomplish the desired outcome only through the technical processing of dead bodies, which stands antithetical to the agriculturalist identity of the swidden rice-growing people. In this context, both acts contain a certain kind of deviation from the quotidian normality.

Hunting may look like a human act of unilateral violence toward animals, but the Iban's main prey, wild boar, is actually a ferocious animal that poses danger to both humans and their dogs. A dream that features being counterattacked by a boar is one of the most frequently narrated dreams among the Iban, and is entrenched as a "culture-pattern dream of fear" that is interpreted as a bad omen. In this sense, the wild boar is an enemy of humans and in fact the practice of hunting shares common elements with that of headhunting in some respects, especially as an act of symbolic substitution. As a small example, there were a few dozen dogs at the longhouse I stayed at for a long period in the mid-1970s, and practically all of them were hunting dogs. Particular dogs, interestingly, were referred to as Polis (police), Komunis (communist), Tuan (lord = white (leader)) for example, indicating the names of strong figures in jungle battles between communist guerrilla forces and government troops.

We must keep in mind that a majority of headhunting expeditions in the past assumed an appropriate "enemy", just as in modern jungle battles, rather than being sporadic killings, and to that extent the killers could end up being killed. In this sense, headhunting means seeing one's own evil in the stranger-other who is supposedly one's enemy, and this type of other who is a stranger has always been a potential source of fear. In Kawai's depiction in Chapter Nine, the Dodoth see the projected image of their own destitution in the Turkana and feel empathy for the inevitability of their need to rustle livestock. By contrast, while it is highly likely that violent hostilities have been historically limited occurrences in the case of the Iban (Wagner 1972), they still view others coming from the outside of their relatively small community – often confined to a river basin – with some degree of suspicion and caution, even today. Their attitude is no different toward unknown Iban people from other areas.

In this way, the stranger-other constitutes the alter ego with different content and meaning than those of companions – others with a low degree of "otherness" – to the Iban ego. If we look at the formation of the alter ego as a process, it involves the transformation of the other into the self or the reverse process, i.e., the formation of a mirror relationship between self and other. *Antu* (spirits) are the Iban's alter ego in this sense, and the Iban see the mirror image of their own ego in the ambivalent existence of *antu* – be it an upstanding or inverted image, or positive or negative in terms of ethical value. *Antu* are positioned as an illusion that transcends an illusion in the meaning world built upon shared understanding. That world is a kind of otherworld to humans living through the five senses. However, these beings sometimes enter into our familiar wakeful life-world from the outside world and interact with us. This possibility for interaction is the aforementioned transcendence of *antu*, and their (supposed) appearance in the wakeful behavioral layer as beings perceivable via the five human senses is the phenomenon that proves this transcendence.

If we look back at our discussion, in Iban communities the appearance of spirits and the behaviors of souls basically occur at night. They are of course rooted in people's real everyday experience of dreaming and narrating these events, and they are all the more susceptible to skepticism because of it. In contrast to their belief in the soul, individual encounters with *antu* cannot be easily shared as truth, whether they occurred in a dream or in waking hours – particularly when they are linked to the benefit or prestige of those who experienced them. In a community situated in a different river basin from the Iban village (longhouse) of my ongoing study, many young people became shamans in the 1980s. They reportedly said that they were motivated to do so by their encounters with *antu* who instigated the process of them becoming shamans in dreams, but many thought that this was a lie and that they were simply motivated by money. For an interaction with *antu* to be regarded as genuine, it needs to be supported by multiple people having similar dreams (as in the case of the episode discussed above) or the successful intermeshing of the logic with calamities and unfortunate events such as someone's death being caused by *antu*.

Although *antu* are perceived through the five senses, only a small number of people claim to "have seen an *antu* itself", instead pointing to various signs of the manifestation of *antu*. An elderly woman I know told me that she had seen one "With my own body", after qualifying her remark with "As I have lived this long". What she saw, however, was merely a large red spherical thing, or an eyeball, on the edge of the forest at night. It is the same with the sense of touch. A man said that one festive evening when he was squatting to urinate (as is customary for Iban men) on the edge of a clothes-drying verandah, a hand had extended through the slatted floor and grabbed his calf. As the sense of touch is a particularly individual sense, there is no other way to share the experience than through narration. The most common sensing of the presence of *antu* by multiple persons at the same time is through "hearing" rather than via tactile or visual sensing, and tends to be a trivial occurrence such as a sudden uproar made by pigs walking under the raised floor of the longhouse. The predominance of hearing in the shared experience of perceiving a physically "nonexistent thing" is similar to the function of hearing in hunting behavior inside the tropical rainforest with a limited field of vision. This is almost an anticlimactic statement, but the five senses that inform individual experience are rather like the gleanings of one's dream experience.

In closing: The evolution of others-as-strangers

The question guiding the discussion in this chapter has focused on others as distinct from "simply other" individuals; or, if you like, "unusual others" as against "usual others". For "the other" in the former sense to stand face-to-face as a somewhat incomprehensible being against "the self" rather than as "simply another" individual, the self must take note of the attributes that are essentially "different" from those of the self. The theory that the formation of the other in general – the "usual other" in this case – entails a certain form of paying attention to the intention or background that is "different" from those of the self regarding the action and behavior of the other individual, who is "similar to" the self, is meaningful in evolutionary behavioral science or developmental psychology, but has a low significance in ethnology. In fact, I wonder if it is at all necessary to establish the notion of "the other" in this sense either in ethnological or even in evolutionary anthropological comparison, for evolutionary anthropology is not circumscribed by evolutionary behavioral science. What is important in our discussion is the formation of "the other" that is distinctly as well as meaningfully "different" from other individuals alongside the experience of relating to this "other".

Looking at individual cases among the Iban, their experiences with spirits are primarily solitary ones, and none of the cases I am familiar with were joint experiences. A solitary experience becomes more of a shared experience when it is narrated and subjected to people's interpretations. However, the sharing of a solitary experience through narration must be repeated on a regular basis. The handing down of a narrative in the form of a story with a firmly fixed plotline (a myth or folktale) alone is weak. What adds a strong degree of realism to the shared experience is the firsthand narration of direct experience based on all five senses (including smell), or at least the secondhand narration of it in the form of hearsay. Of course, this becomes possible on the condition that one can trust the homogeneity between the sensory (five senses) experience of the self and the other close to oneself, that is the other with a low degree of otherness or the "usual other". This trust can be called "sensory communality", and based on that the vicarious sensing at the scene of narration can be called "communal senses".

"The other" in the above meaning is entered into a formative process that requires time when humans bring it to consciousness as an experience through narration and live in the way this experience is rooted in a sensory communality. This is the process of communal understanding and acceptance. Each experience involved in that process is revived as an individual experience founded on communality. The self that narrates this experience and the other individuals who understand and respond to it work jointly to form the other. This process of formation is essentially cyclical, but needless to say, "the other" that is formed thus does not get involved in this work. The formation process also exists outside of the consciousness of each member of the human group involved.

Whether it is a positive or negative mirror image, our underlying ability to create others-as-strangers as the communal self (we) that exists in the other layer is an ability that involves leaping from illusion to imagination. There is actually no need to limit these others-as-strangers to human-like figures. It is conceivable that when we accept the existence of life forms that are analogous to us, i.e., animals (and plants), and expand their understanding of the existence of similar but different beings from among humans to the entire world around us, we come to place interactions between not only humans and non-humans but also between non-humans in the entire plane of interactions. It is self-contradictory, but this entails the diversity of "the other" in the maximum sense possible in the human world. In the case of the Iban it is so even if the range of imagination is not expanded to incorporate interactions between non-humans.

From another angle, is there room to include non-human primates when we consider the existential value of others-as-strangers in the imagination? Or, what kind of evolutionary sequence and momentum does this imaginative development correspond to? An ordinary, conventional answer to these questions, similar to the statement at the start of this section, would be an almost tautological one: "Human-like others emerge because of this imagination". Perhaps we have no way of identifying a specific stage in the evolutionary process of the genus *Homo*, even hypothetically. Apart from the representation of the other as the stranger based on the "comprehensible/incomprehensible" distinction at the level of consciousness, however, we cannot say that non-human primates do not perceive "the incomprehensible" and "the uncanny" (*Das Unheimliche*) on the level of feelings and bodily sensations. Not only primates, but also a wider category of animals may be equipped with the ability to sense a being that is neither the self nor the other and that is "strange" at a level beyond that boundary, so to speak. In a broad sense, it would be one of the abilities acquired evolutionarily for the purpose of detecting and assessing changes in the environment in which they lived (for my recent discussion on death and the evolutionary effects of human imagination, see Uchibori 2017). What was the evolutionary momentum to manifest this sense in the form of illusion, and when did it arrive at representation in the form of a specific stranger-as-other through the retention and sharing of a long-term memory about an illusion? These questions can be traced back to the question of what apes and monkeys dream about and how they perceive their dreams. I wonder how close we are to finding an answer to these questions.

15 A History of the Distance Between Humans and Wildlife

Gen Yamakoshi

Key ideas

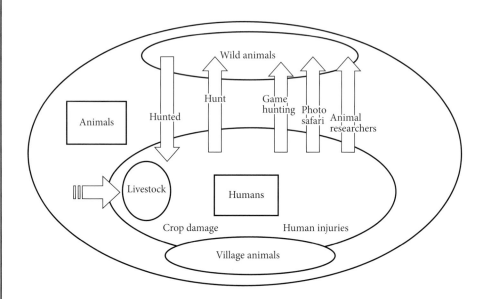

The "we" to which "I" belong can be defined in a multilayered way. This concept of "we" is encircled by the similarly multilayered "others" and constantly threatened by the beings located on the boundary. Where "we" are *Homo sapiens*, "the others" are "(non-human) animals". When we survey the history of mankind for the existence of various interfaces between humans and wild animals, we find that a new relationship in terms of the distance between the two was formed at each turning point, such as human settlement and modernization. The keywords for deciphering the relationship between humans and wild animals in modern times are modern hunting represented by game hunting as well as non-predatory-type animal observation. What is the "strange urge" that has been driving these activities?

Wildlife as "the other"

The "we" to which "I" belong can be defined as "family", "clan", "community", "nation", "modern people", "humanity" and so on in a multilayered way depending on the time and situation. On the other hand, the concept of "we" is surrounded by similarly multilayered "others" and constantly threatened by the beings located on its boundary (e.g., strangers, savage tribes, demonic spirits, foreigners, primitives, artificial intelligence/robots/androids, early humans or apes). Where "we" are humans as a biological species, or *Homo sapiens*, "the others" are "(non-human) animals". This chapter is an attempt to elucidate the relationship between humans and wildlife by focusing on the physical distance between "we" humans and wildlife as "the other", with particular attention on the behavior of the boundary that appears between them in various domains, including hunting, habituation, observation and tourism.

The interface between people and wildlife

The "wildlife problem" is fast becoming a social concern in rural Japan today (Hayama 2001). Particularly in the hilly and mountainous communities impoverished by an aging population, the shrinking labor force involved in hunting and farming has resulted in a failure to prevent the incursion of wild animals such as deer, boars, monkeys and bears that are causing serious crop damage and human casualties. The occasional incursion of these wild animals into urban areas has also been reported, and local governments have been at a loss as to how to control the wildlife habitat. The boundary line between the human habitat and the wildlife habitat is being pushed into the human side, forcing people to redefine the way they interact with fauna regarded as endangered last century.

Damage to agricultural crops and people by wild animals is also a major problem in developing countries in the tropics, but its historical and social context is very different from that in Japan. In Africa, for example, many wild animal species are protected in vast conservation areas, as they are thought to be on the brink of extinction due to decreased habitats and overhunting. Under the auspices of the conservation programs of UN bodies and international conservation groups, wildlife, which can be the source of national revenue from tourism and other activities, are in many cases carefully protected under laws and regulations prohibiting hunting. This has given rise to a sharp conflict between nature conservation and the preservation of people's livelihoods, as local farmers are deprived of a means to prevent crop damage (Meguro 2014).

Meanwhile, an example of a different interface between humans and wild animals is zoonosis. Recent epidemiological and genetic studies have found that major infectious diseases such as Ebola virus, HIV AIDS and falciparum malaria were transmitted from apes to humans (Corbet et al. 2000; Formenty et al. 1999; Liu et al. 2010). Wild bats are suspected to be the reservoir host for the recent Ebola epidemic (Leroy et al. 2005), bringing into question the distance and interface between humans and wild animals from a different angle than direct damage.

These examples demonstrate that when humans share their habitat with wildlife, they need to maintain a certain distance; in other words, getting too close to wildlife involves significant risks (Wolfe et al. 2007). It has been suggested that in the history of humankind humans ran from large carnivores until they "armed" themselves with weapons provided by culture and civilization (Hart and Sussman 2007). It is not hard to imagine that the human/wild animal interfaces at the time were fraught with tension. Nevertheless, at various stages in human history humans went on to build intimate relationships with wild animals by approaching them, crossing the boundary into their habitats and habituating them for all sorts of reasons.

Changes in the human-wildlife relationship over time

Domestication
While there are various theories, it is generally estimated that humans began grain cultivation and animal husbandry by domesticating wild flora and fauna approximately 12,000 years ago (Larson et al. 2014). This means that humans subsisted on hunting and gathering for much of the seven million or so years of our history. The relationship between humans and wild animals during that period would have been one of hostility or deterrence between hunter and hunted, and approaches for other purposes would have been rare.

The subsequent relationship between humans and wildlife was driven into a completely different phase by a major revolution involving the beginning of agriculture and animal husbandry. A prerequisite for animal husbandry is a herd of herbivorous animals habituated enough to allow reproductive management and selective breeding through culling. As Kinji Imanishi pointed out in "Yūboku ron" (1993 [1948]), however, some leaps would have been needed in their relationality to enable the herbivorous animal herd to be sufficiently habituated to range alongside humans instead of avoiding them. While the leading theory at the time was the capture of offspring, Imanishi proposed his unique domestication theory involving humans tracking herbivorous animal herds within a limited ranging area. "When a hunter enters the grazing range of a particular herd and moves with the herd, he may come to think that the herd has been given to him and is owned by him" (Imanishi 1993 [1948]: 226–227).

Regardless of whether Imanishi's theory is right or wrong, humans overcame this particular boundary that entirely separated them from wildlife and habituated and drew wild animals into their domain probably for the first time in the history of humankind.

Settlement and the appearance of the "anthropogenic landscape"

Agriculture that began almost concurrently with pastoralism, together with sedentary life as the cause or consequence of it, redefined the relationship between humans and wild animals in a more ecological manner, unlike the domestication process. When cultivation prompted the spatial concentration of domesticated plants with enlarged edible parts and improved digestibility through selective breeding, wild animals moved into the human domain in search of these crops. This was the start of a similar relationship to that which is causing crop damage today. Animals that gather in cultivated fields can become game for hunting, and some of the theories on the agricultural origin of wild animal domestication, which were alternatives to Imanishi's nomadism theory, argued that the approach by wild animals was the precursor to the origins of pastoralism (Imanishi 1993 [1948]).

As environmental change to the landscape is advanced by human settlement, some wild animals adapt to the newly created artificial environment or anthropogenic landscape. In other words, they are "weed species" (e.g., "weed macaques" – crab-eating monkeys and others – that have adapted to Asian artificial vegetation; see Richard et al. 1989). Some of these animals are given religious and magical significance, and permitted to live in the vicinity of human habitats as sacred animals (Photo 15.1). Numerous examples of this phenomenon are found all over the world, including the deer in Nara Park in Japan and Hanuman langurs at Hindu temples in India. They can be regarded as cases in which wild animals have crossed the boundary to intrude into the human domain, and have indirectly become habituated to an anthropogenic landscape as a result. This is in contrast to the process of wild animal domestication.

Thus, humans who had supposedly been in a hunter-hunted relationship with wild animals as hunter-gatherers invited some species of wild animals into their

Photo 15.1 Sacred chimpanzees of Bossou, Guinea, intrude into the village and eat cultivated papaya

own sphere of daily living as livestock. Alternatively, environmental alteration triggered by the use of fire and expanded by permanent settlement and agricultural development resulted in the appearance of a giant niche called the "anthropogenic landscape", and secondary adaptation to that environment by wild animals saw the intrusion of "village animals" into the humanosphere. In principle, it is possible to say that the habituated animals found in our sphere of everyday living today have come to live near us as a result of these two distinct processes.

The new human-wildlife relationship in the modern age

After a major change triggered by settlement and the beginning of agriculture and animal husbandry 12,000 years ago, the boundary between humans and animals was reorganized once again with the arrival of the modern age. Exchanges of people and goods increased on a global scale along with the Age of Discovery, the slave trade and the colonial period and nations of the Western world encountered exotic wildlife in their rapidly expanding territories. The boundary line between humans and wild animals changed dramatically under these circumstances. Curiously, the change was almost a repeat of the history of human settlement.

Firstly, modern humans armed with modern conveniences called "hunting guns" (rifles) attained the overwhelmingly dominant position in the hunter-hunted relationship with wild animals. Colonial hunting practice was largely a recreational activity and came to be called "big-game hunting", in which hunters collected the heads of wild animals and brought them home as trophies rather than consumed their bodies as a necessity for survival. The symbolic act of confronting pieces of nature to be conquered based on the nature/culture dichotomy can be considered characteristic of Western culture (Cartmill 1995).

While the hunter-hunted relationship was renewed, a new relationship involving wildlife habituation also emerged. Exotic animals, which became the targets of hunting in colonies, had a long history of being exported to faraway cities as rare animals to entertain the ruling classes from ancient times. The expansion of global trade in the modern age turned these curiosities into common entertainment for urban dwellers in the form of mobile zoos and circuses, and became part of the driving force behind the creation of modern zoos (Wakō 2010). This move to take wild animals away from their native habitats and bring them into the sphere of human living by habituating them in a new environment and controlling their consumption and reproduction can be regarded as a re-enactment of the domestication of animals by humans that occurred approximately 12,000 years ago.

One of the relationships with wildlife that we enjoy as a matter of course today is found in the act of "observing" wild animals in their natural habitats. The most common form is wildlife tourism, called "safari" in East Africa, while a smaller specialized form is behavioral and ecological research on wild animals carried out by ecologists. In terms of the history of the relationship between humans and wildlife, the human behavior of visiting places far away from their own habitats and attempting to approach wild animals in order to observe "nature" is quite unique, and did not exist in the nineteenth century. This behavior has a very short history, as it was initiated in the first half of the twentieth century and only popularized after the Second World War. I would like to outline why we adopted this strange behavior of observing wild animals, which is likely a relatively new form of interaction in the history of humankind.

Observation of wild animals

The origin of "nature" tourism

Items of cultural heritage such as literature and paintings confirm that people have appreciated natural landscapes as something rich and beautiful since Greco-

Roman antiquity. However, it has been argued that people showed interest in artificial landscapes that were closely associated with their abundance in life, or so-called pastoral scenes, rather than in "raw landscapes" separated from their everyday living (Kuwahara 1995; Ishikawa 2000). During the seventeenth and eighteenth centuries in the lead up to the modern period, the Alps were gradually transformed in human consciousness from a terrible place that harbored evil spirits into mountains to be climbed/conquered with beautiful tourist spots to be consumed (Nicolson 1989). In the area of aesthetics during the same period, the concept of the "sublime", which was ascribed to vertically configured and commanding landscapes such as steep mountains and waterfalls that moved onlookers, began to draw attention as opposed to the flat and gentle "beauty" of plains and flowering fields in pastoral scenes. In England at the end of the eighteenth century, picturesque tourism involving journeying to experience the sublime landscapes of Wales, including ruins, gained much popularity and it became fashionable for people to go beyond the consumption of literature and paintings and actually travel to see landscapes imbued with the sublime (Morino and Morino 2007).

The movement that started among people who remained in their own domains and consumed sublime "nature" in faraway places through travelogues and landscape paintings gradually transformed into the act of actually travelling to see "nature" through the popularization of tourism. This gave rise to comparisons between landscapes consumed in the form of art and actual landscapes seen at tourist sites, and led to a perverse movement in which natural features in remote places were "improved" to satisfy the desires of city dwellers; in the words of Oscar Wilde (1968: 81), "Life imitates art far more than art imitates life" (Crandell 1993). A paradox brought about by this kind of interaction is still evident today where, for example, residents of "beautiful" villages designated as world heritage are forced to endure inconvenient living conditions in order to cater for the desires of consumers-tourists.

The establishment of nature reserves that began at the end of the nineteenth century throughout the world can be regarded as the realization of "nature" as fiction created by city dwellers. The world's first national park, established in 1872, was the Yellowstone National Park in the western part of the USA. The settlers who migrated from Europe recognized the sublime landscapes of North America far removed from their native pastoral scenes as beautiful unspoiled wilderness (Nash 1967). It is particularly noteworthy that the national park system to protect wilderness was created at the time when America's Westward

Expansion reached the West Coast on the back of the Mexican-American War and made people aware of the vanishing unspoiled frontier. After the controversy over the construction of a dam in Hetch Hetchy Valley, Yosemite National Park, at the beginning of the twentieth century, the movement to not only quarantine nature as it is, but also utilize it for human experience and recreation, gained predominance (Kitoh 1996).

From hunting to observing: The history of East African national parks

The nature reserve system modeled on North American national parks was implemented on a large scale in Sub-Saharan Africa by authoritarian governments under the European and American powers that were strengthening their colonial rule at the time. In reality, this involved the artificial creation of "unspoiled nature" through large-scale infrastructure development by fencing off large tracts of land used by local African people, forcing them out and banning them from using it. Although nature reserves have the connotation of being places untouched by humans, a rather perverse system is involved in their creation, by which large sums of money are invested in their "establishment", boundaries are arbitrarily "created" and "design" is discussed. The perspective that defines the design of these African nature reserves has come from the wealthy classes in Europe and the USA, and has remained extrinsic to the African people from the colonial era to the present day (Yamakoshi 2014).

In the early twentieth century, a curious and dramatic change was taking place in the behavior of visitors toward wildlife in Africa in the history of conservation policy. At the dawn of nature reserves in the early twentieth century, colonialists engaged in the hobby or recreation of hunting wild animals (now called "big-game hunting"). Records show that more than 500 wild animals, including elephants and lions, were killed during the famous East African tour of Theodor Roosevelt, the twenty-sixth President of the United States, in 1909 (Roosevelt 1913).

This big-game hunting form of interaction with wild animals (safari hunting) continues to be pursued mostly by the European and American wealthy class (Yasuda 2013). However, the mainstream tourism activity in East Africa today involves the non-predatory behavior of getting very close to wild animals, observing and photographing them and then going home. The kind of perspective on animals that underpins this photo safari behavior is rarely found in the early twentieth century literature. This suggests that the photo safari perspective came into existence at some point in the twentieth century, and gradually became mainstream by sidelining the safari hunting relationship with animals in response to the advance of photographic technology that saw the miniaturization and popularization of cameras (Steinhart 2006).

To Karen Blixen (under the pen name of Isak Dinesen), who lived in Kenya from the 1910s to the 1930s, wildlife appeared in her famous work, *Out of Africa* (1981 [1937]), solely as the object of safari hunting. Conversely, her essay published in 1960, *A Letter from a King*, carries the following description: "Nowadays great sportsmen hunt with cameras. The practice started while I was still in Africa" (Blixen 1998: 73).

As many non-hunting tourists reportedly visited Amboseli National Park in Kenya during the 1930s (Lovatt Smith 1986), for example, it is suspected that the above change took place around this time. Interestingly, African people viewed the emergent photo safari perspective on wild animals as a strange behavior. Julius Nyerere, a prominent leader for the independence movement of African nations who later became the first President of Tanzania, made the following comment.

> I personally am not very interested in animals. I do not want to spend my holidays watching crocodiles. Nevertheless I am entirely in favor of their survival. I believe that after diamonds and sisal, wild animals will provide Tanganyika with its greatest source of income. Thousands of Americans and Europeans have the strange urge to see these animals, and we must ensure that they are able to do so. (Grzimek 1962)

Around the time of the rise of the photo safari, the wild animals in nature reserves where hunting was banned or restricted due to a sharp decline in their numbers would have become gradually accustomed to tourists who merely photographed them. These days, tourists in four-wheel-drives are able to come within a few meters of various wild animals in many of the East African nature reserves. It is supposed that the animals have been habituated gradually through repeated photo safari-style approaches since the 1930s. As a result of their interaction at a distance, the modern "strange urge" to (only) observe wild animals up close emerged.

I had the opportunity to participate in a photo safari in Nairobi National Park, Kenya, in 2012. Over the course of a few hours, I was able to stop our vehicle in the vicinity of different animals every ten minutes or so and photograph them to my heart's content (Photo 15.2). It gave me the impression that the nature reserve was similar to theme parks such as Disneyland, where people visit one attraction after another, even though it was represented as "unspoiled nature". Considering that this "park" is a facility constructed via a colossal infrastructure development

Photo 15.2 Wildlife tour in Nairobi National Park

in the form of the habituation of wild fauna and the entire ecological system over a period of seventy years or so, it would be perverse to see such a large-scale man-made facility as "unspoiled nature" unchanged from time immemorial.

Habituation of animals by wildlife research

The modern hunter-hunted relationship was sublated in order to protect specific animal populations and gave rise to a new non-predatory relationship consisting of observation and photography. At nature reserves in East Africa, for example, the shift from safari hunting to photo safaris led to the establishment of wildlife tourism as a giant industry. As a result, we have seen the emergence of habituated wild animals that allow the presence of humans in their original habitats.

On the other hand, the field of ecological research that involves observing the societies and ecologies of wild animals in the wild has also developed in parallel to the aforementioned shift. Observational studies of wild animals carried out by researchers were conducted sporadically in the first half of the twentieth century, and only became the standard format after the Second World War, especially from the 1960s. This happened contemporaneously with the sending of humans to the moon under the Apollo Program, and in scientific historical terms this means that the lunar surface and wildlife habitats in the depths of Africa were similarly remote frontiers for humankind.

Paving the way for the popularization of wildlife observation in the 1960s were the studies of wild Japanese macaques conducted by Japanese primatologists under the influence of Kinji Imanishi. In particular, the study of potato-washing culture in Japanese macaques on Kōshima, Miyazaki, had an immeasurable impact on animal ecologists all over the world (de Waal 2002). In order to observe a herd of wild animals directly in close proximity, the observer's presence must be permitted by the targeted group of individuals. Japanese primatologists adopted the method of food provisioning for that purpose. The advantage of food provisioning is that researchers can get closer to the group at a relatively early stage, and in doing so demonstrate to the animals that humans are harmless. After the success and popularization of the food provisioning method, some criticisms were raised about unnatural increases in the population as well as disruption of the "natural" state of behaviors such as increased aggression due to overcrowding in the feeding area. Nowadays, food provisioning is rarely used as a study method and has been replaced by the familiarization method, where the harmlessness of researchers is demonstrated through the patient tracking of animals over a long period, without provisioning them with food.

These habituation methods for groups of specific wild animals came into practice in parallel with the aforementioned photo safari trend, but they developed independently. Interestingly, it is possible to think that the new relationship with wildlife in the form of the habituation of groups achieved by primatologists was an artificial replication of the original habituation of livestock herds (according to Imanishi's theory of nomadic habituation).

Research by habituation initiated by primatologists has developed into an ingenious form of wildlife tourism. In Japan, where this style of research was born, the habituation of wild Japanese macaque troops by food provisioning led to the establishment of monkey parks in Takasakiyama, Ōita, and other locations as tourist attractions during the 1970s and captured public interest during the period of rapid economic growth. Despite a spate of monkey park closures due to declining popularity, the sector continues to maintain a presence as a tourist attraction today. In Africa, forested regions lagged behind savanna grasslands with good visibility and easy four-wheel-drive access to popular animals such as lions, giraffes and elephants. These days, tours to groups of gorillas and chimpanzees habituated to humans through primatological techniques are becoming popular tourism

Table 15.1 Comparison of two types of wildlife tourism in Africa

	Photo safari	Ape tourism
Origin	Hunting management (vehicles)	Research (group/individual tracking)
Habitat	Savanna	Forest
Target	Park, ecological level	Specific population
Approach method	Motor vehicles, large groups of visitors	On foot, small groups of visitors
Price	Relatively low	Relatively high

activities. I shall call these "ape tourism" here, for lack of a better expression. On the back of the success of the habituation of anthropoid groups by primatologists in various places in Africa during the 1960s and 1970s, ape tourism is a relatively new form of tourism in that continent that has gradually developed since the 1980s.

While photo safari on the savanna developed from safari hunting and approaches animals using motor vehicles, ape tourism originates from the habituation of animals by researchers who tracked them on foot. Photo safari brings in large numbers of tourists at relatively low prices, whereas ape tourism is designed to reduce the burden on animals and the environment by limiting the number of tourists at the location and charging a higher price. Ecologically, photo safari achieves habituation at the entire ecological level in the vast reserves, whereas ape tourism focuses on the habituation of individual groups of apes. Thus, in many respects the two types of wildlife tourism provide contrasting activities that reflect their different origins (Table 15.1).

Ape tourism in reality: Chimpanzee conservation at Bossou

Coexistence of people and chimpanzees in Bossou Village

I now present the case of chimpanzees in my research field of Bossou Village in the Republic of Guinea as an example of ape tourism that originates from primatological research. The chimpanzees of Bossou came to be known to the world when the village was found in a scientific study conducted by the French colonial government around 1940 to be an unusual site where villagers protected chimpanzees as their totem in their sacred forest (Yamakoshi 2006). Since then, the University of Amsterdam carried out a short-term study in the 1960s, while a long-running study launched by Yukimaru Sugiyama of Kyoto University in 1976 is ongoing today.

The chimpanzees of Bossou were initially "found" to be mostly unafraid of humans because they had been protected by the villagers. For this reason, it was possible to observe them within a relatively close range from the start of a study without the need for habituation over a long period, which is usually required at other study sites (Yamakoshi 2011). In other words, because the villagers allowed the chimpanzees to live within their sphere of living, they became "village animals" that had adapted to the anthropogenic rural village landscape created by slash-and-burn agriculture that was common throughout the West African tropical forest region.

The relationship between the chimpanzees and the villagers before the start of research was reportedly restrained, where a certain distance was maintained between them while they allowed each other to exist in the same space. Although observation was possible from the start of research, the chimpanzees would flee when trackers approached within ten to twenty meters. It was reported that the villagers accommodated damage to their fields to a certain extent, but in reality they usually chased the chimpanzees away by shouting or throwing rocks when they approached agricultural crops. Women and children were told to run away if they encountered the chimpanzees, as they were believed to be the reincarnation of their ancestors' souls and to have terrifying supernatural powers. It is thought that the villagers maintained a certain distance from the chimpanzees by venerating them and encouraging them to remain deep in the sacred forest.

Since 1970, the Bossou chimpanzees have come to be known internationally thanks to research findings such as the discovery of their tool-using behavior (Sugiyama 1981). Small numbers of tourists have been coming to see the chimpanzees since economic liberalization in the wake of the collapse of the socialist government in 1984. The tourist activity at Bossou adopts the on-foot approach of researchers and follows the typical design of "ape tourism" that limits the object of tourism to the chimpanzee community. The traditional framework that protected chimpanzees at Bossou was based on the sacred forest conceptualization that prevented people from entering it and protected all flora. However, this mechanism protects only the chimpanzees that inhabit the forest and not the entire ecology. The chimpanzees are the only animals that are traditionally exempted from hunting at Bossou. Because the villagers hunt other animals, local fauna other than chimpanzees are very scarce (Yamakoshi 1999).

The habituation of chimpanzees and its problems

As research and tourism continued, the chimpanzees gradually became more accepting of approaching human observers and the distance they maintained as

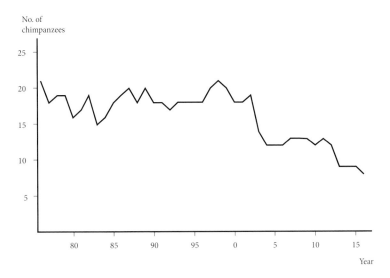

Figure 15.1 Changes in the population of Bossou chimpanzees

"village animals" began to change. For example, during my 1995 study, I attempted to observe the chimpanzees all day, but I was only able to manage two to three hours per day on average and lost sight of them in thick bushes more often than not. However, habituation has progressed rapidly this century and these days the chimpanzees nonchalantly walk right past their observers.

The long-term study that has been running for over four decades combined with ongoing tourism are causing some serious problems for the conservation of the Bossou chimpanzees. After maintaining a stable population of around twenty since the 1970s, a large decline in the twenty-first century resulted in a population of only eight chimpanzees by the end of 2015 (Figure 15.1). There are at least four major conservation problems impacting on the Bossou community of chimpanzees, all of which directly or indirectly stem from the change of distance between people and chimpanzees.

The first problem is the potential for zoonoses. Of the population fluctuations shown in Figure 15.1, a major cause of the decline is the loss of five chimpanzees in a short period of time due to an outbreak of respiratory infection at the end of 2003 (Matsuzawa et al. 2004). The community lost one infant from a similar respiratory disease in 1992. Although an exact causal relationship is unclear, there is more than a small likelihood that the respiratory disease that caused the 2003 mortality was brought in by tourists, researchers or villagers.

The second problem involves increasing damage to agricultural crops such as cassava, rice and orange and other fruit trees as a direct reflection of the chimpanzees' diminishing fear of people (Hockings et al. 2009b).

The third issue is the rising incidence of injuries amongst village children caused by chimpanzees, which have occurred almost yearly since 2000. Such incidents were very rare before the launch of research activities (Hockings et al. 2009a). The second and third problems stem from the escalation of habituation and the loss of the maintenance of an appropriate distance between humans and animals, as the village accommodated research activities and received income from tourists. These issues have raised serious questions about the previous direction of the village's policy to actively utilize its traditional heritage in exchange for revenue and have intensified the division of opinions on this matter in the village, threatening chimpanzee conservation activities as a result.

The fourth problem is a more structural one, involving the aging of individual chimpanzees. The Bossou chimpanzee group is a relatively isolated community separated from neighboring chimpanzee communities by several kilometers of land, as their habitat is highly impacted by the artificially fragmented layout of the sacred forest, swidden fallow plots and cultivation fields in a mosaic pattern (Yamakoshi 2009). Despite the absence of insurmountable geographical barriers separating them from neighboring chimpanzee groups, there have been no confirmed cases of migration from other groups since 1976. On the other hand, there has been a marked tendency for young Bossou chimpanzees to disappear upon reaching sexual maturity, contributing to a significant social decrease in the population, so to speak. As none of the villages around Bossou systematically protect chimpanzees, those in neighboring communities are constantly subjected to hunting. It is suspected that these potential migrants avoid migrating to the Bossou community, which lives in contiguity with the village and is tracked by researchers and tourists day in day out, because they are afraid of humans. Again, this has the same root cause as the preceding three problems in the sense that the act of actively tracking and observing chimpanzees by researchers and tourists has hastened the habituation of chimpanzees and influenced their population structure.

Bossou is currently instituting measures for "de-habituation" in order to stop excessive habituation and reinstitute the appropriate distance that was maintained between humans and chimpanzees in the past. Specific steps taken thus far include keeping a minimum distance of ten meters or so during observation, wearing masks, banning infected people from entering the area and suspending or scaling down non-essential and non-urgent research.

The vulnerability of ape tourism

Ape tourism targeting gorillas and chimpanzees is a relatively new approach to tourism in Africa. As the habituation of great ape groups by primatologists that preceded it gained momentum in the 1960s, it has only a short history of just over fifty years. In this short period of time, however, the "strange urge" of researchers and tourists has led to a gradual shrinking of the distance between the apes and their observers and caused various problems, including injury to people, crop damage and zoonoses, as described in the case of Bossou above. Further, there are concerns for ape communities tracked by humans in various areas in terms of their tendency to gradually reduce in size due to a reduction in the number of immigrants caused by fear of humans. Some say that habituation should be stopped altogether, as it exposes the apes to external threats and makes them vulnerable in the present climate of Africa with pressure from poachers and unstable political conditions.

Although the problems surrounding ape tourism have not become apparent in the photo safari sector on the savanna so far, excessive habituation may eventually cause similar issues. Most of the negative effects of excessive familiarization with humans have much in common with the negative impacts of food provisioning that previously attracted much criticism. It is reasonable to state that the "strange urge" to observe animals up close, which humans realized after all kinds of cultural shifts, has arrived at a period when it needs to be reviewed in light of the experiences of the last half century.

Wildlife as the new others

This chapter has focused on animals, especially wild animals, as the others encircling the outer edge of the definition of humans, and discussed their distance from humans at the ecological boundary zone in terms of manners of avoidance and approach from the perspective of the history of humankind. Unlike the animal species that have been taken into the humanosphere as livestock or the village animals that have adapted to the anthropogenic landscape, the animals that live in habitats remote from humans must have been simply distant beings to humans in the past.

Modernization has brought a new perspective on wildlife. The new modern concept of "wild animals" excluded livestock, assumed the hypothetical condition of a non-artificial environment as unspoiled nature and privileged the animals that live there as "wild". From this perspective, village animals have come to be seen as somewhat inferior animals that have lost their "wild" nature. In other words, the previously nonexistent "wild animals" emerged as the new others to humans, and the act of confronting and hunting them, for example, was given value as a special spiritual experience, as depicted in hunting novels by Hemingway (1966, 1999).

The hunting of wild animals, which was redefined by modernization and developed as safari hunting, has been gradually replaced by photo safari driven by a "strange urge" to observe and photograph wild animals. As a result, the entire local ecology of the African savanna, for example, has been habituated to human observers riding in four-wheel-drive vehicles and has developed into large-scale wildlife tourism. The social and ecological research of wild animals that caught on rather abruptly around the same time also adopted a method to observe animals at close range, habituated the target group to humans and consequently formed the basis for the development of ape tourism. The mighty and sublime wild animals, which had been symbols of nature to be conquered for big-game hunters, were transformed to vulnerable others in need of protection in the second half of the twentieth century.

What do wild animals as others existing outside of human habitation look like nowadays? Following the shift in our perception in the mid-twentieth century, their status as vulnerable beings in need of conservation is expected to be highlighted even further. On the other hand, the aspect of being scientifically unknown others that drew attention in the second half of the twentieth century seems to be losing its appeal perhaps as a result of intensive social and ecological research. Although big-game hunting was thought to have been stamped out as an outmoded activity, there has been a tendency to re-evaluate it as an important source of funds for grass-roots conservation activities, and wild animal hunting itself has been reviewed as an important tool to manage the damage they cause (Yasuda 2013). It appears that our perception of wild animals as others is constantly under review, even today. In view of the rapid changes of the last hundred years or so, the next major shift in our perception may be progressing quietly below the surface in an unexpected way, rather than in an explicit form such as the ape rights movement, for example (Cavalieri and Singer 2001).

16 Toward the Environmental Others: An Ethological Essay on Equilibrium and Coexistence

Kaoru Adachi

Key ideas

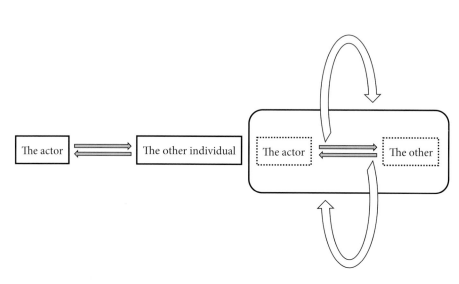

Individual animals that form social groups routinely interact with the other individuals with whom they coexist. If we focus on interaction alone, the other individual is a concrete counterpart who is actually reachable and capable of engaging in an interaction, including a potential one. On the other hand, if we focus on the routine interactions that recursively constrain interactions via the environment as the field, the other individual is not only a concrete counterpart in an interaction, but also the other that is supported by the continuous operation of group formation.

Cultivating "others" in biology

"The other" is a topic that is rarely discussed comprehensively in the field of biology. Ecology and ethology deal with "the other individual" rather than "the other" in a general, conceptual sense. No living organism can exist entirely on its own: it must interact with various elements of the environment around it to survive. Differentiation plays an important role in the process of interaction between the living organism and the environment. It is perhaps no exaggeration to say that a significant part of living is formed by differentiation, but in modern biology this is never explained through the concepts of "the other" or "otherness". For a biological actor situated at the center of a perspective, environmental factors can be grouped into organic and nonorganic, with the former containing conspecific and heterospecific "other individuals". When we consider the evolution of human sociality, the most important environmental element for the actor is the existence of conspecifics. Interaction with conspecifics has been dealt with as an intraspecific communication phenomenon in the field of ethology, and attempts to discuss the evolution of human sociality from the perspective of intraspecific communication usually focus on the question of the precondition for or timing of language acquisition. By contrast, this chapter reviews the history of the study of intraspecific communication in animals and examines the relationship between the behavioral aspect of communication and the ecological aspect of interaction between the actor and the environment. In particular, we shall focus on the effect of *differentiation* as adaptation to the environment that is found in all life forms. The goal of this discussion lies somewhere other than in the view of evolution as an additive process in which something is added to pre-human sociality to achieve human sociality. I aim to discover whether there is an aspect that can elucidate "the other" in the discipline of biology that normally does not deal with this concept outright, by exploring the innate interaction with the environment performed by all life forms.

Communication in animals

Signaling between individuals
In the earliest stage of the development of ethological theory, a phenomenon was discovered in which a species-specific pattern of behavior was caused by a certain stimulus, referred to as a "sign stimulus" (Slater 1994). Among various types of sign stimuli, one used between individual animals is called a "releaser"

and includes, for example, the zigzag dance and the head-down attack posture in three-spined stickleback identified in various model experiments carried out by Niko Tinbergen. The male stickleback is territorial and lures a gravid female into his territory using a pre-mating zigzag dance, whereas he takes a head-down, belly-up posture to repel an intruding male. This threatening action has the effect of driving other males out of his territory. It was discovered that the territorial male stickleback engages in these two completely different types of behavior because color-pattern variations in the form of the swollen silver belly of approaching females and the slim red belly of intruding males trigger the respective patterns of reaction to release the behavior. Various stimuli have been identified as releasers that trigger fighting or courtship displays in many other species. Early ethology uncovered a series of "signals" that transmitted information in communication between individual animals.

In classical ethology, before sociobiology proposed the concept of "inclusive fitness" and recognized that animals evolved their behaviors according to genetic advantage rather than for the benefit of their species, it was thought that both individuals in an interaction mediated by a releaser benefitted by sharing the signaled information and cooperating in dealing with a task. It was understood that communication involved passing information from the sender to the receiver of a signal between two face-to-face individuals, and that the two individuals in this position performed tasks such as fighting and courtship together by practicing communication. Many of the displays exchanged in fighting and courtship appear to be acts of intentionally trying to communicate something, such as calling loudly to one another or demonstrating distinct and showy color movements. In animal communication, the actor individual attempts to convey something to the other individual, while the latter tries to receive the signal by listening to the actor individual's voice and watching its actions. Early ethology described the manner in which two individuals faced one another using a signal transfer model, and supposed that these signs had evolved in order to improve the survival conditions of both parties.

Manipulation and mind-reading

In early ethology, there was a tacit assumption that the actor and the other individual engaged in communication had shared interests in working toward a common goal. It was thought that the ultimate benefit was to contribute to the preservation of their own species by surviving and reproducing by avoiding fatal injury in fighting and succeeding in courtship, mating and producing offspring.

This way of thinking was rejected during the formulation of social biological theory in the 1970s and early 1980s and replaced by the new recognition that all animal behaviors had evolved to maximize benefit for individuals or genes rather than the species as a whole.

With the diffusion of sociobiology, "manipulation and mind-reading" replaced "sign transfer for mutual interest" as an important model in animal communication theory. Krebs and Dawkins (1984) proposed a new communication/signaling model and argued that the signaler gave signals out of its own interest in communication, rather than for the good of the species. The primary function of a signal is to manipulate the other individual's behavior for the signaler's own interests. The other individual receiving the signal is expected to evolve a behavior to read the signaler's intention (mind-reading) in order to avoid being manipulated to their disadvantage. In the manipulation and mind-reading model, communication is still the transfer of information by sending and receiving signals, but the difference is that the actor and the other individual facing them do not share a common interest.

The manipulation and mind-reading model is most applicable to communication between predator and prey, such as mimicry and injury-feigning behavior. Some insects and frogs have body colors such as bright red or starkly contrasting black and yellow to warn predatory birds and mammals that they are noxious prey with poison or the ability to sting. The little ringed plover that nests on the ground behaves as if it were injured and unable to fly to lure an approaching fox or other predator away from its nest. The gazelle found in African grasslands engages in an eye-catching high-jumping display called "stotting" to deter potential predators by demonstrating its fitness. These traits have long been the subject of communication research under the concept of aposematism (warning signaling as an anti-predator strategy).

Communication and social groups

The evolution of communication has been discussed in the context of the evolution of signals transmitted between the actor and the other individual facing them. The view that the signaler manipulates the other individual is applied to communication as a social behavior in group formation. In sociobiology, the ultimate cause of social group formation is individual or genetic benefit. Accordingly, grooming and other affiliative behaviors, fighting, courtship and direct cooperation that are thought to influence the formation and continuation of a group can be discussed using the manipulation and mind-reading model to understand signaling. Communication between individuals does not assume the existence of shared values between the actor and the other individual; it is likely that the actor's manipulation and the other individual's response, that is, adaptation in the transfer of information between the two individuals according to their respective interests, have been driving the design of signals.

In primate species that form social groups, including humans, a large volume of communication takes place within each group. Each communication is constrained by institutional conventions operating within the group and has a recursive relationship with them, as it is this accumulation of communications that formulates the conventions. These institutional conventions are sometimes called "culture" in the groups of some animal species. Modeling in the evolutionary study of animal communication is done basically focusing on the relationship between the actor and the other individual, whereas communication in a social group arises between many individuals where continuous switching takes place between the manipulator and manipulated or the signaler and receiver. It is thought that the sum of dyadic communications cannot be equal to the sociality of the group as a whole, just as a bundle of specific dyadic relationships cannot fully represent the character of the social group as a whole. If we consider the totality of contiguous communications as the foundation instead of reducing a group to dyadic relationships, the other individual that faces the actor in a communication has the potential to exhibit a characteristic that cannot be explained by the dyadic signal model. When we consider the formation of a social group without reducing it to a dyadic relationship, the recursive relationship between communication and institutional conventions is thought to be an important element. In other words, the other individual facing the actor takes on the character of "the other" in the continuum of recursive communications. Next, we examine primate social groups in order to find out what kind of operation of a social group and communication enables the existence of "the other".

Who is "the other"?

Group members
Communication as interaction with the other individual emerges at various levels for gregarious primates. The most fundamental and essential counterpart in interaction for one's survival is the other individual in the same group. Understanding the composition of a social group and its factors was a major goal for early primatology. After a certain period of observation, many primatological studies have found patterns of communication as well as specific relationship

patterns between concerned individuals in a mere aggregation without apparent organization and order.

The challenge for ethology was to observe as many communication patterns as possible, and discover their contexts and social evolutionary significance. I won't go into individual examples here, but the fixed patterns of interaction between members of the same group represent the social structure of the group. Animal sociology has been discussing social evolution by comparing these patterns between different species.

Diverse modes of interaction can be observed, ranging from agonistic to affiliative, dyadic to triadic or more complex and short-term to drawn-out with intervals. Nevertheless, an accumulation of interactions to enable coexistence and to alleviate competition between individuals is observed in many species, and the evolutionary factors of group formation are being investigated. Various fixed patterns found in interactions are sometimes associated with the ecological environment or treated as cultural conventions, but they are equally social in that they recursively constrain the behaviors of members of a social group as an established order.

Adjacent groups

To the observer and perhaps many of the individuals belonging to a group, a clearly distinguishable entity with the second highest degree of social importance after members of the group is a member of the other group in an encounter. Intergroup encounters are hostile in a majority of species. In territorial monkeys, individuals belonging to two adjacent groups face one another on their territorial boundary line and exchange threatening calls or perform charging displays.

In these situations, threat calls are aimed at individuals of the adjacent group and never at those of the vocalizers' own group. The other conspecifics in the group are companions one cooperates with in defending shared resources such as territory and females, whereas the other conspecifics belonging to the adjacent group in the confrontation need to be excluded. Highlighting "the other" in a fight helps bring forth "we" and clarifies the outline of the group. The more developed the group's sociality is and the more structured their organization is, the more clearly one can see "the other". In animals with strong group unity, intergroup encounters have the potential to develop into fierce clashes that result in physical injuries.

The other individuals in adjacent groups are "strangers" and not "acquaintances" one encounters and interacts socially with on a daily basis. One has accumulated routine interactions with the other individuals in one's own group, and the outcomes of these interactions recursively define the relationship between the actor and the other individuals in the form of conventions. In chimpanzees and Japanese macaques, males repeatedly engage in agonistic interactions within their own group, and the outcomes of such interactions are reflected in relative rank relationships. The dominance relationship between specific males is recognized by the other individuals and influences action selection in various interactions that take place within the group. In contrast, the other conspecifics in adjacent groups are the counterparts one suddenly and very rarely comes face-to-face with without any accumulated routine interactions that constitute conventions. An encounter with an individual from an adjacent group happens far less frequently than one with an individual from one's own group, and lacks a sufficient interactional history to facilitate the construction of a certain relationship.

However, it is not that they have no idea what to do when they encounter. An encounter with an individual from an adjacent group proceeds in a manner that is different from referencing the conventionalized relationships between individuals, and sometimes occurs in a more stereotypical fashion than encounters with individuals from one's own group. In many species, threat calls and displays exchanged in intergroup encounters contain ritually fixed patterns.

The other conspecifics have the basic commonality that originates from their conspecificity. Conspecifics share a large proportion of their genetic make-up and have similarities including morphological features such as body size, hair color and body color as well as similar voices, visual displays, cognitive capacity and social behaviors for reproduction and fighting which allow them to communicate within the same species. Moreover, they use the same mode of locomotion such as terrestrial locomotion or arboreal locomotion, and eat mostly the same kind of food. In other words, the other individual may belong to an adjacent group instead of one's own group, but they still have the same lifestyle and social behavioral pattern and therefore are able to communicate in encounters, which in many cases results in agonistic interactions.

What separates the conspecifics of one's own group from those of an adjacent group is the difference in the level of routine interaction accumulation that determines whether a particular individual is an acquaintance or a stranger. The accumulation of routine interactions carries the function of conventions when it manifests in social behavior. Although it is impossible to confirm the abstract notion of "our" group in non-human primates with no language, I have argued previously (Adachi 2017) that groups are constantly generated through the accumulation of interactions, and that the mechanism of accumulation itself operates as a primordial institution. An unknown individual or stranger is an individual who arrives from the outside of the framework of institutional conventions that are constantly produced. This can be called a conspecific that exists outside of the accumulation of routine interactions, even though it has commonalities as an animal belonging to the same species and is potentially capable of communication. Although its capability of communicating is recognized, the conspecific in an adjacent group emerges as a being who is absent from the continual and repetitive routine communications that recursively define the communication.

Transferring individuals

Among the conspecifics that exist outside of the limits of routine interactions, the solitary individual of the transferring sex exhibits a different response from those of other members of an adjacent group. When Itani (1987) classified primate societies according to their phylogeny and constructed a theory for their evolution, he based it on their social structure. Social structure is characterized by the number and sex ratio of adult individuals in a group, as well as the sex of the individuals who transfer out of the group upon sexual maturity.

In Japanese macaques, for instance, male individuals leave their natal group when they reach a certain age. On the other hand, females remain and live in their natal group all their lives, and thus Japanese macaques have a matrilineal social structure. The males who have transferred out of the natal group are called "non-troop males" or "solitary males", and are distinguished from other males within the group. Non-troop males are sometimes divided between troop-following males and non-following males depending on their positioning relative to the troop, and they engage in a diverse range of behaviors from a single male ranging alone to multiple non-troop males gathering and acting together. However, one common feature is that they exhibit patterns of interaction that differ from the social interactions carried out between individuals within the troop (Kawazoe 2016). Non-troop-following males associate with troop-males quite frequently, but they unilaterally groom troop-males during the non-mating season while they tend to be attacked by them during the mating season. Troop-females have a tendency to prefer to mate with "stranger males", and non-troop males achieve successful breeding while dodging the attacks of troop-males.

To the individuals within the group, the transferring conspecifics become stranger conspecifics that exist outside of the group. Just as the conspecifics of adjacent groups, the transferred conspecifics do not participate in the accumulation of interactions within the group, at least to the same extent as the individuals within the group do.

Mixed-species association: Heterospecifics

In the case of conspecifics, there is a recognizable difference in the way they exist inside and outside of the group. What about heterospecific animals? Although it is rare for heterospecifics to engage in social relations in the usual sense, they have been found to interact at various levels when they live sympatrically and use the same environment. In biology, interactions between heterospecifics are divided according to benefit sharing into categories such as mutualism, commensalism, competition and predator-prey. As we are discussing the relationships between different primate species focusing on the group formation action here, we will consider interspecific interactions on the basis of phylogenetic proximity within the order Primates rather than according to the functional benefit-based classification.

In the case of sympatric closely-related heterospecifics, they often use the same resources such as food and habitat and exhibit similar social behaviors such as vocalization and display. In ecology, a group of sympatric heterospecifics using the same resources is called a "guild", and its functional position is examined on the basis of its ecosystem as a whole. In a more extreme case of mixed-species association, some heterospecific primates in the African and South American tropics have been observed to form a group where the two species coexist peacefully over a long period, as if it were a conspecific group. The heterospecifics in a mixed-species association become the important counterparts in interactions that support an accumulation of ordinary social behaviors for the formation of the association, and do not become "stranger-individuals" just because they are heterospecific. Like a conspecific group, a mixed-species association exists through the recursive operation of the accumulation of interactions between individuals within the group as a conventional institution regulating the behaviors of its members (Adachi 2017). Because the group members are heterospecific, the type of interaction is different from that between conspecifics. The frequency of the interactions that are universally conspicuous in conspecific groups such as grooming and intimidation displays is very low. These conspicuous interactions appear to the observer as two individuals face-to-face, directing their attention in the same direction and tackling a common task to be resolved. As I discuss below, however, heterospecifics in a mixed-species association that feeds and ranges together do exhibit behaviors that can be regarded as social relations in a broad sense, including interactions in feeding mediated by the use of the environment, and the relationship between

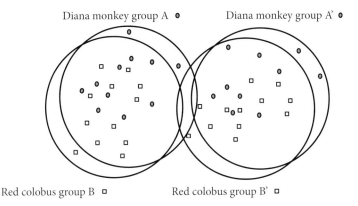

Figure 16.1 A mixed-species association of Diana monkeys and red colobuses and the distribution of conspecific groups in the Taï National Park

the inside and the outside of the framework of accumulation is no different from that in the case of conspecifics. In other words, in a mixed-species association, rather than being accumulated via face-to-face interactions, interactions between constituent individuals are accumulated in the sense that the actor's behavior influences the other individuals via the environment because both the actor and the other individuals use the same environmental resources. Consequently, the other individuals outside of the interactions in a mixed-species association are the conspecifics and heterospecifics in adjacent mixed-species associations outside of the group, and not the heterospecifics within the group.

In the cercopithecine mixed-species associations observed at the Taï National Park in Côte D'Ivoire, heterospecifics from seven different species often form mixed-species groups. Looking at Diana monkeys and red colobuses among them, we can identify a group of Diana monkeys (Group A) as the target group and one of red colobuses (Group B) as its partner group. There is an adjacent group of Diana monkeys (Group A') next to Group A, and an adjacent group of red colobuses that routinely forms a mixed-species association with Group A' (Group B') (Figure 16.1). For the individual Diana monkeys in Group A, their counterparts in daily interactions include the conspecific Diana monkeys in Group A and the heterospecific red colobuses in Group B. On the other hand, the conspecifics in Group A' and the heterospecifics in Group B' are outside of the accumulation of routine social interactions. In the case of mixed-species associations, the distinction between conspecific and heterospecific is not a significant point of difference in terms of the accumulation of routine interactions. Heterospecifics participate in the accumulation of routine interactions in almost the same capacity as conspecifics, while conspecifics can be placed outside of the accumulation of routine interactions as much as heterospecifics.

The routine interactions that support the formation of mixed-species associations include all of the behaviors individuals engage in to coordinate each other's behavior mediated by the environment such as feeding activities and ranging, and not the so-called social behaviors such as grooming and fighting (Adachi 2017). In the mixed-species associations of cercopithecines, whose uses of food resources overlap greatly, interaction with heterospecifics is a necessary part of their daily life in their use of the environment for feeding and ranging, just as in the case of conspecific groups. If an individual's interaction with organic environmental elements (including conspecific and heterospecific others) and the inorganic environment is understood using the concept of "life form" and the "field" of living that enables it, all of the behaviors at the closest level to biological activities such as feeding and ranging become social interactions (Adachi 2013).

Predator-prey

Phylogenetically remote primate groups sometimes use the same environment, while in some cases heterospecifics that are not closely related come to use similar resources through adaptation to the same environment (e.g., duikers or birds and cercopithecines feed on the same fruits in tropical forests). In these cases, it is conceivable that social relationships similar to the aforementioned guild of closely-related species and mixed-species associations are formed leading to the emergence of a field of routine interactions between phylogenetically remote heterospecifics. On the other hand, an extreme case of sympatric animals using different resources is the predator-prey relationship, where one species constitutes a resource to be used by the other species and the field of heterospecific interaction becomes a life-and-death situation. Although it is an everyday situation, what it means is completely different from what an interaction means to conspecifics or heterospecifics with similar lifestyles.

In the case of the aforementioned mixed-species associations at the Taï National Park, sympatric chimpanzees are frightening predators for the constituent cercopithecines, especially Diana monkeys and red colobuses (Bshary and Noë 1997). When cercopithecines in a mixed-species association hear sounds or vocalizations made by chimpanzees, they emit warning calls and raise a clamor in an attempt to deter the chimpanzees from preying on them. The constituent individuals let the predators know that "We are aware of your presence and ready to flee quickly", signaling that the success rate for their hunt will be low. On these occasions, the chimpanzee individuals become the counterpart to be detected and avoided by the cercopithecine individuals.

Here, their communication with chimpanzees as heterospecifics becomes ambiguous. The predator-prey relationship between the cercopithecines in a mixed-species association and the chimpanzees is fashioned through an accumulation of heterospecific interactions. The recurrence of the behavior to emit warning calls upon encountering a chimpanzee group is accumulated conventionally, and this recursively defines the behaviors of the individuals of both cercopithecine and chimpanzee species on the field of their next encounter. The chimpanzees as the predator can be regarded as being situated inside the accumulation of social interactions, but the question is whether this interaction can be seen as a "routine" social interaction.

How routine is an attack by chimpanzees in terms of the formation of a mixed-species association? Where repetitions of recursive interactions operate as conventions and constitute a primordial institution, the feeding activity of closely-related heterospecifics in a mixed-species association is considered to be an important element of their interaction (Adachi 2017). In view of their lifestyle that involves spending the majority of time on feeding and feeding-related ranging, interactions between heterospecifics in feeding behavior can be considered to be sufficiently frequent and recursive to qualify as "routine". On the other hand, attacks by predators occur very infrequently. Encounters with raptors, which are more common predators for cercopithecines, do not happen daily, and encounters with chimpanzees are even less frequent. In the case of my study at the Taï National Park, I witnessed only one occasion of actual contact between chimpanzees and a mixed-species association over an observation period of eighteen months[1].

This question points to the importance of what is "routine" in the timescale of the target individual. In the observer's human timescale, I would like to call the feeding behavior that is repeated daily over many hours "routine", whereas being preyed upon once per year is "non-routine". However, when the significance of a life-or-death predation event is taken into account, it is possible that once per year is not an ignorable frequency to be referred to as non-routine. When we focus on the other individual outside of an accumulation of routine interactions, relevant factors include the timescale of recursive interactions and the rarity of the emergence of the outside, in addition to social structure. I shall discuss this "infrequent event" in the next section.

The place of "the other"

Regarding the modality in which interactions are repeated routinely and the outcomes of the repetitions recursively determine the manners of routine interactions, its functioning as a convention or a primordial institution can also be found in non-human primates (Nishie 2017; Itoh 2017; Hanamura 2017). On the other hand, in human society it is possible to see a modality in which "here, now" sociality realized in day-to-day social interactions forms the foundation of group organization, rather than the conceptualized, higher-order institutional units such as state and nation (Sugiyama 2017). Various individuals become involved in these recursive repetitions, sometimes directly and sometimes latently. The other individual who comes face-to-face with the actor in the process of communication perhaps emerges at the field of group formation as "the other" associated with repeated and recursive interactions, rather than as a mere individual.

Anti-structured social groups

Junichirō Itani (1987) placed the social structure of each species at the foundation of his theory of evolution of primate sociality and called it the Basic Social Unit (BSU). He demonstrated that BSUs could be classified according to the modes of coexistence between adult individuals in the group, including pairs, one-male-multi-female and multi-male-multi-female, and that group composition has a strong correlation with primate sociality. Interactions within the group are repeated in accordance with certain rules, and in turn the repetitions define the coexistence of group members and the group's social structure. In contrast to this view of social structure, Itani also uses the concept of "anti-structure" to explain coexistence in a group that is realized according to a different principle.

The mixed-species association of cercopithecines fits Itani's theory of anti-structure very well (Adachi 2013). In these associations, conspicuous interactions such as grooming and fighting do not take place as frequently as in a conspecific group. Mixed-species associations found at the Taï National Park in Côte D'Ivoire are characterized by a lack of fixed rules governing interactions or a rigid structure, a sustained state of loose association involving different species of animals and a continuously fluctuating association outline through the fission and fusion of groups of different species. A mixed-species association is an assemblage of groups of heterospecifics that is loose and sustained, even though it has no clear internal structure and operates according to a principle that is different from the sociality of conspecific groups supported by rules and structure.

Photo 16.1 A mixed-species association in the Taï National Park
Among the monkeys that form mixed-species associations in the Taï National Park, three particularly closely related cercopithecine species feed on fruit as their stable food. In actual fruit feeding situations, they mutually avoid feeding at the same time in a small treetop space and spread out as if waiting for their turn. The individuals who are far away from the fruit feed on other food within reach such as insects and tree sap while waiting.

I have sought the reason for the viability of mixed-species associations as a group in the function of a chain of feeding behaviors as communication. Communication at the field of feeding leads to feeding niche separation. I have described this process as "living a role", and discussed the social connection between those who use the same environment (Adachi 2017). Cercopithecines who coexist as one group in the same environment simultaneously feed on the same food and on their own menu according to the degree of difference between the species. For example, three species of cercopithecines in one mixed-species association have distinct niches that partially overlap: Diana monkeys eat fruit all the time, Campbell's guenons eat fruit and insects and lesser spot-nosed guenons eat fruit and leaves. The niche regarding "what to eat" is the unique characteristic of each species as the result of their daily feeding behavior, and at the same time functions as a factor that influences interspecific social behaviors in the presence of food in overlapping use at the scene of daily feeding behavior.

In other words, feeding niches in mixed-species associations can trigger social conventions and engender a primordial institution in the sense that "interactions are routinely repeated and the results of the repetitions recursively determine the manners of routine interactions". For cercopithecines that form mixed-species associations, their respective niches (such as frugivorism and insectivorism) work as the role each species assumes in the group, and the viability of such an association as a group is supported by the act of repeating interactions with the other conspecifics and heterospecifics while repeating their feeding behaviors as a form of social communication.

The environment as a "field"

Using the same environment and sharing a "field" of living are important in forming a foundation for feeding behavior to work as communication (Adachi 2017). Communication revolving around feeding means that the individuals who potentially overlap in their uses of common resources mutually adjust their feeding behaviors through living together in the same environment. The "field" of feeding niche separation, or where the repetition of routine interactions takes place recursively, can be regarded as the environment itself that is inseparable from the activities of living organisms that use common resources sympatrically. For the cercopithecines inhabiting the tropical rainforest of the Taï National Park, fruit is the staple food that is an important element of their environment and a "field" that enables communication through feeding, which is the "routine interaction" for cercopithecines in mixed-species associations. In this setting, their action selection itself is a constituent element of the environment, and a feeding individual is simultaneously an actor who uses the environment and an inseparably interconnected part of it.

When we think of a given environment, we recall various ecological factors that influence the survival of living individuals, such as food distribution and quantity, the population or quantity of competitors and predation pressure, but it is important to note that the individuals living in that environment are not given all the information that constitutes the environment. From a microscopic perspective, all sorts of changes are happening over time in the ecological interactions of sympatric conspecifics and heterospecifics in the environment or in inorganic environmental elements, and hence the environment is in a state of constant and continuous flux. Nevertheless, individuals can make it through well "on the whole" in today's environment that is slightly different from that of yesterday by living the role befitting their niche. It is unlikely that cercopithecines in a mixed-species association store the entire accumulation of interactions between conspecifics and heterospecifics – such as past feeding behaviors and fights and mutual concessions on top of feeding trees – in a database somewhere in their brains. For the seasonally fluctuating distribution and quantity of fruit in their habitat, it is more likely that they rely on limited information based on their recent experience and chance such as memories about places they have used for feeding in the near past or food sources they have chanced upon on their ranging route, rather than having a macroscopic perspective on information in space-time[2]. Even though they rely on chance factors or limited history, the individuals are able to survive without making serious mistakes as long as the repetition of interactions continues.

By living in their respective roles according to feeding niches in their routine feeding behaviors, cercopithecines in mixed-species associations coexist and form and dissolve communities. The condition of being absent can be regarded as one of the manifestations of feeding-related communication. The diversity of feeding-related communication largely falls within certain predictable patterns and is observed as species-specific food preferences according to feeding niche separation or behaviors to avoid feeding competition. In their daily lives, cercopithecines in mixed-species associations practice communication revolving around feeding behaviors by following the respective roles prescribed by their feeding niches. On very rare occasions, a behavior that is not predicted by niche theory is selected and observed as a "rare event", but it is understood as a rare pattern that deviates from a role with an "on the whole" compelling force rather than a communication failure.

An order that defines the limit of the communication chain always contains events that will happen beyond that boundary. The inclusive mechanism as an order for achieving niche separation and cooperative coexistence is the foundation supporting its role as an institutional convention. However, the individuals constituting the group can never get a full picture of this mechanism. The "field" of communication mediated by the niche environment constitutes the limit, which the intentions of the individuals living there cannot quite reach. It seems that the other individual acquires the attribute of "the other" only because of this order that exists to circumscribe the totality, including deviations. Here, "the other" tends to emerge at the limit of the communication chain in the environmental "field", and hence can be called "the environmental other".

The ecological theory of non-equilibrium

"Niche" is a concept that evolved in the field of community ecology (Chase and Leibold 2003). One of the ultimate goals of this field is to discover the composition, population and dynamics of the species that inhabit a certain environment in certain spatial and temporal scales. Niche theory proposes that different species with similar niches living in an environment with insufficient resources are potential competitors due to their overlapping resource needs, but they coexist by coordinating their resource uses by mutually making small compromises to their needs. This method of predicting the ecological community structure as an aggregate of niches based on niche separation is called "ecological equilibrium theory", and has been the mainstream of community ecology. There is a contrasting theory called "non-equilibrium theory", which proposes that the ecological community structure is defined by other factors that disturb the environment rather than factors such as interspecific competition and niche separation. Non-equilibrium theory posits that the steady state of the environment assumed by equilibrium theory is rarely reached because natural disasters such as large-scale volcanic eruptions, floods and forest fires, as well as fluctuating predator populations and so on alter the environment at certain intervals, and therefore the state of equilibrium that allows the avoidance of potential interspecific competition cannot be reached.

Stephen Hubbell's unified neutral theory of biodiversity and biogeography (Hubbell 2009) has been conceived under the umbrella of non-equilibrium theories. It hypothesizes that there is neutrality at the individual level in a biological community at a given trophic level, and that a random and neutral process called "ecological drift" structures the community. The theory attempts to predict the logical outcome of this hypothesis and to test its suitability in relation to actual communities. The neutrality hypothesis means that all individuals in all species of a community are equal and ecologically equivalent, and offers an explanation that differs from community structurization by niche separation. The unified neutrality theory is valued for its ability to construct a model for interspecific coexistence at the community level by hypothesizing the neutrality of individuals, instead of the conventional hypothesis of niche separation assuming competition. The theory suggests that community structure is better explained in some cases by non-competitive events on the scale of what Hubbell calls the "metacommunity" traversing local communities, and that there is no ecological competition between different species based on heterogeneity at the local level.

In non-equilibrium ecological theory, it is thought that localized interspecific competition defines the community structure functionally, whereas competition does not occur at the metacommunity level. Coexistence within a community is defined by various events that happen rarely and accidentally, including disturbance factors such as volcanic eruptions, floods and human activities, and fluctuations in predator populations. While niches are constituted by the accumulation of routine and local interactions, non-equilibrium theory is founded on "infrequent" large-scale natural events. Major disasters that happen outside of the principle of regularity cause the extinction of species and increase biodiversity through speciation of the surviving species. The large-scale disturbances to ecosystems that take place far removed from the regularity of living the role prescribed by one's niche become another manifestation of the extreme beyond the chain of routine interactions where we can again find "the environmental other".

Natural harmony

For the group-forming primates, the individuals that constitute a group and coexist in it are the counterparts involved in the accumulation of routine interactions. As we have seen above, the other with individuality is a non-participant being situated outside of the frame of repeated routine interactions, but at the same time this being has the potential to become a participant if the situation changes. The other contains two opposing vectors – one in the direction of an unknown and remote existence and the other in the direction of a proximate being sharing the same characteristics. For this reason, the other's otherness is a relative measure depending on which of the two vectors is given more focus and weight.

In human society, one's own group is called "we" and distinguished from other groups, while its group structure is understood conceptually. The "we" forms categories such as "tribe" and "state" that function as frameworks to spatially and historically control human lives. It is the evolutionary peculiarity of human society that people live while simultaneously referring to the conceptualized framework of their own group as well as sociality in the sense of somehow making it through "here, now".

When we consider primate communities such as mixed-species associations, we find that the inclusive order for the smooth operation of the group's social system is unknown to the individuals belonging to the group, and their individual behaviors are not adapted to follow the inclusive order. The individuals of the species in mixed-species associations follow the ad hoc roles of their niches and achieve success "on the whole". This reminds us of the distinction between "strategies" and "tactics" made by de Certeau (1987). When organisms live day-to-day by cobbling together pieces of information to use as tactics without knowing what the strategy is, "the other" points to the existence of the strategy, which is a set of inclusive rules for the smooth running of the system. Nevertheless, the individuals never refer to the strategy itself. Needless to say, the individual constituents of a social group guarantee the operation of its social system that is kept in harmony as long as they live. This kind of place is the only place where "the other" can function, but it is perhaps safe to say that non-human primates almost never consciously focus on "the other" or "strategies" in their daily living.

Does "the other" ever show signs of its presence to the monkeys in mixed-species associations? The individuals in these associations cannot see the full picture of major disasters such as volcanic eruptions and earthquakes or their metacommunity. However, there are very few occasions when "the other" as an ungraspable inclusive strategy shows its face through an open seam in everyday life, in many cases in the form of a deviation from or a failure of a routine interaction.

One example is when Diana monkeys and olive colobuses, which are the core members of the association and do things together all the time, accidentally dissolve a mixed-species association. I have observed a situation in which a group of olive colobuses in a mixed-species association with Diana monkeys fell into deep sleep during a rest, failed to notice that the Diana monkeys had finished resting and begun to move and were consequently left behind. I am not sure if this occurred because the olive colobuses happened to choose a tree to rest in that was a little distance away from the main Diana monkey group, or because the olive colobuses were particularly tired on that hot day. Faced with the rare event of the dissolution of their mixed-species association, the olive colobus individuals, who seldom vocalized, emitted calls announcing a state of extraordinary emergency. It is thought that the olive colobuses were successfully carrying out repetitive interactions with Diana monkeys on a daily basis, and did not need to refer constantly to the "field" that supported their interactions while they were successful. They were perhaps compelled by the need to return to the stage of assembling the "field" for the first time when they were confronted by the improbable emergency situation of the dissolution of their mixed-species association. This situation emerged as an open seam in their interaction continuum in the form of vocal communication, which I had never heard before, and "the other" supported by an inclusive order covering the entire society showed a small sign of its existence.

The possibility of "the ecological other"

All life forms, including humans, mutually interact with the environment, repeatedly engage in recursive interactions with other individuals mediated by the environment as a field and sometimes exercise their sociality involving coexistence in a group and at other times exist as solitary actors. The inclusive mechanism, which triggers recursive interactions or contains the infinitely repeated interaction as a whole, becomes the absolute externality for the recursively repeated interactions. As an action that causes not only the exterior of the interactions but also the interactions themselves, this action that takes effect in a different phase from the field of interactions seems to be the very factor that transforms the other individual from a mere "other" to "the other". The recursive interactions continue to take place as long as life forms survive, and the entirety of the mechanism constitutes its unreachable limits. In this sense, we can state that "the other" exists on the boundary zone between the finite interactions being repeated daily and the unreachable, infinite whole.

I shall tentatively call the other that is perceived through the use of the environment as a field "the ecological other" or "the environmental other". If we can understand "the other" on the basis of its use of the environment, which is a universally common characteristic of all life forms, "the other" is no longer a uniquely human concept. Historically, many philosophers have grappled with this concept because they have considered the other as an important problem that must be understood if we are to understand human society. It is perhaps no exaggeration to say that humanity, or its characteristic sociality, can be understood as the issue of intentionality toward the other. In attempting to understand human society in terms of its evolutionary foundation, however, I wonder if it is really appropriate to see the other as an additional element acquired only by humans in the process of evolution and thus not found in non-human animals.

The vantage point from which to see the other in human society varies greatly depending on where the other is situated in the gradation of its level of abstraction. In many cases, the most abstract other is mentioned together with the adjective "absolute". It is possible to say that "the absolute other" is a being from a different dimension that is completely unrelated to our everyday social relationships and unapproachable and untouchable by humans; in short, it is a being that can be described as a "god". The belief, albeit vague, that the other refers to a "god" is somewhat ingrained in the subjective appreciation I have as someone not so deeply committed to philosophy or theology. On the other hand, the other as dealt with in phenomenology or psychology is one who is capable of interaction precisely because they are found to share common elements with the self through the process of pre-defining the extent of the self and extracting the other parts from the remainder of the whole (Taguchi 2014). The other as an individual entity that can be touched with an extended hand exists in the world surrounding the self, the owner of the extended hand. The other as an individual entity is a being that has both "sameness" and "difference", unlike the abstract "absolute" other with no individuality. In human society, people have been forming relationships with others with various kinds of "sameness" and "difference" within groups, and at the same time using "the absolute other" as the source of group formation.

Humans have attained evolutionary specificity in that they attach names to others and try to see that which is incognizable. Life forms are able to survive by dealing with the surrounding environment "on the whole" well day by day, without being conscious of the limits of the finite. If "on the whole" (in the sense that things usually go well aside from occasional failures) is a universal trait of life forms, humans may be a formidable species that has cast aside the "on the whole" way of life and embarked on a path toward the theoretically unreachable boundary between the finite and the infinite.

17 Society as a "Story": Work Sharing, Cooperative Breeding and the Evolution of Otherness

Yūji Takenoshita

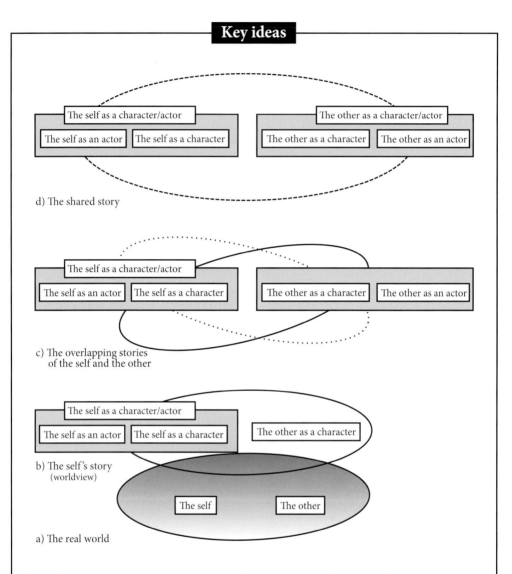

d) The shared story

c) The overlapping stories of the self and the other

b) The self's story (worldview)

a) The real world

The other exists as "a being whose subjectivity is perceived by the self" in the real world (a). Great apes construct a story of the self based on the real world and simultaneously play "the self as a character" as the actor-director ("the self as an actor") and assign roles (casting characters) to others. The other for great apes is understood as "the other as a character" cast in the story of "the self as an actor" (b). Humans discover that "the other as a character" is cast in the story constructed by "the other as an actor" rather than by "the self as an actor" (c). When there are stories of the self and the others layered upon real world events, humans reconcile them and construct one shared saga. The other in humans is "the other as a character/actor" with whom the self shares, directs and performs a story (d).

Defining "others"

As Kawai explains in the Introduction, the authors of this book do not share a strict definition of "other(s)". For this reason, I begin by stating what I refer to as "the other" and what I am trying to discuss in relation to "the other" in this chapter.

In everyday life, we do not perceive other people as akin to mere objects or programmed machines like robots. We see other people as beings with their own purposes and intentions who make autonomous decisions about how to act rather than responding to input from the environment in fixed ways. What I call "the other" in this chapter is "an object in which the self perceives subjectivity".

For humans (or rather, for me), subjectivity is most easily perceived in other individuals belonging to the same species. However, others are not necessarily limited to conspecifics; other organisms can also be others. People who have cats and dogs as pets interact with them as beings with certain levels of subjectivity, although they are not exactly the same as them. Of course, this is not limited to mammals: for some people, birds, lizards, fish, insects and even cactus and other plants can be others. Generally speaking, however, the more phylogenetically remote the species is from humans, or the less involvement or importance it has in our lives, the weaker the level of subjectivity we can perceive in a being in the world around us. The other's subjectivity strongly depends on its similarity to and affinity with the self. Therefore, we discuss the other here from the perspective of "the other who is qualitatively the same as the self" according to Kawai's typology outlined in the Introduction.

Humans are not the only animals that find subjectivity in other beings in the environment. Primates that are closely related to humans, especially great apes such as gorillas and chimpanzees, also treat their conspecifics and humans as beings with their own intentions and purposes, that is, subjectivity[1]. Numerous empirical studies have confirmed this and hence no further explanation is required here.

Accordingly, "the other" in this chapter is found in both humans and non-human primates, and unlike institutions, is not something that emerged somewhere in the evolutionary process of human sociality. Hence, the purpose of this chapter is not to search for the origins of the other. Rather, my aim here is to compare the nature of the other in humans and non-humans, especially great apes that are our closest relatives, and to identify the difference between what the other is for humans and what it is for great apes. Finally, I briefly touch on the transformation process of the other in the evolution of human sociality.

I shall add one more point about my approach here. Some of the chapters in this book discuss the connection between the self and the other, while the rest discuss an understanding of the other. This chapter adopts the latter approach, and discusses what I (the self) understand the other to be.

Theory of mind and the false-belief task

To "perceive subjectivity" means supposing that there is an immanent intention, purpose, emotion or belief behind the behavior of a being. This kind of mental process is called "theory of mind". If we apply this to the aforementioned definition of "the other", the other is a being onto which the self projects theory of mind.

Numerous experiments have been conducted to test if human infants and chimpanzees have theory of mind since Premack and Woodruff (1978) raised the issue. They found that theory of mind develops in humans from around the age of four. In chimpanzees, against the expectations of Premack and Woodruff, positive results have not come easily. Nevertheless, the current understanding is that chimpanzees also have theory of mind, although it is slightly different from that in humans. After reviewing the studies on theory of mind published in the past thirty years, Call and Tomasello (2008) concluded that chimpanzees have theory of mind that differs from that in humans in some aspects. In particular, chimpanzees, unlike humans, do not understand the other's "false belief."

Can chimpanzees understand a false belief?

A "false belief" is an understanding of a phenomenon held by an individual that diverges from fact, due to a lack of information or misrecognition. If an individual understands that another person has a false belief, it constitutes strong evidence that the individual has theory of mind.

Among various tests used for the false-belief task, the most well known is the Sally-Anne test for human infants as outlined below.
1. The following scenes are presented to the test subject by way of a picture-story show, a skit or a video.
    a. There are two children (Sally and Anne) in a room.
    b. Sally puts candy in a basket and leaves the room.
    c. While Sally is out of the room, Anne takes the candy out of the basket and puts it in a box.
    d. Sally comes back to the room.

2. The tester asks the test subject about Sally's belief saying, "Where will Sally look for the candy?" or "Where does Sally think the candy is?".

As the test subject has seen Anne hiding the candy in another place, the test subject knows that the candy is in the box at the time of questioning. However, Sally did not see this happen, and therefore would have the false belief that the candy is still in the basket. Therefore, the correct answer is "the basket". As humans tend to pass the test at around the age of four to seven, it is supposed that theory of mind emerges in humans during this period.

Various tests have been carried out on chimpanzees using non-verbal means. Yet, to date none have produced the conclusive result that chimpanzees can pass the false-belief task.

False-belief task and tactical deception

Despite the above, in light of their behaviors in the wild and in other experimental results, it is doubtful that great apes cannot understand the other's false belief. One of the counterarguments is the fact that chimpanzees engage in tactical deception.

Unlike mimicry in insects and injury-feigning behavior in birds that are genetically programmed, tactical deception involves intentionally performing a misleading act (Byrne and Whiten 2004). For instance, a male chimpanzee shows his erect penis to a desirable female in an attempt to entice her to mate, but he quickly hides his penis with his hands as soon as a dominant male appears nearby. In the case of chimpanzees in captivity, if an individual is the only one who knows where food is, they engage in deceptive acts such as deliberately going the long way around to prevent other individuals from finding out where it is.

It is obvious that this type of "tactical deception" is behavior to manipulate the other's belief and induce the other to have a false belief that is advantageous to the self. The act of hiding one's penis shows a dominant male that "I don't have an erection", while the act of circumventing the whereabouts of food demonstrates that "I don't know where food is". There would be no point in taking these actions if they did not understand the other's false belief.

A similar phenomenon has been confirmed in human infants. There is no shortage of cases in the fields of child-rearing, childcare and preschool education in which infants under the age of three years with supposedly undeveloped theory of mind exhibit deceptive behavior. Uriu (2007) empirically confirmed this through the so-called "hero-and-villain test" as follows.

1. The test subject (infant) is presented with a scene in which a hero, who is the protagonist in a popular children's anime series in Japan, gets in trouble after

a body part that is the source of his power is damaged. All test subjects know that the hero can regain his power by getting a new part.
2. The caregiver provides two boxes and a new part made of paper and tells the test subject to choose one box and hide the new part in it.
3. The caregiver verbally encourages the test subject to help the hero by protecting the part from a villain.
4. The villain appears on the screen and demands the test subject tell where the part is.

The correct answer is to point at the empty box as a rational means to protect the hero's body part. The correct answer rate for older infants (aged four to five), who would be able to pass the false-belief task, was of course 100 percent. However, around thirty percent of younger infants (aged two to three), who would not be expected to understand the false-belief task, also answered correctly. Some children even refused to answer to the villain's question by saying "I don't know" or "No". Although this does not constitute an act of deception and thus is not regarded as the correct answer in the experiment setting, it was an attempt to limit the villain's knowledge. Therefore, it can be said that those who refused to answer tried to manipulate the other's belief.

What does the false-belief task confirm?

The false-belief task is an excellent test method for theory of mind, in that it confirms the existence of theory of mind in subjects who pass the test. However, failing the test does not necessarily mean that the subject cannot understand the other's false belief.

Kimura (2015) illustrated two situations in which the test subject with theory of mind might fail the Sally-Anne test. In one situation the test subject thinks that Sally and Anne are psychics for some reason. In another situation, the test subject is prone to fantasy and believes that humans have an ability to see things remotely. In either situation, it is natural for the test subject to think that Sally is capable of knowing where the candy is without actually seeing Anne move the candy, and hence the correct answer for the subject is "the box".

Through this thought experiment, Kimura pointed out that for humans and other animals to pass the false-belief task, only having theory of mind is not enough. The test subject must have "proper" theory of mind, and the tester determines what is "proper". He called the tester's arbitrary decision an "order of theory of mind". The test subject cannot pass the false-belief task by merely having the ability to guess the other's belief; they must also understand the order of theory of mind held by the experimenter, or in other words, "the commonsense view of the world".

From here, Kimura's argument develops to criticize the anthropocentrism that inadvertently creeps into animal studies. Rather than focusing on this issue, however, I instead examine the false-belief task from a different angle.

The problem of the "order of theory of mind" identified by Kimura is also applicable to both the Sally-Anne test and the hero-villain test[2]. Then, what is the difference between the two tests? Why did children under four years old pass the hero-villain test while they failed the Sally-Anne test?

In my view, the most important difference between the two tests relates to the following two points: whether the test subject knows the characters in and the context of the situation presented, and whether the test subject commits themself to the situation. In the hero-villain test, the children are very familiar with the hero character and understand the relationship between the hero and the villain. They can imagine what will happen if the villain finds out where the hero's replacement part is hidden, they intend to help the hero and their response will influence how the situation will develop.

In other words, what is presented in the hero-villain test is social interaction carried out by a character known to the test subject in a socially meaningful context. Moreover, the situation is presented in a setting where the test subject can commit to and influence the consequences of the interaction.

In contrast, the test subject knows nothing about Sally and Anne or their social relationship, and has no connection to them in the test. The subject does not know what Anne's intention was when she moved the candy to another place. This setup offers almost no "social clue" to help the test subject guess Sally's intention. Moreover, the test subject is a mere bystander and is not allowed to commit to the situation.

When we try to read the other's mind in certain situations in our everyday life, we usually make full use of social clues such as information about the other, the overall context, the known social relationships of the other and their facial expressions and gestures. The Sally-Anne test demands that the test subject guesses the other's mind in a setting totally devoid of these social clues. While this has been done to exclude the possibility that the test subject is simply mechanistically predicting the other individual's behavior based only on visible clues, the test has become an unrealistic and difficult task as a result. In addition, the test subject's answer has no impact on the situation, and hence answering correctly has no meaning to the test subject. This may lead the test subject to be less serious in their answer.

The fact that infants aged three or younger and chimpanzees who have the ability to manipulate the other's belief cannot pass the false-belief task indicates that they invoke their ability to guess the other individual's mind only when they find it meaningful to doing so, and are provided a realistic social relationship and context and an opportunity to commit themselves to that context. In the context of "a dominant male appears when the self is trying to entice a female to mate", for instance, the self can (does) guess the dominant male's mind as follows: "If he sees my penis, he will know that I have been trying to mate with this female and then he will want to attack me". In an experimental setting, however, chimpanzees cannot (or do not) guess the other's mind because there is no social clue at all.

When there is no social clue, one must guess the meaning of the scene (context) before guessing the mind of others on the scene. The individual may recall a specific scene that is similar to the current one from their experience or may refer a generalized understanding of context for the current type of scene. In either case, one must concoct and supplement a context from scratch.

This means that the false-belief task confirms not only if the test subject can guess the other's mind from an existing context, but also if they can construct a context that cannot be read from a provided scene. The ability to construct a context can be paraphrased as an ability to "story-tell" because it resembles fabricating a "scenario" out of a given "scene". Uchida (1990) has shown that human infants begin to create all sorts of stories once they reach the age of four or five: they can create stories in response to a number of scene images by coming up with a time sequence and filling in gaps in the story's development, and the created stories have some degree of similarity[3]. The fact that this story-telling milestone coincides with the age at which they pass the false-belief task supports the argument that what is confirmed by the false-belief task is a "story-telling ability".

Two gaps separating humans from animals

Humans who act out stories
Constructing scenarios recursively
Suddendorf (2014) argues that there is "a tremendous gap between human and animal minds", humans are very different in every aspect from other animals, including great apes, and that this difference has been caused by just two mental abilities that are peculiar to humans – our "capacity for nested scenario building" i.e. the "open-ended ability to imagine and reflect on different situations" and the

"urge to connect our mind (with that of others)". The former allows humans to imagine future or geographically remote situations based on what they experience "here, now", to classify and organize separate experiences according to similarity and to link experiences based on causality. This ability also enables humans to perform mental "rehearsals" prior to taking action, and to immerse themselves in memories by mentally recreating past experiences. Furthermore, humans can imagine what will happen in future, or what would have happened in future if they had behaved differently in the past.

Suddendorf uses the analogy of a theater production to explain these mental processes. The world and the others are compared to a stage and the actors, respectively. The self concurrently is regarded as an actor, director, scriptwriter and executive producer and sets up the stage, writes the scenario, casts the actors and assigns and plays a role. It is not that they create the scenario and characters from scratch. The scenario is formulated as one interpretation of the world one lives in, or a worldview that results from an accumulation of specific social interactions one more or less constantly has with other individuals while living in the real world. The "scenario" here is closer to a "saga" that exists behind phenomena in the course of the accumulation of specific phenomena, as proposed by Ōtsuka (2012), rather than a formal play script. Once a saga is formulated, it is possible to construct a specific context for each scene that fits in the framework of the saga, even when there is no clue to help one guess the context of a scene or the minds of the characters appearing in it.

What Suddendorf calls the "capacity for nested scenario building" is largely synonymous with the story-telling ability mentioned above. By the age of four or five, humans construct a saga about the world they live in based on their past experiences and through the expression of their genetic potential. Then, they begin to understand and live in the world in a way that fits the saga. In other words, humans are acting out stories that are created from the world rather than living in the world itself.

Connecting the minds of the self and others: The duality within self and other
When a human construct a story from the world and tries to direct it, a duality arises within the self between the self as actor/director ("the self as an actor") and the self as a character played in the story ("the self as a character"). Here, the self is both actor and character ("the self as a character/actor"). On the other hand, others only exist as characters in the story constructed and directed by "the self as an actor", i.e., "the others as characters".

However, the others in the real world are not acting out the story constructed and directed by "the self as an actor". The actions of "the others as characters" often deviate from the story of "the self as an actor". On such occasions, "the self as an actor" notices that "the others as characters" are not performing the story they constructed. Here, the self discovers the existence of "the others as actors", who are directing themselves from behind. At this point, the self realizes that the other is a being with character/actor duality, i.e., "the other as a character/actor", just as the self is. For us humans, the other is a being with this character/actor duality.

Once the self understands "the other as a character/actor", they also realize that "the other as a character" is not performing the story of "the self as an actor" as initially assumed. "The other as a character" is in fact a character in another saga. Beyond the self's saga, there are as many layers of sagas as there are others in the world.

Then, the self realizes that the divergence between the story of "the self as an actor" and the actions of "the other as a character" is a discrepancy between the story of the self as an actor and the story of the other as an actor, rather than between the story and reality. This gives rise to the need to reconcile the stories of the self and the other in order to adjust discordant social interactions. I surmise that this is what Suddendorf calls "an urge to connect one's mind with the other's mind".

After reconciling worldviews with numerous individuals, a "shared (common) story" will emerge that does not belong to the self or to any one individual. This shared story is what we make reference to when faced with a false-belief task with no context, such as the Sally-Anne test.

In Chapter Eleven Sugiyama outlined the way the Bemba shifting cultivators compose a shared story by reconciling the individual stories they constructed according to their own interpretations of reality through talking with fellow community members. In humans, a story takes on significance as "that which is actually talked about" between people rather than a mere metaphor.

Great apes live the reality

If the other for humans is "the other as a character/actor", what is the other for great apes such as gorillas and chimpanzees?

If "a nested scenario building ability" and "an urge to connect one's mind with the other's" are uniquely human abilities, as argued by Suddendorf, the other in great apes cannot be "the other as a character/actor" as in humans. However, great apes have the ability to guess/construct the other individual's mind if they are given information about the actual social relationship and context. They seem to recognize the social relationship or structure thus formed, and to engage in social intercourse between individuals based on that recognition. It has been confirmed through mirror self-recognition experiments that chimpanzees have a primordial form of self-awareness (Matsuzawa 2001). Accordingly, it is expected that like humans, great apes also construct some kind of "worldview" in their selves based on the real world. This expectation is at least far more realistic than the view that they live on the basis of ad hoc recognition of the environment day by day. Further, their worldviews constructed in this way seem to be consistent between individuals. Everyone knows who the alpha male is, for example.

Nevertheless, it would be premature to think that they share a single worldview as a story just because there is societal consistency in their worldviews. Their individual worldviews are consistent with each other because they individually refer to the same world in building their worldviews; there is no need for us to think that they actively connect and reconcile the worldviews of the self and others. As in humans, there must be many occasions in great apes when the other's action does not conform to the self's worldview. If Suddendorf is correct, great apes' scenarios do not have a nested structure (recursiveness). When the other's action does not confirm the worldview of "the self as an actor", the self cannot infer "the other as an actor" from it recursively. The other's unexpected action remains no more than the recognition of a discrepancy between the worldview of "the self as an actor" and the other in the real world. This discrepancy can be addressed simply by modifying the worldview of "the self as an actor" to fit reality, or by forcing the other individual to change its action to fit the worldview of the self. In other words, it is enough to reconcile the self's worldview with the real world, rather than the worldviews of the self and the other.

The fact that chimpanzees cannot pass the Sally-Anne test, i.e., that they only guess/construct the mind of a particular individual if they are given the actual social relationship and social context and find themselves placed in that social relationship and context, indicates that chimpanzees only have one worldview of their own. Chimpanzees can understand "the other as a character" cast by the self in the self's worldview, but Sally and Anne, who are almost anonymous characters, cannot be understood according to their worldview. Great apes are always on the stage and do not direct the story from the wings or watch it play out from the gallery.

Difference in the emergence of the other in gorillas and humans

To sum up the discussion so far, the other in humans is understood by the self as "a being with the 'other as a character/actor' duality, like the self", whereas the other in great apes is understood as "the other as a character" with no duality. Let us illustrate this hypothesis based on social interaction in nursing behavior.

Needless to say, nursing for humans and great apes is a process that involves not only raising a child as an individual animal, but also socializing the child. This is common to all social animals. Socialization of an infant means accepting them, a novel, unknown alien, into the community as the other. In that case, the difference in the condition of the other between humans and great apes as discussed above must be reflected in the manner of nursing behavior. We shall compare nursing behavior in gorillas and humans from this perspective below.

Mother and non-mother gorillas relating to a newborn

I have been conducting continuous observation of the interactions between a newly born gorilla, his mother and non-mothers at Nagoya City Zoo since May 2012. Kiyomasa, a male infant, was born by natural delivery to the gorilla community there in November 2011. There were three adult cohabitants, namely, his mother Nene, father Shabarni and older sister Ai by a different father. Ai's female infant named Annie, who had been placed under artificial rearing as soon as she was born in May 2012, joined them from November 2014.

The non-mothers, i.e., father Shabarni and sister Ai, showed a keen interest in Kiyomasa immediately after his birth. When Kiyomasa began to explore the gorilla enclosure alone away from his mother about six months after birth, Shabarni and Ai engaged in various enticement behaviors to arouse Kiyomasa's attention, including showing him a piece of cloth and deliberately lying down in front of him. Despite these frequent enticements, the non-mothers almost never exhibited behaviors that seemed to go "against the will" of Kiyomasa, such as pulling him forcefully toward them or holding him to stop him from leaving, until the age of eighteen months or so. Interactions between Kiyomasa and the non-mothers began with Kiyomasa's voluntary responses to their enticements, and ended when Kiyomasa voluntarily stopped interacting or his mother Nene intervened. The only exception was at feeding time when the non-mothers ceased to interact with Kiyomasa and left him alone, although he seemed to continue to associate with the non-mothers.

After the first eighteen months, Kiyomasa voluntarily attempted to interact with the non-mothers without their enticements. The non-mothers acted very tolerantly in responding to Kiyomasa on these occasions. Shabarni's tolerance was particularly impressive. While Ai sometimes pushed Kiyomasa away gently when he approached, Shabarni never attacked Kiyomasa even when Kiyomasa bit him on the backside in excitement while wrestling or repeatedly messed up the straw bed he had made for himself for napping. Again, the non-mothers rarely acted "against the will" of Kiyomasa during this period.

When I observed the non-mothers use all sorts of enticements to arouse Kiyomasa's attention, they appeared to approach the infant very actively. However, whether an interaction was actually effected or not was completely dependent on whether the infant responded. In this sense, the non-mothers' association with the infant was passive up to this point.

The situation changed when Kiyomasa became increasingly active after the age of two-and-a-half. During this period, the non-mothers began to exhibit agonistic behaviors, including chasing Kiyomasa away or mildly intimidating him, as well as occasional "punishing" acts such as holding Kiyomasa down and softly placing their teeth on his back if he tackled too hard while wrestling.

At first glance, the non-mothers appeared to be teaching "discipline", but actually their interactions with the infant were fickle and inconsistent. They were not punishing Kiyomasa because his behavior was inappropriate according to some norm; they merely attacked in a "sufficiently tempered" way when they found his actions toward them unpleasant. It appeared that the non-mothers basically interacted with the infant at their convenience, while adhering to the principle of affiliativeness and tolerance toward a child. The only exception was when Kiyomasa made little Annie cry. When Annie cried while playing with Kiyomasa, Shabarni always behaved aggressively toward Kiyomasa, not Annie, by holding him down or touching him with his teeth, regardless of how Annie came to cry. Yet, Shabarni's behavior here simply accorded with the silverback's behavioral principle of supporting the loser in a conflict within his group (Yamagiwa 2015b), rather than represented an attempt to teach Kiyomasa something.

Until Kiyomasa was over the age of three, his mother Nene almost never exhibited "enticing", aggressive or punishing behaviors toward him. Her tolerance toward Kiyomasa was similar to that of the non-mothers, but she appeared to seldom entice or respond actively, simply tolerating him in a way, in their mother-child relationship. However, Nene was active at the scenes of interaction between the non-mothers and Kiyomasa. She constantly monitored their interactions and either retrieved her child or attacked the non-mothers if he was exposed to danger, regardless of the circumstances. When an excited Kiyomasa bit Shabarni on the backside during wrestling in the aforementioned example, Shabarni did not retaliate, although he threw his head back and screamed. Nevertheless, Nene rushed toward them as soon as she heard Shabarni's voice and attacked him severely. It is possible to say that the mother always acted as her child's unconditional and undivided ally in his relationships with the non-mothers, and wholeheartedly assisted him in acting as he pleased toward them and his agnate sibling. The non-mothers constantly paid attention to Nene's movements when they interacted with Kiyomasa, and very rarely interfered with her when she came to retrieve Kiyomasa. However, when it came to her interactions with Kiyomasa, although she was more tolerant toward him than the non-mothers, she often gave priority to her own convenience, taking food for herself instead of sharing with him and pushing him away when he came to play while she was lying down to rest.

In this way, there are clear differences in the manner of associating with a child between the mother and non-mothers in a gorilla community. The adults accumulate social interactions with the child under the principle of "dealing with a child at one's convenience with an affiliative and tolerant attitude", which results in promoting the child's physical and social development. The gorilla infant seems to grow up while behaving as they please under the full protection of their mother with the tolerant attitude of the surrounding non-mothers.

Intervention by the mother in child/non-child interactions

In parallel with my observation of the gorillas at the zoo, I conducted observation of mother/child and non-child/child social interactions at gatherings of multiple human mother-child pairs. La Lura, a child and family support center at Chubu Gakuin University, is a facility where children and their parents gather and participate in various activities. I observed a cohort of infants aged between thirty and thirty-six months at this facility, focusing on interactions between them and their mothers as well as other mother-child pairs at the facility.

The human mother's attitude in the co-presence of multiple mother-child pairs at La Lura formed a clear contrast with that of the gorilla mother. The human mother acted in a rather restrictive manner toward her child in interactions with other adults and children, instead of giving them free rein. Further, when acting restrictively toward her child, she often assigned a "character" to them and directed them to play it.

For instance, if a child tried to monopolize a slide by preventing another child from using it, the mother of this child would intervene and chide them by saying, "You must get along with other children". She prompted her child to act in a certain way, such as by saying "Now, tell them 'Let's play together'". Then, the mother of the obstructed child would also intervene by firstly chiding her own child by saying, "You mustn't force your way in without asking", and then prompting them by saying, "Look, (the first child's name) says 'Let's play together'; say 'Yes'". When the children interacted with one another as directed, the mothers praised them by saying, "Well done, let's play together".

In this way, the mothers at La Lura expect their children to play appropriate characters at social scenes and repeatedly prompt them to perform as directed. A large part of the prompting is directed at one's own child, but similar "role expectations" are also directed at other children, albeit to a lesser degree, as demonstrated by the act of praising the other child who, prompted by their mother, said "Let's play together". It seemed to me that once children reached the age of three or so, they voluntarily tried to play their assigned roles while monitoring their own mother and the non-mothers.

A child as the other

Next, I compare the gorillas at Nagoya City Zoo with the humans at the child and family support center according to the aforementioned classification where the human other is "the other as a character/actor" and the gorilla other is "the other as a character".

Both in gorillas and in humans, a newborn is a "stranger" that has appeared in the group. In gorillas, this stranger-gorilla is yet to be placed appropriately in the worldviews of the existing individuals in the group. The only understanding they have is that the mother is the outright protector of the newborn against third parties and the child is the ward of the mother, but no relationship exists between non-mothers and the newborn. In other words, the group members have no idea about what "character" the newborn plays. This is akin to the sudden appearance on stage of a character that is not written into the script one is reading from.

Consequently, the group members must cast the newborn as some character. They need to compose a character based on the newborn's actual behavior. It is likely that the non-mother gorillas at Nagoya City Zoo engaged in seemingly active though actually passive enticement at the early stage of the infant's development in order to see how the "character-less" newborn would behave and to place him in their respective worldviews[4]. As the infant develops and accumulates interactions, their "character" is placed in the non-mothers' worldviews and the infant becomes "the other as a character". This "character" is fluid rather than fixed, and is revised from time-to-time as the child develops. Even with this fluidity, however, group members can understand the child's actual behavior by reference to that character and respond actively as long as the character exists. In light of this, the socialization of a child in gorillas can be regarded as a process by which each member of society assigns a role (i.e. casts a character) within their worldview to a newborn, who has appeared as "the other with no character". During this process, the child themselves may learn to formulate their own worldview and to cast "characters" on the other members of society.

In the meantime, the mother-child relationship begins immediately after birth involving the roles of "the outright protector and the ward"[5]. It is likely that Nene did not engage in enticement with Kiyomasa because she as the mother did not need to check her son's behavior due to the existence of the initial mother-child role establishment.

On the other hand, the interactions between the human mothers and children observed at the child and family support center can be regarded as acts of turning children into "actors". Where children interacted with third parties such as other children or non-mothers, their mothers did not act as their outright protectors. They constantly monitored their children's interactions with third parties, just as the gorilla mother did, but the way they intervened was different. The human mothers monitored their children, intervened when an interaction between their child and another went awry, assigned an appropriate behavior-character on their child and directed them to act accordingly. When one mother began to "direct" in that way, the other mothers often joined in.

On such occasions, it seemed that the mothers subscribed to the shared story of "no dominant-subordinate behavior, no fighting, everyone must get along" and tried to jointly widen the circle of sharing to include their children by making them perform this shared story. Accordingly, it is possible to say that the socialization of children in humans is a process by which group members cooperate in teaching the shared story of the group to the children and coaching them to be actors who perform the story.

It must be noted that although child and family support centers are gaining popularity in contemporary Japanese society, they are a very particular kind of institution from the perspective of human society as a whole. Accordingly, the group formed there is also a relatively particular type of assembly as a human community. I would be going too far if I treated my observations there as universal human phenomena. Especially, the shared story of "not introducing dominant-subordinate behavior, no fighting, everyone must get along" is very characteristic of modernized society such as that of contemporary Japan.

Notwithstanding the content of the story shared within a group, however, teaching children to share it is a phenomenon also found in traditional societies. Hewlett and his co-researchers have reported that in hunter-gatherer societies in Central Africa where teaching children is rare, various cues are used to transmit culture to children such as looking, finger-pointing and verbal prompting, although this occurs infrequently (Hewlett et al. 2011). The contents of communications included not only subsistence technologies such as tool making, tool use and recognizing food and non-food items, but also knowledge about social conventions and institutions such as to whom children are supposed to distribute food, which they learn while helping adults with food distribution, and how to greet people, which is taught to children by prompting, "Do you remember what you are supposed to say in such situation?", when they encounter people. While parents carry out a large part of this teaching, the other members of the group also get involved.

Csibra and Gergely (2011) call the mode of human communication that efficiently transmits shared knowledge "natural pedagogy", and argue that it is the human-specific mentality that is universal to all humans and that human infants are naturally inclined to passively receive teachings from others. In view of these examples, the cooperative transmission of the social group's shared story from the group members to their children, that is, coaching children to be others as characters/actors, is likely to be a phenomenon specific and universal to humankind.

Evolution of the other as a character/actor

In closing this chapter, I would like to offer a brief discussion about the trigger for and process of the transformation of the other as a character to the other as a character/actor in human social evolution.

Cooperative breeding
Hrdy et al. propose "the cooperative breeding model in human social evolution", and argue that the development of cooperative breeding provides the foundation for social and psychological characteristics that separate human society from other great ape societies (Hrdy 2005; Hrdy 2008; Burkart et al. 2009). They hypothesize that while there is no significant difference in social intelligence and cognitive capacity between chimpanzees and humans, the latter often use these abilities in cooperative contexts, whereas chimpanzees use them mainly in competitive contexts. The evolution of cooperative breeding has changed the way these cognitive abilities are used. Suddendorf has also stated that cooperative breeding has been responsible for the development of "two gaps separating humans and

animals" in his hypothesis, although he does not provide a very clear proof of this (Suddendorf 2014).

It sounds logical to think that the members of a society collaborate and cooperate in the form of extending their tolerance toward infants. As we have seen in social interactions surrounding infants in gorillas above, great apes also exhibit a considerable degree of tolerance toward infants. Although the image of chimpanzee cruelty is spreading due to the existence of infanticide, chimpanzees are normally tolerant toward immatures (at least more so than toward adults).

Nevertheless, I disagree with the view that cooperative breeding is the starting point for the mental evolution toward understanding the other as a character/actor and sharing a saga between the self and others for the following reasons.

My observations of gorillas at Nagoya City Zoo demonstrated the strong expression of tolerance by non-mothers toward infants in that species. However, the gorillas initiated interactions with the infant at their own convenience, and no cooperative approach was taken by the mother and non-mothers or among the non-mothers. In this sense, interactions between the mother and non-mothers involving infants in gorillas only "incidentally" assist the infants' development, while they act according to their own intentions or purposes. What they are doing is "collaborating", which cannot be described as "cooperating" in the sense that they do not work together for a shared purpose or intention to raise infants. The cooperative breeding model does not explain the process of transition from collaboration to cooperation. We can predict that extending the application of the tolerance displayed toward infants to other social relations will give rise to collaboration in a broader range of social relations. However, it is unclear what triggers the transformation from collaboration to cooperation.

Another point is that cooperative breeding involves serious risks. Allomothering is one of the common behaviors in cooperative breeding in humans. But Allomothering, i.e. putting childcare in the hands of non-mothers, poses considerable risks to both the mother and the child. In contemporary evolutionary ecology theory, it is thought that primate societies always carry a "potential infanticide risk", and hence protecting offspring from infanticide by conspecifics is one of the important tasks for parents (van Schaick and Janson 2000). The cooperative breeding model of social evolution assumes that the evolution of cooperative breeding preceded other traits of human society such as the division of labor (work sharing) in subsistence activities. However, is it possible for parents to unhesitatingly entrust their child into another's hands in a situation where group members only utilize their social intelligence competitively? Can the child readily entrust themself to a stranger?

Division of labor (work sharing)

For the above reason, it is more reasonable to think that cooperative social relationships in relatively low risk contexts other than child-rearing, including mutual help with transportation and food distribution, existed to a certain extent before the "entrusting of a child to the other", which is the basis for cooperative breeding, became possible. Cooperative breeding does not belong at the starting point of human society. Cooperation and work sharing in relation to food acquisition should be better positioned before the development of cooperative breeding in the chronology of social evolution.

A shared purpose is of paramount importance in cooperation and work sharing. Nishida and Hosaka (2001) have analyzed the hunting behavior of chimpanzees in the Mahale Mountains National Park and argued that group hunting by chimpanzees is more akin to "multiple individual hunts occurring simultaneously", because even though they appear to hunt jointly, there is no role sharing. On the basis of our discussion so far, this is not surprising as chimpanzees are unable to share one another's purpose, although individual members' objectives may coincide occasionally. If, however, they were able to construct a shared "saga" encompassing stages from catching their prey to distributing food and to play their respective parts in it, they would certainly improve their hunting efficiency. The risk of missing out on food because one has accepted the role of a beater and their expectation for receiving a share of food is betrayed later is far less serious than the risk of one's child falling victim to negligent infanticide while being cared for by another. Therefore, the transition from "multiple solo hunts occurring simultaneously" to "cooperative hunting" is considered to be more feasible than that from "collaboration in infant care" to "cooperative breeding".

It is also likely that the merits of cooperative breeding for dependent offspring as well as non-mothers are greater in a society with advanced work sharing than in a society without cooperation and work sharing. In the former, what an immature animal needs to learn to improve their ability in its adulthood depends on the role it plays in that society; in other words, the characteristics that contribute to survival and reproduction of the individual are determined in the individual's social relationships with others. In such situation, it is useful for the dependent offspring to increase opportunities to infer the role others are expecting them to play. Consequently, it becomes desirable that immatures begin to interact with various non-mothers from an early stage and actively share stories with others. For non-mothers, it is desirable that immatures begin to take part in cooperation and work sharing in society as early as possible, be it their own offspring or that of another individual. It would be even more beneficial if non-mothers had opportunities to intervene in the development of another individual's offspring and engage others' offspring in creating a story that is favorable for non-mothers themselves. This is because the reproductive success of an individual in a society with advanced cooperation and work sharing is dependent on the extent to which one can imbue the others with a story that is beneficial for oneself.

In reality, it would be more correct to think that cooperation in livelihood activities (food acquisition) and cooperative breeding co-evolved through reciprocal influence rather than to think that one was completed before the other began evolving. However, considering the higher risk of infanticide in cooperative breeding, I suppose that the evolution of cooperation and work sharing in relation to food acquisition preceded cooperative breeding. In any case, it is likely that the other in humans, or "the other as a character/actor", was formed in the course of the evolution of cooperation for food acquisition and cooperative breeding.

18 The Turing Test in the Wild: When Non-Human "Things" Become Others

Ikuya Tokoro

Key ideas

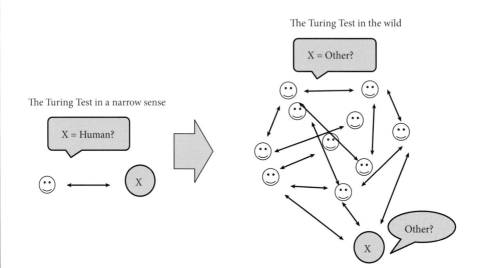

The Turing Test in a narrow sense (left) determines whether Subject X is human or not through an attempt for (dyadic) communication with X in a defined setting. In contrast, the Turing Test in the wild (right) refers to the situation in which a person proceeds with the task of determining whether Subject X is a worthy counterpart to engage in some form of interaction, negotiation or appeal, that is, whether X belongs to Others II (others in a broad sense) in our terminology, while assessing this performatively through their social interactions with X.

Toward non-human others

Plasticity and variability of the human/non-human boundary

This chapter addresses the problem of *non-human* beings as others. Firstly, I briefly explain some issues relating to this problem. Past discourses on otherness in the field of humanities, including cultural (social) anthropology, have tended to hypothesize a framework assuming other humans (conspecifics of humankind) as the denotation of "others" (with some exceptions).

From a more fundamental perspective, including the macroscopic evolutionary historical foundation of humankind, however, we should perhaps more actively examine how various *non-human* beings can become others. What I call "non-human" refers to life forms other than humans in a narrow sense (*Homo sapiens*) (hereafter referred to as "animals", for convenience) as well as various "things" (natural and artificial objects).

The second issue is that we should look at the problem of others from the viewpoint of the plasticity and variability of the boundary between humans and non-humans. More specifically, this concern relates to such matters as the fluctuating boundary between humans and *things*, and *things* that exercise agency. In general, this chapter deals with the question of how we can formulate a theory of others encompassing non-human "things" (animals, natural objects, artificial objects etc.).

In the latter half of the chapter, as an auxiliary line of inquiry in a modified and extended form, I examine the possibility of addressing this phenomenon from the perspective of the evolution of human sociality by using the idea of the Turing Test (imitation game) proposed by mathematician Alan Turing in 1950.

What are others?

Before I consider the problem of "non-human others" (beings other than humans), I touch on the frame of reference in which "others" are discussed in this chapter.

Firstly, if one is asked what "others" are at the everyday or conventional level, one of the standard answers will be "those who are not the self (oneself)". Conversely, the "self" is often assumed to be "that which is not other". The common logic for defining the self and the other seems to be a circular argument (with some exceptions).

Besides the issues and difficulties inherent in a circular and jointly-referenced definition, this type of reasoning seems to be saddled with a major shortfall hindering the more concrete inquiry into actual others (including non-human others) undertaken here. To state the conclusion first, one element missing from the circular definition of "the self" and "the other" (that should not be overlooked) is the existence of "the environment" as a third term.

In other words, the circular definition above is inadequate (at least in terms of our interest here), and "the other" is not "the non-self" as the mere antithesis (or reversal) of "the self". In reality, the non-self (that which is not the self) contains the environment as well as the other. Therefore, not all of the non-self is the other. What we refer to as "the other" in this chapter is not necessarily synonymous with "that which is not the self" (contrary to the common understanding); it is rather a being that is "not the self and not the mere environment".

The other and the environment

Then, the next question revolves around the criteria or characteristics that separate what I call "the other" in this chapter and "the environment" into "that which is not the self" (the non-self) in a broad sense. I conceptualize them as follows here. Among various subjects that are not the self, I shall define "the other" as a subject that is open to the possibility of communication in a broad sense, including negotiation and dialogue, or equivalent interactions with the self. Among the subjects that are not the self (the non-self), those with no possibility of emerging as a subject through communication in a broad sense and similar interactions in principle are more appropriately called "the environment" rather than "the other" from the standpoint of the self.

In short, the other is a being that is of course not the self (the non-self) and is open to the possibility of some form of communication (in a broad sense) or similar interactions with the self, unlike the environment (Figure 18.1).

I would like to add, however, that the distinction between "the self" and "the other" or "the environment" here is highly situation-dependent (context-dependent) and variable. The emergence of a certain physical subject as *the self, the other* or *the environment* depending on the situation is a very common occurrence.

For instance, few would doubt that my body is part of *myself* in my ordinary, everyday situations or awareness. Further, it is commonplace to find skilled cooks and drivers using knives and motor vehicles as if they were extensions of their own bodies, even though they are artificial tools or machines that are not the self in an ordinary sense.

On the other hand, it is not uncommon when one is ill or injured for one's body to emerge as an entity with some kind of remoteness or "otherness", as if it were not the self (the self's body). In this way, the boundary between the denotations

The Turing Test in the Wild: When Non-Human "Things" Become Others

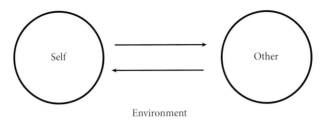

Figure 18.1 The "other" is a being that is open to the possibility of communication

of *the self* and *the non-self* can be regarded as variable and plastic according to the situation or context.

The distinction between *the environment* and *the other* as the subcategories of *those which are not the self* is also highly relative and situation-dependent. As a grounded example, I use the relationship between the ocean and the Sama fishermen of the Sulu Archipelago in the southern Philippines, where I have conducted fieldwork for two years. The Sama people are traditionally known for their excellent fishing skills, including free-diving spearfishing, and for the Sama fishermen the ocean normally emerges as an external space that can be used for transportation and fishing, that is, the environment.

In the event of a storm or other extraordinary weather conditions or an abnormal situation such as a succession of poor catches, however, the Sama appeal or pray to none other than the ocean (or the spirit believed to influence the ocean) to "pacify the storm and the waves". They also swear to the ocean (or the spirit believed to influence the ocean) that they will show their gratitude by performing a ritual if they are given a good catch. In this way, they treat the ocean as the living counterpart in a negotiation or dialogue, rather than just an inert external environment.

In other words, the ocean is normally just the environment for the Sama fishermen, but it is capable of emerging as the other in a broad sense with which they communicate in a broad sense in the form of an appeal, prayer or negotiation in certain circumstances. While "the environment" and "the other" are treated as conceptually distinct in this chapter, we should remember that the boundary between the denotations is variable and not necessarily fixed depending on certain situations.

Others I and Others II

On the assumption that "the other" is distinguished from "the environment" within "the non-self" category as above, I propose that the concept of "the other" should be further divided into two subcategories for the purpose of our discussion here. This step is necessary to allow us to hypothesize a theory of others that includes non-humans (those which are not human).

The two subcategories of the other are the other in a narrow sense (hereafter called Others I for convenience) and the other in a broad sense (Others II). The former, Others I, refers to others with whom the possibility of call-response seems relatively unambiguous and whose relationship with the self is (seems to be) relatively symmetrical and reciprocal among the subjects with whom social interaction, communication, negotiation, dialogue etc. are possible. Typical examples of Others I include other (living) people for a human and conspecifics (especially living ones) for an individual life form.

On the other hand, Others II (others in a broad sense) refers to the subjects with whom attempts at social interaction and communication in a broad sense – negotiation, dialogue, calling etc. – are assumed or supposed to be meaningful for the actor (the self). In other words, Others II includes situations in which the relationship between the self and the counterpart is not necessarily symmetrical or reciprocal (especially from the viewpoint of an outside observer). However, Others I and Others II should be regarded as ideal types or two ends of a spectrum, and the distinction is not necessarily absolute or clear, just as the distinction between the other in general and the environment is not fixed as mentioned above.

In any case, I expect that extending the concept of the other to "the other in a broad sense" (Others II) will create enough room in the denotation of Others II to include the subjects from which responses to calls made by humans are not (objectively or rationally) guaranteed in a normal sense, including dolls, roadside stones and inorganic matter, as well as the subjects such as the dead, gods and spirits as "the nonexistent other" that do not exist physically "here, now".

Aspects of the non-human other

On the basis of the broader concept of the other outlined in the previous section, we begin looking at non-humans (those which are not human) as the other more specifically in this section.

To state the conclusion first, the main argument of the following sections is that non-human beings such as animals and natural and artificial things can emerge in certain social and cultural situations or contexts as subjects the human actor can engage with through interaction or communication (Others I), or at least as subjects to which attempts to call or approach are meaningful for the human actor (Others II).

Animals as the other

Among many kinds of non-human beings, let us examine animals first[1]. It is reasonable to say that in the context of modern Western European society (although a more detailed consideration will find some major exceptions, as mentioned later), mainstream thought viewed animals as automaton-like beings rather than as others capable of negotiation and response akin to humans.

Particularly in the views that developed from the so-called animal-machine theory that became prominent after Descartes, the perspective that animals are living things with human-like minds and senses (or souls/feelings) receded into the background and that which defined them as mindless automatons became predominant. According to Descartes (1997: 78), the dexterity and precision sometimes exhibited by animals do not prove that they have a mentality or mind, but in fact are evidence that they are a kind of mindless machine. Using the textbook expression, this "animal-machine theory" spread throughout Western European society in a more popularized form and wielded its influence aided by the likes of philosopher de Malebranche (1638–1715) (Kanamori 2012: 73–81)[2].

However, a more macroscopic history of humankind is littered with examples that suggest that the animal-machine theory was the exception (peculiarly modern Western European?) rather than the rule. Let us look at some of them.

Firstly, animal burial rituals, animism and totemism in various societies throughout the non-Western cultural sphere, including in the prehistoric age, are prominent examples. In the Mesolithic period, hunter-gatherer peoples at the time treated their prey with awe and adored their companion animals. At the burial sites of Skateholm near the Baltic Sea, dogs were buried with grave goods in formal recognition of their membership to society and bravery. In some cases, dogs were buried with more honor than humans together with precious blood-red ochres and prize catches from a hunt (Fernández-Armesto 2008: 40).

This sensibility can also be found in contemporary hunter societies. For instance, P. Descola, who studies the society of the Achuar people in the Amazon, reports that they respect the animals they hunt. Moreover, they believe that animals and plants are types of "persons" with human-like souls. Animals and plants are considered to be beings with consciousness, intentionality and emotions, and therefore they can communicate (nonverbally) not only with other conspecifics, but also with humans and other heterospecifics (Descola 2013: 4–6).

So far, I have described the animal-machine theory in post-Descartes modern Western European society in opposition to the cultural sphere that views animals as the other in a broad sense. However, I must also mention that there has been a school of thought in the West that recognizes animals as subjects with souls, intelligence and agency and capable of negotiation and dialogue. One example is the so-called "animal trials" that were once practiced in Europe.

In medieval and early modern Europe, there was a practice that involved subjecting an animal that had killed a human to a court proceeding similar to a human murder trial before its execution. It was common until about 300 years ago to give animals practically the same legal rights as humans. The mice that ransacked a barn, the locusts that damaged crops, the birds that defecated on a temple and the dog that bit a person were all tried in court for their "crimes", and local residents funded their defense. Some defendants were even acquitted of their charges (Fernández-Armesto 2008: 55–56).

Needless to say, animal trials took place in the premodern age. However, the sensibility that locates animals as beings with a "mind" similar, if not the same, as that of humans rather than as mindless automatons is not uncommon in secular societies across the world, including contemporary Europe, the US and Japan. The most familiar example must be the relationship between a pet or companion animal and its human master. It is well known that the death of a pet can bring about a profound sense of loss that is comparable to grief caused by the death of a family member (referred to as "pet loss"), and it is not uncommon for the owner to entomb a deceased pet and conduct a funeral for it, even in Europe and the US.

The relationship between pearl oysters and humans at pearl culture farms in contemporary Japan, my own research field, is also very interesting. I have discussed this topic in detail elsewhere (Tokoro 2011; 2018), but in summary, Japanese pearl culture technicians treat the pearl oyster as a being with its own mind and deal with it as if they were interacting or conversing with it rather than treating it as a means to make a profit or a silent and unfeeling object to be controlled.

In the field of biology and modern sciences such as animal psychology, a growing number of studies are being carried out to establish whether not only "advanced" animals such as primates and other mammals, but also squids, woodlouse, earthworms and slime molds are beings with intelligence in a broad sense and (embryonic) "minds" rather than beings driven instinctively, blindly or mechanically (e.g., Ikeda 2011; Moriyama 2011; Nakagaki 2010).

Can non-biological things be the other?

Thus far, we have discussed some examples of the emergence of animals and other life forms as non-human others in a broad sense (Others II) above. Next, we examine whether inert (inanimate) things, i.e., non-biological beings (natural and artificial objects) can be the other in order to further broaden the denotation of the non-human other. This is the question of whether a silent stone by the side of the road or a motor vehicle, for example, can be the other.

Some readers may find it relatively easy to see living organisms as non-human others, while they may have difficulty seeing inanimate natural objects such as stones or artificial objects such as cars in the same way.

Nevertheless, the commonsense dichotomy between organics and inorganics is not necessarily self-evident, as with the case of viruses, and is hardly effective in terms of examining the other from a broader perspective. It has also been pointed out that looking at lifeforms independently of their physical environment is meaningless (Ingold 2000: 20). Next, we shall consider situations in which various inorganic beings emerge as the other (in a broad sense) to humans in more specific contexts.

When natural objects become the other

In anthropology, there have been frequent reports from all over the world of cases in which natural objects and phenomena such as stones, mountains, oceans, the moon, stars, the sun, other celestial bodies and typhoons have been deified. In Japan, it is not uncommon to find stones as objects of worship in Shinto religion. As mentioned above, the ocean (and the waves) is deified by the Sama fishermen in my study field of the Sulu Archipelago, and emerges as the counterpart in rituals and negotiations in certain circumstances.

In these cases, from the perspective of an outside observer, no reciprocity arises in the interactions or negotiations between the actor (human) and natural (in a narrow sense; inanimate) objects such as a mountain or the sea in a narrow sense. Yet, it looks as if an interaction or a dialogue has taken place, at least from the first-person viewpoint of the actor at the scene[3]. It is possible to say that a natural object (or phenomenon) such as the ocean emerges in certain circumstances before the actor as if it were a being with agency, equivalent to a human and with the capacity to be the counterpart in communication or negotiation, that is, the other in a broad sense.

Can artificial objects become the other?

Now we shall examine whether artificial objects can become "the other" in a broad sense, and if so, in what situations.

The phenomenon of an object with a persona outlined by Mauss in *The Gift* is a typical example from classical anthropology. According to Mauss, the idea of a thing itself having a "persona" had been reported in various contexts, such as *the spirit of the thing given* in Maori culture. In early Roman law, the parties to gifting or an exchange were considered to be bound by the spirit of the given thing (*spiritus*) (Mauss 1954).

Another example is the ideas and beliefs surrounding *mono* (things) in premodern Japan. The classical Japanese word *mono* carried the connotation of a being with various spiritual and personal powers and capacities rather than an inert, lifeless thing (object), as suggested by its use in words such as *mononoke* (evil spirit) and *tsukimono* (spirit that possesses) (Tokoro and Kawai 2011: 16; Tokoro 2018).

Even in modern and contemporary Japan, fishermen and aquaculturists are known to erect memorial towers and monuments to pay respect to various animals, and there have been many reports of, for example, whale mounds erected by whalers, memorial monuments for eels, blowfish and chickens and memorial towers and monuments for pearl oysters erected by pearl farmers, where memorial services for these animals are conducted from time-to-time (Tokoro 2011; 2018). What is very interesting is that animals are not the only objects of such memorial services. People have conducted memorial services to pay respect to artificial (human made) objects such as sewing needles, dolls, eyeglasses, abacuses, calendars, brassieres and even computers.

I would like to discuss the case of the masks used in traditional Balinese dance-dramas as an ethnographic example of the clear manifestation of the recognition of the presence of a personal or spiritual character in an artificial object and its ability to exert human-like agency in some situations. According to Yoshida's field study on the masked drama in Bali, the masks used in *topeng* performances are believed to harbor spiritual forces, and on certain occasions various rituals are conducted and offerings are made to the masks. When such a mask is passed on to another performer though succession or gifting, it is said to have the power to drive the recipient to dance. Yoshida explains as follows.

> When actors perform *topeng* as they switch their masks one after another, the masks may literally seem to be "temporal faces". Yet, when we remember that masks are passed on across generations from parent to child and grandchild [...] and that the masks owned by some temples have been worn by generations of local community members in performances, we can see another aspect of masks in which the actors are the masks' "temporal bodies". (Yoshida 2011: 202–203)

A computer as the other

The phenomenon in which an artificial object supposedly devoid of a mind and intelligence, not to mention life, emerges as the other with some kind of personality in the eyes of the person before it is not confined to the "traditional" and "exotic" cultural sphere. In fact, there are cases in the rather highly urbanized social environment of places such as Europe and the US today in which people perceive a sort of otherness in artificial objects, or treat them as the other in a broad sense in interaction or communication in some situations. The most typical example is the computer (or its program, software or AI)[4].

The phenomenon in which a computer program, which is objectively a mere conglomerate of electronic signals and codes, can be perceived as if it were a real person (the other in a narrow sense; Others I) by the person before it has been reported over a long period. The case of a program named Eliza, for example, is very famous.

Eliza is a program developed by Joseph Weizenbaum of MIT from 1964 to 1965. It was initially created to converse with humans for the purpose of conducting psychotherapy, and simulated a therapist in an actual form of treatment called person-centered psychotherapy. The program was built on a very simple mechanism (compared with today's technology) that involved producing a response with a sentence containing keywords extracted from the user's input.

Even though Eliza was mechanically responding with a sentence dictated by a set of simple rules, many of the people who conversed with Eliza had no doubt that they were having a conversation with a real person. Some even felt an emotional bond with Eliza. Interestingly, programs similar to Eliza were later introduced into actual psychotherapy practice in England and elsewhere for the initial treatment of depression patients (Christian 2011: 106–108; Copeland 2013: 244–245).

Programs that converse or interact with humans such as Eliza have been improved continually and applied to recent technologies such as Internet bots (automated dialogue/writing programs). Moreover, in addition to real human traders, computer programs are actually participating in selling and buying shares, currencies and futures as actors in today's financial markets.

Besides financial markets, we now routinely come across situations in which we are unsure if the counterpart in our interaction on the Internet is a person or a computer program. These days, responses to information entered by a person in various electronic transaction or booking services, or advice on "recommended products" in online shops, usually comes from a computer program. Many of the entries in bulletin boards on the Internet are made by automated writing programs (bots) rather than people. In other words, it has become almost normal to not be able to tell whether the other sending a message to us from the other side of the monitor is a real person or an automated program.

The Turing Test as an auxiliary line

In this chapter, we have so far confirmed that various *non-human* beings such as life forms other than humans, natural objects and artificial objects can emerge as a certain type of other depending on the time, situation and context by reference to specific examples from around the world. This fact in turn tells us that rather than being spatially and temporally fixed, the boundary between the environment and inanimate objects and the other to humans is variable and plastic according to the period, culture, situation, scene and context.

In this section, I consider this variability in slightly more generalized and abstract terms. The concept of the Turing Test will be used here to supplement our consideration of how we should interpret the plasticity and variability of the boundary of the other, i.e., the phenomenon in which a particular subject emerges as the other with autonomous agency, intelligence and sometimes a "mind" in a broad sense, or conversely the subject is denied that recognition, depending on the situation and context.

The Turing Test is a concept built upon a kind of thought experiment proposed by a British mathematician named Alan Turing in 1950. To put it simply, it suggests that if humans cannot distinguish between Subject X (computer) and a human in a verbal interaction, Subject X can be regarded as a being that has intelligence equivalent to human intelligence for practical purposes. The test involved people conversing with the subject in a separate room via text messages on a screen, and proposed that the machine could be considered to have intelligence when they could not tell if the subject was a machine or a human[5].

More specifically, the computer in the Turing Test (imitation game) attempts to make the human counterpart in a separate room believe that they are conversing with a real human through text conversation. It is a "game" because if the human counterpart cannot tell if they are conversing with a person or a computer, the computer wins.

Although the Turing Test was initially proposed purely as a thought experiment, attempts have been made to implement it using actual computers (and human judges). The most famous is the Loebner Prize competition, which has been held annually since 1991. Here human judges must determine whether their conversation partner is human within five minutes. In longer tests, the judges evaluate each entry's human-likeness and responsiveness in a fifteen-minute conversation. Prizes are awarded to the "most human-like" programs (Christian 2011).

If we think about it, the Turing Test is a sufficient but not a necessary condition. For example, many young children would fail this test, but this does not mean that they are not thinking (lacking the ability to think). In fact, there have been many occasions at the Loebner Prize and other competitions when real humans in the tests were identified as "non-human" by the judges.

In other words, the Turing Test in a narrow sense uses linguistic communication (conversational) skills as the criterion, and therefore what it is testing is a very narrow aspect of "intelligence", not to mention the "mind" in general, which at most is language-related intelligence or the ability to use language in (adult) humans.

The Turing Test in the wild (the Test in a broad sense)

Generally speaking, Artificial Intelligence (AI) experts tend to have negative opinions about attempts to implement the Turing Test, such as the Loebner Prize. The critics argue that a conversation alone is not a good measure of the interior (the subjective meaning of the interaction), and that this test alone is not sufficient for the assessment of AI, as demonstrated by the aforementioned Eliza case.

Another problem that has been pointed out is that the judges in this type of competition are told in advance that some of their conversation partners will be computers. Moreover, the judges become so engrossed in trying to identify computers that they ask a series of captious questions that turns the test into a kind of witch-hunt (Hoshino 2009).

Despite these problems, however, if we step back from the Loebner Prize and other Turing Tests (in a narrow sense) that are being attempted and return to the original idea conceived by Turing, I believe that the idea he proposed is extremely suggestive in our consideration of computers and other "non-human others".

According to Hoshino (2009: 13), Turing's original intention was to deal with computers fairly (by the same standards) without differentiating them from humans, rather than to judge whether they have intelligence or not via witch-hunt-like interrogations. I shall call this a "symmetry postulate" for convenience. I believe that the symmetry postulate can be a powerful clue when humans recognize and interact with non-human subjects as the other, as discussed below.

Furthermore, it is possible to wonder whether each conversation or exchange we conduct every day is a type of Turing Test (in a broad sense) itself, as suggested by psychologist S. Kanazawa (1999: 12–13). For instance, let us try a thought experiment involving a situation in which all humans other than myself who appear before me (the others) are, theoretically, suspected to be sophisticated but unfeeling robots manufactured by someone (or mindless zombies). It is actually more difficult than we think to "logically" refute this seemingly ridiculous suspicion.

Yet, one completely believes (without clear evidence?) that all subjects called humans around oneself have internal worlds (minds) just like one has in everyday life. It is possible to say that our social intercourse goes smoothly because of this belief. In other words, we humans judge that Subject X called "human" has "passed the Turing Test", and engage in interactions on the assumption that there is a "mind" behind its physical appearance all the time in our day-to-day life (Kanazawa 1999: 12–13).

Now I propose to expand the Turing Test as a metaphor for social, cultural and intersubjective practice that includes our routine interactions with others, rather than continuing to view it as a task to identify computers and humans in a limited setting and framework such as the Loebner Prize competition. Distancing our discussion here from the context of the Turing Test in a narrow sense, I would like to proceed from a viewpoint aligned with Turing's idea of treating objects such as machines and humans on an equal footing (the aforementioned symmetry postulate).

Firstly, let us suppose that members of each society engaging in daily social interactions according to their social, cultural and historical contexts are conducting a certain type of Turing Test in a broad sense (as suggested by Kanazawa). I shall call this test "the Turing Test in the wild" (or the imitation game in the wild)[6].

Let us confirm the difference between the Turing Test in the wild and that in a narrow sense such as the Loebner Prize competition. The latter is conducted in a very specific situation using a specific method for a specific purpose, in that particular judges determine whether Subject X is human (a being belonging to Others I; the other in a narrow sense) or a machine using a specific human language, as explained above.

On the other hand, the Turing Test in the wild refers to the situation in which a person proceeds with the task of determining whether Subject X is a worthy counterpart to engage with in some form of interaction, negotiation or appeal, that is, whether X belongs to Others II (the other in a broad sense) in our terminology, while assessing self-referentially and performatively through their interaction with X.

Unlike the Turing Test in a narrow sense, the Turing Test in the wild is not necessarily limited to verbal interactions in a narrow sense[7]. The Turing Test in the wild does not emphasize the question of whether the subject is human or non-human; it is closer in meaning to the "imitation game" contained in Turing's original idea – the attitude of interacting with Subject X "as if X is the other similar to a human or a human-like being", as Hoshino noted.

Recursivity and arbitrariness in the other

So, what can we say about the other through the metaphor of the Turing Test in the wild? One point is that the question of "whether Subject X is the other or not" is determined (resolved/shown) recursively, self-referentially and performatively through an accumulation of attempts to interact with X. It is obvious that this performative determination of the other carries certain arbitrariness (context-dependency). In other words, what constitutes the other is not necessarily determined by the subject's intrinsic internal and objective traits (e.g., linguistic intelligence). Through repeated interactions with the subject, the subject one can comfortably continue or maintain interactions with as the other is reconfirmed recursively (performatively) as the other.

This performative process of determining the other harbors a certain kind of arbitrariness (context-dependency). Subject X is determined or identified as "the other" not by reference to some absolute criteria; the subject, which is provisionally deemed as "the other" by a person through an interaction in a certain situation, goes on to form the being of the other recursively and self-productively through the interaction.

On the other hand, we must remember that the aforementioned arbitrariness or context-dependency does not mean that individuals can determine whether something is the other in any way they want according to their unfettered subjective views. This is in fact a reality tinged with a kind of externality or "objectivity", if I may say so, in the sense that it is rather a result of intersubjective collaborative work according to the conditions of the society or culture to which these individuals belong, or a result of their way of life that has been established over many years. To paraphrase in more general terms, the question of which subject or object can be deemed as having a mind or a soul is a consequence of intersubjective collaboration in the context of the society, culture and history to which the individual belongs (that has been formed over many years and is called "way of life" or "an attitude toward a soul" in the words of Wittgenstein and Noya), rather than something that can be determined by the individual arbitrarily, and hence it carries certain externality, constraints or historicity (Noya 1995: 74–75; Wittgenstein 1994: 355; Ōmori 1981: 72).

If the question of which subject is deemed as "the other with a mind" is determined context-dependently according to the social and cultural conditions, it is reasonable to say that perceiving a mind in a stone is not necessarily a mistake or a falsehood in a society that has a context in which such a belief is shared and legitimized.

Conclusion: Why humans turn non-humans into the other

In this chapter, I have argued that the possibility of agency and interaction (negotiation and dialogue) in a broad sense is not exclusive to humans, using the expanded concept of the other, including the other in a broad sense (Others II), as a clue, and made reference to recent developments in the non-anthropocentric discourses in a broad sense concerning intelligence, the mind and agency in fields such as cognitive science, biology and anthropology. The discussion seems to point to the prospect that the argument surrounding "the other" in a narrow sense (Others I) is a special case, in a way, that is subsumed under what I call Others II (the other in a broad sense).

In the second half of the chapter, I attempted to expand the concept of the other to include not only non-human life forms, but also artificial and natural objects, instead of confining it to humans in a narrow sense through the metaphor of the Turing Test in the wild.

As our last remaining task, we shall touch on the question of why humans have the tendency to recognize a mind or agency in non-human subjects, even artificial objects, and perceive them as the potentially interactable other.

On this question, we can perhaps draw on some hypotheses in comparative psychology and cognitive science, with Machiavellian intelligence, theory of mind and Donald Norman's proposition in particular as starting points. We shall begin with the Machiavellian intelligence hypothesis and theory of mind.

Loosely speaking, the Machiavellian intelligence hypothesis posits that the major challenge for primates is how to understand, predict, manipulate and outmaneuver the other's action (i.e., the exercise of so-called Machiavellian tricks and tactics) within a group of multiple conspecifics rather than how to deal with the ecological environment. The main argument is that executing successful interactions with others is generally a more complex and sophisticated task than dealing with the ecological environment, and therefore has been a driver for the evolution of more advanced social intelligence (Machiavellian intelligence) (Byrne and Whiten 2004). In other words, it is about the evolutionary historical foundation of sociality in the sense of sympatric coexistence through reconciliation with others or getting along with others by mutually coordinating one another's actions.

This hypothesis is closely correlated with so-called theory of mind. Theory of mind proposes that humans are innately equipped with a system or mechanism for detecting the mental states of others (Baron-Cohen 1997). According to the theory, this system or mechanism is prone to the fallacy of seeing a non-actor as an actor (i.e., misperceiving a mind in a mindless object). This is because, from the evolutionary point of view, it is far more advantageous to one's survival to pay attention to a subject, assume that it is a possible actor with a mind and infer its purpose and next action than to simply ignore it.

This argument is extended to the relationship between humans and artificial objects in cognitive scientist Donald Norman's proposition. According to Norman (2004), humans are predisposed to trying to read emotional responses in everything, whether it is living or not. He points to our long evolutionary historical background as its foundation. Life forms are designed to interact with one another, and the act of reading facial expressions and body language is important in doing so. The ability to infer the internal state of another person has become part of our biological heritage over millions of years. Our ability to notice another person's emotions as well as our tendency to infer emotions even in non-biological objects (anthropomorphism) are consequences of that evolution. While this ability is of great significance when we interact with others, it can make us interpret inanimate objects in terms of human emotions (Norman 2004: 181–182).

The Machiavellian intelligence hypothesis, theory of mind and Norman's argument offer many suggestions for our inquiry into the non-human other problem from the perspective of the evolutionary historical foundations for or background of sociality. However, we must note that some criticisms have been raised against the Machiavellian intelligence hypothesis in recent years, questioning whether it underestimates the roles of ecological, technological and other types of intelligence (other than social intelligence in a narrow sense), or whether it overestimates the competitive aspect of social interaction such as tricking or outmaneuvering others or whether it is a projection of the researcher's own competitive worldview (Boivin 2008: 212–216; Nakamura 2009: 194–196).

Another shortcoming of the above theories from the perspective of biological evolution is that they only provide a weak explanation for the great variability of the denotation of the other in humans when humans are treated as non-humans, i.e., in the opposite direction of treating non-human beings (things, for instance) as humans (others). They leave the question of how to interpret the phenomenon of the dehumanization (objectification) of humans, where real people are excluded from the category of interactable others in certain social or cultural situations while non-humans are included as others in different social or cultural contexts.

The dehumanization phenomenon refers to cases in which Indians and Aborigines were excluded from the proper "human" category in Western Europe, as well as to the extermination of Jews by Nazis and organ transplantation in contemporary society. These examples involve the attitude of seeing fellow humans as objects for unilateral termination and exclusion rather than interaction, or for utilization as resources (e.g., humans as medical resources), instead of seeing them as interactable subjects with minds (others) (an attitude toward a soul).

Another point, which somewhat overlaps with these criticisms, is that the great variability, culturally and historically, of the denotation of "the other" in human evolutionary history is difficult to explain with macroscopic and comprehensive theories such as the Machiavellian intelligence hypothesis. This difficulty indicates the necessity of examining in detail how what I call "the Turing Test in the wild" has been deployed in various situations in specific sociocultural contexts. I shall consider this point on another occasion. In any case, I hope my discussion here has provided some clues about the possibility of a theory of others beyond the conventional anthropocentric framework.

Epilogue
Future Agenda, Others as an Affliction: Tripartite Relationships and the Tetrahedral Model

Takeo Funabiki

This chapter is positioned half a step in front of the other chapters in this volume. The concept of "others" has been contemplated philosophically in terms of afflictions by advanced intellects and artistically represented as incarnations of suffering. The shadow cast by "others" has been darkened with special meaning in terms of Western European modernity that has lasted for a period of a few hundred years, although this is not long in historical terms. We cannot totally ignore "others as an affliction" because it is outside the scope of our discussion on "others". Therefore, I am writing this chapter from a deliberately precarious position, with one foot "out of bounds" and the other not completely removed from the discussion in the rest of the book. We cannot help but notice that this attempt transgresses the bounds or scope of this book, but we commit to this position hoping that the front foot pointing towards the "limits" of society that will be reached eventually will play the role of scout.

The discussion thus far and the preamble

I presented the following arguments in "Human groups at the zero level" (Funabiki 2013; hereinafter called the first thesis) in *Groups: The Evolution of Human Sociality* and "Basic components of institution" (Funabiki 2017; hereinafter called the second thesis) in *Institutions: The Evolution of Human Sociality* that preceded this volume.

In the first thesis, I proposed that "Human beings are able to have relations of mutual understanding with others they meet and face", and that "Let us call [...] the infinite expanse of this position holding the possibilities of such relations a 'field'. Conversely, it is possible to say that the field is carved into scenes by the act of mutual understanding between humans" (Funabiki 2013: 294–295). I went on to reason that in order to form and sustain relations of mutual understanding with not only those on the scenes but also those behind them, "height" in an abstract sense would be needed. When "height" brought about an expanse beyond face-to-face relations and temporal sustainability, society would be structuralized. In the first thesis, I looked at the condition from the reverse position in order to test the idea. In other words, I postulated an extreme situation as an example where even carving a face-to-face scene was impossible, and demonstrated that "height" was needed for the continuation of a human group.

In the second thesis, I considered how "height" would be introduced in terms of the "institution" problem. I inferred that when a relationship between A and B expanded from a face-to-face bipartite relationship to become quadripartite, quinquepartite and so on when additional third parties appeared, mutual understanding between these multiple parties would theoretically become unmanageably difficult. This plays out in our everyday experience as well. Humankind must have discovered a means to overcome this difficulty, because we have built societies on the basis of institutions. I conducted my examination focusing on the stage of transition from a bipartite to a tripartite relationship in a process that illuminated this conjecture from behind. In other words, I raised the question of what sort of being would appear as "the third party" in a tripartite relationship. My expectation was that the answer to this question might help us understand the foundations supporting institutions.

The conclusion drawn from the exercise was that the third party in a tripartite relationship functioned as a third term that "guaranteed" a firmer and longer bipartite relationship. However, whether the third term is pseudo-immortal "gold", the individually dominant and influential "father" or "mother" or the dead father or mother, we cannot have the human society we presently live in that has "gone beyond biological group composition, both qualitatively and quantitatively, and come to possess an incomparably larger scale and complexity" (Funabiki 2017: 297) – which is the issue I have been grappling with since the first thesis – while the substance of the being is important in enabling it to guarantee the bipartite relation. Consequently, I argued that our social institutions would come into existence only when the third term became a symbolic "sign".

I refrain from reiterating the details here, but my conclusion from the second thesis was that all social relations throughout human history have always been and still are bipartite relationships between A and B; that the addition of a symbolic sign "α" forms a triangular relationship, but when C enters it as a third party, it creates three bipartite relationships between A and B, B and C, and C and A; and that each of the three bipartite relationships takes α as the third term and forms a triangle and the three triangles together form a tetrahedron.

As I consider "others" in the wake of the two previous theses, I come to examine the following proposition outlined in the second thesis: "[…] an entity that can potentially form a bipartite relationship with the self. To rephrase, it is currently not the second party but it has the potential to become one. We think that this is the very entity that ought to be called 'other'" (Funabiki 2017: 320).

My investigation may not pose a great difficulty if I proceed along the lines of the argument of the second thesis. However, I sensed something greater than a logical difficulty in discussing "others". This is due to the method I adopted in the first and second theses; I began formulating my theory by referring to characteristic examples of correspondence between the theory and the particulars of social life, and proceeded with my argument and checked its accuracy on the basis of how well the internal consistency of the logic was maintained. Due to the procedural circumvention of the correlation with reality, a consideration of how my conclusions would apply to the historical reality of groups and institutions in humankind became a task outside of the scope of the two theses. However, I had reservations about the methodology of finding clues in ethnographic materials or written works and simply making logical deductions from them by again shelving in this third thesis the concept of "others" that has been expanding its meaning in the philosophical and artistic activities of modern Western Europe.

It may be possible to ignore all the difficulties of addressing others in philosophy due to the fact that this is a social scientific study. Yet, as I myself have always sensed certain psychological pressure from this existence called "others", I would be offending against good morals if I ignored them while writing this thesis, even if that were possible. Further, it would not be a problem for myself alone; doing so would diminish the contemporary meaning that "others" had when we raised the question, as well as tarnish the appeal of the question here as it is in fact written for others. Accordingly, the following discussion entails the task of examining correlations with the philosophical question about others and how effective the two theses, especially the tetrahedral model in the second thesis, are for our consideration of "others".

Others as an affliction rather than a problem

The conundrum about others that began in the modern age is not about simply looking at society from above and arguing about the relationships observed there, such as how the third term works and so on. The argument about others begins with a personal uneasiness, which is "the uneasiness in finding that I don't understand the people around me" at some point in life, whether early or late. It is simultaneously a personal and social problem.

I suppose that Rimbaud's statement, *"Je est un autre"* (I am an other) (2009), contains two meanings in one sentence: I do not understand myself, it is as if I were another person; and I and myself are strangers who do not understand one another. Sartre's statement, *"L'enfer, c'est les autres"* (Hell is other people) (1982), can also be interpreted in two ways: the world is hell because it has people I don't understand in it; or the world could not even be hell if it has no other people. Lévinas's view of others seems to imply that we cannot even claim the sequence of existence as "I before others", because they are not "I" and "I" cannot exist without "others"; it is obvious that we must live on, even if we do not understand others (Lévinas 2005b passim). This may sound coarse, but they all seem to be saying that the "other" is there for "I" to "endure". In other words, the being of others is better described as an incessant "affliction" than a "problem" to be solved.

This may be an oversimplification, but the removal of the fetters of the class system and the weight of religion in modern Europe, and the guaranteeing of the freedom of commerce and movement during China's Sung Dynasty before that, for example, caused a shift from social relationships based on face-to-face familiarity to a situation in which a person routinely interacted with multiple strangers with α as the common third term in many more scenes (as mentioned in the second thesis) in certain regions of the world. Then, perhaps we can say that the difficulty of having relationships with others becomes not only a social difficulty, but also the individual's inner affliction, giving rise to the other as an affliction.

During the ages of hunting and gathering and early agriculture in a simple conceptualization of the stages of civilization, people had the powerful method of "avoidance" if they suddenly encountered a stranger, while any relationship difficulty with a familiar other would have been resolved there and then. Even when hierarchical social orders with "height" were gradually built and the freedom of movement became restricted in the latter part of the agricultural age, difficulties with others were dealt with as personal difficulties through the performance of individual roles under the religion, moral code and class system of the higher-order societies above individual groups. Curiously, as the "freedom" of physical and social movement that characterized the hunting-and-gathering and early agricultural ages returned during the modern age, people had more chances to encounter strangers unexpectedly, but on these occasions it became more difficult to simply avoid by evading them physically or socially. In the case of acquaintances, difficulties are becoming too complicated to be resolved on the spot and hence remain unresolved for a long period.

Japanese novelist Sōseki Natsume (1869–1916) wrote *Michikusa* (Grass on the wayside) in a period in Japanese society called the Meiji era, and had the protagonist of the novel say, "There are very few things in this world that are really finished. Once things happen, they persist forever. Only because they change into all sorts of forms, I as well as others lose track of them" (Natsume 2003: 317). The fact that the Chinese character for "others" in this statement was annotated in ruby characters as "people" is highly suggestive. In this autobiographical novel, all people are stranger-others to Sōseki. In modern Japan, people cannot escape from *seken* ("society" or "social circle" in Japanese), just as Monkey King Goku on the Buddha's palm cannot escape, no matter how much he moves, and "once things happen, they persist forever" as the protagonist says. The affliction named "the other" exists in a place where an ordinary occurrence in everyday social life can become a specific personal problem. All people (others) emerge as "others as an affliction" here.

Is this affliction an appropriate problem to deal with in this book? As I said earlier, I believe that this nasty and sinister problem carries poignancy precisely because of that quality, and although its social or personal resolution may not be the theme of this book, this modern affliction was definitely in the background when the issue of "others" was raised. For this reason, with this point as a clue, we attempt to situate others as an affliction at the level of human sociality, while avoiding the level of personal affliction. We intend to advance the following argument with the intention of exploring the meaning of social others: "'[...] an entity that can potentially form a bipartite relationship with the self… is currently not the second party but it has the potential to become one'; this is the other".

Bipartite relationships: The absence of α in Mbotgote rituals

All social relations and actions are underpinned by ritual activities in the Mbotgote people on Malekula Island (sometimes spelled Malakula) in the Pacific state of Vanuatu (Funabiki 2012). What I see as their "rituals" here are collective activities with three main components, namely, the "spirit", "dance" and "pig sacrifice" according to their verbal representation. A dichotomous framework separating men and women, or more accurately "initiated men" and "the rest of the people", functions as powerful social norms in Mbotgote society. While men and women have separate rituals, those performed by initiated men surpass women's rituals in frequency and scale.

There are two types of male rituals according to their own categorization. One is called *nimangki* and the other is called *nalawan*. The *nimangki* is an open ritual grade-taking system. It is "open" because the names and characteristics of the spirit and dance performances and the ritual killing of pigs can be known to or seen by other groups or women and uninitiated boys within the Mbotgote group. Conversely, the *nalawan* is a secret ritual grade-taking system. It is secret because the names and characteristics of the spirit and dance performances and the ritual killing of pigs cannot be known to or seen by people other than members of the relevant secret society and Mbotgote men who are allowed to participate as novices. *Nalawan* rituals are treated as higher value rituals than *nimangki* rituals in Mbotgote society. There is a common perception that the former is greater in terms of ceremonial cost (for decoration and food preparation) and human energy.

A comparison of these ritual systems with contrasting characteristics in a certain sense highlights the characteristics of others, the theme of this chapter. This relates to the question of how ritual rights and knowledge are transferred. The presence of a second party that appears to the party to the ritual as well as "a third party as the third term" indicates one mode of existence of others.

I shall describe each ritual from the point of view of the man entering a new grade: the "host" for *nimangki* and the "novice" for *nalawan*.

The *nalawan* system of rituals has five or six grades, but the difference between ritual gradations is not our concern here. As the grade rights and knowledge are kept secret, a novice who wishes to enter the system or to advance to a higher grade of *nalawan* either does not exactly know or does not know at all who has the ritual rights and knowledge – he is supposed to not know them, which is the proper attitude to adopt, given the fact that they are secret rituals. The first-grade ritual for boys in Mbotgote society is an initiation involving circumcision. The boys are completely passive, as they cannot perform the initiation ritual by their own volition, and the process begins when they are suddenly abducted by adults to live in isolation for one year in preparation for the ritual. The initiated adult men (although some are still in their early teens) can negotiate the staging of a *nalawan* ritual by indicating their aspiration and readiness, particularly with sacrificial pigs, to the senior men who hold the rights and knowledge of the grade they wish to advance to.

If we describe these relationships using the tetrahedral model outlined in the second thesis (2017: 321), A begins to negotiate with B and C (and theoretically D, E and so on) without knowing whether B or C has the right. Technically, B and C listen to A's aspiration without revealing if they have the right. In this situation,

Epilogue

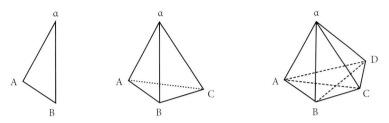

Figure E.1 Tripartite relationships and the tetrahedral model

α can be regarded as the value of the *nalawan* ritual or the power of the spirit. According to my argument in the second thesis, however, α is the symbolic value of the *nalawan* ritual shared by members of the Mbotgote group, rather than a value or power that exists on its own terms. In this sense, even if B or C has the right of access to the grade A is hoping to advance to, B and C are situated at the scene of negotiation as the second party to A, and not as α.

Now, there is a complex problem. The right to host a *nalawan* ritual is in the hands of the elders who have already been through it (grade). The *nalawan* ritual as α is shared by the male population as well as the entire Mbotgote society, including women – the women recognize the value and participate in the final scene of the male initiation ritual in the first grade as female relatives – but the right to decide the staging of the ritual is not shared equally by all members. Only those who have completed the ritual have the right to make this decision.

Suppose A is an NA-1 (i.e., first-stage *nalawan*) right holder who has completed the first initiation ritual, while B is an NA-2 right holder and C is an NA-2 and NA-3 rights holder. A must negotiate with B and C (and other NA-2 right holders) in a weaker position (in the sense that all he can do is ask). If B is in negotiations with C regarding his advancement to NA-3, this means that B is negotiating with C (and other NA-3 right holders) in a weaker position as far as *nalawan* rituals are concerned. In these negotiation relationships, A, B and C are not equal members who support the institution by having *nalawan* rituals as α; it appears as if B and C are personifications of α.

Although B and C to A, as well as B to C, are supposed to be the counterparts with whom a bipartite or even a tripartite structure can be formed via α, it seems that in this situation B and C can influence their relationships with A as if they were not mediated by α. If B and C were behaving as if they were in the position of α as a negotiation "tactic", this would not contradict the group and institutional mechanism proposed in the first and second theses. However, if B, C or other higher-grade rights holders behaved as a personification of α not as a negotiation tactic and refused to negotiate, i.e., refused to transfer rights and knowledge, the *nalawan* rituals would not be shared as α and its meaning space (or value space) could not be effected. The *nalawan* rituals would become rare objects exclusively enjoyed by a limited number of members of society.

Why would they harm their own ritual institution and their Mbotgote society supposedly underpinned by that institution? There is not enough space for me to discuss this negotiation in detail based on the social reality in Mbotgote society at a certain point in time. In short, by not transferring the rights, vested right holders (B and C) are trying to add an aura of rarity to their rights as prestige, rather than attempting to obtain pigs (from A) or gaining a sense of satisfaction with the continuation of the *nalawan* by transferring their own rights and knowledge. Depopulation was a major issue in Mbotgote society in the late 1970s when I was conducting fieldwork there. I shall not elaborate on the matter, aside from highlighting the following for the sake of our discussion here.

While A appeared as a new other to B and C, depopulation and social change led B, C and other members to decide that the tetrahedron with the *nalawan* as α at its apex would not be able to continue expanding to A1, A2, A3 and so on and to think in the following way. The secret ritual system of *nalawan* had preserved its meaning space and value because it was open to the possibility of accepting A1, A2 and A3 as new members, while excluding all non-members. By abandoning that approach and increasing their own rarity by excluding all others as well as the possibility of new entrants, the vested right holders demonstrated that they would rather preserve their own interests as the last people with the experience of the rituals, thus committing the "error" of embodying the *nalawan* as the vested right holders. Here, they refused to allow people (men) other than themselves to emerge as interactable "others" for the purpose of *nalawan* rituals.

The situation with *nalawan* rituals did not occur in the case of *nimangki* rituals. The idea of others found in the latter is rather different. Using the same tetrahedral model, if A wishes to enter n grade (NI-n; the *nimangki* has seventeen grades, far more than the *nalawan*), he is able to consult B, C and others about staging the ritual on an equal footing. This is because a man who wishes to advance to a new grade is entitled to decide when to host the ritual. Of course, a *nimangki* ritual would be meaningless if no one participated in it, so he needs to negotiate with others so that they accept his invitation. As over fifty Mbotgote guests, including men, women and children, typically participate in the ritual, the host has much organizing to do, including preparing food and accommodation. Theoretically, the ritual takes effect as long as two people other than the host are present, and the number of other guests is inconsequential. A ritual exchange for the grade NI-n with A, the host of the ritual, is effected in the presence of one receiver and a mediator who witnesses it (see Figure E.2). Somewhat surprisingly, the receiver does not have to be a current NI-n grade right holder. Neither does the mediator.

Let me elaborate. The receiver is chosen by the host, and can be an NI-n grade right holder or otherwise. Although choosing a current NI-n right holder is thought to be more befitting for the ritual, it does not affect the validity of the acquired right to the grade. It is possible to say that the host can use the opportunity to acquire the right to a certain grade for the purpose of improving or advancing his social relationship with another outside of ritual life, in light of his practical, economic or social debtor-creditor relationship in everyday life. He can choose a counterpart he wishes to give something to (pigs in most cases) on the ceremonial occasion. The payment for *nimangki* rituals between A, B, C and others in Mbotgote society (the entire meaning/value space with the symbolic value of the *nimangki* spirit α at its apex) is made to a certain member who has been chosen as the receiver.

I stated above that the mediator does not have to be an NI-n right holder either. However, there is a strongly held view among the people that it is desirable to choose a mediator from among NI-n right holders. What is important for our discussion here is that the acquisition of the right to the grade is effected even if this does not happen. When a person wishes to enter the NI-n grade, the host A conducts a ritual with the three required components, namely "spirit", "dance" and "pig sacrifice" in the presence of a receiver and mediator, as shown in Figure E.2, openly in front of his people and acquires the right to NI-n when it is acknowledged by all of the participants. Consequently, one can complete the entire seventeen *nimangki* grades without being guided by a senior person.

I would like to touch on two points in order to supplement our discussion about *nimangki* and *nalawan* rituals. In the *nimangki*, it is possible for a host to acquire the right to a certain grade (NI-n) to which no one else has the right, and to have the acquisition recognized by others. The question is, then, if no one present has the experience of hosting the ritual, how can ritual knowledge be passed on to the host who is trying to newly acquire it?

The answer is as follows: memories and knowledge held by those who have participated in past rituals for that grade (NI-n) in some capacity have been verbally communicated and transmitted to the host. The open nature of the ritual means that the content of a given *nimangki* ritual is openly available. More importantly, in the case of the *nalawan*, one may have received some *nalawan*

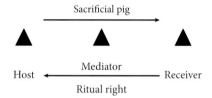

Figure E.2 Three ritual exchange roles in nimangki *rituals*

ritual knowledge from a *nalawan* ritual elder in some form, but one cannot claim to "know" it. On the other hand, *nimangki* ritual knowledge is shared and available to all. One's knowledge may be incomplete or inferred from the content of a ritual for a different grade, but this is not important as long as everyone accepts it.

Another point is that the *nalawan* operates in the manner of a secret society, and therefore its members do not know who knows or what they know. Although the sixth grade is said to be the highest grade, no one can deny that there may actually be a seventh grade. This means that in the *nalawan* system, one cannot know the others that α can be shared with. In other words, this system gives rise to a situation where one cannot know the identity of the "entity that can potentially become the second party", or the other in a bipartite relationship.

So, why is a higher value attached to the *nalawan* in Mbotgote society despite this vulnerability? Perhaps the answer lies in its rarity on the flip side of its vulnerability. I touch on this condition of involving value and rarity in one's potential relationships with others again later. Here, the important point to note is that *nimangki* rituals allow anyone to become the other in the capacity of receiver or mediator. In other words, for *nimangki* rituals, any person can be "an entity that can potentially become the second party", or the other, based on the understanding that anyone can be a substitute for anyone else, even when a senior grade right holder who would otherwise assume an essential role in the ritual (the third term α as an objectified third party in terms of the second thesis) is "absent". The *nimangki* system is a more appropriate social means for making a connection with another person as the other than the *nalawan*.

The bipartite relationship called the "letter"

A letter is a fine example of a thing that is peculiar to a bipartite relationship. Typically, a letter has a sender and a receiver, and everyone else is out of its bounds. The letter is written on the assumption that it will not be read by or known to people other than the two parties. Its oral equivalent would be a private conversation or whispering. However, the letter does not actually exist "socially". It becomes a social entity only when it is read by someone other than the two parties, and then the letter is no longer a letter. This is a little complicated, but as a clear example, a love letter does not exist socially. Someone writes "I love you" to someone else and delivers it so that it will not be read by anyone else. The receiver understands that the matter is between the two parties and keeps the letter at the bottom of a box or burns it, so that it does not appear in a social field. The letter becomes social only when it happens to be found after the receiver's death and read by other people. For instance, a bestselling novel entitled *The Bridges of Madison County* begins when a letter is read by the two children of the deceased heroine. Being read means it has been revealed at the social level. A letter becomes social only when it is no longer a letter.

To link this to our discussion on others, let us explain it from another angle. Not exposing letters "socially" is important for society. The secrecy of private letters is a fundamental human right in contemporary society. Section 2 of Article 21 of the Constitution of Japan stipulates, "No censorship shall be maintained, nor shall the secrecy of any means of communication be violated". In principle, society must not put a hand in that pocket, protecting the privacy of a bipartite relationship.

Thus, if all letters in the world remained as letters, they would not be a topic for our discussion here because they would have been written by a sender and read by a receiver and would not have become social. However, we can discuss them because some letters have been read by third parties such as myself. In other words, we can discuss them because some letters are no longer letters. I have read Paul's *Letters* in *The New Testament* and "Sensei's letter" in *Kokoro*, Sōseki Natsume's novel, which have left their respective bipartite relationships between writer and reader, and are therefore no longer "letters". I shall italicize the letters that have been disclosed and socialized as *letters* to distinguish between the two modes here.

Nevertheless, "Sensei's letter" and "Paul's letters" in our examples are *letters* not because they have been read by third parties and opened to society. They are *letters* because they were actually written as *letters*, intended for reading by third parties in the first place. This contrivance becomes clear when we use the tetrahedral model. The bipartite relationship between A and B mediated by letters cannot expand any further, unless mediated by a third party. The letters are the expressions of the respective inner thoughts and feelings of A and B, for example, and if they ignore one another and do not read them, the letters are erased from existence. Even if the parties read the letters, whether they are affected by their contents and retain something in their minds is a matter for each party, and can be likened to bubbles that appear and disappear in the mind of each person. If the letters exert any action as social or external forces, it is because there is α that is shared by A and B to begin with and functions as, for instance, a norm, commandment or gain; or as we argued in the second thesis, α emerges in response to a desire for the continuation of relationships on an extended social plane and the aforementioned tetrahedron of meaning space (and an institution in another dimension) gives rise to a mechanism by which the letters perform a social function as *letters*.

I read Sensei's testament in *Kokoro* because it was written by Natsume as a serialized novel for a newspaper. The adoption of the epistolary novel style resulted in a duality between the letter inside and the *letter* outside the fiction. While it is a *letter* read by me external to the fiction, Sensei's testament inside the novel was not written to be read by a third party. Not only that, it was sealed repeatedly to make it look like a genuine "letter". Sensei first stated that the letter was written to "I" (the narrator) for the eyes of "I" only; then he stressed that its contents should not be disclosed to his "wife", who had been a party to the matter in the letter; and he asked the narrator as he closed the story "to keep everything to yourself". As another party within the novel named K was dead, and Sensei warned that he intended to kill himself once he finished writing the letter, it was a perfect letter whose contents would remain solely in the head of "I" (the narrator). However, this genuine letter has been "read surreptitiously" by tens of millions of readers so far.

The crux of the epistolary novel technique lies in letting readers read surreptitiously. When Rousseau wrote *Julie, ou la nouvelle Héloïse* (1979–81 [1761]) in a similar style, the epistolary fiction genre was in fashion in Europe. While the thrill of reading *letters* surreptitiously was the reason for its popularity, it was also because the setting for "afflictions" such as the personal "inner life" in relation to "others" was well established by then. *Letters* operate as a device to allow their readers, who are third parties, to feel as if they are the second party, "you", within the novel. In other words, both *Kokoro* and *Julie, ou la nouvelle Héloïse* exert the most powerful action any fiction would aspire to exert on its readers, which is to allow them to mistake fiction for reality, because they are *letters*. The readers begin to read as if they were the recipients of the letters, rather than reading them surreptitiously as a third party. Although there are various devices to maintain the readers' perspectives as second parties – for example, stopping the readers from distancing themselves due to the guilty feeling of "reading surreptitiously"

– the aim is to draw the readers into the bipartite relationship with the writer as "you", the second party.

As this explanation may sound too "literary", I shall frame it in the context of our main argument. In the tetrahedral model, A and B exchange a letter. This action is imagined as communication between what I called "the singulars" in the first thesis. No one else in the world knows the contents of the letter. C appears as a reader. The letter in the novel has of course become a *letter*, but C can set it aside and enter the CA or CB relationship to read it as if C was the recipient. As a fiction, C may have the perspective of α observing everything from above. This can be called the pseudo-author position. The most important point for our discussion is that C as the reader becomes the third party, thus guaranteeing that the letter between A and B has the social nature of a *letter*. Guaranteeing its sociality as a *letter* means that C functions as a social actor who witnesses the *letter* when it, as a transmission from the interior to the interior, disappears as something meaningless or is erased or trampled upon in the social plane – something that ends up worthless. In terms of the aforementioned ritual example, C constructs a meaning space in *Kokoro* and *Julie, ou la nouvelle Héloïse* by assuming the function of the receiver or mediator in *nimangki* rituals. A novel is fictional and not a real society. Whether it is fictional or not a physical reality, however, it is a social reality created by humans as a meaning space, as demonstrated by the tetrahedral model. In comparison, in *nalawan* rituals at the time of my study in 1980, a meaning space with α at its apex was supposed to exist, but the "letter" sent by A wishing to enter remained unread by B and C, or it faded away without becoming a *letter* while A did not know if it had been read.

Paul's "letters" (Shinyaku Seisho Honyaku Iinkai 1996) are also strange *letters*. These letters, which are probably the most widely read letters in history, were sent to various locations to teach, admonish and encourage his followers. We can say that they were *letters* from the time they were penned. The followers who received them and the new converts to Christianity, which was still a new religion with a weak foundation, would have used the letters in talking to their compatriots or debating with their opponents. Paul wrote them on the assumption that they would be used in that way.

In these letters, Paul uses "you" to address people. "You" in his letters is subtly different from the "you" used by Jesus Christ in *The New Testament*. Jesus as the Savior or the Prophet tells "you", the people, what to do. There is a clear line between Jesus and "you" that distinguishes between (the son of) God and people, the Savior and the saved or the Prophet and the receivers of prophecies. From the human viewpoint, there are "we" humans and "you" God on the other side. There is no language to respond on equal terms. A "prayer" would be the closest. On the other hand, "you" in Paul's letters is often used together with "brothers", as in "I came to you, brethren, I…". I surmise that "I (Paul)" as the leader writes a letter to "you", but this "you" is also "we" that includes Paul. This is intended to signify that you the reader and I the writer are brothers in order to draw "you" into the perspective of the joint "first party", while addressing "you" as the second party.

Although Paul had never met Jesus Christ, he reportedly behaved as a powerful leader even while other apostles who had known Jesus personally were still alive. This gives us the impression that Paul, who became Christian after hearing a divine voice, could have used his overwhelming forcefulness to found his own religion as a Prophet or Savior who hears revelations. Such a man, Paul, writes, "Furthermore then we beseech you, brethren, and exhort you by the Lord Jesus" in a little more intricate phrasing (Shinyaku Seisho Honyaku Iinkai 1996: 216). This sentence is structured to say that Paul and "we" around him are "by" (within a tetrahedron) the Lord Jesus (α) and "beseeched" and "exhorted" to have bipartite relationships with "you". We entice you to become the first party equal to us (brethren as the servants of God) by answering this solicitation and appeal.

In terms of the tetrahedral model, although the letters of very forceful Paul seem to be situated in the position of α to A, B, C and so on, Paul addresses other people as those on the same plane as A, B, C… as part of "we", while pointing at α.

By reading Sensei's letter, the readers of *Kokoro* understand it as a socialized *letter* and join Sensei and "I" to become "we" who share in the same affliction. Although Paul's letters appear to have been letters to the Roman and Corinthian follower groups who received them, they in fact came into existence as open letters, or *letters*, that were placed within a fictional bipartite relationship in the form of letters. The significance of these letters lies in the solicitation that it is possible to position I, Paul, and you on the plane of bipartite relationships A, B and C with the Lord Jesus as α, and to become brothers to form a tetrahedron with α at its apex.

We notice that there is a difference in the formation of "we" between these famous "letters" from different time periods, which is meaningful to those of us alive today – we as the discrete singulars who share an affliction in *Kokoro* and we as brothers who try to overcome difficulties relating to propagation and persecution. Let us consider this point from a linguistic perspective.

The inclusive first person and the exclusive first person

Some languages in the Pacific Region, including Mbotgote, feature first person plural pronouns with a distinction between the inclusive first person and the exclusive first person. The former includes the speaker and the addressee in the same "we", whereas the latter excludes the addressee in the first person plural of the speaker. This feature is found in Austronesian languages, Indonesian, Chinese, Ainu and others, and its geographical distribution has been discussed as a distinctive linguistic characteristic. We shall consider the difference in the meaning of these two forms of the first person in line with our argument here.

The people of Vanuatu, including the Mbotgote, have a common language called Bislama (also spelled Bichelamar), which is a branch of so-called pidgin English. In this language, the inclusive first person plural is *yumi*, which derives from "you-me" in English. The exclusive first person plural is *mifala*, which comprises *mi* derived from "me" in English and a Bislama plural suffix *-fala*. They directly express the different natures of the two first person plural words.

Let us look at "we" based on the existence of these two types of first person plural pronouns. As von Humboldt (2006) is known to have discussed this point in *Ueber den Dualis*, I shall offer a general discussion on the linguistic traits of this first person by referring to his pioneering work[1].

Von Humboldt considers that pronouns form the bedrock of language. He thinks that first person and second person pronouns represent a primordial condition that originates from the fact that humans are beings that converse and interact. If there were only first person and second person – which is a purely methodological supposition – language would not have personal pronouns. The first and second person pronouns come into existence reflectively only when humans become aware of a third person and acquire a word for it. This view parallels my understanding of human relationships in the tetrahedral model.

I shall elaborate on this next. Despite the danger of addressing part of von Humboldt's extensive and remarkable argument, I would like to quote the following passage.

> Apart from all physical and sensual relationships, humans yearn for *you* as a counterpart to *I*. (von Humboldt 2006: 33)

This corresponds to the primordial model of a person meeting another person face-to-face in the first thesis. However, besides *you* our languages have a being represented by the pronoun *he* or *she* among people other than *I*. *He* or *she* is not the same as *I*. Borrowing von Humboldt's expression, it is because *I* and *he/she*:

> […] mean *I* and *non-I*. However, *you* are a type of *he/she* who faces *me*. *I* is based on inner perception while *he/she* is based on outer perception but *you* possess the spontaneity of choice. Although *you* is a type of *non-I*, […] it means that not only *non-I* but also *non-you* are contained in *he/she* itself. *He/she* opposes not only either [*I* or *you*] but also both of them. (von Humboldt 2006: 32)

This logic perfectly corresponds to our tetrahedral model. According to the model, a relationship spontaneously (there may be an underlying "yearning") arises between A and B because A and B are different individuals, and it can be described as the condition of the inclusive first person relationship *yumi*. Then, C, or *he* in von Humboldt's passage, appears as not only *non-I* but also *non-you*. In the language of the tetrahedral model, C (*he*) is already a being that cannot be controlled by A (*I*) ("uncontrollable" in the second thesis; Funabiki 2017: 313) in the sense that it has the opposing (meaning opposite in position, not confronting or competing) relationships CA (*non-I*) and CB (*non-you*) independently.

To rephrase in another way, the appearance of C (he) turns AB (we) as *yumi* (inclusive first person) into AB as *mifala* (exclusive first person). Of course, CA and CB become *mifala*, we as the exclusive first person, to B and A respectively. As a world comprising *yumi* "alone" is a mere methodological supposition, the present situation can be explained as follows with A as the subject.

A can form mutual *yumi* with B. However, C's existence is inevitable, and A and B are *mifala* to C. Each of AB, BC and CA is *yumi* within a bipartite relationship and *mifala* to the other party. For the bipartite relationships from A's perspective to acquire an expanse beyond here, or for the scenes that have already spread across the field with D, E, F… (behind B and C, as in the first thesis) to be taken as bipartite relationships (AD, AE, AF) and for the relationships to continue between three or more parties as an "institution", the emergence of α is necessary as well as inevitable.

Others as an affliction and its possibility

While this is hardly an exhaustive discussion, I have considered "others" using the examples of Mbotgote rituals, letters and exclusive and inclusive first person plural pronouns to supplement the tetrahedral model built in the first and second theses, and presented some of its applications.

The conclusion I reached after the first and second theses is that the human relationship is always a bipartite relationship, and a third party cannot have social relationships directly with A and B in their bipartite relationship because social relationships are formed by the layering of multiple bipartite relationships. The third party C enters respective bipartite relationships with A and B, who are in a bipartite relationship, by sharing α with them, and at the same time in doing so forms a social relationship with A and B. The model has been supplemented by the conclusion reached here, as we have confirmed a logical mechanism by which AB emerges as a "relationship" only when C appears, and B becomes "one of the others" to A only when C appears. A notices that B is an other to A only when A has the relationship AC. This can also mean that when "we" is a *yumi*, or an inclusive first person plural relationship, the existence of an "uncontrollable other" that is a source of affliction does not appear. A can see an "other" (C) when A encounters C and at the same time B emerges as an "other" to A.

What we find in *Kokoro* is the exclusive first person plural. The letter was for *yumi*, which were Sensei and "I". The letter was supposed to remain private. In the fictional setting of the novel, however, we are standing in the position of C to the *letter* from the beginning. Sensei and "I" are in the position of *mifala* from the standpoint of we the readers as C. Regardless of whether "Sensei and 'I'" are aware, I (we) form an inescapable spider's web-like *seken* (social circle) by involving "Sensei and 'I'" and mutually overlapping *mifala* with *mifala*. In this place, it is often the "exclusivity" rather than "we-ness" of *mifala* that causes suffering. What we find in Paul's letters is the inclusive first person plural. Paul as A wrote letters to B, which are *letters* assuming C from the beginning. Paul as A addresses B as we as *mifala*. However, Paul's letters are already equipped with a clever device as *letters* to draw C, D, E… into *mifala* as "brethren". The inclusive, Church-like intent to eventually turn all into followers of Christ, *mifala*, manifests clearly in his letters.

Perhaps others as an "affliction" suggested at the start of this chapter lies in a place between *yumi* and *mifala* where "we" cannot be located on the back of the base of the tetrahedral model. We previously paraphrased the affliction as "the uneasiness in finding that I don't understand the people around me", but it is firstly the discomfort of being unable to share α. This may be the problem of a transcendental "god" (α), or a sociological argument about the increasing scale and complexity that arises with the addition of C, D, E and so on. This chapter has not been able to address either of these issues fully. Nevertheless, it is possible to glean some hints. For instance, the new tool called the Social Networking Service

(SNS) that has emerged in our age can be regarded as the *letter* yearning for "others without afflictions" practically and without transcendence.

Now returning to our earlier case, the ritual performance rule for the substitutability of the second and third persons in *nimangki* rituals appears to be innovative. Others, including I, can change their roles in any manner. Although it is not the way everyday social relations operate in Mbotgote society, and it may seem like an expedient to ensure the survival of the rituals, we can see that a certain "invention" has taken place here in contrast with the strict nature of *nalawan* rituals.

I intend to try to place this expedient in the tetrahedron again, and review it from an angle different from the view of others as an affliction. I expect to see the emergence of the "transcendence" problem, which I placed outside of the scope of this chapter. No matter how much it is denied or altered, transcendence never ceases to be the focus of thinking in Western thought. In various societies outside of the West, however, "controllable transcendence" appears to be in the position of α in the tetrahedral model of human relations, despite its logical contradiction in, for example, the rituals of the Mbotgote group and the *seken* of Japan. We plan to consider what its tolerable limit is and whether it can become controllable transcendence without conflicting with the limit.

Notes

Introduction

1 For example, highly solitary animals may make contact only during the mating season.
2 My statement about "species-specific" may sound categorical, but I would like to qualify it by saying that in reality there are a considerable number of cases in which the social structure or social behavior (the manner of interacting with others) differs from one group to the next among conspecifics.
3 See Kimura (2010) for a detailed definition and usage of the word "interaction".
4 It is more appropriate to think that the evolution of sociality referred to here was already manifest at the time of the birth of humankind/hominins rather than emerged with the birth of the human species (modern humans, *Homo sapiens*).
5 The Japanese edition, *Shūdan: Jinrui shakai no shinka*, was published in December 2009 (Kawai (ed.) 2009).
6 The Japanese edition, *Seido: Jinrui shakai no shinka*, was published in 2013 (Kawai (ed.) 2013a).
7 Although *tasha* did not appear in the fourth edition of *Shin meikai kokugo jiten* (1997) at hand, I later found that the word made it into the fifth edition of the dictionary revised the following year (1998). The entry reads: "A person other than oneself who is considered to be a being standing opposed to oneself in some sense; a third person". It is a unique interpretation as usual.
8 A broader notion of "coexistence" is adopted here, including that between humans and animals and between humans and the environment, as well as between humans. This means that it involves a host of contemporary issues such as endangered species and environmental damage.
9 See Funabiki (1997) for details.
10 However, the word "actor" or "subject" is sometimes used to mean the party engaging in an action or behavior, as in Chapter One and Chapter Sixteen.

Chapter 1

1 In addition, when human children are shown a suggested solution to a problem, they concentrate on following the process of the model solution even though they know they can get to the goal very easily (Whiten et al. 1996). In my view, this indicates that human children face a problem by identifying with adults,

and this seems to provide an explanation for some curious traits of human infants and children such as their obedience to adults and conservatism.
2. As I consider that the expression of a need to be approved and a joy of achievement is an important factor in the transformation from anthropoid society to human society, I would like to remain cautious about their existence or otherwise while I wait in anticipation for the appearance of researchers who take an interest in this theme and study it further. With regard to the expression of a joy of achievement, a comparable phenomenon has been observed in bonobos and chimpanzees where every individual at the scene watches with bated breath one individual's act and both the actor and the spectators erupt into huge cheers when the act is successfully performed (de Waal 1987; Kuroda 1982). In a similar example, Sugiyama (1981) reports that when a chimpanzee in Bossou made a great effort to reach a faraway fig branch and finally moved onto it, onlookers cheered loudly and the chimpanzee ran around madly for two minutes on the tree forgetting about eating figs. However, it is not easy to determine whether these were cases of the expression of a joy of achievement. In the case of Bossou, it is normal for a male chimpanzee, upon reaching a large branch full of fruit, to make a fuss by vocalizing loudly for from a few minutes to over five minutes before he starts feeding, regardless of whether he found the branch easily or not, and one interpretation for this behavior is that he is calling females as they are drawn to the uproar.
3. If they are still unattended after such attempts, they become unresponsive to calls and even food (Kuroda 1982).
4. Morphologically, the bonobo is a neotenic-type animal whose upper body in maturity remains at the infant or adolescent stage of chimpanzee, and its attachment to its mother indicates a neotenic tendency in its behavior and disposition as well (Kuroda 1999).

Chapter 2

1. The following conditions are not mutually exclusive nor do they cover all of the existing concepts of others. It is not my intention to say which condition is better than the rest. The task at hand in this chapter is to sort out the situation, albeit insufficiently, in order to determine whether each condition is applicable to animals.
2. There remains the vexing question of what "species" is in a strict sense. The assumption involves the case in which animals are excluded for only the

reason that they are "not human" (without examining other conditions). As we shall see later, the expression "the same species as h" is used so that the same format can be used for animals for the sake of convenience.

3. According to Azuma (2001), humans are demonstrably different from animals in that the former have "intersubjective desire" whereas the latter have only individual or subjective "appetite". It may sound as if the word "intersubjective" does not assume independent individuals. However, Azuma explains that "intersubjective desire" means "the desire of the other is itself desired". If this is the case, it is "I" (ego) who "desires (the desire of the other)" and therefore the existence of "the other" (alter ego) who has desire that is different from "my" desire becomes the fundamental assumption.

4. It derives from a Greek word meaning "those who speak an unfamiliar language" (Maekawa 1998). It is the origin of the English word "barbarian", and is said to have carried a "derogatory" connotation toward outsiders such as Persians as against the Hellenes with a strong sense of community living inside closed *poleis*. According to a presentation given by Sumihiko Kumano, a Japanese philosopher, at one of the meetings of the Otherness Research Project that formed the foundation of this volume, only the Hellenes (i.e., citizens) were considered "human".

5. Naturally, this condition varies depending on the meaning of "to interact socially". The expression here is used to signify interactions that are distinct from, for instance, "physical/chemical interactions". Just as I leave open what can be substituted for X in Condition 1(h) or Y in Condition 2(h), I try to widen the scope of what can be substituted for "to interact socially" here.

6. Even if the parties do not exchange words directly, they have "encountered" and are "co-present" in a broader sense here. If this is included in the meaning of "to interact socially", Condition 3(h)-2 becomes unnecessary.

7. It should be noted that this statement is made only in reference to Condition 3(h). For example, Nagel never doubts that the bat has "experience". Consequently, the bat can be the other if "experience" is substituted for X in Condition 1(h).

8. Just as the aforementioned imaginary companion, some people may argue that it is possible to interact with people on TV. In that case, those on TV become others to the viewers. However, does turning the TV off mean "vanishing" the others at will unilaterally?

9. It may sound similar to Condition 0(a), but it is different in effect. Only chimpanzees can be others to a chimpanzee (i.e., those who resemble oneself)

under Condition 0(*a*), whereas others are non-chimpanzees (i.e., those who are different from oneself) under this condition.
10 Yet, many researchers think that only humans have the ability to "imagine" (e.g., Mitchell (ed.) 2002).
11 Leopards are known to return to a decomposing carcass to eat its flesh.
12 Chimpanzees do not encounter bushpigs and aardvarks very often, as the former are diurnal and the latter are nocturnal. Even when they encounter them, these nocturnal animals run away quickly and chimpanzees have little time to observe them closely.
13 Some may argue that this is simply replacing the mysterious term "others" with another mysterious term "social". The term "others" strongly evokes the term "self" as its opposing concept, and it is considerably difficult to find out directly whether animals have a concept of "self" and if so, what it is. On the other hand, we are able to observe whether animals are behaving socially without finding out whether they have "self", and the term "social" is being used with few objections in animal behavioral science fields as well. Accordingly, the latter term has wider use in evolutionary historical discussions that include animals.
14 Early primatologists in Japan actively exploited this aspect. For instance, Masao Kawai (1964) explained the *kyokan* (empathic) method, one of the unique methodologies of Japanese primatology, as a method "to appreciate the lives of monkeys through experiencing them by living with them, blending in with them, and establishing emotional channels for reciprocal communication". In this case, researchers clearly read "others" into their research subjects. Later on, this type of approach came to be called "anthropomorphism" (Nishida 1999a, among others) with a negative connotation. Yet, it is true that a complete elimination of anthropomorphism makes observation and interpretation extremely uninteresting.

Chapter 4

1 Luhmann (1993) regards social systems as the foundation of his social theory and describes three types of such systems: interaction systems, organizational systems and societal systems. See Kitamura (2014, 2015) for more detailed explanations of communication in interaction systems.
2 I have conducted a detailed analysis of this approach based on the case of the Turkana pastoralists in East Africa who have been the subject of my research over many years (Kitamura, in press).

Chapter 5

1. The phenomenon of infanticide is found in many primate species, but it is peculiar in chimpanzees in that some of the observed cases of infanticide were committed by males who could have been the biological father of the victim in the same group and were accompanied by cannibalism.
2. Affordance is a concept put forward by ecological psychologist J. J. Gibson and refers to resources and information provided to animals by the environment. In ecological psychology, such resources and information are thought to afford opportunities for animal actors to act.
3. The chimpanzees of the Taï National Park, Côte D'Ivoire, are known for collaboration between multiple hunters, who assume different roles in hunting the same prey, in group hunting activity (Boesch and Boesch 1989). This is very triadic in the sense that they understand each other's intentions and cooperate.
4. The evolution of organisms by natural selection is influenced by not only the number of offspring left behind by an individual organism, but also by the successful reproduction by its blood relatives that share the same genes.
5. In this sense, it seems that nepotism has a greater impact on human society, who form larger kinship groups, than in chimpanzees and bonobos.
6. Each primate species has its specific Basic Social Unit (BSU) (Itani 1987). The unit-group is a BSU. In Japanese macaques, for example, an aggregation with a matrilineal structure is the BSU as well as the unit-group. Although the BSU in chimpanzees has the same multi-male, multi-female structure as in Japanese macaques, its constituent members do not aggregate all at once, as individuals constantly merge and separate within the group. Because they constantly form small temporary parties, it is unclear if the term "group" refers to the temporary group or the unit-group. For this reason, Japanese primatologists use the term "unit-group" for the BSU in chimpanzees. Outside of Japan, the unit-group is called a "community" (Goodall 1990).
7. The oldest hominin (the tribe *Hominini*) fossils are of *Sahelanthropus tchadensis*, dated around seven million years old, and found in Chad, Central Africa.
8. In this chapter, early hominins refers to hominins other than the genus *Homo* and early humans refers to early *Homo* species.
9. In view of the evolution of the entire order *Primates*, Nakagawa (2013) points out that female-biased dispersal is a widespread geographic dispersal tendency among all anthropoids and must have been found in early humans as well.
10. The earliest stone tools from 3.3 million years ago were recently discovered in Kenya.

11 The enlargement process of the brain plateaued about 1.8 million years ago and started again around 600,000 years ago (Mithen 2006).
12 Lovejoy (2009) argues that monogamous society existed at the early hominin stage based on very little difference in the size of canine teeth between males and females in *Ardipithecus ramidus*. Nakagawa (2013) also points to the possibility of monogamous society in early hominins.
13 I would like to think that if pair-bonding between a male and a female already existed at the time of early hominins, early hominin couples would have stayed together and ranged together constantly, just as hamadryas baboons do.
14 What Funabiki (2017; Epilogue) calls "α as a sign with a symbolic effect" would not have emerged at this stage. Although communication using some kind of signs might have existed at the *Homo erectus* stage, a further development of cognitive capacity that had been made since *Homo heidelbergensis* would have been needed for the assignment of a symbolic function to signs.

Chapter 6

1 It is generally believed that a subordinate individual utters a pant-grunt at a dominant individual.
2 Because it is difficult to follow chimpanzees in deep undergrowth in the forest, animal trails used by chimpanzees and other animals have been hewed to create a network of research trails about one meter wide.
3 It is possible to say that it (the chimpanzee way of interaction) is characterized by leaving one to the contingency of the counterpart's action, which is beyond one's decision-making capacity, and connecting one's action directly to the counterpart's action. This "leaving oneself to the contingency" of the other's action is made possible by a certain kind of attitude that can be called "hardiness" or "cognitive toughness" in the sense that they have tolerance for being subjected to a state of uncertainty for a prolonged period (Nishie 2010: 394).

Chapter 7

1 See also the argument in Maturana and Varela (1991) that living systems are cognitive systems.
2 Soft vocalization produced at various pitches (Nishida et al. 2010). In terms of a mother and an infant, the latter may whimper in fear when it is separated from its mother or in frustration when breast-feeding is refused, for example, while whimpers are also produced in various other contexts.

Whimpering sometimes escalates to screaming. It appears that whimpering at least draws the attention of other chimpanzees. Cases have been observed where another juvenile comes to groom or hug a whimpering juvenile. I will continue to include this type of note about chimpanzee behaviors as much as possible hereafter, but I must point out that chimpanzee behaviors are highly ambiguous and it is difficult to assign an unambiguous relationship connecting each behavior to its function or meaning.

3 See also Chapter Six by Nishie.
4 String is sometimes used for measuring distances and eventually degrades into the soil.
5 Needless to say, it was also a pressing matter for myself at the start of this encounter. Unlike our life in the city where branches are lopped before they fall and trees are removed before they topple, we never know what will happen in the forest.
6 Nishie (2010) calls these "process-oriented interactions" (see also interactions by long-range vocalization in chimpanzees in Hanamura (2010b), and Chapter Eight by Hanamura) and describes the unique attitude found there as "cognitive toughness" (see also Chapter Six by Nishie). This term aptly reflects the indeterminacy of chimpanzees to humans as well as the uniquely chimpanzee trait.
7 It is typically uttered by a subordinate individual at a dominant individual at the time of their encounter (Nishida et al. 2010). However, the "meaning" of this vocalization is less than clear-cut, as is their rank order (see also Chapter Six by Nishie, Nishie 2017 and Chapter One by Kuroda).
8 An open-mouth kiss differs from a standard kiss, as the mouth is open wide for the duration. Sometimes one party kisses the counterpart's body with its mouth open. This is thought to be performed in a state of social excitement (Nishida et al. 2010).
9 "Cognitive toughness" (Nishie 2010, Chapter Six by Nishie).
10 Yabuta (2008) describes a cross-contextual display, which is a display used in more than one context (such as in fighting and courting), as an evolutionarily-fixed displacement behavior to fill a "pause" (a temporal break taken before an action is carried out for the purpose of risk reduction in animal encounters) and to connect actions. In this chapter, a display is an activity to create an *interstice* for both parties and in this sense the taking of a "pause" itself is regarded as a display.

11 The actual appropriate distance would vary from one species or group to another. Among Japanese macaques, for example, those of Awaji Island are known to maintain a very short distance between individuals.

Chapter 8

1 See Itoh (2017) and Chapter Seven for the seasonal variation of M group's ranging and grouping patterns.
2 Kuroda (2013) finds a communitas type situation in the unification of individuals of the same group mediated by interactions with the individuals of another group, and regards it as an anti-structural aspect underpinning the structure of chimpanzee society. On the other hand, this chapter focuses on the anti-structural nature of their group living itself, where they are usually able to live without such unification.
3 The "enemy" can be another name for others (no longer others) whose otherness cannot be fit into any existing frames of relationship (or institutions) and hence must be destroyed by violence. When encountering strangers, humans have often resorted to the invocation of violence and the generally unilateral reclaiming of such violence into institutions (i.e., legitimization/justification) such as "enlightenment of the uncivilized" and "holy war".
4 When chimpanzees belonging to different groups visually encounter each other in a calmer situation without this type of context, they are able to attempt to engage in a non-hostile association by using their behavioral repertoire. In fact, resident individuals quickly come to repeat non-hostile co-presence with newly immigrated females, who in many cases suddenly turn up alone, although at first some of them show an ambivalent attitude (see Itoh 2013 and Chapter Two by Nakamura).
5 See Kawai (2002b) for a detailed example of the process of materialization of the "enemy" in human society, and Bar-Tal (2011) for numerous examples in human society and a review from a social-psychological perspective.
6 In the case of humans, though much more complex because of the historical and political contexts largely affected or invented by the politics among big powers, we have materialized such boundaries all over the world at least since recorded history by building abhorrent walls or fences, which seem to be increasing especially lately (for various examples see Novosseloff and Neisse 2008; Wiedenhöfer 2013; Spottorno and Abril 2016).
7 There might be cases in which a single group had split into two groups in the

past, as in the case of Gombe, but hostility between them decreased and both groups have managed to survive to date.

Chapter 9

1 I have published a number of studies on the oscillation between the two opposing relationships characterized by hostility and non-hostility (Kawai 2004, 2009, 2013 and others).
2 The Dodoth live in two forms of dwelling, namely, a semi-sedentary robust settlement where they spend a relatively long time (*ere*), and a basic animal camp that undergoes frequent relocation (*awi*: also called "livestock camp" or "satellite camp"). Elderly people, women and children under the age of seven to ten live in the former, while unmarried men and married young men (and occasionally middle-aged men) live in the latter. The majority of livestock are taken to animal camps, while lactating cows supplying milk for human consumption and their calves are left at settlements.
3 However, as well as the Turkana, they often targeted the Jie, their southern neighbors. Similarly, the Jie have raided the Dodoth with relatively high frequency (Kawai 2004).
4 The Dodoth actively work their fields in years with good rain as they have an annual rainfall of around 450 millimeters, enabling them to cultivate sorghum, pearl millet, other cereal crops and maize during the rainy season. Although they appreciate the value of farming, they do not place too much reliance on it as a livelihood because crop failures due to lack of rain are not uncommon.
5 Unlike the Dodoth, the Turkana do not have a semi-sedentary "settlement" (*ere*) with huts inside a robust enclosure. The Turkana have a dual residence system, like the Dodoth, with a "large camp" (*awi napoleon*) where married couples, young children and old people live and an animal camp (*awi*: satellite camp) for each animal species where unmarried men and women live but, unlike the Dodoth, they never build mud-walled and thatched-roofed huts at these camps.
6 A similar phenomenon is found among the camel-herding peoples of "proto-Rendille-Somali (PRS) culture" in East Africa, including the Rendille, Garre, Gabra and Sakuye (Schlee 1989).
7 Sagawa, who has been surveying and studying the pastoral Daasanach people in southwestern Ethiopia, describes a quality almost the same as "peoples oriented toward subsisting on livestock rearing" (Sagawa 2011).
8 Such patterns include surrounding an animal camp before dawn and

ambushing at particular points near watering places or on routes to grazing areas.
9. The Dodoth's western neighbors are the farming people of Acholi, and their northeastern neighbors are the Ik whose main livelihoods are hunting and honey collecting. The Dodoth either have almost no relationship with them or tend to treat them as "weaker" peoples. These attitudes are clearly different from the way they relate to the Turkana and other pastoralist neighbors. To the Dodoth, the Acholi and the Ik are more like "strangers-others" existing on an entirely different plane than the others discussed here (Kawai in print).
10. This tendency is called "independence syndrome", a widely known characteristic of East African pastoral peoples.

Chapter 10

1. Translator's note: I have used "responsibility" for both *sekinin* (responsibility) and *seme* (charge, liability) (see Note 2) in the translation as it is generally used in English without regard for this particular distinction, aside from avoiding the use of active verbs to collocate with "responsibility".
2. This chapter adopts the concept of subjectivity as outlined in Lévinas's *Sonzai no Kanata he* (1999b) that differs from the way it is used in *Zentaisei to mugen* (Lévinas 2005a, 2006) (Kumano 1999, 2012). However, I have quoted passages from the latter in the beginning as I consider that they overlap to the extent that the primordial sociality involves the imposition of an infinite responsibility by the Other on one who approaches the Other, as well as the questioning of one's freedom in light of the Other's infinite demands, and that this sociality is the very condition of human subjectivity. In the Japanese language, the word *sekinin* (responsibility) is used in the quote from the former for *responsabilité* according to Gōda's translation, whereas the word *seme* (charge, liability) is used in the rest of the chapter following Kumano's use (1999, 2012). This is because I agree with Kumano's view that Lévinas's *responsibilité* is "more passive than all passivity and never a thing to 'take on' actively" (Kumano 2012). While I owe much of my interpretation of Lévinas in this chapter to Kumano (1999, 2012), I am solely to blame for all errors arising from my misinterpretation.
3. This chapter is a companion piece to my article on trauma in Lévinas's work on the Other (Omura, 2018).
4. When I actually asked an elder what "a wise, good person" would be, he gave me an answer to the effect that "a person with the breadth of mind to laugh

and who can even laugh at themselves to make others laugh". This pertains to the qualities we have been discussing such as being open to others, avoiding hostility, not invading others' autonomy, being willing to share generously in dealing with others and dealing with any situation resourcefully and flexibly with equanimity and calm. In other words, being both affectionate and reasonable is the requirement for "real Inuit".

5 In her ethnographic studies, Briggs (1968, 1970) memorably describes the strong vigilance exercised by the Inuit against domination and control. We can also surmise their strong vigilance against the exploitation of their actions to treat the other as "the Other" from the recurrence of this theme in their myths and folklore (Boas 2011; Saitō et al. 2009). A typical example is the story of Atanarjuat, which was made into a film by Isuma Igloolik Productions that won the Caméra d'Or at Cannes. During my fieldwork, the most common criticism I heard whispered against someone was "He wants to be a boss", which also points to their vigilance in this regard.

6 This problem compares with Luhmann's double contingency (1993). By the way, I have a strong sense that the problem of betrayal in interaction is missing from Lévinas's argument. Squarely addressing my intuition was the starting point of this chapter. If every subject is already and always responding to the call of the Other and burdened with a responsibility for the Other, theoretically all human beings are burdened with a responsibility for the Other. However, we cannot rule out the appearance of some subjects who ignore or reject this responsibility. In fact, it is no exaggeration to say that the history of humankind is one of betrayals by shirking responsibility for the Other. This act of betrayal and eliminating and diminishing the Other to an object of domination and control has been discussed and criticized as "Orientalism" in postcolonial and postmodern anthropology (Omura 2005). One of the goals of this chapter is to squarely face the human act of shirking responsibility for the Other.

7 The Inuit people have been exposed to waves of dramatic change in all aspects of life since they were transitioned from their seasonally migrational lifestyle to a sedentary one under the Canadian government's assimilation policy of the 1950s and 1960s. Consequently, they live in a consumer society just like ours today. Yet, Inuit subsistence activities have not lost their importance as the basis for their life and identity. Their methods have certainly changed greatly, and many of the hunters combine wage labor with subsistence activities. This is because hunting and other subsistence activities are now highly mechanized with the use of high-powered rifles, snowmobiles,

FWD buggies, metal boats with outboard motors and other equipment, and they need cash to acquire and maintain these items as well as to purchase fuel and ammunition. Nevertheless, subsistence activities are practiced actively to the extent that "Those who do not engage in subsistence activities are not considered to be Inuit" (Omura 2013; Stewart 1995, 1996). While the purchase of processed food with cash income has become a common practice, animal meat acquired in subsistence activities is favored as "real food" (*niqinmarik*) that is essential for the preservation of their ethnic identity, and the sharing of the hunted meat continues to function as one of the keystones in maintaining their social relationships (Kishigami 1995, 1996, 2007; Stewart 1995; Wenzel 1991).

8   A social group that forms the basis for Inuit social relations is a kinship group called *ilagiit*, and an extended family group called *ilagiimariktut* (real *ilagiit*) within it functions as the basic unit for everyday social relations. The *ilagiit* is a group of "related people who may go away but come back and then share food, help each other, and stay together" (Balikci 1989: 112), suggesting that food sharing is a core practice of a social group. The *ilagiimariktut* refers to "members of an extended family group who live in the same place and have close relations in economic and other activities, i.e., those who form a concrete social group. As a result, the latter (*ilagiimariktut*) is generally comprised of one's parents, siblings, wife, children, grandchildren, uncles, aunties, grandparents and cousins" (Kishigami and Stewart 1994). Associations are formed that have this *ilagiimariktut* at their core and that transcend kinship groups – quasi-kinship relationships, such as adoption, and voluntary associations, such as name-saking relationships and avoidance relationships. In this way complex social relationships are created with extended family at their core.

9   The fear of someone in the extended family group trying to dominate and control the others by monopolizing and dispensing all food always exists. The fear of a despot who eliminates and diminishes the others as "the Other" to an object of domination and control is a recurring theme in myths and folklore (Boas 2011; Saitō et al. 2009), and remains the worst fear of the Inuit people.

10 Therein lies the vulnerability of the Inuit subsistence system. The system cannot eliminate freeloaders who consume food without making any contribution. Elders reported that there actually were some freeloaders, but they were not subjected to any social sanctions except that people criticized them behind their backs. Freeloaders often appear in Inuit myths and folklore (Saitō et al. 2009).

11 See my companion article (Omura 2018) for a detailed discussion of the process in which children are made aware of their responsibility for others.

Chapter 11
1 "The other" can be created at the individual level in the sense that one recognizes a being with a subjectivity that is different to one's own. However, we concentrate on the collectively formed "other" in this chapter, and the individual-level "other" is referred to as "the other individual", unless otherwise stated.
2 With the analogy of drama used by Zuddendorf, Takenoshita considers what "the other" is for a human who is "a being who acts out a narrative" and finds in the self the duality between the self as the actor and director (self = actor) and the self as the character performed in the narrative (self = character). This framework has something in common with Hermans and Kempen's idea of the dialogical self quoted here.
3 These monographic descriptions below are based on data collected from the 1980s to the late 1990s. The worship rituals of ancestral spirits such as finger millet harvesting, net hunting and occasional gathering of *ngulu* spirit mediums had been maintained as Audrey Richards mentioned in 1939 until the late 1980s. However, those rituals related to net hunting and the gathering of *ngulu* spirit mediums disappeared after the drastic change of the government's land policy and the national economic system, due to the introduction of the Structural Adjustment Program.
4 The post-colonial land system of the country has been community ownership based on this political structure. The headman is recognized by the chief and given the authority to use the land in the area at the same time. It had been customary until recently that villagers were able to cultivate and use the land in the area freely, but they could not own it privately (Oyama 2011).
5 Zambia stopped reporting ethnic group-based population statistics after it became independent in 1964. The currently available statistics are based on routinely spoken languages.
6 Anger must be expressed verbally in a public forum. It is said that if anger remains unexpressed in public and the person who has that anger utters it privately, the angry words turn into witchcraft and invoke the ancestral spirits' anger (Sugiyama 2017).
7 I found out about this episode in the following year.
8 For instance, in the healing ritual for a young woman conducted in December

1985, it was said that the young woman suffered misfortunes because a relative on her husband's side had aroused anger in the ancestral spirits. The accused male relative protested his innocence, but he was persuaded by other relatives to go to the woman's village and participate in her healing ritual. As a result of the healing ritual and medicine from a town clinic, she recovered (according to an interview with the woman in 1987). If a patient is diagnosed with witchcraft carried out by the illicit lover of their spouse, the witch doctor uses witchcraft to countervail it rather than calling for the attendance of the lover.
9 In matrilineal society, a maternal uncle and the sons of his sisters are in a structurally competitive relationship over political power (Turner 1972).
10 It also relates to the other as the suffering subject and the afflicted other (see the Epilogue by Funabiki).

Chapter 12

1 Just as in Japan, they remove the cover (a cloth or casket lid) and view the face to pay their final respects.
2 Kokuritsu Kagaku Hakubutsukan "Dai kao ten" (Great exhibition of faces), http://www.kahaku.go.jp/special/past/kao-ten/kao/kao-index.html (accessed 18 October 2015).

   Regarding facial expression recognition, it has been reported that an experiment by a Kyoto University team has found that humans begin to acquire the ability to read the other's thoughts by "reading the face" from around the age of three-and-a-half (before they acquire the ability to guess the other's mind through language at the age of four to four-and-a-half). A similar experiment on chimpanzees found no attentive face watching. This does not necessarily mean that chimpanzees "do not read faces"; it only means that they did not attentively watch the other's face under certain conditions of the experiment (*Mainichi Shimbun*, 5 November 2015).
3 Nihon Kao Gakkai (Japanese Academy of Facial Studies) was established in 1995 with a broad-based membership of researchers, including psychologists, anthropologists, engineers, dentistry researchers and neuroscientists (http://www.jface.jp/jp).
4 The worldwide Islamic revivalist movement is wielding influence in various forms in Thailand as well. Da'wa comes from the Arabic word Da'wah, meaning "calling others to Islam", and originally referred to the proselytizing

of non-Muslims to Islam. In the Islamic revivalist movement, however, Da'wa has developed as mission work within Muslim societies (Kosugi 2002). In Thailand, in most cases Da'wa refers to Tablighi Jama'at or Jama'ah Tabligh. The Da'wa movement is characterized by repetitive acts and simplified teachings. The Da'wa movement upholds the "return to Sunni Islam" as the ultimate goal. Sunni is an Islamic lifestyle that views the life of the Prophet Muhammad as the ideal. Accordingly, the *Ahadith* as the records of the words and actions of Muhammad is treated as an important guide, and the six articles of faith and five pillars of Islam, the central faith of Islam, also carry detailed rules to be followed in daily life.

5 According to Ōtsuka (2004), the Islamic revivalist movement here refers to the social and cultural phenomena that position Islam as the basis for identity in response to the influences of Western-style modernization on twentieth-century Muslim society. The term is used differently than Islamism, which refers to the political ideology and movement of those who choose Islam as their political ideology and engage in a reformist movement on that basis (Ōtsuka 2004: 10–15).

6 This chapter draws mainly on data collected in two fortnight-long surveys conducted in Mae Sot in December 2012 and December 2013. They are supplemented by findings from a village of Muslim-Buddhist mixed residents in Satun Province, southern Thailand, where I have been carrying out ethnographic research since 1989 on an ongoing basis.

7 Lévinas's "face" is that of the unreachable other. Lévinas explains this as follows. "In it [the face] the infinite resistance of a being to our power affirms itself precisely against the murderous will that it defies; because, completely naked (and the nakedness of the face is not a figure of style), the face signifies itself" (Lévinas 1999a: 361). An individual does not exist first; the existence of the other allows the individual to exist. The "face" emerges there, mediated by death as the ethics of "You should not commit murder". In philosophy, discussions surrounding the face have two main streams, namely Lévinas-like *non-phenomenal* ethics and Merleau-Ponty's lineage of *phenomenological* theory of perception (Kobayashi 1998: 232).

8 The use of veils in Muslim women began to draw attention from 1975 in the international proliferation of women's studies inspired by the United Nations Decade for Women. It has been discussed in terms of the progression from deveiling as women's liberation in the midst of modernization from the end

of the nineteenth century, to reveiling in the current of Islamic revival that started in Egypt in the 1970s (Nakayama 1999; Ōkawa 2000; Shioya 2012; Gotō 2014).

9 There are broadly two groups of Muslims in northern Thailand: a community of Indian, Pakistani and Bangladeshi Muslims and a community of Chinese Muslims from Yunnan Province. As the Da'wa movement began in India and Haji Yusuf Kan himself was Indian Muslim, it gained ground among South Asian Muslims first and eventually spread to Chinese Muslims.

10 Muslims entering into Mae Sot are Myanmar Muslims from the Thai-Myanmar border area. The Rohingya are another group of Muslims living near the Myanmar-Bangladesh border.

11 At a Burmese-speaking *talim*, there were twenty-three participants (twenty-two of whom wore face-covering veils) on 31 August 2012 and twenty-six participants (all wore veils) on 27 December 2013. I participated in a Thai-speaking *talim* on 22 December with twelve female participants, of which four were Burmese Muslims. They all wore face-covering veils and all Thai Muslims were collected by their husbands after the meeting with no service of tea or sweets. I had the impression that the Burmese-speaking *talim* was more active.

12 All names used in this chapter are pseudonyms.

13 A Thai Muslim woman at the meeting translated it from Burmese into Thai.

14 Thin Indian-style flat bread or crepes made from flour and water and rolled with sugar or condensed milk inside. They are often sold at food stalls with hot-plates operated by South Asian people.

15 One baht is equivalent to approximately 3.4 yen, as at October 2015. One hundred baht is about one third of the minimum daily wage for laborers.

16 E. Gotō (2014) describes the aspect of wearing a veil for God with regard to the phenomenon of increased veil (hijab) use among contemporary Egyptian women.

17 The offering of prayer five times a day is the second duty of Muslims among the five pillars of Islam. The prayer times are: Fajr between the first light of dawn and sunrise, followed by Dhuhr at midday, Aṣr in the afternoon, Maghrib at sunset and Isha'a between the disappearance of the white twilight and Fajr.

18 Chiba explains as follows. "In *Ethica*, the first step to expand 'the body's power of acting' is an 'affection' from other bodies. [...] triggered by this affective incitement, our bodies are inclined toward a different condition. Our 'pleasure

or pain, joy or sorrow' will increase or decrease according to the intensity of sunlight. This type of sustained becoming is the 'affect'" (2013: 347).
19 Luhmann places the difference between the self and the other in a primordial situation in which the "social" comes into existence. See his argument on double contingency (Luhmann 1993).

Chapter 13

1 While there are a large number of philosophical studies on others, I shall mention a study by Schütz (1967) discussing *the other* from a sociological perspective.
2 Of course, not all practices can be separated along the lines of morality and instrumentality.
3 See also Chapter Eighteen by Tokoro for a perspective similar to a practical approach that emphasizes context-dependence.
4 For instance, Masao Yamaguchi's (2000) center-periphery argument is a typical example of the structural approach, but its core is a peripheral existence, i.e., the stranger.
5 Sahlins's (1972) argument attempting to typify exchanges can be interpreted as the typification of *the other* via exchange practices.
6 Funded via a Grant-in-Aid for Scientific Research on Innovative Areas (2).
7 Accessed on 13 June 2015 at http://www.mext.go.jp/component/a_menu/science/detail/__icsFiles/afieldfile/2010/12/22/1300741_001.pdf.
8 For the bonding-type negative social capital to operate efficiently, it requires an enemy (sacrificial goat). It is not that negative social capital strengthens bonds and results in the exclusion of outside groups; rather, bonds within the group are strengthened by creating an enemy for exclusion outside of the group (Tanaka 2013). Unfortunately, we cannot find this perspective in theories on social capital.
9 See Wolf (1965) for patron-client relationships and Nicholas (1965) for factions.
10 See Tanaka (2014a) for a discussion on whether prostitution/sex work is considered to be work.
11 See Tanaka (2012) for further details on honor killings.
12 According to Basu (2013).
13 Strictly speaking, occupational group-based castes are divided into many local groups (sub-castes), which have been endogamous.
14 See Grossman (1995) on psychological resistance to killing at the time of war.

We must not generalize that the act of killing does not accompany moral relationships. In many hunter-gatherer societies, people do not employ the tactic of depersonalizing animals. On the contrary, animals that are the targets of hunts are understood as beings with rich personality, as mentioned by Omura in Chapter Ten and Tokoro in Chapter Eighteen. They maintain their personality (animal identity?) when they are slaughtered and cooked until they are eaten and digested. For many hunter-gatherer peoples in Mongolia, Siberia and the Arctic, there is an individual called the Master Spirit among large game animals (Konagaya 1994). Each animal they hunt is seen as a messenger of the Master. After an interaction between a hunter and an animal, the animal is killed. The animal is regarded as a gift from the Master and the human is obliged to offer a counter-performance. What is found here is a gifting relationship between the human and the Master over an individual animal. The killing of the animal by the hunter signifies the continuation of the relationship between humans and the animal Master, rather than the end of the relationship between a human and an animal. Nevertheless, the relationship between the animal Master and human beings should not be regarded as an insider relationship. As I mention below, it is perhaps more appropriate to regard the animal Master as the stranger.

15 Although it is possible to see the Jews in extermination camps as outsiders, there was no long-term relationship between them and their Nazi captors.

16 As in the world portrayed by Kazuo Ishiguro in *Never Let Me Go* (2005), or the boy under "protection" in *Get the Gringo* (2012), a US film directed by Adrian Grunberg.

17 We can suppose that the "Master Spirit" mentioned in Note 11 above is one of such beings.

Chapter 14

1 In the area I have surveyed, it is said that each family (household) has one plant of this invisible "flower", which grows at the base of one of the four pillars supporting a firewood shelf above the hearth in each living room. Damaging this pillar is taboo, as doing so is thought to cause conflict in the community. In other areas, it is conceptualized as a clump of plants rather than one "flower" (Uchibori 2002; Uchibori and Yamashita 2006).

2 An ordinary Iban person, that is to say, not a shaman, told me "The world looks different to shamans from that to *iban*". The word *iban* has the connotation of "non-shamanic" person. Besides shamans, the bards who chant ritual songs

at ceremonies – called *lemanbang* – refer to infiltration into another layer, although it is purely in the process of narration. Unlike shamans, they do not go into a trance state, even as a formality. Yet, they chant a phrase that invokes "the return of the soul" after chanting the main story of the song (Uchibori 2006). The soul referred to here is closer to a "life force" rather than an agent who can act (see Note 4).

3   The explanation that the soul leaves its wakeful-state station during dreaming is fundamentally contradictory, as it is unclear as to how to reconcile that with the temporary separation of the soul and body at times of illness, or with the permanent separation after death. The persistence of this contradiction or ambiguity without contention proves that the folk theory about the soul is not logically integrated. A historical example of turning inconsistency into something consistent can be found in ancient Greece, and I would have liked to have called this section "Plato in the tropical rainforest" to play on it (Ide 1967).

4   It is clear from this that *semengat* in the Iban language is not a mere vital force or life substance. As suggested by the ritual act of *kering semengat* (to "strengthen the soul" by biting a woodman's knife or another iron article), however, some say that multiple souls reside in different parts of the human body (Jensen 1974). It is possible to find a more or less substantive aspect there. The word spelt and pronounced *semangat* in Malay corresponds to *semengat* in Iban, but the Malay word is largely used to indicate "spirit", as in a spirit of chivalry or the Japanese spirit. It is certainly different from the Iban's concept of the word in this regard, but it is not totally unrelated. I used *semengat* for nearly forty years until I spelt it as *semangat* for the first time in 2014 (Uchibori 2014). I did so preemptively in response to a movement to revise the orthography of the Romanized Iban language, but one Iban cultural activist pointed out to me that it was incorrect. It is very interesting to know that some activists loathe equating *semengat* in Iban with *semangat* in Malay conceptually in today's political climate, but I shall refrain from discussing this here as it is beyond the scope of this section.

5   I would like to point out that the word *utai* somehow corresponds to the Japanese expression for an evil spirit, *mononoke* (literally "the power of a thing") (see Freeman (1967) for the incubus that attacks women).

6   It contains a vast number of stories and began to attract the attention of literary historians early on (Chadwick and Chadwick 1932–40). In Sarawak, dozens of stories have been collected and published by public and private literary agencies

so far, and it is considered to form the nucleus of "objectified" Iban culture, as new works are being created even today. A public holiday was established by the government at the end of the 1970s on which an event called *Gawai Dayak* (the festival of the Dayak peoples, including the Iban) is held, involving the staging of beauty contests across Sarawak. The contest winners in the Iban communities are called Kumang. The winners of contests for young males, which are less of a drawing card, are called Keling.

7 "Cumbersome" was the word used by an elderly man, who was also an expert on Iban rituals and a local authority on bird augury, and this feeling, a dislike for the need to take various ritualistic measures against *antu*, including *petara*, is certainly one of the motives for their conversion to Christianity.

Chapter 16

1 It is possible that the predator chimpanzees did not approach the mixed-species associations because they were watched by human observers, and the same may apply to the aerial predators.
2 It is highly likely that there is a process for storing the memory of feeding places in something similar to a cognitive map, but that for referencing all data history is improbable. From my personal experience, this is perhaps the same for humans who supposedly have advanced cognitive capacity.

Chapter 17

1 Life forms that are phylogenetically remote from humans such as insects may have some subjectivity recognition system that is different from ours, but this constitutes "the other that is dissimilar to the self", which is outside the scope of our discussion here.
2 If the infant being tested were a nonconformist who likes the villain better than the hero, their correct response would be to happily reveal the hiding place.
3 For example, children somehow formulate a story similar to *Little Red Riding Hood* when presented with the pictures of "a girl", "an old woman", "woods" and "a wolf".
4 In addition to the newborn, they may be trying to evaluate the "character" of the mother, i.e., establishing "what kind of mother" she is, at the same time. This is equivalent to the "exploratory action" toward unspecified others mentioned by Nishie in Chapter Six.
5 It is considered that infant abandonment, which is occasionally found in primate mothers under captive conditions, occurs when this initial setting is faulty.

Chapter 18

1 Needless to say, *Homo sapiens* is an animal species, but the word "animals" in this chapter refers to non-human animals for the sake of simplicity.

2 It should be noted, however, that the "animal-machine theory" since Descartes contained a certain kind of ambiguity from the beginning. It is commonly believed that Descartes' imaginary enemy was the traditional teleological or animistic view of nature of Aristotle and others, and that Descartes established his mechanistic view of nature by discarding all anthropomorphic understanding and teleological elements to stand against it. Despite this "common knowledge", science historian G. Canguilhem asserts that the rejection of teleology and anthropomorphism by the mechanistic explanation of life forms is mere pretense; the mechanistic view actually presupposes teleology and anthropomorphism (Yamaguchi 2011: 11; Canguilhem 2002: 129–130). If this is the case, I must say that the commonly accepted conflict between the Cartesian animal-machine theory and the so-called animism or anthropomorphic understanding of animals is too simplistic. Notwithstanding, I must defer our discussion on this point to another occasion due to lack of space. See also Kubo (2015: 28–31) on this point.

3 For example, there are common sayings among the aforementioned Sama people, such as "the rough sea calmed down while I recited a charm".

4 Another typical example is robots. See Kubo's study on robots (2015).

5 Turing was a gifted mathematician who pioneered the concept of computing machines and built the foundations for computer science. The Turing Test was first proposed in his article "Computing machinery and intelligence", published in the philosophy journal *Mind*. While Turing described it as the "imitation game", I shall use the more general designation of the Turing Test for convenience. As Hoshino points out, however, it is reasonable to say that the original purpose of the Turing Test was a thought experiment to treat humans and computers on fair (equal) ground, which is in the opposite direction from the commonly accepted idea that it is a "test" to clearly distinguish and separate computers from humans. Much of the description of and discussion on the Turing Test presented in this chapter draws on Christian (2011), Shibata (2001) and Kanazawa (1999), in addition to Hoshino (2002, 2009).

6 As you would have guessed, "wild" here carries the connotation of "outside the laboratory, in the field, under actual everyday conditions" rather than a negative meaning such as "savage" or "inferior".

7 They also include non-verbal physical interactions as well as those not mediated by language or to which language is not central, such as rituals and various physical interactions.

Epilogue

1 Information about this reference was imparted by Motomitsu Uchibori.

Bibliography

Adachi, K. (2003) "Kongun to iu shakai" (The society of mixed-species associations). In M. Nishida, K. Kitamura and J. Yamagiwa (eds), *Ningensei no kigen to shinka* (Origin and evolution of human nature). Kyoto: Shōwadō, 204–232.

Adachi, K. (2013) "The sociology of anti-structure: Toward a climax of groups". In K. Kawai (ed.), *Groups: The Evolution of Human Sociality*. Melbourne: Trans Pacific Press and Kyoto: Kyoto University Press, 21–41.

Adachi, K. (2017) "Living one's role under institution: Ecological niches and animal societies". In K. Kawai (ed.), *Institutions: The Evolution of Human Sociality*. Melbourne: Trans Pacific Press and Kyoto: Kyoto University Press, 265–286.

Agamben, G. (1999) *Remnants of Auschwitz: The Witness and the Archive*. English Translation of G. Agamben (1998) *Quel che resta di Auschwitz: L7archivio e il testimone*, D. Heller-Roazen (trans.). New York: Zone Books.

Azuma, H. (2001) *Dōbutsukasuru posutomodan: Otaku kara mita Nihon shakai* (Otaku: Japan's database animals). Tokyo: Kōdansha Gendai Shinsho.

Baba, H. (2009) *NHK Shiru wo tanoshimu Kono hito kono sekai: 'Kao tte nandarō?* (NHK's The joy of learning: What is the "face"?). Feb–Mar 2009 issue. Tokyo: Nihon Hōsō Kyōkai.

Balikci, A. (1989) *The Netsilik Eskimo*. Long Grove: Waveland Press.

Bar-Tal, D. (2011) *Intergroup Conflicts and Their Resolution: A Social Psychological Perspective*. New York: Psychology Press.

Bar, N. and E. Ben-Ari (2005) "Israeli snipers in the Al-Aqsa Intifada: Killing, humanity and lived experience". *Third World Quarterly*, 26(1): 133–152.

Baron-Cohen, S. (1997) *Jiheishō to maindo buraindonesu*. Japanese translation of S. Baron-Cohen (1995) *Mindblindness*, T. Nagano et al. (trans.). Tokyo: Seido Sha.

Basu, N. (2013) "Honour killings: India's crying shame". *IPS* 2013/11/30. Accessed on 14 August 2015 at http://www.ipsnews.net/2013/11/op-ed-honour-killings-indias-crying-shame/.

Bateson, G. (1972) *Steps to an Ecology of Mind*. Chicago: The University of Chicago Press.

Blixen, K. (1998) *Sōgen ni ochiru kage*. Japanese translation of K. Blixen (1960) *Shadows on the Grass*, K. Masuda (trans.). Tokyo: Chikuma Shobō.

Boas, F. (2011) *Primitivu āto*. Japanese translation of F. Boas (1927) *Primitive Art*, K. Omura (trans.). Tokyo: Gensō Sha.

Bodenhorn, B. (1989) *The Animals Come to Me, They Know I Share: Inuipiaq Kinship, Changing Economic Relations and Enduring World Views on Alaska's North Slope*. PhD thesis, Cambridge University.

Boehm, C. (2014) *Moraru no kigen: Dōtoku, ryōshin, rita kōdō ha donoyōni shinkashita noka*. Japanese translation of C. Boehm (2012) *Moral Origins*, T. Saitō (trans.). Tokyo: Hakuyōsha.

Boesch, C. (1991) "The effects of leopard predation on grouping patterns in forest chimpanzees". *Behaviour*, 117: 220–242.

Boesch, C. and H. Boesch (1989) "Hunting behavior of wild chimpanzees in the Taï National Park". *American Journal of Physical Anthropology*, 78: 547–573.

Boesch, C., C. Crockford, I. Herbinger, R. Wittig, Y. Moebius and E. Normand (2008) "Intergroup conflicts among chimpanzees in Taï National Park: Lethal violence and the female perspective". *American Journal of Primatology*, 70: 519–532.

Boivin, N. (2008) *Material Cultures, Material Minds: The Impact on Human Thought, Society and Evolution*. Cambridge: Cambridge University Press.

Briggs, J. L. (1968) *Utkuhikhalingmiut Eskimo Emotional Expression*. Ottawa: Department of Indian Affairs and Northern Development, Northern Science Research Group.

Briggs, J. L. (1970) *Never in Anger: Portrait of an Eskimo Family*. Cambridge: Harvard University Press.

Brody, H. (1975) *The People's Land: Whites and the Eastern Arctic*. New York: Penguin Books.

Bruner, J. S. (1998) *Kanō sekai no shinri*. Japanese translation of J. S. Bruner (1986) *Actual Minds, Possible Worlds*, K. Tanaka (trans.). Tokyo: Misuzu Shobō.

Bruner, J. S. (1999) *Imi no fukken: Fōku saikorojī ni mukete*. Japanese translation of J. S. Bruner (1990) *Acts of Meaning*, N. Okamoto et al. (trans.). Tokyo: Minerva Shobō.

Bshary, R. and R. Noë (1997) "Red colobus and Diana monkeys provide mutual protection against predators". *Animal Behavior*, 54: 1461–1474.

Burkart, J. M., S. B. Hrdy and C. P. van Schaik (2009) "Cooperative breeding and human cognitive evolution". *Evolutionary Anthropology*, 18: 175–186.

Burkert, W. (1989) *Homo Necans: The Anthropology of Ancient Greek Sacrificial Ritual and Myth*. Berkeley: University of California Press.

Byrne, R. and A. Whiten (2004) *Makyaberi teki chisei to kokoro no riron no shinka ron: Hito ha naze kashikokunatta ka*. Japanese translation of R. Byrne and A. Whiten (1988) *Machiavellian Intelligence: Social Expertise and the Evolution of Intellect in Monkeys, Apes and Humans*, K. Fujita et al. (trans.). Tokyo: Nakanishiya Shuppan.

Call, J. and M. Tomasello (2008) "Does the chimpanzee have a theory of mind? 30 years later". *Trends in Cognitive Sciences*, 12: 187–192.

Canguilhem, G. (2002) *Seimei no ninshiki.* Japanese translation of G. Canguilhem (1952) *La connaissance de la vie*, Y. Sugiyama (trans.). Tokyo: Hōsei Daigaku Shuppan.

Carsten, J. (1995) "The substance of kinship and the heat of the hearth: Feeding, personhood and relatedness among Malays in Pulau Langkawi". *American Ethnologist*, 22(2): 223–241.

Carsten, J. (2000) "Introduction: Cultures of relatedness". In J. Carsten (ed.), *Cultures of Relatedness: New Approaches to the Study of Kinship.* Cambridge: Cambridge University Press.

Cartmill, M. (1995) *Hito ha naze korosu ka: Shuryō kasetsu to dōbutsu kan no bunmei shi.* Japanese translation of M. Cartmill (1993) *A View to a Death in the Morning: Hunting and Nature Through History*, R. Uchida (trans.). Tokyo: Shinyō Sha.

Cavalieri, P. and P. Singer (2001) *Ōgata ruijin-en no kenri sengen.* Japanese translation of P. Cavalieri and P. Singer (1993) *The Great Ape Project: Equality beyond Humanity*, Y. Yamauchi and T. Nishida (trans.). Tokyo: Shōwa Dō.

Chadwick, H. M. and N. Chadwick (1932–1940) *The Growth of Literature*, 3 vols. Cambridge: Cambridge University Press.

Chase, M. and M. A. Leibold (2003) *Ecological Niches: Linking Classical and Contemporary Approaches.* Chicago: University of Chicago Press.

Chiba, M. (2013) *Ugokisugite ha ikenai: Jiru Durūzu to seisei henka no tetsugaku* (Do not move too much: Gilles Deleuze and the philosophy of becoming). Tokyo: Kawade Shobō Shinsha.

Christian, B. (2011) *Kikai yori ningen rashiku nareruka.* Japanese translation of B. Christian (2011) *The Most Human Human*, S. Yoshida (trans.). Tokyo: Sōshi Sha.

Clastres, P. (2003) *Bōryoku no kōkogaku: Mikai shakai ni okeru sensō.* Japanese translation of P. Clastres (1997) *Archéologie de la Violence*, M. Marimo (trans.). Tokyo: Gendai Kikaku Sha.

Copeland, B. J. (2013) *Chūringu: Jōhō jidai no paionia.* Japanese translation of B. J. Copeland (2013) *Turing: Pioneer of the Information Age*, K. Hattori (trans.). Tokyo: NTT Shuppan.

Corbet, S., et al. (2000) "env sequences of simian immunodeficiency viruses from chimpanzees in Cameroon are strongly related to those of human immunodeficiency virus group N from the same geographic area". *Journal of Virology*, 74: 529–534.

Crandell, G. (1993) *Nature Pictorialized*. Baltimore: The Johns Hopkins University Press.

Csibra, G. and G. Gergely (2011) "Natural pedagogy as evolutionary adaptation". *Philosophical Transactions of the Royal Society B: Biological Sciences*, 366: 1149–1157.

Davis, M. H. (1999) *Kyōkan no shakai shinrigaku*. Japanese translation of M. H. Davis (1994) *Empathy: A Social Psychological Approach*, A. Kikuchi (trans.). Tokyo: Kawashima Shoten.

de Certeau, M. (1987) *Nichijōteki jissen no poietīku*. Japanese translation of M. de Certeau (1980) *L'invention du quotidien*, T. Yamada (trans.). Tokyo: Kokubunsha.

de Fontenay, E. (2008) *Dōbutsu tachi no chinmoku: "Dōbutsusei" wo meguru tetsugaku shiron*. Japanese translation of E. de Fontenay (1998) *Le silence des bêtes*, K. Ishida et al. (trans.). Tokyo: Sairyūsha.

de Waal, F. (1987) *Seiji wo suru saru*. Japanese translation of de Waal (1982) *Chimpanzee Politics*, T. Nishida (trans.). Tokyo: Dōbutsu Sha.

de Waal, F. (1993) *Nakanaori senjutsu: Reichōrui ha heiwa na kurashi wo donoyōni jitsugen shiteiruka*. Japanese translation of de Waal (1989) *Peacemaking among Primates*, T. Nishida and T. Enomoto (trans.). Tokyo: Dōbutsu Sha.

de Waal, F. (1994) *Seiji wo suru saru*. Japanese translation of F. de Waal (1982) *Chimpanzee Politics*, T. Nishida (trans.). Tokyo: Heibon Sha Library.

de Waal, F. (1998) *Rikoteki na saru, tanin wo omoiyaru saru: Moraru ha naze umareta noka*. Japanese translation of F. de Waal (1997) *Good Natured: The Origins of Right and Wrong in Humans and Other Animals*, T. Nishida and R. Fujii (trans.). Tokyo: Sōshisha.

de Waal, F. (2002) *Saru to sushi shokunin: Bunka to dōbutsu no kōdōgaku*. Japanese translation of F. de Waal (2001) *The Ape and the Sushi Master: Cultural Reflections of a Primatologist*, T. Nishida and R. Fujii (trans.). Tokyo: Hara Shobō.

de Waal, F. (2006) *Chinpanjī no seijigaku: Saru no kenryoku to sei*. Japanese translation of F. de Waal (1982) *Chimpanzee Politics: Power and Sex Among Apes*, T. Nishida (trans.). Tokyo: Sankei Shimbun Shuppan.

de Waal, F. (2010) *Kyōkan no jidai he: Dōbutsu kōdōgaku ga oshietekureru koto*.

Japanese translation of F. de Waal (2009) *The Age of Empathy: Nature's Lessons for a Kindly Society*, H. Shibata (trans.). Tokyo: Kinokuniya Shoten.

de Waal, F. (2014) *Dōtokusei no kigen: Bonobo ga oshietekureru koto*. Japanese translation of F. de Waal (2013) *The Bonobo and the Athiest*, H. Shibata (trans.). Tokyo: Kinokuniya Shoten.

Deccan Herald (2004) "Choices, not for 'her'". 22 October.

Derrida, J. (2014) *Dōbutsu wo ou, yueni watashi ha (dōbutsu de) aru*. Japanese translation of J. Derrida (2002) *L'animal que donc je suis* (The animal that therefore I am), S. Ukai (trans.). Tokyo: Chikuma Shobō.

Descartes, R. (1953) *Hōhō josetsu*. Japanese translation of R. Descartes (1637) *Discours de la méthode* (Discourse on the method), T. Ochiai (trans.). Tokyo: Iwanami Bunko.

Descartes, R. (1997) *Hōhō josetsu*. Japanese translation of R. Descartes (1637) *Discours de la méthode*, T. Tanigawa (trans.). Tokyo: Iwanami Bunko.

Descola, P. (2013) *Beyond Nature and Culture*, J. Lloyd (trans.). Chicago: University of Chicago Press.

Dinesen, I. (1981) *Afurika no hibi*. Japanese translation of I. Dinesen (1937) *Out of Africa*, S. Yokoyama (trans.). Tokyo: Shōbun Sha.

Ekman, P. and W. V. Friesen (1987) *Hyōjō bunseki nyūmon: Hyōjō ni kakusareta imi wo saguru*. Japanese translation of P. Ekman and W. V. Friesen (1978) *The Facial Action Coding System*, T. Kudō (trans.). Tokyo: Seishin Shobō.

Erikson, E. H. (1959) *Identity and the Life Cycle*. New York: International Universities Press.

Erikson, E. H. (1973) *Aidentitī: Seinen to kiki*. Japanese translation of E. H. Erikson (1968) *Identity: Youth and Crisis*, N. Iwase (trans.). Tokyo: Kanazawa Bunko.

Evans-Pritchard, E. E. (1937) *Witchcraft, Oracles and Magic Among the Azande*. Oxford: Oxford University Press.

Fernández-Armesto, F. (2008) *Ningen no kyōkai ha doko ni arunodarō?*. Japanese translation of F. Fernández-Armesto (2004) *So You Think You're Human?*, M. Hasegawa (trans.). Tokyo: Iwanami Shoten.

Fienup-Riordan, A. (1983) *The Nelson Island Eskimo: Social Structure and Ritual Distribution*. Anchorage: Alaska Pacific University Press.

Formenty, P., et al. (1999) "Ebola virus outbreak among wild chimpanzees living in a rain forest of Côte d'Ivoire". *The Journal of Infectious Diseases*, 179: S120–S126.

Freeman, D. (1967) "Shaman and incubus". *Psychoanalytic Study of Society*, 4: 315–343.

Freeman, D. (1970) *Report on the Iban*. London: Athlone Press.
Freeman, D. (1981) "Some reflections on the nature of Iban society". An occasional paper of the Department of Anthropology, Research School of Pacific Studies, Australian National University, Canberra.
Fukui, K. (1993) "Tatakai to heijunka kikō: Sūdan nanbu Nārimu no kachiku ryakudatsu no jirei kara" (Fighting and leveling mechanism: A case of livestock raiding in Narim, South Sudan). *Shakai jinrigaku nenpō* (Annual for social anthropology), 19: 1–38.
Fukui, K., et al. (2004) "Tokushū: Hito ha naze tatakau noka" (Special feature: Why people fight). In K. Fukui (ed.), *Kikan minzokugaku* (Quarterly journal of ethnography), 109: 4–62.
Fukushima, M. (1998) "Sai no kōgaku: Minzoku no kōchikugaku eno sobyō" (On the technology of difference: Outline of a theory of ethnicity construction). *Tōnan Ajia kenkyū* (Southeast Asian studies), 35: 898–913.
Funabiki, T. (1997) "Jo: Communal to Social, soshite shinmitsusei". In T. Aoki et al. (eds), *Iwanami kōza bunka jinruigaku dai 4-kan Ko kara suru shakai tenbō* (The outlook of society from the individual perspective, Iwanami cultural anthropology series Vol. 4). Tokyo: Iwanami Shoten, 1–24.
Funabiki, T. (2012) *Living Field: Monograph and Models Concerning Human's Social Design, Based on the Mbotgote in Malakula Island, Vanuatu*. Tokyo: University Museum, University of Tokyo.
Funabiki, T. (2013) "Human groups at the zero-level: An exploration of the meaning, field and structure of relations at the level of group extinction". In K. Kawai (ed.), *Groups: The Evolution of Human Sociality*. Melbourne: Trans Pacific Press and Kyoto: Kyoto University Press, 309–322.
Funabiki, T. (2017) "Basic components of institution: Understanding institution according to triangular and tetrahedral models". In K. Kawai (ed.), *Institutions: The Evolution of Human Sociality*. Melbourne: Trans Pacific Press and Kyoto: Kyoto University Press, 309–323.
Furnham, A. F. (1988) *Lay Theories: Everyday Understanding of Problems in the Social Sciences*. Oxford: Pergamon Press.
Furuichi, T. (1991) "Fukei shakai wo gyūjiru mesutachi: Pigumī chinpanjī no bokenteki jun'i kōzō" (Females who rule a patrilineal society: The matriarchal rank structure in pygmy chimpanzees). In T. Nishida, K. Izawa and T. Kanō (eds), *Saru no bunka shi* (Chimpanzee cultures). Tokyo: Heibon Sha, 561–581.

Gell, A. (1998) *Art and Agency: An Anthropological Theory*. Oxford: Oxford University Press.
Goodall, J. (1986) *The Chimpanzees of Gombe: Patterns of Behavior*. Cambridge: Harvard University Press.
Goodall, J. (1990) *Yasei chinpanjī no sekai*. Japanese translation of J. Goodall (1986) *The Chimpanzees of Gombe*, Y. Sugiyama and T. Matsuzawa (trans.). Kyoto: Minerva Shobō.
Goodall, J. (1994) *Kokoro no mado: Chinpanjī tono 30 nen*. Japanese translation of J. Goodall (1990) *Through a Window: My Thirty Years With the Chimpanzees of Gombe*, K. Takasaki et al. (trans.). Tokyo: Dōbutsu Sha.
Gotō, E. (2014) *Kami no tameni matou vēru: Gendai Ejiputo no josei to isurāmu* (The veil worn for God: Contemporary Egyptian women and Islam). Tokyo: Chūō Kōron Sha.
Grossman, D. (1995) *On Killing: The Psychological Cost of Learning to Kill in War and Society*. New York: Black Bay Books.
Grzimek, B. (1962) "African national parks: The position today". In W. Engelhardt (ed.), *Survival of the Free: The Last Strongholds of Wild Animal Life*. New York: G. P. Putnam's Sons, 101–113.
Hacking, I. (1999) *Gūzen wo kainarasu*. Japanese translation of I. Hacking (1990) *The Taming of Chance*, H. Ishihara and S. Omoda (trans.). Tokyo: Bokutaku Sha.
Hall, E. T. (1970) *Kakureta jigen*. Japanese translation of E. T. Hall (1966) *The Hidden Dimension*, T. Hidaka and N. Satō (trans.). Tokyo: Misuzu Shobō.
Hallowell, A. I. (1955) *Culture and Experience*. Baltimore: University of Pennsylvania Press.
Hamada, S. (1988) "Kotoba, shimboru, jiga: 'Watashi' toiu monogatari no hajimari" (Language, symbol and self: The beginning of the story of "I"). In N. Okamoto (ed.), *Ninshiki to kotoba no hattatsu shinrigaku* (Developmental psychology of cognition and language). Kyoto: Minerva Shobō, 3–36.
Hamilton, W. D. (1971) "Geometry for the selfish herd". *Journal of Theoretical Biology*, 31: 295–311.
Hanamura, S. (2010a) "Chinpanjī no chōkyori onsei wo kaishita kōi setsuzoku no yarikata to shikaigai ni hirogaru ba no yōtai" (Long-distance calls by chimpanzees: How they connect actions and organize their social field beyond visual contact). *Reichōrui kenkyū* (Primate Research), 26(2): 159–176.
Hanamura, S. (2010b) "Gūyūsei ni tayutau chinpanjī" (Contingency that sways chimpanzees). In D. Kimura, M. Nakamura and K. Takanashi (eds),

Intarakushon no kyōkai to setsuzoku: Saru, hito, kaiwa kenkyū kara (Boundary and conjunction of social interaction: Studies in non-human primates, humans and conversation). Tokyo: Shōwadō, 185–204.

Hanamura, S. (2015) "Fission-fusion grouping". In M. Nakamura, K. Hosaka, N. Itoh and K. Zamma (eds), *Mahale Chimpanzees: 50 Years of Research*. Cambridge: Cambridge University Press, 106–118.

Hanamura, S. (2017) "When keeping one's ears open for the distant voices of others: The process-oriented convention in chimpanzees and institution". In K. Kawai (ed.), *Institutions: The Evolution of Human Sociality*. Melbourne: Trans Pacific Press and Kyoto: Kyoto University Press, 165–195.

Haraway, D. (1991) *Simians, Cyborgs and Women*. London: Free Association Press.

Hart, D. and R. W. Sussman (2007) *Hito ha taberarete shinka shita*. Japanese translation of D. Hart and R. W. Sussman (2005) *Man the Hunted: Primates, Predators, and Human Evolution*, N. Itō (trans.). Kyoto: Kagaku Dōjin.

Hasegawa, G. (2009) "Fīrudo nōto: Kapitto barē ryūiki Iban no kubikari to yōkai gurashi" (Field notes: Head-hunting and *gerasi* in the Iban in Kapit valley). *Nihon Malēshia kenkyūkai kaihō* (JAMS News) (Japan Association of Malaysian Studies newsletter), 42: 42–43.

Hasegawa, M. (1983) *Yasei nihonzaru no ikuji kōdō* (Nursing behavior in wild Japanese macaques). Tokyo: Kaimei Sha.

Hasegawa, T. and M. Hasegawa (2000) *Shinka to ningen kōdō* (Evolution and human behavior). Tokyo: Tokyo Daigaku Shuppan Kai.

Hayaki, H. (1990) *Chinpanjī no naka no hito* (The human inside the chimpanzee). Tokyo: Shōkabō.

Hayaki, H. (1991) "Seinenki no owari: Chinpanjī no wakamono ga taitokusuru mono" (The end of adolescence: What adolescent chimpanzees learn through experience). In T. Nishida, K. Izawa and T. Kanō (eds), *Saru no bunka shi* (Chimpanzee cultures). Tokyo: Heibon Sha, 371–388.

Hayama, S. (2001) *Yasei dōbutsu mondai* (Wildlife issue). Tokyo: Chijin Shokan.

Hayek, F. A. (1967a) "The result of human action but not of human design". In F. A. Hayek, *Studies in Philosophy, Politics, and Economics*. London: Routledge and Kegan Paul.

Hayek, F. A. (1967b) "Dr. Bernard Mandeville". *Proceedings of the British Academy*, 52: 125–141.

Hayek, F. A. (1973) *Law, Legislation and Liberty, Volume 1: Rules and Order*. Chicago: University of Chicago Press.

Hemingway, E. (1966) *Afurika no midori no oka*. Japanese translation of E.

Hemingway (1935) *Green Hills of Africa*, K. Nishimura (trans.). Tokyo: Mikasa Shobō.

Hemingway, E. (1999) *Kenia*. Japanese translation of E. Hemingway (1999) *True at First Light*, M. Kanehara (trans.). Tokyo: Artist House.

Hermans, H. (2004) "The dialogical self: Between exchange and power". In H. Hermans and G. Dimaggio (eds), *The Dialogical Self in Psychotherapy*. East Sussex: Brunner-Routledge, 13–28.

Hermans, H. and H. Kempen (1993) *The Dialogical Self*. Kindle edition.

Hewlett, B. S., H. N. Fouts, A. H. Boyette and B. L. Hewlett (2011) "Social learning among Congo Basin hunter-gatherers". *Philosophical Transactions of the Royal Society B: Biological Sciences*, 366: 1168–1178.

Hiraiwa-Hasegawa, M., R. W. Byrne, H. Takasaki and J. M. E. Byrne (1986) "Aggression toward large carnivores by wild chimpanzees of Mahale Mountains National Park, Tanzania". *Folia Primatologica*, 47: 8–13.

Hockings, K. J., G. Yamakoshi, A. Kabasawa and T. Matsuzawa (2009a) "Attacks on local persons by chimpanzees in Bossou, Republic of Guinea: Long-term perspectives". *American Journal of Primatology*, 71: 1–10.

Hockings, K. J., J. R. Anderson and T. Matsuzawa (2009b) "Use of wild and cultivated foods by chimpanzees at Bossou, Republic of Guinea: Feeding dynamics in a human-influenced environment". *American Journal of Primatology*, 71: 636–646.

Hosaka, K. and M. Nakamura (2015) "Male-male relationships". In M. Nakamura, K. Hosaka, N. Itoh and K. Zamma (eds), *Mahale Chimpanzees: 50 Years of Research*. Cambridge: Cambridge University Press, 387–398.

Hosaka, K., A. Matsumoto, M. A. Huffman and K. Kawanaka (2000) "Mahale no yasei chinpanjī ni okeru dōshu kotai no shitai ni taisuru hannō" (Reactions to dead bodies of conspecifics by wild chimpanzees in the Mahale Mountains, Tanzania). *Reichōrui kenkyū* (Primate Research), 16(1): 1–15.

Hosaka, K., E. Inoue and M. Fujimoto (2014) "Responses of wild chimpanzees to fresh carcasses of aardvark (*Orycteropus afer*) in Mahale". *Pan Africa News*, 21: 19–22.

Hosaka, K., K. Matsusaka and S. Hanamura (2015) "Vocal communication". In M. Nakamura, K. Hosaka, N. Itoh and K. Zamma (eds), *Mahale Chimpanzees: 50 Years of Research*. Cambridge: Cambridge University Press, 533–543.

Hosaka, K., T. Nishida, M. Hamai, A. Matsumoto-Oda and S. Uehara (2001) "Predation of mammals by the chimpanzees of the Mahale Mountains, Tanzania". In B. M. F. Galdikas, N. E. Briggs, L. K. Sheeran, G. L. Shapiro and

J. Goodall (eds), *All Apes Great and Small Vol I: African Apes*. New York: Kluwer Academic/Plenum, 107–130.

Hoshino, T. (2002) *Yomigaeru Chūringu: Konpyūta kagaku ni nokosareta yume* (A Turing revival: An unfulfilled dream of computer science). Tokyo: NTT Shuppan.

Hoshino, T. (2009) *Chūringu wo uketsugu: Ronri to seimei to shi* (Turing's heritage: Logic, life and death). Tokyo: Keisō Shobō.

Hoskins, J. (2006) "Agency, biography and objects". In C. Tilley and W. Keane et al. (eds), *Handbook of Material Culture*. London: SAGE Publications, 74–84.

Hrdy, S. B. (2005) *Mazā neichā I & II*. Japanese translation of S. B. Hrdy (1999) *Mother Nature: Maternal Instincts and How They Shape the Human Species*, M. Shiobara (trans.). Tokyo: Hayakawa Shobō.

Hrdy, S. B. (2008) "Evolutionary context of human development: The cooperative breeding model". In C. A. Salmon and T. K. Shackelford (eds), *Family Relationships: An Evolutionary Perspective*. New York: Oxford University Press, 39–68.

Hubbell, S. P. (2009) *Gunshū seitaigaku: Seibutsu tayōseigaku to seibutsu chirigaku no tōitsu chūritsu riron*. Japanese translation of S. P. Hubbell (2001) *The Unified Neutral Theory of Biodiversity and Biogeography*, T. Hirao et al. (trans.). Tokyo: Bunichi Sōgō Shuppan.

Hutchinson, S. (1996) *Nuer Dilemma: Coping with Money, War, and the State*. Berkeley: University of California Press.

Idani, G. (1991) "Waka mesu no aidentitī: Bonobo no shūdan kan iseki wo megutte" (The identity of a young female: Intergroup transfer in bonobos). In T. Nishida, K. Izawa and T. Kanō (eds), *Saru no bunka shi* (Chimpanzee cultures). Tokyo: Heibon Sha, 523–542.

Ide, T. (1967) "Girisha jin no reikon kan to ningen gaku" (Ancient Greek view of the soul and anthropology) (D.Lit. thesis from 1935). In *Ide Takashi chosaku shū bekkan 1* (Collected works of Takashi Ide supplementary volume 1). Tokyo: Keisō Shobō.

Ikeda, Y. (2011) *Ika no kokoro wo saguru: Chi no sekai ni ikiru umi no reichōrui* (Exploring the mind of the squid: The primate of the ocean in the world of intelligence). Tokyo: NHK Shuppan.

Imamura, H. (1982) *Bōryoku no ontorogī* (The ontology of violence). Tokyo: Keisō Shobō.

Imanishi, K. (1993 [1948]) "Yūboku ron" (An essay on nomadism). In *Zōho ban*

Imanishi Kinji zenshū (Collected works of Kinji Imanishi enlarged edition). Tokyo: Kōdan Sha, 214–285.
Ingold, T. (2000) *The Perception of the Environment*. London: Routledge.
Ishikawa, Y. (2000) *Tabi no ekurichūru* (An essay on travel). Tokyo: Hakusui Sha.
Isobe, T. (1998) *Dōtoku ishiki to kihan no gyakusetsu* (The paradox of morality and norm). Kyoto: Akademia Shuppan Kai.
Itani, J. (1983) "Kazoku kigen ron no yukue" (The future of the theory of the origin of the family). In *Kazoku shi kenkyū 7* (Studies on the history of the family 7). Tokyo: Ōtsuki Shoten.
Itani, J. (1987) *Reichōrui shakai no shinka* (The evolution of primate society). Tokyo: Heibon Sha.
Itō, T. and H. Hirabayashi (1997) "Kōshakaiteki kōdō no hattatsu" (Development of prosocial behavior). In K. Inoue and Y. Kubo (eds), *Kodomo no shakaiteki hattatsu* (Social development in children). Tokyo: Tokyo Daigaku Shuppan Kai, 167–184.
Itoh, N. (2003) "Matomaru koto no mekanizumu" (Mechanism of assembling). In M. Nishida, K. Kitamura and J. Yamagiwa (eds), *Ningensei no kigen to shinka* (Origin and evolution of human nature). Kyoto: Shōwadō, 233–262.
Itoh, N. (2010) "Mure no idō ha donoyōnishite hajimaru noka?" (How does a troop of chimpanzees begin to travel?). In D. Kimura, M. Nakamura and K. Takanashi (eds), *Intarakushon no kyōkai to setsuzoku: Saru, hito, kaiwa kenkyū kara* (Boundary and conjunction of social interaction: Studies in non-human primates, humans and conversation). Tokyo: Shōwadō, 275–293.
Itoh, N. (2013) "A group of chimpanzees: The world viewed from females' perspectives". In K. Kawai (ed.), *Groups: The Evolution of Human Sociality*. Melbourne: Trans Pacific Press and Kyoto: Kyoto University Press, 111–119.
Itoh, N. (2017) "Duality of the mode of coexistence and action selection: Groups and the emergence of 'institutions' in chimpanzees". In K. Kawai (ed.), *Institutions: The Evolution of Human Sociality*. Melbourne: Trans Pacific Press and Kyoto: Kyoto University Press, 141–163.
Itoh, N. and M. Nakamura (2015a) "Mahale flora: Its historical background and long-term changes". In M. Nakamura, K. Hosaka, N. Itoh and K. Zamma (eds), *Mahale Chimpanzees: 50 Years of Research*. Cambridge: Cambridge University Press, 150–173.
Itoh, N. and M. Nakamura (2015b) "Female-female relationships". In M. Nakamura,

K. Hosaka, N. Itoh and K. Zamma (eds), *Mahale Chimpanzees: 50 Years of Research*. Cambridge: Cambridge University Press, 399–409.

Iwata, K. (1973) *Sōmokuchūgyo no jinruigaku: Animizumu no sekai* (An anthropology of the grass, the trees, the insects and the fish: The world of animism). Kyoto: Tankō Sha.

James, W. (1993) *Shinrigaku*. Japanese translation of W. James (1890) *The Principles of Psychology*, H. Imada (trans.). Tokyo: Iwanami Bunko.

Jensen, E. (1974) *The Iban and Their Religion*. Oxford: Oxford University Press.

Kakeya, M. (1983) "Netami no seitai-jinruigaku" (Ecological anthropology of envy). In R. Otsuka (ed.), *Gendai no jinruigaku I, seitai jinruigaku* (Anthropology of today I, ecological anthropology). Tokyo: Shibundō, 229–241.

Kakeya, M. (1987) "Netami no seitaigaku" (Ecology of envy). In *Sozo no sekai 61* (World of creation 61). Tokyo: Shogakukan, 56–83.

Kakeya, M. (1994) "Yakihata nōkō shakai to heijunka kikō" (Shifting cultivation society and the leveling mechanism). In R. Otsuka (ed.), *Kōza chikyū ni ikiru (3), shigen heno bunka tekiō* (Lectures on living on the Earth (3), cultural adaptation to resources). Tokyo: Yūzankaku Shuppan, 121–145.

Kanamori, O. (2012) *Dōbutsu ni tamashii ha arunoka* (Do animals have souls?). Tokyo: Chūkō Shinsho.

Kanaya, O. (1975) *Sōshi: Dai 2 satsu "Gaihen"* (Zhuangzi: Vol. 2 "Outer Chapters"). Tokyo: Iwanami Bunko.

Kanazawa, S. (1999) *Tasha no kokoro ha sonzaisuru ka: "Tasha" kara "watashi" heno shinka ron* (Are there other minds: A theory of evolution from "other" to "I"). Tokyo: Kaneko Shobō.

Kanō, T. (1986) *Saigo no ruijin'en: Pigumī chinpanjī no kōdō to seitai* (The last ape: Behavior and biology of the pygmy chimpanzee). Tokyo: Dōbutsu Sha.

Kanō, T. (2001) "Ningen no honsei ha aku nanoka? Birya no shakai karano kentō" (Are humans inherently evil? A view from bonobo society). In T. Nishida (ed.), *Hominizēshon* (Hominization). Kyoto: Kyoto Daigaku Gakujutsu Shuppan Kai, 33–81.

Kawai, K. (2002a) "'Chimei' toiu chishiki: Dodosu no kankyō ninshiki ron josetsu" ("Place name" as knowledge: Theory of environmental recognition). In S. Satō (ed.), *Yūbokumin no sekai* (kōza seitai jinruigaku dai 4 kan) (Pastoral nomads in East Africa (ecological anthropology series Vol. 4)). Kyoto: Kyoto Daigaku Gakujutsu Shuppan Kai, 17–85.

Kawai, K. (2002b) "'Teki' no jittaika katei: Dodosu ni okeru reidingu to tasha hyōshō" (The process of materialization of "enemy": Raiding and the representation of the other in Dodoth). *Afurika repōto* (Africa report), 35: 3–8.

Kawai, K. (2004) "Dodosu ni okeru kachiku no ryakudatsu to rinsetsu shūdan kan no kankei" (Raiding and intergroup relationships in the Dodoth). In J. Tanaka et al., *Yūdōmin (nomaddo): genya ni ikiru* (Nomads: Living in the African wilderness). Tokyo: Shōwadō, 542–566.

Kawai, K. (2006) "Kyanpu idō to chō uranai: Dodosu ni okeru rinsetsu shūdan tono kankei wo meguru shakai kūkan no seisei kijo" (Camp relocation and divinatory reading of animal intestines: The mechanism for the Dodoth's social space generation surrounding their relations with neighboring communities). In R. Nishii and S. Tanabe (eds), *Shakai kūkan no jinruigaku: Materiariti, shutai, modaniti* (Anthropology of social space: Materiality, agency and modernity). Tokyo: Sekai Shisō Sha, 175–202.

Kawai, K. (2013) "Forming a gang: Raiding among pastoralists and the 'practice of cooperativity'". In K. Kawai (ed.), *Groups: The Evolution of Human Sociality*. Melbourne: Trans Pacific Press and Kyoto: Kyoto University Press, 167–186.

Kawai, K. (2017) Institutionalized cattle raiding: Its formalization and value creation amongst the pastoral Dodoth). In K. Kawai (ed.), *Institutions: The Evolution of Human Sociality*. Melbourne: Trans Pacific Press and Kyoto: Kyoto University Press, 219–238.

Kawai, K. (ed.) (2009) *Shūdan: Jinrui shakai no shinka* (Groups: The evolution of human sociality). Kyoto: Kyoto Daigaku Gakujutsu Shuppan Kai.

Kawai, K. (ed.) (2013a) *Seido: Jinrui shakai no shinka* (Institutions: The evolution of human sociality). Kyoto: Kyoto Daigaku Gakujutsu Shuppan Kai.

Kawai, K. (ed.) (2013b) *Groups: The Evolution of Human Sociality*. Melbourne: Trans Pacific Press and Kyoto: Kyoto University Press.

Kawai, K. (ed.) (2017) *Institutions: The Evolution of Human Sociality*. Melbourne: Trans Pacific Press and Kyoto: Kyoto University Press.

Kawai, K. (in print) "Teki to tomo no hazama de: Uganda Dodosu to rinsetsu minzoku Turukana tono kankei" (Between enemy and friend: The relationship between the Dodoth and the neighboring Turkana in Uganda). In I. Ōta and T. Soga (eds), *Afurika sabanna juku: Bokuchikumin no ikikata ni manabu* (Learning from the pastoral way of life in the African savanna). Tokyo: Shōwadō.

Kawai, M. (1964) *Nihonzaru no seitai* (Ecology of Japanese monkeys). Tokyo: Kawade Bunko.

Kawazoe, T. (2016) "Association patterns and affiliative relationships outside a troop in wild male Japanese macaques, *Macaca fuscata*, during the non-mating season". *Behavior*, 153(1): 69–89.

Kimura, D. (2010) "Intarakushon to sōtai zushiki" (Interaction and reciprocity schema). In D. Kimura, M. Nakamura and K. Takanashi (eds), *Intarakushon no kyōkai to setsuzoku: Saru, hito, kaiwa kenkyū kara* (Boundary and conjunction of social interaction: Studies in non-human primates, humans and conversation). Kyoto: Shōwadō, 3–18.

Kimura, D. (2015) "Sonzai no motsure" (Entangled presence). In D. Kimura (ed.), *Dōbutsu to deau II: Kokoro to shakai no seisei* (Animal encounters II: Generation of minds and societies). Kyoto: Nakanishiya Shuppan, i–xvi.

Kishigami, N. (1995) "Extended family and food sharing practices among the contemporary Netsilik Inuit: A case study of Pelly Bay". *Hokkaidō Kyōiku Daigaku kiyō 1-bu B* (Journal of Hokkaido University of Education Vol. 1B), 45(2): 1–9.

Kishigami, N. (1996) "Kanada kyokuhoku chiiki ni okeru shakai henka no tokushitsu ni tsuite" (Characteristics of social change in the Canadian Arctic). In H. Stewart (ed.), *Saishū shuryō min no genzai* (The gatherer-hunters today). Tokyo: Gensō Sha, 13–52.

Kishigami, N. (2007) *Kanada Inuitto no shoku bunka to shakai henka* (Food culture of the Canadian Inuit and social change). Kyoto: Sekaishisō Sha.

Kishigami, N. and H. Stewart (1994) "Gendai Neturikku Inuitto shakai ni okeru shakai kankei ni tsuite" (Indigenous social relations in a contemporary Canadian Inuit society). *Kokuritsu Minzokugaku Hakubutsukan kenkyū hōkoku* (Bulletin of the National Museum of Ethnology), 19(3): 405–448.

Kitamura, K. (1991) "'Fukai kanyo' wo yōkyūsuru shakai: Turukana ni okeru sōgo sayō no 'keishiki' to 'chikara'" (Society that demands "deep engagement": The "form" and "force" of interaction in Turkana). In J. Tanaka and M. Kakeya (eds), *Hito no shizen shi* (Natural history of humans). Tokyo: Heibon Sha, 137–164.

Kitamura, K. (1996a) "'Byōdō shugi shakai' toiu nosutarujia: Busshuman ha byōdō shugisha deha nai" (The nostalgia of egalitarianism: The Bushmen are not egalitarian). *Afurika kenkyū* (Journal of African studies), 48: 19–34.

Kitamura, K. (1996b) "Shintai teki komyunikēshon ni okeru 'kyōdō no genzai' no keiken: Turukana no 'kōshō' teki komyunikēshon" (The experience of the "collective present" in physical communication: "Negotiative" communication among the Turkana). In K. Sugawara and M. Nomura (eds), *Komyunikēshon to shiteno karada* (Body as a means of communication). Tokyo: Taishūkan Shoten, 288–314.

Kitamura, K. (2008) "'Shakaitekinarumono' toha nanika? Tasha tono kankeizuke ni okeru 'ketteifukanousei' to 'souzouteki taisho'" (What is "social"? Undecidability and creative coping mechanisms in the process of making relations with others). *Reichōrui kenkyū* (Primate Research), 24: 109–120.

Kitamura, K. (2013) "From whence comes human sociality? Recursive decision-making processes in the group phenomenon and classification of others through representation. In K. Kawai (ed.), *Groups: The Evolution of Human Sociality*. Melbourne: Trans Pacific Press and Kyoto: Kyoto University Press, 59–77.

Kitamura, K. (2014) "Shima ni kurasu hitobito ga taisetsu ni shiteiru koto: Okayama ken Shiraishijima no jirei kara" (Communication in interaction systems among islanders: The case of Shiraishi Island, Okayama Prefecture). *Bunka kyōseigaku kenkyu* (Studies in cultural symbiotics, Graduate School of Humanities and Social Sciences, Okayama University), 13: 43–60.

Kitamura, K. (2015) "Sōgo kōi shisutemu no komyunikēshon: Hito to dōbutsu wo tsunagitsutsu hedateru mono" (Communication in interaction systems: A mode of communication common to human and non-human animal societies). In D. Kimura (ed.), *Dōbutsu to deau II: Kokoro to shakai no seisei* (Animal encounters II: Generation of minds and societies). Kyoto: Nakanishiya Shuppan, 143–159.

Kitamura, K. (in press) "Higashi Afurika bokuchiku min Turukana no jiko kōteiteki na ikikata wo sasaeteiru mono: 'Monogoi' no komyunikēshon wo chūshin ni'" (The foundation of the self-assured attitude of the Turkana pastoralists in East Africa). In I. Ōta and T. Soga (eds), *Sabanna juku* (Savanna school). Tokyo: Shōwadō.

Kitoh, S. (1996) *Shizen hogo wo toinaosu* (Rethinking conservation). Tokyo: Chikuma Shobō.

Knapett, C. (2005) *Thinking Through Material Culture: An Interdisciplinary Perspective*. Philadelphia: University of Pennsylvania Press.

Kobayashi, Y. (1998) "Kaisetsu" (Commentary). In K. Washida, *Kao no genshōgaku: Mirarerukoto no kenri* (The phenomenology of the face: The right to be seen). Tokyo: Kōdansha Gakujutsu Bunko, 228–235.

Kojima, K. (2004) "'Uru otoko' to 'kau onna': Josei muke seikan massāji wo megutte" ("Male sellers" and "female customers": Sexual massage for women). M.Phil. thesis, the Graduate School of Human and Environmental Studies, Kyoto University.

Konagaya, Y. (1994) "Shuryō to yūboku wo tsunagu dōbutsu shigen kan" (Views on animal resources that connect hunting and nomadic life). In R. Otsuka (ed.), *Kōza chikyū ni ikiru (3), shigen heno bunka tekiō* (Lectures on living on the Earth (3), cultural adaptation to resources). Tokyo: Yūzankaku Shuppan, 69-92.

Kosugi, Y. (2002) "Dāwa" (Da'wah). In K. Ōtsuka (ed.), *Iwanami Isurāmu jiten* (Iwanami Islam dictionary). Tokyo: Iwanami Shoten, 589-590.

Krebs, J. and R. Dawkins (1984) "Animal signals: Mind-reading and manipulation". In J. R. Krebs and N. B. Davies (eds), *Behavioural Ecology: An Evolutionary Approach*, second edition. Oxford: Blackwell Scientific, 380-402.

Kubo, A. (2015) *Robotto no jinruigaku: 20 seiki Nihon no kikai to ningen* (Robot anthropology: Machine and human in Japan of the twentieth century). Kyoto: Sekai Shisō Sha.

Kubo, Y. (1997) "Tasha rikai no hattatsu" (Development of an understanding of others). In K. Inoue and Y. Kubo (eds), *Kodomo no shakaiteki hattatsu* (Social development in children). Tokyo: Tokyo Daigaku Shuppan Kai, Chapter 6.

Kumano, S. (1999) *Revinasu nyūmon* (Introduction to Lévinas). Tokyo: Chikuma Shobō.

Kumano, S. (2002) *Hēgeru: "Tanaru mon" wo meguru shikō* (Hegel: Thoughts on "that which is other"). Tokyo: Chikuma Shobō.

Kumano, S. (2012) *Revinasu: Utsuroiyuku mono heno shisen* (Lévinas: A gaze at the transient). Tokyo: Iwanami Shoten.

Kummer, H. (1971) *Primate Societies: Group Techniques of Ecological Adaptation*. Chicago: Aldine-Atherton.

Kummer, H. (1972) *Reichōrui no shakai*. Japanese translation of H. Kummer (1975) *Primate Societies: Group Techniques of Ecological Adaptation*, H. Mizuhara (trans.). Tokyo: Shakai Shisō Sha.

Kurimoto, E. (1996) *Minzoku funsō wo ikiru hitobito: Gendai Afurika no kokka to mainoriti* (Peoples living in ethnic conflicts: Contemporary African states and minorities). Tokyo: Sekai Shikō Sha.

Kurimoto, E. and S. Simonse (1997) *Conflict, Age and Power in North East Africa: Age Systems in Transition*. Oxford: James Currey.

Kuroda, S. (1982) *Pigumī chinpanjī: Michi no ruijinen* (Pygmy chimpanzee:

Unknown ape). Tokyo: Chikuma Shobō. (New edition published in 1999 by Ibun Sha).

Kuroda, S. (1999) *Jinrui shinka saikō: Shakai seisei no kōkogaku* (Reconsideration of human evolution: Archeology of the emergence of the hominid society). Tokyo: Ibun Sha.

Kuroda, S. (2013) "Collective excitement and primitive war: What is the equality principle?". In K. Kawai (ed.), *Groups: The Evolution of Human Sociality*. Melbourne: Trans Pacific Press and Kyoto: Kyoto University Press, 273–292.

Kuroda, S. (2015) "Reichōrui wo kansatsusuru: Seitaiteki sanyo kansatsu no kanōsei" (Observing primates: The potential of ecological participant observation). In I. Tokoro (ed.), *Fīrudowāku heno sasoi: Hito ha naze fīrudo ni ikunoka* (An invitation to fieldwork: Why do people go out into the field). Tokyo: Gaikokugo Daigaku Ajia Afurika Gengo Bunka Kenkyū Sho, 132–148.

Kuroda, S. (2017) "The evolutionary foundations of institutions: Rule, deviation, identity". In K. Kawai (ed.), *Institutions: The Evolution of Human Sociality*. Melbourne: Trans Pacific Press and Kyoto: Kyoto University Press, 393–412.

Kurosaki, M. (1998) *Tetsugakusha Kurosaki no yūutsu: Tonari no andoroid* (The melancholy of philosopher Kurosaki: The android next door). Tokyo: NHK Shuppan.

Kuwahara, T. (1995 [1944]) *Tozan no bunka shi* (Cultural history of mountaineering). Tokyo: Heibonsha Library.

Larson, G., et al. (2014) "Current perspectives and the future of domestication studies". *Proceedings of the National Academy of Sciences of the United States of America*, 111(17): 6139–6146.

Latour, B. (2008) *Kyokō no "kindai": Kagaku jinruigaku ha keikokusuru*. Japanese translation of B. Latour (1991) *We Have Never Been Modern*, K. Kawamura (trans.). Tokyo: Shinhyōron.

Lee, R. B. (1979) *The !Kung San*. New York: Cambridge University Press.

Leroy, E. M., et al. (2005) "Fruit bats as reservoirs of Ebola virus". *Nature*, 438: 575–576.

Lévinas, E. (1974) *Autrement qu'etre ou au-dela de l'essence.* Paris: Le Livre de Poche. English translation (1991) *Otherwise than Being or Beyond Essence*, A. Lingis (trans.). Dordrecht: Kluwer Academic Publishers.

Lévinas, E. (1999a) "Sonzai ha Kongentekika" (Is ontology fundamental?). *Levinasu korekushon* (Levinas collection), M. Gōda (ed. & trans.). Tokyo: Cyhikuma

Gakugei Bunko, 343–363. (Original from "L'ontologie est-elle fondamentale?" in *Revue de Métaphysique et de Morale*, 56, janvier-mars, 1951).

Lévinas, E. (1999b) *Sonzai no Kanata he*. Japanese translation of E. Lévinas (1974) *Autrement qu'etre ou au-dela de l'essence*, M. Gōda (trans.). Tokyo: Kōdan Sha.

Lévinas, E. (2005a) *Zentaisei to mugen (Vol.1)*. Japanese translation of E. Lévinas (1961) *Totalité et infini*, S. Kumano (trans.). Tokyo: Iwanami Bunko. English translation (1969) *Totality and Infinity: An Essay on Exteriority*, A. Lingis (trans.). Hague: Duquesne University Press.

Lévinas, E. (2005b) *Zentaisei to mugen (Vol.1A, Vol.3B)*. Japanese translation of E. Lévinas (1961) *Totalité et infini*, S. Kumano (trans.). Tokyo: Iwanami Bunko.

Lévinas, E. (2006) *Zentaisei to mugen (Vol.2)*. Japanese translation of E. Lévinas (1961) *Totalité et infini*, S. Kumano (trans.). Tokyo: Iwanami Bunko. English translation (1969) *Totality and Infinity: An Essay on Exteriority*, A. Lingis (trans.). Hague: Duquesne University Press.

Liu, W., et al. (2010) "Origin of the human malaria parasite *Plasmodium falciparum* in gorillas". *Nature*, 467: 420–425.

Lovatt Smith, D. (1986) *Amboseli: Nothing Short of a Miracle*. Nairobi: East African Publishing House.

Lovejoy, C. O. (2009) "Reexamining human origins in light of Ardipithecus ramidus". *Science*, 326: 74e1–74e8.

Luhmann, N. (1993) *Shakai shisutemu riron 1*. Japanese translation of N. Luhmann (1984) *Soziale Systeme. Grundriß einer allgemeinen Theorie*, T. Sato (trans.). Tokyo: Kōseisha Kōseikaku.

Luhmann, N. (1995) *Shakai shisutemu riron (Vol. 2)*. Japanese translation of N. Luhmann (1984) *Soziale Systeme. Grundriß einer allgemeinen Theorie*, T. Sato (trans.). Tokyo: Kōseisha Kōseikaku.

Maekawa, H. (1998) "Shito genkōroku ni okeru Barubaroi" (Barbaros in the acts of the Apostles). *Kirisutokyō kenkyū* (Studies in Christianity), 60(1): 83–98.

Masing, J. (1980) "Timang and the Iban cult of head-hunting". *Canberra Anthropology*, 1(2): 59–68.

Masud, M. K. (2000) "Introduction". In M. K. Masud (ed.), *Travellers in Faith: Studies of the Tablighi Jama'at as a Transnational Movement for Faith Renewal*. Leiden: Brill, viii–lx.

Matsumoto, T. and H. Hayaki (2015) "Development and growth: With special reference to mother-infant relationships". In M. Nakamura, K. Hosaka,

N. Itoh and K. Zamma (eds), *Mahale Chimpanzees: 50 Years of Research*. Cambridge: Cambridge University Press, 313–325.

Matsuzawa, T. (2001) *Primate Origins of Human Cognition and Behavior*. Tokyo: Springer.

Matsuzawa, T., et al. (2004) "Wild chimpanzees at Bossou-Nimba: Deaths through a flu-like epidemic in 2003 and the green-corridor project". *Reichōrui kenkyū* (Primate Research), 20(1): 45–55.

Maturana, H. R. and F. J. Varela (1991) *Ōtopoiēshisu: Seimei shisutemu toha nanika*. Japanese translation of H. R. Maturana and F. J. Varela (1980) *Autopoiesis and Cognition: The Realization of the Living*, H. Kawamoto (trans.). Tokyo: Kokubun Sha.

Mauss, M. (1954) *The Gift: Forms and Functions of Exchange in Archaic Societies*. English translation of M. Mauss (1925) *Essai sur le don: forme et raison de l'échange dans les sociétés archaïques*, I. Cunnison (trans.). London: Cohen and West.

Mead, J. H. (1991) *Shakaiteki jiga*. Japanese translation of J. H. Mead (1982) *The Individual and the Social Self*. M. Funatsu and N. Tokugawa (trans.). Tokyo: Kōseisha Kōseikaku.

Meguro, N. (2014) *Samayoeru "kyōzon" to Masai: Kenia no yasei dōbutsu hozen no genba kara* (Wandering "coexistence" and the Maasai: From the frontline of wildlife conservation in Kenya). Tokyo: Shinsen Sha.

Mitani, J. C., D. P. Watts and S. J. Amsler (2010) "Lethal intergroup aggression leads to territorial expansion in wild chimpanzees". *Current Biology*, 20: R507–R508.

Mitchell, R. W. (ed.) (2002) *Pretending and Imagination in Animals and Children*. Cambridge: Cambridge University Press.

Mithen, S. (2006) *Utau neanderutāru: Ongaku to gengo kara miru hito no shinka*. Japanese translation of S. Mithen (2005) *The Singing Neanderthals: The Origins of Music, Language, Mind and Body*, J. Kumagai (trans.). Tokyo: Hayakawa Shobō.

Miyawaki, Y. (2006) *Henkyō no sōzōryoku: Echiopia kokka shihai ni kōsuru shōsū minzoku Hōru* (Imagination on the frontier: The Hor ethnic minority resisting Ethiopian state rule). Kyoto: Sekai Shisō Sha.

Mizokami, S. (2008) *Jiko keisei no shinrigaku: Tasha no mori wo kakenukete jiko ni naru* (Psychology of identity formation: Forming one's identity among others). Kyoto: Sekai Shisō Sha.

Mori, A. (1977) "Intra-troop spacing mechanism of the wild Japanese monkeys of the Koshima Troop". *Primates*, 18: 331–357.

Morino, S. and K. Morino (2007) *Pikucharesuku Uēruzu no sōzō to henyō* (The creation and transformation of picturesque Wales). Sagamihara: Seizan Sha.

Moriyama, T. (2011) *Dangomushi ni kokoro wa arunoka: Atarashii kokoro no kagaku* (Do woodlice have minds?: A new science of mind). Tokyo: PHP Saiensu Wārudo Shinsho.

Nagel, T. (1989) *Kōmori dearu toha donoyōna koto ka*. Japanese translation of T. Nagel (1974) "What is it like to be a bat?", H. Nagai (trans.). Tokyo: Keisō Shobō.

Nakagaki, T. (2010) *Nenkin: Sono odorokubeki chisei* (Slime molds: Their amazing intelligence). Tokyo: PHP Saiensu Wārudo Shinsho.

Nakagawa, N. (2013) "The function and evolutionary history of primate groups: Focusing on sex differences in locational dispersal". In K. Kawai (ed.), *Groups: The Evolution of Human Sociality*. Melbourne: Trans Pacific Press and Kyoto: Kyoto University Press, 79–110.

Nakamura, M. (2003) "Dōji ni 'suru' kezukuroi: Chinpanjī no sōgo kōi kara miru shakai to bunka" (Grooming at the same time: Society and culture viewed from chimpanzee culture). In M. Nishida, K. Kitamura and J. Yamagiwa (eds), *Ningensei no kigen to shinka* (Origin and evolution of human nature). Kyoto: Shōwadō, 264–292.

Nakamura, M. (2009) *Chinpanjī: Kotoba no nai karera ga kataru koto* (Chimpanzees: What they have told me without language). Tokyo: Chūkō Shinsho.

Nakamura, M. (2013) "A juvenile chimpanzee played with a live moth". *Pan Africa News*, 20: 22–24.

Nakamura, M. (2015a) "Mori no naka de dōbutsu to deau" (Encountering animals in the forest). In D. Kimura (ed.), *Dōbutsu to deau I: Deai no sōgo kōi* (Encountering animals I: Analyzing encounters). Kyoto: Nakanishiya Shuppan, 79–81.

Nakamura, M. (2015b) *"Sarugaku" no keifu: Hito to chinpanjī no 50-nen* (Genealogy of Japanese primatology: 50 years of people and chimpanzees). Tokyo: Chūō Kōron Sha.

Nakamura, M. (2015c) "Home range". In M. Nakamura, K. Hosaka, N. Itoh and K. Zamma (eds), *Mahale Chimpanzees: 50 Years of Research*. Cambridge: Cambridge University Press, 94–105.

Nakamura, M. and N. Itoh (2005) "Notes on the behavior of a newly immigrated female chimpanzee to the Mahale M group". *Pan Africa News*, 12: 20–22.

Nakamura, M. and N. Itoh (2015a) "Overview of the field site: Mahale Mountains and their surroundings". In M. Nakamura, K. Hosaka, N. Itoh and K. Zamma (eds), *Mahale Chimpanzees: 50 Years of Research*. Cambridge: Cambridge University Press, 7–20.

Nakamura, M. and N. Itoh (2015b) "Conspecific killings". In M. Nakamura, K. Hosaka, N. Itoh and K. Zamma (eds), *Mahale Chimpanzees: 50 Years of Research*. Cambridge: Cambridge University Press, 372–383.

Nakayama, G. (2007) *Shikō no yōgo jiten* (Dictionary of philosophical terms). Tokyo: Chikuma Shobō.

Nakayama, N. (1999) "Sukāfu ni miru Isurāmu no tayōsei: Toruko O mura no jirei yori" (Diversity of Islam in scarves: The case of O village in Turkey). In K. Suzuki and M. Yamamoto (eds), *Yosooi no jinruigaku* (The anthropology of dress). Kyoto: Jinbun Shoin, 147–169.

Nakayashiki, C. (2014) "Kita Indo Chibetto kei shakai ni okeru senkyo to shinzoku: Supiti keikoku ni okeru shinzoku kankei nirin no jirei kara" (The modern election system and indigenous kinship relationships: The case of Nirin in a Tibetan society in North India). *Bunka jinruigaku* (Japanese journal of cultural anthropology), 79(3): 241–263.

Nakazawa, N., S. Hanamura, E. Inoue, M. Nakatsukasa and M. Nakamura (2013) "A leopard ate a chimpanzee: The first evidence from East Africa". *Journal of Human Evolution*, 65: 334–337.

Nash, R. F. (1967) *Wilderness and the American Mind*. New Haven: Yale University Press.

Natsume, S. (1994 [1915]) *Michikusa* (Grass on the wayside). *Sōseki zenshū* (Complete works of Sōseki), Vol. 10. Tokyo: Iwanami Shoten.

NHK (1998) *Ikimono chikyū kikō: Afurika Ginia no mori, oya kara ko he dōgu wo tsutaeru chinpanjī* (Travelling the world of animals: The Guinean forests of Africa, tool use transmitted from chimpanzee parents to their offspring). Broadcast on 12 January on television.

NHK Enterprise 21 (2000) *Kanzi to Panbanisha: Tensai zaru ga miseta kyōi no kiroku* (Kanzi and Panbanish: Amazing records of genius apes). NHK video, broadcast 13 February on television.

Nicholas, R. W. (1965) "Factions: A comparative analysis". In M. Banton (ed.), *Political Systems and the Distribution of Power*. London: Tavistock, 1–22.

Nicolson, M. H. (1989) *Kuratēru sōsho 13 Kurai yama to eikō no yama: Mugensei no bigaku no tenkai*. Japanese translation of M. H. Nicolson (1959) *Mountain Gloom and Mountain Glory: The Development of the Aesthetics of the Infinite*, K. Oguro (trans.). Tokyo: Kokusho Kankō Kai.

Nishida, T. (1968) "The social group of wild chimpanzees in the Mahali Mountains". *Primates*, 9: 167–224.

Nishida, T. (1973) *Seirei no kodomo tachi* (Children of spirits). Tokyo: Chikuma Shobō.

Nishida, T. (1979) "The social structure of chimpanzees of the Mahale Mountains". In D. A. Hamburg and E. R. McCown (eds), *The Great Apes*. Menlo Park: Benjamin/Cummings, 73–121.

Nishida, T. (1981) *Yasei Chinpanji Kansatsuki* (Observations on chimpanzees in the forest). Tokyo: Chukoshinsho.

Nishida, T. (1998) "Yakusha atogaki" (Translator's afterword). In F. de Waal, *Rikoteki na saru, tanin wo omoiyaru saru: Moraru ha naze umareta noka*. Japanese translation of F. de Waal (1997) *Good Natured: The Origins of Right and Wrong in Humans and Other Animals*, T. Nishida and R. Fujii (trans.). Tokyo: Sōshisha.

Nishida, T. (1999a) "Reichōruigaku no rekishi to tenbō" (The history and future of primatology). In T. Nishida and S. Uehara (eds), *Reichōruigaku wo manabu hito no tame ni* (For the students of primatology). Kyoto: Sekaishisōsha, 2–24.

Nishida, T. (1999b) *Ningensei ha doko kara kitaka: Sarugaku karano apurōchi* (Human origin: Primatological approach). Kyoto: Kyoto Daigaku Gakujutsu Shuppan Kai.

Nishida, T. (2008) "Chinpanjī no shakai" (Chimpanzee society). *Inochi no kagaku wo kataru 4* (Discourse on life science 4). Tokyo: Tōhō Shuppan.

Nishida, T. (2011) *Chimpanzees of Lakeshore: Natural History and Culture at Mahale*. New York: Cambridge University Press.

Nishida, T. (2012) *Chimpanzees of the Lakeshore: Natural History and Culture at Mahale*. Cambridge: Cambridge University Press.

Nishida, T. and K. Hosaka (2001) "Reichōrui ni okeru shokumotsu bunpai" (Food distribution in primates). In T. Nishida (ed.), *Hominizēshon* (Hominization) (kōza seitai jinruigaku 8). Kyoto: Kyoto Daigaku Gakujutsu Shuppankai, 255–304.

Nishida, T., K. Hosaka, M. Nakamura and M. Hamai (1995) "A within-group gang attack on a young adult male chimpanzee: Ostracism of an ill-mannered member?". *Primates*, 36: 169–180.

Nishida, T., K. Zamma, T. Matsusaka, A. Inaba and W. C. McGrew (2010) *Chimpanzee Behavior in the Wild*. Tokyo: Springer.

Nishie, H. (2010) "Sōgo kōi ha owaranai: Yasei chinpanjī no 'jōchō na yaritori'" (Never-ending interaction: "Redundant" interaction among wild chimpanzees). In D. Kimura, M. Nakamura and K. Takanashi (eds), *Intārakushon no kyōkai to setsuzoku: Saru, hito kaiwa kenkyū kara* (Boundary and conjunction of social interaction: Studies in non-human primates, humans and conversation). Tokyo: Shōwadō, 387–396.

Nishie, H. (2017) "Who is the alpha male?: The institutionality of dominance rank in chimpanzee society". In K. Kawai (ed.), *Institutions: The Evolution of Human Sociality*. Melbourne: Trans Pacific Press and Kyoto: Kyoto University Press, 121–140.

Nishii, R. (2012) "Dōin no purosesu toshiteno komyuniti, aruiha 'seiseisuru' komyunitī: Minami Thai no Isurāmu fukkō undo" (Community as a process of mobilization, or community generation). In K. Hirai (ed.), *Jissen toshiteno komyunitī: Idō, kokka, undo* (Community as practice: Mobility, state, movement). Kyoto: Kyoto Daigaku Gakujutsu Shuppan Kai, 273–309.

Nishii, R. (2013) *Jōdō no esunogurafī: Minami Tai no mura de kanjiru, tsunagaru, ikiru* (An ethnography of emotions: Feeling, connecting and living in a southern Thai village). Kyoto: Kyoto Daigaku Gakujutsu Shuppan Kai.

Norman, D. A. (2004) *Emōshonaru dezain*. Japanese translation of D. A. Norman (2004) *Emotional Design: Why We Love (or Hate) Everyday Things*, A. Okamoto et al. (trans.). Tokyo: Shinyō Sha.

Novosseloff, A. and F. Neisse (2008) *Des Murs Entre les Hommes*. Paris: La Documentation Française.

Noya, S. (1995) *Kokoro to tasha* (Mind and otherness). Tokyo: Keisō Shobō.

Noya, S. (2012) *Kokoro to tasha* (Mind and otherness). Tokyo: Chūō Kōron Sha.

Nuttall, M. (1992) *Arctic Homeland: Kinship, Community and Development in Northwest Greenland*. London: University of Toronto Press.

Ohta, I. (1986) "Turukana zoku no goshūsei" (Reciprocity among the Turkana). In J. Itani and J. Tanaka (eds), *Shizen shakai no jinruigaku: Afurika ni ikiru* (Anthropology of natural societies: Living in Africa). Kyoto: Academia Shuppan Kai, 181–215.

Ōkawa, M. (2000) "Vēru ron ni miru Chūtō Musurimu josei kenkyū no genzai: Isurāmu shugi to 'kindaika' no shiten kara" (The current state of Middle Eastern Muslim women's studies seen from the discourse on the veil: From the viewpoint of Islamism and "modernization"). *Shakai jinruigaku nenpō* (Annual for social anthropology), 26: 187–203.

Okuno, K., M. Yamaguchi and S. Kondō (2012) *Hito to dōbutsu no jinruigaku* (Anthropology of humans and animals). Tokyo: Shumpūsha.

Ōmori, S. (1981) *Nagare to yodomi* (Flow and stagnation). Tokyo: Sangyō Tosho.

Omura, K. (2005) "Bunka tayōsei heno tobira: Bunka jinruigaku to senjūmin kenkyū" (A door to cultural diversity: Cultural anthropology and indigenous research). In T. Honda, H. Kuzuno and K. Omura (eds), *Bunka jinruigaku kenkyū: Senjūmin no sekai* (Cultural anthropological studies: The world of indigenous peoples). Tokyo: Hōsō Daigaku Kyōiku Shinkō Kai, 29–55.

Omura, K. (2012) "Gijutsu no ontorogī: Inuito no gijutsu fukugō shisutemu wo tōshite miru shizen=Bunka jinruigaku no kanōsei" (The ontology of technology: Considering the potentiality of natural-cultural anthropology through an analysis of the Inuit technological-complex system). *Bunka jinruigaku* (Japanese journal of cultural anthropology), 77(1): 105–127.

Omura, K. (2013a) "The ontology of sociality: 'Sharing' and subsistence mechanisms". In K. Kawai (ed.), *Groups: The Evolution of Human Sociality*. Melbourne: Trans Pacific Press and Kyoto: Kyoto University Press, 123–142.

Omura, K. (2013b) *Kanada Inuito no minzokushi: Nichijōteki jissen no dainamikusu* (The ethnography of Canadian Inuit: The dynamics of everyday practices). Osaka: Osaka Daigaku Shuppan Kai.

Omura, K. (2018) "Shakaisei no jōken toshiteno torauma: Inuito no kodomo heno karakai wo tōshita tasha karano yobikake" (Trauma as a condition of sociality: The call of the Other through the teasing of Inuit children). In M. Tanaka (ed.), *Torauma: Gainen no rekishi to keiken no rekishi* (Trauma: A history of its concept and a history of its experience). Kyoto: Rakuhoku Shuppan, 147–180.

Ōtsuka, E. (2012) *Monogatari shōhi ron aratame* (Narrative consumption theory revised). Tokyo: Ascii Media Works.

Ōtsuka, K. (2004) *Isurāmu shugi toha nanika* (What is Islamism?). Tokyo: Iwanami Shinsho.

Oyama, S. (2002) "Shijō keizaika to yakihata nōkō shakai no henyō" (Market economy and the transformation of shifting cultivation society). In M. Kakeya (ed.), *Afurika nōkōmin no sekai* (The world of African agricultural peoples). Kyoto: Kyoto Daigaku Gakujutsu Shuppan Kai, 3–50.

Oyama, S. (2011) "Zanbia ni okeru shin tochi hō no seitei to Benba nōson no konkyūka" (Enactment of a new land law in Zambia and impoverishment of Bemba rural villages). In J. Itani and M. Kakeya (eds), *Afurika chiiki kenkyū to nōson kaihatsu* (African area studies and rural development), Chapter 5-2. Kyoto: Kyoto Daigaku Gakujutsu Shuppan Kai, 246–274.

Patterson, F. and E. Linden (1984) *Koko, ohanashi shiyō*. Japanese translation of F. Patterson and E. Linden (1981) *The Education of Koko*, A. Tsumori (trans.). Tokyo: Dōbutsu Sha.

Premack, D. and G. Woodruff (1978) "Does the chimpanzee have a theory of mind?". *Behavioral and Brain Sciences*, 4: 515–526.
Propp, V. (1975) *Minwa no keitaigaku*. Japanese translation (from Russian) of V. Propp ([1928] 1958, 1968) *Morphology of the Folktale*, S. Oki (trans.). Tokyo: Hakuba Shobō.
Putnam, R. D. (1993) *Making Democracy Work: Civic Traditions in Modern Italy*. Princeton: Princeton University Press.
Putnam, R. D. (2000) *Bowling Alone: The Collapse and Revival of American Community*. New York: Simon & Schuster.
Reed, E. S. (2000) *Affōdansu no shinrigaku*. Japanese translation of E. S. Reed (1996) *Encountering the World: Toward an Ecological Psychology*, N. Hosoda (trans.). Tokyo: Shinyōsha.
Richard, A. F., S. J. Goldstein and R. E. Dewar (1989) "Weed macaques: The evolutionary implications of macaque feeding ecology". *International Journal of Primatology*, 10(6): 569–594.
Richards, A. I. (1939) *Land, Labour and Diet in Northern Rhodesia*. London: Oxford University Press.
Richards, A. I. (1950) *Bemba Witchcraft*. Rhodes-Livingstone papers 34. Northern Rhodesia: Rhodes-Livingstone Institute.
Rimbaud, A. (2009 [1871]) *Lettres du Voyant, Œuvres complètes* (Bibliothèque de la Pléiade, n° 68). Paris: Editions Gallimard.
Roberts, A. (1974) *History of the Bemba*. New York: Longman.
Roosevelt, T. (1913) *Rūzuberuto shi mōjū gari nikki*. Japanese translation of T. Roosevelt (1910) *African Game Trails: An Account of the African Wanderings of an American Hunter-Naturalist*, F. Yamaguchi (trans.). Tokyo: Hakubun Kan.
Rosaldo, R. (1993) *Culture and Truth: The Remaking of Social Analysis*. Boston: Beacon Press.
Rousseau, J.-J. (1979–1981) *Shin Eroīzu*. Japanese translation of J.-J. Rousseau (1761) *Julie, ou la nouvelle Héloïse*, T. Matsumoto (trans.). *Rusō zenshū* (Complete works of Rousseau) Vols. 9 and 10. Tokyo: Hakusui Sha.
Rowell, T. E. and D. K. Olson (1983) "Alternative mechanisms of social organization in monkeys". *Behaviour*, 86: 31–54.
Sagawa, T. (2011) *Bōryoku to kantai no minzokushi: Higashi Afurika bokuchiku shakai no sensō to heiwa* (Ethnography of violence and hospitality: War and peace in East African pastoralist society). Kyoto: Shōwadō.
Sahlins, M. D. (1972) *Stone Age Economics*. New York: Aldine.
Saitō, R., N. Kishigami and K. Omura (eds) (2009) *Kyokuhoku to shinrin no kioku:*

Inuitto to hokusei kaigan Indian no āto (Memories of life in the Arctic and forest: The art of the Inuit and Northwest Coast Indians). Kyoto: Shōwadō.

Sakamaki, T. and M. Nakamura (2015) "Intergroup relationships". In M. Nakamura, K. Hosaka, N. Itoh and K. Zamma (eds), *Mahale Chimpanzees: 50 Years of Research*. Cambridge: Cambridge University Press, 128–139.

Sakamoto, H. (2010) "Nihon no sōsharu kyapitaru no genjō to rironteki haikei" (The current state of social capital in Japan and its theoretical background). In Kansai Daigaku Keizai Seiji Kenkyūjo (ed.), *Sōsharu kyapiraru to shimin sanka* (Social capital and citizen participation). Osaka: Kansai Daigaku Keizai Seiji Kenkyūjo.

Sartre, J.-P. (1982 [1943]) *Huit Clos, Théâtre complet* (Bibliothèque de la Pléiade, n° 512). Paris: Editions Gallimard.

Savage-Rumbaugh, S. (1993) *Kotoba wo motta tensai zaru Kanzi* (Kanzi, a genius monkey with language). A book version of a television documentary, E. Kaji (trans.). Tokyo: NHK Shuppan.

Schlee, G. (1989) *Identities on the Move: Clanship and Pastoralism in Northern Kenya*. Manchester: Manchester University Press.

Schütz, A. (1967) *The Phenomenology of the Social World*. English translation of A. Schütz (1932) *Der sinnhafte Aufbau der sozialen Welt*, G. Walsh and F. Lehnert (trans.). Evanston: Northwestern University Press.

Sharma, V. (2008) "'Honor Killings' cause concern", *The Hindu*, 29 August.

Shibata, M. (2001) *Robotto no kokoro: 7-tsu no tetsugaku monogatari* (The mind of robots: Seven philosophical tales). Tokyo: Kōdan Sha Gendai Shinsho.

Shinyaku Seisho Honyaku Iinkai (1996) *Shinyaku seisho IV Pauro shokan* (The new testament IV The letters of Paul), T. Aono (trans.). Tokyo: Iwanami Shoten.

Shioya, M. (2004) "Jawa ni okeru vēru chakuyōsha no zōka to sono haikei" (An increase in the number of veil wearers in Java and its background). In I. Tokoro et al. (eds), *Tōnan Ajia no isurāmu* (Islam in Southeast Asia). Tokyo: Tokyo Gaikokugo Daigaku Shuppan Kai, 287–309.

Simonse, S. (1998) "Age, conflict and power in the Momyomiji age system". In E. Kurimoto and S. Simonse (eds), *Conflict, Age, and Power in North East Africa: Age System in Transition*. Oxford: James Currey, 51–78.

Singer, P. (2011) *Dōbutsu no kaihō: kaiteiban*. Japanese translation (revised) of P. Singer (1975) *Animal Liberation*, K. Toda (trans.). Kyoto: Jimbun Shoin.

Skeat, W. W. (1900) *Malay Magic: Being an Introduction to the Folklore and Popular Religion of the Malay Peninsula*. London: Macmillan.

Slater, P. J. B. (1994) *Dōbutsu kōdōgaku nyūmon*. Japanese translation of P. J. B.

Slater (1987) *The Encyclopedia of Animal Behavior*, T. Hidaka and H. Momose (trans.). Tokyo: Heibon Sha.

Soga, T. (2002) "Kokka no soto kara uchigawa he: Rakuda bokuchikumin Gabura ga keikenshita senkyo" (From the outside to the inside of the state: The impact of an election on the camel pastoralist Gabra). In S. Satō (ed.), *Yūboku min no sekai* (The world of nomadic peoples). Kyoto: Kyoto University Press, 127–174.

Soga, T. (2013) "Perceivable 'unity': Between visible 'group' and invisible 'category'". In K. Kawai (ed.), *Groups: The Evolution of Human Sociality*. Melbourne: Trans Pacific Press and Kyoto: Kyoto University Press, 219–238.

Soga, T. (2017) "The formation of institutions". In K. Kawai (ed.), *Institutions: The Evolution of Human Sociality*. Melbourne: Trans Pacific Press and Kyoto: Kyoto University Press, 19–38.

Spottorno, C. and G. Abril (2016) *La Grieta*. Bilbao: Astiberri.

Steinhart, E. I. (2006) *Black Poachers, White Hunters: A Social History of Hunting in Colonial Kenya*. Oxford: James Currey.

Stern, D. (1983) "The early development of schemas of self, other and 'self with other'". In J. D. Lichtenberg and S. Kaplar (eds), *Reflection on Self Psychology*. New Jersey: Hillsdale, 49–84.

Stewart, H. (1995) "Gendai no Netsurikku Inuitto shakai ni okeru seigyō katsudō" (Subsistence activities in modern-day Netsilik Inuit society: Physical survival, cultural survival). *Dai 9-kai hoppō minzoku bunka shinpojiumu hōkokusho* (Proceedings of the 9th International Abashiri Symposium). Hokkaido Museum of Northern Peoples, 37–67.

Stewart, H. (1996) "Genzai no saishū shuryōmin ni totteno seigyō katsudō no igi: Minzoku to minzoku gakusha no jiko teiji gensetsu wo megutte" (The meaning of subsistence activities for modern-day hunters and gatherers: Surrounding self-presented discourses of ethnic peoples and ethnologists). In H. Stewart (ed.), *Saishū shuryōmin no genzai* (The gatherer-hunters today: Changes in and reproduction of subsistence culture). Tokyo: Gensō Sha, 125–154.

Stöhr, W. and P. Zoetmulder (1965) *Religionen Indonesiens*. Stuttgart: Kohlhammer.

Suddendorf, T. (2014) *Genjitsu wo ikiru saru, kūsō wo kataru hito: Ningen to dōbutsu wo hedateru tatta futatsu no chigai*. Japanese translation of T. Suddendorf (2013) *The Gap: The Science of What Separates Us from Other Animals*, T. Teramachi (trans.). Tokyo: Hakuyō Sha.

Sugiyama, Y. (1981) *Yasei chinpanjī no shakai* (Wild chimpanzee society). Tokyo: Kōdansha.

Sugiyama, Y. (2004) "Kieta mura, saisei suru mura: Bemba no nōson ni okeru noroi jiken no kaishaku to ken'i no seitōsei" (Village that disappears, village that revives: The interpretation of witchcraft cases in Bemba rural villages and the legitimacy of authority). In H. Terashima (ed.), *Byōdō to fubyōdō wo meguru jinruigakuteki kenkyū* (Anthropological study on equality and inequality). Kyoto: Nakanishiya Shuppan, 134–171.

Sugiyama, Y. (2013) "The small village of 'We, the Bemba'". In K. Kawai (ed.), *Groups: The Evolution of Human Sociality*. Melbourne: Trans Pacific Press and Kyoto: Kyoto University Press, 239–260.

Sugiyama, Y. (2017) "The Institution of 'Feeling': On 'Feeling Inside' and 'Institutionalized Envy'". In K. Kawai (ed.), *Institutions: The Evolution of Human Sociality*. Melbourne: Trans Pacific Press and Kyoto: Kyoto University Press, 349–370.

Taguchi, S. (2014) *Genshōgaku toiu shikō: "Jimeina mono" no chi e* (Phenomenological thinking: Toward a knowledge of the obvious). Tokyo: Chikuma Shobō.

Takeshita, H. (1999) *Kokoro to kotoba no shoki hattatsu: Reichōrui no hikaku hattatsugaku* (The early development of mind and language: A comparative study of primate development). Tokyo: Tokyo Daigaku Shuppan Kai.

Tamura, U. (2009) "Toruko no teiki ichi ni okeru urite-kaite kankei: Kokyaku kankei no koteika wo megutte" (Buyer-seller relationships in Turkish periodic markets: An analysis of clientelization). *Bunka jinruigaku* (Cultural anthropology), 74(1): 48–72.

Tanabe, S. (2013) *Seirei no jinruigaku: Kita Tai ni okeru kyōdōsei no poritikusu* (An anthropology of spirits: The politics of cooperativity in northern Thailand). Tokyo: Iwanami Shoten.

Tanaka, M. (2007) "Kahei to kyōdōtai: Sriranka tamiru gyoson ni okeru fusai no zōyoteki shigensei wo megutte" (Currency and community: On the gift-like nature of debts in a Tamil fishing village, Sri Lanka). In N. Kasuga (ed.), *Kahei to shigen* (Currency and resources). Tokyo: Kōbundō, 59–107.

Tanaka, M. (2012) "Meiyo satsujin: Gendai Indo ni okeru josei heno bōryoku" (Honor killing: On the violence against women in contemporary India). *Gendai Indo kenkyū* (Contemporary India), 2: 59–77.

Tanaka, M. (2013) "Agency and seduction: Against a Girardian model of society". In K. Kawai (ed.), *Groups: The Evolution of Human Sociality*. Melbourne: Trans Pacific Press and Kyoto: Kyoto University Press, 293–308.

Tanaka, M. (2014a) "'Yatto honto no kao wo misete kureta ne!': Nihonjin sekkusu wākā ni miru nikutai, kanjō, kannō wo meguru rōdō ni tsuite" ("You are showing me your real face at last!": On manual, emotional and erotic labor in Japanese sex work). *Contact Zone*, 6: 30–59.

Tanaka, M. (2014b) "Shinguru wo hitei shi shinguru wo kōtei suru: Nihon no sekkusu wākā ni okeru kokyaku to koibito tono kankei wo megutte" (Denial and affirmation of singlehood: On Japanese sex workers' relationships with clients and lovers). In W. Shiino (ed.), *Shinguru no jinruigaku 2: Shinguru no tsunagu en* (An anthropology of singles 2: Connection between singles). Kyoto: Jimbun Shoin, 79–99.

Tanaka, M. (2015) "Suriranka no minzoku funsō to shūkyō: Sōsharu kyapitaru ron no shiten kara" (Ethnic conflicts and religion in Sri Lanka: From the perspective of social capital theory). In Y. Sakurai et al. (eds), *Ajia no shakai sanka bukkyō: Seikyō kankei no shiza kara* (Engaged Buddhism in Asia: From a state-religion relationship perspective). Hokkaido: Hokkaido Daigaku Shuppan Kai, 309–336.

Thompson, J. L. and A. J. Nelson (2011) "Middle childhood and modern human origins". *Human Nature*, 22: 249–280.

Tinbergen, N. (1957) *Dōbutsu no kotoba*. Japanese translation of N. Tinbergen (1953) *Social Behavior in Animals*, M. Watanabe et al. (trans.). Tokyo: Misuzu Shobō.

Tokoro, I. (1999) *Ekkyō: Sūrū kaiiki sekai kara* (Border transgressions: From the world of the Sulu maritime world). Tokyo: Iwanami Shoten.

Tokoro, I. (2011) "'Mono' no gyoshigatasa: Shinju yōshoku wo meguru aratana 'hito/mono' ron" (Uncontrollability of mono: A new perspective on 'humans/mono' surrounding cultured pearls). In I. Tokoro and K. Kawai (eds), *Mono no jinruigaku* (The anthropology of mono/things). Kyoto: Kyoto Daigaku Gakujutsu Shuppan Kai, 71–89.

Tokoro, I. (2018) "Mono beyond control: A new perspective on cultured pearls". In I. Tokoro and K. Kawai (eds), *An Anthropology of Things*. Kyoto: Kyoto University Press and Melbourne: Trans Pacific Press, 81–95.

Tokoro, I. and K. Kawai (eds), (2011) *Mono no jinruigaku* (The anthropology of mono/things). Kyoto: Kyoto Daigaku Gakujutsu Shuppan Kai.

Tomasello, M. (1999) *The Cultural Origins of Human Cognition*. Cambridge: Harvard University Press.

Tomasello, M. (2006) *Kokoro to kotoba no kigen wo saguru*. Japanese translation of M. Tomasello (1999) *The Cultural Origins of Human Cognition*, T. Ōhori et al. (trans.). Tokyo: Keisō Shobō.

Tomasello, M. (2008) *Kotoba wo tsukuru*. Japanese translation of M. Tomasello

(2003) *Constructing a Language*, Y. Tsuji et al. (trans.). Tokyo: Keio Gijuku Daigaku Shuppan Kai.

Tomasello, M. (2013) *Hito ha naze kyōryokusuru noka*. Japanese translation of M. Tomasello (2009) *Why We Cooperate*, K. Hashiya (trans.). Tokyo: Keisō Shoten.

Trivers, R. (1991) *Seibutsu no shakai shinka*. Japanese translation of R. Trivers (1985) *Social Evolution*, Y. Nakajima et al. (trans.). Tokyo: Sangyō Tosho.

Tsuru, S. (1998) "Levinasu no tasha ron" (Otherness by Lévinas). *Hattatsu ningengaku ronsō* (Bulletin of the Laboratory of Developmental Psychology of Osaka Kyoiku University), 1: 99–105.

Tsuru, S. (2012) "Levinasu ni okeru chōetsu wo kiten toshita rinri to shūkyō" (Ethics and religion from the transcendence of Lévinas). *Osaka Yakka Daigaku Kiyō* (Bulletin of Osaka University of Pharmaceutical Sciences), 6: 27–36.

Tsutsui, Y. (1979) "Saiaku no sesshoku" (Worst contact). In *Uchū eisei hakurankai* (Universal hygiene expo). Tokyo: Shinchō Bunko, 127–158.

Turing, A. M. (1950) "Computing machinery and intelligence". *Mind*, 49: 433–460.

Turner, V. (1972) *Schism and Continuity in an African Society: A Study of Ndembu Village Life*. Manchester: Manchester University Press.

Uchibori, M. (1980) "Iban zoku no minwa (jō, chū, ge)" (Folk tales of the Iban people 1, 2, 3). *Gekkan gengo* (Language monthly), 8(10): 82–94; 8(11): 86–95; 8(12): 88–97. Tokyo: Taishū Kan.

Uchibori, M. (1996) *Mori no tabekata* (Between the longhouse and the forest). Tokyo: Tokyo Daigaku Shuppan Kai.

Uchibori, M. (2002) "Bungai". *Encyclopaedia of Iban Studies*, 4 vols. Kuching: The Tun Jugah Foundation and Borneo Research Council.

Uchibori, M. (2006) "Koe to kotoba no chikara: Boruneo Iban no saimon wo megutte" (The power of voices and words: On ritual incantations of the Iban, Borneo). *Shizen to bunka soshite kotoba* (Nature, culture and language), 1: 74–80.

Uchibori, M. (2013) "Kokoro ha shintaiteki ni shika katarenai: Kokoro, inochi, tamashii ha karada no doko ni arunoka" (The mind can only be spoken of through the body: Where are the mind, life and soul situated in the body?). In K. Sugawara (ed.), *Shintaika no jinruigaku: Ninchi, kioku, gengo, tasha* (An anthropology of embodiment: Cognition, memory, language, other). Kyoto: Sekai Shisō Sha, 76–101.

Uchibori, M. (2014) "When *Semangat* becomes *Antu*: An essay on Iban ontology". *NGINGIT*, Kuching: The Tun Jugah Foundation, 5: 27–32.

Uchibori, M. (2017) "An institution called death: Towards its *arche*". In K. Kawai (ed.), *Institutions: The Evolution of Human Sociality*. Melbourne: Trans Pacific Press and Kyoto: Kyoto University Press, 39–58.

Uchibori, M. and S. Yamahita (2006 [1986]) *Shi no jijruigaku* (Anthropology of death). Tokyo: Kōbundō, Kōdansha.

Uchida, N. (1990) *Sōzōryoku no hattatsu: Sōzōteki sōzō no mechanizumu* (The development of imagination: The mechanism of creative imagining). Tokyo: Saiensu Sha.

Uno, K. (2012) *Durūzu: Mure to kesshō* (Deleuze: Aggregates and crystals). Tokyo: Kawade Shobō Shinsha.

Uriu, Y. (2007) "Uso wo motomerareru bamen deno yōji no hannō: Go shinnen kadai tono hikaku kara" (Young children's responses to a deception task: Compared with responses to the false-belief task). *Hattatsu shinrigaku kenkyū* (The Japanese journal of developmental psychology), 18: 13–24.

Van Schaick, C. P. and C. H. Janson (eds) (2000) *Infanticide by Males and its Implications*. Cambridge: Cambridge University Press.

von Humboldt, W. (2006) *Sōsū nit suite*. Japanese translation of W. von Humboldt (1827–1829) *Ueber den Dualis*, S. Muraoka (trans.). Tokyo: Shinsho Kan.

Wagner, U. (1972) *Colonialism and Iban Warfare*. Stockholm: Obe-Tryck Sthlm.

Wakō, K. (2010) *Dōbutsu en kakumei* (The zoo revolution). Tokyo: Iwanami Shoten.

Washida, K. (1998) *Kao no genshōgaku: Mirareru koto no kenri* (A phenomenology of the face: The right to be seen). Tokyo: Kōdansha Gakujutsu Bunko.

Watanabe, M. (2015) "Shō torihiki ni okeru 'kake' to 'furendoshippu': Katomanzu no kankō shijō, Tameru ni okeru hōshoku shōnin no jirei kara" (The "bet" and "friendship" in economic transactions: A case study of jewelry merchants in Thamel, the tourist market of Kathmandu). *Bunka jinruigaku* (Cultural anthropology), 79(4): 397–416.

Wenzel, G. (1991) *Animal Rights, Human Rights*. London: University of Toronto Press.

Whiten, A., D. M. Custance, J.-C. Gomez, P. Teixidor and K. A. Bard (1996) "Imitative learning of artificial fruit processing in children (*Homo sapiens*) and chimpanzees (*Pan troglodytes*)". *Journal of Comparative Psychology*, 110: 3–14.

Wiedenhöfer, K. (2013) *Confrontier: Borders 1989–2012*. Göttingen: Steidl.

Wilde, O. (1968) *Kyogen no suitai*. Japanese translation of O. Wilde (1891) *The Decay of Lying*, M. Yoshida (trans.). Tokyo: Kenkyu Sha.

Wilson, E. O. (2000 [1975]) *Sociobiology: The New Synthesis*. Cambridge: Belknap.

Wilson, M. L., S. M. Kahlenberg, M. Wells and R. W. Wrangham (2012) "Ecological

and social factors affect the occurrence and outcomes of intergroup encounters in chimpanzees". *Animal Behaviour*, 83: 277–291.
Wittgenstein, L. (1994) *Tetsugaku tankyū*. Japanese translation of L. Wittgenstein (1953) *Philosophische untersuchungen*, T. Fujimoto (trans.). Tokyo: Taishūkan.
Wolf, E. R. (1965) "Kinship, friendship, and patron-client relations in complex societies". In M. Banton (ed.), *Social Anthropology of Complex Societies*. London: Tavistock, 21–62.
Wolfe, N. D., C. Panosian Dunavan and J. Diamond (2007) "Origins of major human infectious diseases". *Nature*, 447: 279–283.
Wrangham, R. and D. Peterson (1996) *Demonic Males: Apes and the Origins of Human Violence*. Boston and New York: Mariner Books/Houghton Mifflin Company.
Wrangham, R. W. (1999) "Evolution of coalitionary killing". *Yearbook of Physical Anthropology*, 42: 1–30.
Yabuta, S. (2008) "'Shakaisei' ha reichōrui ni tokuyū no genshō ka" (Is "sociality" a uniquely primate phenomenon?). *Reichōrui kenkyū* (Primate Research), 24(2): 133–136.
Yamagiwa, J. (2007) *Bōryoku wa doko kara kitaka* (Origins of violence). Tokyo: Nihon Hōsō Shuppan Kyōkai.
Yamagiwa, J. (2015a) "Evolution of hominid life history strategy and origin of human family". In T. Furuich, J. Yamagiwa and F. Aureli (eds), *Dispersing Primate Females: Life History and Social Strategies in Male-Philopatric Species*. Berlin: Springer.
Yamagiwa, J. (2015b) *Gorira* (Gorillas). Tokyo: Tokyo Daigaku Shuppan Kai.
Yamagiwa, J. (2015c) *Gorira dai-2-han* (Gorillas, second edition). Tokyo: Tokyo Daigaku Shuppan Kai.
Yamagiwa, J. (ed.) (2007) *Hito ha donoyōnishite tsukurareta ka* (How humans were made), Hito no kagaku (Human science) series 1. Tokyo: Iwanami Shoten.
Yamaguchi, H. (2011) *Hito ha seimei wo donoyōni rikaishitekitaka* (The history of people's understanding of life). Tokyo: Kōdan Sha Sensho Mechie.
Yamaguchi, M. (2000) *Bunka no ryōgisei* (Ambiguity of culture). Tokyo: Iwanami Shoten.
Yamakoshi, G. (1999) "'Shinsei na mori' no chinpanjī: Ginia Bossou ni okeru hito tono kyōzon" (Chimpanzees in the "sacred forest": Coexistence with people in Bossou, Guinea). *Ekosofia* (Ecosophia), 3: 106–117.
Yamakoshi, G. (2006) "Yasei chinpanjī tono kyōzon wo sasaeru zairai chi ni motozuita hozen moderu: Ginia Bossou mura ni okeru jūmin undō no jirei

kara" (A conservation model based on conventional wisdom supporting coexistence with wild chimpanzees: A case of civic movement in a village, Bossou, Guinea). *Kankyō shakaigaku kenkyū* (Journal of environmental sociology), 12: 120–135.

Yamakoshi, G. (2009) "Ginia nanbu shinrin chiiki ni okeru sonraku rin no seitai shi: Dōnatsu jō shinrin no kinō to seiin" (Ecological history of village forests in the woodland of southern Guinea: The function and origin of the doughnut-shaped forest). In K. Ikeya (ed.), *Chikyū kankyō shi kara no toi* (Questions from the environmental history of the Earth). Tokyo: Iwanami Shoten, 208–216.

Yamakoshi, G. (2011) "The 'prehistory' before 1976: Looking back on three decades of research on Bossou chimpanzees". In T. Matsuzawa, T. Humle and Y. Sugiyama (eds), *The Chimpanzees of Bossou and Nimba*. Tokyo: Springer, 35–44.

Yamakoshi, G. (2014) "Shizen hogo" (Conservation). In Nihon Afurika Gakkai (ed.), *Afurika jiten* (Encyclopedia of African studies). Kyoto: Shōwa Dō, 614–623.

Yasuda, A. (2013) *Mamoru tame ni korosu? Afurika ni okeru supōtsu hantingu no "jizoku kanōsei" to chiiki shakai* (Kill to protect? The concept of game hunting "sustainability" and local community in Africa). Tokyo: Keisō Shobō.

Yoshida, Y. (2011) "Kamen ga geinō wo hagukumu: Bari tō no topen butōgeki ni chūmokushite" (Masks nurturing the performing arts: Topeng, a Balinese masked dance drama). In I. Tokoro and K. Kawai (eds), *Mono no jinruigaku* (The anthropology of mono/things). Kyoto: Kyoto Daigaku Gakujutsu Shuppan Kai, 191–210.

Yoshizawa, N. (2002) *Sekai no hakanasa no shakaigaku: Shuttsu kara Rūman* (A sociology of the transience of the world: From Schütz to Luhmann). Tokyo: Keisō Shobō.

Zamma, K. (2011) "Responses of chimpanzees to a python". *Pan Africa News*, 18: 13–15.

Index

Subjects

absence of the face *see* "face"
academic disciplines 66
acquaintances 115, 180, 204
activation of difference 201
adaptation 360
adolescents (*inuuhuktut*) 242
adult (*inirniit*) 241
affection (*naglik-*) 241
affliction 428
agency 409, 416, 422
all possible but invisible relationships *see* "relationship"
allomothering 404
alpha male *see* "male"
alter ego 342
alterity 243, 253
altruism 305
amalgamation 227
ancestral spirits 263
animal 409, 413–414
  animal behavioral science 55
  animal carcass 62
  damage to agricultural crops and people by wild animals 349
  discourse on animals in anthropology 52
  pet animal 53
  strange urge to see animals 356
  village animals 352, 360
animism 333
anthropogenic landscape 352
anthropology 6, 8
  cultural anthropology 50
  discourse on animals in anthropology 52
  ecological anthropology 7
  economic anthropology 313
  resource anthropology 308
anthropomorphization 15
anti-cohesiveness (*hishūchūsei*) 165, 168, 171
anti-social 247
anti-structured social groups *see* "social group"

antu (spirits) 333, 342
approachable/unapproachable other *see* "other/otherness"
approval
  approval for co-presence 30, 33, 38
  request for approval 33
  seeking approval 35, 37, 39
approving others *see* "other/otherness"
artificial objects 409
associate 268
Atanarjuat 453
atypical 266
auditory co-presence 181, 192, 198
automatic/physical response 65
autonomous "individual" *see* "individual"
autonomy 241

"bare others" *see* "other/otherness"
begging 74
behavioral layers 331
betrayal 453
"big-game hunting" 353, 355
bipartite relationship *see* "relationship"
boundaries 450
boundary 192, 201, 205
boundary between self and other 259, 285, 299
Buddhists 285

call-response 181
cannibalism 73
cercopithecine 375
change the rules and reorganize "We" 31
character 401
  character/actor duality 396–397
chiefdom 263
child as the other *see* "other/otherness"
children (*nutaraat*) 241
chitemene system 264
circuit for sympathy 232
client 314–315

Index 499

coexistence 1, 219, 232, 359, 371, 382, 384, 423
 coexistence of I and the other 300 *see also* "other/otherness"
 coexistence principle 28
cognition
 cognition of the other 55, 115, 222 *see also* "other/otherness"
 cognitive toughness 147
cohesiveness 165
 lack of cohesiveness 167
collaboration 247, 404
collective
 collective consumption 103
 collective excitement 28, 43
 collective others 261 *see also* "other/otherness"
communal dining 238, 247–248 *see also* "extended family group"
communication 93, 286, 403
communitas-like collective excitement 43
communitas-like situation 43
companions 195
comprehensible others *see* "other/otherness"
computer 417–420
concept of others *see* "other/otherness"
conditions giving rise to others *see* "other/otherness"
consideration 223, 231, 233
constructing scenarios recursively 394
consumption 353 *see also* "habituation"
contingency 128, 147
control 244, 248, 253 *see* "domination"
cooperation 404
cooperative breeding 403
cooperative hunting 405
co-presence 1, 8–9, 36, 38, 93, 130, 196–198, 258
cosmology 286
cultural anthropology *see* "anthropology"
culture 370
currency 306

Da'wa movement 286–287, 295–296
dead 285, 301
debt 316
deep engagement 33, 35, 74
demand approval 33

demon 334
 demon spirit 329
deviant 45
deviation 28, 39, 45–46
dialogically 277
difference between one species and another 63
differentiation 367
dilemma 240, 243–44, 247, 250
 deferring the dilemma 247
dissolve or split "We" 31
division of labor *see* "work sharing"
domestication 246, 350, 353
dominant-subordinate relationships *see* "relationships"
domination 244, 248, 253
dream 332, 336, 346

egalitarian 107
ego
 problem of ego and alter ego 51
embodiment 305
emoit as "enemy" 230
emotion 221
empathic understanding of the other *see* "other/otherness"
empathy 6, 19, 112, 207, 220–222, 232, 261
empirical sciences 3, 6
encounter 151–152, 156, 158, 165–166, 168, 170, 172
 non-face-to-face encounters 181 *see also* "face"
 repeated encounters 154
enemy 76, 199, 201–202, 223, 450
"enticement–order" 247
environment 367
equality 233
 equality principle 28, 42–43, 45
equilibrium 382
erotic massage 315
erotic masseur 315
ethics 6, 228, 252, 256
ethnographic materials 427
ethology 327
evolution 3, 5, 16
exploit 248
exploration 152–158, 160, 164–165, 170–172, 189, 192, 195, 198
extended family group 238, 245, 454

extermination camp 319
extraordinary sense 289

face 285, 299
  face covering 293
  face-covering veil (*pit na*) *see* "veil"
  face-to-face interaction 75
  absence of the face 286
  non-face-to-face encounters 181
  non-face-to-face interactions 200
faction 313
false belief 390
falteringness (difficulty) of interaction 131
familiarization method 358
family 120
female
  newly immigrated females 204–206
field 151–152, 164–165, 172, 376, 380–381
  field research 6
first person plural pronouns 439
fishing 245
fission-fusion 97, 132, 168, 170–171
flower 328
food provisioning 358
food sharing 99, 103, 245
frames of relationship *see* "relationship"
freedom
  freedom of refusal 102
  freedom to move 43
friendly 76

gap 260
gathering 245
  non-structured gathering 258
genital rubbing 38, 44
genito-genital rubbing 38
Gerasi 334 *see also* "*antu* (spirits)"
gift 306, 310, 313, 316
goal-oriented 199, 202–203 *see also* "process-oriented"
goods 352
greeting 37
gregariousness 220
group 12, 151, 164, 166, 168, 170–172
  group living 205
  structured group 259
  unit-group 19, 56, 96, 98, 116–117, 132
Groups: The Evolution of Human Sociality 2, 8, 425

habituation 61, 350, 353, 358, 361–362
  consumption 353
  domestication 246, 350, 353
  reproduction 353
headhunting 73, 339, 341
here, now 9, 378, 383
hero-and-villain test 391
heterogeneous others *see* "other/otherness"
higher-order identity 224
home range 184–185
hominins 117
homogeneous others *see* "other/otherness"
honor killing 316–318
hostile (non-hostile) relationship/
  interaction *see* "relationship"
human evolution 7, 17, 115, 119, 424
hunter-gatherer 402
hunting 59, 245, 342

ideal personality 240
identity 221
ikat cloth 329
ilagiimariktut (real *ilagiit*) 454
ilagiit 454
imaginary companions 54
incidence of injuries amongst village
  children caused by chimpanzees 362
incomprehensible others *see* "other/otherness"
incomprehensible whole 132
independent beings 229
indeterminacy 151–154, 157–158, 160–161, 163–165, 167–168, 171–172
individual 2
  autonomous "individual" 51
inequality principle 42–43
infanticide 404
infants 33–35
  infants (*inuuhaat*) 241
inhibition 228
initiation 430
insiders 306
institution 12, 128–130, 199, 373
  institutional conventions 370
  natural institutions 122
  proto-institutions 10, 228
Institutions: The Evolution of Human Sociality 2, 8, 425
instrumentality 305

Index 501

interaction 225
　interaction systems 93
　non-face-to-face interactions 200 *see also* "face"
　readiness (possibility) for interaction 131
intercorporeality 72
intergroup encounters 57, 371
intergroup relations 182, 184, 202
intergroup transfer 207
inter-individual relationship *see* "relationship"
interpersonal relations *see* "relationship"
interspecific relationship *see* "relationship"
interstice (*sukima*) 153–154, 156–158, 160–162, 164–165, 168, 170
intersubjectivity 72, 114
involvement 81
Isuma Igloolik Productions 453

Japanese primatology 4
joy of achievement 33, 35
Julie, ou la nouvelle Héloïse 436

known other *see* "other/otherness"
Kokoro 441

lack of cohesiveness *see* "cohesiveness"
lack of need for approval 34
language acquisition 100, 106
letter 435
"letter" as bipartite relationship 434
life form 376
life-world 247
limit 442

Machiavellian intelligence hypothesis 423
male
　male group 36–38
　alpha male 133
　non-troop male 373
　solitary male 204
manipulation 369
matrilineal social groups *see* "social group"
matrilineality 264
membership of the same group 205
mind 5
　mind-reading 369

miombo woodland 263
mixed-species association 374
modern age 352
"modification of the self" 72
monolithic existence 230
morality/moral 6, 228, 305
multilevel societies *see* "society"
Muslim women 286, 301
mutuality
　mutual approval 36, 41
　mutual dependency 221
　mutually referable relationship framework 146–147

nalawan 430
narrative 261
　narrative for reunification 276
　narrative of division 272
natural institutions 122 *see also* "institution"
natural objects 415
natural pedagogy 403
nature reserves 354
"nature" as fiction 354
"nature" tourism *see* "tourism"
need for approval 33–34, 36
nested scenario building 394
net hunting 273
newly immigrated females 204–206
niche 379, 381
nimangki 430
non-equilibrium 381
non-face-to-face encounters 181 *see also* "encounter ", "face"
non-face-to-face interactions 200
non-human 52, 345
　non-human beings 409, 418, 424
nonlinguistic vocalization 200
non-mother 398, 400
non-structured gathering *see* "gathering"
non-troop male *see* "male"
norm 246
nuna 247

on the whole 380, 383
ontology 252, 256, 330
order of theory of mind 392 *see also* "theory of mind"
organ transplantation 305

Orientalism 453
other/otherness 3, 14, 113, 130–132, 202, 239, 243, 252, 305, 389, 453
    other as a character/actor 396, 406
    others as groups 50, 56, 58
    others as individuals 50, 55
    others who can refuse 107
    other with no character 402
    others with whom we could potentially interact 53
    others-as-strangers 345
    approachable/unapproachable other 258, 266, 269
    approving other 30, 34–38
    "bare others" 17, 128, 130, 148, 152
    child as the other 401
    coexistence of I and the other 300
    cognition of the other 55
    comprehensible others 72
    concept of others 29, 66
    conditions giving rise to others 50
    empathic understanding of the other 115, 222, 233
    heterogeneous others 4
    homogeneous others 4
    incomprehensible others 31, 33, 39–41, 43, 45–46, 73
    known other 333
    qualified other 128, 130, 148, 151–152
    recognizing otherness 45
    spectrum of approving others 30
    stranger-other 327, 337
    violent incomprehensible others 40
    ways to deal with otherness 180, 203
Others I 411, 422
Others II 411, 422
othering 2–4, 11, 276, 305, 312, 318, 404
outsider 306, 313

pant-grunt 133
pant-hoot 137, 181, 186, 204
paradox 300
pastoralism 246
patrilineal social structure / patrilineal social groups / patrilineal society 28, 36, 42–43
patron-client relationship 313 see also "relationship"

Paul's letters 437, 441
peace 226
peering behavior 44–45
permanent settlement 352
personal reform 286
personality 240
personhood 330
perspectives 331
pet animal see "animal"
phenomenology 305
philosophical problem 50
philosophy 427
"photo safari" 355–356, 363–364 see also "safari"
physical synchronization 222
picturesque tourism see "tourism"
polyphonic dialogue 261
"potential infanticide risk" 404
predator-prey interactions 376
primatology 6, 8, 12, 14–15, 358
primordial human societies see "society"
problem of ego and alter ego see "ego"
process-oriented 181, 192, 195, 199, 202–203 see also "goal-oriented"
prostitution see "sex work"
proto-institutions 10, 228 see also "institution"

qualified other see "other/otherness"

raiding 219, 226
rank order 37, 40, 42
readiness (possibility) for interaction 131 see also "interaction"
"real food" (*niqinmarik*) 238, 249, 454
"real Inuit" 240, 453 see also "ethnic groups index"
"reason" (*ihuma-*) 241
reciprocal altruism 5–6, 221
recognizing otherness see "other/otherness"
recurrent 170
recursive process 97, 165
reference standard 84
relatedness 311
relationship
    all possible but invisible relationships 139, 144

Index 503

bipartite relationship 426
dominant-subordinate relationship 246
frames of relationship 199
hostile (non-hostile) relationship/
    interaction 219, 223, 227
inter-individual relationship 15
interpersonal relations 230
interspecific relationship 65
patron-client relationship 313
relatives 115
renewed world 46
repeated encounters see "encounter"
repetitiveness 168
reproduction 353 see also "habituation"
request for approval see "approval"
resource anthropology see "anthropology"
responsibility 239, 252, 452
robotic pets 54
role 379
    role expectations 401

sacred forest 362
safari 353
    safari hunting 357, 364
    "photo safari" 355–356, 363–364
saga 224, 395, 405
Sally-Anne test 390
savanna 358
seeking approval see "approval"
seken ("society" or "social circle" in
    Japanese) 429
self 113, 202, 344
    self as a character 395
    self as actor/director 395
self-recognition/self-awareness 15, 397
self-other-object model 77
self-productive process 108
self-restraint 43
seme (charge, liability) 452
sex work 314, 315
sexuality 316
shaman 328
sharing 265
sign 153–154, 160, 164
    sign stimulus 367
    symbolic "sign" 426
"singulars" 437
sniper 319

social capital 309
social clue 393
social counterparts 66
social facilitation 94
social group
    anti-structured social groups 378
    matrilineal social groups 42
social inhibition 94
social interaction 11, 53
social structure of *Pan* 36
social system 238
sociality 2, 5, 239, 252–253
socializing the child 398
societal foundation 93
society
    society where they can stay apart from
        one another 204
    multilevel societies 119
    primordial human societies 106
sociobiology 52
solidarity 43, 196, 289
solitary male see "male"
somebody 137
    yet-to-be encountered (specified/
        unspecified) somebody 144
soul 329
speech overlap 105
spirit (*tagniq*) 245
spontaneous order 129
story 395
    stories of relationships 198
    story-telling ability 394
    shared (common) story 396
strange urge to see animals 356 see also
    "animal"
stranger/stranger-ness 115, 180, 187, 198,
    203, 205, 207, 307, 320
    stranger-other 327, 337 see also "other/
        otherness"
    strangers' voices 186, 207
strategy 383
structured group see "group"
subjectivity 239, 243, 252
subordination 246, 248, 251–252
subsistence 238, 240, 245, 453–454
    subsistence system 238
supracommunal pastoral value-sharing
    sphere 224

suspension 138
synchronization 111

tactics 383
   tactical deception 391
telling/retelling 263
tetrahedral model 430 *see also* "bipartite relationship", "tripartite relationship"
The New Testament 435
theory of mind 6, 45, 115, 119, 390–393, 423
third term 78
tool-using behavior 360
tourism
   "nature" tourism 353
   picturesque tourism 354
   wildlife tourism 364
transcendence 270, 442
transfer 58, 373
trapping 245
triadic interaction 114
triadic relationship 77
tripartite relationship 426 *see also* "bipartite relationship", "tetrahedral model"
trust 246
   trust and collaboration 247
Turing Test 418–421

unapproachable other 258
unclean 76
unified neutral theory 382

unit-group 56, 132 *see also* "group"
"unspoiled nature" 355

veil 286, 288, 291, 295–296, 300–301
   face-covering veil (*pit na*) 288
village animals 352, 360 *see also* "animal"
violent incomprehensible others *see* "other/otherness"
visage 90
voluntary choices 102

war 183, 225
ways to deal with otherness *see* "other/otherness"
"we" consciousness/framework/*we*-ness 9, 13, 31, 39, 46, 122
weaning infant 32
wildlife/wild animal 349, 357
   wildlife tourism *see* "tourism"
witch 321
witchcraft 264
work sharing 405
worldview 245
wraa calls 186, 190, 192, 206
written works 427

yet-to-be encountered (specified/unspecified) somebody *see* "somebody"

zoonosis 350, 361

Ethnic groups

Bemba 258
Bushmen 103
Daasanach 85
Dodoth 219
Gabra Malbe 79
Gabra Miigo 78
Iban 328

Ilongot 86
Inuit 240
Jie 224
Mbotgote 429
Sama 411, 463
Turkana 85, 219

Organisms

ant 64
ape 350
bonobo 34–39, 43–44
bushpig 62
chimpanzee 28, 34–35, 37–39, 42–43, 49,
    112, 132, 151–152, 154, 158, 161–168,
    170–172, 180, 199, 358–359, 363, 396
diana monkey 375
genet 62
gorilla 358, 363, 396, 398
great ape 391, 396

Homo 118
Homo sapiens (human) 1, 49, 199, 349
Japanese macaque 111, 358
leopard 60
non-human primate 1
Pan 27–28
red colobus 58, 375
social insects 64
three-spined stickleback 64
warthog 61

Personal names

Blixen, Karen (Dinesen, Isak) 356
Briggs, J. L. 240, 453
Carsten, Janet 311
Dinesen, Isak *see* "Blixen, Karen"
de Waal, Franciscus Bernardus Maria 15,
    221, 358
Ekman, P. 285
Erikson, E. H. 27, 30
Evans-Pritchard, Edward Evan 321
Freeman, D. 330
Goblin 40–41
Goodall, Jane 40–41
Hegel, Georg Wilhelm Friedrich 228
Hallowel, A. I. 331
Hewlett, B. S. 402
Hubbell, Stephen 382
Humboldt, Friedrich Wilhelm Christian
    Karl Ferdinand Freiherr von 439
Imanishi Kinji 7, 350–351, 358

Itani Jun'ichirō 7, 27–30, 36, 42, 120, 165,
    373, 378
Kumano Sumihiko 239
Lévinas, Emmanuel 30, 74–76, 239–240,
    243, 252, 285, 300, 452, 457
Luhmann, Niklas 300–301, 453
Mead, G. H. 27, 30
Nakayashiki Chihiro 312
Natsume Sōseki 435
Putnam, Robert 309
Rimbaud, Jean Nicolas Arthur 428
Rousseau, Jean-Jacques 436
Sartre, Jean-Paul Charles Aymard 428
Suddendorf, T. 403
Sugiyama Yukimaru 359
Tylor, Edward Burnett 333
Tinbergen, Niko 368
Washida Kiyokazu 299

Places and Organizations

Auschwitz 305, 319
Bossou Village 34, 359
Canadian Arctic 240
child and family support center at Chubu Gakuin University 400
Gombe 40, 182, 201
India 317
Mahale 49, 132, 154, 168, 171, 181, 183
Malekula Island 429
Myanmar 287
Nairobi National Park, Kenya 356
Sarawak 328
southern Thailand 291
Taï National Park 375
Uganda 219
Wamba 38